The Jewish Enlightenment

JEWISH CULTURE AND CONTEXTS

Published in association with the Center for Advanced Judaic Studies
of the University of Pennsylvania

David B. Ruderman, Series Editor

A complete list of books in the series is available from the publisher.

The Jewish Enlightenment

Shmuel Feiner

Translated by Chaya Naor

PENN

University of Pennsylvania Press

Philadelphia

DS
113
.F4413
2004

Publication of this book was made possible by a grant from the Lucius N. Littauer Foundation.
Originally published as Ma'apechat ha-neorut, tenuat ha-Haskalah ha-Yehudit ba-mea ha-shmune esre

10   9   8   7   6   5   4   3   2   1

Published by
University of Pennsylvania Press
Philadelphia, Pennsylvania 19104-4011

Library of Congress Cataloging-in-Publication Data

Feiner, Shmuel.
  [Mahpekhat ha-ne'orut. English]
  The Jewish enlightenment / Shmuel Feiner ; translated by Chaya Naor.
    p.   cm. —Jewish culture and contexts
  Includes bibliographical references and index.
  ISBN 0-8122-3755-2 (cloth. : alk. paper)
    1. Jews—Intellectual life—18th century. 2. Haskalah—History—18th century. 3. Jewish learning and scholarship—History—18th century. I. Title. II. Series
  DS113 .F4413   2003
  296'.094'09033—dc22   *2003061057*

For my wife, Rivka

Contents

Preface

The historian of Jewish modernization is faced with the formidable challenge of recreating in all its vitality the dramatic and convoluted historical development that gave birth to the contemporary Jewish world. One of the most fascinating and telling areas to explore regarding the aspirations of the Jews to drastically alter their values, modes of thought, and collective future is that of the elite of maskilim (enlightened Jews). This book is devoted to the history of the eighteenth-century Haskalah (Enlightenment) movement, weaving it into the broad and prolonged story of the changes that affected the Jewish people in the modern era. It provides a wide-scope reconstruction of the historical development and its ideas, and describes the public storms and the initial shocks that attended modernization.

The book opens in the early eighteenth century, with the story of several young men in European Ashkenazi society, who embarked on a conscious, deliberate course to change their cultural environment. They were motivated by a sense of intellectual inferiority, as well as by the strong desire to partake of the domains of knowledge of a cultural renaissance—the redemption of science and philosophy—the entrance to which had been denied them by those holding the keys to the traditional library. In relation to the state of knowledge and those who monopolized it, this was a subversive trend that began to break new ground for an alternative route. In the last quarter of the century, over a period of twenty years (1778–1797), this cultural trend crystallized into the Haskalah movement. With the intensification of the maskilim's revolutionary demands for an autonomous status and the right to speak out on current issues and to shape culture, the critical and modernist character of the Haskalah became clear. As soon as it did, the guardians of the existing order sounded an alarm, and an inevitable struggle ensued between the two competing elites—the rabbinical-traditional elite and the innovative maskilic elite with its liberal worldview. The front lines of the Jewish culture war, then, were already drawn. The unity of the pre-modern Jewish society, at least in the minds of its members, was shattered once and for all. In the history of Jewish culture, the modern era opened, marked by controversies, conflicts and schisms.

When I entered the field of historical research, I was intrigued by the subject of the Haskalah movement. I realized that by attempting to fully understand it and all its ramifications, the scholar and student would gain a compass for navigating the complex map of the various paths of modernization. The Haskalah is a dynamic phenomenon of transition from tradition to modernity, and its bearers are the maskilim. Each and every one of them experienced, in his own way, a profound cultural conversion. Hence one must try to comprehend the mind and soul of the maskil, his qualms, his rebelliousness, and his special traditional-secular language. Generations of research have greatly enriched the picture of the eighteenth century. The accepted model, which placed the Haskalah in Germany and Moses Mendelssohn at the epicenter of the changes of the modern era, has been undermined, since the formulation of other and different models of modernization, in which the movement is not seen as the agent of change, such as the model of the Sephardi diaspora in Western Europe, "Port Jews" in Italian Trieste, or British Jewry.

My intent in this book is to show that, despite this, the value of the Haskalah should not be underestimated. On the contrary, the enlightenment movement led by the maskilim in Europe represented the conscious process of modernization and signified the point of departure of the major trends in intellectual history and in the history of the Jewish public sphere from the eighteenth century and thereafter. In my previous book, *Haskalah and History*, I attempted to prove that the ideology of the Haskalah was responsible for a series of manipulations of the past in all of the movement's metamorphoses, in particular in nineteenth-century Eastern Europe. That book centered on one of the most influential inventions of the Haskalah—the "modern age" in Jewish culture. The historical space of the present book is confined to the eighteenth century. It describes in detail—and I hope with the sensitivity it merits—the process in which the modern and secular intellectual elite came into being.

I was faced with three main tasks in writing this book. The first was to uncover new historical sources that would enable me to paint a complete picture of the Haskalah movement. By examining letters, contemporary newspapers, documentary material spread throughout the issues of *Hame'asef*, unknown manuscripts, neglected figures, and forgotten books, I was able to present as full a picture as possible, and on more than one occasion to observe the maskilim from a variety of vantage points: through their self-consciousness and their experiential worlds, through the eyes of their adversaries and through the testimony of observers outside of Jewish society.

My second task was to reinterpret the Haskalah movement and to explain its historical significance. To a large extent, I was inspired by the insights offered by the recent research on the European Enlightenment and was helped by freeing myself of the perception of the Haskalah as a movement of German Jewry only. I felt it was particularly important to properly present the role played by Mendelssohn, who had been unjustly accorded the status of the father or the founder of the Haskalah; to connect the history of ideas and the social history of the Enlightenment; and to avoid linking the Haskalah to an analysis of political and social phenomena, such as emancipation, religious reform, and assimilation.

My third task was to weave the story of the Haskalah movement as a chronological story line, since by reconstructing it along the time axis, I was able to avoid leaving it solely within the realm of ideas. I chose to tell the story of the movement beginning with its emergence as the early Haskalah, through its development and its attempts at institutionalization, and ending with its dissolution at the end of the century. As I strove to reconstruct the story of the Haskalah, to tie all the threads together and to listen to the orthodox counterreactions, I came to realize that this was indeed the story of a revolution.

I collected the vast amount of documentation that underpins this book over many years. I reread the known sources and made every effort to search in dark corners and discover new ones. I was assisted by the treasures found in many libraries, including the Bodleian Library at Oxford, the British Museum Library in London, the Rosentalean Library in Amsterdam, the Weidner Library at Harvard University, the main archive on Jewish History in Jerusalem, and the National and University Library in Jerusalem, which has the richest, most complete collection on the Haskalah and has served for me as an excellent laboratory for historical research since I first began my studies at the Hebrew University.

I began writing the Hebrew version of this book in 1996, at the Harvard University Center for Jewish Studies, to which I had been invited as a Harry Starr Fellow. Several chapters were written while I was a research fellow at the Hebrew University Institute for Advanced Studies in Jerusalem and a fellow in the research group on the Haskalah at the Center for Jewish Studies of the University of Pennsylvania. I finished writing it in the summer of 2000, in the department of Hebrew and Jewish studies of the University College in London, to which I was invited as a fellow through the generosity of John Klier and Ada Rappaport-Albert.

The thriving research on the Haskalah movement, the appearance of articles and books on various issues related to the modernization of European Jewry and the Haskalah, the conduct of various research projects, and the organization of a series of international conferences and seminars enabled me to base the book on an intellectual space that branched out and crossed geographical boundaries. In recent years, a group of scholars from Israel, the United States, and Europe has been carrying on a fascinating discourse, and each of them has been making his own contribution to solving the riddles of Jewish modernization.

I am grateful to all my colleagues and friends, with whom I held discussions over the years that enabled me to write this comprehensive book. I should like to make special mention of several historians who have shown a keen interest in my research, and whose reactions, criticism, encouragement, and good will have been a source of inspiration: David Sorkin of the University of Madison, Michael Heyd and Shmuel Werses of the Hebrew University of Jerusalem, and Michael Meyer of Hebrew Union College. I owe a special debt of gratitude to David Ruderman of the University of Pennsylvania, who was helpful in arranging for the translation and publication of this book in the University of Pennsylvania's new series.

I received generous grants for the translation of this book from Mr. Felix Posen, who has always shown a special interest in studies on the modernization and secularization of the Jews, and from the Littauer Foundation. I am indebted to them, for without their assistance this book could not have been published.

For several years, research on the eighteenth-century Haskalah movement has been a major project of the Samuel Braun Chair for the History of the Jews in Prussia, at Bar-Ilan University, and the Chair has generously assisted me in the translation and publication of this book.

Introduction: The Jews and the Enlightenment

The Haskalah movement had no less a historical impact on the Jews than did the French Revolution on the history of Europe. A conscious and deliberate revolution began as soon as the first maskil mounted the public Jewish stage and proclaimed the independence of the republic of maskilim: Listen to me! I bear a reformist and redemptive vision that will be fulfilled in this world; I speak of an all-embracing criticism of the ills of existing Jewish life, and I have a detailed plan for the rehabilitation of our society and culture. I come armed with new knowledge, am attentive to European culture, and am capable of reading the changing map of history and correctly and precisely interpreting its codes. My senses are particularly attuned to the changes of the time and I hold a compass that helps me navigate between the paths of present and future without repeating the errors of the past.

The maskil had no troops behind him. His audience was small and selective, and he himself usually lacked any recognized religious-rabbinical authority. Nor, for the most part, did he possess the attributes of the high social class—capital and illustrious lineage. His only weapons were knowledge, a quill, and a bottle of ink, as well as a powerful urge to immortalize his words in print and to disseminate them widely. Nonetheless, he represented a new, unprecedented elite, which felt it was its duty to chastise and educate the public, and to promote alternative ideas. It was here that the revolution burst forth; here the historical process of a shift in sovereignty in the Jewish community began: an intellectual elite appeared that confronted the rabbinical, scholarly elite of the Jewish ancien régime and competed with it. The emergence of this elite in no way resembled the popular militant assault on the Bastille, which in France symbolized the revolt against the monarchy. But it was similar to what occurred on June 17, 1789, when a bourgeois elite of professionals and intellectuals, leaders of the Third Estate announced that from then on it would be the "National Assembly," and claimed sovereignty in France. This political-declarative act shattered the foundations of the ancien régime, which, until then had rested on the king's absolute sovereignty and on the privileges of the aristocracy and the church. True, the relatively small elite of maskilim in the eighteenth century did not enjoy the support of a broad popular camp, nor did the traditional leadership of rabbis and community leaders vacate their seats for the maskilim. But, had it not been for that revolutionary emergence of a new Jewish intelligentsia, no modern public sphere of Jewish culture—the new book market, the new ideological and religious movements of the nineteenth and twentieth centuries and their debates, and the press as a forum for political and cultural discourse—none of these would have been created in the modern era. This intelligentsia was secular insofar as its source of authority and the texture of its ideas were concerned (although it was multifaceted in its commitment to tradition), and at its center stood the modern Jewish intellectual.

The implications of this revolution, which took place in Europe from the eighteenth century, were truly remarkable. The internal Jewish public debate now left the Torah study halls, synagogues, community council meetings, rabbinical responsa, books of ethics and sermons, and moved into the multilingual periodicals, literary clubs, the republic of letters, and private homes. One of the results of this process was the creation of a new Jewish library. The religious establishment's monopoly on knowledge was broken and so too was its monopoly on the guidance of the community, on criticism and moral preaching, on education, and even on the most intimate aspects of life—dress, manners, and family.

The path of the Haskalah, like that of the French Revolution, was far from smooth. From the outset, it was divided by various trends, some more extreme, others more moderate, and its strengths and achievements varied according to time and place. Nor was it free of internal rivalries and dialectic processes that greatly unsettled many maskilim, hurling them from one position to another—from a zealous militant awakening to plans for fundamental reform, to incisive soul searching, disillusionment, denial, to a return to conservatism, to a search for harmony, and in some cases also to rapprochement with the orthodox opponents of the Haskalah. It was a multifaceted movement, in which the old and the new contended with one another over the changing ratio of its components. The Haskalah is often depicted as being elusive, difficult to describe precisely, but this is merely a typical expression of an historical interim period—a transition that reflects the maskilic dualism, its shaky path along the thin line separating the traditional and the modern, and its attempt to employ checks and balances to guide the Jews on their journey into a changing world.[1]

This book reconstructs the story of the Jewish revolution of enlightenment, in particular the formation of the republic of maskilic writers in European Jewry, as it gradually developed throughout the eighteenth century. The founders of this republic provided an avenue of secularization for Jewish society and culture, formulated the first modern ideology to emerge in Jewry, sowed the seeds of Jewish liberalism, and sparked the orthodox counter-reaction that culminated in the outbreak of a *Kulturkampf*. The story of the maskilic revolution in the Ashkenazi communities between Vilna and Amsterdam is a chapter of history best viewed from within, enabling the reader to see how it developed and influenced the traditional cultural patterns, religion, and society of eighteenth-century European Jewry. Many of the problems that confronted the maskilim, in particular the key question of whether it was legitimate to introduce nonreligious knowledge into Jewish culture, were unique. They stemmed from the Jewish context and in part were also a subject of discussion and polemics in the pre-modern era (for example, the medieval debate on the legitimacy of philosophy). The Haskalah's confrontations with its opponents within Jewry constitute one of the most fascinating chapters in the history of the dramatic and traumatic encounter between the Jews and modernity. But the basic assumption here is also that the Haskalah was the Jewish case of the European Enlightenment, and as such cannot be isolated from eighteenth-century Europe. Even if the classical culture of the Enlightenment, such as Diderot's and d'Alembert's *Encyclopédie*, Montesquieu's, Voltaire's, and Rousseau's writings, Hume's philosophy, Hogarth's paintings, Fielding's novels, and Mozart's music filled but a secondary role in the Haskalah, there was nonetheless a great similarity in mentality, values, worldview, self-consciousness, and rhetoric, which justifies classifying the Haskalah as part of the culture of the Enlightenment, or the *Aufklärung*, as it is known in German.

What was the Enlightenment? This question was posed by some who lived in the period, in the famous discussion held in Prussia in 1784 on the pages of the periodical of the German circle of the Enlightened, the *Berlinische Monatsschrift*. The reply of the famous philosopher from Königsberg University, Immanuel Kant, was a classic one. He refrained from suggesting any philosophical characteristics for the doctrine of enlightenment, emphasizing instead the immense mental upheaval it was causing at the time: "Enlightenment is man's release from his self-incurred tutelage. Tutelage is man's inability to make use of his understanding without direction from another. Self-incurred in this tutelage when its cause lies not in lack of reason but in lack of resolution and courage to use it without direction from another. *Sapere aude!* Have courage to use your own reason!—that is the motto of enlightenment."[2] The explosive nature of this brief definition lies in its sweeping criticism of the "old" world, in which man, out of pessimism and passivity, allows the existing order to dictate his life and those possessing religious and spiritual authority to determine for him what is truth. In contrast, the enlightened man is an autonomous, rational, and skeptical person, who has the power to free himself of the shackles of the past and authority, and to pave new and better ways for himself and for all of humanity.

Kant's consciousness that the Enlightenment is the most dominant progressive historical process of the eighteenth century was shared by many members of the European elites. This critical and activist—but also optimistic—ethos was cherished by members of the aristocracy and the bourgeoisie: scholars, publishers, writers, journalists, university professors, scientists, physicians, and lawyers, as well as senior government officials in France, in the German states, in Scotland, Italy, and other countries in Europe from the beginning of the century. Together they formed an imagined, informal intellectual community of writers and readers—the "literary republic" of the Enlightenment. Its members were partners in the project of enlightenment, which was conducted through the written and printed word, primarily in French, but also in German, English, and Italian. On the local level, the institutionalized or private meeting places of the citizens of this republic were academies of science, lodges of the Freemasons, reading societies, cafes, and literary salons.[3] The knowledge they accumulated and attempted to disseminate (in particular, the new Newtonian science, rational philosophy, and world history), the humanistic sensitivity and rational thought became power in their hands, and with it, they strove, with varying degrees of zeal, to transform the world in which they lived. The search for knowledge and truth was not limited to scholarship for its own sake; rather it was a means of formulating an ideological agenda for an optimistic, utopian purpose—to improve man's condition, freedom, and morality, and to enhance his happiness.[4] Although there was a broad range of opinion in this republic, in Isaiah Berlin's view: "There was a wide area of agreement about fundamental points: the reality of natural law (no longer formulated in the language of orthodox Catholic or Protestant doctrine), of eternal principles by following which alone men could become wise, happy, virtuous and free."[5] The clergy monopoly on knowledge was broken, and the intellectuals committed to enlightenment now demanded a share in it for themselves. They challenged the validity and usefulness of traditional knowledge. In fact, as soon as there was a secular intelligentsia, large enough and strong enough to pose a threatening challenge to the clergy, the Enlightenment contributed to the sweeping secularization of the European intellectual world and its elite.[6] The men of the eighteenth-century Enlightenment, Robert Darnton claimed, were "the secular apostles of civilization, in opposition to the champions of tradition religious orthodoxy."[7] These "apostles" developed a self-consciousness of "us" against "them," and some of their most prominent and enthusiastic spokesmen launched a *Kulturkampf*, criticizing, with heavy irony and sarcasm, institutions, prejudices, and superstitions, and calling for freedom and religious tolerance. For example, Candide, Voltaire's hero in the most incisive philosophical novel of the Enlightenment, asks "What sort of world is this?" and the reply he hears is "Something very mad and very abominable." And on another occasion, despairing of the human species, Candide wondered whether "men have always massacred each other as they do today, always been liars, cheats, faithbreakers, ingrates, brigands, weaklings, rovers, cowards, enviers, gluttons, drunkards, misers, self-seekers, carnivores, calumniators, debauchers, fanatics, hypocrites and fools?" Only Eldorado, the utopian land of gold that Candide and his friends discover, is totally devoid of those fanatic monopolists of knowledge: "monks, to teach, to dispute, to govern, to intrigue and to have people burned who are not of their opinion."[8]

Such relatively radical trends were particularly typical of the French Enlightenment, while in Germany, the main arena in which the Haskalah developed, political and religious criticism was far more moderate. Immanuel Kant, the Prussian citizen who formulated the revolutionary version of the Enlightenment, was also the one who limited it to the expression of views, being totally opposed to any breach of discipline on the part of Prussian citizens or any Christians. "Only one who is himself enlightened," Kant wrote about the king of Prussia, Frederick the Great, "is not afraid of shadows, and has a numerous and well-disciplined army to assure public peace can say: 'Argue as much as you will, and about what you will, only obey!'"[9] The philosopher Moses Mendelssohn, who was also a Prussian citizen but enjoyed fewer rights because he was Jewish, preceded Kant in replying to the question, "What is Enlightenment?" He was, however, considerably more cautious.

If it is not possible to disseminate a certain truth that is beneficial to man and embellishing, without totally demolishing the principles of religion and ethics that dwell in him, then the disseminator of Enlightenment, to whom virtue is dear, should behave with caution and moderation, and he would do well to suffer the prejudice rather than to expel together with it the truth that is inseparably bound up with it . . . the misuse of Enlightenment weakens the moral sense, gives rise to obstinacy, egotism, heresy and anarchy.[10]

Undoubtedly these words of warning about the Enlightenment, which already bear the seeds of the Counter-Enlightenment, were not merely a declaration of faith in the existing order and religion. They also contained a forceful expression of the awareness of the two Prussian intellectuals, Kant and Mendelssohn, five years before the French Revolution, that if the Enlightenment were not restrained by its thinkers and proponents, it would carry a revolutionary potential, one that threatened to shatter the old regime to bits.

The Enlightenment assailed the Jews from without and within, posing enormous challenges to them that left a deep imprint on their history. The "rationalist shift," as Jacob Katz termed it, in political and philosophical thought enabled an approach that advocated a secular state, moved the public debate about the place of the Jews in the society and state from Christian theological tracks to secular-rationalistic tracks, and influenced emancipative legislation.[11] The emergence of the idea of religious tolerance, one of the outstanding by-products of the Enlightenment, allowed intellectuals and statesmen to consider, for the first time, persuasive reasons for eradicating discrimination against the Jews, to present it as one of the prejudices that prevailed in the dark era of religious fanaticism, and to arrive at diversified programs for integrating the Jews into the secular state. These programs were based on two models: the relatively moderate model of enlightened absolutism, which called for the transformation of the Jews as a prerequisite for giving them rights (for example in the Austrian empire), and the far more radical and sweeping model, of legislative emancipation in revolutionary France.[12]

However, from the outset, the rationalist shift turned out to be a double-edged sword. The deistic criticism of Christianity, which began in the seventeenth century and reached its peak with Voltaire in the eighteenth century, also dialectically made basic assumptions about the negation of Judaism and criticism of the Jews, assumptions not based on religious reasoning, as in the past, but rather on secular historical observation. A new examination of the Bible and of Jewish history led many of the deists to an evaluation of the Jews that contradicted many values of the Enlightenment—Judaism is a religion of superstitions, of cruel commandments attributed to God, of the manipulative rule of priests, and of barbaric behavior opposed to humanism and morality.[13] Of course, there was not complete agreement among the deists, and a great divide separated, for example, John Toland and Voltaire. In 1714, Toland suggested that the Jews be allowed to become British citizens, and wrote a harsh accusatory essay against Christianity, holding it responsible for the prolonged suffering of the Jews.[14] In contrast, Voltaire concluded his satirical essay on Jewish history, in his 1764 *Philosophical Dictionary*, with the famous sentence, "In short, we find in them only an ignorant and barbarous people, who have long united the most sordid avarice with the most detestable superstition and the most invincible hatred for every people by whom they are tolerated and enriched. Still, we ought not to burn them."[15] But there is no overlooking the fact at the height of the Jean Calas affair, during which Voltaire angrily lashed out at Christian fanaticism, he somewhat tempered his sweeping criticism of ancient Judaism. In his 1763 "Treatise on Toleration," Voltaire argued, this time without his typical cynicism, that a perusal of the Bible and the ancient Jewish historical sources would also reveal, beneath the murkiness of horrifying barbarism, some rays of light of universal tolerance.[16] Most of the thinkers and statesmen who related to the question of the Jews on the basis of Enlightenment criteria laid down the same condition, explicitly or implicitly—the Jews must change. Rights, recognition, acceptance, and a change in the traditional hostile attitude toward the Jews would be given in exchange for a commitment on their part to undergo rejuvenation—to be reeducated, to internalize the values of Enlightenment, to be Europeanized, and to totally expunge the flaws in their culture, religion, and morality.[17] Kant, for example, went even further, and at the end of the eighteenth century, expected the Jews to almost totally abandon their traditional religion and the rituals of the practical commandments, as a prerequisite for receiving civil rights in the state.[18]

The Enlightenment entered the world of traditional pre-modern Ashkenazi society bearing a contradictory message—a promise to abolish the legal restrictions on Jews and to take them out of the ghetto, along with a direct threat to their religious and cultural heritage. Enlightened public opinion and the modern state laid down a series of demands for the removal of the obstacles that hindered the Jews' integration into society and the state and the weakening of their communal autonomy. However, the far more significant challenge posed by the Enlightenment was the double message of hope and threat that it bore from within: the promise of a joyful era, a kind of redemption on earth, and a real alleviation of the hardships of exile, on the one hand, and the undermining of the "old order," a blow to rabbinical hegemony and control over knowledge and education, and indirectly also to the lifestyle dictated by religious norms, on the other. Many chapters in the modern social and cultural history of the Jews are no more than recapitulations of the argument between those who welcomed the Enlightenment, seeing in it a promise, and those who had no doubt that it was the worst enemy ever to rise up against Judaism. Although rationalist criticism had already been leveled from within Jewry in the seventeenth century, it was confined to the Western Sephardic diaspora and to fascinating, but rather exceptional heterodox figures like the deist Uriel D'Acosta and the famous pantheist Baruch Spinoza, who questioned the divine authority of the Bible and criticized what to their minds were the superstitions in Jewish religion. But this threat posed by several audacious individuals, who did not form any movement or develop any ideology directed at the overall Jewish public with the aim of fundamentally changing it, was met by communities that generally succeeded in ousting deviants from their midst or silencing them with the threat of excommunication.[19]

In the eighteenth century, it was the Haskalah movement that posed a far more significant challenge to the traditional society and its elite leadership, in the name of Enlightenment values. Its spokesmen demanded tolerance and freedom of opinion in Jewish life, broke the religious monopoly on knowledge and public guidance, built a new library, and did their utmost to alter the Jewish educational system. Moreover, they saw themselves as an alternative elite, one that was dissatisfied with the existing reality, and proposed a new public discourse and a different agenda. The maskilim internalized various values of the Enlightenment and based the transformative ideology of the Haskalah on their criticism of the existing situation and on the great vision of a rehabilitated Jewry.

The maskilim's revolution of enlightenment was unquestionably one of the most important formative events in the history of European Jewry. However, eighteenth-century Jewry was not marked by stability; nor did it stagnate while it awaited the advent of the Haskalah. The "tradition and crisis" model depicts a long period of continuity, until Moses Mendelssohn and his "disciples" appeared upon the scene and shattered the foundation of the leadership by force of rationalism and their association with the social frameworks of the German intellectual elite. But, in reality, this was a particularly dynamic century. For both Christians and Jews, it was not only the "century of enlightenment." For the Ashkenazi Jews, it was a century of division, of the emergence of separate camps and the beginning of the internal struggle over hegemony. It was the century in which the uniformity and totality of the traditional world was smashed, from without and from within. From without: the differentiation in the legal status of the Jews under various rulers and regimes in Europe, manifested, for example, in the divergence between the expulsion of Prague Jewry by the Catholic empress Maria Teresa, in the 1740s, and the majority vote granting emancipation to Jews in the National Assembly of Paris in the 1790s. And from within—moderate and radical Sabbatianism, Pietism, Hasidism, rabbinical opposition to Hasidism, the early and the late Haskalah, acculturation, apostasy, and orthodoxy.

The number of Jews in Europe ranged from between about seven hundred thousand early in the century to more than a million and a half toward its end (out of more than two million Jews in the entire world). Some of the more prominent Jewish figures of the eighteenth century were the Vilna Gaon, who represented the ethos of talmudic scholarship at its height and zealously defended it against the threat of the pietistic, enthusiastic religiosity of the Hasidim; Moses Hayim Luzzatto (the Ramhal), who represented Kabbalistic religiosity that purported to be divinely inspired and was seen as a threat to the accepted religious order; Jacob Frank, the idolized, libertine leader of a radical Sabbatian sect in the middle of the century; the Jerusalem rabbi Moses Hagiz, who waged a fierce battle against the Sabbatians and apostates; Israel Ben-Eliezer, better known as the Baal Shem Tov, the miracle worker and expert in magic from Medzibezh, regarded by the Hasidic movement as its founding father; the Berlin philosopher Moses Mendelssohn; the poet, linguist, and commentator on the Bible Naphtali Herz Wessely; the physician and philosopher Marcus Herz, who was a student of Kant's; the well-known rabbis and rivals Jacob Emden and Jonathan Eybeschütz; the Berlin intellectual Rahel Levin, whose home became a cultural salon; and many others.

In the eighteenth century, Jewish life in Europe was marked by polarized trends that aroused tremendous fervor. Throughout the entire century, an underground Sabbatian movement existed, which legitimated religious-radical permissiveness and evoked no end of scandals; circles of talmudic scholars were supported by philanthropists; messianic anticipations and calculations of the end of days excited mystics and rationalists alike; wealthy elites became increasingly acculturated and adopted the bourgeoisie ethos of Europe in the lifestyle and aristocratic culture of the Baroque and Rococo periods. Secularization was expressed in the lifestyle of the urban economic elite in Germany, Austria, Bohemia, Holland, and England. It was reflected, for example, in the renewed interest in medieval Jewish philosophy, one of whose most ardent disciples was Moses Mendelssohn of Dessau.[20] The reprinting, after two hundred years, of Maimonides's *Guide for the Perplexed* (1742) in the Jesnitz printing house near Dessau, was a symbol of this interest and a source of inspiration.

Polish Jewry continued to supply community rabbis and teachers to Ashkenazi Jewry in the states of Germany, in France, Holland, and Austria. In journeying from Lithuania to Prussia in the 1770s, the scholar Solomon Maimon, who would later become a German philosopher, followed a well-known geographical and cultural path. Even though his purpose was a radical cultural conversion, he was regarded in Germany as a Polish talmudic scholar.[21] Despite these meetings and contacts, the cultural boundary between the Jews of Eastern Europe and those of Central and Western Europe became even more clearly defined toward the end of the century. This process was greatly furthered by the partitions of Poland (1772–95) between Russia, Austria, and Prussia, and the political changes introduced by enlightened absolutism in Central Europe (in particular Joseph II's tolerant legislation, 1781–89). Of course, the spread of Hasidism in Eastern Europe and the inception of the Haskalah in Central Europe also contributed to the erection of the cultural barrier, which grew higher and higher, between the two parts of Ashkenazi Jewry, in the last quarter of the century.[22] In any event, the processes of modernization during this period had not yet considerably weakened the strength of the community or the authority of its leadership, nor had it as yet freed the Jews from the restrictions the state had imposed on them. Even the lives of individualists and proponents of Enlightenment, like Mendelssohn and Maimon, were constricted by the special legislation that discriminated against the Jews and reduced their opportunities for employment; consequently they had to rely on the help of wealthy Jews and community institutions.

Paradoxically, although the Haskalah has become one of the chief topics of modern Jewish historiography, so that there is hardly a historian who has failed to include it when depicting Jewish modernization, a book devoted entirely to the history of the eighteenth-century Haskalah movement has never been written. Since Jost and Graetz in the nineteenth century, and Michael Meyer, Raphael Mahler, Jacob Katz, and Michael Graetz in the twentieth, the Haskalah has been assigned a central role in the many changes that German Jews have undergone in the modern age.²³ Exceptional attention has been devoted, of course, to Moses Mendelssohn, and Alexander Altmann's monumental biography is unquestionably a major contribution to the study of the Haskalah.²⁴ However, it seems that, in most instances, the Haskalah has been harnessed to fill the particular role assigned it in the historical narratives. The historical Mendelssohn has become the mythological Mendelssohn, symbolizing either the marvelous, truly admirable fulfillment of German Jewry's vision of emancipation or, on the contrary, the commencement of the descent into the abyss of apostasy and assimilation (as Mendelssohn was represented in orthodox historiography, on the one hand, and in national historiography, on the other). The Haskalah was often enlisted to tell the story of the Jews' social integration. It was regarded as the source of the religious reform movement and as the creator of the new Jewish education. It played yet another role, particularly in literary research, from the publication of Joseph Klausner's classic book *The History of the New Hebrew Literature*, as the reviver of the Hebrew language and the catalyst of the modern Hebrew literature that began with Naphtali Herz Wessely and reached its peak with the poets, novelists, and writers of articles in Eastern Europe in nineteenth-century Hebrew periodicals.²⁵

In the last decades of the twentieth century, the historical frameworks that embraced the Haskalah were greatly broadened, and new, more profound insights regarding it were proffered: the geographical framework was broadened to include communities such as Trieste in Italy (Lois Dubin), Shklov in Belorussia (David Fishman), Prague in Bohemia (Kestenberg-Gladstein and Hillel Kieval), Hungary (Michael Silber), Holland (Joseph Michman), and England (David Ruderman), and detailed studies have been devoted to fascinating key figures, other than Mendelssohn, like Isaac Euchel (my study), Solomon Maimon (Liliane Weissberg et al.), Wessely (Edward Breuer), Marcus Herz (Martin Davis), and Mendel Lefin (Nancy Sinkoff).²⁶ Scholars of Haskalah literature, including Moshe Pelli, Yehudah Friedländer, and Shmuel Werses, have in recent years mapped the diverse field of literary genres that the maskilim employed, examined the links between Hebrew literature and European Enlightenment literature, and noted how various historical events resonated in Haskalah literature.²⁷ Altmann's book did not provide an answer to the enigma that was Mendelssohn. In the 1990s, scholars like Allan Arkush and David Sorkin turned to new, opposed directions. Arkush attempted to uncover the "real" Mendelssohn, whose Jewish thought, he believes, served merely as a mask for his deism. And Sorkin placed Mendelssohn within the contexts of the German "religious Enlightenment."[28] Steve Lowenstein's important, exhaustive historical-social study on the Berlin community underscored the "Berlin Haskalah's" ties to an affluent elite and more precisely assessed how much weight the maskilim really carried in the community in contrast to the traditional element.[29] Sorkin pursued an innovative, particularly fecund direction, in taking a comparative view of the Haskalah. He found an analogy between it and other religious enlightenment movements in Germany, and drew a distinction between the early Haskalah, which was marked by intellectual rejuvenation, and the politicization of the Haskalah in the 1770s—a process that characterized both the Catholic and the Protestant enlightenments in eighteenth-century Germany.[30]

Notwithstanding all the above, the only work that attempted to comprehensively describe the Haskalah in a special monograph is still Shimon Berenfeld's *Dor Ta'hapukhot* (*A Generation of Upheavals*), which came out in Warsaw in 1897. Although it provides a great deal of information and is arranged chronologically, this book would not satisfy the present-day reader, not only because of the great progress made in research since then, but also because of Berenfeld's tendentious approach and his lack of sympathy for his subject. It is written with admiration for Mendelssohn but with criticism—at times with aversion—toward those same maskilim who "multiplied apostasy and licentiousness among the Jews" and dared to show contempt for the sanctities and sages of the nation. He also guided his readers in how to distinguish between what was admirable in the Haskalah and what was abhorrent in it. The book's orientation was nationalistic, and its author's position was postmaskilic, a tendency characteristic of Berenfeld, the former Galician maskil who at the time was an historian residing in Berlin, as well as of other writers like him, who near the end of the nineteenth century increasingly became cultural pessimists and often attacked the Haskalah, guided by post-Enlightenment attitudes.[31]

Over two hundred years after Mendelssohn and more than one hundred after Berenfeld, the question being asked is whether research on the Haskalah is still relevant. Does the Haskalah have any significance for the scholar and his readers in the early twenty-first century, and what is the historical narrative into which the Haskalah fits? To grapple with the issue of relevance and significance, one must first look at the intellectual and methodological changes that have occurred in the discussion and treatment of the European Enlightenment in the last two or three decades. Although the Enlightenment had already been subjected to the criticism of Romanticism and Conservatism, until recently it was still perceived as representing the value system of Western culture. The "age of lights" earned many flattering epithets, and conservatives and "enemies of the Enlightenment" were the only ones who refused to ideal-ize it. That was the situation until postmodernism challenged many of the basic conventions that Western civilization had inherited from the eighteenth-century age of Enlightenment. The postmodernist trend in Western culture put the Enlightenment to a new test, from which it emerged in surprising and particularly uncomplimentary garb. Several of the fundamental paradigms of the Enlightenment were shattered, in particular the polarization between humanism and barbarism, between reason and madness, and between knowledge and ignorance. Is good really based on rational knowledge, while evil is embodied in ignorance and irrational darkness? In the critics' view, the knowledge that the Enlightenment presumed to present as universal actually stemmed from various interests and was under the monopolistic hegemony of males and of European whites. Not only did the Enlightenment fail to liberate the human spirit; it stifled it, and also led to man's alienation from his environment and his spontaneous nature. When the French Revolution's stage of terror was blamed on the Enlightenment, the reputation of the proponents of reason was stained, and they were then charged with anarchism, oppression, and discrimination. In the wake of the breakdown of the great ideologies, truths that had been regarded as incontrovertible were being questioned: did reason, the expanding knowledge, and new science really make the world a better place? Was the concept of human progress, which the maskilim had cultivated, realistic, or was it no more than wishful thinking or a futile belief?[32]

In a rather rare response by an historian to the challenge of postmodernism, Robert Darnton recently vigorously defended the values of the Enlightenment and rejected the notion that it is identified with modernism as a whole. To counter this criticism, which is far from the reality of the eighteenth century and is anchored in the problems of the Western world in the second half of the twentieth century, Darnton strongly suggested that the Enlightenment be restored to its historical dimensions. In his opinion, it should be viewed as an historical movement, with a beginning, middle, and end, promoted by ardent intellectuals who wanted to change moods, patterns of thought, and traditional institutions.[33] This view has great significance for research on the Haskalah too, and it fits in with the new tendency to classify the various avenues through which the Jews experienced modernization. Now that Tod Endelman, in his illuminating examination of the English case of Jewish modernization, has challenged the Germanocentric model and Jacob Katz's "tradition and crisis" narrative, there is no longer any doubt that the Haskalah is not synonymous with modernization; rather it represents one of the routes it took.[34] Recently, this tendency has been coherently articulated by Shulamit Volkov, who distinguishes between unexpected and involuntary processes of change and "conscious and explicit efforts by the Jewish public throughout the European continent to adapt to the changes taking place around it and to alter—according to a program—the social structure and cultural milieu in which it lived."[35] Such distinctions and subdivisions between the various avenues of modernization assign the Haskalah a limited role in the "project of modernity," as the movement that initiated the deliberate, conscious process of modernization in the eighteenth century. Nonetheless, they free the Haskalah of any sweeping "responsibility" for processes such as assimilation, legal emancipation and the emergence of modern nationalism, and for the first time make it possible to write a balanced history of the Haskalah as an historical movement, based on Darnton's suggestion, and to study its revolutionary aspects in the broad context of eighteenth-century European Jewry.

From an opposite direction, albeit one with similar implications, the Enlightenment's values are also threatened by its enemies, the fundamentalist streams. In essence, these are antimodernist and antirationalist streams, and their slogans challenge each and every one of the conceptions of the Enlightenment, beginning with the very perception of man and his autonomous status in the world, and ending with political conceptions relating to rights, freedom, and equality. In certain aspects, these trends also gain a particular expression in Jewish and Israeli life. As we shall see later, the orthodox claim that the Haskalah is an extreme manifestation of apostasy and assimilation originated as soon as the Haskalah movement itself came into being. This criticism has never died out, and is one of the hallmarks of militant ultra-orthodox historiography in the present as well, particularly in the *Kulturkampf* being waged in the State of Israel. In actual fact, the Haskalah was the opening battle of the Jewish *Kulturkampf*, whose later stages are still being experienced by Jews in Israel at the beginning of the twenty-first century. The dilemmas that the Haskalah provoked when it first began to grapple with the challenge of modernity have not yet been completely resolved, and some are still very much alive after more than two hundred years. The Haskalah can be most appropriately introduced into the historical narrative that reconstructs the complete, tortuous, and traumatic story of the *Kulturkampf*, in an attempt to sensitively penetrate the world of those representing the various camps and to understand the intensity of the upheaval the Jews experienced in their encounter with modernity.

These are a few of the questions and conclusions that arise from the intellectual discourse on the Enlightenment in general and on the Haskalah in particular. It is also important to place alongside them the new methodological approaches, which began to emerge in Enlightenment research a quarter of a century ago, or even earlier, and which have only recently begun to resonate in Haskalah research too. Historians of the present generation no longer accept the generalization implied by the labels, such as the "Age of Reason," which were attached to the eighteenth century; they no longer agree with the concepts of the basic studies on the Enlightenment, like that of Ernst Cassirer, that depict the Enlightenment as a cohesive, uniform ideological and philosophical doctrine. They also reject the insights of Peter Gay, who, in his monumental work, represented the *philosophes* as "one family" of renowned authors who shared the same aims and the same values. First and foremost, we should turn again to Robert Darnton, who in his studies on the book and reading culture in eighteenth-century France, in his fascinating studies on underground literature, and his major work, *The Business of Enlightenment*, on the publishing history of the *Encylopédie*, formulated replies to totally new questions. He no longer asked what the Enlightenment thinkers said or wrote in their famous works, but rather what the Enlightenment was, how it was disseminated, who its consumers were, what its scope was and how it was understood by the readers.[36] The work of the German sociologist and philosopher Jürgen Habermas gave a particularly strong impetus to Enlightenment research. He described the emergence of an imagined community of readers in eighteenth-century Europe and the construction of a modern, democratic "public sphere," secular in nature, within which an Enlightenment project took place.[37]

The aim of these new questions is to clarify the identity of the proponents of Enlightenment ideas and of the unifying and organizational frameworks of their literary republic. They also turn the spotlight on the anonymous secondary agents, who filled a key role in disseminating the ideas, but were not in the front ranks of the movement, were overshadowed by the great figures, and hence have not received any attention until now. The relatively limited scope of the Haskalah and the small number of existing historical sources render it difficult to write a comprehensive historiographical study. Nonetheless, this book attempts to write the history of the Haskalah with sensitivity in regard to newly raised questions and insights in Enlightenment research. The discussion will focus less on the development of ideas and more on the maskilim themselves and their steadfast attempts to overcome the stubborn opposition and gain a central place for themselves in the Jewish public discourse.

Was the Enlightenment a single movement, with one philosophy and shared values? This assumption, which was commonly accepted, has been discredited. Instead of speaking about a coherent ideological system of the Enlightenment, scholars now tend to speak in general terms only about attitudes and mentalities. The expansion of the boundaries of research beyond the classic cases of France and Germany has revealed the singularity of the various enlightenment movements that evolved in different countries. In 1981, an important collection of essays edited by Roy Porter and Mikulis Teich was published. Its title, *Enlightenment in National Context*, already implies recognition of the existence of singular enlightenments national and local in character, whose specific traits are revealed in a comparative study, rather than the existence of a single, unified movement.[38] It is surprising that the Haskalah has not been included in this multinational context. But this can be explained by the fact that it is almost totally nonexistent in the general studies on the European Enlightenment. European historiography usually mentions the Haskalah only in the context of Germany and Moses Mendelssohn, the "German Socrates," who was always regarded as an integral member of the German *Aufklärung* in the generation of Lessing, Dohm, and Nicolai, and not necessarily as a maskil who played a significant role in internal developments in the Jewish world. He is depicted as a symbol of the Prussian religious toleration, which made possible his acceptance into the enlightened elite despite his being Jewish. This phenomenon undoubtedly should be related to in a more balanced manner.

The reaction of the scholar of French Enlightenment Robert Darnton to the postmodernist criticism also includes a protest against what he regards as the exaggerated multiplicity of Enlightenment studies—the extension of the territory from France to instances of radical, religious, Pietist, and conservative enlightenment, or to Russian, Austrian, and Jewish enlightenment. In this way, Darnton asserts, the Enlightenment becomes everything and in fact nothing.[39] The demand to limit the Enlightenment, at least insofar as the Jewish case is concerned, is misleading and also precludes the opportunity to understand the Enlightenment in its entire scope. The Haskalah, as a instance of national enlightenment, took place in circumstances peculiar to the Jews, since they were a minority devoid of any political or territorial framework; the maskilim were a minority within a minority and hence had to build their literary community. Unlike the Enlightened in Germany, for example, the maskilim were not government officials, members of the academy, or clergy. Their collective identity differed from the traditional Jewish identity, which was based on religion and on communal autonomy, on the one hand; yet, on the other hand, it was not an assimilated identity, indifferent to or alienated from Jewish society and its future. Nor was this a specifically Jewish-German or Prussian movement, although in the years when it flourished, the Berlin community was the maskilim's major focal point, so that an overall definition of the Haskalah as the "Berlin Haskalah" is apparently misleading.[40] By means of the written word, in particular in the *Hame'asef* periodical, the maskilim, within a few years, founded a literary republic of writers and readers within the Ashkenazi communities of Europe. The Haskalah's dualistic identity resulted from its link to religious culture and the Hebrew language, as well as from its identification with the new agenda and project of rejuvenation and regeneration of Jewish culture. It is actually the Haskalah's singularity that makes it a fascinating, important test case for an understanding of the Enlightenment in its national contexts, and just as it is fitting to examine the Haskalah using tools and concepts from Enlightenment studies, so it is both fitting and productive to include it in the picture of European Enlightenment.

The Jewish Enlightenment attempts to fill the void and to reconstruct for the first time, as faithfully as possible, the story of the eighteenth-century Haskalah movement, which originated when a climate of humanism, of rational scientific and philosophical thought was created in Europe. Its further development was based on the early maskilim, who were endowed with tremendous curiosity, a quasi-erotic passion for new knowledge, and a sense of affront in the face of the Jews' intellectual inferiority. During the early stages of the Haskalah, and even long before a maskilic agenda and transformative programs were formulated, modern "authors" began to break into the public arena. Undoubtedly, however, the outbreak of the *Kulturkampf*, centered around the program for new Jewish education proposed by Naphtali Herz Wessely in 1782, was the formative event in the history of the Haskalah movement. Moses Mendelssohn, even if he was not the main protagonist in the story of the Haskalah, certainly played a key role in it. During those same years, he formulated his concept of tolerance that was highly significant in his disputes with Christian enlighteners and underpinned his expectations and demands of his Jewish co-religionists. The 1780s were the years the Haskalah flourished—the new intellectual elite were engaged in shaping the public sphere, disputing orthodox positions, and building an alternative library and an organization of maskilim that aspired to far-reaching expansion. At this stage, the results of the maskilim's revolution were already evident. As an antithesis to the rabbinical elite, the maskilic elite took shape—sometimes in defiance, but always striving to make its mark and to propose alternative ways.

The Haskalah's momentum was halted at the end of the century in its two centers, Berlin and Königsberg, but a new generation of maskilim transferred the Haskalah's formulas of modernization to other places, and in the nineteenth century the revolution of enlightenment found a particularly broad scope of activity among the scholarly elite of East European Jewry.

Anyone wishing to uncover the roots of the Haskalah can justifiably point to the influence the Enlightenment's challenges had on the Jews, to the spread of the idea of religious tolerance in state and society, to the rise in the standard of living and changes in lifestyle that characterized court Jews and the Jewish bourgeoisie and gradually broke down some of the barriers that had traditionally separated Jewish and Christian life. There was also the need for an intellectual-rationalistic response to the religious challenge of Sabbatian messianism, of the enthusiastic groups of Kabbalists, and the threat of religious permissiveness and apostasy. But there can be no doubt that the genetic code of the Haskalah was, from the early eighteenth century, inscribed in the minds of several young men, from the religious elite, who had a burning passion for new knowledge, then considered foreign and superfluous. For these young men, the Haskalah was a life-shaping, enthralling experience, just as Kant defined it: "Man's release from his self-incurred tutelage."

PART I

A Passion for Knowledge

Chapter 1

Intellectual Inferiority: The Affront

In the winter of 1702, a young Jewish student walked through the corridors of the faculty of medicine at the University of Frankfurt-on-Oder, his heart consumed by a sense of despair and frustration. Shmuel Shimon Ben-Yaacov, a native of Raudenai in Lithuania, had come to the Prussian University from Opatow, Poland, where he lived, to fulfill his dream of studying medicine. Like other Jewish students at German universities, from the end of the seventeenth century, Shmuel had received a well-grounded religious education (before coming to Prussia, he studied for two years in Rabbi Meir Frankel's *beit midrash* [house of study] in Pinsk), and like them he needed a special permit from the rulers of Prussia, to study in the academic institution.[1] Not only did Shmuel Ben-Yaacov have to cope with the enormous challenge academic studies posed, he also had to endure the pain of loneliness and the distressing sense of being doubly exiled—as the only Jewish student in the university that year, alone in a foreign, Christian world. He might have been able to overcome his misery if he could only find one other student of his faith, so they could give one another support and, in their spare time, study religious literature as they had been accustomed to doing in their youth. When he learned that a Jewish student, Isaac Wallich of Koblenz, from a highly respected family of physicians, was enrolled at Halle University that year, he hastened to send him an emotional letter, suggesting that Isaac transfer to Frankfurt University and join him there. Within a few weeks, he received a reply.[2]

These two young men, who were apparently in their later teens, wrote their letters in mellifluous scholarly Hebrew, in ornate, embellished rhymed prose, interspersed with biblical verses, and in talmudic patterns of language. In them, they expressed their fervent desire to excel in their studies. They wrote of their boundless admiration for the new science, whose treasures were revealed to them at the German university, and their favorable impression of the diverse cosmopolitan student body, which even included students from faraway, exotic China. In particular, they wrote about their passion for knowledge: "The fervor that the Almighty has imprinted upon me lusts and yearns to quench its thirst in the *chokhmot*, and most of all, to light a torch to guide me in the *chokhmah* of medicine," the student from Frankfurt wrote. And his friend from Halle lavished extravagant praise on the skills and innovative ideas of the well-known professor Friederich Hoffman (1660–1742), whose teachings he thirstily imbibed: "Had you not seen his genius at length, it would have seemed incredible. It bursts forth in every *chokhmah* and lore and nothing is hidden from him, he inquires into all mysteries, not only is his erudition vast in the science of medicine but he also has knowledge in the esoteric wisdoms and in all other inquiries." Professor Hoffman had such a great affection for the Jewish student Isaac that he took him under his wing, concealing from him none of his innovative methods of healing, contrary to the conduct of other physicians at the time.[3] And "he tells me of all the remedies and singular secrets that he has acquired and devised . . . that he will not disclose to one among thousands," Issac Wallich proudly wrote.

Each of these two young men was the only Jewish student in his university, and each sought a companion with whom to converse and study. "Oh, my brother, how much we would inquire into every wisdom and discretion as the good Lord allows us," Shmuel wrote to the student in Halle, "in religious study, in all its categories, sorts, and distinctions, as well as in matters of wisdom from the holy books of our ancestors or from the books of the gentiles written in their languages." However, all entreaties to Wallich pleading with him to transfer from Halle to Frankfurt to rescue him from his lonely state and be a companion were of no avail. Wallich was already then in an advanced stage of his studies, living comfortably in the home of the wealthy Jewish banker Asher Markus, and enjoying his patronage, and he saw no reason to leave the faculty of medicine, then considered the best and most modern in Germany. He was enthralled by Halle University and its vibrant, tolerant atmosphere, and he suggested that Shmuel join him there: "We will be together, what can remain that we shall not inquire into, what can be too difficult for us to overcome, what can be too hard that we shall not learn it, and what can be beyond our grasp to acquire it." With these words, Wallich tried to tempt his inexperienced friend, tendering him but a taste of the intellectual experience they could expect to share.[4]

Wallich could more easily bear the psychological anguish of a young Jew alone in a foreign, Christian environment, because he had grown up in Germany, in a family many of whose sons had studied medicine in a European academic institution (mainly in Italy). Shmuel, in contrast, was from Poland-Lithuania, where Jews rarely attended universities, even though it was necessary if the community were to have doctors. Nonetheless, they were both aware that they had taken an unusual, daring step in enrolling at a university, which exposed them to intellectual challenges and a Christian environment, and knew all too well that they were among the first Jewish students in Germany. Throughout the entire eighteenth century, only some three hundred Jews studied in Germany, and from 1678 to 1730, only twenty-five Jews were enrolled in five universities. Wallich had far more self-confidence, and he boasted to the somewhat more timid student in Frankfurt that he was not afraid to walk about freely in public: "As I wear my sword upon my hip as do all the medical students, there is no one who will tell me what to do." This was certainly exceptional and pretentious behavior in a university which only seven years before had first opened its doors to Jewish students. Wallich tried to embolden Shmuel, advising him to overcome his sense of inferiority and his awe of his Christian environment. "Unquestionably we two represent an unusual, relatively rare phenomenon as Jewish students in the heart of Christian institutions of higher learning," Isaac stated. "And since this fact arouses surprise and wonder, we must show a large measure of self-confidence." Realizing that he was breaking fresh ground and shattering the accepted image of the Jew, Wallich declared that the time had come to remedy the anomalous situation in which members of the Jewish minority in Europe were merchants while all the scientific and humanistic knowledge was left solely in the hands of the ruling Christian elite.

The Restoration of Jewish Honor

The voices of the two medical students that we hear from between the lines of the letters they wrote to one another in 1702 were the first to articulate the battle cry of the early maskil: no more Jewish inferiority in Europe's new world of knowledge! The voice of another early maskil, Isaac Wetzlar (1680–1751), from Celle, was heard only in 1749, in the unpublished manuscript of his book, *Libes briv*, two years before his death. Wetzlar was a wealthy merchant and businessman who traveled widely throughout Europe, but he had also received a broad Jewish education. He owned an extensive library, which contained printed books from the sixteenth and seventeenth centuries as well as manuscripts, and his erudition in *musar* (ethical) literature and in Jewish rationalist philosophy of the Middle Ages and the Renaissance was very impressive. None of those who read the relatively numerous copies of Wetzlar's manuscript had any reason to doubt his piety. Nonetheless, his criticism, often sharply cynical in tone, of the religious elite and the serious flaws that he saw in the education, society, and leadership of Ashkenazi Jewry in Europe, was very scathing. Wetzlar cloaked his critique with his good intentions, because supposedly his only desire was to modestly fulfill the commandment "Love thy brethren as yourself," and he prefaced nearly every criticism he wrote with the sanctimonious phrase, "Because of our many sins."

Wetzlar saw himself as an outsider, not part of the traditional religious elite, and the role he undertook was that of an observer, an eyewitness with a sense of responsibility, traveling between communities, seeking the truth and reporting on the flaws he sees. He tried to convey his messages in his book *Libes briv*, written in spoken Yiddish, which was also the language of the popular literature. His aim was to reach all groups in Jewish society, and bypassing the men, he also sought paths to the hearts of the women—a rather rare phenomenon at the time. Wetzlar warned the Jews to be wary about the new Kabbalists, expressed his concern that the gentiles would mock the meager knowledge of the Jewish masses and their vulgar behavior in the synagogue, called on them to teach girls Hebrew and the Bible, decried the numerous errors in Hebrew in the new books, stressed the importance of the natural sciences, and warmly recommended the study of Jewish philosophy. More than anything else, he condemned the corruption and ineptitude of the Rabbinate and denounced the deplorable level of contemporary scholars. This scourge was so appalling that from time to time, popular, anticlerical protests burst forth—justifiably, in his view. Simple Jews hurl public criticism against those who are responsible for the Torah and are distorting it. With my own ears I heard, Wetzlar wrote, "that scholars are among the most contemptible people, doing the worst deeds." Among the ideal types he mentions favorably in *Libes briv*, one, rarely found according to Wetzlar, stands out above all others. This is the intellectual Jew, who observes nature and ponders the great wonder and beauty of the divine creation. Several years later, this type was the subject of further development and idealization in the Hebrew periodical *Kohelet musar* (The Preacher), published in Berlin in the 1750s by two early maskilim: the young Moses Mendelssohn (1729–86) and his friend, Tobias Bock, an early maskil, whose identity is not yet altogether clear.[5]

In the 1780s, a fire in the city of Slonim totally destroyed Rabbi Shimson ben Mordechai's library, including manuscripts he had written himself. Unfortunately, this prevents us from hearing the voice of this scholar, who served as the rabbi of the Slonim community and later as the rabbi of Königsberg, and in the family tradition was known as "A scholar and Kabbalist, an astronomer and philosopher, accomplished in all seven sciences, the author of many books, on the exoteric and the esoteric, and the *chokhmot*."[6] In the middle of the century, the rabbi from Slonim spent some time in Hamburg and brought science books back with him. He became well known as a man who secretly studied the sciences, read German, and kept a library rare in its diversity. In the early 1770s, Solomon Maimon (1753–1800) walked from Nieshviz to Slonim in midwinter to borrow German scientific and medical books from the rabbi's library. His study of these books in physics and optics brought the young Maimon one step closer to his future entry into enlightened culture. As a result of the medical knowledge he acquired then, he began to think himself superior to the "ignorant boors" around him and to jeer at the superstitions and irrational beliefs of the Jews in Lithuania among whom he had lived until then.[7] According to the tradition of the Epstein family, the Gaon from Vilna also sent the rabbi of Slonim a letter, in which he requested that he send him some books from his library.[8] In 1778, he was among the advance subscribers to the German translation of the Torah (the *Bi'ur*) by Moses Mendelssohn. That same year, another well-known early maskil came to him—the *dayan* (a justice in a rabbinical court) from Minsk, Baruch Schick of Shklov (1774– 1808), who on his way from a meeting with the Gaon in Vilna, to Germany and Holland, passed through Slonim. Rabbi Shimshon wrote an enthused approbation for Schick's partial translation into Hebrew of Euclid's geometry, commending the writer for having undertaken a project that would bring honor to the Jewish people and might dissuade the gentiles from mocking the Jews for their lack of knowledge.[9] These words reflect the early maskilim's sense of intellectual inferiority in relation to European scholars, as well as the hope that the Jewish cultural world would expand in the near future. These feelings, often expressed by the early maskilim, also resonate in the writing of one of the first Jewish students in a German university—Tobias Cohen (1653– 1729), born to a Polish family in Metz. In his introduction to his science and medical book, *Ma'aseh Tuvyah* (1707), he explains how he was motivated by his encounter and that of his friend Gabriel ben Moshe of Brode, with Christian scholars and students at Frankfurt-on-Oder University in 1678–79 to try to rehabilitate the reputation of the Jews. He was bitterly frustrated by the fact that he lacked the proper knowledge to cope with the new cultural world:

So that we may reply to the nations of the world who open their mouths without measure and speak of us arrogantly, saying you have no mouth with which to answer us, nor the impudence to raise your heads in matters of faith, and you have lost your wisdom and intelligence of yore, as I have heard the calumny of many in the days of my youth. And in truth the men of the house of learning [Frankfurt University] do us great honor and each and every day debate with us on matters of faith at length as is their wont. And at times they have reproached us, saying where is your wisdom and intelligence? It has been taken from you and given to us, for you have no knowledge . . . and thus they reproached us every day. We were filled with shame instead of glory, and had it not been for the mercy and help of the Almighty, we could not have raised our heads to answer them. For we had no experience in such debates. Although we were, thank God, proficient in the verses of the Talmud and the *midrashim*, in debates with them we were appallingly deficient. Then the spirit of jealousy came upon me and I took an oath that with God's help I would write a book containing some *chokhmot* and knowledge that I may answer those who reproach me and show them that not to them alone were the *chokhmot* given.[10]

We hear the voice of another early maskil in an encomium in verse written in Amsterdam in 1766 to the author of the book *Amudei bet Yehudah* (Pillars of the House of Judah), the physician Judah Hurwitz (1734–97), a native of Vilna who studied medicine in Padua. This Hebrew poem was written by the poet, writer, and linguist Naphtali Herz Wessely (1725–1805), better known as the author of the pamphlets *Divrei shalom ve'emet* (Words of Peace and Truth), which were disseminated from Berlin at the beginning of the 1780s, as an ardent response to the Jewish legislation (Edict of Toleration) of the Austrian emperor Joseph II. In 1766, Wessely was still living in Amsterdam, in the company of Sephardi and Ashkenazi men of letters, and was already well known as a scholar of the Hebrew language and author of the grammar book *Gan na'ul* (Amsterdam 1765–66). Others in this circle in Amsterdam were David Franco-Mendes (1713–92), Isaac Hacohen Belinfante (1720–80), David Wagenaar, and from 1767, Shlomo Dubno (1738–1813). In 1740, a society of scholars and literary men (Chevrat Mikra Kodesh) was founded there, and in the 1760s, Mendes and Wessely's group often met in the home of Shmuel Baruch Benavente to study together, among other works, Maimonides's *Guide for the Perplexed*.[11] The society maintained contacts with its counterpart in Berlin. When Mendelssohn's widely acclaimed book *Phädon* was published in 1767, several scholars in Amsterdam persuaded David Wagenaar to translate this philosophical work on the afterlife from German into Hebrew. Several years passed before Wagenaar sent Mendelssohn the manuscript of his translation (which was never published) for his opinion. In his accompanying letter, Wagenaar sent special regards to Wessely, then living in Berlin, from the members of the Amsterdam society. Whenever one of them published a book, the others were in the habit of appending poems of friendship to it, to encourage the author and express their identification with his aims. Wessely wrote his encomium, which was printed on the frontispiece of *Amudei bet Yehudah* in honor of the "wise and perfect maskil," Judah Hurwitz, who had recently been warmly welcomed into the group. This was a kind of poetic approbation for a very special book, one that proposed a rationalist religion in response to the challenge posed by both mysticism and skepticism.[12] Two years later, in a letter to Mendelssohn, Wessely articulated his harmonistic religious approach, one that combined Torah, science, and philosophy and concurred with Hurwitz's view: "All truths are from one God, faith, the Torah and the true tradition, nature and philosophy, they are all from the one Shepherd, all are God-given truths, and blessed is he who strengthens beliefs with rational proofs."[13]

We have now heard four voices, representing the subtypes of the early Haskalah. The first voice was that of university students and physicians, who created the basis of the new (and in fact, almost the only) Jewish academic intelligentsia, which emerged in the eighteenth century, and were among the first to grapple with the challenges of the new science and of religious skepticism. The second voice was that of the merchant and social critic Isaac Wetzlar. He represented the cultured bourgeoisie, merchants and men of wealth, who possessed broad Jewish and European knowledge, with a rationalist orientation and the desire to correct flaws in Jewish society, a desire apparently influenced to a large extent by the economic and political rationalism of absolutist and mercantile Europe. The third voice represented the early maskilim who were members of the religious elite—community rabbis, preachers, and talmudic scholars. The fourth and last voice, resonating through Wessely's words, represented the independent intellectual, who has no diploma but no longer belongs to the circle of talmudic scholars, and whose interests lie in the fields of literature, poetry, and linguistic and biblical studies.

These four early maskilim were well versed in all facets of the religious culture, but they had explicitly rejected or deliberately ignored the Kabbalistic trends of Judaism. All four had an affinity—direct or literary—with the intellectual world of Europe (in particular of Germany) in the era of the Enlightenment, and revealed their sensitivity to the place and images of the Jews in that world. Above all, the four represented a prototype of the new Jewish intellectual—the author, the poet, and the man of science. Over the years, this type carved out a path for himself, acquired dominant positions in society, and played a role in the intellectual elite, in contrast to the traditional elite. The encomiums written by poets like Wessely can easily be seen as a secular alternative to the rabbinical approbations. Although rabbinical approbations also appeared in books written by early maskilim, they had only a religious validity, while the poet provided a literary approbation. He judged the work and its author based on their quality, not on their religious contribution. As we shall see later, a conscious decision to forego rabbinical approbations amounted to a rebellious defiance of the rabbis.

"Precursors of the Haskalah" or "Early Maskilim"?

Although the names and writings of many of the early maskilim are scattered in various studies on the Haskalah, their appearance is relatively marginal and often takes the form of a brief biographical lexicon. They are almost always related to as isolated figures whose connection to the overall context is problematic and confusing. The absence of an integrative discussion of the early maskilim is striking in view of their varied achievements—Hebrew texts in mathematics, geometry, physics, astronomy, and medicine, studies on the Hebrew language, and reprintings of medieval and Renaissance books on science and philosophy. From a later perspective, the early Haskalah was seen to be lacking in cohesiveness and very hard to pin down; hence, it was classified as the crude precursor of the Haskalah, and its proponents were defined as the "precursors of the Haskalah."

From then on, things became complicated. If engaging in "external *chokhmot*" and publishing nonreligious books are the criteria of "enlightenment," then when did the Haskalah begin? With the Italian Kabbalist and poet Moses Hayim Luzzatto and his 1743 play *Layesharim tehilah*?[14] As early as the Western Sephardic diaspora in the seventeenth century, especially in Amsterdam? Or perhaps even earlier, in Italy during the Renaissance?[15] Or with the rabbis Emden and Eybeschuetz, who were regarded by several scholars as pre-Mendelssohnian German maskilim? Or with Tobias Cohen, the physician and author of the impressive book *Ma'aseh Tuvyah*?[16] Or did it in fact begin with the Gaon of Vilna, whose encouragement of translations into Hebrew of science books was related in the winter of 1777 to Baruch Schick?[17]

It is possible that the historical concept that underlies the term "precursors of the Haskalah" is in itself an anachronism, one that every historian must be wary of. Perhaps the more fitting criterion is not the actual encounter with new ideas or a positive attitude toward new knowledge, but rather the internalization of new modes of thought and the formation of an ideology that could propose alternative norms for the society.[18] And perhaps one should not be overly impressed by rabbis who praised the study of the *chokhmot* or by scholars who took the trouble to print an out-of-date science book that bore only faint traces of modern science. It seems that nearly every scholar of the Haskalah movement has related to these questions. And each and every one of them has created a structure into which he introduced the "precursors of the Haskalah" or its pioneers and forerunners—those who heralded Mendelssohn in Germany and the nineteenth-century maskilim in Eastern Europe.[19]

The truth of the matter is that the "precursors of the Haskalah" are a nineteenth-century invention, intended to prove that the Haskalah movement had immanent roots and to present it as a continuous trend throughout Jewish history, one that is not contradictory to the tradition. The maskilim's self-consciousness of introducing a cultural and social approach that seemed to them an innovation and a breakthrough led them to invent the "precursors" as a moderating concept, one which gave them legitimation.

The first to invent this concept was Moses Mendelson-Frankfurter of Hamburg (1784–1862), a maskil of the second phase of the Haskalah movement. In the mid-nineteenth century, he composed what amounted to a lexicon of "precursors," ranging from rabbis Emden and Eybeschuetz and the Vilna Gaon to the *dayan* Baruch Schick, Rabbi Shimshon of Slonim, Israel Zamosc, and Raphael Levy of Hanover, a teacher, mathematician, and astronomer. The man known as the "second Mendelssohn" wrote this lexicon, first printed in *Orient* in 1848 (although it had been written early in the century), in order to stress the sustained innovativeness of Jewish intellectuals in past generations and the enlightenment of scholars in the traditional society. All this in order to reject the claims made by the new reform rabbis about the backwardness of traditional Jewish culture.[20]

The second "inventor" was Isaac Baer Levinsohn (1788–1860), the main figure in the Haskalah movement in Russia in the second quarter of the nine-teenth century. In his 1828 book *T'eudah beYisra'el* (A Testimony in Israel), Levinsohn constructed a glorious lineage for the Haskalah, which included Tobias Cohen, Moses Hayim Luzzatto, Rabbi Hayim Bachrach, Israel Zamosc, the Vilna Gaon, and many others. They all joined an imposing gallery of schol-ars that continues an uninterrupted dynasty from antiquity. Levinsohn wanted to convince his conservative readers, members of the East European scholarly elite, that the Haskalah was not revolutionary or opposed to tradition. At the most, it was restorative, with the aim of restoring past glory, and was definitely not alien to Judaism.[21] The moderate maskil Shmuel Yosef Fuenn went even farther than these two. In his 1881 *Safah lene'emanim* (Language for the Faith-ful), he published a detailed, comprehensive chronological lexicon that con-tained the names of scores of scholars from previous generations. He supported the view of the moderate maskilim, that "the light of the religious and scientific Haskalah" had never been extinguished, and that the founding fathers of the Haskalah were unquestionably Mendelssohn and the Vilna Gaon.[22]

This invention of "the precursors" is so transparent that no contempo-rary scholar need invest any special effort to refute it. Nonetheless, in recent years only a few attempts have been made to resolve this problem. Several his-torians, in particular Salo Baron and Yitzhak Baer, have ventured beyond the "inventors" of the "precursors," and have been tempted to see the "new spirit" and the religious skepticism, which characterized Jews in sixteenth- and seventeenth-century Italy and Holland, as portents of the eighteenth-century Haskalah. In contrast to them, Yosef Kaplan stated that "it would seem appro-priate to draw a clear line of separation between the world of the Sephardi Jews of Amsterdam in the seventeenth century and the Jewish world in the second half of the eighteenth century in the centers where a great change took place with regards to tradition."[23] In his view, there is no affinity or continuity between seventeenth-century Sephardic intellectuals, whose Haskalah never matured, and the eighteenth-century Berlin Haskalah movement. They are separated by two major characteristics. The former had no ideology of chang-ing Jewish society, and they exploited their natural command of European cul-ture, of languages and the values of the environment that they acquired from their native countries and education, as a means of actually strengthening the authority of Jewish tradition. These "new Jews" in the centers of Western Sephardi Jewry "did not need to break down any walls that separated them from the culture of the European environment; they came to Judaism immersed in the cultural values of the countries of their origin."[24]

Recently, Immanuel Etkes has systematically examined the validity of the term "precursors of the Haskalah in Eastern Europe," and, based on coherent methodological distinctions, dismissed the myth that the Vilna Gaon was a proponent of the Haskalah.[25] Without rejecting the validity of this term, Etkes suggests that the phenomenon should be observed with great caution and precision, and viewed, as he defines it, "as a new direction first exhibited in the spiritual life of Polish-Lithuanian Jewry in the second half of the eighteenth century, a kind of interim phenomenon between the traditional way of life and the Haskalah movement in its mature manifestations."[26] However, this interim phenomenon, which characterized a thin layer of society, was not stable, in his view. One can discern in it a constant ascent on the ladder of the Haskalah, from a less developed to a more developed model of "precursors." At the foot of this ladder are the Gaon of Vilna (a "distant precursor") and Rabbi Solomon of Chelm, and at its head is the mature Haskalah (the Galician maskil Menahem Mendel Lefin, 1749–1826).

Another new approach was proposed by David Fishman. His study focused on Rabbi Baruch Schick of Shklov (1744–1808), Rabbi Judah Leib Margolioth (1751–1811), and Rabbi Benjamin Rivlin (1728–1812). He proposed a new definition, "an enlightened variant of *mitnagedim*," one more appropriate, in his opinion, to the middle-of-the-road position taken by these men, who belonged to the rabbinical elite but also engaged in science. Fishman's meticulous study on Baruch of Shklov is extremely important, not only because it showed how Schick combined science and Kabbalah, but also because it attested to the changes that occurred in his views over the years. Until he met with Mendelssohn's circle in Berlin, no traits of "Haskalah" can be attributed to him, and there is no basis for defining him as a "precursor of the Haskalah." However, in Fishman's view, he later unwittingly internalized several of the Haskalah's values, to the point that the epithet "a maskilic rabbi" fit him.[27]

The confusion about the "precursors" is also reflected in the character of Rabbi Jacob Emden (1698–1776). In contrast to those who regarded Emden not only as a "precursor of the Haskalah," but as a pre-Mendelssohnian maskil, Jacob Schacter states that Emden was one of the last great scholars of the Middle Ages, not one of the first modernists. In an extensive discussion, Schacter looks at the extent to which Emden was really open to *chokhmot* and how anxious he was to obtain books and knowledge outside of the religious culture. He concluded that despite the resemblance he bears to the maskilim, Emden cannot be regarded as a "precursor of the Haskalah" because of his total commitment to the tradition. Nonetheless, Schacter does not overlook the inner tension between Emden's consciousness of the "new" and his adherence to the "old."[28]

David Sorkin examined the historical role of those doctors and rabbis who were members of the small group described as Mendelssohn's teachers: the physician Avraham Kisch of Prague, Israel Zamosc, and Aaron Gumpertz. Sorkin does not accept the simplistic approach that prevailed in the research on German Jewry in the generation before Mendelssohn. He puts forward two arguments: first, the maskilim in this generation belonged to the mainstream and were not perceived as moving against the tradition; second, their efforts were aimed first and foremost at rejuvenating the Jewish intellectual world by offering a new interpretation, based on internal sources that had been neglected, on the literal, *peshat* meaning of the written text, and on auxiliary sciences and external sources.[29] Sorkin used the term "early Haskalah" to account for the entire phenomenon, and justifiably included in it Mendelssohn himself.[30]

David Ruderman made a different suggestion, in an attempt to circumvent the historiographic problem so as to evade its limitations and to discuss actual content. In his comprehensive book on the Jews in relation to the new science, he devoted a special chapter to Zamosc, Gumpertz, and the physician Mordechai Gumpel Schnaber-Levison (1741–97). Instead of focusing on their affinity with the Haskalah, as "precursors" or in any other way, Ruderman proposed an examination of their thinking about science and philosophy, against the background of the developments in these fields from the sixteenth century, as a result of the "continuous encounter of the Jews with the scientific culture of Europe" and as a response "to particular developments within the scientific culture of the eighteenth century."[31]

These suggested solutions for the issue of "precursors" are important because they relate seriously to the persons and texts in question and attempt to examine the issue as an historical phenomenon, whether as an "interim phenomenon," a "bridge," or an "early" phenomenon. The view that men like the Vilna Gaon and Rabbi Emden are not "precursors of the Haskalah" also helps clarify the historical countenance of that intellectual trend. Still, several problems remain in theories about the "precursors." Most of these theories regard the "early Haskalah" as almost totally dependent on the later Haskalah, and they gauge the former according to the qualities and attributes of the latter. They tend to describe the phenomenon by means of a biographical lexicon, and most of them divide the early maskilim into two paths that never intersect—the precursors of the West on the one side and those of the East on the other. While it may have been easy to fit secular figures, like physicians, into the increasing modernization that preceded the Haskalah, it was very confounding in relation to men from the rabbinical elite who tended to take an interest in *chokhmot*. The focus on the writings of the early maskilim and the identification of select passages and sentences that refer to *chokhmot* and "inquiry" still fail to thoroughly address the subject in a satisfactory manner. Very few scholars have acknowledged the need to examine the changes that early maskilim underwent over the years, which led them to utterly change their outlook. Another problem is how to arrange the early maskilim chronologically: whether to place them, as is generally done, in the early stages of the Haskalah process, or to relate to them according to the nature of their activity, since, as a matter of fact, there were early maskilim active during the mature Haskalah, and in Germany even during the years of its decline.

The solution proposed in this book for the issue of the "precursors" does not consist only of a change in name, that is, by replacing the definition "precursors" by that of "early maskilim." Rather it lies in a definition of this historical phenomenon as an autonomous trend, which is not dependent on the mature Haskalah movement. The early Haskalah was an important trend in the history of the development of the Jewish intellectual elite in the eighteenth century, although certainly not the dominant one. Probably only after this trend is thoroughly examined in its own right will it be possible to clarify whether it was one of the roots of the Haskalah movement.

The early Haskalah existed in various places in Jewish Europe, from Courland and Lithuania to Amsterdam and London. It was active for a number of generations (particularly in the second half of the century), and Sephardim like Moses Luzzatto (1707–47) and the poet and scholar from Amsterdam David Franco-Mendes took part in it, each in his own way, but it was primarily Ashkenazi. One did not belong to the early Haskalah only on the basis of complete commitment or formal membership. Since it was not a distinct, organized movement, those who followed this intellectual path, in full or in part, were not, in most cases, identified as belonging to a trend with clear-cut features. In defining a Jew as an early eighteenth-century maskil, one does not necessarily divest him of his traditional definition—as a rabbi, talmudic scholar, or preacher. As long as the "maskil" did not give up his previous lifestyle and was identified in Jewish society as a particular type on his own, he belonged to both worlds. Rabbi Jacob Emden, for example, absorbed the spirit of the early Haskalah to a large extent; he grappled with his strong leanings toward the expanding world of knowledge offered by the European Enlightenment culture, and even admitted as much in his autobiography, *Megilat sefer* (Scroll of the Book). However, he curbed these leanings because of his deep religious conviction that science and enlightenment, and philosophy in particular, were a dangerous threat to the traditional world. In his autobiographical confession, again and again Emden stressed his twofold sense of shame—

toward the scholars in his Jewish environment for neglecting his Torah studies, and toward the non-Jews for his ignorance of European culture. Finally, he allotted his free time, hours he was not obliged to devote entirely to Torah study, to general knowledge: "I am careful not to read or peruse them, other than in a place where it is forbidden to ponder matters relating to the Torah."[32] As we shall see later, Jacob Emden was not the only one who suppressed his desire for enlightenment.

Most of the literary activity of the early maskilim took place between the 1740s and the beginning of the 1780s, before the mature Haskalah crystallized. However, the term "early" does not demarcate only the pre-maskilic chronological phase; it also denotes a series of characteristics that make it possible to define this historical phenomenon and to point out the various types that represented it. The early Enlightenment is already a well-known term in the study of the Enlightenment movement, particularly in relation to the German *Aufklärung*, so we can borrow it for the Jewish phenomenon, although there is only a partial similarity between the two.

In the periodization of the *Aufklärung* movement in Germany, the end of the seventeenth century and the beginning of the eighteenth century are defined as the early phase, the *Frühaufklärung*. This phase is represented by intellectuals, most of them writers and thinkers from the universities of Protestant Germany, who proposed key ideas afterward developed in the later Enlightenment. The most prominent of these men were Samuel Pufendorf, Christian Thomasius, Gottfried Leibniz, and Christian Wolff. Among the contributions they made to the Enlightenment culture were their introduction of German as the language of literature and academic study in place of Latin, their conception of the humanistic ideal according to which men of reason would learn to know nature and themselves, and their conviction that man's purpose in life is to educate himself to attain personal and moral perfection. This intellectual elite believed, in general, that enlightenment is compatible with religion. They perceived God as present in the world, and sharply rejected atheism. Nonetheless, the seeds of the secularization of thought were also sown in these circles.

Christian Wolff (1679–1754) was the first to demand autonomy for philosophy ("the science of the possible," as he defined it), arguing that it deserved the status of an independent science, not that of an introduction to theology. He drew a distinction between eternal and rational truths and those that originate in the holy scriptures. This idea was a source of direct inspiration for the Jewish philosophers of the early Haskalah, first and foremost Moses Mendelssohn. As a philosopher, Wolff preached a religion that is tenable—natural theology. He demanded of the theologians that they adopt rationalistic philosophical thought, which he maintained had supreme intellectual authority, and he endowed the Enlightenment philosopher with autonomy. The early Enlightenment was disseminated through books, periodicals, and moral weeklies, and its expanding readership was hungry for knowledge about the world and for guidance on how to properly mold their lives, with positive bonds to the state, to religion, nature, and human beings.[33] The gap between the early European Enlightenment and the early Haskalah resulted from several causes: it was impossible to create an academic Jewish intellectual elite because the gates of academia were closed to Jewish teachers; there were very few Jewish philosophers, and it was necessary to legitimate the acquisition of general knowledge, which seemed to contradict the ideal of total dedication to Torah study. But the two did have something in common: trends of rationalization, eagerness to create a new literature in the language of the original culture, negation of the connection created by their opponents between enlightenment and education and the loss of religious faith, and stress on the aim of educating and molding men and women.

A perusal of the new research on the Enlightenment movement can also be helpful in studies on the early Haskalah. Thus, for example, Michael Heyd's conclusion that opposition to religious enthusiasm was one of the roots of the Enlightenment can also be apt to an analysis of the Haskalah, both the early and the mature.[34] Early maskilim, like Rabbi Shlomo of Chelm, Isaac Wetzlar, Israel Zamosc, Judah Hurwitz, Judah Leib Margolioth and Baruch Schick, all met with enthusiastic Kabbalists or with Sabbatians and Hasidim. And as we shall see later, these encounters unquestionably had a formative influence on their rationalistic views and their aspiration to improve and purify the Jewish religion, even if they were not directly affected by the spirit of the European Enlightenment.

However, it is vital to divert attention from the search for references to *chokhmot* (an approach that links the early maskilim particularly to the Haskalah's educational reforms and new curriculum) to the inclusion of the early Haskalah in a broader process—the emergence of the secular Jewish intellectual elite. Among the many definitions of "intellectuals," here we can adopt the broadest, like that of Edward Shils, who defined intellectuals as members of the social group that, more than any other, engages in intellectual pursuits, is endowed with intellectual faculties, is interested in the abstract, the absolute, and questions about nature and man, and aspires to the truth. Intellectuals are primarily active in producing and disseminating "high culture," and in endeavoring to influence the way in which society's image is shaped, out of a sense of mission, and often also out of a sense of unease in the face of the existing social reality.[35]

Secularization in Europe was characterized, among other things, by the process in which the elite, which drew its authority from a supernatural source, gradually relinquished its divine and clerical authority in culture and morality to elites that drew their authority from human experience and reason.[36] The Enlightenment's trend of secularization manifested itself, for example, in ousting theologians from key positions in the world of knowledge and study and rendering literature autonomous, free of religious considerations or authority.[37] A similar process occurred in Jewish society. The maskilim were the first secular intellectuals. The author, the physician, the philosopher, the student, and the periodical editor represented a new secular type of Jewish intellectual, who did not lose their commitment to faith, the study of Torah, and the observance of the commandments. This type was no longer defined by his talmudic scholarship or his rabbinic and community role, but rather by his ideas and intellectual capacity. The new elite became autonomous and gradually broke away from the rabbinical elite, which until then had enjoyed total exclusivity in the world of the book, knowledge, and the spiritual guidance of the Jews.[38]

And yet, many of the early maskilim maintained their ties to the rabbinical elite. Very few intellectuals were completely independent; Mendelssohn is a good example of one such intellectual, since he acquired his status as a philosopher first of all in an extra-Jewish society and culture. Maskilim who held rabbinical positions saw themselves and were seen by those around them as an integral part of the traditional elite. Obviously, some of them did endeavor to strengthen religious faith and to enhance the status of talmudic scholars, and regarded atheistic or deistic trends in Europe as a destructive threat to human patterns of behavior. Unlike the later maskilim, the early maskilim had no self-awareness of being "new Jews," living in a progressive historical era, better than its predecessors; nor did they develop coherent ideologies of transforming Jewish society. They had not yet been confronted by political challenges and demands posed by the state and by intellectuals for the overall rehabilitation (*Verbesserung*) of the Jews and their integration into society as citizens, like those faced by maskilim from the early 1780s. Nonetheless, some early maskilim were already pinning great hopes on a momentous change in European society's attitude toward the Jews. Nor did they present themselves as an alternative leadership of the public, or create institutionalized organizational frameworks. However, they did represent, consciously or otherwise, the starting point of that new, still immature elite: they sought universal knowledge about the world and mankind, were determined to nurture rationalistic Jewish thought, criticized flaws in Jewish society, and religion, denounced ignorance and superstition on the one hand, and heresy and religious permissiveness on the other, were sensitive to changes and crises among Jews in their generation, and were exposed to the Enlightenment culture—through direct contacts with Christian scholars or through books.

Chapter Two
The Early Haskalah and the Redemption of Knowledge

Intense curiosity and a strong drive to acquire knowledge not easily accessible within the culture of the traditional Jewish society were the hallmarks of the early maskilim. From the vantage point of the twenty-first century, it is hard to appreciate how much audacity these men needed to venture into the realms of the forbidden extra-Jewish and extra-religious knowledge. To satisfy their passion for knowledge, they had not only to cross barriers of language and social norms, but also to cope with the fear of undermining their religious faith. When a young Jew took a step like this it often had a subversive cultural and social implication: there was a significant difference between merely reading a book and studying medicine at a university where the student was exposed to the new science. To appreciate the momentous significance of this step, we need to listen with sensitivity to the voices of those intellectuals of the time describing their passion for knowledge as a spiritual, even a religious experience that carried a special meaning.

"The uncontrolled mob inside me has a strong craving to learn the science of medicine," Benjamin Wolf Ginzburg, a medical student at Göttingen University, wrote in 1737 to Rabbi Jacob Emden in Altona. He used biblical associations and images that signified unrestrained passion for something forbidden. Although in principle Rabbi Emden was opposed to Jews pursuing academic studies and stressed the religious dangers lying in wait for a Jew in a European university outside the confines of the community, he was unable to conceal his envy of the young student who was in the company of scholars, surrounded by books of science. He urged Ginzburg to find in academia answers to questions that had been troubling him, for example, how reliable alchemy was as an exact science. At the end of his long halakhic response, which gave the student permission to observe an anatomy lesson on the Sabbath, Emden was unable to contain his own desire for knowledge. He concluded with words that reflected his erotic attraction and frustration: "Like you, I also crave to enter into a covenant with the sciences and to cleave unto them with love; I long to delve into the depths of scientific research, to uncover its secrets, to quench my thirst and to take my pleasure." But to his misfortune, "the sciences have despised me and have not let me come into them after the manner of all flesh and have banished me, driving me away with both hands, as if I were a worthless person."[1] Indeed, on many occasions similar feelings were voiced by frustrated rabbis whose occupation and status did not permit them to venture into the new spheres of knowledge they so longed for. Unfortunately they had to content themselves with writing enthusiastic approbations for books written by others and with making general declarations about their support of the early maskilim.

The Erotic Seductiveness of Knowledge

In the "war of books" waged between modernistic maskilim and the traditionalists, the forbidden book had a very subversive meaning. The maskilim utilized it as an agent of the modern era and as a weapon with which to demolish a world of traditional scholarship, in which cracks had already begun to appear, while the guardians of tradition dreaded its poisoned arrows. The power of the quasi-erotic attraction of the forbidden book is mentioned, for example, in an instance related by Rabbi Judah Leib Margolioth. Visiting the home of a religiously observant friend, he was surprised to discover there one of these "prohibited" books, whose author was already infamous as a man of weakened religious faith. To his astonishment, he saw that the book was in a state of deliberate neglect, "placed on a bench, nude and unbound, covered with dust and ashes." Margolioth, amazed by the double message—the very existence of the book, on the one hand, and its harsh neglect, on the other— queried his host: If you like this book, "why do you not cover its nudity?" and "If you dislike it, why do you not observe the ruling by burning and burying it?" The book owner's reply revealed at one stroke how intensely seductive that tattered forbidden book was, a temptation that for very good reason was aptly depicted in erotic terms: "Brother, know that what happened to me in taking [this book] was akin to lust for a beautiful maiden; I desired it and was seduced into buying it. And as it befits upright men to urge their good inclinations to overcome their bad inclinations, my heart told me to treat this book according to the commandment of the Torah [Numbers, 21, 10–14], as a man of Israel ought to conduct himself with a comely maiden." For this reason, he did not refrain from acquiring the book and bringing it into his home; for the very same reason, he treated the book, which had become both enticing and threatening, an object of disgrace—by tearing off the binding, placing it on a bench, and abandoning it to the dust. He did this in the hope that in this ugly and abject form, the book would seem contemptible in his eyes and his longing to read it would subside. It is similar to the case of a man who desires a woman taken captive in the turmoil of war, and she sits in his home, weeping and mourning, in the hope that she will lose her sexual attractiveness: "Then I will be disgusted by it, and will set it on fire, and the disgrace will be gone from my home."² However, Margolioth rejected this sanctimonious pretext, and demanded that the book owner suppress his desire without further ado, and not put himself to the test of temptation. If the book is still in your possession, Margolioth insisted, that means "your heart still yearns for it," and you are sure to throw off all restraint in your great desire for it. Hence, you must banish it from your house immediately.

The image of the alien and the external, of the sciences, of Christian apostasy, and in particular of philosophy, as a loose woman, an illegal wife, a rival of the Torah, which is the legal wife, or as a predatory prostitute, exploiting the weakness of the male, was often employed before the eighteenth century.³ The scholarly elite's encounter with science and philosophy was attended by a struggle against desire, guilt feelings, and a persisting attraction to the forbidden. Anyone who had attained his place in society by claiming that he was the embodiment of the supreme aspiration of Torah study day and night had to explain to himself and to his peers any deviation from this absolute ideal. In his well-known introduction to *Mirkevet hamishneh*, written in the rhymed, ornate prose characteristic of the baroque style of Hebrew writing, Rabbi Shlomo of Chelm (1715–1781) told of his attraction to science:

My heart clamored for the delights of wisdom, and I came unto her, and there were twelve springs of water and seventy palm trees, in the wisdom of whole numbers and fractions and of algebra, lovely and pure, and the wonders of geometry . . . and with my little finger I lightly touched the science of nature and what lies beyond it, to explore the seven columns, and walk among them, in the book *The Guide for the Perplexed*, in grammar and logic.⁴

But the rabbi apologized immediately after these words, explaining that although he was attracted to the sciences, he did not forget his priorities ("I did not replace the main thing by things of secondary importance") but took care to set aside to nonreligious knowledge only those free hours he was not obliged to devote to the study of the Torah.

The rabbi of Berlin, Zevi Hirsch Levin (1721–1800), known for his good relations with Mendelssohn, adopted a similar approach. He wrote a three-page approbation for the two-volume book printed by Baruch Schick of Shklov in Berlin in 1777, *Amudei hashamayim* (The Pillars of the Sky), a volume on astronomy, and *Tiferet adam* (The Glory of Man), on anatomy. Like Shlomo of Chelm, Rabbi Levin took care to point out that "The Torah is in itself a realm likened to a lady, to whom the sciences are as maidservants," and yet this in no way justified ignorance. Although the traditional approach legitimized the study of science for the purpose of clarifying certain *halakhot*, or because of the historical "fact" that ancient Judaism was the source of the sciences—a well-known view that appropriated extra-Jewish knowledge and permitted its internalization—in his view, this did not suffice. Hence, he confessed to his sorrow and frustration at his own ignorance: "While in my youth I drew somewhat near to the gates of science like someone dipping his toe in the sea, only what is needed for an understanding of the *halakhot*, yet the major themes and strong proofs were concealed from me."[5]

This marked tendency of attraction to the *chokhmot* in Jewish Ashkenazi culture began in the first half of century; Benjamin Ginzburg and Shlomo of Chelm were preceded, among others, by Tobias Cohen, author of *Ma'aseh Tuvyah*, the previously mentioned medical students Shmuel Ben-Yaacov and Isaac Wallich, Meir Neumark, Shlomo Zalman Hanau, and Raphael Levi of Hanover.

Meir ben Judah Loeb Neumark (apparently born in 1688) was not yet twenty years of age when he began translating German and Latin books of physics, astronomy, geography, and history into Hebrew. The son of the manager of the Hebrew printing house in Berlin at the turn of the eighteenth century, Neumark moved to Frankfurt and studied in Nikolsburg, Moravia, under the patronage of the court Jew, David Oppenheim, a well-known rabbi and collector of books. Oppenheim encouraged him to try his hand at translation, which he regarded as highly important, and after seeing one sample of Neumark's translations, urged him to continue. Although all Neumark's translations were edited and prepared for publication, none were actually printed. Two of them, *Tokhen hakadur* and *Tekhunot havaya*, on astronomy and physics, remained in manuscript form in Oppenheim's library, and they attest not only to the young man's impressive intellectual endeavors, but also to his purpose. He was anxious to disseminate knowledge about all aspects of the world, to publicize the newest scientific and geographical discoveries, and to open a window on the world for the Jewish reader, based on the most recent European literature. Fluent in European languages and a member of the wealthy elite, Neumark was responsive to extra-Jewish knowledge, and provided his readers with a list of reasons for justifying "the study of the external *chokhmot*." He made no effort to conceal his attraction to European culture: "I found no rest until I took up books that thoroughly and correctly explain everything, and those I chose to translate into our holy tongue."[6]

Shlomo Zalman Hanau (1687–1746) was of the same generation as Neumark. He spent most of his life in Hamburg and Amsterdam, but in his old age lived in Berlin and Hanover. In 1708, only twenty-one years of age, he published his first book, *Binyan Shlomo*, on Hebrew grammar. He unabashedly revealed his intellectual passion, raising to a sublime level the medieval term "inquiry," which in the eighteenth century became one of the code words of rationalism and of the Jewish Enlightenment (that rarely used the term "Haskalah"):

The Almighty has instilled in man's heart intelligence and wisdom and the sense to understand and know what is good and what is bad until he nearly attains the state of the angels . . . so that he may through the depth of his thought and his artifice plumb the very nature of the matter and comprehend the innate value of inquiry and study until in his wisdom he conceives of that which is hidden from the eye of every living thing, no bird of prey knows the path there; the falcon's keen eye cannot descry it, and no human being knows its value.[7]

Nothing can withstand the critical power of "inquiry," Hanau asserted. He proved his claim by citing examples from the words of commentators and rabbis, whose ignorance of the language caused them, in his view, to misunderstand the Bible. But at the beginning of the century such an audacious comment was far too radical, and the young man was resolutely called upon to apologize on a special page affixed to the printed copies of his book. Hanau's apology took the form of a personal confession of a man repenting his deeds:

The author said: Here I have stumbled, erring in the opinions I voiced of these writers; I have spoken too freely and have shown disrespect to sages (although I did not do so in rebellion or treachery, nor did I entertain any abominable thoughts in contempt of [these] sages. . . . I merely meant to excite the minds of my readers and to encourage them to study). Hence I come to ask their forgiveness.[8]

In particular, he begged the forgiveness of Rabbi Issac Abarbanel, the commentator Abraham Ibn Ezra, and other sages, whom he had dared to criticize and to expose some of their grammatical errors. Hanau also admitted that he had wrongly strayed from the straight and narrow path and promised he would not fall back into his wicked ways: "Verily I stand here and repent these things; my errors are incomprehensible; my intemperance shall not cause my mouth to utter such things again and God will atone for me."

Hanau's character can be reconstructed from his introduction to his book *Tzohar hateivah* (The Window of the Ark/Word) (1733), one of the most widely circulated Hebrew books in the eighteenth century. From the age of forty-six, he already allowed himself to imply his defiance of his critics and to argue that the promise to repent he had been forced to make was not really sincere, and that he was still committed to his rational views. He declared that the investigator must remain resolute and fixed on his views, and not give in to persecutions and attacks; certainly he ought not to pay heed to the loud voices of those representing "imagination"—an irrational and uncritical trend. The scholar must be an intellectual, bent on a great mission, based on the reasoning of his intelligence: "This is the learning of man which the light of his intelligence will illuminate and beautify, to make his entire purpose to perfect others, and to influence them by his own splendor . . . and he must not cast off the burden of study and the labor of inquiry that relies on his reason, nor to be content with that which the imagination draws forth at first sight, but must endeavor to thoroughly probe in his investigation."[9]

Indeed, this one example substantiates the claim that to fully probe the historical significance of the early Haskalah, one must do more than emphasize positive references to the *chokhmot*. The self-awareness of the early maskil, the *choker*, or philosopher, is far more important. Even if he were not yet cut off from the scholarly elite, he did strive to define his own intellectual endeavor, which, at this stage, was focused on his aspirations as a writer and philosopher and on his commitment to the rational criteria of science and his professional specialization. These traits and this self-awareness gradually set him apart from the intellectual elite, which at the time was almost exclusively made up of talmudic scholars.

One of the first to achieve the autonomous status of a Jewish philosopher and man of science was Raphael Levi of Hanover (1685–1779), a contemporary of Neumark and Hanau. He apparently acquired a knowledge of European languages, mathematics, and philosophy through his own efforts, although his yeshivah studies in Frankfort-on-Main were his only formal education. At first, he worked as a bookkeeper for the court Jew, Wolf Oppenheimer of Hanover. Then for six years he lived under the protection and in the home of the philosopher Leibniz. Afterward, he earned his living as a mathematics and astronomy teacher, gathering around him pupils as well as many admirers. These contacts with the Jewish mercantile and financial elite and with non-Jewish intellectuals enabled him to be independent. His books in Hebrew, printed during the 1750s and '60s, which included various astronomical calculations, many timetables, and drawings, he signed with the title "The engineer, the astronomer and philosopher, Raphael Halevi of Hanover."[10] The declared purpose of his research was religious, for example to clarify Maimonides' complex rulings on the sanctification of the new moon. In his introduction to the astronomy book *Tekhunot hashamayim*, he stated that the aim of the book was to make its readers knowledgeable in astronomy, so that the Jews may "learn from it and thus understand the grandeur of the Creator and master of the heavens."[11] He left behind a manuscript in which he calculated the End of Days based on Daniel's prophecy, and declared that anyone who does not believe in the Messiah is a heretic. At the end of that manuscript, he added several guidelines to enhance the devoutness of prayer.[12] Despite his piety and his messianic expectations (traits that also characterized Christian scholars in the early modern era), Raphael Levi can be viewed as a man of the European Enlightenment, whose world was the new world of science and philosophy. This is evinced not only by his teacher-student relations with Leibniz, but also by his portrait. The picture is one of a typical eighteenth-century scholar in European garb (a wig and fashionable collar), alongside him the symbols of science—measuring instruments, a globe, a telescope, writing utensils, and of course, books.[13] On his passion for knowledge, his total dedication to science, and his desire to redeem astronomy and the other *chokhmot* the Jews had neglected, Levi wrote:

In this last generation, in the travails of the long exile, we have almost entirely lost our ancient sagacity, and no one is inclined to study and probe these profound matters, so much so that we have plummeted from the highest peak to the very lowest abyss. Now instead of being superior to all the gentiles in our fame and glory, we have become objects of shame, mocked by all the nations. And I turned to seek out wisdom . . . I have seen that wisdom has an advantage over stupidity . . . and I grew very zealous, anxious to remove the taint of shame from our faces. I did not rest or desist from my efforts, turning nights into days until I filled many booklets with all of human wisdom, all the sciences, the natural, the philosophical and the divine, all beautifully arranged, from beginning to end, and all based on rational proofs.[14]

This suggests that Raphael Levi had written lengthy manuscripts on a wide variety of subjects, although only those on astronomy were published. After Mendelssohn's book *Phädon* was published, Levi, then eighty years of age, kept up a correspondence with him, one that reflected a dialogue between two Jewish philosophers, both faithful to Leibniz's teachings. In a 1767 letter Mendelssohn apologizes to Levi, in the tone of a student apologizing to his teacher, for his relatively popular book, which an expert like Levi was apt to find simplistic, and the two discussed the possibility of translating it into Hebrew.[15]

Aaron Gumpertz (1723–69), the scion of a wealthy Berlin family that belonged to the elite of affluent court Jews, another early maskil, in the 1740s was one of Mendelssohn's personal guides in his first foray into European culture. Gumpertz, unencumbered by any commitment to the rabbinical elite, was eager to acquire the protection and patronage of a teacher who was a notable Enlightenment figure, as Raphael Levi had received from Leibniz. In 1745 Gumpertz wrote to one of the luminaries of German literature, Professor Johann Gottsched, entreating him to become his teacher and patron in his Leipzig home. In his letter, Gumpertz described himself as a compulsive scholar, an autodidact who had already learned quite a lot, but who was troubled by the fact that there were many areas he had not yet studied and was eager to greatly expand his knowledge. Other than his religious studies, Gumpertz wrote, he had learned French and Latin, mathematics and the natural sciences, and now yearned to "imbibe the nectar of the sciences with a superb teacher like yourself."[16] This attempt to obtain academic patronage was unsuccessful, but Gumpertz, who even before the age of twenty had lived under the patronage of the French deist and adventurer the Marquis d'Argens and served as his secretary, did not despair. In the 1740s he found other patrons, including the president of the Prussian Royal Academy of Sciences, Pierre Louis Maupertuis, but twenty years later he had still not satisfied his hunger for knowledge. In *Ma'amar hamada* (Treatise on Science), a Hebrew introduction to science and philosophy and an apologetic essay on these subjects, intended for the scholarly elite, he wrote about his total dedication to his studies: "I shall undertake to learn the philosophical, natural, and divine sciences, as far as my feeble mind will enable me." Gumpertz's craving for more and more knowledge kept him from succumbing to the temptation of the easy self-indulgent life he could have enjoyed as the son of one of the richest Jewish families in Germany.[17] Moses Mendelssohn admired Gumpertz and warmly recommended his *Ma'amar hamada*, which comprehensively surveyed the "sea of *chokhmot*."[18]

The Redeemers of the Neglected Sciences

These Jewish intellectuals, who developed their formal or informal scholarship and their scientific and philosophical world by associating with non-Jewish intellectuals, represented only one end of the broad spectrum of the early Haskalah. At the other end, we find, for example, the model of the author who wrote with total dedication but under conditions of hardship, worries, and penury.

One such was Shlomo Dubno (1738–1813), a teacher, collector of books, linguist, and biblical scholar from Poland, who, in the 1760s and '70s lived in Amsterdam and Berlin. In a letter of complaint to Mendelssohn, he wrote about his scholarly pursuits: "I have given no sleep to my eyes or slumber to my eyelids, several midday meals at work I have not eaten, and many suppers I have forgone, and several nights of labor I have counted, until I arrived at the reward of my endeavors." At the time, Mendelssohn was engaged in his *Bi'ur* project (a German translation of the Pentateuch with a new Hebrew commentary). In his youth he had been a zealous scholar in Berlin, arriving from Dessau in 1743, where he became a merchant, community leader, and renowned philosopher. Dubno entreated him to note how "I have neglected my livelihood these past four years to persevere wholeheartedly in my work on this book, and have taken no pity on myself or on my only son." He did not conceal his envy of Mendelssohn, who did not have to spend every waking moment on his literary endeavor, but devoted only the pleasant morning hours to it before leaving for work at his commercial enterprise. Dubno recounted all his troubles to Mendelssohn, expressing his frustration at the fact that copies of Shlomo of Chelm's book *Sha'arei ne'imah*, which Dubno had printed in Frankfurt in 1766, "lie here in a corner, there is no demand for them, no interest in them, and many have I given as gifts to young men."[19] But none of these troubles deterred Dubno, an ardent book collector and merchant, who devoted his entire life to writing and printing books. The list of books in his library, which he compiled in Amsterdam in 1771, is a representative inventory of the Jewish book culture; it includes more than 350 books, including those written by early maskilim, which Dubno collected, sold, and distributed in his travels between Amsterdam and Vilna.[20]

The bookshelf of the early maskilim, which took shape throughout the eighteenth century, in particular in the second half of that century, is impressive and surprising in its scope and diversity. Many of these books were modest in size, of poor quality print, and their florid rabbinical or baroque style (in particular ornate, rhymed prose, replete with allusions, riddles, and associations) did not arouse much interest in later generations. But the sheer number of books the early maskilim brought to the printing press attests to the efforts they invested in building this alternative library. A representative list would include books on medicine and anatomy by Tobias Cohen, Baruch Schick, and Moses Marcuse; on linguistics by Shlomo Hanau and Naphtali Herz Wessely; on science—astronomy, mathematics, and chemistry—by Gumpertz, Worms, Raphael Levi, Jonathan of Ruzhany, Baruch Schick, Judah Leib Margolioth, and Pinhas Hurwitz; on philosophy by Israel Zamosc, Napthali Ullman, and Mendelssohn; and on ethics by Judah Hurwitz and Judah Leib Margolioth. Although these early maskilim usually did not coordinate the subjects of their books with one another, it would be a mistake to assume that it is a random collection of books. This was a creative endeavor with a twofold purpose: to move neglected layers of Jewish culture from the sidelines to the center by reprinting out-of-print books, and to purify and improve Jewish culture and religion, as well as here and there to remedy the flaws of Jewish society—the patterns of behavior and the moral code of its members.[21]

How may we correctly understand the meaning of the early maskilim's literary activity? First, it is important to note how they cautiously walked the tightrope between the legitimate and the forbidden. Second, one must examine the books on language, science, ethics, and philosophy printed during the eighteenth century to see whether they reflected a real change in the accepted traditional values and the patterns of literary activity, study, and cultural creativity. The very act of printing nonreligious books embodied a defiant—sometimes even a subversive—critique of the neglect of these important fields of knowledge. It would be correct to say that an assertive departure from this neglect was one of the distinctive features common to all the early maskilim. At the beginning of the century, in 1707, Tobias Hacohen had already cautioned against the neglect of scientific knowledge and the serious harm it caused to the image of the Jews. Yonathan ben Yosef, who fled the plague in Lithuanian Ruzhany in 1710, and ten years later printed his book *Yeshuah beYisrael* (Salvation in Israel) in Frankfurt, regarded himself as no less than the redeemer of astronomy ("Now, at this time, for our many sins, minds have dwindled, the skill of counsel has perished among our people, and wisdom has fled from them, for these many days they have not utilized her, so this wisdom lies in a corner, her face grown over with thorns, covered over with nettles").[22] Raphael Levi declared that his mission was to redeem "all of humankind's *chokhmot*," and Rabbi Shlomo of Chelm denounced the fools that discredit the study of the sciences and complained about their grievous neglect: "For the light has failed to shine for our people and its sun has set . . . and why should you turn aside from her, for she is your wisdom and your intellect, in the eyes of the nations."[23]

When the early maskilim were hard at work writing books in Hebrew, they regarded themselves as no less than the revivers of the language and the purifiers of the biblical text. Shlomo Zalman Hanau depicted himself as leading the renaissance of grammar: "Once I saw that this wisdom is hidden and neglected. No one inquired into it or sought it." He imputed to the "wisdom of grammar" immense significance in the development of intellectual ability and the refinement of Jewish culture, which centered on the Torah.[24] His student Naphtali Herz Wessely (whom Hanau taught linguistics in Copenhagen) adopted a similar approach. In his book *Gan na'ul* (A Locked Garden), printed in Amsterdam in 1765, Wessely offered his readers much more than a reference book to familiarize them with Hebrew roots. It was, in his words, a tool for clarifying and purifying the Bible for the purpose of truly comprehending it, for without a well-grounded knowledge of the language, the words of the Bible could never be properly understood. Like Hanau, who also influenced Wessely's sense of fulfilling the destiny of an author and scholar, he declared, "Since my youth I have loved the truth, and my heart seeks to find the true way." He regarded his book as a barricade against fools, on the one hand, and heretics ("wise men in their own eyes") on the other, since both of them fail to grasp the real truth.[25]

Kohelet musar, the Hebrew weekly edited by Tobias Bock and Moses Mendelssohn, which came out in Berlin for a short time in the middle of the century, also battled against the neglect of the Hebrew language. It suggested to its readers the idea of a real cultural revolution, like the one being conducted, in its view, in Europe—expansion of the classic language to a level that would enable the creation of a variegated secular literature, not restricted merely to religious content. Mendelssohn, who had already been living in Berlin for more than ten years, was then taking his first steps towards acceptance as an acknowledged member of the literary republic of Germany's enlightened. His first philosophical writings and his friendship with the author and playwright Gotthold Ephraim Lessing, who was instrumental in Mendelssohn's acceptance into Berlin intellectual circles, helped him attain a place in the German world of culture. As opposed to the generally accepted view, in the 1750s and '60s, Mendelssohn still regarded himself as belonging to Jewish society and culture, and in *Kohelet musar* he joined Tobias Bock in an endeavor to change the self-awareness of young Jews.

"And the Jews will see that our language is fit for every possible occasion, to lift our voice in weeping, to sing songs to gladden hearts, or to chastise the wicked at the gate," the editors of *Kohelet musar* wrote, conscious of their pioneering endeavor. It was incumbent on the Jews to engage in cultural activism, in keeping with the cultural trend of Enlightenment-age Europe: "We will learn from the other nations and their languages. They did not rest or leave off until they expanded the boundaries of their language. And why should we be as dreamers, loving to slumber and not do as they did with our own language, which is worthier and earlier in time?" Indeed, the endeavor to revive German and dislodge Latin from literature and academia was one of the distinctive features of the early Enlightenment in Germany.[26] Moreover, *Kohelet musar* provided its readers with a sphere of life that had hardly any legitimation in the traditional culture. The weekly called on the Jews to fill their lungs with the air of natural life, to freely observe the beauty of nature, to smell the fragrance of blossoms in spring, to nurture their sense of aesthetics and harmony. It is also their right to delight in a world that is, as Leibniz taught, the best of all possible worlds created by God. Man, "God's finest creature," is at the center of nature, and it is unthinkable that the Jew, of all people, should repress his humanistic traits:

In all my days on this earth, I have never seen a man pass through a field in which the plants are budding whose eyes did not wander from its beginning to its end. God gave man an eye with which to see, to be filled with pleasure as he beamed at the glory of all creatures. . . . And you are that human being! For your sake God has done His deeds. Because of you, meadows are clothed with grain, and under your feet every growing thing buds and blossoms.[27]

Man can discover the majesty of the Almighty and His powers by observing the creation of the great architect of the world. It is not only legitimate to take pleasure in the beauty of the world from a humanistic point of view; it is tantamount to a religious commandment.

From the beginning of the eighteenth century, the popular *musar* book *Kav hayashar* (The Straight Measure) was published in a number of editions, in Hebrew and Yiddish. It depicted the reality in gloomy, ominous colors and called on the Jews to be wary of innumerable forces of evil that were conspiring to do violence to their souls. The author of the book, the preacher Zevi Hirsch Koidonover, warned: "If only you knew how many evil demons are lying in wait for a quarter of the blood in your heart, you would certainly bind your heart and soul to the Creator, may He be blessed."[28]

Other early maskilim revealed the sensitivity to aesthetics in language, literature, nature and daily life that developed in the 1740s and '50s. For example, in 1766, Judah Hurwitz described the ideal house of the *chakham*—a spacious home embellished with works of art, where people listen to music, and alongside it a luxuriant garden, in which the learned homeowner strolls alone, taking pleasure in "the lushness of the *chokhmot.*" The aspiration for literary aesthetics was taken to new heights in Hurwitz's *Amudei bet Yehudah.* In addition to its rhymed prose and multiple linguistic embellishments, the book is presented to the reader as a splendid building in the elegant baroque style: a marble palace with large halls, offices, many rooms, and doors through which the reader can enter and stroll pleasantly. We can find other examples of literary aesthetics in Hanau's *Binyan Shlomo* and Wessely's *Gan na'ul.* They all invited the reader to take pleasure in his reading, to enter through the many doors opening wide before him, to stroll around the building and discover the surprises awaiting him behind each and every gate, or to peek through the "windows" of the locked garden.

In addition to discovering nature, aesthetics, and harmony in the world, the circles of early maskilim in the 1740s also called for the revival of the tradition of rationalist philosophy. The turning point came when Moshe Wolf in Jesnitz, near Dessau, published several new editions of out-of-print books, among them *Guide for the Perplexed*, which he printed in 1742. To appreciate the importance of its reprinting in Jesnitz, we need only note the formative influence of this medieval philosophical work on two philosophers, Moses Mendelssohn and Shlomo Maimon, who through it were exposed to the beguiling power of philosophy. We can assume that if the reprinted *Guide for the Perplexed* had not come into Mendelssohn's hands, he would have had a hard time becoming a philosopher of the German Enlightenment. Even if we are skeptical about the tale that Mendelssohn got his famous humpback because in his youth he was constantly bent over, concentrating intently on the *Guide*, the maskilim did learn from Maimonides the rhetoric of knowledge, his appeal to his fellow Jews to develop their intellect and learn to know God, and the ideal of the intellectual perfection of man. The rationalist messages formulated in the twelfth century were easily incorporated into the slogans of the eighteenth-century Haskalah.

In 1744, the book *Ruach chen*, a philosophical dictionary attributed to Judah Ibn Tibbon, was printed in Jesnitz. The publishers presented it as a reference tool for an understanding of the *Guide*[29] and appended to it a commentary by Israel ben Moshe Halevi of Zamosc (1710–72), an important early maskil, who showed a great deal of interest in the sciences and medieval philosophy, and also wrote a commentary on the *Kuzari* and on Bahya Ibn Paquda's *Chovot halevavot* (Duties of the Hearts). In the 1740s, he moved from Poland to Germany, where, as an independent scholar, he joined the circle of Gumpertz and Mendelssohn, which was supported by the wealthy patron Daniel Itzig, and became one of the militant defenders of "inquiry." In his apologetics on the *chokhmot*, Israel Zamosc represented the struggle the early maskilim saw themselves as waging—wisdom against folly. He invested much effort to prove that the knowledge the members of his circle were trying to introduce into Jewish culture would in no way endanger religious faith. In his first book, *Netzach Yisrael*, written in Galicia and printed in Frankfurt-on-Oder in 1741, he had leveled criticism at the flaws of traditional scholarship and the method of *pilpul* (the casuistic discussion of the Talmud). "Owing to this, we are sick at heart, our eyes grow dim, for the true study whose path has been made desolate," Zamosc lamented in the introduction to his book, which was a sharp denunciation of the rabbinical elite to which he had belonged. Many were in the habit, he added, of "despising all science and all knowledge unknown to them . . . and go so far as to call the sciences nonsense and folly."[30] In *Ruach chen*, he furiously assailed the "accursed insolent ones, the ignorant brutal men, many with us in this generation, who . . . [are] foolish to think that piety will decrease among those knowledgeable in the sciences."[31]

Zamosc's *Ruach chen* amounted to a defense of science and philosophy. He held that it was within the power of human intelligence to controvert the imagination to which the masses were inclined, to nullify false thoughts and to properly guide people in overcoming obstacles, in marked contrast to the traditional guidance based solely on religion. In his commentary, he included scientific knowledge (Galileo's telescope, the vacuum), but cautiously avoided taking a stand on major issues that had theological implications, such as the truth of Copernican cosmology. On the one hand, he admitted that Copernicus's view is "closer to the ways of astronomy," and that most of the gentile scholars support it, while on the other hand: "anyone getting so much as a whiff of his view is disgusted by it, regards it as opposed to the spirit of the Torah and the teachings of the Sages, as a heretic notion." He also left unresolved the question whether revelation was a subjective mental experience, which occurred when the mind was momentarily in "darkness," or perhaps an objective, realistic sight.[32] Although Israel Zamosc clearly implied what his view was on these sensitive issues, he was careful to avoid openly stating it, probably because he was regarded with suspicion, perhaps even persecuted because of his dedication to the *chokhmot*. This is evinced not only by his introduction to *Netzach Yisrael*, but also in his correspondence with Rabbi Jacob Emden in 1764, and the apologetic, defensive manner in which he introduced himself to the rabbi: "You may have heard many loud voices diminishing my worth and enlarging my shortcomings. But God knows that my entire purpose was to draw the waters of truth from the source of His wisdom."[33] We see then that early maskilim were already being denounced as deviants because of their passion for knowledge and their intellectual daring.

The all-embracing plan of the physician Anshel Worms of Frankfurt (1695–1769) merits special consideration. He wanted to print a series of books that, taken together, would comprise a complete corpus of scientific, philosophical, and religious knowledge, but very few of these volumes were actually printed. In 1722, when he was a twenty-seven-year-old student of medicine and philosophy at the University of Frankfurt, he had already published an algebra textbook "to open the gates of understanding to the nation which walks in the dark." In his literary introduction to the book, Worms depicted his intense attraction to knowledge and his self-image as a redeemer of the neglected *chokhmot*, by describing a utopian prophetic dream: Algebra appears in his vision in the figure of a beautiful maiden, who miraculously survived a shipwreck and was cast upon the beach of a spacious, flowering island. The maskil, as a hero destined to know the sciences, saw himself as the first to "know" (in the biblical sense) the maiden Algebra, whom he discovered in a state of neglect: "a virgin, very fair to look upon, whom no man had known, lying there her face pressed to the ground." The Jewish man of science fell in love with her, was strongly attracted to her sexually and restored her to life ("I emptied her of the water she had swallowed and anointed her body with oils and perfumes . . . until the breath of life was within her"). The maiden Algebra loved him in return and promised her savior that she would reveal all her secrets to him, because "you have rescued me and with your right arm have pulled me from the miry clay; had it not been for you, I would have been plunged into a deep pit, and now I shall walk in the land of the living."[34]

More than forty years passed before another book by the savior of the neglected sciences and the redeemer of virgins was published. "I have set my table, poured my wine, and placed upon it the bread of the Presence, lit up by several [of my] essays," Worms declared in 1766, stating that his aim was to reach a point where "in the paths of Zion which until now have been in darkness for the Jews, there shall be a bright light wherever they turn."[35] His book

Seyag laTorah (A Fence Around the Torah), which systematically dealt with the Masoretic tradition and the precise, pure wording of the Torah, was intended to serve as only one link in his great project. The seven chapters of the literary project were defined as "philosophical works," and included Hebrew grammar, the Masoretic tradition and biblical commentary, logic in general and talmudic logic in particular, metaphysics, the theoretical and practical sciences (geography, history, astronomy, geometry, mechanics, algebra, optics, and music), physics, and, finally, "practical philosophy and natural law." According to Worms, he had already written most of these chapters, and their wide distribution was being delayed only due to the printing costs. In his introduction, he therefore called on "the lovers of the sciences and the devotees of knowledge" to help him finance his project. But three years later he died, leaving behind only a few of his writings.

The physician from Frankfurt, like other early maskilim, was very sensitive to the inferiority of the Jews in these fields of knowledge in the age of Enlightenment. "You have become brutish and ignorant, like a stupid man who knows not how to wage a battle and to engage in combat in the war of religion and the argumentation of the sciences," Worms rebuked all those who did not properly appreciate the importance of the intellectual elite that was capable of coping with the challenges of the Enlightenment. However, Worms himself, as a rationalist who clung to tradition, was also aware of the challenges posed by modern philosophy and deistic views. He stated this explicitly in referring to the new philosophies, which because of their radical approach, were in his opinion a threat to religious faith:

Men such as Spinoza, Hobbs, Edelmann, and their ilk are going about praising themselves in the towns and districts, demanding respect and mocking every man of religion, the circumcised and the uncircumcised, who relies on the holy words written by the finger of God rather than on his own wisdom. If anyone believes that intelligence must submit to the words of the Almighty, King of the earth, they deride him, opening their mouths wide.[36]

Confronting Skepticism: The Noble Savage

The need to grapple with the challenge of the skeptical Enlightenment was also an important factor in the development of the early Haskalah, since it induced the maskilim to try to present a rationalist Jewish approach replete with wisdom and inquiry. In 1766, the very same year that Worms's book was printed, Judah Hurwitz proposed an original way of coping with contemporary skeptical approaches that challenged accepted religious views. In his book *Amudei bet Yehudah* he placed in the mouths of his heros rationalist replies to skeptical theology. Hurwitz, who had been exposed to the Enlightenment culture of his time, created for this purpose a fascinating literary character, one unique to Jewish culture—a noble savage, devoid of any of the influences of tradition or religion, whose path to Judaism passed only through study and rational persuasion. In his responses to the challenges of the Enlightenment's skepticism and its criticism of religion, Hurwitz defended the Torah and the commandments, but his replies also had the very opposite effect: they introduced the Jewish reader for the first time to the radical ideas of Enlightenment; they made him more aware of the very existence and intensity of religious skepticism, and were directed toward a rationalization of Judaism.[37]

Amudei bet Yehudah, Hurwitz's most important work, employs a religious debate in order to denounce all types of heresy. The debate is placed in a picturesque literary setting, which is of interest in itself, and its plot is set in an undefined historical period, during which "there is rampant skepticism and apostasy." Its two protagonists are pious philosophers: one (named Itai Hagiti) is speculative, the other (Chushai Haerki) pragmatic, relying on his experience and senses. The two flee to a secret place in nature, far from human habitation, and in the company of "lions and tigers . . . animals of the forests," they spend their time on varied pursuits: Torah, Talmud, Kabbalah, "sayings and rules of ethics from the disciples of philosophers," as well as science— astronomy and geography. Chushai, who excels at empirical thought and a sensual approach, observes "the deeds of the awe-inspiring Almighty in everything He created in His world," and from his observation of the divine creation, arrives at conclusions. Itai, on the other hand, excels at rationalist, abstract thought, and "to them applies his logic."[38] The most original and intriguing literary character Hurwitz introduces to the religious debate is that of the "noble savage"—Ira HaYe'ari—an addition that attests to the strong impact the eighteenth-century Enlightenment had on the world of this physician and early maskil.

One of the roots of the Enlightenment is the Europeans' encounter with the exotic inhabitants of the "new world." Eighteenth-century colonialism further expanded European acquaintance with America and the Pacific islands, with Africa and Asia. Riveting travel books attracted enormous attention; Daniel Defoe's novel *Robinson Crusoe* (1719), describing a meeting on a deserted island in the southern Caribbean between the European Crusoe and the native, Man Friday, is but one of these popular books depicting characters of "savages." The impact on the Enlightenment of the discovery of strange new cultures in the "new world" was immense; it affected religious views, intellectual vibrancy, literature, and Europe's self-image.

At first, the inhabitants of Africa and the American Indians were regarded as barbaric savages, walking about naked and no better than wild beasts, so that there was even some doubt whether their bodies contained a soul and if they could be seen as human creatures. Later, the view of them changed to one of admiration, and the image of the "noble savage" began to take shape—a natural, simple, innocent, happy man whose traits, thoughts, and lifestyle had not been corrupted by European civilization and religious dogma.

The challenges posed by the discovery of new tribes, religions, and customs were very great indeed. The writers and philosophers of the Enlightenment learned from these, for example, the relativity of cultures and religions, and pointed to the need for a change in the view that until then had regarded Europe and Christianity as the be-all and end-all of existence. To deists and free thinkers, the Indians were proof of the truth of their concept of a rational, moral, natural religion that has no need of revelation and ritual. In his well-known book *Christianity Not Mysterious*, John Toland, one of the fathers of British deism, presented his "Indian test" to examine the validity of the religious truth of Christianity. By doing so, he wished to illustrate and substantiate his concept of "common notion," which in his view is the acid test of any religious truth, namely, how would the Indian understand the principles of Christianity, using the universal tools of thought inherent in him? Defoe's Robinson Crusoe, for example, was amazed to discover how difficult, or perhaps impossible, it was to explain the principles of Christianity to a "savage" endowed with "natural" thought. Writers, like Montesquieu in his *Persian Letters* (1721), placed sweeping criticism of European Christian civilization, from social ethics to the conduct of government and church, into the mouths of "noble savages" and other exotic peoples such as Chinese, Persians, and Egyptians. Admiration for the simplicity and vitality of the "natural man"—embodied, for example, in the "savages" of the Pacific islands—made him, in the eighteenth century, the symbol of an egalitarian model society, free of sexual inhibitions or religious hypocrisy, like the people Swift's Gulliver encountered on his travels.[39]

At a very early stage of European colonialism, several "savages" were taken on a tour through the cities of Europe and shown to the public, evoking cries of wonder from spectators in cities like London and Paris. In the early 1760s, Samson Occum (1723–91) became very famous. A Mohawk Indian persuaded by missionaries to convert to Christianity, Occum was the pupil of the clergyman Eleazar Wheelock, who taught him English, Greek, Latin, and of course Christian theology, and he later became an influential preacher in the colonies of New England. In 1765, Occum was brought to England, where he aroused enormous excitement.[40]

There is no way of knowing whether Hurwitz read Defoe and Swift or whether he was familiar with the life story of the Indian Occum, who was then on tour in Europe. However, the story of Ira HaYe'ari, discovered on a deserted island very much like Robinson Crusoe's, is related in *Amudei bet Yehudah.* The frame story and the concepts of this tale are unquestionably drawn from the literature of travels in the "new world." Hurwitz provided his readers with the figure of the "savage" in "Judaized" garb, suitable both to the Jewish background and to the book's polemical aims: Ira HaYe'ari is a "savage," "a man of the forest," who astounds everyone when he is transformed from a barbaric, ignorant man of nature into an educated, believing Jew. His first appearance in the book exhibits all the ingredients of the "savage" as they appeared in the travel books of the period:

And on that day, they [the scholars, Itai and Chushai] went forth to gather wild herbs so that they might eat, and from afar they saw a man standing, entirely naked and unashamed, pulling up the wet grasses that are good for human consumption, and digging up the roots that are fine for the human temperament, and when the wild man saw the two, he ran from them, and hid within the forest, in the manner of a stupid man. And they also removed their clothes, and naked walked about there all day, until the wild man came like a beast, to the place where he had stood, come to dig for the roots of the earth. And Itai went and showed himself to him in a vision, and made him a sign, and the man came to him, and stood before him, and Itai gave him of his bread, and the food was to his liking. And thus the scholar did unto him, until the savage followed after him, like a calf after the cow.[41]

The instinctive reaction of the two scholars was, of course, to enslave the savage and make him their servant, but they rejected this notion at once. Instead of behaving like the colonialists, they decided to take pity on the wild man and to undertake an amazing challenge: "To make this rough, wild creature appealing, to turn him into a man of knowledge and true feeling." This savage, who embodies materiality, naturalness, and a tabula rasa, is about to receive a "Pygmalion-like" education, not only to become a full-fledged member of human civilization, but also to become a Jew! In this way, Hurwitz was able to employ him as an effective weapon in his literary diatribe against the deplorable status of religion and morality and against other flaws that were marring Jewish society and culture. Not only would Ira HaYe'ari prove that it is possible to soundly educate the natural man and to mold him by means of knowledge and reason, but also through him, a utopian model of the Jew would be presented. This man has attained truth, wisdom, and piety without being exposed to the tradition of his forefathers or compelled to convert to Judaism:

To enlighten the blind Hebrews, who have refused to walk in the straight paths, and perhaps of the man of the wilderness I shall make a remedy, to bind him up with the Hebrew, who walked contrary to the Lord, my fortress . . . when they see a God-fearing savage who has learned to speak, with wisdom and morality . . . this man became a model for the men of the inferno.[42]

The use made of the noble savage motif in *Amudei bet Yehudah* was in fact more similar to the way orthodox Christianity exploited it to strengthen faith, based on the example of the Indian Occum, than to the use made by freethinkers to undermine religious faith. Nonetheless, the task of educating Ira haYe'ari is prescribed with special care, out of an awareness of how difficult it was to explain any positivistic religion to a "natural man" in a manner that seems reasonable to him. Since Ira is meant to serve as a utopian model, he can not be forcibly converted to Judaism, as Christian missionaries often converted "savages" in the "new world." He must be guided and counseled so that he accepts Judaism out of his free choice and rational judgment, in other words, according to the fundamentals of the universal natural religion inherent in every human being. In this way, Ira HaYe'ari's conversion, perhaps unintentionally, became the "Indian test" of the Jewish religion: would it be consistent with natural reason?

The guidelines laid down by Itai, the rational philosopher of *Amudei bet Yehudah*, were abundantly clear. "Please take Ira HaYe'ari," he told his comrade who was in charge of the savage's education, "and teach him *chokhmot* and morals, according to the Torah and its proper laws, so nothing shall come to pass by chance, by trickery or deceit, or the way a beast is taught, with rage and anger . . . that is not the way of our pleasing Torah, nor is it the path of wisdom. You must retain the free choice, choice of the truth of our Torah, of love and piety." For this education to achieve its aim, the "savage"'s teacher must permit his novice, innocent pupil to ask any question that comes to his mind: "Allow him to speak, to say what he will, on any subject, as a maskil and a friend, and it is your duty to provide him with a satisfactory reply." Ira's elementary education begins with the study of language, Hebrew writing and grammar, the prayers, and *"chokhmot* and morals," and ends with a study of the Torah and the commandments and everything required in order to worship God. In the education of this natural man, they took special care to avoid referring to any religious experience, divine inspiration, or ecstatic religiosity of the kind that characterized the Kabbalists, whose conduct Hurwitz counted as one of the causes of the contemporary religious crisis. In contrast, they utilized the faculties of reason: "Not with the fancies of the sense," not "seeing visions," but "the intellect and morality are the sources of logic."[43]

Needless to say, the task met with great success, and Ira HaYe'ari became an intellectual as astute and quick-witted as his two teachers. After having been prepared to enter human society in general and Jewish society in particular, although his outward appearance was still that of a "savage," the three returned to the Jewish community. The two wise scholars exhibited him to an excited Jewish multitude, just as Indians were being shown to the public in European cities at the time: "And when they came into the city, with the savage, the entire city was astounded by the awesome sight, seeing a naked man come forth from the forests, and all the people came and stood looking upon them." To further intensify the exotic surprise, Chushai explained to the crowd that this very "savage," the essence of "man" by the nature of his creation, is going to teach them how to correct their minds and deeds. "Hear all you people, who marvel at the clay and shapeless mass, and do not look to see if there is form and soul in the world," Itai declared as he introduced the outlandish man to the astonished Jews:

I have seen that you wonder about the soul of this wild man, and do not know that he possesses a soul and form, that he is a man of morals and Torah, and you may think he has no wisdom or morality because he is not dressed like a gentleman or aristocrat . . . Hence, know my brethren, the man you see here with me, is the tree of the field . . . he will teach the misguided souls wisdom, he will set the crooked mind straight, with wisdom, reason and good sense.[44]

At this stage of the frame story of *Amudei bet Yehudah*, the debate ensues in which Ira HaYe'ari supplements his worldview and his values in relation to humankind and the Jewish religion in a series of penetrating questions. Since he has been given the right to raise any question, Ira serves as a mouthpiece for the arguments of the skeptics. Thus, in his "orthodox" book, Hurwitz allows Ira to express doubts and queries that clash with the social and cultural norms of European and Jewish reality. Just as it is hard to know whether Hurwitz knew about Occum, there is also no way of knowing whether he read the popular dialogues between the Huron Indian chief Adario and the French baron Lahontan, which appeared in several languages and in many editions. In any event, there is a marked similarity between the questions posed by Ira and those by Adario, who adopted a rationalistic, deistic approach and cast serious doubt on the moral, social, and religious norms of Christianity.[45] The Jewish "savage" wondered at the fine manners, so lacking in any natural or existential benefit, of human beings who take care to eat only refined foodstuffs and delicacies, wear stylish fashionable clothing, and live in fancy, spacious homes. He called into question the need to eat meat and drink wine, so injurious to man's health. Nor did he refrain from religious skepticism, challenging the degree of moral justice to be found in the considerations of divine providence and pointing to the bitter fate of righteous men. He also was amazed at how irrational religion was when he first heard of the belief in reincarnation: "How strange that is to me, that the soul of man should be reincarnated in dogs and swine."[46]

The "Indian test" of the disciples of natural religion, like Defoe, Toland, and Lahontan, also came up for discussion in *Amudei bet Yehudah*. Would only those whose forefathers had been vouchsafed divine revelation be granted redemption and an afterlife? What would be the fate of other believers such as the Christians or the tribes of the "new world," or even the Chinese, who had never heard of the monotheistic religions? In particular Ira found it hard to accept the fate of the seven peoples of Canaan, and Hurwitz places in his mouth a skeptical, daring question: "Why did the Torah decree that every last soul of the seven ancient nations be slaughtered like cattle?"

The "Indian test" also served Moses Mendelssohn, at first in the late 1760s, in his public debate with the Swiss clergyman Johann Casper Lavater, about whether Judaism met the test of reason in comparison to Christianity, and later in the 1780s in his book *Jerusalem*.[47] Mendelssohn, who believed Judaism was tolerant of other religions, that it adhered to the principles of the universal natural religion and did not deny the achievement of perfection or divine reward to those to whom God had not granted special revelation, thought that every person has the rational faculties to arrive at the truths of natural religion. In Mendelssohn's view, it was utterly absurd "to send missions to the lands of India or to Greenland, to preach to those far-off peoples to accept our religion. In particular, the latter nation, which, according to the descriptions we have of it, correctly practices the law of nature."[48]

Hurwitz's reply, which preceded Mendelssohn, was totally different. His "savages"—Indian, Chinese, or the seven biblical peoples of Canaan—have been endowed, at the most, with a moral sense, the ability to freely choose, and definitely do not have any religious consciousness. His religious tolerance was restricted to "men of reason," the Christians only, and was totally nonexistent in relation to "savages." In contrast to Mendelssohn, who rejected the speculative argument that exemplary universal figures like the Greek Solon and the Chinese Confucius be required to convert to Judaism, the heros of Hurwitz's book endeavored to persuade "the savage man" to accept the truth of Judaism, out of a belief that he could be truly reformed only by becoming a Jew. In contrast to their compassion for Ira himself, the candidate for Judaization, their basic approach, which justified not only the killing of the seven peoples of Canaan but also the massacre of the natives of the "new world" by European colonialists, is indeed surprising. While the Christians, "who believe in the renewal of the world and in resurrection, and other essentials, as we do" (principles they learned from the Jews, as Hurwitz put it) are assured of divine reward and are worthy of being treated with tolerance,[49] the inferiority of other peoples is irremediable. Hurwitz's intellectual attempt to grapple with the heresy of the Jews caused him to depict the "savages" as an extreme model of heresy, which degrades them to a level below the status of human beings. This is how Hurwitz responds to the challenge of the natural religion encapsulated in the "Indian test":

In the lands of wilderness to which the word of our Lord and His religion have not reached . . . when all the beasts of the forest go prowling; the young lions roar for prey, to devour the believer in the God of the world, truly when the men of Europe conquered them, they slaughtered them mercilessly, for they did not see they were any better than the beasts, as we know from the history of the world of the kings of Edom and Spain, and had the Lord given them into our hands as he did the seven nations, surely He would have commanded us not to permit a single one of them to live, for the same judgement applies to each of them.[50]

Ira HaYe'ari, himself a former "savage," at first raised objections, employing a Mendelssohnian argument: "How are those whom the word of God never reached to blame?" However, he understandingly accepted the very non-Mendelssohnian reply: "Know that in truth these men are unlike human beings, and it is forever their nature that their souls are mixed with the soul of beasts." The travel books taught Hurwitz that the "new world" was replete with moral and sexual debauchery, and hence it was the immoral corruption of the "savages" that "placed them outside of human nature" and justifiably doomed them to perdition. God punished them by depriving them of His revelation. Thus, out of the wealth of images of the "noble savage" in the European Enlightenment culture, Hurwitz chose that of the "barbaric savage" or the "atheistic savage," who could only rise to the level of man by converting to the religions of revelation. To close the last crack in the wall, Ira, the skeptic and rationalist thinker, asked whether perhaps the Chinese are an exception, since "all the travel and geography books marvel at their rich, highly developed civilization, which they established without any direct contact with Europe." From the reply, it is clear that Hurwitz viewed even the ideal image of the Chinese in a totally different light. In his opinion, the Chinese are worse than the Indians in their moral corruption, because their awareness of their sins only increases their responsibility and intensifies their evilness: "For the understanding of their nature draws them to magnify the iniquity of their souls and to multiply their vices a thousand-fold . . . in the manner of every wise man to be more wicked than the fools who have never seen the light."[51]

Hurwitz undoubtedly drew on contemporary European culture in devising the character of Ira, his literary hero, as a "savage" who becomes a "noble savage" and also a believing Jew. However, his character also attests to the limitations of his assimilation of Enlightenment culture. Ira, who rises from bestial barbarity and total ignorance to become a wise Jew, does exemplify the possibility of reshaping a man by means of education, enlightenment, reading, and persuasion. And Hurwitz even took the daring step of placing in his mouth skeptical, critical questions, in which he put forward the very claims of naturalistic and philosophical heresy he was trying to combat, since the declared aim of *Amudei bet Yehudah* was to break the "teeth of the heretics" and to eradicate the "views of the philosophers." Nonetheless, his final conclusion was that the divine revelation to the Jews is the only basis for religious truth that exists in the world, and that it is also the religious truth underlying Christianity. Hence, only a "savage" who has had the benefit of seeing "the light of the Torah," only a "savage" who has become a Jew deserves to be called a man, while all the other "savages" deserve to be liquidated. Although Hurwitz adopted this orthodox stance, which ostensibly does not acknowledge the validity of the natural religion, he obviously needed to rationalize Judaism and its commandments so that he could ask skeptical questions and provide satisfactory answers to them, thereby convincing the natural man of the overriding superiority of Judaism. In *Amudei bet Yehudah*, Hurwitz tried to provide a rationalistic backing for the religious position so that it would seem reasonable and acceptable to a man just emerging from his natural state, to present Judaism to him as a truth devoid of mystery which he would freely choose based on his reason.

Some of Hurwitz's readers failed to understand his complex approach, which involved the use of skeptical arguments to support an orthodox position. From various testimonies that reached him, the German Orientalist Tychsen learned that Hurwitz had been suspected of being himself a heretic naturalist. Hurwitz hastened to print a two-page apologetic clarification that he attached to all the copies of *Amudei bet Yehudah* that had not yet been sold. Under the heading, "A Field of Reason," he defended the appropriateness of the daring questions he had placed in the mouth of "the Jewish savage," claiming that his critics had not fully understood him and that his sole motive was to defend the faith: "I would not turn the house of the Lord into a den of thieves."[52]

Shaping Rational Thinking

Another frame story that presents a theological debate appears in the book *Tov veYafeh* (Good and Nice), printed by the Galician rabbi Judah Leib Margolioth in Frankfort-on-Oder in 1770, in which he purported to demonstrate to his readers "with good taste and reason, the existence of God, Divine Providence, reward and punishment, based on intelligent proof."[53] This story, typical of the baroque *musar* literature, presents a debate between two brothers, Jedaiah and Shemaiah, each of whom represents a different religious awareness. Jedaiah knows of the existence of God "through inquiry, knows the Creator by way of 'know thy father', and this is the sect of philosophers," while Shemaiah "knows of the existence of the Creator only through tradition and hearing." Margolioth's sympathy obviously lies with the inquiring philosopher. The words he places in Jedaiah's mouth echo his own personal experiences and quandaries as a rabbi and early maskil, and we cannot go wrong by regarding him as Margolioth's literary alter ego.

These two literary young men grew up as prodigies in the study of the Torah, as erudite scholars in Talmud and halakhah. As their natural curiosity grew, they expanded their intellectual world and turned to the natural sciences, quickly discovering how meager their extra-religious knowledge was. Like Adam and Eve, who tasted of the forbidden fruit of the Tree of Knowledge, the two understood "that they were still naked in the hidden wisdom and were ashamed." Jedaiah, responding to the challenge, called to his brother, "Come, let us acquire wisdom! Let us leave the house of study and travel to search for a wise teacher, so that we shall no longer suffer from intellectual inferiority." Jedaiah suggested to his brother: "Let us go forth on a pilgrimage to find a man who will deliberate with us and teach us. He is a great philosopher, renowned in his generation, we shall draw upon the wellsprings of his salvation and imbibe its waters."[54] This was clearly an allusion to the philosopher Moses Mendelssohn, who in those very years had earned much fame for his book *Phädon.* Many years before the Haskalah crystallized in the 1780s, it had become popular to pay visits to Mendelssohn in Berlin, and Margolioth himself had met him there once.

Shemaiah, the figure of the disciplined believer, demurred, preferring to remain in his home to continue studying what was required of him from the traditional religious books, rather than to be exposed to science and philosophy. Jedaiah remonstrated with him, out of his youthful eagerness and passion for wisdom, arguing that wisdom is not acquired by accepting existing knowledge, but rather by daring, by seeking new experiences, wandering, and inquiring. Fourteen years before Immanuel Kant, Margolioth understood that the highest barrier to enlightenment lay in the fact that men were by nature too indolent to think independently and to utilize existing human reason. Through his literary character, Jedaiah, he uttered for his Jewish readership the rallying cry of the Enlightenment: Have the courage to use your own reason, gain your release from submission to every authority![55] In his attempt to persuade Shemaiah to join him on his journey to the renowned philosopher, Jedaiah did not hesitate to express a rather radical thought: religious faith acquired through free choice, a religion that the believer adheres to of his own free will, is preferable to religious conduct resulting from coercion and habit.

In the end, the brothers part. Shemaiah remains in the house of study and Jedaiah leaves on his journey. He satisfies his thirst for knowledge, "having found what he was lacking in the hidden wisdom," and returns to his home, a new man who has undergone a cultural change. He is now like Moses, who has descended from Mt. Sinai, holding the Torah in his hand and the inspiration of the Divine Presence lighting up his face: "And it came to pass at the end of two years, he became a winged eagle, and Jedaiah knew that the skin of his face shone and a light glowed within him." Shemaiah did not have an easy time adapting to his philosopher brother's new character. At first, he took umbrage at what he regarded as his brother's arrogance, and he tested him to see if he provided rationalist answers to timely questions, in particular the skeptical questions of atheists and deists, who cast doubt on the existence of God and divine providence. But he finally broke down and admitted that the philosopher had surpassed him and, with self-effacement, said to him: "Now I know, my brother, that you are like a tree planted by the rivers of water, while I am a parched tree, for the waters of the springs of wisdom have not flowed upon me, and my intelligence is so meager that I cannot flee the arrows of evil inclination that have come towards me to bar my way."[56]

In Shemaiah's confession, Margolioth not only sided with the philosopher, depicting him as a desirable religious and intellectual ideal, but he also claimed that the current problem of religious skepticism had to be combated with answers based on reason, and there are a number of such answers in *Tov veYafeh*. However, Margolioth wrote *Tov veYafeh*, as he did his later books, out of religious faith, as a member of the rabbinical elite, and the religious experience is central to it. One of his declared values was the search for closeness to God and for what in His eyes was the good path; another was a disavowal of life in this fleeting, transient world.[57] However, in the course of the dialogue between Shemaiah and Jedaiah, a growing tendency emerged toward rational religious instruction, similar to the education given to the "savage man." After the philosopher cited evidence of the existence of God from the medieval books of philosophy, *Chovot halevavot* and *Guide for the Perplexed*, and advocated uprooting "the materialism of the masses," he was asked whether philosophical inquiry was permitted and legitimate for the religiously faithful. The seductive nature of philosophy, Shemaiah claimed, is like the taste of sweet honey, but it is the duty of the faithful to refrain from tasting philosophy, for its seductiveness is like that of a whore covering her face. Is not "inquiry into the essence" of God opposed to His will? Is not "what our forefathers have told us of His existence" sufficient? Jedaiah hastened to reply that philosophical inquiry is not only permissible, but also essential, in particular in order to grapple with heretics, for they will accept no evidence to which reason does not attest.

However, although Margolioth declared through his literary hero that rationalist theological study was of the utmost importance, he also added a caveat, thus becoming entangled in an internal contradiction: those *chokhmot* that do not help prove the truth of God's existence and His uniqueness ought to be "off limits" for Jews, and on the most vital subjects, scientific investigation is insufficient unless it is accompanied "by the faith that preceded it in the tradition." This relative retreat by Margolioth following his statement of support for philosophy is not really surprising, and it is evident time and again in his books. Although he regards Aristotle as an unfailing source of knowledge, intellectual insights, and moral precepts, he is also capable of pointing out the dangers of adopting Aristotle as a consummate model of rationalism in general. The same man who several years later invested much effort in writing a book of natural science (*Or olam*), wrote in *Tov veYafeh*: "As for these other *chokhmot* that [do not prove] the oneness of God, I admit that I am disgusted to see our people commit harlotry with the daughters [*chokhmot*] of Moab and idolators."[58] Several pages later, Margolioth changed his approach once again, and exhorted men "to first study the sciences to gain self-knowledge and for the benefit of mankind."[59]

But the picture of the early maskil that emerges from this book is that of a very hesitant person—his quandaries and indecisiveness are exposed to the reader and his tendency to waver between two contrary positions can be both surprising and confusing. And yet, in the eighteenth century, Margolioth had already given his readers the key to understanding his words: the theological and philosophical questions that he raised for discussion had no unequivocal, fixed answers. They were contemporary questions, and hence should be taken more as evidence of his personal grappling with them than as an orderly doctrine. Even those like Margolioth and other early maskilim, who had a strong desire to gather "the honey of wisdom" and also urged others to do so, could not ignore the real presence of all types of heresy, which hovered like a shadow over the discussion about the legitimacy of rationalistic inquiry, a discussion the likes of which had probably taken place in Jewish culture hundreds of years before the eighteenth century. Hence, the literary Shemaiah, Margolioth's conservative voice of a man who toes the line, poses contentious arguments to Jedaiah, the philosophical voice of a man who strives for change and has a passion for knowledge. In our time, he says to him, there is a growing number of heretics who attack the foundations of our religion, among them deists who deny God's involvement in this world ("There are many servants nowadays breaking away from their master, the Lord of the earth and the heavens, saying the Creator has risen to the heights and to His majesty, and hence has left the earth and no longer watches over them"). Some no longer believe in personal providence, others are materialists who deny the afterlife of the soul, relating to the Torah as to an earthly, human law, claiming that "man has no preeminence over a beast."[60]

Another example of the way rationalist thought was shaped is the attempt by Moshe Steinhardt, the son of the Fürth rabbi, to use the publication of *Chovot halevavot* in Yiddish in 1765 as an opportunity to provide his readers with some scant knowledge of the new science and philosophy. To the Yiddish edition of the book, Steinhardt added an appendix containing a German translation in Hebrew letters of the first chapter along with his own interpretation. He claimed that only the German translation could preserve the author's original intention, and hence it was preferable to the translation into the vernacular. Mendelssohn's followers in the 1770s had a similar motive in initiating the German translation of the Bible in Berlin.[61]

This trend, which also characterizes the early Haskalah, began with the Hebrew-German dictionary of the Bible published by Judah Leib Minden of Berlin several years before Steinhardt's translation. His book *Milim leElohah* was an early attempt to purify and improve biblical study, to free it of dependence on poor translations, which in Minden's view "in many places misled [students] from the text, and garbled the pleasant words of our Torah in a stammering language far from the language of the people that we speak."[62] But Steinhardt was even more audacious. He did not hesitate to state his intention to interpret the first chapter of *Chovot halevavot*, which is a philosophical discussion of the foundations of faith and includes ideas about the world and nature, according to Copernicus's cosmology because, he argues, only that approach is consistent with reason. "And I have set up signposts for you," he writes in his introduction:

These are natural and divine remarks [in the German version of the introduction: natural science and divine philosophy] which I have been justified in making. And these include the advice that you should accept Copernicus' view that the earth and everything on it is one with the heavenly bodies . . . as they move, so does it move, turning around and around on the girdle of the constellations, and as it turns on its diameter, it makes day into day and night into night.

Steinhardt realized he was being very daring, and he wrote with the self-consciousness of an intellectual faithful to reason and insisting upon its preeminence. Nevertheless, he did not conceal his fear that the Jews were not yet ready to accept the fruits of scientific progress and that they would be met with mockery and resistance:

And I know in my own mind that if these things should reach one as yet unaffected by the light of science and has seen none of its results, he will jeer at my words and think me a fool who believes in the impossible. But this knowledge is not opposed to the religion or to common sense, and why should I think my intelligence errs, and chase after the imagination, which has always misled men. So I shall remain on my guard and be prepared to verify this knowledge with mental, nearly prodigious, proofs. And it is for any man among our people who does not follow the counsel of those who speak, but has been reared on the sciences, that I have prepared this translation of mine.[63]

There is no way of knowing what happened between 1765 and 1773, when Steinhardt's father Joseph's first tirade denouncing the sciences and philosophy first appeared in printed form. At the time, he had supported his son's translation into German of a chapter of *Chovot halevavot*, and had written an approbation of his interpretation, which was based on science and German philosophical terminology.[64] The rabbi of Fürth may have realized only later the potential danger of adopting Copernican cosmology and accepting reason as the supreme judge, a position clearly implied by what his son had written. The issue surrounding Copernicus posed a challenge throughout the eighteenth century, and a relatively large number of early maskilim related to it, from Tobias Cohen in the first decade of the century, through Raphael Levi in the 1730s and Israel Zamosc in the 1740s, to Wessely in the 1760s.[65] In any event, Rabbi Joseph Steinhardt's words were an extremely scathing reaction to the emergence of the new intellectual elite. The strong emotion underlying his criticism and his trenchant invective suggest that, in the wake of his son's book, he was filled with a vivid sense of the danger posed by that same elite, who, in their presumptuousness, were challenging the traditional rabbinical elite:

The whole of my complaint is directed against those who render our Torah ephemeral and of lesser consequence, and take interest only in insignificant, worthless matters, in philosophy and science that exist in the basest world, who in their self-aggrandizement claim they are the wisest of men, more than all the loftiest of rabbis, to whom they say they are superior, and their despicable, vapid views are opposed to the words of the Sages . . . but in their ideas they have strayed from the true path . . . they are wise only in doing evil and to do good they know not . . . may their portion on earth be cursed, their skulls be crushed . . . a fire not blown shall consume them, the wicked shall be as thorns thrust away that cannot be taken by hands, and they shall be completely burned with fire in their place and shall remain in the congregation of the dead. . . . And who is simpleton enough to believe in their devious words, their vain and foolish visions, can they persuade an educated man to believe that they are wiser than our great rabbi R. Moshe ben-Maimon [Maimonides] who never strayed, either to the right or the left, from the words of our Sages, although he was well-versed in all the sciences.[66]

It is no wonder that many of the attempts to revive and redeem philosophy were made by students and doctors, who had been exposed to European philosophy in their studies. In 1762 a medical student at the Berlin Collegium Medico-Chirorgicum appealed to Mendelssohn to write a commentary to Maimonides's book on logic, *Bi'ur milot hahigayon* (Logical Terms), to make it easier for scholars not yet familiar with European literature to study philosophy. This student, Shimshon Hakaliri, a native of Jerusalem,[67] was an interesting type of early maskil: a scholar who specialized in teaching Maimonides's rulings on the consecration of the new month (in actual fact, a chapter on the science of astronomy in the halakhic corpus of *Mishneh Torah*, which, as I mentioned, was also Raphael Levi's introduction to science). In his travels he passed through Turkey and Italy until he arrived in Germany. He, like Israel Zamosc, found a home and patronage with one of the wealthy families that supported scholars—the Ephraim family. And like other early maskilim, he was greatly perturbed by the neglect of science and philosophy. He was distressed by the fact that Maimonides's important text on logic had not been printed for nearly two hundred years: "and this wisdom has been cast into a corner, its face grown over with thorns, nettles covering it all."[68]

Mendelssohn met the challenge, by writing *Bi'ur milot hahigayon*, and Hakaliri printed it in 1764, in the city where he had been accepted for the completion of his medical studies—Frankfurt-on-Oder—without noting Mendelssohn's name as the commentator. Mendelssohn, angered by this omission, issued a new edition a year later, at the suggestion of a medical student in Berlin—Dov Baer of Dohlinow, son of the rabbi of Wysokie in Lithuania.[69] The important point here is not only the desire to redeem Maimonides' text, but the attempt to actually infuse it into the bloodstream of traditional scholarship, thus changing its face. Logic, Mendelssohn wrote in his preface, is essential for rational thought and improves the very nature of man: "A lover of the truth would do well to examine them [the rules of logic] to arrive at their truth and essence, to habituate his mind to this kind of inquiry that will regulate his thinking and teach him to follow a level way and walk in the paths of righteousness." Hence this study shapes man and his personality, improves the quality of his discourse and thought and enhances his human virtues. Scholars should, therefore, devote a number of hours to improving their minds, and also include *Bi'ur milot hahigayon* in their program of studies. Mendelssohn assured his potential critics that the book says nothing about religious faith, nor does it present any danger of distracting the reader from Torah study or attracting him to an alien culture. But, he adds, it is enormously important to introduce rational thinking into the religious lesson plans.[70]

One of the most succinct, coherent, and up-to-date science books written by early maskilim was *Ma'amar haTorah vehachokhmah* (A Dissertation on the Law and Science), by the London medical student Mordechai Gumpel Schnaber-Levison. It ventured to defend the new science in general and Copernicus's and Newton's theories in particular.[71] "To inquire into the natural and theoretical sciences and what can be attained from the Divinity," in his view, was tantamount to a commandment. To the hesitant, he said it was unthinkable that the Torah or the words of the Sages would contain anything contradictory to reason. Schnaber recommended that no one should commence talmudic study without first learning the "inner logic of the Talmud," so that he may understand "its literal meaning and its logic" without his "mind being twisted." He went even further toward the natural religion when he suggested that what was imperative in nature was identical with the will of the Creator. The seven Noachic commandments, for example, were presented in *Ma'amar haTorah vehachokhmah* as being the result of reason and social agreement: "And this was what they commanded that if we always safeguard and pay heed to nature and behave properly toward it, we will do no wrong, for everything that Nature requires is also the will of the Creator." Only after humankind fell into a decline was there a need for explicit commandments issued by the Creator, and their main purpose was to cultivate minds so they would "not believe in anything that does not derive from reason and would acknowledge the existence of the Creator, may He be blessed, based on rational proofs and theoretical premises."[72] Schnaber, the physician and early maskil, adhered to quite subversive rationalist positions, and in the final analysis he believed that reason and "the book of Nature," whose secrets the new science was deciphering, were man's principal guides.

Joined to this rationalistic trend was a struggle against superstition, a subject that particularly troubled the physicians, who, in the eighteenth century, thought of themselves as acting in the spirit of the Enlightenment.[73] Tobias Cohen had already begun to engage in this struggle, in the medical part of his *Ma'aseh Tuvyah*, in which he strongly recommended preventive medicine, in particular a proper diet and hygiene. Cohen informed his readers of the natural and environmental causes of disease and suggested natural remedies. For example, he devoted a long chapter to ringworm, which he said was particularly widespread among Polish Jewry. While still a student in Padua, he received despairing letters from one of the leaders of the Lvov community, asking for a remedy to relieve his suffering from this disease. In Cohen's opinion, the cause of the disease was the polluted environment, which he reported on, having seen it with his own eyes:

The land is more fertile than all the other lands of the gentiles, but full of filth and rubbish . . . their homes stink and their clothes are dirty, and they do not comb the hair of their heads or their beards even once a year . . . they eat strange food, mostly beans and cucumbers . . . they drink a kind of brandy that burns both the heart and the soul, and ale and other alcoholic beverages, drinks that are improper since they undoubtedly cause various aliments, fill the head with smoke, causing all manner of maladies, dizziness, contractions, and sometimes paralysis, and needless to say, madness, befuddlement, ringing in the ears, and sickness of the eyes.[74]

In Poland, ringworm was often treated with magical remedies because of the belief that it was caused by the sorcery of demons. Tobias mocked these rampant superstitions and vigorously objected to them: "Even if there were no demons and had never been created, they ought to have been for the people of this country, for there is no other country or community where so many people deal in commerce connected with them—amulets, oaths, names and dreams—my spirit will not be joined to their company." In his opinion, the only remedy for this disease is a natural one, and in his book he offers a recipe for home preparation of the remedy and precise instructions for treatment.[75]

To prevent the spread of an epidemic that broke out in Poland and threatened to penetrate eastern Prussia, in 1770 the Jewish doctors of Berlin published guidelines for the maintenance of good health, based on their professional authority: "Tested medicines from great physicians who have gained renown in several universities."[76]

Vigorous opposition to magical medicine is also expressed in *Sefer refu'ot*, written in Yiddish by the doctor Moses Marcuse, who was apparently born in Slonim in 1743 and studied at Königsberg University in 1766. The book was printed in Poritzk in 1790 for the Jews of Poland and Lithuania.[77] The university-educated Jewish doctors took a stand in favor of science and reason and against popular medicine and the miracle-working shamans. Hence they often represented a critical, even a subversive religious and social trend.[78] Marcuse set forth his aims in his apology for having written his book in spoken Yiddish:

In this book I wish to save each year several thousand people from all manner of people who will only cause them harm—for example, old women, ineffectual midwives, murmurers of incantations against the evil eye, miracle workers, the ignorant and wicked, pourers of wax, diviners who can guess at any illness, preachers selling remedies for the price of a good meal, or the price of a small donation, and from witch doctors, who have made themselves, or have been made by old women, into doctors.[79]

In Marcuse's campaign to improve public health, hygiene, and nutrition and to prevent disease, he was scathingly critical of the existing situation and demanded that the living conditions be rationalized, taking into account nature, the environment, and medical guidelines. It is no wonder that he was among those Jewish representatives who proposed some wide-ranging reforms in the economy and education of Jews in the final years of the independent Polish monarchy.

The sense of intellectual inferiority and affront that motivated the early maskilim was alleviated to some extent through the redemption of the neglected sciences and the inception of rational thought. The passion for knowledge was not satisfied merely by the expansion of fields of study; it also inevitably meant that concepts, values, and patterns of life had to be put to the test of criticism. The criticism of the early Haskalah was met with opposition by the spokesmen of the rabbinical elite, who were determined to keep the tradition intact, and exposed subversive tendencies among men such as Hanau, Hurwitz, and Zamosc. Although the extent of deviation from the religious culture, from the legitimate texts and the definitions of what was permissible and what was forbidden, was not very great, yet from the new library created by the early maskilim a novel, unprecedented type emerged—the modern author who was no longer identified with the rabbinical elite.

Chapter Three
The Secular Author in the Public Arena

In their books, quite a few early maskilim also undertook to fill the traditional role of moralists for the society at large, a role that until then had been the exclusive province of *magidim* (preachers) and rabbis. Such a new sociocultural function was filled, for example, by the journal *Kohelet musar*, which consciously presented itself to its readers as the modern alternative to the traditional preachers, who frequently put the fear of God into their listeners.

This initial attempt by Mendelssohn and his friend Tobias Bock in the 1750s in Berlin, was important for several reasons. First, its editors preached morality to Jewish society in the literary form (the moral weekly) that was popular in the early European Enlightenment, particularly in England and Germany. Second, in this Hebrew periodical, they imparted some of Wolf's and Leibniz's philosophical ideas to Jews. Third, and this is the main point, *Kohelet musar* was an initial, conscious attempt to suggest the writer as an alternative to the traditional preacher, and to depict him as a spiritual figure providing guidance and dictating proper behavior to the Jewish public. From now on, the writer would draw his authority as a "chastiser at the city gates," not from a religious source or a community position, but by virtue of his being an intellectual, with writing skills and a desire to provide guidance to his society.

Apparently it was the satirical social criticism, printed in the second issue of *Kohelet musar* and directed at the wealthy pretentious elite, indifferent to the plight of their fellow Jews, that evoked the ire of the "zealots" and caused the periodical to cease publication. Mendelssohn's German biographer was probably exaggerating when he wrote that "the rabbis, those pious members of the Jewish church, went berserk in the full sense of the word, raising such a hue and cry that the modest scholar had to back down, and the publication of the periodical was discontinued." Nonetheless, there is some ground for assuming that it was the pressure of the community leaders that blocked the project initiated by Bock and Mendelssohn (then in his mid-twenties) to engender cultural change. This early literary-journalistic endeavor, despite its failure, is one more expression of the fact that the early maskilim were conscious of belonging to a new type of intellectual elite, which drew its authority from a secular source.[1]

On the Verge of Separation from the Rabbinical Elite

A sweeping, far sharper critique was included by Israel Zamosc in his book *Nezed hadema.* The date of its writing is not known, but it reflects life in the Jewish society in Poland and Germany until the author's death in Galician Brody in 1772. In 1741, Zamosc was already regarded as a new, suspicious type of intellectual, and he was denied the possibility to serve as a guide of the public since he was not an official member of the rabbinical elite. This case is of significance in any attempt to trace the process in which the new intellectual emerged after breaking away from the traditional scholarly elite. Israel Zamosc's monologue, filled with his rage and frustration at being rebuffed by circles of the scholarly elite, shows that the early maskil, who "had never been appointed either as a rabbi or a member," was already fighting to gain recognition and the legitimate right to venture into the public arena:

Even though they may count me a slanderer of my people, a boisterous rebel, and in a loud voice call to one another, saying: have you seen that man and heard his speech, his audacity and obstinacy, how he has begun to rise to the high places on the field at the head stone . . . as if he were an elder, full of wisdom, as if the generation were an orphan and Jewry were a widower . . . and boldly presumes to say: I shall remove the impurities of those of my generation . . . and they ask one another: who is this nobody who has clothed himself in majesty, girded himself in the strength of his righteousness, what way has the spirit of God passed to speak unto him, or whose son is this young man, who in his ornate speech, makes himself known to us, what is his name and what is the name of his son, so we may know . . . he has never been appointed not as a rabbi nor as a member, and why does he see himself today higher than all the people, and think he is raising the banner of Torah, as if he had come forth from the lion's den and from the mountains of the leopards and ventures to judge the beast of the forest.[2]

In Berlin, Israel Zamosc joined a circle of scholars, thereby coming out of his isolation and acquiring the confidence to express himself in his book in the fiery rhetoric of a prophet of doom to chastise Jewish society at large. "Listen, oh mountains, for I speak justly," Zamosc opened, "hear my rebukes, the strong foundations of the earth, I stand here at the top of the hill . . . for a fire has gone forth from Heshbon, a flame from the city of Sihon, it has blazed in my nostrils and set the foundations of my body on fire."[3] In rhymed, ornate prose, replete with associations from the world of the religious culture, Zamosc settled accounts with various types he had encountered in the Jewish society of Eastern and Central Europe. In a jeering, satirical tone, he exposed their deplorable moral state and denounced their evil deeds. In his scathing criticism, he did not spare the type known in the Enlightenment as the religious hypocrite and the charlatan, particularly those whose religiosity had an ecstatic cast. One of these types, the ascetic Hasid, was the object of a particularly scornful rebuke: "Come out, come out, you bloody man, desist from deceiving people, for it is God that you are deceiving, in your iniquity you have stumbled. . . . You have lifted up your eyes on high, against the Holy One of Israel, You have estranged yourself, and God is alien to your heart, and how can you find favor when the oppressed are shedding tears and the voice of your brothers' blood cries out."[4] During his first stay in Berlin, in the 1740s, Zamosc had already attracted the attention of German theologians and intellectuals, like Friedrich Nicolai. This militant intellectual was inspired by the exacting ideal of an elite of rationalist scholars, one free of all the flaws that marred the existing elite, which, in its hypocrisy, had, in his view, succumbed to the pursuit of delights and pleasures. He believed that only a new, purified elite was worthy to take over the leadership of the community.[5]

The early maskil had a strong sense of crisis, was dissatisfied with the reality, and intensely desired to carve a path between the seekers of the truth and those groups he believed threatened "science"-related subjects, and frequently felt angry and frustrated too. The encounter of these rationalist intellectual men of letters with Kabbalist circles, Sabbatians and ecstatic Hasidim served to further reinforce their belief in the preeminence of reason. In the mid-eighteenth century, Rabbi Shlomo of Chelm's criticism of the neglect of the *chokhmot* was voiced together with his well-known words harshly condemning enthusiastic Kabbalists for their ignorance and mad behavior:

And many of them lack even the slightest portion of knowledge, and have not striven to learn either the esoteric lore or the Gemarra, Rashi's commentary and the *Tosafoth*. These are cunning men who wail loudly, skipping over the mountains, with prayers and supplications, in song and dance, in chants and melodies . . . behaving bizarrely, clothed in white, the fringes [of their garb] with a thread of blue like On the son of Peleth . . . with groans that break half of a man's body, waving their hands to and fro, swaying like the trees of the forest.[6]

In 1766, Judah Hurwitz also drew a gloomy picture of a serious all-encompassing crisis in the society and the religion. In his view, two contending sects were the cause: the sect of the "men of pride" and that of the "men of heresy." One of these two "defiled camps" was that of the enthusiastic Kabbalists and Hasidim, who claimed to have a direct link to the heavenly worlds: "They erred like a half-blind drunkard staring at the heavens and calling it water . . . and spoke out deceitfully, saying, we are the most superior of men"; and the other is that of the rationalist heretics, "philosophizing in falsehoods and fraud."[7] Like other early maskilim, Hurwitz also vigorously objected to these two sects, convinced of the need to fight against them. He regarded himself as a *chakham*, whose chief enemy is folly in all of its varying forms. In a time of crisis, he claimed, when "the darkness of folly grows ever denser," the writers, not the rabbis or the *tzadikim*, are actually the ones capable of remedying the situation. He formulated the task of the writers in the most militant of terms: "And with their pens, the maskilim went forth to shoot down the stupid, and with the swords of their tongues struck down the simpletons . . . and when the clouds of folly rose, the light of pure reason shone forth, and the children of Israel had light in their dwellings."[8]

Baruch Schick was another critic of the sanctimonious Jews, who hypocritically made an outward show of being pious. Although he was attracted to Kabbalah, and many of its doctrines are included in the science books he published, in the 1770s he saw a direct link, albeit not a true identity, between the "haters of science," the fools who mock at the *chokhmot* and persecute the *chokrim* (philosophers) who inquire into them, and the pseudo-pious, "who pose as humble sages, lie in wait in ambush for the blameless, speak loftily with proud hearts, despise anyone who says to them that he possesses a good virtue or wisdom . . . put on the garb of a humble, pious man, and mislead people."[9] Rabbi Judah Leib Margolioth, an active rabbi of a congregation, preacher, and early maskil, also joined in this trend. In addition to his criticism of the community leaders and rabbis whom he accused of having abused their positions and oppressing the poor classes, he viciously lashed out at the fraudulent miracle workers and those who "show themselves openly as the highest of pious men, holy and purified . . . spend long hours at prayer, shaking their heads, in the height above and in the depths."[10]

These examples are not limited only to East European Jewry, or to those early maskilim who moved westward, from Poland to Germany. The philosopher Napthali Herz Ullman, who was born in Mainz and lived in Amsterdam and The Hague, greatly admired the major German philosophers of the early Enlightenment. He recounted an incident in which a Jew, pretending to be possessed by a dyybuk, came to the courtyard of the synagogue, behaving madly—shouting, weeping and throwing stones at his chest: "He made weird movements with his limbs and fell upon his face as if his soul had left his body." Ullman laughed at the man, observing his behavior with scorn, and the rabbi of the community exposed him as a rogue and imposter. This experience pushed Ullman even further into the arms of the new rationalist philosophy and to a worldview that sided with the philosophers in the controversy between "the religious who walk aimlessly and the intellectual philosophers of our nation."[11]

In their new sociocultural status, authors (under the label *choker*) were in some danger. As we have seen, some of them were already conscious of their identity as writers, not as moralists or scholars of the traditional type. The physician Judah Hurwitz, for example, was the target of criticism and persecution, and was denounced as a heretic after he published his ideas in *Amudei bet Yehudah*.[12] Israel Zamosc's reputation was also tarnished, and that may have been why he fled from Galicia to Germany in the 1740s. As the presence of this new type—the Jewish intellectual—was more keenly felt, hostility toward him increased. The physician Anshel Worms complained in the 1760s, in the name of the *chokrim*: "My ears are ringing for I have heard the calumny of many, fear on every side, the voice of a charging bear and a roaring lion they taunt us, calling us by the name of *chokrim*, and always saying in their hearts . . . the language of the philosophers is filled with venom and the fierceness of crocodiles to twist words and expressions." He reacted angrily, inveighing against "the masses who despise and abhor the philosopher and think him a heretic and apostate, in any case, a man free and unrestrained in his thinking who scarcely values the words of the Prophets." He had to defend himself against the claims of the opponents of philosophers that the *chokrim* had left the scholarly elite because they lacked sufficient knowledge in the Talmud and the halakhah to belong to that elite: "They have lied, saying he who innocently follows the path of the sciences is not a student of the Talmud and has no knowledge of the religion or its law."[13]

In a like manner, Schnaber-Levison, as a student in London in the early 1770s, tried to confute the traditionalists' tendency to equate the new intellectuals with libertines and apostates. However, he was probably unsuccessful, and when similar accusations were leveled at him in the course of this polemic he left for Hamburg.[14]

Another case is that of the "refugee" from the opponents of philosophy, Naphtali Ullman. He fled to Holland in the 1760s, his heart full of bitterness and resentment toward his persecutors, who had denounced him as a heretic and deist: "How greatly I have suffered owing to the most arrogant of liars in our land, who want to uproot wisdom from the world, abuses and maltreatment and great cruelties that can barely be contained in one book or language." According to Ullman, "they rise up against the astute philosophers who possess the just faith and accuse them of being deists who deny the truth of the Torah."[15] Ullman defined himself as a philosopher who belonged to the "sect of Wolf's disciples." He was one of the early maskilim, like Tobias Cohen, Raphael Levi of Hanover, Aaron Gumpertz, Mendelssohn, and Schnaber-Levison, who achieved a large measure of intellectual autonomy. Although most of his works in philosophy, original books and translations of Wolf's writings, remained in manuscript form, his importance should not be underestimated: he too embodies the new type of Jewish philosopher who is also a man of the Enlightenment. Like Mendelssohn, whom he greatly admired and with whom he corresponded, Ullman endeavored to prove that modern philosophy is consistent with the Jewish religion. He emphasized, more than other early maskilim, the commitment of the Jewish philosopher to come to terms with the new teachings of the German Enlightenment, and disagreed with those who felt one could earn the title of a philosopher merely by studying medieval Jewish philosophy.

More than anyone else, Ullman tried to sharpen the boundaries between the new elite and the traditional elite. One daring expression of this attempt was his refusal to follow the common practice and to request the approbations of rabbis for his book *Chokhmat hashorashim* (Wisdom of the Roots). This book of philosophy, the only one he succeeded in publishing, is a 400-page work on ontology, which he finished writing in 1777.[16] In his declaration of independence as a philosopher, Ullman heaped scorn on the institution of rabbinical approbations. He remarked that it was absurd to request approbations for a book that contained universal truths, which stood on their own and needed no supernatural or religious-authoritative stamp of approval to give them validity. "Any matter that has incontrovertible proof," Ullman wrote on the frontispiece of his book, from which rabbinical approbations were intentionally absent, "is the complete truth which testifies to itself and has no need of any approbation." And if this reason did not suffice, then the rabbis' ignorance of the subject of the book furnished further grounds for the omission of any approbation:

These are the rabbis who are famous throughout the land for their knowledge and teaching of the Torah and the commandments, for their theoretical scholarship and the profundity of their erudition, their prowess in the halakhah, so they are left with no leisure time to observe the wonders of nature and the divine secrets as rational proofs, but only the tradition will serve as proof for them instead, as it does for all the rest of the masses of the faithful of Israel.

If it had been a talmudic book, and Ullman claimed he could write such a book as well, there would have been some reason to bow down before the rabbis and plead for their approbation, but in a nonreligious book the author must preserve complete autonomy: "But this inquiry is given only to the *chokrim* who are proficient at attaining the true proof, by seeking and probing each and every inference and analogy that constitute the proof."[17]

Ullman's personal rebellion against religious authority was an exceptional case in which a philosopher openly defied the rabbinical elite. This may have been a result of the affront that left a psychological scar on him after he was persecuted in Mainz, the city of his birth, for engaging in the study of philosophy. However, we have already seen that even relatively minor deviations, for example, the detection of several linguistic errors by interpreters of the Torah, met with protests, as in the case of Shlomo Hanau, early in the century, when he was compelled to publicly apologize and repent. It is incorrect to assume that traditional Judaism was flexible enough to provide a certain degree of legitimacy to the "external *chokhmot*" as long as those engaged in them did not embrace any new values and ideologies. The representatives of the religious elite in Ashkenazi society continued throughout to press for the total negation of the *chokhmot* and to caution against them. In fact, many early maskilim who realized that their approach ran contrary to prevailing norms, encountered real resistance. It was in fact easier to gain some legitimacy for science than for philosophy, which was perceived as a theological threat, and the opposition to the early maskilim who engaged in philosophy was much greater than that against those who engaged in the natural sciences. However, their moralistic opponents frequently coupled these two areas of knowledge, fearing that by approving an ostensibly neutral field of knowledge they would open the way to the legitimation of one that posed a theological threat.

Moses Mendelssohn warmly recommended *Ma'amar hamada*, published by Aaron Gumpertz, while Rabbi Jacob Emden, who throughout his lifetime wavered between two opposing positions, attacked it vigorously and thoroughly denied the claim that the *chokhmot* were necessary for Jews as well. Gumpertz's entire purpose, Emden argued, against this work on science, in 1768, was "to distract the children of Israel from studying the Torah and learning their religious obligations, since the life span of Methuselah would not suffice for reading and studying all the external books that he advised the children of Israel to peruse."[18] However, in opposing the trends of the early Haskalah, as they were reflected in *Ma'amar hamada*, Emden was motivated by more than this seemingly pragmatic reason; his aim was to curb "the rebellious wicked, who throw off all restraint." Thirty years after he was reconciled to Ginzburg's medical studies at Göttingen, he was assailed by a sense of danger:

Heaven forbid that a man of Israel should engage permanently in the external *chokhmot*, and this [prohibition] is according to the word of the Almighty, and needless to say he who goes to their houses of study, watching daily at their gates, in this way causes the [mating] season of the loving doe to be called off, and finally abandons her entirely to embrace a loose woman . . . as experience has time and again proven those who drew near to the door of her home have spurned the wife of their youth and will come no more unto her to know her. From the permitted they came to the forbidden, and as they increased so they sinned, to think lightly of the commandments. They moved not from there until they began to deny the Torah and the prophecy.[19]

Conscious of how enticing the temptation was, Emden employed erotic images to describe the attraction to external knowledge and the need to avoid succumbing to it. He wanted to caution against the seductive charms of science, that he equated with "the alien woman," and stated unequivocally that Jews had no need of it. Hence, he advised against spending too much in non-religious study (although he did not totally negate such study), and urged his readers to avoid any infringement of the supreme commandment of total devotion to the study of Torah, the one and only "legal wife." In fact, in the 1730s, Emden already felt compelled to repudiate medicine based on his considerations as a halakhic authority. In *Igeret bikoret* (A Letter of Criticism) he declared: "Let thousands of such physicians and their words be set aside and vanish but not [to harm] a single letter of our Torah . . . Heaven forbid that our perfect Torah should be likened to their idle talk or that one should believe in their utterances and trust their wisdom, what is this wisdom of theirs, it cannot withstand the power of the wisdom of our rabbis of blessed memory, the sages of the truth."[20]

The correspondence between Mendelssohn and Rabbi Emden in 1772 on the issue of early burial is a test case in this controversy. At the time, this disagreement remained the subject of their private correspondence and was publicized only in the 1780s, when the Haskalah took shape. It was connected with the duke of Meklenburg's demand that the local Jews behave according to the recommendations of physicians and stop burying their dead on the same day, as was their practice. In distress, the heads of the community applied to Mendelssohn and Emden, hoping to obtain some grounds to help them in their struggle against what they regarded as an edict that banned the observance of a custom prescribed by Jewish law.[21] The fundamental differences of opinion between the two are more important here than the historical affair itself. Mendelssohn endeavored, as was his wont, to show that the new science could be reconciled with the religious sources, and hence that the conclusions of scientists could be accepted and support for them could be found even in the Talmud. In contrast, Emden's opposition was uncompromising. The rabbi and the early maskil seem to have taken totally divergent paths. The rabbi, who in moments of weakness, had also revealed his craving for the new science, now expressed an unrelenting, orthodox position, claiming that science could not be a consideration in any aspect of the religious culture: "Heaven forbid that we should pay heed to them in connection with the laws of the Torah, for then, Heaven forfend, its foundations will be weakened and its pillars will tremble . . . [for] there is no real substance in the words of a doctor that are devoid of Torah." In relation to Mendelssohn, Emden adopted a menacing tone: "Lest angry fellows do you harm, upon hearing that you pay heed to the nonsense of strangers and think of changing a Jewish custom."[22] While the polemic remained in their personal correspondence until the 1780s, and Mendelssohn's status and prestige protected him against any persecution, this test case attests to the extreme sensitivity of the rabbinical elite, which was constantly on guard against the danger of apostasy and which, even before the Haskalah coalesced into a movement, reacted violently to the intrusion of any scientific considerations into the heart of religious culture.

Patrons and the First Circles

To reconstruct the character of the early Haskalah one must look at the entire eighteenth century and at a varied, relatively scattered number of intellectuals who moved from place to place. It began in the early part of the century, through initiatives undertaken by individual physicians and scholars who were greatly perturbed by the neglect of the Hebrew language and sciences; it continued with the revival of Jewish philosophy in the 1740s and '50s; and it reached its peak in the 1760s and '70s, with the growing number and diversity of books printed by early maskilim and their attempts to establish contacts among themselves. From the outset, several subtypes emerged among them—the most common were university-educated men of science (particularly physicians) and scholars from the rabbinical elite. Some of them remained rabbis and preachers within their society of origin, and a few succeeded in acquiring an autonomous status as writers and philosophers. The degree of their commitment to the early Haskalah varied, ranging over a broad spectrum. At one end was the curiosity and passion for knowledge of a rabbi, like Jacob Emden, who found it difficult to justify even to himself his attraction to extra-Jewish culture, and who, in the end, erected barricades against the Haskalah. At the other end, there was the mature self-consciousness of a philosopher, like Naphtali Ullman, who demanded recognition as an independent intellectual cut off from the rabbinical elite.

Early maskilim who were unable to achieve economic independence, for example, as doctors, merchants, or rabbis, sought patrons among the financial elite of court Jews and wealthy merchants, who employed medical students or scholars and writers as tutors in their homes or as clerks in their places of business, provided them with housing and sometimes also with a residence permit, and financially supported the publication of their books. This kind of relationship between wealthy Jews and intellectuals, which generally was not long-lasting, but nearly always was a precondition, without which the early maskilim could not free themselves of their past, also existed in the later Haskalah.[23]

In Berlin in the 1770s, the list of subscribers to the book by "the learned engineer, Abraham Yosef Mentz of Frankfurt-on-Main," or to the book published there by Baruch Schick of Shklov, included the names of distinguished members of the Berlin community—physicians, community leaders, wealthy merchants, educated merchants like David Friedländer (then in his twenties), and "the renowned scholar Moses of Dessau."[24] In addition, people from Poland and other cities in Germany subscribed. The sycophantic poems lauding members of the affluent elite, who helped intellectuals and men of letters, reflect their authors' consciousness of the social gap between the two groups. Wessely, for example, one of the most adept of his contemporaries at writing poetry commissioned for various occasions and fawning poems of gratitude, was excessive in paying tribute to the wealthy merchant Berman Friedländer, who had bought his book *Yain levanon* (The Wine of Lebanon). Belittling his own value, he wrote, "I knew that you would surely forget me . . . and that merchants, distinguished men of the land, would command your attention . . . how easy it is to forget a man like me! But I did not know you, there is also room for an ardor for reason in your heart, and if some part of it is given over to peddlers, you will not give all of it to them."[25] In some instances, the patrons were non-Jewish intellectuals and academics, like Leibniz, who was Raphael Levi's patron, and d'Argens and Maupertuis, who assisted Aaron Gumpertz. It was the German author and playwright Lessing who introduced Mendelssohn in the 1750s into Berlin literary society. And David Friedrich of Megerlin, a professor at Frankfurt University, wrote an introduction in Latin to Worms's book in the 1760s.

Most of the early maskilim were born in the states of Germany, Poland, and Lithuania, but the literary activity existed mainly in Germany or near the Hebrew printing houses in various places in Europe. Ostensibly this was a random assortment of personalities and books, but in actual fact there were mutual ties between the early maskilim, and their intellectual activity was conducted in several centers, the most important of which were unquestionably the printing houses, where they could publish books in Hebrew: Jesnitz in the 1740s, and in the coming decades—Berlin, Amsterdam, The Hague, Frankfurt-on-Main, Frankfurt-on-Oder, Hamburg, and Königsberg. The process of publishing books was a long and tedious one. It involved traveling with the "book of subscribers" to raise money to defray printing costs, and trips to distant printing houses where the writers had to stay nearby for fairly long periods, while their books were being printed, generally in the homes of affluent Jews. The trips to the printing houses, the efforts to find patrons, and the demand for positions as doctors, rabbis, preachers or tutors—all required the early maskilim to spend much time on the roads of Europe. Yehudah Hurwitz, for example, was born in Vilna, studied medicine in Padua, printed his books in Königsberg, Amsterdam, Prague, and Grodna, collected subscriptions to his books in most of the communities of Germany, and earned his livelihood as a doctor in Lithuania and Kurland. Schnaber-Levison was born in Berlin, studied in London, lived for a time in Stockholm, and finally settled in Hamburg. Baruch Schick of Shklov, the *dayan* of Minsk, traveled westward several times, passing through The Hague, Berlin, Prague, Vienna, Frankfurt, Brody, Lissa, and even London.

Real circles of maskilim and meeting places, although informal, were active in Amsterdam (Franco-Mendes, Wagnaar, Hurwitz, Shlomo Dubno in the 1760s), in Berlin (Zamosc, Gumpertz, Mendelssohn, Tobias Bock in the 1740s and '50s, and in the 1760s also the teacher from Glogau, Avigdor Levi, the medical student Dov Baer of Dohlinow, Hertog Leo [Zevi Hirsch Lifschitz, the community secretary] and others). The campuses of the universities where Jewish students were enrolled also served as meeting places. Shlomo Maimon, for example, who left Lithuania in the 1770s, describes his meeting in Königsberg with a group of Jewish students. His acquaintance with them made him sharply aware of the cultural gap between the new intelligentsia that was taking shape in universities and the Lithuanian talmudic scholars. His description provides important evidence of the patterns of life and self-consciousness of the members of this circle, who defined themselves as a new elite, a distinctive phenomenon in contemporary Jewry. They wore European clothing, were fluent in German and well-versed in philosophy and science, read the newest books of the Enlightenment culture, and also had a good command of the Hebrew language.[26]

Many examples exist of the personal and literary ties among the early maskilim. Baruch Schick, in his well-known introduction to Euclid's *Geometry*, quoted from Israel Zamosc's *Netzach Yisrael*, in his own books drew on Raphael Levi's *Tekhunot hashamayim*, and during his visit to Berlin apparently met with Wessely. Shlomo Dubno received the manuscript of *Sha'arei ne'imah* from Shlomo of Chelm when he visited Lvov and published it; Judah Leib Margolioth inserted in his book *Beit midot* (House of Ethics) things written by Wessely in *Gan na'ul* and by Zamosc in *Nezed hadema*. Shlomo Hanau taught Wessely Hebrew grammar in Copenhagen, and Gumpertz and Zamosc taught Mendelssohn languages and medieval Jewish philosophy in Berlin. Schnaber-Levison, in his *Ma'amar haTorah vehachokhmah* was influenced by Gumpertz's *Ma'amar hamada*. Wessely wrote a paean to Judah Hurwitz, and at the front of *Amudei bet Yehudah* Hurwitz proudly printed a letter of recommendation from Mendelssohn.

Many early maskilim who were interested in philosophy—for example, Naphtali Ullman, David Wagenaar from Holland, and Raphael Levi from Hanover—came to visit or corresponded with Mendelssohn, who had gained fame in Germany. "My heart swells, as I fondly recall the bygone days when my soul was in the council of my master," an early maskil from Breslau (probably Jacob Jaroslav) nostalgically wrote about his meetings with Mendelssohn. Afterward, he continued carrying on his correspondence with him on philosophical questions.[27] Isaac Euchel (1756–1804), who was born in Copenhagen and in the 1780s, as we shall see later, was the most energetic activist of the Haskalah and the founder of societies of maskilim, studied with Raphael Levi in Hanover in the 1770s and organized a local group of maskilim there, which met to discuss questions of the Hebrew language and the Bible.[28]

Only a small portion of the correspondence between early maskilim is extant and a large part of it was conducted by Mendelssohn. One example—an exchange of letters between Wessely in Copenhagen and Mendelssohn in Berlin in 1768—will give the reader a glimpse into that literary republic in its formative stages and some idea of the intellectual vigor, literary dynamism, and passion for knowledge of its members. Mendelssohn sent Wessely a copy of his book *Phädon*, which had earned him fame, and addressed him as a personal friend and colleague for a philosophical discussion. He was well aware of Wessely's religious conservatism and wondered whether he would regard his philosophical book, written in German, with suspicion; how would he receive a book that was consummately secular in nature, and "All of its posts and pegs are made of the lead of inquiry and its interior inlaid with the restrictions of human reason"? The reply from Copenhagen showed how eager Wessely was to be counted among the members of the new elite, despite his caution and religious devotion. He commended Mendelssohn's attempt to show that Copernican cosmology was acceptable even according to the Sages, praised the virtues of *Phädon*, defended philosophy, and regarded as a personal insult Mendelssohn's doubt about his readiness to accept "inquiry" or his ability to understand the philosophical book: "For I had the book in my hand about one day, and due to my great desire to thirstily imbibe its words I read it from beginning to end, and how sweet was its wondrous flowery language." As a man who had read Plato's *Republic*, Wessely proudly asserted, he had no trouble understanding the abstract ideas of *Phädon*, and was thinking of translating it into Hebrew.[29] The first organized group of maskilim, Chevrat Dorshei Lashon Ever, the Society of Friends of the Hebrew Language, was founded only in 1782 in Königsberg, by new maskilim, most of them born in the second half of the 1750s, as we shall see in the following chapters. However, the process of a change in values, for the sake of which societies were founded, "not to observe the religious commandments, but to disseminate Enlightenment and to achieve rationalist aims," according to Jacob Katz's definition, had already begun with those informal meetings, letters, and mutual literary borrowings of the circles of early maskilim.[30]

Three Avenues of Development

Now, in light of the description of personalities and events in the previous sections, we can better assess the significance of the new intellectual awakening of the early Haskalah. It was characterized by a passion for knowledge and reading, a critical approach, an aspiration to purify, improve, and reform, to nurture repressed texts, to encourage rationalist thinking, to expand the Hebrew language, to pay more attention to nature and to aesthetic values, and to print more and more books, not necessarily religious literature. All these aspirations were marked by a tendency to undermine the foundations of the existing order and in particular to weaken the status of the religious elite. It was their recognition of the failings of the Ashkenazi rabbinical culture that aroused these early maskilim to engage in new forms of literary activity. They strove for rationalism, humanism, nature and science, to counteract ignorance, folly, religious enthusiasm, and the exaggerated fantasies of the Kabbalists. Out of the belief that it was possible to design a rational version of Judaism and to remedy the inferiority of the Jews in the age of Enlightenment, the early maskilim, nearly all of whom were an integral part of the religious culture, molded an alternative to the rabbinical elite in the form of the new Jewish intellectual. The intellectual's declaration of independence, which began to take shape at the start of the century, became an increasingly conscious one in the middle of the century. This independence was expressed in the gradual entry of Jewish intellectuals in the eighteenth century into the world of the European Enlightenment, which led to the expansion of Jewish culture beyond the religious culture and to the separation of the maskilim from the traditional elite. This process reached its peak in the 1780s, when a new generation of maskilim unified around a program of reforms, joined together to disseminate the Haskalah, and acted out of a modern self-consciousness, as Jews who consider themselves members of the "modern era." There were several early maskilim who, at the end of this dialectical process, actually adopted an orthodox position; however, this later reaction to the phenomena of enlightenment and secularism in no way invalidates the part they played in the historical process of the early Haskalah. They contributed to the secularization of the intellectual elite and were one of the manifestations of the enlightenment revolution in Central and East European Ashkenazi Jewry.

Nonetheless, the directions the early maskilim turned to were different and even opposed, and did not necessarily lead to the Haskalah movement, as one might perhaps have expected they would. The route taken by those early maskilim, who were born between the 1720s and 1750s and were also active in the 1780s, split into at least three avenues: Jewish intelligentsia, orthodoxy, and leadership of the mature Haskalah movement.

The first avenue led to the continued expansion of the Jewish intelligentsia. The maskilim were always intellectually and socially drawn to the non-Jewish intellectual and scientific world, but their formal education enabled them to live in the Jewish world as well. These maskilim gradually separated from the traditional elite and took on an identity of their own as doctors, intellectuals, or philosophers. For example, Mordechai Gumpel Schnaber-Levison emphasized his independence, on the one hand, and his affiliation with the professional group of physicians, on the other. He used the foreign name of Gompert Levison and the title of a physician, his official position with the king of Sweden: "of the society of physicians and a doctor at the General Medical Asylum of the Duke of Portland in London and professor for the King of Sweden, Gustave III."[31] When the members of Chevrat Dorshei Lashon Ever publicly announced in 1783 on the pages of *Nachal habesor* that they had organized and would soon be publishing *Hame'asef*, Schnaber sent them a letter of support. He mentioned his rights as the author of *Ma'amar haTorah vehachokhmah*, encouraged them, and urged them not to be intimidated by those "ignorant Jews" who would try to stand in their way. The newly established periodical treated the "scholar, physician, and professor Levison" with great respect and acceded to his request to print in one issue a chapter of his book, in which he decried the neglect of the Hebrew language.[32] Marcus Herz, who studied at Königsberg, Berlin, and Halle, found his purpose in life in his profession as a physician. Owing to the profession he acquired and the fascinating lectures on science and philosophy that he delivered in closed circles, he gained a large measure of social prestige in Berlin high society from the 1770s, despite the fact that he came from a low social class.[33] In 1785, Baruch Schick took a surprising step toward intellectual independence when he joined the Judeo-Christian Masonic lodge in Vienna, the "Asiatic Brethren," with its Kabbalistic and mystic elements, and in it was dubbed "Peter son of El-Chai."[34] Undoubtedly, Mendelssohn was the most independent and well known of all. His achievements and prestige within and outside the Jewish community endowed him with the status of an unquestioned authority. Many waited to hear his views on matters of religion and state, and the maskilim of the 1780s greatly admired him and were largely responsible for fostering his mythological image, during his lifetime as well as after his death.[35]

Some early maskilim broke off completely or partially from the Jewish social and cultural environment. They took the route of cultural conversion from the scholarly elite to the Enlightenment, and reached intellectual maturity in the 1760s and '70s, before the organized Haskalah movement, which offered an address and an identity to the enlightened Jews, was forged. They did not join the ranks of the later maskilim, making only a marginal contribution to the Jewish revolution of enlightenment, because they aspired to belong to the non-Jewish enlightened intelligentsia. One such maskil was Isachar Behr Falkensohn (1746–1817). Born in Kurland in the 1760s, he joined the Berlin circle of early maskilim, along with his relative Israel Zamosc, his patron Daniel Itzig, and the philosopher he greatly admired, Moses Mendelssohn. In the 1770s, Falkensohn studied medicine at Leipzig and Halle and became well known in the German literary republic as a poet in the German language owing to his book *Poems by a Polish Jew*. He described himself in one of his poems as a fashionable European who had adapted to the manners of the bourgeoisie—he was clean-shaven, dressed according to the latest fashions, and wore a powdered wig. In the 1780s, he worked as a physician in Russia, and in 1781 finally broke off completely from the Jewish environment when he converted to Christianity in St. Petersburg.[36]

Another Jewish poet who secured a place for himself in the German literary sphere and gained recognition and esteem was the merchant from Breslau, Ephraim Kuh (1731–90). He also did not play a substantial role in the enlightenment project of the maskilim, although he did maintain some relations with Mendelssohn and Solomon Maimon.[37]

The early maskil Joseph Levin had an even greater desire to engender drastic change in the lifestyle of the Jews. The son of a rabbi, born in 1740, he came to Prussia from Moravia in 1761, where he earned his living as a tutor in Berlin and Potsdam. In 1772, he sent a detailed memorandum to King Frederick II, in which he tried to persuade him that an end should be put to the control of Jewish education by Polish teachers, which was harmful both to the Jews and to the state. He proposed that he be authorized to establish a government educational system that would replace the Poles with other teachers, would teach texts aimed at molding the pupils' rationalistic views, and would produce moral citizens, beneficial to the state. His proposal was received with suspicion and coolness by Prussian officialdom, and rejected. Only a few months later, Levin converted to Christianity in a public ceremony held in a Berlin church.[38] Zalkind Hurwitz (1751–1812), on the other hand, was much more successful. He was born in a small village near Lublin and in 1772 traveled to Berlin to find employment as a tutor. In Germany and France, he very rapidly became a convert to Enlightenment, and thanks to his talents and scholarship was given a position in the royal library in Paris. In a debate held on the Jewish question, he won the Academy prize for his apologetic essay, *Apologie des Juifs*, and gained admission to the literary republic of French scholars. He exploited this position to express his belief that the Enlightenment should promote the emancipation of the Jews, and in 1790 was one of the heads of the Jewish delegation that petitioned the revolutionary leadership to grant equal rights to the Jews.[39]

The second avenue taken by early maskilim paradoxically led to orthodoxy, the adversary of the Enlightenment. When early maskilim, who still belonged to the religious elite, encountered trends of acculturation, the maskilic criticism of the 1780s and 1790s, and instances of apostasy and permissiveness, some of them reacted by withdrawing from their moderate positions. They regretted having been tempted to appreciate the "sciences" or having advocated the rationalization of Judaism. The Galician wine merchant, Dov Baer Birkenthal from Bolichov (1723–1805) was one of those who hungered for knowledge, had a good command of European languages (in his case, Polish, Latin, and French), and read quite a lot of nonreligious literature. Like other early maskilim, he denounced phenomena of ecstatic religiosity, jeered at the miracle workers that dealt in magic ("charlatans that deceive people and threaten them with demons and ghosts"), and fought against the Frankists. In his youth, he had stated, "Some members of our community have begun to spread gossip about me and doubt my faith, saying that I am engaging in this study, Heaven forbid, not for the honor of God," and as a result he abandoned his nonreligious studies. When, many years later, he came across some Jewish libertines, "Young Ashkenazi men, close-shaven, and accustomed from their youth to the pleasures of this world and ignoring some of the commandments," he regretted having been attracted to those books "which in the eyes of our people are very loathsome, and we call them 'unfit books'."[40]

As the early maskilim met more and more young scholars who were becoming freethinkers, ostensibly proving that there was some connection between the Haskalah and apostasy, they became persuaded that it was justified to erect obstacles against "inquiry." The case of Rabbi Judah Leib Margolioth provides a "window" through which to observe the frustrations and quandaries of an early maskil who belonged to the religious elite, but wondered time and again whether it was proper to taste the "honey" of science and philosophy, and finally decided against it. A close scrutiny of his path as an intellectual attracted to the early Haskalah reveals a circuitous route that began when he burst into the world of the Enlightenment and ended when he expressed remorse, retreated in panic and took refuge in a fideistic religious approach.[41]

A third avenue also came out of the early Haskalah: one root of the mature Haskalah that took shape in Berlin and Königsberg from the end of the 1770s. The consummate representative of this avenue is Naphtali Herz Wessely. He followed the development of the group of young maskilim, was accepted by them as an experienced advisor, and represented himself as their patron. As a matter of fact, it was Wessely who launched the maskilim's ideological struggle in his programmatic work *Divrei shalom ve'emet* (1782–85). Its message reverberated far more loudly than the author himself had anticipated it would, as we shall see in the coming chapters. Wessely became a constant advisor to the editors of *Ha-ma'asef*, although a certain distance was always maintained between them, between the early maskil born in the 1720s and those born in the 1750s and '60s, so that it would be a mistake to think that he was a regular member of their circle. However, when Wessely summed up the path he had taken, he did not hesitate to take credit for the breakthrough whose fruits were by then evident. At the opening of the Hebrew translation of Mendelssohn's *Phädon*, which appeared exactly twenty years after the publication of the original work and more than thirty years after the publication of his own first book, *Gan na'ul,* in Amsterdam, Wessely reviewed the intensive maskilic activity and in particular praised the books printed by Chevrat Chinukh Ne'arim (the Society for the Education of Youth) in Berlin. With evident self-satisfaction and the patronizing pride of a "father of the Haskalah," Wessely wrote in 1787:

Now my soul rejoices at seeing plants of Lebanon growing in the cities of Ashkenaz . . . Such spices had not been known heretofore until I brought the first fruits of my heart as an offering to the Lord . . . I have been the cause of much good, since I began to speak a little to the best of my power in these matters . . . for this I have prayed and for this my soul waits, that our writings will be the path which every valiant and wise man shall follow to add of his own knowledge in these studies.[42]

PART II

Jewish *Kulturkampf*

Chapter Four

The Wessely Affair: Threats and Anxieties

On Shabbat HaGadol, the special Sabbath before the Passover fes-
tival, David Tevele, rabbi of the Lissa community in Western Poland, rose to
the pulpit of the great synagogue to deliver a scathing sermon. "I deplore the
act of this man, a hypocrite and evildoer, a boor, the worst kind of layman, by
the name of Herz Wessely from Berlin." The rabbi, in thunderous tones,
voiced his swift public reaction to the slim pamphlet *Divrei shalom ve'emet*,
published in Berlin in the winter of 1782. "Proud and haughty is this enemy of
the Jews who is a threat to our very lives . . . he is excommunicated, banned,
and cursed with a blowing of the shofar and the extinguishing of candles, for
he is accursed and damned, cut off from the Congregation of Israel." The
rabbi went on to vent his rage before the congregation, in a tearful voice: "My
heart shall moan like a harp . . . oh, that my head were waters that I might
weep day and night for the daughter of my people . . . it is true that today is a
holy sabbath, dedicated to God, when weeping is not permitted, but I am overcome by floods of tears and am weary of holding them in."[1]

Orthodox Counterreaction

Rabbi Tevele's sermon was a crucial milestone in the history of the orthodox
reaction to the threat of a modernist awakening in Jewish society, and in its
written form, it constitutes the first distinctly orthodox text. The rabbi's dramatic and emotional response is particularly noteworthy. It is a reflection of
deep anxiety, attended by physical as well as emotional expressions (weeping,
trembling, loud cries) and extreme invective and denunciations heaped on the
heads of those who posed the threat that aroused this outburst. David Tevele's
response was not exceptional. Three months later, when copies of the sermon
came from Lissa and were received by Rabbi Pinhas Halevi Hurwitz in Frankfurt-on-Main, he too was greatly agitated. In an admonitory moralistic sermon, delivered to his congregation on the eve of the first day of Tammuz, he
described his mental state resulting from those same threats to the Jews that
were emanating from Berlin. "When I heard about and saw this sight, I was

so alarmed, I began to tremble and my knees struck one against the other."[2] Other testimonies tell of the panic that also spread through Lithuanian Vilna. According to the rumors that reached Tevele and were taken at face value by all those who participated in the polemic, the news was that "In the community of Vilna, a great city of God, they burned this book in the city streets, and at first hung it by an iron chain in the courtyard of the synagogue." The rabbi of Lissa applauded this act of despoiling Wessley's "open letter," which was tied to the pillory (the *kuna*) that stood near the entrance to the Vilna synagogue (based on his information, at the express instruction of the Vilna Gaon himself, whom, like many of the religious elite, he greatly admired). Later, *Divrei shalom ve'emet* was burned as a heretical book, just as, ten years earlier, the writings of the Hasidim, the Gaon's detested foes, were burned and ridiculed in ceremonies held at the same spot, under the supervision of that same authoritative and charismatic rabbi.[3]

That same Sabbath when Rabbi Tevele delivered his sermon in Lissa, Wessely was also attacked by the rabbi acknowledged as the most senior religious authority of that generation, Rabbi Yehezkel Landau (1713–93), in his own Shabbat HaGadol sermon in Prague. As a matter of fact, the rabbi of Prague was the first to react publicly to *Divrei shalom ve'emet*. In an earlier sermon, the full text of which was not preserved, delivered on the eve of the first day of Shevat (January 1782), apparently only a few days after Wessely's pamphlet had come off the Hebrew printing press in Berlin, Rabbi Landau had already marked him as an enemy of Judaism. Although, in obedience to the laws of the country, he had refrained from issuing an explicit writ of excommunication against Wessely, he did pronounce him in his sermon as "damned, accursed, and banished from the Jewish people," and called for the expulsion "of this evildoer, Herz Wessely." But Landau was not satisfied merely to deliver a sermon to his congregation. He hastened to enlist the support of other rabbis in the Austrian empire (the rabbis of Pressburg in Hungary and Nikolsburg in Moravia). He was particularly concerned about the possibility that Wessely might pay a visit to Vienna, the capital of the empire, where he would be assisted by some wealthy enlightened Jews (such as Wessely's contact there, the affluent and influential Nathan Orenstein), and was liable to seriously impair the relationship between the traditional Jewish leadership and the members of Emperor Joseph II's administration. In a letter that he hastened to send off to Vienna, Rabbi Landau, who had apparently heard rumors about Wessely's impending visit to that city, asked the heads of the community to make sure that "no Jew will welcome him or invite him into his home, but that each one, fearing divine retribution, will avoid any contact with this evil heretic, and anyone despising and rebuffing him will be rewarded by a heavenly blessing." The things he read in the eight chapters of *Divrei shalom ve'emet* had sufficed to induce him to harshly judge Wessely as a heretic. "That pamphlet in itself," Rabbi Landau wrote in his letter to Vienna, amounts to "a denial of the Torah, a mockery of the written and the oral Law, and reflects the view that they are of no value or benefit." And even more than that— Wessely's words, which attest to the fact that he is an atheist who abjures any religion, also cast suspicion on him as belonging to that same menacing, dangerous sect of adherents of the natural religion of eighteenth-century Europe: "that evildoer mocks the faithful of all religions, which proves that in his heart he is not a believer of any religion or creed, but is one of those *Naturalisten* [naturalists]."[4]

Divrei shalom ve'emet was, then, the stimulus that incited the first battle in the history of the Jewish *Kulturkampf*. In the events of 1782, the Haskalah, which was impinging for the first time on Jewish public opinion, evoked feelings of frustration and anxiety that fueled the reaction of the orthodox camp, which went on the defensive and at the same time launched an attack using verbal aggression and counterthreats. What were these threats? Why did they produce such existential anxiety among those faithful to the tradition? Why was this anxiety so profound in particular among the rabbinical elite? Why was Wessely, who until then had never been accused of religious laxity, and who certainly was not a freethinker, now so mercilessly persecuted? And what was the fundamental innovation that aroused so bitter a controversy and first shaped both the orthodox self-consciousness and the maskilic self-consciousness?

That eight-page pamphlet, based on its form and its author's intentions, was, in fact, more of an open letter than a book. No date or place of publication was noted on it, and the author's signature appeared at the end, not at the beginning, which was the usual practice. The pamphlet was written by the fifty-seven-year-old author, Hebrew linguist, and biblical scholar Naphtali Herz Wessely. The most threatening aspect of this programmatic article was the author's opinion of what should be the content and nature of Jewish education. But this was just one of the threats that faced the religious elite in the eighteenth century.[5] It was preceded by at least five other threats. We enumerate them here so as to better understand why the sensitivity and anxiety of the orthodox were heightened in the face of the accumulated threats.

The first threat had already emerged in the seventeenth century, in the form of the enthusiastic and messianic mystics who joined the Sabbatian underground, and in the course of the eighteenth century aroused several embarrassing scandals by their radical and anarchistic behavior and their religious and sexual permissiveness. As Elisheva Carlebach showed in her description of the case of the well-known adversary of Sabbatianism, Moses Hagiz, the orthodox reaction to and struggle against Sabbatianism was, in the first half of the eighteenth century, already marked by certain patterns and characteristics, for example, a tendency to barricade themselves in *emunat chakhamim* ("the belief in the Sages") and to adopt a fiedistic religious position, which called for belief in God and in the written and oral Torah, leaving no room for questions, proofs, or skeptical inquiry.[6]

The second threat was a more distant one. It came from the European world of the eighteenth century in the form of the rationalistic, skeptical, and naturalistic heretic doctrines of the radical Enlightenment, which many Jews were acquainted with. The all-European threat encompassed the third threat—that of rationalistic Jewish heresy. Those who espoused this heresy, most of whom were completely anonymous, came out against the authority of the Sages and the oral Torah and subverted the authority of the contemporary rabbis.[7]

The fourth threat was described in detail about forty years ago by the historian Azriel Shohet. He produced a great deal of evidence from Germany in the first half of the century, attesting to the struggle waged by the religious elite—rabbis, preachers, and moralists—against the acculturation of the Jews (in particular in urban communities like Hamburg and Berlin). This acculturation was expressed in their lifestyle: the way they spent their leisure time, their language, art, purchases, mode of dress, and other aspects of life in aristocratic and bourgeois Europe.[8] The fifth threat was posed by those students, physicians, and sons of the members of the religious elite, who were the early maskilim and whose activities and intellectual pretensions did not go undetected by the rabbis of the generation, as we noted in the previous chapters.

When Rabbi David Tevele and Rabbi Landau of Prague first held Wessely's pamphlet *Divrei shalom ve'emet* in their hands, they were already aware of all these threats. Rabbi Tevele, born in Brody (died in 1792), was a typical representative of the rabbinical elite. He was of the same generation as the Gaon of Vilna, Wessely, and Mendelssohn, and the son of a rabbi who fought against the Frankists. In his religious writings, Rabbi Tevele quoted from the teachings of the Gaon of Vilna and Dov Baer the Magid of Mezhirech, as well as from the *Zohar* and the Lurianic Kabbalah. He maintained ties with the rabbinical elite in Europe; while he was still in Brody, he was involved in the stormy controversy between rabbis, in the 1760s, about the validity of the Cleve divorce; he granted approbations to many books; and he corresponded with Rabbi Yehezkel Landau, whom he regarded as the greatest rabbi of the generation. As rabbi of the Lissa community, he enacted regulations in the 1770s against the influence of French fashion on the dress of women in his community.[9] He was very familiar with the array of threats that confronted the traditionalists and, like Landau, he apparently also accused Wessely of belonging to the "sect of naturalists." What was it that evoked his harsh reaction? What heightened his frustration? What fueled the anxiety that gripped him when he stood at his pulpit on Shabbat HaGadol, in 1782 to deliver his sermon decrying *Divrei shalom ve'emet*?

The rabbi's rhetoric was extremely aggressive. He hurled invective at Wessely ("this man"), calling him wicked, accursed, vile and worthless, stupid, oafish, simpleminded and vulgar, loathsome, and heretical. One might have expected such bellicose rhetoric in the reaction to a much more serious threat than the proposal of a new curriculum for the traditional educational system, such as the one made in *Divrei shalom ve'emet*, which included a foreign language, science, history, and geography. In the 1782 polemic, no one denied the importance of these areas of knowledge, nor was anyone totally opposed to the demand made by the state (Joseph II), on the one hand, and by the maskil Wessely, on the other, that these be included in the accepted religious curriculum. Even those rabbis who attacked Wessely acknowledged the necessity of neutral extra-religious knowledge (languages and science) in the professional training of merchants and craftsmen, although they would have had it restricted to a very small measure of basic knowledge. "For truly all parents would wish to provide their children with every *chokhmah* and science, every craft and occupation," the rabbi from Lissa contended, at least in principle.[10]

What, then, caused Rabbi Tevele to adopt an antimodernist position and to react in such a radical, agitated, orthodox manner? First, he was beset by great anxiety in the face of what he interpreted as a threat to the supreme value of Torah study. In his eyes, the idea of permitting the student to choose between various tracks in Jewish education, as Wessely proposed, was a grave danger. He feared that the rabbinical-talmudic track would become just one of many, and that in addition to it, the students could select other tracks that would ensure them of a livelihood. In 1782, Wessely declared, "We were not all created to be talmudic scholars and to deal in the profundities of religion and to teach, for the Almighty has distinguished among men, and given unto each that he may specialize according to his interest and his abilities."[11] He attempted to introduce new criteria into education, rejecting the traditional educational ideal, which held that a Jew's highest achievement was the attainment of the rank of a *talmid chakham*, a rabbinic scholar, and allocated all educational resources from early childhood to religious studies. Wessely advocated the ideal of enlightenment, which recognized the individual's right to fulfill his potential in his own autonomous fashion. His approach actually meant no less than the secularization of education, culture, and social values. From then on, if Wessely's program were to be adopted, the study of Torah and the taking of a rabbinical post would be one of the options open to members of Jewish society, rather than a sweeping imperative that was binding on all. In fact, only a few actually realized the ideal of talmudic scholarship even in the pre-modern traditional society, becoming members of the "community of scholars." But any other occupation or course in life, even that followed by rich merchants whose wealth financed the traditional community, was recognized as a necessity recognition only after the fact.[12] Now, Wessely, in his *Divrei shalom ve'emet*, was trying to turn the reality that existed after the fact into one that was desirable from the outset. He based his approach on the change in the government's policy, heralded by Joseph II's Edict of Toleration, and aspired to encourage the economic, perhaps even the political normalization of the Jews. He called on the Jewish community to recognize the need and the value of nonreligious life pursuits and to cooperate in devising an innovative curriculum for schools that would prepare Jewish youths for a variety of patterns of life.

A change in the curriculum would have far-reaching implications. Wessely and other maskilim who pointed out that traditional education had many limitations and found fault with the qualifications of the Polish teachers linked their proposed change to the maskilic utopia. They believed that the educational programs would hasten the arrival of a joyous era that was already on the threshold. In their vision of the future, the maskilim did not aspire to see a total invalidation of the traditional values, nor did they want to deliberately injure the religion, its commandments and the value placed on talmudic study. However, they were dissatisfied with the traditional patterns of life and the educational processes designed to prepare students to fit into this way of life, as their fathers and forefathers had done.

The maskilim placed a special emphasis on the moral rehabilitation of the Jews, and internalized the educational ideal of the *Bildung*, one of the hallmarks of the German Enlightenment. They wanted the Jews' enlightenment to express more than the acquisition of scientific and humanistic knowledge about the world and mankind and the normalization of their economic life (so fewer of them would engage in commerce and as many as possible would be integrated into the productive sectors of the economy, benefiting the society and the state); they also wanted it to contribute to the Jews' personal development. The Jew, they felt, ought to become a rational and moral being and a citizen who places his skills at the disposal of the society and the state.[13] Of course, the fact that they suggested the maskilic ideal of a rational, moral being as an alternative to the rabbinic scholar carried the meaning of secularization.

The religious ideal of *musar* literature was transformed by the maskilim into a universal secular ideal: the moral individual. Nonetheless, the maskilic *musar* literature written by Isaac Satanow (*Sefer hamidot* [Book of Ethics], 1784), Wessely (*Sefer hamidot*, 1786), Mendel Breslau (*Yaldut vebacharut* [Childhood and Adolescence], 1786) and others did not abandon religious faith. Moreover, their doctrine of *midot* was broad enough so that it could also include a commitment to Torah and *mitzvoth* (commandments), and the point of departure of the maskilic *musar* literature was man's obligations to God and to His Torah. What made it innovative was that it extended the obligations to external spheres—the state and its rulers, the citizens of the state, and man as a human being. Wessely, for example, recommended that the Jews "draw knowledge and good morals from the primary source, from the depths of the Torah's language."[14] Isaac Euchel, the most important maskil in the 1780s and '90s, who contributed greatly to the organizational molding of the Haskalah movement in its formative stages, drew a distinction between *philosophische Moral* and *theologische Moral*. He asserted that the Torah provides a set of general moral principles, whereas philosophy only enables one to delve into the details. He suggested that the Jewish educator first present to his students "philosophical morals," and only thereafter should he return to the religious texts to show that the "theological morals" of the Jews are consistent with the "philosophical morals." In his view, the Jews have three guides available to aid them on the path to perfection: wisdom (in the sense of the totality of knowledge accumulated by humankind), rational morals (acquired through reason), and the Torah (that originates in divine revelation).[15]

The maskilic utopia did not call for the Jews to abandon their life patterns or their existence as a separate society, as a culture that draws upon the religious texts or a religion that requires the observance of the commandments. However, in actual fact, it did call for the Jewish identity—in which religious life, the Torah and the *chakham* comprise an entire, satisfying world—to be split. The maskilim envisaged three identities—a Jew, a human being, and a citizen. If these identities were to be combined in the life of the Jewish individual and that of the entire Jewish society, a complete whole would be produced.

As a Jew, the individual is required in the maskilic utopia to preserve a link to the various levels of the religious culture, including the Talmud. The unique culture of the Jews would be expanded and enriched in the essential encounter with the "sciences," by renewed attention to the Hebrew language, by the revival of literature and poetry, and by the methodical approach to the "Torah of God," to be adopted in the new schools. A methodical study of the Hebrew language would help provide an understanding of the biblical text; the study of history would place the biblical events into their broad context; geography would endow the Torah with a realistic dimension; and the natural sciences would arouse in the Jew a sense of "the majesty of the Lord, His power and greatness, so that the glory of the Lord will grow in his heart and he will fear Him."[16]

As a human being, the Jew would join the family of humankind: he too would aspire to mold himself into a moral being, free himself of folly and superstition, acquire the knowledge that men have gained by force of their reason and experience, and adopt the humanistic values of the Enlightenment. From the "teachings of man," the Jew would learn "how to enjoy all things under the sun," and how to find his happiness in this world. As a citizen, and as a loyal subject of the modern absolutist state that aspires to mobilize all its residents for its sake, the Jew will also contribute to the "benefit of the political collective." The knowledge of languages and sciences will serve him in achieving a practical goal—economic success in his commercial ventures and in his association with others.

This fusion of human being, citizen, and Jew would bring about the yearned-for normalization. The Jews would be rehabilitated and revitalized, their negative image in the eyes of non-Jews and the state would be improved, the Jewish nation would have its lost honor restored, and it would be accepted into the family of enlightened nations.[17]

Clearly, Wessely was cognizant of the need to relate positively, with an integrative approach, to extra-Jewish spheres: that of the state and its citizens and that of humanity as a whole. His plan was to fulfill this need by reforming the traditional educational system, doing away with the exclusivity of the religious studies track. It seems that the preacher from Lissa was all too aware of the significance of this program. He foresaw that it would lead to the dissolution of the traditional educational system based on Torah study and would considerably erode the value of this study: "If, Heaven forbid, his words are heeded, there will not remain one Jewish child who will not turn his back on the laborious study of the Torah." If the door were to be opened wide, permitting every child the freedom of choice, and if the study of Talmud had to face open competition, the religious track would surely come out second best, even among those students possessed of a scholarly aptitude.[18]

The preacher therefore felt compelled to go on the defensive against Wessely's integrative curriculum (in his well-known terms the religious knowledge originating from a divine source, "the teaching of God," versus human knowledge originating in autonomous reason, "the teaching of man") and to object vehemently to the primacy Wessely had assigned to extra-religious learning in the maskilic curriculum. Still, even these reasons did not suffice to justify such a scathing and panic-stricken attack, nor do they explain the rabbi's attempts to expand the circle of protest by circulating his sermon throughout Poland and even outside its borders. In his Shabbat HaGadol sermon, Rabbi Tevele, with orthodox sensibility, keenly discerned the fundamental deviations from the tradition contained in *Divrei shalom ve'emet*. In addition to exposing the future implications of the maskilic educational revolution for the structure of the society and angrily defining it as a subversive program, he was perceptive enough to identify the new, revolutionary modes of thought reflected in it. For example, he warned his listeners against the historicization of the Bible and the attempt to place giants from the ancient Jewish past in an historical context that would render them of no greater value than ordinary men. He entrenched himself in the position that held that the entire Torah was secret, mysterious, not susceptible to a rationalistic or realistic reading, and opposed the view that Torah study was not sufficient to mold men and prepare them for life. Rabbi Tevele went even further, accusing Wessely of being a rationalistic heretic, a deist who believes in the natural religion: "He has no part or share in the God of Israel," because "he adheres to alien views like those of the naturalists."[19] This grave accusation was groundless, as we have seen, and certainly it could not be proved, or even insinuated, from anything written in Wessely's work. And, as a matter of fact, the rabbi did not develop it further in his sermon beyond this single sentence. However, there were real grounds for another key threat that Rabbi Tevele identified, one that ran like a thread through his entire sermon.

The Subversive Intellectual

Who are you Wessely? Rabbi Tevele asked again and again: who are you, "a man poor in knowledge, the worst kind of layman," who has offered "hasty counsel to innocent, wise, and intelligent men" as if you were "an eminent scholar"? Who has appointed you a spokesman for the Jews? The rabbi from Lissa definitely regarded Wessely's approach as an unprecedented threat, which, for very good reason, caused him and his rabbi colleagues to tremble and to marshal their finest rhetorical powers to preach against him. Rabbi Tevele identified Wessely as the representative of the elite of writers, the new intellectuals, who drew inspiration from the European Enlightenment and were sensitive to its criticism of the existing order. The modern Jewish writers incorporated extra-Jewish knowledge into their books, called for the rational-ization and normalization of Jewish life in Europe, showed their appreciation of values like tolerance and freedom, and were highly conscious of being mod-ern men, living in a new historical era that had embraced all of Europe. It was not only the contents of *Divrei shalom ve'emet* and Wessely's criticism of the traditional educational system and its exclusive religious curriculum that aroused the preacher's ire and anxiety. Rabbi Tevele was also angered by the temerity of a writer who did not belong to the traditional elite of rabbis and scholars, who drew their authority from their erudition in the Torah, their ability to write religious books and to hand down halakhic rulings, as well as from their rabbinical positions. And yet, Wessely had the political presumptu-ousness to try to mobilize Jewish public opinion throughout the land to sup-port his educational program.

This new type of intellectual, as we have seen, had begun to emerge early in the eighteenth century, from within the early Haskalah. *Divrei shalom ve'emet*, however, reflected a genuine change, despite the fact that it was not a theoretical book, but merely a pamphlet, a journalistic article. It was written before the Hebrew periodicals were founded and was sent as an open letter to various communities for the declared purpose of mobilizing support for his program.

Wessely opened a Jewish public discourse of a new type, a kind of "maskilic preaching," which was critical, optimistic, employed the rhetoric of progress and future promise, was oriented to "the modern," preoccupied with worldly issues, contained persuasive arguments about the need for reform, and proferred a picture of the future. This new form of preaching, unlike the traditional form, did not call for greater piety or religious devotion; it included no threats of divine punishment or the frights of hell; nor did it promise a reward in the next world. The "author" forged his way into the public sphere and demanded his audience's attention to this new discourse. Rabbi Tevele was not unmindful of the political challenge Wessely was posing to the leadership of the rabbinical elite through this daring, unprecedented act.

Wessely was not a philosopher of the same stature as his friend Mendelssohn, nor did he offer any abstract insights or ideas derived from the European Enlightenment. But his booklet *Divrei shalom ve'emet* was far more than a program for an educational change, although it was written in relatively simple language, in an effort to make his ideas clear to every Hebrew reader (an aim that in the eighteenth century called for the reader's ability to read and comprehend religious texts, a skill often acquired only after the basic stages of study in a *cheder* or *talmud Torah*). In effect, it was an essay influenced by Enlightenment concepts about man, who through his reason shaped his social world and life and developed his latent potential without relying on divine revelation or religious guidance.[20] In truth, the heading *torat ha'adam* (human knowledge) would have been more fitting for Wessely's revolutionary work, while the title *Divrei shalom ve'emet* denoted only the form of the pamphlet (a letter, based on the Book of Esther) and its purpose—to serve as an agent for mobilizing Jewish public opinion.

The author's dissatisfaction with the self-definition of the Jew, who for generations had been isolating himself from the society of his fellow men, and the desire to see him break out of this isolation resonate from each of the eight chapters of *Divrei shalom ve'emet*. Although, for Wessely, the Jew, with his unique culture, Torah, and commandments, was manifestly the proper model, in *Divrei shalom ve'emet* he issued the great clarion call of the Haskalah—be a man, too! He then enumerated each of those attributes "that make one worthy of being called a man." His trenchant criticism of the traditional society, its values, education, and leadership, left no room for doubt—in his view, in the course of centuries, the Jews had forgotten they were born first as human beings before they were Jews.

Man, in Wessely's description, is endowed with reason, capable of constructing his own world without dependence on heavenly revelation or divine instructions. He acquires knowledge and experience, develops science, builds states, improves the economy, makes inventions, and expands human knowledge. Man is capable, through his senses, of gaining knowledge from the environment, perfecting himself and revitalizing himself time and again, like a tabula rasa, an idea drawn from the English philosopher John Locke. From it, the enlightened drew an enormous measure of optimism and faith in the ability of education to improve men's minds and faculties. Echoing the well-known words of Lessing, the German dramaturge and friend of Mendelssohn, in his 1779 play *Nathan der Weise*, a plea for tolerance, Wessely called on his brethren to change the order of their priorities: from now on, it is incumbent on each and every one to realize that he is first and foremost a man, and only then a member of his people and his religion. "*Torat ha'adam* is prior in time to the supreme laws of God," Wessely stated, and hence it is wrong for the Jews to avoid the society and culture of other human beings and to seclude themselves within the bounds of their religious culture. The Jews too are social creatures, and hence their social circle of reference cannot be limited to their own society. Wessely's criticism was extremely harsh, and it is not hard to identify its target. The author was referring to the rabbinical elite, challenging the foundations of its existence, pointing to its idleness and shortcomings:

> He who lacks *torat ha'adam*, although he has learned the laws and teachings of God and lives according to them, is deficient on two counts. One, his society is burdensome to other men, and in all his comings and goings, he will err in the customs of men, his words on worldly matters are lacking in intelligence, and his actions in all things under the sun are vain and soon diminished for they are of no service or benefit to other people. And two, although the laws and teachings of God are much loftier than "human knowledge," they are connected and intertwined . . . hence he who is ignorant in the laws of God but is versed in human knowledge, although the Sages of Israel will not derive pleasure from his light in the study of the Torah, the rest of humanity will take pleasure from him. And he who is ignorant of human knowledge, although he knows the laws of God, will bring no joy to the sages of his own people, nor to all other men.[21]

While in the distant past, in their independent state, the Jews lived like other nations and maintained their state based on *torat ha'adam*, the crisis of exile distanced them from normal life and plunged them "into the darkness of this folly that is pitched above us." Wessely places the blame on the rulers of Europe, who sorely humiliated the Jews in their countries, oppressing their spirit and excluding them from politics, science, and culture. However, in the late eighteenth century, the leaders of the Ashkenazi rabbinical elite share in the blame, particularly at a time when the spirit of tolerance was growing in Europe. Since, in Wessely's view, every man of intelligence could discern the signs of an historical shift, after the Austrian emperor had proclaimed legal reliefs and a program to improve the status of the Jews in his empire, there was no longer any justification for the traditional social and cultural isolation, just as there was no room for a pessimistic mood or despondency.[22] "It would behoove you to cast off the ways of depressed spirit in which you walked when you lived in affliction," Wessely called out to the Jews of Europe. He urged them to oust the Polish teachers, "who speak in a poor tongue and have taught us rude and common phrases" and perpetuate ignorance and isolation; to shun the Yiddish language, which only exacerbates their segregation; to adopt the "language of the land"; to teach their children the sciences, ethics, and other vital knowledge; to write new textbooks for their children—all this to redress the historical neglect that led to this lamentable anomaly of Jewish life. Thus the Jews would be rehabilitated and return to the society of all human beings. Moreover, as a result of educational reform, religious studies would regain a status of respect, and young Jewish businessmen would be less inclined to show indifference to religious obligations or to leave Judaism entirely. Wessely described how the very first encounter of these Jews with European culture, untempered by a reformed education, threw them straight into the open arms of atheism and into the bosom of the "society of those who have forgotten God."[23]

In later stages of the polemic, when, defensive and apologetic, he faced the rabbis, Wessely claimed that he failed to understand why he had aroused their ire. At that time, however, he was unquestionably aware of the revolutionary trend introduced in *Divrei shalom ve'emet*. He made no attempt to conceal the innovative nature of his unprecedented program, and was prepared to receive skeptical reactions. "All beginnings are difficult," he wrote at the end of his open letter, "and all the more so to bring forth new things in our community, since for several generations, our fathers and forefathers have not been accustomed to them."[24] Nonetheless, he hoped that his words of reason would persuade the Jewish leadership, at least those living under the rule of Joseph II, to hasten to cooperate in establishing reformed schools. Wessely was so confident in his ability to convince the contemporary rabbis to revamp their traditional approach and to understand that the human being takes precedence over the Jew and that an educated man takes precedence over a talmudic scholar, that he was not afraid to attack the traditional ideal: "The Sages have said (*Midrash raba*, *Leviticus*, chapter 1) 'A *talmid chakham* (who knows the laws and Torah of God) who is lacking in knowledge (good manners and civility) a carcass is better than he', and that is a parable . . . for one who has no knowledge will give no pleasure to the Sages of Israel nor to the sages of the other nations, for he puts his Torah to shame, and other men despise him."[25] These challenging words, which demolished the ideal image of the talmudic scholar, were in the eyes of the rabbinical elite a provocation that could not go unanswered.

The key question was, therefore, what grounds were there for the authority of the secular intellectual, who had no formal or traditional authorization. He did not represent himself as a religious figure, and he was perceived as an intruder who threatened the monopoly of the traditional elite and was competing with it. So the rabbi from Lissa cried out in his Shabbat HaGadol sermon:

> How did he dare, this man lacking in all sublime wisdom, other than the fundamentals of the Hebrew language, the literal meaning of the Bible, and a rudimentary knowledge of the Scriptures and the commentaries. He has no part or share in the profundities of the Talmud, the early commentaries or the Oral Torah . . . how does he have the audacity to say "I shall offer them counsel" . . . how does this man who does not possess any of the foundations of wisdom come forth to teach us the [proper] curriculum and to instruct this people in the ways of God, and the deeds they must do . . . the weak will say I am strong and the blind will say walk at my feet, I will show you the way.[26]

Rabbi Tevele could hardly fathom how this independent author and intellectual, who came from outside the traditional framework, could be presumptuous enough to offer himself as a guide to the Jewish public. This step of Wessely's was totally unacceptable to him; he regarded it as an attempt to subvert the foundations of the rabbinical elite, of which he was the consummate representative and which he fervently wanted to protect. The rabbi of Lissa reminded his listeners that he had met Wessely seven years earlier, when he had come to request an approbation for his book *Yain levanon*. Already then his suspicion and doubts were aroused, and at first he had refused to grant him the approbation, "since a man so shaken out and emptied of all the profound wisdom of the Talmud and the ancients surely is not one of the sages of Israel." This sentence probably best reflects the full intensity of Rabbi Tevele's anxiety. After he himself had written an approbation for Wessely, he was determined to deny him the legitimation of an author and to disassociate him from the intellectual elite, because only "the sages of Israel," those men well-versed in the Talmud and the halakhah, are the legitimate and acknowledged members of that elite. He had relented and agreed to grant the approbation only after other rabbis in Lissa had urged him to do so, claiming there was no cause for concern, since Wessely's grammar book was not a halakhic work. Of course, in hindsight, the rabbi very much regretted having given his approbation, and announced that he was rescinding it. Just as someone who does not know how to play a musical instrument himself, but has only heard music and song, would not presume to serve as a music teacher ("is it conceivable that a man who knows not the art of music but has only heard the sound of singers and musicians, would instruct them in the art of drawing their bows and playing their instruments?"), so it is unthinkable that someone who has not acquired the tools of the profession (who is not "a talmudic scholar") would intrude into the exclusive territory of the elite.[27] Rabbi Hurwitz of Frankfurt presented a similar argument in his sermon against Wessely: "Woe to that shame, alas, to that disgrace! That the most insignificant of men, a contemptible fellow devoid of any wisdom, who does not know even the general form of the subject, should presume to tell talmudic scholars, the watchmen of the world, how they should behave."[28]

Wessely's opponents were infuriated by the sentence in *Divrei shalom ve'emet* that quoted from the midrash: "A *talmid chakham* who lacks knowledge a carcass is better than he." It was interpreted as a grave, direct affront to the rabbinical elite. "Who are you reviling, who are you defaming?" And how have you dared to "cast aspersions upon the great sages?" the Rabbi of Lissa lashed out at Wessely, how had he failed to respect the authority of the rabbis, first among them Rabbi Yehezkel Landau, the only one with the right to speak in the name of the Jews living under Austrian rule, and who is perhaps also the official spokesmen of all Jews, by virtue of his religious authority and his rabbinical position in the Prague community? Wessely ought to have turned at least to his community rabbi in Berlin, Zevi Hirsch Levin, before daring to mount the public stage and call on the public to follow him. "As if there were no (other) guide there until this layman appeared to lead the flock like a wise shepherd," Rabbi Tevele upbraided Wessely.[29]

In Tevele's view, Wessely's threat endangered the entire rabbinical elite. Therefore he did not hesitate to react in his Polish community to ideas about cultural policy that emanated from Vienna, the capital of the Austrian empire and from Berlin, the capital of the Prussian kingdom. He was in fact calling for the supra-local solidarity of members of the rabbinical elite against the laymen trying to subvert it. By circulating copies of his Shabbat HaGadol sermon, he was hoping to enlist the heads of that elite in a counterattack. These copies did reach many communities, but as we shall see later, this intrusion into other countries turned out to be an impediment to Rabbi Tevele.

Obviously, then, Rabbi Tevele astutely identified the essence of the maskilic threat, expressed in the appearance of the secular, subversive intellectual. In his Shabbat HaGadol sermon, he adopted an anxious orthodox position in an attempt to defend the sector of scholars ("the sect of those studying the laws of God"), the honor of the Torah and of God. In this opening battle of the Jewish *Kulturkampf* between the orthodox and the modern, the fierce political and cultural rivalry over hegemony in Jewish society was launched. On one side, the old elite, warning against any deviation by the laymen usurpers, and on the other, the new elite, imbued with a sense that the future was theirs.

This initial battle of the Jewish culture war, which reverberated from London and Amsterdam in the West to Vilna and Lissa in the East, was, of course, not conducted in an historical vacuum. To understand the role of *Divrei shalom ve'emet* as an agent of change that generated internal Jewish power struggles, one must realize what the historical backdrop to the publication was. The second half of the 1770s and the early 1780s was a particularly stormy period: the demographic growth of Europe in that century reached its peak (from 120 million at the beginning of the century to 190 million at its end); in Britain the industrial revolution, which would transform the entire world, took its first steps; in Boston and Philadelphia the patriots marched toward political independence and formulated the basic documents of the new American democracy, in which they adopted rallying cries of the Enlightenment to justify their rebellion against British rule; and in Paris and Versailles the monarchs faced the threat of the approaching revolution. The Enlightenment culture was already the dominant culture among the European elite, despite the churches' conservative protests. During those years, several of the most important works of the late Enlightenment were published, such as Adam Smith's *Wealth of Nations* (1776), Lessing's *Nathan der Weise* (1779), Rousseau's *Confessions* (1782), and Kant's *Was ist Aufklärung?* (1784). Paris maintained its status as the capital of Enlightenment and French was regarded as the language of high culture. These were the peak years of the *Aufklärung* in Berlin, Königsberg, Hamburg, Frankfurt, and other cities in Germany. Universities, periodicals, cafes, and reading societies served as meeting places for enlightened intellectuals. Professors, physicians, publishers, playwrights, and government officials coalesced into a secular elite that created a large corpus of literature and attracted a growing readership.[30] The monarchic rulers of Europe also wanted to acquire the image of enlightened men. Frederick the Great, king of Prussia, Empress Catherine II of Russia (the two rising European powers in the eighteenth century), and the Habsburg ruler Joseph II maintained close ties with the Enlightenment philosophers, employed academy graduates as officials and advisors, and supported the sciences and arts. And although they did not change the class structure of their states or the dynastic absolutist form of rule, they did introduce various reforms.[31]

Naphtali Herz Wessely was also a man of the eighteenth-century Enlightenment. Although he was committed to the tradition, observed the commandments, and in his literary work was engaged mainly with Hebrew texts—a commentary on Leviticus in the framework of the *Bi'ur* project, a book on ethics for schoolchildren, the sweeping biblical epic *Shirei tiferet*, and others—he was fluent in German, read newspapers and philosophy books, dressed in the rococo fashion (a wig, its curls falling on the back of his neck, and clean-shaven), and showed great interest in events occurring in Europe.[32] The stations of his life provided him with an all-European vantage point: his family on his father's side had survived the 1648–49 pogroms in the Ukraine; he himself had traveled between the commercial cities of Hamburg, Copenhagen, and Amsterdam, and moved to the Prussian capital of Berlin, where he engaged in commerce. Wessely had a broad view of reality, was actively involved in Jewish affairs, and in particular endeavored to learn about the true situation of the Jews in general (their political, economic, and cultural status) and to single out their problems. Based on his progressive and optimistic consciousness, he depicted an extremely dynamic European world: the expansion of knowledge, technological achievements, discoveries, and inventions. He attributed particular importance to the growing emergence of religious tolerance, which began in sixteenth-century Holland and seventeenth-century England, and spread during his own lifetime throughout all the countries of Europe: the Russia of Catherine II ("word of whose courage, wisdom, and acts of generosity has spread throughout all the nations"); the Poland of Stanislav Poniatowski; the Denmark of Christian VII; the Sweden of Gustav; the France of Louis XVI ("who expanded the hearts of his subjects through his goodness and his generous deeds"); the lands under Joseph II; and the Prussia of Frederick II, the most enlightened and liberal ruler of them all. These are the fervent words Wessely wrote about Frederick: "Our lord, the King of Prussia, may his glory be exalted, has seen that it befits a king to rule over free men, not over slaves . . . and that culture, wisdom, and knowledge cannot exist in his land if men are afraid to speak the truth."[33] Regarding Wessely as a writer who also wrote poetry when the occasion called for it, leaders of Jewish communities sometimes asked him to compose accolades in verse for the rulers of Europe to be submitted to them as a gesture of loyalty. Indeed, the Hebrew poet of enlightened absolutism wrote poems of praise to the kings of Denmark, Prussia, and Russia, and reacted to political events in poetic language. For example, he was commissioned by the communities of Shklov and Mohilev to write such a paean on the occasion of Catherine's visit to the new regions of White Russia, which Russia had annexed in the first division of Poland in 1772.[34]

In *Divrei shalom ve'emet*, Wessely also included what amounted to a report on the state of the Jewish nation. Although his description of the situation was partial and tendentious, it was written in the first person and reflected the writer's own political consciousness—the sense of responsibility and involvement of an intellectual Jew who has no official status. It was based on Wessely's perception of the reality in the last quarter of the eighteenth century, when considerable change had taken place in Jewish life in the diaspora. The Jews were no longer persecuted as they had been in the past, and although they were still a nation of merchants, new opportunities were being opened to them. Insofar as culture, language, and patterns of education were concerned, Wessely discriminated between Jewish communities in the Muslim East and the Sephardic communities of Western Europe, on the one hand, and Ashkenazi Jewry, on the other. While Ashkenazi Jewry was benighted, still living according to the old norms of isolation, particularly in Poland, Sephardic Jews were already living in the present and were geared for the future. They spoke the languages of their countries of residence, maintained more natural commercial ties with non-Jews, and their manners were those generally accepted in their societies. Wessely especially admired the Jewish community of Italian Trieste, with which he maintained close ties during the polemic surrounding *Divrei shalom ve'emet*, as we shall see, and Sephardic Amsterdam, with which he was very familiar during the years he lived in that city. His links to the Sephardim were so strong that towards the end of his life, when he returned to Hamburg, this Ashkenazi Jew asked to be buried in the Portuguese section of the Altona cemetery.[35]

The most promising ray of light that he saw in the Ashkenazi world came from Berlin, the city in which he lived. He wrote that it was the major Jewish community that fostered *torat ha'adam*, and was very proud of the fact that some of her sons had already made a name for themselves in the world of Enlightenment. This is how he applauded his old friend and the greatly admired symbol of the Haskalah:

It is known to one and all that the wise rabbi and illustrious scholar, Moses from Dessau, is renowned among the gentiles for the books he has written in the German language, as well as for his research and his splendid command of that language. He is praised in most of the lands of Europe, and high officials and the sages of the nations when passing through here, first pay a visit to his home, to meet with him and bask in his company.

But Mendelssohn was not alone in the society of Berlin maskilim, which numbered other luminaries: David Friedländer (1750–1834), from the wealthy elite and the scion of an affluent family of merchants in Königsberg; the physician Marcus Bloch (1723–99), a contemporary of Wessely and Mendelssohn, an expert in the field of ichthyology and a member of several European scientific and medical societies; and the physician and philosopher Marcus Herz, a graduate of Königsberg University and a student of Immanuel Kant, whose lectures on logic and physiology were attended by "aristocrats and dignitaries."[36] The author of *Divrei shalom ve'emet* saw himself, then, as the representative of the Berlin circle of maskilim and the spokesman of the promising new era.

Chapter Five

Projects of Enlightenment and Tests of Tolerance

Wessely was hardly a reliable witness of the reality that existed during his lifetime. On the one hand, his optimism was exaggerated and he depicted the kings of Prussia in ideal terms, attributing to them more tolerance than they actually demonstrated. On the other hand, he provided only a partial description of the Jewish world in the early 1780s, omitting several of the key processes that took place in the life of European Jews in the last third of the century. The Jewish population increased more than two and a half times from the beginning of the century, and the proportion of European Jews in world Jewry grew from 65 percent to close to 80 percent. In Königsberg, Breslau, and Berlin, the Prussian cities in which the first circles of maskilim were formed, the Jewish communities were relatively small, numbering only a thousand to three thousand, while the Jews of Poland and Lithuania (at the end of the century, most of them under Russian rule) formed the major portion of European Jewry.[1]

In his description of the condition of the Jewish people in the 1780s, Wessely scarcely referred to the emergence of the early Haskalah, although he himself was one of its important representatives, perhaps because he was still only vaguely aware that the new elite was gradually acquiring status in Jewish society. He made no mention of the continued existence of the Sabbatian movement in Poland and the Habsburg Empire, nor of the frenzied activity of Kabbalists and pietistic Hasidim in Germany, like the circle of Rabbi Nathan Adler in Frankfurt. He also was not aware that the Hasidic movement in Eastern Europe was gaining in strength and swelling its ranks in the 1770s; nor did he know about the fierce campaign that was being waged against Hasidism in Lithuania from 1772 under the inspiration of the Gaon of Vilna. As a result of the first partition of Poland, which also took place in 1772, many Polish Jews were transferred from the backward kingdom under aristocratic rule to the absolutist regimes of the centralized state—Russia, Prussia, and Austria. This development had far-reaching implications in international relations, which affected thousands of Jews.

Most of the Jews of Europe still maintained the patterns of life of a conservative traditional society at the end of the eighteenth century. They were faithful to religion, to traditional texts and education, community, and rabbinical leadership; continued to speak Yiddish and wear the traditional clothing. In contrast, among the elite circles of merchants and affluent Jews in the major European cities (London, Amsterdam, Vienna, Berlin), the trend of acculturation, which had begun among the court Jews and merchants in the previous century, further intensified.[2]

In Wessely's own environment, acculturation was particularly marked among the wives and daughters of wealthy families. These women, who grew up in the homes of wealthy merchants, commercial agents, and physicians, received a modern European education from private tutors (one way in which young students and maskilim earned their livelihood). They spoke fluent German and French, preferred their European names (Dorothea, Henrietta, Angelica) to their Jewish names (Brendel, Sheindel, Goldeche), dressed according to the dictates of the latest fashions, knew how to dance and play musical instruments, read sentimental novels, and enjoyed attending concerts, theater, and opera. It was from this social circle that the Berlin salon ladies came in the last two decades of the century. In Moses Mendelssohn's home, too, the daughters were raised by their mother, Fromet, as modern European women. During that time, Mendelssohn had begun working on his *Bi'ur* project, the German translation of the Pentateuch, while Fromet was in charge of their daughters' upbringing—introducing them to social life and encouraging them to learn languages, music and to attend the theater.[3]

Although none of these trends in the life of European Jewry were included in Wessely's picture of the situation, he did aptly describe what was taking place among the outstanding Jewish intellectuals in Berlin, where he lived. At the time of the controversy aroused by *Divrei shalom ve'emet*, other endeavors were being made in Berlin to promote the Enlightenment of the Jews, such as the founding of an innovative Jewish school and initiatives taken there and elsewhere to apply the principle of religious tolerance to the Jews. Against the background of these efforts, Wessely's own initiative took on a revolutionary meaning and fit in well with others, taken by both Jewish and Christian intellectuals, that were intended to transform Jewish life. These changes also explain why the maskilim, who defended Wessely and his positions during the fierce debate that raged around him, reacted so sharply. Before tracing the permutations of that controversy, we will describe some of the other endeavors to imbue Jewish society with the concepts, values and patterns of the Enlightenment.

The Jewish Free School

The first Enlightenment project undertaken in the Berlin community was the establishment of the school Chinukh Ne'arim in 1778, which served as one of the sources of inspiration for Wessely's program to reform Jewish education. The Freischule, the free school (that is, one that did not charge any tuition fees) was intended for the children of poor Jews and was the first modern school in the Jewish world. For the first time in Ashkenazi Jewry, an educational institution included languages, science, and the culture of European society.[4] The enlightened Prussian intelligentsia had great expectations for the school, regarding it as an extremely important expression of Jewish Enlightenment that heralded a social transformation. For example, F. Gedike, a member of the supreme consistory of the Lutheran church and a key figure in Berlin's flourishing intellectual life, suggested to his readers, in an article printed in 1784 in the *Berlinische Monatsschrift*, that they should view the Freischule as an example of self-enlightenment at its finest.

It amounted to an affirmation of the words of Immanuel Kant, who that same year in the same periodical, had defined Enlightenment as an action, taken independently by man as he matures and throws off the yoke of tutelage; enlightenment is motivated by free rational thinking. Now it seemed that the sons of the Jewish nation, at the very lowest ebb for hundreds of years, were now rising to a high level of enlightenment, engaging in self-building (*Bildung*) and in developing free thought. Under the encyclopedic entry, "Jews," in a 1784 work, the Freischule was cited as an example of the spread of Enlightenment among the Jews. It read: "This is the first educational institution of this kind, which prepares Jewish youth for adulthood as moral human beings, as subjects who are a benefit to the state, and as good neighbors in society."[5]

Although the school was a reformative Enlightenment project par excellence, it was not actually founded by maskilim, nor was it run according to their educational utopia like the model outlined by Wessely in his *Divrei shalom ve'emet*. Although maskilim were involved in various stages of its existence and pinned great hopes on it as an institution of the Haskalah, the Freischule was the outcome of a philanthropic initiative of wealthy Berlin families. Seventeen years before its establishment, a Jewish school of a new type had been planned by Daniel Itzig (1723–99) and Feitel Heine Ephraim (1703–75), men of great wealth, who were leaders of the Berlin community and patrons of early maskilim. They had amassed their wealth during the Seven Years' War (1756–63), as a result of the commercial and financial services they had rendered to Prussia. In 1761 they submitted a plan for the establishment of a school for poor children to the "general administration" of the land. The two stated as their motive for founding the school as "to make the Jews more beneficial to the country." In it, the boys would receive a basic education (Torah, reading and writing in German and French, mathematics, sciences), be taught manners and hygiene, and be given regular meals. The necessary permits were obtained in 1762, but the philanthropic institution was never opened, apparently because at the time the two men dissolved their business partnership.

In 1775, Benjamin, Feital Ephraim's son, opened a free school in a branch of his lace factory, where children were taught the basic skills of reading and writing. The Berlin publisher and author Friedrich Nicolai linked this school together with the Freischule in a survey entitled "Jewish institutions for the poor." There was a good reason for doing so, since both institutions were established by wealthy men in the community as part of the welfare system and for philanthropic purposes—in particular to solve the problem of indigenous Jews.[6]

What was the background to these projects? Men of wealth enjoyed a special legal status—a "general privilege" that exempted them from the restrictions on residence and employment, as well as all the other restrictions Frederick the Great had imposed on Berlin's Jews in 1750. They played a key role in promoting the mercantile economy in Prussia, maintained close ties with the ruling class, and acquired a European education through private tutors. As a result, they identified with the values and basic principles of the absolutist state—the primacy of the state's interests, the good of the state, and the importance of productive economic activity. Philanthropy was an integral part of their economic activity and their positions as leaders of the community who also supervised it on behalf of the government. They undertook to prepare the weaker, more problematic groups in the society, such as orphans, the poor, and lawbreakers, to become useful citizens in the future. Reformative education which made its students productive citizens and endowed them with virtues, like the Prussian *Volkschule*, was one of the means of attaining this end.[7]

The Freischule was founded by the brothers-in-law Isaac Daniel Itzig (1750–1806) and David Friedländer as a private family institution. It was defined from the outset as a free school, and its budget came from a basic fund and monthly contributions from other wealthy families. The head of the family, Daniel Itzig, donated the basic fund required to establish the school and purchased the building in 1782, each year adding five hundred taler to the institution.[8] The government recognized the philanthropic nature of the Freischule, and granted it a tax exemption and a permit to establish a Hebrew printing house. At first, the printing house was a workshop next to the school (*Die orientalische Buchdruckerei*), but later it was very instrumental in disseminating the maskilim's books. The school's philanthropic character was also reflected in the fact that its two founder-principals received no salary. Chevrat Chinukh Ne'arim was founded in parallel with Chevrat Talmud Torah, which operated on behalf of the community's charitable societies, since it also provided education for the children of the poor. There was a salient difference, however. In the former case, wealthy Jews, who traditionally provided financial support for institutions of the rabbinical elite like the *kloiz* (the house of study for select pupils, financed by generous affluent Jews), were supporting institutions to train productive Jews who would be of benefit to the state. Although, even at the end of the century the Itzig and Ephraim families still set up funds to support houses of study for needy talmudic scholars in Berlin, they apparently now gave preference to the reform of Jewish society over excellence in talmudic studies.

As a matter of fact, one of the two founders, David Friedländer, was a central figure in the Berlin circle of maskilim, closely involved in their activities and in the debates they conducted with their opponents; moreover, throughout his life, he regarded himself as one of Mendelssohn's faithful followers.[9] Friedländer wished to promote the knowledge of German among the Jews and its use as the language of speech, prayer, and literature. For him, the Freischule was more than a philanthropic project. He designed its curriculum in its early years, and in 1770 wrote a "reader for Jewish children," to serve as the first textbook in the new school. The reader was in German and included a selection of sources for learning the language and memorizing the principles of the natural and universal religion (a prayer in German to God, who is the source of truth and love) and of the Jewish religion (Maimonides's thirteen principles). The religious texts were presented in the reader as a source of universal, humanistic morals. Although only a small number of pupils, probably no more than a few dozen pupils at the Freischule, which was in its early stages at the time, studied from the reader, Zohar Shavit was correct in noting its revolutionary nature as an Enlightenment text: "For the first time in the history of European Jewish history, a book was published to serve as a textbook in a modern Jewish school."[10]

In the letter written by Itzig and Friedländer to the king of Prussia in 1784, the two, in explaining the need to found the Freischule, also related to the rehabilitation of the Jews. They combined philanthropic aims, to give Jews the opportunity to rise on the economic scale, with educational aims, to mold a useful citizen and a moral person: "to make the Jews men of culture and to educate them to become useful subjects of the state."[11] In 1782, a short time after the appearance of Wessely's open letter, Friedländer helped him to disseminate *Divrei shalom ve'emet* by translating it into German. However, Friedländer left his personal imprint on Wessely's work; his translation introduced changes from the original, which underscored the translator's own radical position. For example, Friedländer was in favor of reducing the religious curriculum, and unlike Wessely, also unhesitatingly advocated the supremacy of the "man" and the "citizen" over the "Jew."[12] As we shall see later, Friedländer also played an important role in organizing the reaction of the maskilim and their supporters against the rabbis who attacked Wessely. However, during the 1780s and even more so in the 1790s, Friedländer's positions became more extreme. He apparently abandoned his management of the school in the mid-1780s and invested his major efforts in obtaining political rights for the Prussian Jews.

Very little information is available about the Freischule's activity during its early years. Most of the details about the school in the fifth year of its operations were provided by Wessely, who praised the institution and its founders and regarded its establishment as one of the achievements of the Berlin community at the time:

The distinguished leaders of this holy community . . . have gone to the trouble to found an institution here that they have called *Chinukh ne'arim*, where Jewish children learn Bible and the German translation, and Hebrew grammar, to read and write German and French, mathematics and geography. For children of the poor it is free, and children of the rich pay a fee. And we have seen the fruits of their labor, for students who have learned all of these subjects have already graduated from this school, and have been a great help and succor to their families. Some have become teachers to their younger brethren who are beginning their studies, others have become the bookkeepers of merchants. And others are students of Mishnah and Talmud, succeeding at this as well, spending most of the day learning Talmud, and only in the afternoon hours does the school open its doors, when all may come to study the above-mentioned subjects. There were also those who looked upon this institution with disfavor, for they thought its founding would be in violation of the Torah and lead to the abandonment of the religion. But now that they see what its true nature is and how fine it is, many wish to send their sons there to study, so that the number would have reached five hundred, had there only been room for that many, but now they can only take in seventy boys.[13]

Based on this description, the Freischule did not meet all the maskilic expectations that Wessely had set forth in *Divrei shalom ve'emet*. It was instead a supplementary philanthropic school, which operated only in the afternoon hours, while some of its students received a traditional education in the morning. But Wessely's report about the community's opposition to its establishment, for fear that it would be detrimental to the religion, is interesting, in view of the relatively skimpy curriculum and the small number of hours of study. Even though the first modern Jewish school can hardly be seen as the fulfillment of the maskilic vision, still it was undoubtedly an Enlightenment project. In the Freischule, the process began in which traditional education was taken out of the hands of the Polish teachers and transferred to professional teachers, who, in the case of the Berlin school, were both Jews and Christians. Friedländer, and after him, Wessely, Isaac Satanow, and others, began writing special books for teaching in the school. In essence, they created a primary model for the institutionalization of education in a school, which at first was a supplement to, and later also a secular replacement for, the Talmud Torah and the cheder. For the first time, an extra-religious curriculum was offered in a regular setting, even to those who could not afford to hire private tutors for their children. The educational ideal of the school was relatively modest and did not go beyond training graduates to engage in teaching or work as clerks for the wealthy, nor did it set any transformative goals for itself, such as training an elite that would be an alternative to the rabbinical elite. Nonetheless, Wessely was able to point with pride to the Berlin school when he tried to persuade the Jewish leadership elsewhere that there was an urgent need for educational reform.

The heads of the Freischule, who were also the leaders of the community, were very proud of the institution. Each year, they held public examinations, in which the students displayed their achievements to an audience of invitees from the Jewish community and the enlightened Christian elite of Berlin (for example, teachers at the *Gymnasium*). Everyone present in the examination hall was entitled to pose questions to the students to test their knowledge in mathematics, the natural sciences, and languages—French and German. Friedländer invited Mendelssohn and probably Wessely too to the semiannual public examination in 1782. Another invitee was the author and acerbic satirist August Cranz (1737–1801), who had a hand in stirring up the Jewish *Kulturkampf* in the early 1780s. An expanded version of Cranz's enthusiastic report about his visit to the Freischule was sent to the editorial board of the Hebrew periodical *Hame'asef* in Königsberg, which printed the description in one of its first issues. The report gives us a rare glimpse into the modern Jewish classroom in Berlin:

It is now mid-year, the date set for the general examination to test what the boys have learned and achieved. In this school hall, the heads of their community gather, including the scholar, R. Moses ben Menahem (Mendelssohn) and many Christian learned men . . . the Jewish boys walk about freely in their room, and each person attending has the right to ask them whatever he wishes. And here the first boys have come forth to be examined in the science of geometry, and all those hearing were amazed at how well they replied to every question asked of them. And how they solved all the profound questions in the calculation of interest and the exchange of currency, with such brilliant proofs. Afterward we asked them to explain the underlying reason for their words, and it appears they have not merely learned by memorizing rules, but through intelligent comprehension. After them, came others to show their knowledge in cosmology and geography, and the boys showed they knew the latitude and longitude of every place on the globe and when the sun rises and sets, and the like . . . After them came others to be tested in their knowledge of languages, and one read a chapter in the Bible and then translated it according to the rules of grammar and syntax into German, and the other translated from French into German, and a third showed his fluency in the science of geography, and others in their penmanship, and yet others in lovely drawings displayed to all present.[14]

Religious Tolerance

The purpose of holding a public examination of seventy Jewish pupils, in the presence of the leaders of the community, was to prove to the wealthy Jews that their financial contribution to the school's maintenance was producing sterling results. Since the founders of the Freischule greatly admired Mendelssohn and felt his renown also reflected on them, his presence at the examination, along with that of a number of enlightened Christian scholars, was very meaningful. It conveyed the impression that the young generation of Jews was integrating into the Enlightenment world of knowledge and also created a climate of religious tolerance. Indeed, Cranz summed up the report of his visit to the school with much enthusiasm and optimism. If until then, he concluded, the state had treated the Jews as a despicably exploited, alien, Asiatic nation, the Jews were now taking measures themselves to turn their coreligionists into people who would be greatly beneficial to the state in the future.[15]

"The toleration of those that differ from others in matters of religion is so agreeable to the Gospel of Jesus Christ, and to the genuine reason of mankind, that it seems monstrous for men to be so blind as not to perceive the necessity and advantage of it in so clear a light," the philosopher John Locke stated in his *Letter Concerning Toleration* in 1689. The time has come, he argued, "to distinguish exactly the business of civil government from that of religion and to settle the just bounds that lie between the one and the other." The church, he wrote, is "a voluntary society of men, joining themselves together of their own accord for the public worshipping of God, while the commonwealth seems to me to be a society of men constituted only for procuring, preserving, and advancing their own civil interests." Coercion by the ruling authority has no validity and is opposed to reason if it is applied to the realm of faith and opinion: "The care of souls cannot belong to the civil magistrate, because his power consists only in outward force; but true and saving religion consists in the inward persuasion of the mind, without which nothing can be acceptable to God."[16] Some of the fundamental criteria of the Enlightenment were based on Locke's approach to toleration, which he articulated in his Letter. It changed the concept that had existed for generations concerning the rivalry between religions, which claimed to possess the sole truth, endeavored to gain political control over the churches and their adherents, and to expel those who "erred" in their beliefs.[17]

Religious toleration was unquestionably one of the central issues of the European Enlightenment. The eighteenth-century philosophers called for religious toleration and vigorously opposed fanaticism and the persecution of religious minorities. A number of factors led them to adopt this approach. These philosophers engaged in rational and secular thought; recognized the unity of the human race on the basis of natural law; and had encountered the cultures of the new world, which apprised them of the versatility and relativeness of religions and led them to deny the superiority of the Judeo-Christian culture. Moreover, at the time the deistic beliefs of adherents of the natural religions, which negated any difference between the various positivistic religions, were gaining in strength, and anticlerical stances and the influence of humanism were more widespread. "What is toleration?" Voltaire asked in 1764 in his *Philosophical Dictionary*, and replied: "It is the prerogative of humanity. We are all steeped in weaknesses and error; let us forgive one another's follies—that is the first law of nature . . . It is clear that every individual who persecutes a man, his brother, because he does not agree with him, is a monster."[18]

Just as Locke himself cited the Jews as an example of a religious minority that ought to be tolerated by the state, they became a touchstone in the discussions of Enlightenment philosophers on tolerance. This, of course, had some practical political implications, leading to changes in the legal status of Jews in European countries.[19] The concept of religious tolerance was not, however, absolute, sweeping or unconditional. For example, for political reasons connected with the reality in England, Locke excluded Catholicism from those religions that were deserving of tolerance. But he was also suspicious of atheists, and stated: "Lastly, those are not at all to be tolerated who deny the being of a God. Promises, covenants, and oaths, which are the bonds of human society, can have no hold upon an atheist."[20] When the fundamental concept of tolerance clashed with the prejudices of the Christian culture toward the Jews, the intellectuals were divided in their views. While some demanded that the principle ought to apply to all human beings, others wished to make the political toleration of the Jews conditional upon their economic and moral rehabilitation.

The rationalistic shift in relation to the Christian religion and its institutions in the eighteenth century did not always lead to a religiously tolerant attitude toward the Jews, as is evident from the famous case of Voltaire. He fought zealously and uncompromisingly against the misdeeds of the church, criticizing it in the most sarcastic, acerbic terms, but as far as the Jews were concerned, he argued that their centuries-long corrupt character was irremediable. His deistic critique of Christianity went hand in hand with his trenchant criticism of Judaism and the Jews. Voltaire used rationalistic and secular arguments to depict the Jews as possessing values and beliefs that were diametrically opposed to the Enlightenment. The secular character of this anti-Jewish position armed the opponents of tolerance with new weapons. In this connection, Jacob Katz's explanation seems a salient one; he relates to the dialectic that influenced Enlightenment intellectuals in the seventeenth and eighteenth centuries, and led them from their criticism of Christianity to anti-Jewish positions.[21] Nonetheless, there is no ignoring the fact that public opinion voiced many more protests against the long-lasting oppression of the Jews, along with explicit demands that they be treated as human beings.

Katz placed this historical development at the center of the upheaval that totally changed the relations between Jews and Christians in Europe, and explained how a neutral social sphere was created that for the first time enabled Jews and Christians to meet in a common milieu on the basis of tolerance. The weakening of class ties on the one hand, and of the dominant status of the Christian religion, on the other, made room for new models of socialization. One of these was applied in the new frameworks of the supra-class intelligentsia, "the elite of the spirit," because its cosmopolitan values provided an opportunity, at least in theory, for those Jews who met the intellectual requirements of that elite, to join it.[22] As a matter of fact, in nineteenth-century German Jewish historiography, the neutral encounter between the Christian and the Jewish intellectual is depicted as an exemplary expression of the new era in Jewish history. The historian Heinrich Graetz opened the age of Jewish revival with Mendelssohn's appearance on the stage of history and the story of his friendship with the tolerant humanist Gotthold Ephraim Lessing.[23] For historians from Graetz to Katz, the game of chess between the two in a Berlin cafe in the 1750s told the story of the emancipation and integration of the Jews in Germany and in Europe in general.[24] In Graetz's approach, the story is one of the achievement of a much sought-after objective that led to the revival of the Jewish nation, while Katz viewed it as a decisive expression of the crisis experienced by the traditional society. However, even Katz, who coined the concept of the "neutral society," was forced to admit that meetings of this kind at the end of the eighteenth century were relatively rare and only a few Jewish intellectuals took part in them.[25]

Nor is there any doubt that the concept of a neutral society was influenced by Mendelssohn's remarkable life story. It even seems to have been patterned on Mendelssohn, who gained widespread recognition as the most prominent modern Jew in the age of Enlightenment and religious tolerance. Mendelssohn himself never tried to conceal his inferior position or his frustration at the demeaning Prussian laws and edicts, signed by the supposedly enlightened ruler, Frederick the Great, that made life so oppressive for the Jews. Moreover, the king of Prussia refused to acknowledge him as a bona fide Prussian intellectual and blocked his appointment to the Academy of Sciences in the 1770s. Nonetheless, Mendelssohn did enjoy the religious toleration that existed in Berlin in the late eighteenth century; he was a popular member in the clubs of the enlightened, a close friend of some of the more important among them, and Christian members of the academy and men of letters frequently visited his home.[26] The question of religious tolerance for a man like him, who aspired to be recognized as a philosopher by the republic of enlightened scholars, was particularly crucial. Throughout his entire life, the issue, which he regarded as both a personal-existential and a national one, continued to perturb him.

In 1754, as an early maskil and a philosopher making his debut in the circles of enlightened Germans, Mendelssohn had come forward to defend the honor of the Jews, in an article of protest published in *Theatralische Bibliothek*, a periodical edited by his friend Lessing. It was a letter to Aaron Gumpertz, in which he reacted strongly to Johann David Michaelis's critique of Lessing's play *Die Juden*. How was it possible, Mendelssohn expostulated, that Michaelis could deny the very possibility that the Jewish nation was capable of producing even one decent person? How could it be that only now the Christians were discovering that at least one Jew could be included in human society, and why was the degree of toleration they were granting the Jews still so limited? "I would have expected far more from learned men," Mendelssohn wrote. Michaelis's critique is a grave affront to Jews and a disappointment to the enlightened, and, Mendelssohn asserted, it shakes his belief in the ability of Christian scholars to rise above their prejudices. The young Mendelssohn (then twenty-seven) expressed his sense of insult with cynicism and frustration: "Let them continue to oppress us, let them continue to restrict our lives as free and happy people, let them even expose us to the scorn and mockery of the world, as long as they do not deprive us entirely of virtue [*Tugend*] . . . which is the sole refuge of the abandoned and the forgotten."[27]

Mendelssohn's involvement in the *Divrei shalom ve'emet* polemic was connected with his struggle to see the principle of tolerance applied throughout European society. In his view, this would assure the civic place of the Jews in society at large and their religious freedom, as well as the freedom of activity of Jewish intellectuals. The struggle for toleration was foremost in his mind from his first appearance in the public sphere until his dying day.

In 1769, an incident occurred that brought Mendelssohn great pain, a traumatic experience that haunted him from then on. Only two years had passed since the publication of *Phädon*, his philosophical work on the immortality of the soul, which had earned him fame and prestige among the intellectuals of the German Enlightenment. And now the young Swiss pastor with a Christian-millenarian vision, Johann Caspar Lavater (1741–1801), wounded him grievously by publicly betraying their friendship.[28] Lavater had visited Mendelssohn in his home on several occasions, trying to draw him into theological discussions. After he had succeeded in inducing Mendelssohn to say something positive about Jesus' moral stature, Lavater believed that the conversion to Christianity of the most famous Jew in Europe was imminent, and that this would touch off a wave of conversion among the Jews, which in turn would inevitably lead to their redemption. In the summer of 1769, Mendelssohn received by mail a copy of a new translation from French to German of a book by C. Bonnet. When he opened the book, he was distressed to find a dedication to him by the translator Lavater, who mentioned their talk in Berlin about Jesus and issued a theological ultimatum to him. Lavater challenged Mendelssohn to refute Bonnet's persuasive proofs of the truth of Christianity with counterarguments, or to behave as Socrates would have and admit he was unable to do so. He would then be compelled to reach the only possible conclusion—conversion to Christianity.

Although public opinion denounced Lavater's act as unseemly, the affair stirred a great deal of interest, and Mendelssohn was forced to defend his position publicly. His reply shows how offended he was by Lavater's betrayal of the friendship he thought they had shared. The publication of words spoken in a friendly conversation, particularly by a man who had promised to keep them to himself, angered and embarrassed Mendelssohn: "What could possibly have motivated you," he wrote in his reply, "to single me out against my will in order to drag me into the arena of public controversy, which I had hoped never to enter?"[29] Mendelssohn made it clear that the very ultimatum posed to him was despicable in his eyes, and there was not even the slightest chance that he would abandon the faith of his forefathers.

In his reply to Lavater, Mendelssohn devoted his main points to a presentation of Judaism as the religion of tolerance and to a criticism of the Christian religion, which in his view was far removed from the religious tolerance of the Enlightenment. While Christianity was a missionary religion, Judaism did not presume to convert anyone who was not born a Jew: "Proselytizing . . . is completely alien to Judaism."[30] The Jewish doctrine of revelation is not binding on anyone except the Jews themselves: "All other nations were enjoined by God to observe the law of nature and the religion of the patriarchs. All who live in accordance with this religion of nature and of reason are called the 'the righteous among other nations'; they too are entitled to eternal bliss."[31] Judaism is tolerant and recognizes the value of the natural religion and the inferior political condition of the Jews is caused by the intolerance of the Christians. "I am a member of an oppressed people which must appeal to the benevolence of the government for protection and shelter—which are not always granted, and never without limitations." Moreover, Mendelssohn expostulated, pointing out his inferior status: "As you know, your circumcised friend may not even visit you in Zurich, because of the laws of your own home town."[32] Nonetheless, Mendelssohn persisted in his belief that religious tolerance served as a firm foundation for friendship with other Christian intellectuals, with whom he maintained close contact. Hence, he still looked upon this neutral relationship, which unfortunately Lavater had attempted to shatter, as an ideal of the Enlightenment:

It is my good fortune to count among my friends many an excellent man who is not of my faith. We love each other sincerely, although both of us suspect or assume that we differ in matters of faith. I enjoy the pleasure of his company and feel enriched by it. But at no time has my heart whispered to me, "What a pity that this beautiful soul should be lost . . . " Only that man will be troubled by such regrets who believes there is no salvation outside his church.[33]

The Lavater affair ended with Mendelssohn's moral victory. Enlightened public opinion tended to take his side, and even Lavater himself admitted he had exceeded the bounds of good taste, and although he did not recant, he did apologize to Mendelssohn. However, as a result of the affair, Mendelssohn realized that religious tolerance could not be taken for granted, even among his fellow members of the Enlightenment circle in Germany. Authors of anti-Jewish writings printed during the affair took the opportunity to attack Mendelssohn as a Jew. Despite his strong desire to avoid any discussions on theological matters and to devote himself entirely to philosophy, he realized that if he were to continue defending rationalist religion, claiming that the Torah was consistent with reason and calling for tolerance, he now had to underpin his positions with apologetic, ideological, and theological arguments.

Mendelssohn's intellectual distress had an immediate effect on his health. Shortly after the Lavater affair he fell ill, growing extremely weak, but his doctors were unable to diagnose his illness. Marcus Bloch, his personal physician, prescribed a severe diet and complete rest, ordering him to avoid all intellectual activity. Bloch and Mendelssohn's other admirers were convinced that the pressure of the months of the affair had damaged his health. His biographer, Isaac Euchel, described Mendelssohn's condition in the early 1770s with the following words: "His strength was very much diminished, because his mind was sorely depressed by the pressures of his work, and in addition, the quarrelsome words, invective, and conspiracy had so exhausted him, that he could no longer engage in any logical thought without suffering pain in one of his limbs or dizziness in his head." Owing to his illness, he read very little and wrote nothing. According to one testimony, Mendelssohn spoke about his boredom during that time: "To shorten the hours spent on trivial matters, I would stand in my room, looking out the window, and count the roof tiles of the neighbor's house opposite mine."[34]

In a personal letter he wrote about ten years after the affair to the Benedictine monk Peter Adolph Winkopp of Erfurt, Mendelssohn described with rare candor his existential distress as an inferior Jew living in Berlin. In what is known as a tolerant country, I live in a condition in which intolerance presses upon me from every direction, Mendelssohn admitted. For him, as a private Jew, not as a well-known philosopher, intolerance was not at all theoretical. It was an experience of everyday life in Berlin:

Sometimes I go out of an evening for a stroll with my wife and children. Papa! Those innocent children ask, what are those boys yelling at us? Why are they throwing stones at us? What have we done to them? Yes, dear Papa, one of them says, they are always chasing after us in the streets, cursing us—Jews! Jews! Is just being a Jew enough reason for those people to curse us?[35]

"And I," he wrote with a sense of helplessness, "can only lower my eyes and mutter to myself: People, people, when will you stop doing these things?"

The Lavater affair stirred up a storm in the neutral sphere of the German republic of the Enlightened, of which Mendelssohn was a popular, highly regarded member. Mendelssohn's Jewish associates also followed the controversy with great interest. Wessely, who at the time lived in Copenhagen, and in any case was far from those Christian circles in which Mendelssohn felt at home, saw fit to translate Mendelssohn's reply to Lavater into Hebrew, in the early 1770s, so that his position in the controversy could be published and disseminated. The translation, however, was not printed at the time, apparently at Mendelssohn's request, because it was not complete and Wessely had in several places misunderstood Mendelssohn's intent. Wessely was not satisfied merely to translate the reply, but added his commentary to it, one replete with words of admiration for Mendelssohn and his ability to successfully repel the attack on Judaism. Although Wessely did not use reasoning based on the philosophy of natural religion, he, like Mendelssohn, did embrace the principle of tolerance. In his commentary, he defended the concept of Judaism as a non-proselytizing religion, one that had a positive attitude toward the sages of all the nations. Wessely praised Mendelssohn for also having successfully refuted the claim made, during the controversy, that a Jew could not be a close friend of a Christian without trying to persuade him to convert to Judaism.[36] Ten years later, Mendelssohn defended Wessely against the rabbis who attacked him, this time emphasizing his demand for religious tolerance within Jewry.

At the end of the 1770s, numerous works were published in Germany on religious tolerance in general and toward the Jews in particular. A high point in the attempt to grapple with this issue was Lessing's well-known 1779 play *Nathan der Weise.* Its dramatic plot, which took place against the backdrop of the Crusades, was merely a literary frame intended to bring home to the audience the idea of religious tolerance. In his play *Die Juden* in 1749, Lessing had already tried out the notion of portraying a Jew as a virtuous hero, but in *Nathan der Weise,* he was more explicit. The Jew in that play is a character modeled on Mendelssohn, whose battle for tolerance in the Lavater affair is given literary expression. The parable of the "three rings," around which the play revolves, places the three historical religions—Judaism, Christianity, and Islam—on an equal footing. Each has received the ring of religion from Father-God, and none will ever know who possesses the true ring. It would be more correct to say that all the rings are true from the standpoint of the intent of the bestower and the belief of the holder, and hence the interfaith struggle over religious truth and primacy is futile. The lines Lessing put into his hero's mouth—"We did not choose a nation for ourselves. Are we our nations? What's a nation then? Were Jews and Christians such, e'er they were men?"— called for a dramatic change in public opinion in relation to the Jews.[37] It was a step forward toward the secularization of the relations between religions— Christians and Jews would no longer be measuring one another through the prism of their respective religions or based on the lengthy history of hierarchical relations, but would be observing one another through the prism of humanism, reason, and natural law.

Lessing paid a personal price for having strongly advocated religious tolerance; he was accused of being a hireling of the Jews or an enemy of Christianity. This accusation shows how daring his play was in terms of that time period in Germany.[38] The sharp distinction that Lessing drew between the Jew and the man was of course at the core of his demand for tolerance toward the Jews by Christians. However, three years later it served as the basis for Wessely's ideology of *torat ha'adam* and his demand for the transformation of Jewish life.

Dohm: *On the Civil Improvement of the Jews*

Two years after the publication of his play, Lessing was joined by two German deists from Berlin in his call for tolerance of the Jews and a demand for a significant improvement in their political status. The first was August Cranz, whom we have already met as a guest and an enthusiastic observer at the public examination of the the the Freischule pupils held in 1782. Interestingly enough, starting in the seventeenth century, deism led to two contradictory positions in regard to the Jews. The English deists constantly depicted Judaism in an unfavorable light, and Voltaire followed this same line, denying any possibility that the abject moral stature of the Jews could ever be changed. In contrast, the German deists generally held more liberal views. For example, Cranz is best known for having induced Mendelssohn to justify his objections to conversion to Christianity and his adherence to Judaism in his *Jerusalem*. In actual fact, Cranz also fought hard to gain entry for the Jews into Christian society as equal members. As a deist, he distinguished between the pure, original Judaism, which was close to the natural religion, like that of the Karaites, and the clerical, intolerant talmudic Judaism. He also displayed much interest in the transformation of the Jews and their introduction to Enlightenment culture.[39]

Another German deist made a much stronger impression on public opinion. Christian Wilhelm von Dohm (1750–1820), a member of a Berlin enlightened circle, was a high official in the Prussian government, and a friend of Mendelssohn's. In 1780 he began to produce one of the major texts in the project of religious tolerance of the German Enlightenment. Dohm was well aware that he was writing a text that was revolutionary, no less so than Lessing's *Nathan der Weise*. His treatise *Über die bürgerliche Verbesserung der Juden* (On the Civil Improvement of the Jews) cautiously moved along the thin line between theology and politics, as Dohm himself wrote to his publisher and friend, Nicolai, while he was writing it. He added that perhaps it would be best to consult the censor before printing the essay or, alternatively, to print it outside of Prussia. The implied criticism in it about the serious flaws in the Christian state's treatment of the Jews could easily have been interpreted as political criticism, and Dohm admitted that he was writing the essay with great caution and an awareness of the most sensitive points in it.[40] It was published in September 1781, and four months later was on Wessely's desk while he was writing *Divrei shalom ve'emet*. It gave Wessely added confidence that his reading of the new reality was not merely wishful thinking, but that religious toleration was in fact a principle upheld by many lovers of humanity. He did not conceal his surprise and delight at the fact that such a politically bold work had been published in Frederick the Great's Prussia. He shared his enthusiastic response with his readers in these words:

Under this benevolent government, the state minister Dohm has written an essay defending the Jews, challenging the states that rule us harshly, denying us all good things because of our belief. And this is a very fine essay, written with much wisdom and acute understanding. And it is also favorably received by state officials and by the sages of the nations. And if anyone had written such an essay two hundred years ago, what would have been said about it then?[41]

Dohm's *On the Civil Improvement of the Jews* was written within the framework of the Enlightenment project. But while Dohm was its author, the text reflects a social dynamic of meetings, correspondence, rewrites, and finally controversy and polemics. It all began in 1780, when Herz Cerfberr, a very distinguished Alsatian Jew, addressed an urgent appeal to Mendelssohn in Berlin to help the Jews of Alsace to combat the wave of anti-Semitism that had broken out there, by writing a memorandum to be submitted to the Council of State. The purpose of this apologetic-literary document was to place the immediate plight of French Jews within the broader context of Jewish existence in Europe. Mendelssohn, who knew Dohm from the Berlin circle of enlightened men and probably also had heard that he planned to write a history of the Jews, asked him to compose the requested memorandum. Dohm agreed, and submitted the memorandum to Cerfberr against payment of a fee, but the French government that ruled during the last days of the ancien régime was not impressed by it. The Jews of Alsace were forced to wait another eleven years (September 1791) until the Revolutionary National Assembly concluded that the Jews inevitably had to be granted political equality. In the meantime, Dohm began work on his more extensive treatise, which was published in Berlin late in the summer of 1781, by Nicolai (who was in close touch with Dohm while he was writing it, as was Mendelssohn, who read the drafts).[42]

On the Civil Improvement of the Jews was a particularly powerful piece of writing because it made the Jews a test case for the validity of the ideas of the Enlightenment. Dohm was a historian trained to conduct a comparative examination, a deist whose attitude to the positivistic religions was disinterested and historical. He was a man of the Prussian nation who had adopted the attitude of the modern state toward its economic and political interests, a humanist and a rationalist. As such, for him the limitations placed upon the Jews and the inferior status assigned them on the periphery of society was an unacceptable anomaly. As Robert Liberles rightly stated, in undertaking the role of defender of the Jews, Dohm was in fact writing a fundamental work on the tolerance of the Enlightenment. He admitted as much himself:

[My essay] is not actually for the purpose of presenting the position of the oppressed Hebrews, but rather of humanity and of the governments. I did not wish to arouse pity for them nor to ask that they be accorded better treatment, but only to show that human, healthy and rational thinking, as well as the interest of the civil society, demand such an improved treatment.[43]

As soon as the kings of Europe were persuaded that a man's religion has no effect on economics and politics, because they are conducted on the basis of earthly, rational considerations, and not theological or ecclesiastical ones, they would integrate the Jews into the state. Dohm's treatise contains a detailed plan for such an integration, which consists mainly of political rights to be granted to the Jews by the state together with the regeneration and transformation of the Jews with the aid of the state: economic productivization on the one hand, and an improvement of their morals and education, on the other. According to Dohm, this plan was contingent on a dramatic change in the thinking of both Jews and Christians, in particular with regard to separating the "Jew" from the "man"—the same concept that underpinned *Divrei shalom ve'emet* and aroused such vehement opposition. Judaism is no different in character than any other religion, Dohm asserted, that believes it possesses the sole truth and is hostile to all other religions. The Jews are not to blame for their sorry moral state or their exclusion from the productive mainstream of society; rather this is a natural outcome of the abominable policy implemented toward them for centuries. "That policy," Dohm contended, "is a remnant of the barbarism of past centuries, a consequence of a fanatical religious hatred. It is unworthy of our enlightened times and should have been abolished long ago."[44] Any and every human society would have sunk to the condition of the Jews if they had been treated in a similar fashion. Therefore, the state must rise above differences in religion, enable freedom of opinion, and tolerate within it members of all religions without restricting their freedom of worship and faith:

so long as their laws are not contrary to the general principles of morality and do not permit antisocial vices, they do not justify their persecution . . . The only prerogative of the government would be to have an exact knowledge of these principles . . . and the actual influence of these on their actions [and] to endeavor to weaken the influence of these principles, by general enlightenment of the nation, by furthering and advancing its morals independently of religion, and in general, to further the refinement of their sentiments. More than anything else, a life of normal civil happiness in a well-ordered state, enjoying the long-withheld freedom, would tend to do away with clannish religious opinions. The Jew is even more man than Jew, and how would it be possible for him not to love a state . . . He would look at his country with the eyes of a long misjudged, and finally after long banishment, reinstated son. These human emotions would talk louder in his heart than the sophistic sayings of his rabbis.[45]

These lines quoted from Dohm's essay link the tolerance of Jews required of the state with the deist utopia of the Enlightenment. Not only would the Jew regain his lost honor as a man, but the policy of toleration would inevitably give birth to the new Jew, the Jew of the Enlightenment, whose religion scarcely affects his civil life. There was more than a trace of paternalism in the approach of the Enlightened, who believed it was possible—even essential—to redress the flaws of the society and to reshape it according to what their notion of good, even if the members of that society had not yet recognized it them-selves. Dohm did suggest, however, that the autonomy of the Jewish commu-nity be preserved and the rabbis be permitted to use the sanction of excommunication to impose their will on its refractory members, in opposi-tion to Mendelssohn's view, because he regarded the community as a religious body and did not feel that the autonomy of its leaders was related to the civil and personal status of its members. However, in his vision of the future, Dohm saw a new Jew: a man of virtuous character; a Jew who had cast off the image of the wily merchant seeking easy profits, and who, through a healthier diet and training for hard physical labor, would take on the image of an artisan or peasant; a Jew whose body was more robust, closer to that of "our decent citizen and the inhabitants of our cities"; a Jew who would find stability in his way of life, would be loyal to the state and have a European education. None-theless, the time was not yet ripe to admit Jews to public office, because "the too mercantile spirit of most Jews will probably be broken more easily by heavy physical labor than by the sedentary work of the public servant; and for the state as well as for himself it will be better in most cases if the Jew works in the shops and behind the plow than in the state chancelleries."[46]

The last months of 1781 and the winter of 1782 were a particularly inten-sive time for the intellectuals in Berlin involved in writing about and reacting to the issue of religious toleration in general and the regeneration of Jewish life in particular. Dohm finished writing *On the Civil Improvement of the Jews* in August 1781, and it was printed by Nicolai's publishing house in September. In the following months, the French translation of the pamphlet was prepared; it was published at the beginning of 1782. Although Mendelssohn was involved throughout the writing of Dohm's essay, he did not accept Dohm's position regarding the continuation of traditional Jewish autonomy, particularly the right to punish members of the community for religious infractions, and had already planned his reaction. He asked the physician Marcus Herz to translate into German Menasseh ben Israel's book *Teshu'at Israel* (Vindiciae Judae-orum, Vindication of the Jews), written in the seventeenth century in defense of the Jews' right to return to England. Mendelssohn wanted to publish it, along with a *Preface* in which he would put forth his position on the question of tolerance toward the Jews and his vision of the future existence of Jews in a tolerant state.[47] In the meantime, he asked his friend, the merchant Moshe Wessely in Hamburg, Napthali Herz Wessely's brother, to write a review of Dohm's essay that would refute the view supporting the rabbis' continued right to impose excommunication.[48]

Dohm's pamphlet was therefore at the center of the public discussion and he collected reactions in order to print them in the second half of the essay. In October 1781, from his court in Vienna, Emperor Joseph II issued an edict known as the Edict of Toleration toward the Jews of Bohemia, and in January 1782, another Edict of Toleration toward the Jews of Austria. Excerpts from these edicts were published in the press and news of them reached Berlin as well. The enthusiasm among Jews reached a high pitch because it seemed to them that the debate about toleration had finally been given real political expression. From that moment, the documents emanating from Vienna became a part of the overall discussion. Although most of the restrictions on Austrian Jews, in particular on those in Vienna, were not removed, the solemn declarations included in the Edict of Toleration resembled some of the positions presented by Dohm in Berlin only several months earlier: the desire to make the Jews happier, more useful citizens of the state; annulment of the discriminatory laws based on the church's desire for separation; and a reformative plan for the Jews, which consisted mainly of compulsory education in the language of the land and of morals—in general schools or in special schools that the Jews were entitled to establish for themselves.[49]

The Edicts of Toleration created a special problem for the Jews of the Austrian Empire, since they were required to begin establishing modern schools. The intellectuals of Berlin, however, regarded the edicts as a further step in the public discourse about the status of the Jews. Early in February 1782, Mendelssohn sent the complete version of the Edict of Toleration to the publisher Nicolai, suggesting that he print it as an appendix to *Teshu'at Israel*, which he was about to publish. "What Dohm feels about it, I have deeply felt myself," Mendelssohn wrote to him. "After all, I cannot express my view as plainly and candidly as I would like. Hence I prefer to be altogether silent."[50] Unquestionably, the Edicts of Toleration, in particular the widely publicized one referring to the Jews of Vienna, which was very disappointing in comparison to Dohm's and Mendelssohn's vision of Enlightenment. Moreover, the emperor's clear allusions to his hope that the Jews would convert to Christianity within two decades could hardly evoke the enthusiasm of Dohm the deist and Mendelssohn the Jew. Wessely, on the other hand, ignored all the shortcomings of the Edict of Toleration, and in January 1782 had already begun writing his *Divrei shalom ve'emet*. In it, he compared the Austrian emperor to a divine emissary: "You have seen that God is good. He has raised up a great man, a savior to mankind, the exalted emperor, His Majesty, Joseph II."[51] And now, in his well-known *Preface* to Menasseh ben Israel's book, completed on March 19, 1782, Mendelssohn, swept up by the sequence of stormy events, was unable to conceal his delight at the current developments, as he linked Lessing, Dohm, and Joseph II all together:

Lessing and Dohm, one as a philosophical poet and the other as a philosophical political scientist, had given thought to the great purpose of Providence, which embraced the prerogatives of humanity as a whole, and the admirable monarch not only has accepted these principles in their broadest sense, at this very time, but in keeping with his wide field of activity, he has also drawn up a plan, whose implementation requires more than human powers, and now he is beginning to execute it.[52]

Although Mendelssohn wrote his preface to Menasseh ben Israel's work as a critique of Dohm's pamphlet, in order to reject his approach to the regeneration and productivization of the Jews and to promote the approach granting rights to the Jews irrespective of any prior internal reforms, he also used the occasion to discuss the issue of religious tolerance. Mendelssohn was in total accord with Dohm's view that tolerance was a matter relating to the rights of all humankind. Hence he praised Dohm for having described the problem of anomalous Jewish existence in the state as an individual case of the fundamental universal question:

It is not his intent to defend Judaism or the Jews; he is arguing the case of humankind and defending its rights. It is our fortune that this argument has also become our argument, and it is impossible to demand the rights of humankind without at the same time demanding our rights. The eighteenth century philosopher discerned no difference in doctrines or views, but considered every individual simply as a human being.[53]

However, following the declaration of universal tolerance, which in the contemporary public discourse referred to Christian tolerance of other religions and of deists and atheists, Mendelssohn was the first to point out that a problem might actually be raised by the side meant to gain by the introduction of tolerance. He opined that it was possible that the Jews might themselves place obstacles in the way of their improved civil status in the state. He publicly admitted for the first time to his associates in the public discourse in Germany that he had some doubts about the tolerance of his fellow Jews and feared that in the new enlightened age, the Jewish leaders might not display a large measure of tolerance internally, toward the members of their community.

Therefore, Mendelssohn's *Preface* is devoted primarily to his attempt to persuade Dohm that in order to rehabilitate the Jews it was necessary to abolish the religious-ecclesiastical power of the traditional Jewish autonomy over its members. Mendelssohn presented a most liberal and radical position in the *Preface*. In the desired future state, guided by the principle of tolerance, every individual would have the natural right to hold religious beliefs as he would any other opinion, immune to the rule of a government agency or community or ecclesiastical coercion: "True, divine religion does not abrogate to itself any power over opinions and propositions . . . it knows no power other than the power to convince by reasoning and to make one happy through convictions held." As he had argued ten years earlier to Lavater, who had deviated from the principles of tolerance by expecting the Jews to convert to Christianity, and as he had endeavored at the very same time to reply to the Orientalist from Göttingen University, Michaelis, who had questioned the very possibility that Jews could be integrated as citizens based on Dohm's program, thus he now turned inward with great concern. "True, divine religion needs neither arms nor fingers to be effective; it is all mind and heart," Mendelssohn explained his demand that the rabbis be completely denied the right to excommunicate ideological and religious deviants from the Jewish community. And he added: "All societies may have the right to expel members, religious groups do not. For it is diametrically opposed to their nature and aim . . . on what grounds, then, can we deny admission to dissenters, separatists, disbelievers or sectarians. Reason's house of prayer has no need of closed doors."

Mendelssohn did not conceal his fear that the right of religious coercion and excommunication would be abused. "I see no possibility of blocking or restraining the fanaticism of false religion," he wrote with great anxiety, "the clergy are not sufficiently enlightened so that there is no danger in granting them this privilege."[54]

At the end of the *Preface*, Mendelssohn no longer concealed from the reader the object of his remarks. He addressed an emotional appeal, albeit one marked by great pessimism, to the leaders and rabbis of contemporary Jewish communities to take part in the European Enlightenment's project of religious tolerance. He urged them to relinquish of their own accord the coercive authority they possessed, in the hope that they would "show the same love and tolerance toward their brothers that they themselves had so passionately sighed for." Mendelssohn expected that they would respond fairly, measure for measure, to the religious tolerance that the Jews were now being accorded by the Christians. "Oh my brothers, too keenly have you felt the bitter yoke of intolerance, and perhaps you have found some compensation in exerting against those who were within your jurisdiction the pressure which you suffered from." Mendelssohn offered a psychological explanation for the tyranny of the rabbis toward their communities: "Vengeance always seeks satisfaction, and when it can find nothing else to feed upon, it will feed upon itself. Perhaps the general example misleads you." Now the times have changed, and the ridiculous idea that "religion can only be established by a rule of iron" has passed from the world:

Thank the God of your fathers, who is the God of all love and mercy, that this delusion is gradually vanishing. Nations are now tolerating one another; and they also show a measure of kindness toward you—an attitude which, with the help of Him who fashions the hearts of men, may ultimately grow into genuine brotherly love. Oh, my brethren, follow the example of love, just as you formerly followed that of hatred. Emulate the virtues of the nations whose vices you had previously felt impelled to imitate. If you would desire protection, tolerance, and sufferance from others, then protect, tolerate, and suffer each other. Love and you will be loved.[55]

Mendelssohn's great apprehension that the rabbis would remain intolerant in an age of religious tolerance was not merely prescient or theoretical. From his own personal experience, he was able to point to at least one clear address—the Lithuanian rabbi Raphael Suesskind Kohen (1722–1803), who from 1775 was the rabbi of the Altona-Hamburg community. His involvement in two affairs that were close in time, his attempt to persuade rabbis to ban Mendelssohn's *Bi'ur* in 1779, and his struggle against Netanel Posner, who rebelled against the halakhah and rabbinical authority in 1781, marked him as an enemy of the Enlightenment. The first tests of tolerance within Jewish communities produced very worrisome results as far as Mendelssohn was concerned.[56]

Mendelssohn's *Bi'ur* of the Pentateuch

For six years beginning in 1778, Mendelssohn was totally immersed in his work on a translation of the Pentateuch into German and printing a new edition of the five books of the Torah along with a new commentary written by maskilic "commentators" whom he had enlisted to work on this project. Although he never stopped complaining of his weakness and failing health, Mendelssohn succeeded in gathering a rather impressive team of scholars who helped him complete this expensive and complex project.

Mendelssohn related the history of this project in a letter to Avigdor Levi of Prague in mid-1779. It began with a suggestion made by Shlomo Dubno, the Polish maskil, who was an outstanding scholar of the Hebrew language and was employed as a tutor for nine-year-old Joseph Mendelssohn. In his letter, Mendelssohn underscored the importance of the translation as a counterweight to the Christian translations of the Bible, but played down his own role in the project:

I translated the Bible into German, not out of pride in the task or to make a name for myself, but for my children that God had bestowed upon me . . . And here, by the will of God, there came to my acquaintance the learned Shlomo Dubno to whom I entrusted my son Joseph that he might take daily lessons from him in Hebrew. And when this Rabbi learned of my translation, it found favor in his eyes, and he urged me to publish it for the benefit of Jewish children, who had need of a biblical commentary and translation in German that would surpass and replace the misleading books of the Gentiles.[57]

Nonetheless, when a month later he told his friend August Hennings, a member of the Danish government in Copenhagen, about the project, Mendelssohn revealed much greater transformative expectations of this work. He then referred to it as much more than a learning aid for students or a counterweight to the writings of Christian biblical scholars: "This is the first step to culture from which, alas, my nation has held itself so aloof that one might almost despair of any possibility of improvement [*Verbesserung*]."[58] This was unquestionably an Enlightenment project, and those engaged in it had high hopes for it. It reflected several innovative changes: it was meant to serve as an agent of change—to replace the Yiddish and the Christian translations of the Bible; to make Torah the chief object of study rather than the Talmud; to convey the sacred wording of the Bible in a European language—high German; to express the need for a new commentary. Above all, this was a collective literary project, the first of its kind.[59] Of course, in its dimensions and subversive aims, the *Bi'ur* project was nothing like the well-known *Encyclopédie* of the mid-eighteenth-century French philosophers, but it was nonetheless one of the first literary projects of the Haskalah, one initiated and executed by intellectuals, who were not members of the rabbinical elite, in an attempt to break into the Enlightenment culture.

Many people participated in the *Bi'ur* project. First, Mendelssohn himself, who translated into German and wrote the commentary for several of the Books, and Shlomo Dubno, who wrote the commentary for the Book of Genesis (except for the first chapter of Genesis, for which Mendelssohn wrote the commentary). In addition, Aaron Friedenthal of Jaroslav in Galicia (the Book of Numbers); Herz Homberg of Bohemia (Deuteronomy); Naphtali Herz Wessely (Leviticus); Shalom of Mezerich (the unacknowledged author who wrote the masoretic notes for the last three Books, after Dubno quarreled with the managers of the project, affronted by what he understood as their denial of promises made to him, and abruptly left the project); and Saul Mendelssohn, Moses' brother, who was in charge of the proofreading and printing. Because there were so many editions, it was necessary to appoint a financial manager: "to supervise those engaged in the work, to examine expense accounts and receipts, and even to distribute the copies of the subscribers."[60] Jermias Bendit, a wealthy merchant from Berlin, was assigned this task. The original budget to finance the project was obtained about two years before the first volume of the *Bi'ur* came out, when about five hundred people subscribed to it in advance. A list of the subscribers shows that the *Bi'ur* project was very widely circulated—to nearly every corner of Jewish Europe. Although about a quarter of the subscribers were wealthy Berlin Jews, there was much interest in the Mendelssohnian Bible even beyond Germany, and there were subscribers from France, Italy, Austria, Bohemia, Holland, Denmark, England, and Poland-Lithuania.[61] A prospectus, *Alim literufah*, containing a sample translation and commentary, along with his introduction and a solicitation of prospective purchasers, was published in Amsterdam by Dubno in 1778, the same year in which Chevrat Chinukh Ne'arim was established.

Once again it was Wessely who hastened to ally himself with his esteemed friend Mendelssohn. He wrote an encomium in his honor to explain to the public why the *Bi'ur* was urgently needed.[62] Wessely's *Mehalel re'a* (Praise for a Friend) can be read as a typical composition of the early Haskalah—a poem of friendship that serves as a kind of poetic approbation, replete with rapturous language and effusive praise of Mendelssohn and the *Bi'ur*. However, in this 1778 poetic essay he also voices his dissatisfaction with the shortcomings of Jewish education, a criticism that reached its peak four years later in *Divrei shalom ve'emet*. Still, it was not only the Austrian emperor's tolerant policy that prompted Wessely to write his dramatic pamphlet in 1782. In *Mehalal re'a* he had already broached ideas that appeared in *Divrei shalom ve'emet* which had obviously been forming in his mind for several years beforehand. In 1778, he wrote in the introduction to his paean to the *Bi'ur*:

Ignorance has become widespread among our people, so they know not, nor do they comprehend the difference between the teaching of the ancients and the teaching of the later generations, and they think it is a simple matter to study the Bible, and in their view, every stupid youngster can understand it . . . and they think little indeed of Hebrew grammar . . . they send their children to school at the age of four or five, to teachers of Bible, without even taking note that they speak with a stammering tongue, and sometimes do not even know how to read properly . . . and they will teach these tender children the word of God in their one way for a year or more, and when that time is up, will inform their parents: your children have already succeeded in learning Mishnah and Talmud, so it is no longer fit to teach them Bible . . . Hence their words are bothersome to these lads, and press upon them like a heavy burden, and most of them, when they grow up, will cast off the yoke of Talmud, and as they turn aside from it, nothing will remain with them, neither Torah nor the elements of Jewish faith, neither knowledge nor morals nor refinement. They do not even know how to read Hebrew and hence will not understand the words of the prayers they utter each day.

Wessely at this point did not develop his distinction between *torat ha'adam* and *torat haShem* (teachings of God), and his main concern was the reform of the traditional curriculum of *torat haShem*. However, in 1778 he called, for example, for the orderly study of the German language and pointed out the advantages accruing to all those fluent in it. For this reason, he warmly recommended Mendelssohn's project:

Here I am, still amazed by the illness of my people . . . and nearly despairing, and now in front of my eyes, pages bearing a remedy [Alim literufah] . . . I saw and was joyous and told my mind to return to a state of calm . . . for Mendelssohn's translation far surpasses all the German translations that we have seen and heard of until now, written by Jews as well as by Gentile scholars . . . and there will be a clear path for the teachers of children, on which they can lead the children of Israel.[63]

The purpose of Alim literufah was, of course, to sign up potential subscribers so that their money would cover the printing costs. But a short while before the Bi'ur was publicized through this prospectus, rumors were heard about rabbis' opposition to the project. The fact that the prospectus, with its sample translation, did not include the customary rabbinical approbations had aroused their suspicions. Mendelssohn, after learning from Avigdor Levi that Rabbi Yehezkel Landau of Prague was displeased by this omission, wrote a letter of explanation in which he admitted that he regarded the Bi'ur as a different type of work, which had no need of rabbinical approbations. Hence the rabbi, who was acknowledged as one of the greats of the generation, had no cause to feel affronted. "We have never seen that the rabbinical authorities have taken an interest in a book written in Judeo-German, to agree to its printing, or to protest to its author," Mendelssohn argued. With these words, Mendelssohn was attempting to remove the Bi'ur project from the domain of rabbinical control and to place it in the domain of non-religious literature. The German translation of the Bible and the new commentary were paradoxically regarded as secular literature, over which the rabbinic elite had no sole authority. "If I should ever write a work in Hebrew," Mendelssohn promised, "I shall surely ask the Sages of Israel and receive their permission and approbation, as I am obliged to do." In the meantime, he was convinced that the Bi'ur was exempt from such an obligation.[64]

As a matter of fact, Shlomo Dubno had already received three approbations in 1778, all based on Alim literufah. One was from Rabbi Hirschel Levin, the head of the Berlin community's court and a friend of Mendelssohn's; the second was from Rabbi Saul Berlin, Zevi Hirsch's son, who served as rabbi of the Frankfurt-on-Oder community and later was known to be an covert maskil; the third was from the bet din (rabbinical court) of Berlin. But Mendelssohn only printed these approbations when the Bi'ur was completed in 1783, and in the meantime he chose not to mention their existence. In any event, after the books of the Pentateuch began to come out, Mendelssohn again heard a rumor that Rabbi Landau of Prague was furious and planned to ban the Bi'ur. He asked his contact in Prague, Avigdor Levi, to inform him whether there was any truth in the rumor, surprised that anyone would pronounce such a precipitate, sweeping sentence, one for which there were no grounds. Probably Mendelssohn's sense of being a victim, persecuted for his views, troubled him even more than his concern about the fate of the project. "What have they seen concerning this matter and what has come unto them when they sentenced me without trial and lawful process?" he asked, deeply insulted, admitting that he was threatened by a wave of opposition, even of hatred. Mendelssohn's blunt defiance of the rabbis who were threatening him is of particular importance—"Let them curse, I shall bless!" he wrote in a letter in the summer of 1781. Even if this defiant cry was not made in public, it was meant to mark the boundaries of the rabbis' intervention in the new projects of the maskilim.[65]

While Rabbi Landau's protestations reached Mendelssohn only in the form of rumors, the opposition of Rabbi Raphael Kohen of Hamburg-Altona was out in the open. From mid-1779, various persons knew that he was threatening to excommunicate Mendelssohn and applying to rabbis in different locations in an effort to organize a united rabbinical front against the *Bi'ur*. Mendelssohn was informed of this effort by his brother-in-law Moses Fürst, who lived in Copenhagen. Hennings, Mendelssohn's Danish friend, who like Lessing, Dohm, and others was an avid supporter of religious tolerance, was Mendelssohn's contact regarding steps taken by the rabbi from Altona, since the Jewish community was then under the control of the Danish monarchy. The correspondence between the two during the summer of 1779 shows that a storm was brewing around the *Bi'ur*, even though it had not yet been published, and its opponents had only seen the prospectus, *Alim literufah*.[66] "The zealots shall not deter me from my work or cause me disquiet," Mendelssohn wrote to the worried Hennings. His fears were mollified by the fact that the rabbi from Altona had not yet taken any serious public steps such as banning the work, but he was concerned that he might be reserving his weapons until the *Bi'ur* appeared in print. His Danish friend offered to involve the authorities in order to block the fanaticism and "theological despotism" of the Altona rabbi by police measures, but Mendelssohn asked him to refrain from intervening; he believed the truth would win out in the end in the ideological battle over public opinion, and that it was still necessary to put to the test the question of whether to violate the principle of tolerance to defend oneself against intolerance. To deter any action by Rabbi Raphael Kohen, Mendelssohn recommended that, if possible, subscriptions to the *Bi'ur* be taken out in the name of the Danish king, Christian VII, the heir to the throne and other state officials. This Hennings succeeded in arranging, thereby greatly enhancing the prestige of the maskilic literary project and giving it a measure of immunity.

Several days later (July 17, 1779) a brief news item appeared in a Hamburg newspaper reporting from Altona that the local rabbi had placed under a ban any Jew who read Mendelssohn's translation of the Torah.[67] It is reasonable to assume that this piece of news was intended to publicly expose Rabbi Kohen's plot, to dissuade him from taking such a step, or perhaps to prompt officials of the Danish government to deal with him. Hennings regarded the affair as a test of enlightened men's ability to forestall intolerance without themselves exceeding the bounds of tolerance or violating the principle of freedom of thought, and hence he wrote to Mendelssohn recommending that the rabbi of Altona leave the state. In any event, a ban of the *Bi'ur* was never more than a threat, since none was ever issued in Altona. In September 1779, Mendelssohn was able to inform Hennings: "My rabbis have been rather quiet of late. What has caused their silence I do not know. It was surely not some better understanding on their part. Judging from a correspondence that came into my hands by chance they seemed to be rather determined not to change their mind. As for me I have no intention of either challenging or ridiculing them."[68]

The threats of a ban of the *Bi'ur*, rumors of which reached Berlin from Altona in 1779 and from Prague in 1781, were all too familiar to Wessely, and once again he came out in defense of his friend. In the summer of 1781, only shortly before the publication of *Divrei shalom ve'emet*, Wessely wrote an essay in defense of the *Bi'ur*, which remained in manuscript form and has only recently been uncovered.[69] Wessely was particularly agitated, after finishing his commentary on Leviticus. The book had just come off the press, and in view of the rumors about its anticipated ban, he found it necessary to widely publicize the great benefit to be gained from the *Bi'ur*. The essay, which Wessely as yet untitled, opened like *Divrei shalom ve'emet*, stressing the lofty status of "man" and his inherent potential:

Since man alone was created in the image of God, and possesses the spirit of life and innumerable powers, among them the powers of the mind and its traits, such as the power of wisdom and intellect, understanding and cognition, hence he has the ability to rise above the customs of the world, indifferent to the charms that the heart is drawn to, in his ways to resemble the ways of the Almighty, to do good works, to show mercy, and to act as great men of renown have done from time immemorial.

But those men of renown endowed with reason and lofty morals must carry their people with them. They must assume positions of leadership out of a sense of public responsibility: "The man of intellect will help all the people in his generation, and those in the following generations, for each and every generation shall enjoy the fruits of his enlightenment and the products of his reason." Wessely pinned high hopes on the *Bi'ur*; hence he was very troubled by the controversy it had aroused, and began, in this manuscript, which very soon grew into *Divrei shalom ve'emet*, to develop the public role of the enlightened Jewish intellectual: "a scholar, a virtuous man, rationalistic in his thinking, whose goal is 'the success of all men in this world'." He saw this type as one of the "great men of renown" in the overall culture, who, within the Jewish nation, is engaged in the "wisdom of the Torah." Nonetheless, his aims are not the same as those of the members of the talmudic rabbinical elite; rather they are pure morals and thought and an orientation to practical life. This role that the maskil undertakes calls for much courage and requires him to pay the social price demanded of "great men who deliver sermons to congregations and write books to teach the people knowledge and devoutness." Facing his opponents, he "will not falter at his labor, and will not fear their scorn, but will only stick firmly to his integrity and will not weaken."

In uttering these words of encouragement and depicting the model of the maskil as one of the "great men of renown," Wessely was referring to Mendelssohn and the *Bi'ur* project. "And "this spirit," Wessely wrote out of boundless admiration and esteem, "has also entered into this man, my friend and colleague, the accomplished sage, the famous scholar, our honored master and teacher, Moses Mendelssohn, and has emboldened him to translate God's Torah into the German language, a tongue in which young men in these regions are fluent." He depicted Mendelssohn in the likeness of Moses, who was a shepherd acting out of his profound, sincere concern for the "abandoned lambs," neglected for many generations by inexpert and irresponsible shepherds—the traditional teachers. Wessely depicted the *Bi'ur* as a transformative project par excellence, whose aim was to redress the wrongs of the past in Jewish education and to bring about significant change: "I shall level the track before them to place in their mouths the words of God in a pristine language that the boys will hear and understand, so that a different spirit may come into them, a good, pleasant spirit, and what till now has been like a heavy burden for them will be pleasing to their minds."

This manuscript of Wessely's, which was never published, can be read as a first draft of *Divrei shalom ve'emet*. It contains trenchant criticism of the traditional curriculum and the Polish teachers, and a sharp protest against the disastrous "great stupidity" that exists in the field of education: the Bible was being neglected; the rules of Hebrew grammar were ignored; students were skipped from the Torah to the Talmud before they were prepared to understand it; the teachers, who were dilettantes, felt self-satisfied about their pointless casuistry, which was totally contrary to common sense. But this essay contains far more than a critique on education. Wessely was vexed by the intellectual insularity of the rabbinical culture and the talmudic scholars, but his anxiety was also aroused by the deists ("the scoundrels who say our hand is uppermost and it is not God who has done all these deeds . . . who do not believe in God's providence over His creatures"). Consequently, he demarcated the boundaries between the various trends of the Jewish elite and finally shaped his ideal type—the "true maskil." This maskil is endowed with the natural traits of moral commitment, in addition to his broad knowledge. He must "first fill his mind with the studies of the sciences and knowledge about what is just and what is evil, and shall know the fundamental beliefs and elements . . . so he will feel in his mind purity of virtue and the glory of divine matters." This manuscript did not yet include the distinction Wessely later drew between *Torat haShem* (the teachings of God) and *Torat ha'adam* (the teachings of man, or human knowledge). But Wessely had already demanded autonomy for the maskilim in those fields of knowledge that were outside the sphere of halakhot: those doctrines and beliefs on which the rabbis of the last generations had not written books. In this way, Wessely continually more clearly demarcated the maskilim's autonomous intellectual space, without denying the talmudic elite its traditional roles. The members of this elite were responsible for maintaining the halakhic tradition, and their role was to "vindicate the many and to light the way like stars in the midst of this night of exile." In contrast: "those studies relating to the ways of God and the ways of the human mind, and how the young may lead a pure life, all these leave to the wise-hearted in each and every generation to teach the people knowledge and piety."

After allocating a place of their own to the "wise-hearted" maskilim, Wessely described his comprehensive transformative curriculum in this draft of *Divrei shalom ve'emet*, written mainly because of the controversy aroused by the *Bi'ur* and before the Edicts of Toleration were published in Vienna. He suggested a complete program of studies for Jewish education: all the sciences, history, geography, mathematics, and so on. His justification for the inclusion of every subject in the curriculum was twofold: it would be an aid to an understanding of the Torah and a benefit in everyday life. At this point, Wessely did not demand that the new curriculum be binding on all the students, and stressed the primacy of Torah study. However, he developed an approach that was subversive from the standpoint of the traditional values: "For God has differentiated between men and their faculties." Hence a multitrack system should be created that takes account of varying abilities and defines an equal basis for all, one that would serve as a springboard for outstanding students and a foothold in Judaism, and as a barrier against heresy for the weak students. In Wessely's view, the *Bi'ur* that had just been published would provide a common framework of this kind. And as a paraphrase of the words of Mendelssohn, who defined his German translation of the Pentateuch as "the first step toward culture," Wessely wrote in this manuscript: "And as for this translation, it is the first step to all these good things, if enlightened people will use it for the benefit of those who come to the schools."

The Posner Affair

While, in Berlin, Wessely was engrossed in writing his defense of the *Bi'ur*, religious tolerance among the Jews was put to a second test in the Altona-Hamburg community. This time too Rabbi Raphael Kohen, refusing to accept the principle of tolerance, adopted punitive and coercive measures in his struggle against those who committed offenses against the religious tradition.[70] In the spring and summer of 1781, evidence was presented to the rabbi and the Altona-Hamburg *bet din* about a businessman, Netanel Posner (who called himself Samuel Marcus in his contacts with gentiles), who was publicly defying various religious rules, questioning the jurisdiction of the *bet din* to try and punish him, and attempting to reject the community's authority over him. Even after his excommunication, Posner did not conceal his contempt but publicly demonstrated his indifference to it. After he had publicly scorned the words of the Sages, claiming that they had distorted the instructions of the Torah, Rabbi Kohen warned him that he would impose a more severe ban on him, from which he could redeem himself only by a series of acts of confession and atonement:

Now you, the holy people of God, see how far things have gone, that this man denies the Torah and the words of the Sages, has become irreligious, inciting and instigating honorable men. Hence we, this *bet din*, have issued a judgment, in honor of our Lord and in honor of our sacred Torah, that this man is banned from two worlds, and we declare we have placed the said ban upon him, which is cited in the *kol bo* book (the conventional text of excommunication), in all the synagogues, that he be excluded and shunned by all, that no one may have commerce with him nor sit within his four walls until such time as he will come before us, before this *bet din*, and receive repentance from us, according to the law and our holy Torah.[71]

Netanel Posner was not the type of obstinate Jew, a *gavra alima* (a violent man who accepts no authority) who appeared from time to time in the traditional community, nor was he one of the maskilim. Posner was a representative of the Jewish-German bourgeoisie that had begun to emerge from the circles of court Jews and the wealthy elite in the seventeenth century. Its contacts with the European milieu had greatly influenced this bourgeoisie and led it to various degrees of acculturation. Although Posner was one of the advance subscribers to Mendelssohn's *Bi'ur*, his financial assistance to the Berlin maskilim's literary project did not mean he had joined the circle of maskilic writers, nor that he was adopting their ideology. The picture that emerges from the documents about the Posner affair is one of a Jew who earns his livelihood from the stock exchange, is clean shaven, fashionably dressed (a wig and a snood), and leads an active social life (balls, theater). This lifestyle was typical of that rising bourgeoisie, which did not forego any of the pleasures of life in the European city. Posner's outspoken remarks against the Sages were apparently a spontaneous expression of his freethinking ideas and his deist views, a position he tried to conceal, but one Rabbi Kohen had no trouble in detecting.[72]

In the wake of the ban, Posner applied to the Danish government for help. Rabbi Kohen prepared a memorandum of reply and was forced in the end to rescind his punitive measures. The rabbi was not divested of his right to issue bans, but this privilege was restricted and placed under government control, and he was warned not to exaggerate in taking steps against Jews who violated religious rules. The man who, in the last months of 1781, made the public and the Danish authorities aware of the Posner affair was none other than August Cranz, that same energetic champion of enlightenment and tolerance who constantly kept his finger on the pulse of events in the Jewish world. Armed with the wording of the complaint lodged by Posner, Cranz wrote a memorandum to the Danish heir to the throne, Prince Friedrich, entitled *Über den Missbrauch der geistlichen Macht* (*On the Misuse of Ecclesiastical Power*). He called upon the Prince to restrain Rabbi Kohen, whom he called "The great Pope and Inquisitor" of Altona.[73] Cranz's aim was to expose the affair in the Altona-Hamburg Jewish community to public opinion and to the Danish authorities, as an example of what could happen when religious tolerance was wrongly applied. It is unthinkable, he asserted, at a time when religious tolerance has been accepted as a general principle, enlightenment is dominant and humanism is the guiding principle for decision-makers, that Rabbi Raphael Kohen should be permitted to wield his power of coercion under the very nose of the secular state.

Cranz's memorandum was a most extreme piece of writing, filled with comparisons between the actions of the rabbi and the tribunal of the Catholic Inquisition, which sentenced heretics to burn at the stake, and descriptions of the penalty of excommunication as an extremely cruel inhumane act. Cranz objected to the very existence of anachronistic Jewish autonomy and demanded that the state restrict it. He called on the government to assume secular authority in order to protect respectable citizens like Netanel Posner, who had fallen victim to the persecutions of zealous rabbis, and whose civil status had been adversely affected because of his religious views. Can there be a more absurd situation, Cranz remarked, than this, when in a Christian state, the Jewish church possesses sovereignty and such vast powers, the likes of which were not given to any other religion? Only the natural religion, he asserted, in no way harms the happiness of the state's citizens, nor does it impair their freedom. Cranz took this opportunity to protest against the expulsion order issued by the Hamburg senate against George Schade, the author of a book on the natural religion. The clergy ought to instruct the members of their congregations to recognize the truth and to cultivate high moral standards, but they must do so only by persuasion not coercion. Any form of coercion or punishment for beliefs and views is intolerable.[74]

Mendelssohn learned about the Posner affair from Cranz's memorandum and from rumors about the Danish authorities's involvement in it, and he was deeply concerned. At the very same time, in the early months of 1782, he had to contend with Dohm's recommendation that the Jews be permitted to retain the powers of self-rule even after their reform and improved civil status. Now, the news of this affair further strengthened his conviction that one could not rely on the rabbis' tolerance. "I do not want to investigate to what extent the complaints voiced in public against a certain famous rabbi about this kind of misuse were or were not justified," Mendelssohn wrote in his *Preface*.[75] He knew he could rely on Cranz's approach to religious tolerance, which was influenced by Locke, insofar as the division of powers between the secular and the ecclesiastical authorities was concerned. But Mendelssohn was very embarrassed and troubled when Cranz publicized the Posner affair and cited it as an example of intolerance. Indeed, this affair was a slap in the face for anyone lauding the encouraging signs of tolerance, manifested by Lessing, Dohm, and Joseph II, as Mendelssohn had done in his *Preface*. In view of Rabbi Kohen's actions, it was hard for Mendelssohn to argue against religious fanaticism, ecclesiastical rule and discipline ("Ah! Even after hundreds of years, humankind will not be healed from the whip lashes these monsters have struck at it!"), at the very time when he was endeavoring to prove to Dohm that the Jews had a tradition of tolerance: "I do not find that the wisest of our forefathers ever did claim to possess the right to exclude individuals from religious practices."[76]

In his distress, Mendelssohn could only hope that the dreadful rumors about the Posner affair would turn out to be groundless. In the meantime, he was forced to publicly acknowledge the harsh reality: "The clergy are not sufficiently enlightened so that they can be given such a privilege [the right to impose ecclesiastical discipline] without any danger." There was still some hope that enlightened rabbis would willingly relinquish their coercive power and the use of the penalty of excommunication. Thus, at the end of his *Preface*, signed on March 19, 1782, Mendelssohn wrote: "I have that confidence in the more enlightened among the Rabbis and elders of my nation, that they will be glad to relinquish so pernicious a prerogative, that they will cheerfully do away with all church and synagogue discipline, and let their flock enjoy, at their hands, even that kindness and forbearance, which they themselves have been so long yearning for."[77]

Ironically enough, only a short while later, it became clear that Mendelssohn's earnest hopes had been premature and overly optimistic. Only four days after he wrote these lines, calling upon the rabbis to willingly embrace the principle of tolerance, Rabbis Landau and Tevele attacked Wessely and his pamphlet, *Divrei shalom ve'emet*.

Chapter Six
The Rabbinical Elite on the Defensive

Despite the rumors from Altona-Hamburg about the affair involving Netanel Posner and Rabbi Raphael Kohen, the atmosphere in the small circle of maskilim in Berlin in the winter of 1782 was one of elation.[1] Within the brief period of several months, there were many encouraging signs that could arouse the optimism of anyone who believed in the Enlightenment and its practical implications for the fate of the Jews. One after another, Dohm's *On the Civil Improvement of the Jews* and Joseph II's Edict of Toleration were published. The Freischule had been established and was earning the esteem of German intellectuals. The five books of the *Bi'ur* prepared by Mendelssohn and his collaborators were gradually coming off the press. In January of 1782, a short time after excerpts from the Edicts of Toleration had been published in the press, Wessely wrote his *Divrei shalom ve'emet*.

Elsewhere, too, ambitious young maskilim were active. Wessely sent an open letter to various communities in his attempt to enlist favorable public opinion for his *torat ha'adam* program. The student and private tutor Isaac Euchel (1756–1804) initiated the establishment of a modern school in the Königsberg community.[2] Euchel, thirty years Wessely's junior, also adopted an unprecedented, subversive method to try to persuade the heads of the community that radical changes in Jewish education had to be made. At the end of 1781, he published an open letter to the members of the community, entitled *Sefat emet* (Language of Truth), in which he appealed to the local rabbi. He drew a bleak picture of the crisis in Jewish education and culture, caused by an excessive concentration on study of the Talmud:

My brethren, lovers of the truth and seekers of justice! . . . take a good look at the boys of our Jewish people . . . see how they are like a flock without a shepherd, without knowing or understanding the word of God and His Torah, they have found no guide in the Bible, and speak Hebrew with a stammering tongue. They did not linger long in studying the Mishnah for they thought lightly of it . . . but in the Talmud they thought they had gained success . . . most of these youngsters leave school when they are thirteen years of age, wander about the streets in search of a livelihood to satisfy their physical needs, they forget the little they have learned . . . they abandon their Torah, and falter in their piety.[3]

In *Sefat emet*, Euchel circulated his program to the members and leaders of the community, proposing that they "establish a special school for all members of our community, to properly educate the youth." In this school, the teachers would be "educated, astute men with a knowledge of language." All the members of the community were asked to state their opinion, pro or con, in letters to be submitted to the local rabbi. After a few months, Euchel would open the envelopes and present the results of the poll to an assembly of community leaders: "Once I have the opinions of the majority of the people in our community on this matter, I shall present them at an assembly of all the leaders and prominent members of the community; they shall examine the results and based on them, reach their decision."[4] It was no easy matter for a young private tutor, then only twenty-five, to interfere in the affairs of the community. Euchel's initiative for the establishment of a new institution to cope with the crisis in education came from outside the circle of authoritative decision makers. His attempt to enlist the support of prominent community members through a democratic public poll, for which he was responsible and whose rules would be binding on the community leadership, also posed a problem. Nonetheless, his activity was one more expression of the maskilic elite's consciousness of public responsibility and its demand that it be allowed to play a role in the overall leadership.

"To Publicize the Wickedness of the Evil Man, Herz Wessely"

Euchel's program was never implemented. There is no way of knowing whether this was because of opposition to his presumptuous plan to conduct a poll instead of conforming to the accepted decision-making process, in particular to his intent to avoid addressing the rabbi, expecting him to accept the majority view. In any event, this affair did not make an impact on the public at large. In contrast, immediately after the publication of *Divrei shalom ve'emet*, in the winter of 1782, the Wessely affair began to snowball.[5] The first reaction came from Prague, when, in January 1782, Rabbi Yehezkel Landau delivered a sermon applauding the Edict of Toleration issued by the Emperor Joseph II and denouncing *Divrei shalom ve'emet*. He then called on several other rabbis in the Austrian empire to join him, so they too "will like me publicize the wickedness of the wicked Herz Wessely, may his name be publicly damned."[6]

About two months later (on March 23, 1782) Landau renewed his attack in a Shabbat HaGadol sermon. Although his personal denunciation of Wessely, "a wicked man . . . worse than a carcass," was uttered without the specific mention of a name, and constituted only a small part of his sermon, he gave vent to his great fear that the heretics would gain strength now that government schools (*Normalschulen*) were being established and the Jews were being encouraged to follow an extra-religious curriculum. In his sermon, he described heresy as a dangerous onslaught by of three enemies: the libertine Sabbatians ("the Shabbetai Zevi sect . . . who commit all the offenses mentioned in the Torah"); the hedonists, who are indifferent to the religious commandments; and the rationalist philosophers, for whom Wessely was a spokesman. In the third group, Landau also identified Jewish deists who deny the words of the Sages and even "try to dissuade young boys from studying the Oral Law." Now, in his view, Wessely had burst into this alarming "topsy-turvy world" with his heretical challenge "that the Torah is worth nothing, and a carcass is better than learners of Torah." He did add that the new schools, established by the order of the Austrian government, were a welcome blessing, because a nation that lives from commerce has to teach its sons proficiency in the language of the state, and added that this should be done professionally: "Do not assume that you know how to speak German, for one can only say he truly knows if he has a knowledge of the grammar of the language." For this reason, no one should oppose the emperor's instructions, but neither should one ignore the danger that the study of German was liable to accelerate a process that would culminate in heresy. Like his contemporary, Rabbi Leib Margolioth, Landau cautioned against such a sweeping process: "Take great care, you pious Jews, lest the study of the German language lead you to read other books that are of no benefit in studying language, but that only delve into questions of faith and Torah, and by doing so, God forbid, plant doubts in your hearts as to faith." It is not surprising that a large portion of that Shabbat HaGadol sermon was devoted to reinforcing the religious faith of Landau's audience in Prague. He recited to them the principles of Jewish faith (Creation, Providence, reward and punishment, revelation), and stated: "We must caution against inquiring into matters relating to faith, and all the words of the scholars, whether Jews or men of other nations are sheer nonsense in a matter that is beyond the reach of human understanding, and the crux of that matter is faith, not intelligence nor inquiry." Expressing hope mingled with apprehension, Landau concluded his sermon by calling on the new schoolteachers to avoid crossing the line separating legitimate, necessary enlightenment, and heresy:

I do not suspect teachers in the government schools, Heaven forbid, of doing such a grievous thing . . . for it would be contrary to the desire of the exalted sovereign who established [these schools] only that the boys might learn the language, writing and reading, arithmetic, morals and good manners, but not to speak evil of our religion, and if in any city or state some teacher should be found who commits such a deceitful offense, you shall not heed his words.[7]

On that same Shabbat HaGadol, when Rabbi Landau was delivering his sermon in Prague, Rabbi David Tevele of Lissa delivered his own irate sermon. More than any other rabbinical counterreaction, this sermon was at the very core of the Jewish *Kulturkampf* that erupted in the winter of 1782. Although the rabbi of Lissa lived in Poland, far from the sphere of the Austrian emperor's authority, he also tried to enlist the state on his side, in order to separate the threat posed by *Divrei shalom ve'emet* from the Edicts of Toleration, which in no way ran contrary to traditional Jewish life. He opened his sermon with ingratiating words addressed to the rulers of Austria and Poland and praise for the Edicts of Toleration. He claimed that Wessely had not only distorted the government's program ("perverts the counsel of His Majesty") and introduced into it an interpretation that the legislator, Joseph II, had never contemplated, but he also "deserves to be cursed by the monarchy for he has confused the hearts of our people with his rash and vain words."[8] With these words, the rabbi was openly accusing Wessely of a lack of faith, of treachery and incitement of the Jewish public against the monarchy. However, very soon the tables were turned, and Rabbi Tevele himself faced a serious personal threat.

Many copies of the sermon were circulated, reaching various communities in Europe only a few weeks after the Passover holiday. According to Wessely, he received the full text of the sermon in Berlin on May 1, only a week after he had printed the second half of his *Divrei shalom ve'emet*. "People came to me holding a scroll, on which the aforementioned sermon was written, one full of wrath and indignation, barbs and death from beginning to end."[9]

In the small circle of intellectuals and wealthy enlightened Jews in Berlin of the early 1780s, the sermon evoked anger and bewilderment. News of Rabbi Tevele's reaction on Shabbat HaGadol and rumors that *Divrei shalom ve'emet* had been publicly burned and its author excommunicated rapidly reached Berlin. During the Passover holiday itself, a few days after Tevele's words had been uttered in the Lissa synagogue, Wessely already knew he was being threatened by at least three Polish rabbis: Rabbi Tevele of Lissa, the Gaon of Vilna and Rabbi Joseph of Posen, Rabbi Landau's son-in-law. In Wessely's words, "Men to whom this letter was loathsome, spoke out against me, calling me a knave and villain."[10] A week had passed since the sermon and the Prussian minister of education, Karl Abraham, Baron von Zedlitz, began to inquire among the leaders of the Berlin community whether there was any truth in the rumors that a Jew by the name of Wessely was being persecuted and threatened with expulsion from the city because of a book he had written. Was it possible that such a step, which contravened the spirit of tolerance, could be taken against Wessely?[11]

If Wessely was in a distressing situation, confronted by rabbis threatening to organize a broad front against him, then Moses Mendelssohn's embarrassment was far more harrowing. Only four days before Rabbi Tevele's sermon, he had completed his *Preface*, which had vigorously opposed the coercive powers of the Jewish community. Still shaken by the rumors about the Netanel Posner affair in Altona-Hamburg and the harsh measures taken by Rabbi Raphael Kohen, he had called on the rabbis to relinquish their punitive powers in the name of religious tolerance. And now, within only a few days, Rabbi Tevele had delivered his sermon and at one fell swoop had shattered Mendelssohn's hopes. In a letter he wrote to David Friedländer (April 17), Mendelssohn expressed his concern that the new affair would be taken as further evidence of the Jews' lack of religious tolerance. He feared that Wessely's persecution would be understood as the rabbinical leadership's opposition to the rights of freedom of thought and freedom of the press, recognized in Enlightened Europe as the natural right of free men. What would the Christians say about us? Would they accuse us of obstructing the right of free expression by force? To him, this thought was repugnant and unbearable.

Mendelssohn complained of his distress to Friedländer, reminding him that more than ten years earlier he had been involved in the Lavater affair and had been given permission to write whatever he wished. Anyone who but knew how to write, Jew or Christian, enjoyed a broad freedom, thanks to the Prussian king's magnanimity, and now the Jews were attempting to deny this right to someone who wanted only to improve Jewish education. The first, immediate step to be taken, Mendelssohn felt, was to find out whether any pressure was being exerted on the rabbi of Berlin, Zevi Hirsch Levin, to induce him to expel Wessely from Berlin. If so, he had to be prevented from doing so. Mendelssohn knew that some rabbis had sent letters to Rabbi Levin, who intended to raise complaints about Wessely before the community leaders. Nonetheless, at this stage, Mendelssohn wanted to avoid a head-on clash with his friend Rabbi Levin. As we have already learned, Mendelssohn's fundamental approach was to try and persuade with words and logic, rather than to bring about a situation in which rabbis would be scorned and their disgrace exposed.[12] Mendelssohn suggested that Friedländer speak to the heads of the community and, in particular, dissuade Rabbi Levin from mentioning the affair in a public sermon. He also tried to indirectly advise Rabbi Levin how to reply to the rabbis who were demanding that he severely punish Wessely. He ought to say to them outright: here in Germany we have freedom of printing for all, and it is unthinkable to prevent anyone from expressing his views.[13]

Thus, the principle of tolerance was once again being put to the test, this time on the internal Jewish scene, and the maskilim were well aware that the Jews could not afford to fail. It is no wonder that Mendelssohn was tirelessly involved in all the consultations and actions that he and his friends in Berlin took, in the spring of 1782, to defend Wessely and to denounce Rabbi Tevele and the others who were attacking him. Nonetheless, all during that time, he was careful not to come out publicly against the rabbis.

Even before he read the full version of Rabbi Tevele's sermon, Wessely set about defending himself in public. Deeply offended and alarmed by the rumors about plans to persecute him, but still spoiling for a fight, he composed a tract in defense of *Divrei shalom ve'emet*. He was then receiving encouragement not only from his close friends in the Berlin circle of maskilim, but also from leaders and rabbis of communities in northern Italy, in particular Trieste. This community, which was under Austrian rule and about to establish a school in compliance with Joseph II's instructions and with the guidance of the governor, Count Zinzendorf, had asked Mendelssohn to serve as its advisor. He in turn referred the people of Trieste to Wessely and sent them a copy of *Divrei shalom ve'emet* (in an Italian translation by Elijah Morpurgo, an intellectual and a great admirer of Wessely). In doing so, he opened a channel of communication between Berlin and Trieste, in which the main subject discussed was the new education. The enthusiastic reception of his book in Trieste greatly raised Wessely's spirits, and his tract of defense, *Rav tuv livnei Israel* (April 24, 1782), the "second epistle" in the *Divrei shalom ve'emet* series, was written in reply to the heads of the Trieste community.[14]

Two contradictory voices rose from Wessely's defensive tract. One was the apologetic voice of an injured man who fails to understand what sin he has committed and why he is being attacked. He tried his utmost to show how his opponents had misunderstood and misjudged him, and above all, that he was in all aspects a God-fearing Jew who upheld the absolute supremacy of the Torah over any other value. The other voice was the militant voice of a maskil whose self-identity had been thrown into sharper focus by the attack. He does not hesitate to proclaim his autonomy of thought and his right to express his view freely and courageously, and replies to his critics with a counterattack that has anticlerical undertones.

In his first voice, the frightened, offended voice of a pious Jew who has the highest regard for the rabbis' position, Wessely nonetheless repeated the main points of his program for curricular changes in Jewish education. Nor did he retract his support for the historical shift being led by the gracious monarchs with tolerance and humanism. However, to demonstrate his moderation and his adherence to the tradition, he reduced the innovative aspects of his program as far as he could. He apologized for the offensive expression he had used in relation to talmudic scholars ("a talmudic scholar who has no knowledge, a carcass is better than he") and explained what exactly he had meant by the term "knowledge" (moral virtues, not learning in the "external studies" as his critics had thought). Wessely took pains to clarify that *torat haShem* was substantively different than *torat ha'adam*, and anyone who believed he had placed the two side by side, rather than one above the other, had simply misunderstood. He limited the recommended time for study of the sciences and other nonreligious subjects in the ideal school to only a few hours, and then primarily for outstanding students, stressing that he had no intention of burdening the students with a demanding curriculum that required them to study numerous subjects. Nothing should be done at the expense of Torah learning ("To deflect them from learning Torah, because of these studies, such a thing will never come to pass within Jewry"). He did not plan to include philosophy in his curriculum; he admitted that this might pose a danger to religious faith: "The wise of heart have no need of the science of philosophy (which is called metaphysics), for he knows his God from His Torah and his faith, and the knowledge of the divine is in his heart. And for the layman whose knowledge is inadequate, it is liable to undermine the foundations of his faith." Although pious sages must study philosophy, A far be it from me to introduce children and students to these studies before the light of the Torah and of knowing belief can shield them."[15]

But in the end, Wessely's second, militant radical voice, which was certain of the rightness of his path and demanded that the three rabbis restore his honor, won out. The Trieste Jews, needing no inducement to introduce change, since their natural lifestyle reflected Wessely's notions of the desirable pattern of Jewish life (knowledge of languages, literary creation, high moral standards, respectable contacts with non-Jews), gave him their support, and this encouraged him to believe that all the Jews would adopt his program in the end. His self-image was that of a peerless warrior who had truth on his side and would not back down in the face of his foes:

There were men among them who found this letter odious, opened their mouths to speak ill of it and spoke of me as one of the basest of men . . . and I shall pay it no heed . . . far be it from me to do such a thing, to flatter the men of our generation, to defend our inadequacies, to say peace when there is no peace, and if archers secretly struck at me, I remained silent, as a man who hears not . . . And what am I? The smallest of men within Jewry, and yet, with the help of God, I shall not desist from doing what I must, I shall show no favor to anyone.[16]

Wessely confronted the rabbis, who in his view had misconstrued *Divrei shalom ve'emet* and distorted its meaning, heaped invective upon his head, and "stirred up all the Jewish communities because of this letter, as if, God forbid, I had set fire to the entire Torah." With the self-confidence of a "layman" who believes he is in the right, he challenged the authority of his critics, the rabbis who rested upon their status and their titles:

I have heard the shame and the invective of these rabbis . . . for the way of love they know not, not a single one of them speaks any opinions or arguments based on knowledge, to advise me of the truth or to hear what I may reply to their reproofs, but they whisper in secret, and dispatch letters of animosity to one another. And I hold my tongue, not because I am in awe of a rabbi who has taught me wisdom, for I have never learned from them or others, the little wisdom I possess I have been taught by my brain, with the help of Him who endows men with knowledge. Nor am I in awe of the title of rabbi, for this title does not attest to greatness of spirit, but greatness of spirit does enhance the title of rabbi . . . all the more so, if the rabbi vilifies hatefully, not according to the law of the Torah . . . and what has the rabbinate to do with this matter, we are all laymen before God Almighty and His Torah.[17]

Wessely found the courage to free himself of the "fear of rabbis"; he declared his independence from their authority and his right to freedom of thought. Then this maskilic writer who had no access to the synagogue pulpit attempted to submit the controversy to the decision of Jewish public opinion. *Rav tuv livnei Israel*, like its predecessor *Divrei shalom ve'emet*, served as a means of communication for Wessely, since a periodical that would present his position publicly had not yet been established. He called on his adversaries to stop hiding behind their rabbinic titles and to publicly present their position, by printing and distributing it. Since he knew that *Rav tuv livnei Israel* would reach the Polish rabbis within a short time, toward its conclusion, he issued an ultimatum printed in large, bold letters: within three months he expected a well-reasoned public reply in which they would clarify the reasons for their opposition to *Divrei shalom ve'emet*. If they failed to reply, their silence would be taken as an admission of their error, and no one would pay further attention to what they had to say.

Wessely's aim was to take the discussion out of the closed rooms of the community rabbis and leaders, out of the religious courts, and move it to the public sphere, using the media of open letters, pamphlets, and in the near future—the press. He demanded that the right of decision be transferred to the "court of the House of Israel"—that same anonymous readership that is interested and cares deeply about these burning issues. He hoped in doing so to dispossess the rabbis, who were using their traditional authority to impugn and excommunicate, of their exclusive right to render decisions:

Now, in the name of the God of Israel, I charge with an oath those three rabbis, who have heaped upon me words of fury and animosity, to provide their evidence in a letter and in print, to state what evil or crime they found in our letter *Divrei shalom ve'emet*. And what moved their hearts to so dishonor me in the synagogues and the congregations of Israel . . . for until now we have heard nothing of reason on this matter, no substantial arguments, nothing other than the sound of a voice uttering vituperation. And *I have set a date three months hence beginning from today*. And when their words arrive, the entire house of Israel will judge who is in the right. For these rabbis are not ministers or judges over us, but are our adversaries, and must act according to the law of the Torah, to hear the judgement of the house of Israel. And if they do so, we have already said that we forgive them all their offenses. If that date should pass, and no man replies with words of reason, and they do not hasten to justify their actions, all they have done, all their schemes to lord it over the people . . . Then all of the Jews will know they have no reply to offer. And their silence will be taken before God and His people as a total admission of the justice of what is written in our first letter. (emphasis in original)[18]

The news of the creation of a rabbinical front against him, the threats to expel him from Berlin, and the rumors about his excommunication and the public burning of copies of *Divrei shalom ve'emet* greatly alarmed Wessely. This painful experience brought him closer and closer to the views on religious tolerance held by his friend Mendelssohn. When he read Mendelssohn's *Preface*, published only a month before he wrote his *Rav tuv livnei Israel*, Wessely could not help identifying with his criticism of religious persecution, in particular his appeal to the rabbis to stop "persecuting their brethren for every matter, large or small, with bans and excommunication and words of defamation and disgrace." For this reason, Wessely chose to end his counterattack with a Hebrew translation of the paragraph in the *Preface* in which Mendelssohn called on the rabbis to embrace the principle of religious tolerance and to forgo using their power of excommunication.[19]

This furor took place even before anyone in Berlin knew the exact contents of the sermon. When Mendelssohn received a copy, his agitation grew. Several days later (May 7, 1782) he sent a copy of *Rav tuv livnei Israel* to Trieste, and wrote to Joseph Galico, the secretary of the community:

God knows how my heart within me turns over, my bowels writhe in anguish upon hearing of the evil ways and perverse words of our brethren, the Jews, who live under the Emperor's rule . . . for they try with all their might and their force to disobey the counsel of the wise ruler and to turn his desire into anger, for Heaven forbid, he will call us a people lacking in wisdom, and say we have no need of fools who know not what is good for them . . . and here my close friend Herz Wessely, may he enjoy a long life, who is well known to all pious Jews and renowned for his precious writings . . . now men of enmity have arisen against him, harassing him and giving him no peace, as if, God forbid, he had incited and seduced the entire community of Israel.[20]

Mendelssohn was deeply concerned about the image of the Jews in enlightened Europe and hoped that the Austrian emperor ("a benevolent ruler to his people") would be advised of the views of those who supported the policy of tolerance so he might know that "not all the Jews are alarmed by and reject the good, heaven forbid." At the time, Mendelssohn pictured the battlefield of the Jewish culture war as one in which two camps confronted one another—one said "aye" to Joseph II and the other said "nay." The latter camp was made up of the "fools," Wessely's persecutors, who were attempting to evade the emperor's directives. Mendelssohn's identification with Wessely was unqualified. He came to his defense, heaping lavish praise on his literary work and his moderate character, and complaining of the injustice done to him: "He has ever followed the path of the righteous, never inclining to follow devious paths, neither in his scholarly studies nor in his actions, as all his books will testify, and now he stands upright, endeavoring to strengthen the weak and to awaken the lazy from their slumber with words of peace and truth." In his opinion, the arguments of Wessely's persecutors were baseless, and theirs appeared to be a malicious campaign of revenge ("heartless folly, and they know not their right hand from their left") against Wessely, because he had succeeded in exposing the rabbis' flaws, and now, panic-stricken, they were trying to conceal them. In order to persist in the struggle, Mendelssohn tried to enlist the support of the Trieste community, and hence wrote his letter to Galico, in which he had a hard time controlling his rage.

At that stage of the struggle between the rabbis and Wessely and his supporters (early May 1782), Wessely already knew how broad the opposition to his pamphlet was: not only the three rabbis from Poland, but Rabbi Yehezkel Landau had also joined the camp of his enemies. And the opposition did not stem only from their criticism of *Divrei shalom ve'emet*; it also concerned Mendelssohn and his *Bi'ur*. And at the same time attempts were being made to enlist other rabbis in the fray.

The postal system, which was growing very efficient at the end of the eighteenth century, transmitted letters rather speedily, and in addition to the printed publications, letters, some of which were copied and circulated, became one of the arenas in which the battle was fought. Information was rapidly passed to both sides and influenced the course of the controversy. Wessely too wrote to Trieste:

> I very much regret that when this letter [*Divrei shalom ve'emet*] reached Prague, they spoke ill of it, and found it loathsome, and the Rabbi, head of the rabbinical court [Yehezkel Landau] came out against it in the synagogue in language as sharp as a razor, and also against the translation of the Torah by our beloved scholar R. Moses Mendelssohn, with words strange to hear, that neither taste nor smell of wisdom.[21]

Wessely, like Mendelssohn, pulled out all the stops, and at least in his letters allowed himself to attack the rabbis, because as far he was concerned, he was now waging an antirabbinical struggle par excellence. He also understood that what stood in the balance was the traditional authority of the rabbis countered by the demand for change voiced by writers and maskilim. Many members of the rabbinical elite derive their authority from Rabbi Landau, because their education is so flawed and they are so cut off from practical life that they are incapable of thinking for themselves:

Since from their youth they possess nothing but their Talmud, in which they have learned the laws governing kashrut and forbidden foods, the laws relating to women and to trade, and other than that they know only the house and the street they live in, not those subjects that the Torah does not relate to, nor any general learning, and certainly none of the sciences, some of which man needs to have some knowledge of.

Hence, the danger posed to them by a maskil like Wessely was particularly threatening. The struggle against him amounted to a struggle for their continued dominance, which was now endangered, and even those who knew that Wessely was in the right could no longer refrain from attacking him:

Since everything is strange to them, they believe they alone are worthy of governing the communities of Israel, and not only of Israel, but of all the peoples of the land . . . and some of them who understand that we are in the right, have become enraged with me for having drawn the attention of the Jews to these [shortcomings], for they fear their imagined honor will be sullied when these become known. Hence they have come forth with keen swords against our letter, *Divrei shalom ve'emet*, and written words of vilification against it to all the Jewish communities in Poland and Germany.

An Ultimatum from the Seven Berliners

As the Wessely affair grew more tangled, emotions rose to a high pitch. Enlightened public opinion learned the details of the affair ("wise men and intellectuals are all crying out to us asking to know what caused these rabbis to find fault with such delightful words"). Zedlitz was not the only one to react; in Copenhagen, August Hennings also had something to say on the subject. In an exchange of letters with Mendelssohn on the question of tolerance, he cited Wessely's persecution as a negative example.[22] A contemporary of Wessely's had this to say about the affair: "it caused a sensation among the Jews and members of other religions, it appeared in translations into German, Dutch, French and Italian that were read by everyone with relish."[23]

Rabbi Levin, the rabbi of Berlin, received letters denouncing Wessely as a man who "desired to destroy and uproot the entire House of Israel," and urging him to take steps to block him. Among these letters, one by Landau, whose views were growing more extreme, has been preserved. Based on Landau's information (up to mid-May 1782), the chief rabbi of Berlin had joined the attack against Wessely without taking account of "the few leaders of his city" who were Wessely's supporters, and hence he felt certain that Levin would help him mobilize as broad a front as possible to condemn Wessely as a heretic. Even after reading Wessely's second version, elucidated in his *Rav tuv livnei Israel*, the rabbi of Prague still persevered in his opposition, hurled slurs and invective upon Wessely, and refused to respond to his ultimatum that called for a reply within three months. "Now I have been handed this second pamphlet printed by the above instigator," Landau wrote to Rabbi Levin, "and everything said about the first pamphlet holds true for this second one, which is full of deceit and fraud and comes in stealth. May malignant leprosy fasten on to his tongue, and he is not worthy of a reply." Landau was infuriated by Wessely's rebellious claim that he was not subject to the will of the rabbis who had preached against him on Shabbat HaGadol. His fury grew even greater when he read the paragraph Wessely had translated from Mendelssohn's *Preface* and used to support his plea for tolerance. In his view, Mendelssohn, in printing in German his public appeal to the rabbis to willingly embrace the value of tolerance and to forbear using the power of their authority, was informing on the rabbis and showing his contempt for them: "Now I see that every offense we have found him [Mendelssohn] to be guilty of was all true. He has declared of himself that he has no share in the God of Israel nor in His Torah, and that every man may do as his heart desires. Moreover, he has printed his words in a foreign tongue, and to the monarchs he has spoken ill of the Sages of Israel."[24]

According to Wessely's testimony, the group of Berlin maskilim reacted strongly, greeting the rabbis' aggressive attack with contempt: "I and our cherished scholar R. Moses [Mendelssohn], and many who are with us here, jeer and shake our heads upon hearing of such villainous words and strange behavior."[25] But they also decided to take action. Mendelssohn urged those in Berlin who shared his views to embark on a counteroffensive, and they gladly agreed. Until now it has been difficult to precisely reconstruct the course of events; but a recently discovered document provides the missing link. It enables us to better understand Rabbi Tevele's angst and how frightened the rabbis were by the growing power of the new elite and its ability to mobilize public opinion for both a defensive and an offensive.

While Wessely and Mendelssohn were reporting to Trieste about the course of events (May 7, 1782), the maskilim of Berlin were preparing their next move in the battle. Only three or four days after the report to Trieste, seven Berliners, leaders of the Jewish community, wealthy men and maskilim, spoke out in defense of Wessely. The seven were representatives of the wealthy elite: Daniel Itzig (then the chief leader of Berlin Jewry); the cotton industrialist Isaac Benjamin Wolf, Aaron Joresh and Joel Halle; the two founders and principles of the Freischule, Itzik Daniel and David Friedländer (the latter was also the accountant of the Jewish community and had recently finished his translation of *Divrei shalom ve'emet* into German), and Moses Mendelssohn, who was greatly agitated by Tevele's sermon, so irreconcilable with his concept of tolerance. The seven signed an extremely aggressive letter of complaint, evidently coauthored by Mendelssohn and Friedländer. It was sent to the lay leaders of the Lissa community in mid-May 1782.[26] Another letter in a similar vein, which is not extant, was sent to the Posen community, whose rabbi, according to Wessely, was one of the three Polish rabbis who had denounced him.[27] Although this was not an official letter on behalf of the Berlin community, some of its signatories, including Mendelssohn, filled key positions in the city's communal establishment, serving three-year terms of office beginning in 1780. The three rabbis were evidently unaware of this fact, and they expected the support of the Berlin communal establishment.[28]

The letter of complaint sent from Berlin demanded that the leaders of the Lissa community reprimand their rabbis for having stirred up such a furor and launching an unjust campaign of vilification against Wessely: "Your rabbi, head of the religious court, was the first to slander us, to bring grievous trouble upon us, for he has attacked a man of our community, the honorable scholar Naphtali Herz Wessely, and has sent letters full of hostility and hatred to several Polish rabbis to heap contempt and shame upon this honorable man and his letter, *Divrei shalom ve'emet*."

When a copy of the sermon reached Berlin, their indignation reached a new height, for they read how Rabbi Tevele had "cursed and defamed [Wessely] with opprobrious invective, which is counter to the law of our holy Torah, and also has pronounced his sentence, saying "burn his books, and as for the author of *Divrei shalom ve'emet*, let him be trampled into the mud for he is banned and excommunicated, and let anyone encountering him, shun him." The rabbi of Lissa was severely rebuked and disparaged in this counter-letter, and he was resolutely charged to provide the reasons for his claims in the spirit of the ultimatum Wessely had submitted to him a short time before in *Rav tuv livnei Israel*. This challenge, recently published by Wessely, was also appended to the "letter of the seven," so that Rabbi Tevele would not be able to evade the issue by claiming he did not have the text in front of him. The seven signatories categorically demanded that the rabbi retract his words and apologize for having dared to sully Wessely's name. Moreover the letter threatened that if Rabbi Tevele were to refuse, or if the Polish community were to grant him its backing and protection, the seven would have no choice but to apply to the authorities: "We shall do whatever is in our power, to save our friend from the hands of his enemies, and who knows how far this can go, and this should suffice for wise men like you."

The seven signatories wished to impress the leaders of the Lissa community with the severity of their rabbi's actions by suggesting that the events had implications for intercommunal politics. The personal affront to Wessely and the venomous propaganda against him spread by the rabbis of Poland (the news that *Divrei shalom ve'emet* had been burned in Vilna at the Gaon of Vilna's orders only added fuel to the flames) were depicted as an affront to the entire Berlin community and as defamation of its members. In their opinion, there was no basis for criticism of the fitting and sound contents of Wessely's letter, and they gave him their unanimous support ("for these are words of truth that find favor with every man who has eyes to see, a mind to understand and ears to listen to open reproof"). Moreover, Rabbi Tevele had rudely intervened in a matter that went far beyond his sphere of jurisdiction: "who had the arrogance . . . to attack a resident of another community which does not heed your bidding, and of all men, a member of this community who is a famous scholar, well known for his precious books, who is now held in esteem by all the wise-hearted of our time." Out of patriotic sentiment for their city, Berlin, and a large measure of disgust for the intolerant leader of a Polish community, the seven protested against Tevele's excommunication of Wessely and his arrogant impudence in calling upon others to persecute Wessely: "Are we the Lissa's rabbi's creditors that he presumes to judge us, as if we were under his sway?"

If he did not apologize at once, the seven threatened, or if the lay leaders of Lissa failed to understand the grave significance of the excommunication and to reprimand their rabbi, they would use their political connections to lodge a complaint with several senior political officials: the Polish king, Stanislav Poniatowski, who had already been sent a German translation of *Divrei shalom ve'emet* prepared by Friedländer; Prince Anton Sulkowsky, the Polish aristocrat who ruled the city of Lissa; and the Polish diplomatic legate (the permanent consul) in Berlin.[29] In a threatening tone and in no uncertain words, the seven cautioned: "For you know well that we are able to enter the court of His Majesty, and the court of the great Duke Sulkowsky and to plead with words of reason about everything that has been done in a city under their governance to a man who is one of our close associates."[30] These were not empty threats. In their business affairs with the Polish government, affluent Berlin Jews had established certain connections with men who possessed political power.

The readiness of these seven leading figures from Berlin to enlist in the struggle against Wessely's persecutors was of far-reaching import. In this distinctly maskilic text, the seven, men of letters and of wealth, had adopted an explicit modernist position that supported Wessely's reformist program. With enormous self-confidence, they criticized the representatives of the traditional rabbinical elite and united in defense of the maskil and writer, a close friend and associate, and the representative of the few intellectual modernists who had then emerged in Jewish society. For the first time, a group coalesced, composed of men who thought of themselves as modernists and dared to speak out, in the name of freedom of expression and toleration against the rabbinical elite, which regarded enlightened Jews as heretics and attempted to stifle their revolutionary initiatives.

A few days later the writer and satirist August Cranz, an interesting character from the German enlightened circle, joined the campaign of pressure on Rabbi Tevele. He lived under the protection of Frederick the Great in Berlin and closely followed the battle between the supporters and opponents of toleration being waged by the Jews. Cranz was particularly intrigued by Mendelssohn's approach to the issue of religious toleration. He regarded that as the most crucial issue, since as a man of the Enlightenment he had nothing but contempt for clerical forces, superstition, and religious fanaticism. In the summer of 1782, he was active in the cause of toleration by putting pressure on Mendelssohn to thoroughly clarify his commitment to religious tolerance, and by intervening to block the rabbi now publicly known to have violated the principle of toleration. About the time of the struggle against Rabbi Tevele, Cranz (June 12, 1782) had finished writing his anonymous pamphlet, *Das Foreschen nach Licht und Recht* (The Search for Light and Right), in which he delivered what amounted to an intellectual-theological ultimatum to Mendelssohn. He placed him in a predicament the likes of which he had encountered only once before, in the Lavater affair: If he adheres firmly to the concept of toleration put forth in the Preface to *Teshu'at Israel*, if he claims that Judaism is averse to religious coercion, and if he is avowedly opposed to the penalty of excommunication—how can he explain his attachment to the religion of his fathers? What prevents him from taking one more step and becoming a Christian?[31]

This provocative pamphlet was printed no earlier than September 1782. In the meantime, Cranz had intervened in the Wessely affair. Only twelve days after he finished writing it (June 24, 1782), Cranz completed another one, the material for which he had received from the group responsible for the "letter of the seven." In this sixty-page pamphlet, a continuation of his *Über den Missbrauch der geistlichen Macht*, Cranz addressed Prince Sulkowsky of Lissa directly.[32] Following on the Posner affair, to which he had dedicated the first part of the pamphlet at the end of 1781, Cranz now placed the Wessely affair before the public. He depicted it as a second test case of whether the Jews were accepting the principle of religious toleration. Cranz quoted to the Polish prince several excerpts translated into German from Rabbi Tevele's sermon to apprise him of the serious nature of Wessely's persecution and excommunication. Employing the finest Enlightenment rhetoric, Cranz depicted the affair (which is how Mendelssohn saw it too) as a crucial test case in the struggle against religious dominance, fanaticism, and intolerance. This pamphlet had the effect of further exacerbating the orthodox camp's anxiety.

Scholars, in addressing the Cranz-Mendelssohn affair, have tended to characterize the German maskil as a second-rate writer, a "hired pen," who served anyone who paid him for his services. He is often also depicted as an unworthy adversary of Mendelssohn's, even though Mendelssohn wrote *Jerusalem*, his most important work on Judaism, as a reaction to his challenge. It seems probable, however, that Cranz was in fact an outstanding representative of the German Enlightenment.[33] An anticlerical deist, in his numerous writings, he fought the battle of Enlightenment with fervor and sharp rhetoric. Nonetheless, modern enlightened men in Berlin (for example, the publisher, Friedrich Nicolai) had serious reservations about him. After having drawn the inescapable conclusions from Enlightenment ideology about the status of persecuted religious minorities, Cranz did not hesitate to consistently side with the Jews and even dared criticize the Prussian state's treatment of them. He was particularly incensed by the Rabbi Tevele affair, having seen in it all the flaws of a system that allowed the use of religious sanctions to deny freedom of expression. He employed many arguments taken from the deist arsenal and the terminology and slogans of the Enlightenment to support his appeal to Prince Sulkowsky to take note of what was happening in his city of Lissa. He maintained that intolerance, religious fanaticism, prejudice, delusions, and the clergy's abuses had exceeded all bounds in this case. In his eyes, Tevele's persecution of Wessely was motivated by fanatic aggressive drives, and was irreconcilable with humane feelings and the law of justice and integrity commonly accepted in every enlightened European state. Cranz greatly exaggerated in describing the rabbi's threats to Wessely as tantamount to declaring that he was outside the law, and that anyone who killed him would be blessed. It is unthinkable, he wrote to the Polish prince, "that in our enlightened times, in a century of light," we should remain silent about such a horrible act by a Jewish rabbi, an act that is suffused with the evil spirit of the Inquisition and casts dark clouds over the Enlightenment.[34] In this pamphlet Cranz reaffirmed his advocacy of civil equality for the Jews and religious tolerance on the part of the state, but also severely censured the intolerance of the Jewish rabbis.

Cranz, one of Mendelssohn's most ardent admirers, presented him to the Polish prince as a highly praised, top-ranking philosopher of the eighteenth century. But this time too, even before *The Search for Light and Right* was published (Cranz had misled Mendelssohn into thinking that its author was Josef Edler von Sonnenfels of Vienna), Mendelssohn had been backed into a corner. In his strident criticism of Rabbi Tevele (as well as of another fanatic rabbi, Raphael Kohen), Cranz employed Mendelssohn's own arguments in his *Preface* against the coercive power of any religious-ecclesiastical authority. He praised this position, but also embarrassed Mendelssohn. What was the use of all the reasons brought by a great philosopher in objecting to religious fanaticism if he was incapable of subduing the fanatics? There is no choice, then, but to seek the intervention of the authorities if the power of persuasion is of no avail.[35]

The vigorous actions of the Berliners in support of Wessely's cause in the summer of 1782 undoubtedly exacerbated the controversy. The reactions of the orthodox grew more extreme as their anxieties intensified. After the "letter of the seven" reached Lissa, Rabbi Tevele turned in desperation to the rabbi and laymen of Berlin, pleading with them to do something to halt those conspiring against him. This letter of his (apparently written in June 1782) is the only evidence of Rabbi Tevele's distress now that the affair had begun to snowball and he was the one being persecuted. Even after he read *Rav tuv livnei Israel*, in which Wessely tried to clarify his arguments to the Polish rabbis and to persuade them that he was a man of integrity and a God-fearing Jew, Tevele still did not retract his total disavowal of Wessely and his views. He derisively rejected Wessely's ultimatum, claiming that he would not have bothered to react to the affair if he had not been threatened by the slander of the seven men of Berlin, in particular Cranz's public appeal to Sulkowsky: "For today a Gentile there has lifted his heel against me, printing words of slander to inform against me before His Excellency the Duke here, falsely accusing me of things that never entered my mind." Tevele denied that he had declared Wessely's person and property as "fair game," a legitimate object for abuse, and hinted that he had not excommunicated him. He did not conceal his apprehension that Cranz's pamphlet would get him into trouble with the law, especially since he feared that Wessely's ultimatum, which gave the three Polish rabbis three months (till the end of July) in which to reply to him, might have some legal validity. Hence, he hoped that his letter to the Berlin community might be regarded as some sort of official reply to that ultimatum, and that if he were put on trial by the Polish authorities, he could at least expect support from Berlin. And yet, by no means was he prepared to recant his words; in his view, Wessely was a deviant and a heretic.

I am deeply concerned lest under the law and customs of the Gentiles, it is incumbent upon us three to reply within these three months, hence I say unto you men that the second letter [*Rav tuv livnei Israel*] printed by the author of *Divrei shalom ve'emet* was before my eyes, and you must surely know that he did not correct any of his earlier distortions, but I have no desire to argue with him, as it is written, do not answer a fool as his folly deserves. Heaven forbid, let no one think my silence is an admission, but I judge my silence to be more comely than my speech. Yet all that I said of him, I still maintain, and I say the man has become licentious and is a heretic.[36]

Earlier, Rabbi Tevele had turned to Rabbi Landau in Prague, sending him a copy of the threatening letter of the seven from Berlin and asking for his help. Rabbi Landau hastened to write to the heads of the Berlin community and to Rabbi Zevi Hirsch Levin, wielding all of his influence to persuade them to use their authority against the seven. His letter also merits special attention, because in it he takes up arms against the threat posed by the incursion of a subversive unauthorized elite into the realm of rabbis and talmudic scholars. Rabbi Landau vehemently protested against any disregard of the authorities—the publication of libelous writings without obtaining the permission of the lay leaders and without first consulting the local community rabbi. Moreover, he took umbrage at the unprecedented demand made by men "who are not learned scholars" that the Rabbi of Lissa apologize to them and explain the meaning of his sermon and his ban of excommunication. "It was not only the honor of the above-mentioned rabbi that they sullied," Rabbi Landau went on to say, "but that of all the other rabbis and rabbinical authorities of the generation, for Rabbi Tevele is not alone in this, since most of the rabbis have recognized this man, Herz Wessely, as a heretic."[37]

Now again, all the threats and counterthreats were being aired. Rabbi Landau was, of course, also sensitive to the rationalistic heresy in his time. In his Shabbat HaGadol sermon in Prague he had already cautioned that *Divrei shalom ve'emet* was guaranteed to breed heresy and had accused Wessely of being a subversive apostate. Like Rabbi Tevele, he too was particularly perturbed by the damage being caused to the rabbinical elite and hastened to come to its defense. If anyone had to apologize, Rabbi Landau contended, it was Wessely, and it was up to the rabbis of Berlin to return him to the right path. He brought pressure to bear on the community leaders to prevent the seven from turning to the authorities, and moreover, to compel them to ask the rabbi of Lissa for his forgiveness, for, in Landau's opinion, he was the injured party in the affair. If the "natural" religious and communal order was not restored in this way, then, the rabbi threatened, the rabbinical elite would come to Tevele's defense: "If anyone should raise a hand against this rabbi, then many other rabbis will demand that his honor be restored." And he went on: "Be on your guard to forcefully warn these men not to intervene in a matter that does not concern them but affects only the rabbinical authorities of the generation, not the men of means, and I am confident in your ability to stand in the breach."

Rabbi Landau's letter is of great significance as an orthodox text. Written at the height of the affair, it was marked by strong feelings and a sense of panic and urgency. In it, the Tevele-Wessely controversy was depicted as an existential struggle: "I call on you from my affliction, I cannot hold back my words, I appeal to you my brethren and friends, do not be the last to restore the religion of the Lord of the world and to save the religion of the Torah from this man, our enemy." Indeed, in the summer of 1782, Rabbi Landau was conducting a defensive war: "the rabbinical authorities" versus "men who in the main

were not learned Torah scholars," but merely "men of means"—as he called
them with the elitist contempt of a man who knows his self-worth and the
import of his status—who are knowingly trying to erode their opponents' traditional authority.[38]

Rabbi Levin Flees Berlin

Wessely gained a large measure of confidence from the backing he received in
Berlin. He really believed that the "letter of the seven" would give added force
to his ultimatum and that Jewish public opinion would realize he was in the
right, either as a result of the rabbis' reply or their silence, which would be
taken as an admission. In his letters to the Trieste community, whose support
also contributed to his optimism, he again assailed the obscurantism of the
Polish rabbis, and their religious policy that preferred ignorance and obedience to wisdom and independence.

The folly of some students of Talmud in these territories has so increased, that they
care naught for the honor of the Torah or the honor of Jewry, they do nothing to raise
the prestige of the Jews among the nations, nor to save their sons from the veil of
stupidity that is obscuring the world from them. Their strongest desire is that the Jews
shall acquire no knowledge or morals so that the entire nation will heed their words
blindly. So that they may dominate the people of the Lord in keeping with the spirit of
their pride and the tempest of their rage.[39]

At the same time, Landau and Tevele were doing their utmost to impugn
Wessely and to persuade other rabbis to speak out against him publicly. The
only one in Germany to do so was Pinhas Hurwitz (1730–1805), the rabbi of
Frankfurt. After David Tevele sent him a copy of his sermon, Hurwitz also
entered the anti-maskilic fray. In a sermon he delivered to his congregation on
the eve of Rosh Chodesh Tammuz (June 12, 1782), he ferociously attacked not
only *Divrei shalom ve'emet* but the entire maskilic movement, as he viewed it
in its early stages: the problem was not one deviant individual, an apostate,
who could be excommunicated, but an entire group that was coalescing ("an
ugly association, whose dispersal is desirable"). This group was disseminating
heretic books that should best be burned, as he had heard had been done, and
rightly so, in Vilna. In his sermon, the Frankfurt rabbi linked his criticism of
Divrei shalom ve'emet ("which seized on schoolchildren to lead them astray,
from the path of the Almighty to the path of heresy") to criticism of the *Bi'ur*.
He also took the opportunity to settle accounts with Mendelssohn for the
stand he had taken against the rabbis' coercive authority. But Rabbi Hurwitz,
like the others, understood that the major threat came from the presumptuous

attempt of reformists bereft of any traditional authority to circumvent the rabbinical elite:

See now how you must keep a distance from them lest you are snared in their trap, do not heed them, look and see that all their books turn on their desire to lay down improvements and rules of conduct for rabbinic scholars. Woe to that shame, woe to that disgrace! How can this man, the least of all men, so despised and despicable, bereft of all wisdom, who is not a talmudic scholar, presume to tell rabbinic scholars, how they should behave![40]

A week after the sermon, Hurwitz wrote to Rabbi Tevele in Lissa that he had done what Tevele had requested. He had delivered a sermon in the great synagogue in Frankfurt publicly condemning Wessely, he had forbidden anyone to possess his books, and had also issued a special polemic writ against him: "We have prepared a public notice to be placed in all the synagogues, new and old, condemning and castigating those heretic books and others like them, and issued several restrictions to ban them from Jewry, and we are prepared to continue to persecute these defilers and make them known to all."[41]

Mendelssohn, unaware of what was happening in Frankfurt, was convinced that the Wessely affair would end with a maskilic victory: the entire enlightened group of Jews (*der venünftigere Theil der Nation*) had sided with Wessely, the Polish rabbis had been silenced, and their attempt to enlist support among the German rabbis had failed.[42] The rabbi of Berlin, however, was in an extremely awkward situation. Greatly distressed and frustrated by his predicament, Rabbi Zevi Hirsch Levin decided on an extreme, surprising, and unprecedented action. He was unable to face up to the irreconcilable pressures brought to bear on him—to take steps against Wessely, as the rabbis urgently and aggressively demanded, or to refrain from any step against him, as the signatories of the "letter of the seven" urged him. Mendelssohn was his friend and neighbor, Rabbi Landau was the senior representative of the rabbinical elite of which he himself was a member, and he also perceived Cranz's public exposure of the affair as an act of harmful slander. In the end, Rabbi Levin felt that the step taken by the seven amounted to a challenge to his status, and saw it as a personal affront too, so he decided to leave his position as rabbi and the Berlin community without any prior notice. Four days after the Ninth day of Av in 1782, Levin secretly left Berlin, traveling alone, leaving a letter addressed to the lay leaders of the community with the instruction that it be opened only six days hence.

Rabbi Levin had been considering resigning for a long time. He was already in despair about the religious permissiveness that attended Jewish acculturation in Berlin. Only the pleas of his congregation, the raise in his salary, and the belief that he was the sole person capable of limiting the damage to the faith had kept him from carrying out his threat to resign until then. But the Wessely affair was more than he could bear.

Now some new men have arrived who have found allies to vilify their religion . . . they have grown angry with their shepherds . . . and they will judge God's law, these foreigners with uncircumcised flesh or Jews with uncircumcised hearts. They have also begun to speak of ill-gotten gain and have commissioned a stranger [Cranz] to employ his pen to inform on us to the authorities, and what have I to do here when my eyes see and my ears hear how they heed not my words, so I become as a mute, not opening my mouth. Upon my word, I would better choose death . . . I have faith in you honorable men that you will not feel I have sinned in hastening to leave, without bidding you farewell and embracing you, as custom dictates, and will surely understand that this way is best for me, for who knows how far things may go, and these men are stronger than I. If I should reply and they should speak out, we will be disgraced in the eyes of our neighbors.[43]

In these words in the explanatory letter he left to his congregation, Rabbi Levin specified the very real threat facing the orthodox camp and shared the anxiety that the worrisome changes taking place in the Jewish world were arousing among the orthodox. Further on in his letter of resignation, he wrote: "I was greatly alarmed by the rumors I heard that while there are still many remaining God-fearing Jews, the number of unlearned men on the margins of our society have much increased in number . . . and they commit unspeakable deeds and people report to me of their abomination."

Rabbi Levin's observation that the God-fearing Jews were a weakening group and his spontaneous decision to flee from pressures to seek refuge in Palestine were a typical orthodox reaction. Since the rabbi fled without informing anyone of his intention, the leaders of the community had no opportunity to pressure him any further. His astonishing action amply attests to the panic that had seized him. Levin stopped a short distance from Berlin, apparently at an inn, and sent his wife instructions about how to handle several matters he had left behind. He urged the Berlin lay leaders to assist his wife so that she and their children might join him soon, before the hard winter set in, on a journey to a safe haven—Palestine. The community leaders, including Mendelssohn and Friedländer, were stunned but decided not to forgo the services of their rabbi who had fled. After his wife agreed to divulge the rabbi's hiding place, they sent him a letter, in the name of the entire community, imploring him to return to his rabbinical post.[44] How could he have even considered taking such an extreme, rash step, the lay leaders asked. They expressed their amazement that such a respected rabbi should abandon his wife and children, expose himself to the dangers of travel ("the weakness of his body, broken by prolonged suffering, the delicateness of his gentle temperament is known to him and to us as well"), without informing the lay leaders, who had always respected and supported him, of his intentions. The lay leaders were particularly concerned about the shame this would bring upon the community: "for we are greatly astounded by the plan decided upon by our master and teacher, the crown of our community, to leave us and to travel far without giving any thought to say—my journey will bring disgrace upon this great city, shaming it in the eyes of all of Jewry on that day when they hear I have forsaken my post as rabbi, and have concealed from them the day of my departure, as well as all reasons and causes for it." It was not right to abandon a community of four thousand because of a small minority that had aroused his anger, they argued. Change your mind, they urged him: "Reconsider the evil you thought of doing to yourself and to your household, to your students, and to the members of the community, who love you. Return to us as in days gone by." Even if neither he nor they had the power to impose our authority on those "who wander in the wilderness," he should bear in mind, they reminded him, that they are the ones who bear the community's major financial burden.[45]

The story of Rabbi Levin's flight soon became widely known, and within a few weeks several copies of his letter of resignation were circulated. A witness to the affair, Mendelssohn's friend the Benedictine monk Peter Winkopp, described the mounting tension in the community between the "fanatic Poles" and the "enlightened Germans," and its sensational climax—Rabbi Levin's desertion. According to his information, the rabbi had left for Warsaw.[46] The major West European communities—Amsterdam and London—had also learned of the Wessely affair. In correspondence between two merchants, brothers of the Prager family, Jacob in Amsterdam reported to his brother in London that Wessely's *Divrei shalom ve'emet* was stirring up a furor among the rabbis, but there was no doubt that Wessely was the justified party in this conflict.[47]

Rabbi David Tevele spared no efforts in trying to enlist broad support, and to this end, sent copies of his Shabbat HaGadol sermon to Berlin, Prague, and Frankfurt, and to the rabbi of Amsterdam as well. There a copy came into the hands of Rabbi David Tevil Schiff, rabbi of the London community. In a letter he sent from London to his brother in Frankfurt (20th of Elul, 1782) Schiff related the news he had learned about the latest events in the affair, and asked him to mail him the notice that Rabbi Horowitz of Frankfurt had circulated:

Everyone here has learned that the rabbi has left Berlin. And I have seen a copy of the letter that the rabbi left there before departing, with instructions to open it six days after he left the city. Rumor states he left for Vienna, and from the letter it seems he is planning to travel to the Holy Land. I have also seen a copy of what the rabbi of Lissa wrote on this matter, vilifying and cursing R. Herz Wessely and condemning the letter he has printed . . . and from the content of the letter and the rabbi of Lissa's sermon, in Posen and in Vilna, they have followed the instructions of the Gaon of Vilna, and have burned R. Wessely's letter in the city streets, and it is also written that the rabbi of Prague delivered a sermon on the matter in Prague. Now, of course, he must remain silent in public, and does his deeds secretly to incite the other famous rabbis of communities. And in the wake of all these incidents, it is obvious that the rabbi of Berlin could not remain at his post and had to leave. If you can send me a copy of the notice, I should be glad to receive it.[48]

In the end, the appeals of the Berlin lay leaders had the desired effect, and Rabbi Levin was persuaded to return to serve as their rabbi, a position he filled for another eight years until his death in 1800. However, before he returned he sent a letter of reply from his hiding place, in which he explained why he had had no choice but to relinquish his post and to flee. Rabbi Levin agreed to return on one condition—that the community leaders would help him to restrain those men who were responsible for his decision to flee Berlin, or at least to obtain their promise that they would refrain from conducting a public campaign that was liable to seriously injure the rabbinical elite. In an appeasing, apologetic letter he appealed to the lay leaders: "If you can but place some restriction to prevent them from gaining the power to uproot religious institutions." He added, "If you truly desire to induce me to change my mind and return to you, then although it is impossible to rectify what has already been done, promise to do your utmost to ensure that they will write no more letters of oppression to take the name of the Lord in vain and to scorn the Torah and its sages."[49]

After the autumn of 1782, no real steps were taken in this cultural campaign. No one caused Wessely any harm and his feeling of being persecuted gradually dissipated. Rabbi Levin returned to Berlin; Rabbi Tevele apparently was content with the steps he had taken thus far to denounce Wessely. The affair that had flared with great intensity throughout the spring and summer of 1782 finally subsided. But the importance of this initial campaign in the Jewish *Kulturkampf* cannot be overstated. The modern Jewish intellectual, born in the eighteenth-century early Haskalah, entered the public sphere for the first time in 1782. He made his appearance as a writer-maskil who demanded a place in the social and cultural leadership and contended with the rabbinical elite, with the backing of a supportive social group. At the very time this secular intellectual was first attempting to influence public opinion, the first enemy of the Enlightenment appeared. He was not prepared to accept a split in the spiritual elite, nor was he prepared to grant legitimacy to an intellectual who was not a rabbinical scholar or lacked proven proficiency in the Talmud and the religious rulings. The rabbi of Lissa's sermon was the first distinctively orthodox text, because Rabbi Tevele, with his keen senses, was the first to identify the threats that modernity posed to the traditional religious elite.[50] At first, he was taken aback by the very temerity of a man, representing only himself, in presuming to forge a new path. Then he mobilized all of his rhetorical powers and his connections with other rabbis to defend the elite to which he belonged against the foreign intruder, to demonize and denounce him as a heretic so he would be denied any authority whatsoever. It seems that at this historic moment in Jewish history a series of battles were launched in the *Kulturkampf* between the modernist maskilim and the orthodox enemies of the Enlightenment.

Chapter Seven
On Religious Power and Judaism

Neither side won a decisive victory in the 1780s campaign of the culture war. Nonetheless, the aftereffects of the Wessely affair continued to be felt for at least three more years. Wessely carried on defending his positions in two more epistles of the *Divrei shalom ve'emet* series; Mendelssohn had the affair in mind when he wrote *Jerusalem*, his most significant work; and for other maskilim it was an important, formative episode that sharpened their identity as intellectuals striving with the conservative forces. The question of the hour was whether the rabbinical elite would succeed in maintaining its status despite the maskilim's revolutionary challenge.

Saul Berlin's *Ktav Yosher*

The controversy and the competition for favorable public opinion was conducted by circulating letters, copies of sermons, and printed pamphlets. A rabbi secretly wrote his reaction to the Wessely affair in a trenchant critique, the first maskilic satire. This covert piece of writing, published only after the author's death, was written by Rabbi Saul Levin-Berlin (1740–94), rabbi of the Frankfurt-on-Oder community, and the son of the rabbi of Berlin, Zevi Hirsch Levin. A scholar in his own right, Berlin's education, family ties, and position made him a full-fledged member of the rabbinical elite, but secretly he was a maskil. Until nearly the end of his life, he found it hard to change his lifestyle; he never publicly revealed his true leanings nor did he identify himself as a maskil. In his writings, he always hid behind a pseudonym and disguised his true opinions, presenting them as pious views in works that appeared to be totally scholarly in nature. He apparently also allowed his father to believe he was leading only the life of a rabbi and talmudic scholar.[1] Unlike his father, who in 1782 was in the eye of the storm, the target of pressures that led him to take the side of his fellow members of the rabbinical elite, the rabbi of Frankfurt identified with Wessely, and devoted his finest talents as a scholar and radical, enlightened anti-clerical critic to Wessely's cause.

The satire *Ktav Yosher* (A Certificate of Integrity) was written around 1785 but remained in manuscript form. It was probably read by many, but not everyone knew that the man behind the pen name "Avdun ben Hillel Hayi-duni" was Rabbi Saul Berlin. David Friedländer did identify Berlin as the author and wrote his name on his copy of the satire, noting that it was written at the time Wessely was being persecuted. *Ktav Yosher* was printed in Berlin a short time after the author's death in London, in 1794, when the Berlin maskilim were still active.[2]

In *Ktav Yosher*, Berlin assailed the religious and social institutions, in order to unmask them and to condemn all ignorance, wrongdoing, hypocrisy, malice, and corruption. This secret maskil and deist, who served as a community rabbi and was regarded as the finest representative of the social and religious ideal, used the Wessely affair as the linchpin for his sweeping criticism of the world of the elite into which he was born. *Ktav Yosher* adopted an ironic, radical tone to scorn and denigrate the social stratum which in traditional society, wielded control over religious writings, religious faith and rulings, and education. The author introduced himself to his readers as "a member of the elite, one of the great men of the generation, a luminary in Torah and wisdom, also knowledgeable in the Kabbalah." Since he knew and liked Wessely, he was particularly vexed by the war being waged against him and tried in *Ktav Yosher* to clarify why there was so much opposition to *Divrei shalom ve'emet*. In it, an ignorant teacher from Poland and one of the great rabbis of the rabbinical elite explain to him what Wessely's offense was, and then he finds a way to persuade them that Wessely's pamphlet, surprisingly enough, is really a sacred book, which contains nothing less than Kabbalistic secrets. *Ktav Yosher* takes the doctrine of Kabbalah to absurd lengths, depicting it in a derisive light, debasing it, and totally depleting it of its sacred nature.[3]

To perceive the irony and the satirical criticism of *Ktav Yosher*, the reader had to be a scholar; otherwise, he would fail to comprehend the many associations and allusions sprinkled throughout the text, in particular those from the Talmud and the halakhic literature. To such a sophisticated, scholarly reader, Berlin attempted to reveal the shortcomings of the teachers and the rabbis and what he regarded as the public's primitive conception of the Jewish religion. The Polish teacher, one of the characters in the satire, is very much afraid that Wessely's program may deprive him of his livelihood: "Most of the teachers are from Poland, like me, who have had to travel far from their home country because there is neither bread nor clothing in their homes, and how are we to know how to speak German fluently . . . and according to this man's counsel, we should all be exiled from this land." The Polish teacher's religious approach negated the value of any non-religious culture ("all of the sciences are as a drop in the ocean and a grain of sand in comparison to one issue in a halakhic dispute between Abbayeh and Raba. And our Talmud contains all the wisdoms"), scorns the books of the gentiles, sanctifies ridiculous customs, clings absurdly and masochistically to the suffering of the diaspora and the persecutions of the Jews, and takes foolish pleasure in the superiority of the Jews— "the world was created for us." The teacher denounces Mendelssohn, rejects the study of Hebrew grammar and foreign languages for fear of heresy, advocates the beating of students so that from a young age they will fear and respect talmudic scholars, and presumes to have the shamanic powers of a miracle worker ("I know how to remove an evil eye with incantations, to cure fevers by writing on almonds, and to pour lead for those sick with terror"). In the critic's eyes, "the great rabbi" who, in the satire, speaks out against Wessely, is no better than the teacher. He faithfully represents talmudic scholarship that employs casuistry, and enthusiastically makes the paradoxical argument that "the fact that we do not study the sciences, that is our wisdom and intelligence in the eyes of the nations."

Ktav Yosher does not spare its criticism from any of the fields of traditional religious study—the basic studies in the *cheder* taught by the teachers, the higher talmudic and halakhic studies of the scholars, the religious book culture, and in particular, the Kabbalah. In Saul Berlin's view, the Kabbalah can be used to clear up every problematic talmudic text, and every "shocking article," which is literally a piece of lewd pornography, is interpreted as esoteric in meaning and turned into divine speech. Ironically enough, Wessely's persecutors, who, fearful of any challenge to the existing order, close their ears to the voice of reason that rises from a literal reading of *Divrei shalom ve'emet*, are prepared to eagerly accept it when it is disguised by the satirist in the "emperor's new clothes" and represented as a veil for meaningless Kabbalistic secrets.[4]

Although *Ktav Yosher* was intended to speak in defense of *Divrei shalom ve'emet*, Saul Berlin was poles apart from Wessely in his personality, style, aims, and biting criticism. Wessely was a reformist insofar as Jewish education and the future ideal were concerned, but showed much sensitivity about his image in the eyes of the rabbis. Berlin was a radical revolutionary who went much further, not hesitating to harshly criticize the flaws of the rabbinical elite. In his *Ktav Yosher*, he stripped away all the rabbinical culture's layers of pretense, exposing its turpitude and total failure. Unlike Wessely, Berlin did not propose a program to remedy the flaws, nor did he suggest the alternative of employing enlightened educators; he was content to reveal, in his mocking, sarcastic style, the serious defects of traditional society: the teachers, the rabbis, the Talmud, the Kabbalah, the popular beliefs, the ignorance, coarseness, superstition, violence toward pupils, the imperviousness to reason and the sciences, the late halakhic literature and casuistry, the sense of superiority to the gentiles. The Wessely affair had made all the abuses and shortcomings of the rabbinical culture and its proponents widely known, and now *Ktav Yosher*—perhaps the most radical and pessimistic work written in maskilic circles in the 1780s—declared an all-out war against this culture. As we shall see later, Berlin persisted in his subversive criticism of the rabbinical culture, which reached its apogee in the polemic against Rabbi Raphael Kohen of Hamburg in the late 1780s, and in the scandal caused by Berlin's halakhic work, *Beshamim rosh*, in the early 1790s.

It is not surprising that Berlin did not believe that Wessely's reformist program would provide a solution to the wretched state of rabbinical culture, although he did support Wessely against the rabbis who persecuted him. In the last chapter of *Ktav Yosher*, Berlin addressed Wessely directly, criticizing him for having taken an initiative which was contrary to Mendelssohn's policy. In his view, reform would not result from the spread of Enlightenment ("how could you think of saying now the House of Israel is like all the nations and seducing all of the people to eat again from the fruit of the tree of knowledge?"), but rather it would come from "redemption"—the liberation of the Jews by a state decision, as their mutual great "teacher" had called for in his writings addressed to general public opinion. Berlin advised Wessely to leave the public stage at this point: "And you ought to go to your destiny . . . and do not be alarmed by the raucous noise of the masses rising against you, for your action is pleasing to the Almighty, and your enemies too will accept it, but do not continue to speak of it, look and see what is written in the *Zohar* about Moses and the Messiah, and you will find that only such a man is capable of clearing the way. And you shall have justice but little fame, and wrong-doers will no longer torment you." He found Wessely's action too rash and ill-considered, because the Jews, in his view, would become open to non-Jewish culture and the normalization of their lives not only because of internal reform but in particular because of a real change in their legal status.[5]

Mendelssohn's *Jerusalem*

During 1783, Mendelssohn grew more and more disillusioned with Joseph II's Edicts of Toleration. He began to suspect that the ruler's policy was not intended to achieve true tolerance and a pluralistic society of the future, but rather a "union of religions," and he did not see that this would produce the desired solution. "A union of faith is not tolerance. It is the very opposite!" Mendelssohn wrote in *Jerusalem*, and addressed a cry of despair to the rulers of Europe:

For the sake of your happiness and ours, do not use your powerful prestige to give the force of law to some eternal truth that is immaterial to civic well-being; do not transform some religious doctrine to which the state should be indifferent into a statute of the land! . . . At least, prepare the way for your more fortunate descendants to reach that height of culture, that universal human tolerance for which tolerance is still sighing in vain! Reward and punish no doctrine, hold out no allurement or bribe to anyone for the adoption of a particular faith.[6]

Mendelssohn began writing *Jerusalem* in September 1782 and published it in 1783. For generations, it has been regarded as his most important book and as the public, well-reasoned declaration of his unreserved attachment to the Jewish religion and its commandments. But it was also his most pessimistic work, in particular when compared to the preface he wrote to Menasseh ben Israel's book. Although only a short time had elapsed between *Jerusalem* and the *Preface*, the change that took place in Mendelssohn's position is unmistakable. Within a few short months, his belief that he was privileged to witness "the joyous hour in which the rulers' hearts are disposed to grant us human rights to the full and proper degree," was replaced by the suspicion that the enemy of the freedom of thought was putting on "the mask of meekness . . . feigning brotherly love , while secretly he is at work forging the chains with which he plans to shackle our reason so that, taking it by surprise, he can cast it back into the cesspool of barbarism."[7]

This extreme swing in his mood, from optimism to skepticism, was unquestionably caused by the challenge Cranz flung at him in his anonymous pamphlet *The Search for Light and Right*: "You, good Mr. Mendelssohn, have renounced the religion of your forefathers. One step more, and you will become one of us."[8] "This objection," Mendelssohn admitted, feeling profoundly insulted, "goes right to my heart."[9] His biographer Alexander Altmann has already shown that Mendelssohn wrote *Jerusalem* in reaction not only to Cranz's pamphlet, but also to other criticism voiced by some of his close associates, which he felt obligated to relate to. For example, August Hennings, his friend from Copenhagen, who closely followed the struggle between the proponents of tolerance and of intolerance in Jewish society, strongly argued in the spirit of deist criticism against the penalties demanded in Jewish law against those guilty of religious offenses.[10] But it was undoubtedly the publication of Cranz's pamphlet in September 1782, along with the postscript by the military chaplain from Berlin, David Moerschel, that impelled Mendelssohn to divulge his true opinion about revelatory religions in general.[11]

Cranz misled Mendelssohn by signing his pamphlet with the letter "S" and noting Vienna as the place of publication, to create the impression that the author of this public provocation was the Jewish convert to Catholicism Josef Edler von Sonnenfels, a university professor who exerted much influence on the reformist policy of the Austrian court. If Mendelssohn believed that

Sonnenfels was behind *The Search for Light and Right*, then he understood it, Jacob Katz contends, as a semi-official interpretation by the Catholic ruler of the objective he wished to achieve with his Edicts of Toleration.[12] But even if Mendelssohn knew the author was Cranz, he could not help being disappointed by the fact that more than ten years after the Lavater polemic, enlightened intellectuals were still expecting him to draw nearer to Christianity. As a matter of fact, Cranz the deist did not intend to call on Mendelssohn to convert. Although he mentioned the Lavater affair and left the impression that he was renewing the Swiss pastor's ultimatum, his true objective was to test the principle of religious tolerance.[13]

The Search for Light and Right was written with the enormous zeal of an enlightened writer who believed in the revolutionary historic transformation taking shape before his eyes at the end of the eighteenth century. Religious tolerance, reason, and humanism were overcoming the persecutions, superstition, and strong-armed oppression of human freedom. The persecuted minorities that, in his view, were benefiting from that revolution included the Jews of Prussia and England, and from now on a new dawn would break for the Jews in the lands of the Austrian emperor Joseph II. There was a clear need for the Jews and Christians to draw closer to one another, although the Christians were not the only ones who had to show tolerance. The Jews bore a good share of the blame for the estrangement between Jews and Christians. The Mosaic doctrine was opposed to the principle of tolerance because it was based on punishing sinners and contained laws—such as those pertaining to the Sabbath and marriage—that separated the Jews from their Christian neighbors. Therefore, the Torah was an obstacle in the way of truly realizing the Enlightenment's cosmopolitan vision of the future—the removal of all religious and ethnic divisions.

In this pamphlet Cranz also reminded Mendelssohn of an issue that perturbed both of them—the rabbis who persecuted free-thinking Jews. In a footnote, he referred to his polemical tract *Über den Missbrauch der geistlichen Macht* (On the Misuse of Ecclesiastical Power), written against Rabbi Raphael Kohen. Now that Mendelssohn had so clearly championed religious tolerance and argued against the rabbis' authority to punish and excommunicate, Cranz, who truly revered Mendelssohn, expected the Jewish philosopher to become a reformist leader and to carry all the Jews with him. A rational critique proves that the laws in Judaism that prevent the desired intermixture between the Jews and their neighbors were established down in historical circumstances that no longer exist, he opined. If Mendelssohn were true to his principles, he ought to free his people from those halakhic restrictions. "You have opposed the right to excommunicate a member of the Jewish community and argued that the rabbis are authorized only to persuade, not to coerce," Cranz held forth to Mendelssohn, "and in doing so have overturned the cornerstone of your forefathers' religion. If so, how can one understand what prevents you from publicly admitting that you no longer adhere to it."[14]

Jerusalem was not an apologetic work arguing against the temptation to convert to Christianity. It was a philosophical work, rooted within the fervent culture of the German Enlightenment. Its purpose was to defend the principle of religious tolerance, against the background of the incidents provoked by the rabbis of Altona, Prague and Lissa, and it proposed a version of tolerant Judaism suitable to life in a pluralistic, tolerant state. The sub-title that Mendelssohn chose for *Jerusalem*: *On Religious Power and Judaism*—is similar to the title Cranz chose for his two pamphlets attacking the rabbis Kohen and Tevele. From this title it is obvious what Mendelssohn's major aims in this book were: to fundamentally explain why no ecclesiastical authority should be granted the power of coercion, and to demonstrate to his critics why there is no contradiction between faith in the Jewish religion and the principle of tolerance.

At the beginning of *Jerusalem*, Mendelssohn expresses his great trepidation: "Enormous evil has resulted from the clash of these forces [state and religion]; more threatens yet to come." Based on Locke's ideas about the essential difference between a political organization and an ecclesiastical organization and their modes of operation, elucidated in his *Letter Concerning Toleration*, Mendelssohn resolutely repeats his demand that the religious authority be denied the right of coercion. This right, in his view, is reserved solely to the political authority for the purpose of regulating man's relations with his fellow citizens:

The state commands and coerces, religion teaches and persuaded. The state issues laws, religion issues commandments. The state possesses physical power and uses it when necessary; the power of religion is love and charity . . . civil society, viewed as a moral person, has the right of coercion; in fact, it has secured this right through the social contract. Religious society neither demands the right of coercion nor can it possibly obtain it by any contract.[15]

At the very most, the state can maintain its vigilance, at a certain distance, to ensure that "no doctrines will be spread which are detrimental to public welfare or which, like atheism or Epicureanism, might undermine the foundations of society." Moreover, the state ought not to make "civil unity" conditional upon "a union of faiths." Employing this argument in favor of pluralism, Mendelssohn attempted to persuade the "rulers of the earth" that in a tolerant state it was proper to allocate a place to members of the Jewish religion as well ("diversity is obviously the plan and goal of Providence"), despite Cranz's claims that the Jewish laws separate the Jews from Christian society. If this union is nonetheless made a condition for citizenship, then the

Jews will be compelled to forgo it: "if we can be united with you as citizens only on the condition that we deviate from the law which we still consider binding, then we sincerely regret the necessity of declaring that we shall renounce our claim to civil equality and union with you. And everything the humanitarian von Dohm has written will in this case have been in vain."[16]

Mendelssohn depicted the Christian world, as he did in his reply to Lavater, as one in which even the most enlightened men are incapable of casting off their religious fanaticism, in contrast to Judaism which is faithful to the principle of religious tolerance. He did admit that, regrettably, many Jews did conceive of Judaism as Cranz described it: a religion which is "a structure of strict ecclesiastical laws." But he added that he did not share this view: "If such an obvious contradiction between the word of God and my own reason actually existed, I would probably be able to silence my reason. Nevertheless, my unresolved questions would continue to perturb me in the recesses of my heart and would gradually turn into doubts."[17] The identity between state and religion existed only until the destruction of the Temple. In the ancient era, "Every act of civic service became, at the same time, a true act of divine worship . . . every offense against the respect for God, the Lawgiver of the nation, was a crime against the [civil] sovereign . . . whoever desecrated the Sabbath willfully, nullified, as far as He was concerned, a fundamental law of civil society." Hence, the perpetrators of such offenses could be punished as guilty of offenses against God, for the state and religion were one authority, although even then the punishments were not harsh. However, he pointed out, since the destruction of the Temple, the duty of observing the commandments has become a personal obligation and no one has the right to impose their observance on anyone: "The civil bonds of the nation have been dissolved. Religious offenses are no longer a crime against the state. Our religion, as religion, knows no punishment, no penalty save the one the repentant sinner voluntarily imposes upon himself. Religion knows no coercion, prods us but gently, affects only mind and heart."[18]

It was not only the breakdown of the Jewish state that prevented punishment for religious offenses and brought the Jewish religion closer to the principle of tolerance. Mendelssohn held that Judaism was also the religion closest to the natural religion, whose universal and rational principles included the existence of God and the immortality of the soul. It is a religion that has no need of a special divine revelation in order for its truths to be engraved in the minds of men. Christianity rests upon dogmas, principles of faith that obligate the believer, even if they do not seem rational to him and are contrary to reason, while Judaism has no such dogmas: "I believe Judaism knows nothing of a revealed religion in the sense in which Christians define this term. The Israelites possess a divine legislation—laws, commandments, statues, rules of conduct, instruction in God's will and in what they are to do to attain temporal and eternal salvation."[19] Through reason, God reveals universal and eternal truths to Jews and to all of humankind. Only the historical truths (such as the stories of the Patriarchs, miracles, and the exodus from Egypt) and the commandments as they were revealed on Mt. Sinai set Judaism apart from other religions. Despite this essential difference between the Jewish and Christian religions, the Jews belong to the realm of human freedom. God did not impose faith on them with threats of punishment; rather he left the religious truths to the judgment of the intellect. Only the laws, addressed to man's will, were given in revelation, and their purpose was to guide his reason to the divine verities and to ensure the happiness of the individual and of humankind. However, the most important point is that there is nothing in Judaism that imposes beliefs and views:

> But all these excellent notions address themselves not to our ability to believe but to our capacity to understand and reflect. Among the precepts and ordinance of the Mosaic law, there is none saying, "You shall believe," or "You shall not believe." All say, "You shall do" or "You shall not do." You are not commanded to believe, for faith accepts no commands; it accepts only what comes to it by reasoned conviction.[20]

This great freedom does not relate, of course, to the obligation to observe the commandments. Since the commandments are the core of Judaism and the law was given in a revelation from a divine source, reason can neither criticize nor annul it unless there is another divine revelation that unequivocally proclaims its abrogation. Thus, Mendelssohn rejected Cranz's deist criticism of the Jewish law, removed it from the realm of historical thought and granted it absolute validity. Naturally, it never occurred to him to release the Jews from the laws, which in Cranz's view were no longer valid in the new Europe.[21] As far as the continued existence of the Jews in the European state was concerned, the pessimistic Jewish philosopher did not offer a vision in *Jerusalem* that would inspire hope in the hearts of his fellow Jews. With enormous skepticism about the possibility of properly applying the principle of tolerance when voices calling for a "union of religions" were being heard, Mendelssohn's recommendation to the Jews was to bear the double burden in the meantime with perseverance and submission, until that same overall human tolerance would be achieved in the future. Thus, he advised them:

> Adopt the mores and constitution of the country in which you find yourself, but be steadfast in upholding the religion of your fathers, too. Bear both burdens as well as you can. True, on the one hand, people make it difficult for you to bear the burden of civil life because of the religion to which you remain faithful; and, on the other, the climate of our time makes the observance of your religious laws in some respects more

burdensome than it need be . . . Persevere nevertheless; stand fast in the place which Providence has assigned to you; and submit to everything which may happen, as you were told to do by your Lawmaker long ago.[22]

In the months to come, Mendelssohn's disillusionment intensified. In personal letters, he disclosed how disappointed he was by what he regarded as Enlightenment's failure to banish prejudice and fantasies with the clear light of reason. When, for example, Herz Homberg notified him that the emperor had prevented his appointment as a lecturer in Vienna, Mendelssohn did not conceal his disappointment and sense of personal insult: The same thing happened to him, he told Homberg. The Royal Academy of Sciences elected him as a member, but the king did not give his approval. Why was the principle of tolerance not being implemented? To that he had no reply.[23]

Rabbinical Reactions

Jerusalem evoked a spirited discussion among the enlightened public, and its readers were outspoken in their criticism. Mendelssohn, however, had cause to be gratified, at least by the interest his book aroused and in particular by the response he received from the renowned philosopher, Immanuel Kant of Königsberg, who was pleasantly surprised by the book's boldness. Kant conveyed his compliments to Mendelssohn orally, through David Friedländer, who met him on one of his trips to Königsberg, as well as in a personal letter. "I consider your book," Kant wrote to him, "a true manifesto which calls for a great reform that will affect the Jewish nation as well as other nations." "I would not have imagined that it were possible to reconcile the Jewish religion with unlimited freedom of conscience [*Gwissensfreiheit*], as you have done in your book."[24] Obviously, Mendelssohn's concept of religious tolerance and freedom made a strong impression on Kant, and he acclaimed it enthusiastically.

Mendelssohn's *Jerusalem*, unlike Wessely's *Divrei shalom ve'emet*, did not stir up an internal storm, nor was it a factor in the *Kulturkampf* of the 1780s, but Mendelssohn waited expectantly for an orthodox counterreaction.[25] *Jerusalem* was probably not perceived as a threat because it was written in German and its direct addressee was outside the bounds of Jewish society. Mendelssohn's version of a tolerant Judaism, close to the natural religion, not distinguished by commandments, rather than by articles of faith, was concealed among the pages of a philosophical work whose significance was not yet fully comprehended. Nonetheless, many rabbis continued to oppose Mendelssohn, and although this opposition was not expressed in public, it circulated through word of mouth. A report from Hamburg in 1785, for example, referred indignantly to Mendelssohn's enemies in that city and hinted that Rabbi Raphael Kohen was the chief among them.[26]

Only a few years later, a rabbi did openly criticize *Jerusalem*. It was Rabbi Judah Leib Margolioth, one of the early maskilim, then a community rabbi in a part of Poland under Prussian rule. His polemic against Mendelssohn was contained in his book *Atzei eden*, written in the early 1790s and published in Frankfurt-on-Oder only in 1802.[27] There is no way of knowing whether Margolioth was familiar with the German original, but he apparently drew his knowledge of Mendelssohn's concept of Judaism in his philosophical thought from excerpts translated into Hebrew included by Isaac Euchel in his biography of Mendelssohn, first published in serial form in *Hame'asef*.[28]

Margolioth faithfully reconstructed the course of the events. First "von Dohm, advisor to the king of Prussia" had published a work in which "he thought well of the Jews." Afterward, Mendelssohn published his response, in which he opposed the preservation of the communal right of coercion and the excommunication of religious dissenters. Finally, Cranz printed his anonymous booklet, in which he "wrote about the author of *Jerusalem*, and stated, as he put it, that the mask had fallen from Moses' face, that he now stood revealed before the eyes of his community, so every man can see that he has cast off the cords that bind him to the Jewish religion and severed the reins of the law."[29] Margolioth had met Mendelssohn in Berlin in the 1770s and held him in great esteem. But now he emphasized the dangers that, in his view, could result from Mendelssohn's concept of Judaism—his tolerant attitude toward religious deviance and his attempt to bring Judaism closer to the natural religion. Margolioth was apprehensive about the division between "temporal happiness," which is the responsibility of the state that has coercive powers, and "eternal happiness," which is the responsibility of the clergy, who possess only the power of persuasion. Moreover, he rejected Mendelssohn's claim, in the spirit of the natural religion, that "eternal truths" were not given in the divine revelation on Mt. Sinai. In *Atzei eden*, he appealed to the preachers, the traditional vanguard of the scholarly elite, to marshal their forces in the face of the new maskilic elite, and in particular called upon them to undertake the urgent mission of fighting resolutely against these ideas.

In his view, Mendelssohn's concept of natural religion was tantamount to deism—a challenge to the validity of the Torah and the commandments, the ruin of rabbinical authority and an ideological refuge for skeptics.[30] The division between beliefs and opinions and laws and commandments is not a genuine division, Margolioth asserted, because the Torah desires to coerce and to punish dissenters from the faith as well. Mendelssohn's liberal view that "anyone who has transgressed because his heart was seduced by his reason to deny beliefs and views" ought not to be punished, would ultimately lead to heresy and legitimize it. While the scholar who wrote *Jerusalem* may have been aware of the deist potential inherent in his philosophical arguments, and knew very well "that this issue he raised was capable of, Heaven forbid, causing the destruction of the Jewish religion, whose foundations are perfectly constructed on what, as is well known, we were given on that occasion with thunder and lighting, signs and wonders that are beyond the ways of nature," Margolioth believed that Mendelssohn's division between laws that originated in revelation and beliefs and views that originated in reason, which he thought would solve the problem of religious coercion, would only exacerbate it.

In his final words, Margolioth, in an attempt to give Mendelssohn the benefit of the doubt, asserted that *Jerusalem* can be regarded not as an incitement to heresy or as an expression of skepticism, but merely as an error, a one-time lapse, or the distinguished philosopher's use of arguments that were not his own. To explain this lapse on the part of the Berlin philosopher, Margolioth suggested that one should consider the peculiar circumstances in which Mendelssohn found himself in the circles of the German enlighteners. He was very much under the sway of the rationalist philosophers, had a sense of inferiority and self-effacement in relation to the Christian intellectuals, and was compelled to give them replies they would find acceptable.[31]

Margolioth's Mendelssohn is not the author of *Jerusalem*, whose true views emerge clearly from the book; rather he is the man Margolioth had met personally and wished to defend. He found it difficult to believe that Mendelssohn conceived of Judaism as a tolerant, rationalistic religion, devoid of any coercive elements, as he depicted it in *Jerusalem*, and he interpreted this approach as arising from Mendelssohn's need to defend Judaism to the non-Jewish world.[32] On this issue, Margolioth felt that the approach taken by Dohm, who agreed to the continuation of Jewish religious autonomy and did not demand that it be deprived of the power of coercion in religious matters, was far preferable. He charged Mendelssohn with responsibility for an historical error: providing an opening for heretics to justify their heresy. Moreover, the philosophical leeway provided by Mendelssohn paved the way for those who slighted the commandments to become religiously permissive: "for this scholar has set free every religious transgressor, providing a sanctuary where all corrupt men could hide, saying they do so in their unyielding zeal for philosophy."[33]

Another major spokesman of orthodoxy, who continued to conduct a campaign against Wessely and Mendelssohn, was Rabbi Eleazar Fleckeles (1754–1826), a disciple of Yehezkel Landau, and a popular preacher in Prague. From 1783 to 1785, Fleckeles delivered many sermons in Prague synagogues, devoting considerable portions of them to his declaration of war against any reforms in Jewish education and the new trends introduced by the maskilim, who aspired to effect far-reaching changes in Jewish culture. Although much younger than Wessely and Mendelssohn, and actually the same age as the young maskilim, Fleckeles bitterly remonstrated against the new generation that sought to trample the world of values of the former generations. His trepidation about the Haskalah was part and parcel of his anxiety about religious permissiveness, an outcome of the acculturation of the wealthy elite in Prague, as well as in other urban communities in Central and Western Europe. He branded all the maskilim as "contemporary apostates," who no longer heeded the instructions of the rabbis but scorned them and strove to utterly destroy the old world.[34]

In the fall of 1783, Fleckeles attacked the *Bi'ur* project, denouncing it as sacrilegious and an act contrary to the halakhah. "The translator's main purpose," Fleckeles accused Mendelssohn, "was to gain fame for himself among the Gentiles, as a man who does not believe in the traditions and commentaries of our Sages."[35] To support his criticism of Mendelssohn's Bible translation, he cited the words of his mentor, Rabbi Landau. They both publicly expressed their opposition to the translation, in an approbation they granted in 1785 to another German translation of the Bible, in a far simpler language than Mendelssohn's, which was printed by Susmann Glogau:

For that translator [Mendelssohn] deeply immersed himself in the language using, as he did, an extremely difficult German that presupposes expertise in its grammar. Now since the children will find it hard to understand it, the teacher will have to spend most of the time in explaining German grammar, and by then the day is gone and the children have studied no Torah.

The two rabbis were less opposed to the translation per se, and more to the catastrophic results of studying Bible from the *Bi'ur*:

Now that this translation is in demand by teachers of children, it induces the young to spend their time reading Gentile books in order to become sufficiently familiar with refined German to be able to understand the translation. Our Torah is thereby reduced to the role of a maidservant to the German tongue.[36]

In these campaigns of the Jewish *Kulturkampf*, anxiety was a key motif in the orthodox rhetoric. Rabbi Landau and Tevele's sermons still reflected a certain degree of agreement as to the necessity for extra-religious knowledge, albeit limited in scope. In contrast, Fleckeles's sermons represented the "books of the gentiles" as an out-and-out threat. He marshaled his powers of rhetoric to demonstrate how insidious this danger was and to terrify the audience listening to his sermon. The establishment of government schools in Joseph II's

Austria, and Wessely's propaganda advocating them were depicted as acts of heresy. "They are all slaughterers, slaughtering children given to them by God," Fleckeles lashed out at the parents of pupils in these schools, claiming that they were sacrificing their children to the Moloch of this new education.[37]

Agonizing over the neglect of Torah study, Fleckeles demanded that its immense value be recognized: the study of Torah should not be abandoned for the sake of the "books of the gentiles," which contrary to maskilic propaganda, were of no benefit in acquiring virtues and piety. Anyone who studied "books of the apostates" would surely cause the Torah to be forgotten, prevent redemption, and endanger his soul. "We were created only for the Torah, which is our life," Flekeles averred again and again, repeating the orthodox rallying cry. He cautioned: "My children, both large and small, distance yourselves from external wisdom, for it is very, very far from any good reward and close to the gates of death."[38] Fleckeles attempted to take the revolutionary concept of *torat ha'adam*," which Wessely had introduced into the new discourse, and place it in a religious context. Consequently, he paraphrased the opening lines of *Divrei shalom ve'emet*:

When a child knows how to talk, his father teaches him Torah, namely, the Torah of man [human knowledge] that teaches some etiquette and civility, in keeping with the child's ability. Therefore, it is said from whence comes the Torah; it was commanded to us by Moses, and not the Torah of man in etiquette and knowledge, constructed on shaky foundations, as is customary in our generation, when a child knows to call on his father and mother, his father teaches him the Torah of evil man.[39]

Even when Fleckeles tried to fill his listeners with fear, he was unable to conceal his sense of despair brought on by the crisis the scholarly elite was undergoing. He believed that the Haskalah was corrupting even the finest of its advocates:

Even the great scholars, who were well versed in the sacred word of God, studied diligently and interpreted His laws and teachings, have turned their backs on the Torah and worship, and have pursued the vanities of alien sciences, which lead man into the deepest of pits which are not the source of living waters, but rather of scorpions, vipers, serpents who will consume them . . . Hence the Torah will be neglected and the wisdom of the scribes will be perverted, and talmudic scholars weakened and depleted.[40]

Rabbi Fleckeles' sermons were printed, unlike Landau's and Tevele's Shabbat HaGadol sermons and the rabbis' letters in the Wessely affair, which were circulated in handwritten copies. Fleckeles's book, which came out in two parts in 1785 and 1787 in Prague (part 3 was printed only in 1793), along with approbations by several rabbis, including Rabbi Landau, was at the time the rabbinical elite's only public expression in the culture war. Fleckeles's *Olat chodesh* was in fact the first printed orthodox piece of writing, and throughout the 1780s it stood alone vis-à-vis *Divrei shalom ve'emet* and other maskilic writings, which appeared in *Hame'asef* from 1784. The maskilim quickly realized that the *dayan* from Prague, who later became the community rabbi, was one of their bitterest adversaries, and after Fleckeles's book was published, David Friedländer was harshly critical of it.[41]

In the meantime, the maskilim were able to find some consolation in the views of the moderate and exceptional rabbi of the Regensburg community in Bavaria, Isaac Alexander, who in the 1780s sided with the Enlightenment and believed its values to be consistent with Judaism.[42] The publisher, Friedrich Nicolai, a major figure in Berlin literary circles, who had met Rabbi Alexander, said he would not have expected to find such qualities in a rabbi.[43] The rabbi's mastery of philosophy and knowledge of the sources of classical culture enabled him to write a number of works in German. In one of them, *Salomo und Joseph II* (Solomon and Joseph II), printed in Vienna in 1782, Alexander praised the Austrian king, comparing him to King Solomon.[44] For the rabbi of Regensburg, Joseph II was the exemplar of a perfect ruler: an ideal embodiment of Plato's philosopher king, a friend of God, and a supporter of wisdom, philosophy, justice, brotherhood, and humanism. Above all, Alexander believed he was worthy of admiration for his policy of religious tolerance, whose major benefactors, in his view, were the long-persecuted Jews. In 1784, Alexander's book was favorably reviewed in the German section of *Hame'asef* along with Mendelssohn's *Jerusalem*. The critic concluded his review by stating, "We bring you this slim volume because it is a work by the first contemporary rabbi to write in German, and because we realize that his words arise from the pure fount of emotion that seeks his nation's good. If only all the rabbis thought as he does!"[45]

Wessely and the Italian Rabbis

The reaction of this Ashkenazi rabbi, who supported the modernistic trends and was knowledgeable about the Enlightenment culture, was exceptional, yet it drew very little attention during the stormy events of 1782. Toward the end of that year, in an effort to clear his name, Wessely embarked on a personal struggle against the rabbis who had attacked him. He did not turn to Rabbi Alexander for help, but placed his trust in the Italian rabbis. Although in *Rav tuv livnei Israel* Wessely courageously stated he did not feel he was subject to the rabbis' authority and even issued them a three-month ultimatum to publicly expose their feebleness, it was his wish to finally gain rabbinical backing and a halakhic ruling to absolve him of the charge of heresy that had been made against him, so deeply aggrieving him. Through the contacts set up between Berlin and Trieste and Gradisca, Jewish communities in Italy, then under Austrian rule, he received encouraging letters from seven rabbis—the chief rabbi of Trieste, Isacco Formiggini, and rabbis from Ferrara, Venice, Ancona, and Reggio. Wessely was particularly heartened by the support of his chief contact in Italy, Rabbi Elijah Morpurgo, a leader of the Gradisca community. An admirer of Mendelssohn, he was involved in what was going on in the Berlin maskilic circles, and was enthusiastic in his desire to help Wessely. From far away, he empathized with the persecuted Wessely's distress and also tried to mobilize support for him outside of Italy—among rabbis from the capital of the Ottoman Empire.[46] Only in the spring of 1784, when the dust raised by the *Divrei shalom ve'emet* controversy had settled, did Wessely publish these sympathetic views in his "Third Epistle"—*Ein mishpat*.[47]

In *Ein mishpat*, Wessely continued to address Jewish leadership as if he were a major player in forming public opinion. He wrote this work too as an open letter, in an attempt to enlist broad support for his views. However, unlike the two previous pamphlets, printed in 1782, it was more in the nature of a personal defense than a daring ideological work. Wessely had lost much of his earlier zeal and was now ready to pay a heavy personal price for having confronted the rabbinical elite as a representative of the new intellectual elite. The feeling he projected was that of a man unjustly persecuted, prepared to do almost anything in order to be cleansed of the stain of guilt, and he now attributed much importance to the rabbis' opinions. "For almost two years, I have borne the scars of the unjust attack by a number of rabbis who failed to understand my true intent," Wessely contended again and again. He was wounded by the silence and the indifference with which the rabbis had received the ultimatum he had published in *Rav tuv livnei Israel* and complained bitterly of their ingratitude: "Everything I did was for the general good, and how is it that I am portrayed in such a negative light?" And he added: "My image has been almost irremediably smeared." Rabbi Tevele's sermon was read by a great many, "and it was heard far and wide, and became a taunt in everyone's mouth and the song of the drunkard . . . and is this my reward for my labors for the sake of God's people"?[48]

Hurt and aggrieved, Wessely compared himself to Moses, Maimonides and Luzzatto—all fine, just men, who were objects of suspicion and baseless accusations. He denied that he had done anything to exacerbate the dispute with the rabbis and disassociated himself from his Berlin friends' efforts to defend him. I was never motivated by thoughts of revenge, Wessely declared, and neither the letter of the seven from Berlin nor Cranz's pamphlet dedicated to Prince Sulkowsky were written at my instigation.

It never occurred to me to retaliate; no epistle of a vexatious character was written by me; only two epistles have come from my pen. Everything else was written either by some fellow-Jew or by writers not of our faith [Cranz]. I did not ask for this in any shape or form. Everything printed on this matter was not of my doing, except the epistles bearing my name.[49]

The only thing he could still do to defend his good name, without having to pursue the polemic any further, was to publish the words of the Italian rabbis. He hoped their praises would make it unnecessary for him to come out directly against the rabbis who had attacked him. As a matter of fact, none of the letters written by the Italians actually criticized those rabbis; in his reply, the Italian rabbi Ishmael Cohen sided with Wessely's opponents, but Wessely did not publish it. Lois Dubin has analyzed the affair at length from the Italian viewpoint; according to her, while Wessely did receive a sympathetic, encouraging response from the Italians, it did not amount to maskilic support.[50] Joseph II's cultural policy and the establishment of *Normalschule* did not arouse any ferment in Italy; no maskilic circles were formed, nor was a *Kulturkampf* incited. At the same time that the maskilim in Berlin were mobilizing to unleash a strong protest against Rabbi Tevele of Lissa, a new Jewish school was founded in Trieste (May 1782), and the rabbis actively participated in its establishment. The Jews of Italy were fluent in Italian, well-versed in European culture, and aware of the need to teach languages and sciences. In their special culture, neither the Austrian policy nor the Wessely curriculum was perceived as a revolutionary step or a threat to the existing order. The legitimacy of extra-religious knowledge, the encounter with European culture, and the status of the intellectual who is not a talmudic scholar, issues so central to the *Kulturkampf* provoked by Wessely, were not particularly crucial in Italy. In that social and cultural reality, it was not necessary to weaken or discredit the religious elite in order to gain a certain degree of modernization. In the Italian communities, where Jewish acculturation was already a natural, enduring process that had encountered no rabbinical opposition, there was no need for the emergence of the militant maskil or for the development of a maskilic ideology aimed at changing the nature of society and culture.

A careful reading of the opinions of the Italian rabbis reveals this singular characteristic with great clarity. They favorably received *Divrei shalom ve'emet* only because they completely identified with Wessely's proposed curriculum, even adding reasons to enhance the legitimacy of "external learning." Even those who were perplexed by the opposition of the Polish rabbis who had attacked Wessely tried to at least understand why they were so alarmed by the curtailment of religious studies, and proposed a certain compromise. None of the Italians actually accepted Wessely's maskilic principles, and they all explicitly or implicitly rejected the separation he had drawn between *torat ha-Shem* and *torat ha'adam*." Rabbi Formiggini, whom Wessely praised in particular, voiced some criticism of the curriculum proposed in *Divrei shalom ve'emet* and identified with the anxieties of the Polish rabbis:

My heart tells me that these rabbis feared that that which is most important, namely, the study of Torah, would be rendered of secondary significance, while that of lesser importance, namely the study of sciences, would be rendered of greater significance, and that, Heaven forbid, the Torah would be forgotten by the Jews . . . if we were to confuse their minds with the study of sciences and languages, they would not gain the one but lose the other, and the child would remain confounded, lacking in all knowledge, a loser on both counts.[51]

If we were to describe the ideal Jewish education based on the opinions of the Italian rabbis, it would differ substantially from the form of education Wessely envisioned. The rabbis demanded that in the early stages of education the curriculum should focus only on sacred studies and Hebrew, and that only later would a limited number of hours be devoted to nonreligious study. Wessely's reactions to these views, recorded in the footnotes he added to *Ein mishpat*, were pathetic and apologetic, and revealed by his willingness to retreat from his earlier positions. Wherever the rabbis suggested that extra-religious knowledge ought to be limited, he hastened to state that that was precisely his original intent. For example, "Who would disagree with that? Heaven forfend, that anyone should find in our letter even the slightest hint that the young child should be taught foreign languages, such as Greek, Latin, French, or Italian before he is well versed in the Torah." Wessely did not even shrink from printing the letter from Rabbi Israel Bassan of Reggio, in which he expressed his misgivings about the furor Wessely had so rashly aroused: "If at the very beginning, it had been possible to advise our rabbi and teacher [Wessely], then I would have said to him: write nothing and publish nothing." In the margins of that letter, Wessely admitted that he was already anxious to see the end of the affair. He still had to publish his detailed reply to all of Rabbi Tevele's arguments, he asserted, and then he could leave the whole affair behind him. "After I have justified myself, I will forget everything that has taken place, and will never recall it again."[52]

In the fourth and last "epistle" in the *Divrei shalom ve'emet* series, written in 1784 but only printed in the spring of 1785, Wessely's revolutionary fervor had almost entirely dissipated. Under the appeasing title *Rehovoth*, which evoked in the reader an association to the end to a dispute (based on Genesis 26: 22), Wessely declared that he was opposed to any form of factionalism and wanted to be accepted by all sides.[53] Nonetheless, in *Rehovoth* he grappled with the criticism hurled at him by Rabbi Tevele of Lissa, by no means prepared to say he had changed his mind or that he felt the criticism was justified. In this fourth epistle, he still fought against ignorance and other flaws in Ashkenazi Jewish education and again defended the innovative curriculum he had proposed three years earlier. His purpose in it, however, was to demonstrate his moderation ("not that I have become a different person") and to prove that his words were compatible with the Polish rabbi's positions and not contrary to Jewish tradition. He averred that only an incorrect reading of *Divrei shalom ve'emet* had so infuriated the rabbi. What he had learned about the faulty manner in which the new curriculum had been introduced into government schools in Austria also contributed to his reservations about the whole project. "It pains me to say," he wrote, "that the emperor's law has been established, but that of the Torah has been abandoned." Mendelssohn's translation was not being used in teaching Torah ("This was tantamount to decreeing that the youths should not study Scripture at all"), no proper textbooks on faith and morals had been written in Hebrew, and too many hours were being devoted to a study of the German language.[54]

Wessely consoled himself with the fact that only a few rabbis had joined the campaign conducted against him by the Polish rabbis, and those who attacked him did not do so for any substantive reasons: "Those men who quarrel with me did not speak from their hearts, I think, but because of the counsel of others. Some men incited them against me. Who knows what evil words these sycophants and speakers of lies have written about me, not because of the letter I wrote, but out of malice and envy of one another." And in 1785, feeling insecure and anxious to reduce the damage incurred by the affair, Wessely tried to portray it as an error and to derive some conciliatory lessons from it: "It is best to behave calmly at all times, not in the heat of wrath or in a deluge of anger, not to wage war with the seekers of peace, not to spill out the jewels of the crown at every street corner." The "house of Israel" in the diaspora is deprived of any central leadership and is at the mercy of the rulers, and hence it must never become embroiled in internal wars. Consequently, it is best "to search for peace by candlelight, to tie the tents of Jacob with the bonds of love and peace between men, so we may each protect one another."[55]

The early maskil, Wessely, who in 1782 had burst onto center stage and borne the full brunt of the intense orthodox counter-attack, did not persevere in his role as a trailblazer. This is clear from a letter he sent in early 1786 to Elijah Morpurgo, which amounted to his swan song as far as that first campaign of the *Kulturkampf* was concerned. Wessely was wounded and disappointed by what he viewed as a sundering of his connections with the Italian scholars. His personal condition had deteriorated following his wife's death and his worsening financial situation, and this aggravated his dejected mood.[56]

None of the rabbis to whom Wessely had sent his *Ein mishpat*, which included the opinions of those rabbis, reacted to it or even acknowledged its receipt. Only Morpurgo wrote one letter to him (during the winter of 1784), and to his surprise Wessely found no mention at all in it of *Ein mishpat* or of *Rehovoth*. The silence of the Italians was a hard blow for Wessely and he was deeply insulted by it: "I wonder about you and the scholars of your land, I am too ignorant to understand why I have not received a single word about the eight letters I wrote to Trieste in the summer of 1784." And he asked whether it was possible that the scholars of Italy had already tired of dealing with this matter, or had changed their minds and had withdrawn their support of him. Why "have they deprived me of their respect by failing to answer me, for I have done them no wrong, and there is no word on my tongue that, Heaven forbid, insults their honor?" He concluded by stating that these were his last words on the painful affair: "For I have done everything I had to do and will speak no more about this quarrel."[57] Wessely, the man behind the new critical discourse of the Haskalah, who in 1782 had issued a revolutionary challenge to the rabbinical elite in the name of the elite of maskilic writers, was then sixty-one years of age. He continued to engage in his extensive literary activity and closely followed what was happening in maskilic circles, but left it to other, younger maskilim to stand at the helm of the Haskalah's major initiative to create a full-fledged movement.

PART III

The Maskilic Republic

Chapter Eight

The Society of Friends of the Hebrew Language

The year 1782 was a particularly difficult year for Wessely, from the moment he touched off a fierce debate in Jewish public opinion with his *Divrei shalom ve'emet*. At the end of that year, he received a surprising letter from Königsberg in Eastern Prussia. The writers of the letter, "A society of friends—maskilim and seekers of truth," signed it with the name "Chevrat Dorshei Leshon Ever" (Society of Friends of the Hebrew Language), and asked Wessely for his patronage and a few articles for the monthly that their maskilic circle planned to publish in the near future. They introduced themselves to him as a circle of ambitious intellectuals, including scholars proficient in the religious sources and students knowledgeable in the sciences, and in Greek and Latin literature. They regarded Wessely as no less than an admired prophet, who had engendered an enormous cultural transformation, and flattered him by writing: "From the moment your pamphlets were circulated throughout the land, you have ignited the hearts of maskilim with the fire of your song . . . for like a seer you have spoken."[1] In addition to the support he had received from his friends in the Berlin community and his admirers in the Italian communities, Wessely could now take much encouragement from the letter sent him by these young maskilim. He regarded it as an expression of trust in him as well as in the views he had publicly stated during the culture war waged against him.

However, the letter from Königsberg also marked one of the most decisive moments in the history of the Haskalah movement. In early 1782, Wessely, at his own initiative, had come out with a detailed and exciting program for an innovative new order, and in doing so had challenged the traditional elite. When this had distressing consequences for him, Jews from Berlin's intellectual and economic elite rallied to his defense, stridently protesting against the violation of his freedom of expression and the insult to their community's honor. At the end of that year, the first cohesive group of intellectuals was organized. This group aspired to be at the forefront of an all-inclusive cultural transformation and to found the Haskalah's literary republic.

Establishing a New Public Sphere

The new sociocultural history tends to look for the significance of the Enlightenment in a far broader area than the world of ideas of the philosophers—the consummate bearers of intellectual history.[2] The new historiography has shifted the emphasis from a description of the individual phenomenon to a study of the social structures, and has added new subjects to historical research, such as "public opinion," the "reading culture," and the "public sphere." As a result, a series of new questions has arisen as well: Who were the bearers of the Enlightenment's ideas? In which social and institutional settings was the life of the Enlightenment conducted? How were its ideas disseminated? What was the influence of printing and of printed books on the changing social reality? And what impression did these ideas leave on various social groups?

It seems that the main focus of investigation has been to find along what lines the writers community was organized and how it functioned. The German philosopher and sociologist Jürgen Habermas was the main source of inspiration for this direction in Enlightenment research. In *The Structural Transformation of the Public Sphere*, first published in 1962, he noted the emergence of a literary republic in eighteenth-century Europe, which he regarded as a bourgeois phenomenon of enormous cultural and political import. Private educated persons, possessed of critical-rationalistic thought and nourished by the flourishing world of books, became the producers and consumers of culture, and established in various European cities a network of institutions (reading clubs, salons, Freemason lodges, cafes) and means of communication (letters and periodicals). In addition to the local groups of intellectuals, a kind of independent, cosmopolitan, all-European republic of talented writers emerged, which operated in a virtual space without any personal contact between its members. This was an exceptional development, one subversive in nature, in particular in absolutist states like France and Germany. The members of the literary republic also engaged in public criticism, thus becoming the shapers of cultural taste and the spokesmen of "public opinion," so much so that they could no longer be ignored.[3] The new writers of the Enlightenment viewed themselves as authoritative judges. The revolutionary consciousness of these intellectuals is best expressed in the words of Chrétien Malesherbes, a liberal minster in Louis XVI's government, in a 1775 speech delivered to the French Academy. Roger Chartier, an eminent historian of the Enlightenment's literary republic, who examined its revolutionary significance, quotes Malesherbes:

A tribunal has arisen, independent of all powers and that all powers respect, that appreciates all talents, that pronounces on all people of merit. And in an enlightened century, in a century in which each citizen can speak to the entire nation by way of print, those who have a talent for instructing men and a gift for moving them—in a word, men of letters—are, amid the public dispersed, what the orators of Rome and Athens were in the middle of the public assembled.[4]

Until now, the new questions of sociocultural history have scarcely related to the place of the Jews in the Enlightenment revolution.[5] It is true that, compared to England, France, and the German states, the dimensions of the Jewish literary republic were minute, and it barely reverberated in the European public sphere. But these new questions can be extremely helpful in arriving at a full description of the Haskalah and an understanding of the revolutionary significance of the emergence of the new maskilic elite in Jewish society and culture. Who were the maskilim? Where did they meet one another and where did they conduct their activities? How was the literary republic of the Haskalah constructed and how were channels of communication established between its members?

In this part of the book, the reader's attention will be drawn to the maskilim's collective experience, to the friendships that were forged in their circles, and in particular to their efforts to establish an organizational setting that had a public status and would enable the new elite of critical writers to exert their influence through the written word. In the 1780s, the maskilim also began to establish a Jewish tribunal of their own. Its members set out to judge flaws in Jewish life based on a new *Weltanschauung* and to speak directly to the public through the printed word, above the heads of the traditional spokesmen.

When the letter from Chevrat Dorshei Leshon Ever asking for his patronage reached Wessely, he realized at once that something unprecedented was taking place in Königsburg, and he excitedly hastened to reply, apparently on the very same day. In his response, he did not conceal his enthusiasm, highly praised the founders of the society and wished them every success in their pioneering venture. His reply included the following:

In the midst of the night, be you the first among all the young men of Israel, to illuminate us with the glowing light of truth and of rational inquiry. You shall be a model to all the young men of your age, enlightened by wisdom, and all those who take up their pen and those who seek justice shall try to emulate you. And many shall run to and fro, and knowledge shall increase . . . and you shall be blessed for you have shown them the path they should follow.[6]

He had already conjured up a vision of how the circles of writers and readers would grow and expand, and how the planned periodical would make the Königsberg community the focus of all literary and scholarly activity that would develop Hebrew culture. He expressed his readiness to help the young men and suggested that they correspond on a regular basis.

However, he also wanted to guide them from afar under his patronage, which had in it more than a trace of condescension, so that the zeal of youth would not lead them to level unwarranted radical criticism. Wessely, the moderate early maskil, was sensitive to the spread of religious criticism in the European and the Jewish society in the eighteenth century. He was apparently trying to shape the young literary republic in light of the personal lessons he had learned from the *Divrei shalom ve'emet* controversy, and particularly out of a desire to avoid a direct confrontation with the rabbinical elite. In his view, the editorial board of the maskilic periodical soon to be published ought to exercise great caution to avoid impinging on religion and faith. It must display a large measure of responsibility and abstain from doing anything to undermine devoutness and morals. The publication of biting social or anticlerical satires, so typical of the Enlightenment culture, should not be permitted; nor should any mythological literary articles, or any articles erotic in nature that might inflame the passions, be included in the periodical.

Wessely was undoubtedly apprehensive about any orthodox counter-reactions of the type he had himself experienced. However, he failed to take two facts into account. First, that he himself was the one who had provoked the conflict between the maskilim and the traditional elite. Second, that it was his public appeal to the Jewish leadership to respond favorably to Joseph II's reformist policy that first exposed his aspiration to shape Jewish public opinion and to open a debate between diverse views that would take place in a new type of arena. *Divrei shalom ve'emet*, the revolutionary pamphlet, whose significance Wessely tried in vain to play down, cried: "Jew, dare to be a man!" In actual fact, the pamphlet heaped radical, sweeping criticism on the basic values of Jewish life in the traditional society, in particular on the cultural and social barriers between Jews and non-Jews.

The founding of Chevrat Dorshei Leshon Ever as a society of maskilim was no less a subversive act than Wessely's pamphlet. Hence, this event in modern intellectual history merits our special attention. Who were the young men who were behind the letter Wessely received? In the absence of any orderly archival sources, we can only partially reconstruct the history of the society. We can, nonetheless, learn quite a bit about its aims and activity. First, a short time after its establishment, it already had at its disposal the Hebrew-German periodical *Hame'asef*, which printed news about the society and letters from its members. Second, letters written by the members were printed or left in handwriting, and they also left literary material (in particular poems written for festive events in their lives).

Chevrat Dorshei Leshon Ever of Königsburg was one of hundreds of reading and literary societies that emerged in various German cities in the eighteenth century, in particular in its last two decades. These were the active social nuclei of the Enlightenment in Germany, the frameworks of the producers and consumers of culture, who were the bearers of the ideological world constructed by the written word. The aim of these societies was to foster various maskilic values: the dissemination of knowledge by reading; the acquisition of virtues; the promotion of science, literature, and the arts; and the improvement of education and health. They filled the function of a social club, at which the members read books and periodicals, read aloud their original work, held debates, and spent their leisure time drinking coffee, tea, and chocolate and playing billiards, chess, and cards. Some of these societies published periodicals. Most of them had detailed bylaws that defined their method of operation, their membership fees, their various offices and positions, and how new members would be admitted. The shared desire to exchange views and to acquire knowledge brought under one roof young men from diverse social groups. The "reading society" was a voluntary club of individuals who were involved in public issues and ran their society democratically—very different from the rules of the political game in the monarchic and class-defined state.[7] The Berlin Wednesday Society (Mittwochgesellschaft), for example, was organized at the same time as Chevrat Dorshei Leshon Ever in Königsburg, and from 1783 also began to publish a periodical—the *Berlinische Monatsschrift*.[8]

Although Chevrat Dorshei Leshon Ever was modeled on the German society, Aufklärungsgesellschaft (Society of Enlightenment), and its composition and goals were similar to those of the exclusive Literarische Freundschaftzirkel (Literary Society), it had a singular nature. It was intended for Jewish intellectuals, for "young Israelites" and was devoted to promoting the interests of "the Jewish nation." While the German Enlightenment societies included among their members an impressive number of government officials, representatives of the learned professions, and professors,[9] the membership of Chevrat Dorshei Leshon Ever was comprised mainly of the sons of merchants, teachers and students.

The establishment of voluntary societies was not in itself an exceptional feature of Jewish life in the eighteenth century. The traditional society had many such organizations, with orderly bylaws, whose purpose was to promote religious and social aims: societies for the study of Torah at various levels and charitable societies.[10] Influenced by the growing interest in Kabbalah, mystics, eager for communion with the Divinity, organized in study houses of scholars and Hasidim and in secret societies of Kabbalists, and they also often anchored their association in bylaws. For example, the exclusive society of Moses Hayim Luzzatto (Ramhal) was founded in Padua, Italy, in the 1730s ("they all united as one man to engage in the pure worship of their Creator"), and the Ahavat

Shalom (Love of Peace) society was founded by twelve Kabbalists in Jerusalem in the middle of the century ("for the sake of the unity of God, the holy one, blessed be He, and His divine presence to bring satisfaction to our Creator").[11] These societies were founded on the basis of bonds of love and friendship, mutual aid in time of trouble, and religious devotion, at times accompanied by messianic pretensions. Their members were asked to keep their activity secret and never to mention the bylaws.

Chevrat Dorshei Leshon Ever was unique in the fact that it was not a "holy society," but rather one secular in nature, in the wording of its bylaws, and in its aims. None of its members belonged to the rabbinical elite; it did not serve any religious or community purposes, nor did it base any of its programs on religious legitimacy. It reflected the maturity of unofficial circles of early maskilim, at least one of which was already active in Berlin in the 1750s, as we learn from the periodical *Kohelet musar*. Among the letters sent to the editors of that periodical, one related a marvelous experience of a society of friends and scholars who engaged together in reading, writing, translating, and exchanging views ("How good for a man and how pleasant to sit in the company of his fellows, for he nourishes his loved ones, and pours out to them the searchings of his heart"). The letter also describes the members' traits: "They are all well-read, able to understand the splendor of rhetoric," and among them are physicians and brilliant scholars.[12] More detailed information is available about another early society for the purpose of promoting Hebrew culture, multilingual poetry, and the Bible. Called Amadores das Musas (Lovers of the Muses), the society was founded in Amsterdam in the 1760s, and the main figure in it was Wessely's close friend, the early maskil David Franco-Mendes.[13]

A Maskilic Association in Königsberg

Chevrat Dorshei Leshon Ever began with the friendships formed among ten young bachelors in their twenties, who lived in Königsburg. They were scions of wealthy merchant families, tutors in the homes of the high and middle-class Jewish bourgeoisie or students in the city's famed university, one of whose illustrious professors was the renowned philosopher Immanuel Kant. Some of these young men, in particular Isaac Euchel, the founder and guiding spirit behind Chevrat Dorshei Leshon Ever, had attracted Kant's special attention while studying at the university and were about to embark on an academic career.[14] Solomon Maimon's memoirs provide us with a glimpse into one of the student apartments in Königsburg at the end of the 1770s. Maimon, a Lithuanian maskil with a thirst for knowledge, had fled the miserable life he abhorred back in his "benighted" country. His first stop was in Königsberg, where a Jewish physician sent him to an apartment he was renting to Jewish students, who had already adopted the German language and fashionable clothing, and probably were clean shaven. They roared with laughter at the sight of this "man from Polish Lithuania of about five-and-twenty years, with a tolerably stiff beard, in tattered, dirty clothes, whose language is a mixture of Hebrew, Yiddish, Polish, and Russian." The members of the group, however, knew how to appreciate the intellectual skills and philosophical thought that Maimon exhibited, and helped him continue on his way to Berlin.[15]

When Chevrat Dorshei Leshon Ever was founded, the Königsberg community numbered only 665 Jews (172 of whom were "servants," without the status of permanent residents). The community was founded around a nucleus of protected Jews with broad commercial rights. The wealthy Friedländer family provided comfortable living conditions for young, ambitious intellectuals and, like other families from Berlin, supported maskilic projects in education and the printing of books. Without this vital support and patronage, the German Haskalah could not have become firmly established, and its importance was particularly evident when these wealthy Jews rallied to Wessely's support in 1782. The Freischule, the first modern Jewish school of Chevrat Chinukh Ne'arim, founded in Berlin in 1778, was established through the philanthropic initiative of the Itzig and Friedländer families too.

The Friedländer family also extended its patronage to Isaac Euchel. In the list of Königsberg Jews he is recorded as a tutor in the home of Meir Friedländer (1745–1808), the brother of David Friedländer of Berlin (the husband of Blimchen neé Itzig) and one of six children of the founder of the successful family business, Joachim Moses Friedländer (1712–76).[16] This prominent family ranked high in the Königsberg elite of merchants, bankers and financiers. A year prior to Euchel's arrival there, Moses Mendelssohn, connected with families of the financial elite since the time he came to Berlin as a youth, was a guest in the Friedländer home. These affluent patrons of the Haskalah fostered a circle of young maskilim, tutors and students. These maskilim used the rich libraries in their patrons' homes to good advantage, and some of them received scholarships for university study.[17] Euchel commended these wealthy Jews' readiness to contribute to the enlightenment of their nation, and he apparently also succeeded in beginning his academic studies in 1781 with the support of theFriedländer family.[18]

In the second half of the century, the Prussian merchant community underwent rapid processes of acculturation and enlightenment, expressed in their adoption of the fashion of dress and manners of high society, their social ties with the non-Jewish milieu, and their growing interest in politics and culture. Many Jewish homes boasted large libraries that contained the very latest publications. These families wished to educate their children according to the newest "noble principles" of the European Enlightenment.[19] However, this ideal picture portrayed by outside observers does not fully reflect the image of the community. The traditional social group still played a dominant role in it, as is evident from Euchel's failed attempt in 1781 to bypass the local rabbi and found a modern school through a democratic decision. The traditional group, which took a dim view of these developments, tried to block them, with some success, at least in the early stages.[20]

This failure apparently had the effect of coalescing the Königsberg group, and it certainly made Euchel all the more determined to inculcate the Jews with new attitudes and aims. The members of the group had much in common: they were young, unencumbered by families, passionately eager to acquire knowledge, and attracted to the world of books. They also came from a similar cultural background: they were fluent in Hebrew and the religious sources, from the Torah to the Talmud and Jewish philosophy, on the one hand, and also well-versed in Enlightenment culture and European languages, on the other. They also revered Moses Mendelssohn and were well acquainted with his writings. These shared traits and interests deepened their ties of friendship and bridged the social gap between tutors, who were regarded as servants of the house and whose legal status entitled them only to temporary residence in the city, and the sons of rich, well-connected families. The group created a social and cultural framework of its own, in addition to the family, religious, and communal frameworks. Its members met frequently in their homes to discuss linguistics, Hebrew, the Bible, and the "books of the ancients." Some of them wrote original articles and took advantage of their meetings to read them aloud to the others. At first, they thought only of sending their writings to the two scholars they most admired—Mendelssohn and Wessely—but then they came up with the revolutionary idea of founding a periodical to present their ideas and the fruit of their literary endeavors to a broader readership. At this stage, the members decided to institutionalize their group and to establish an administrative staff to manage it.

Chevrat Dorshei Leshon Ever was founded on Sunday, December 11, 1782, at an official meeting held four days before their letter was sent to Wessely.[21] The members elected four "heads" to manage the society and to edit its periodical. Two from the group of students and tutors—Isaac Euchel and Menachem Mendel Breslau—and two from the group of sons of upper-class families—Shimon Friedländer (1764–1818), Joachim Moses' youngest son, and Sanwil (Shmuel) Friedländer (1764–1837), one of his grandsons. Euchel and Breslau were appointed as editors of Hame'asef and the other two, only eighteen years old, were made responsible for management and accounting. Chevrat Dorshei Leshon Ever opened its doors to additional candidates from the Königsberg community. All those interested in joining were asked to apply in writing to Sanwil Friedländer, who would invite them to the next meeting, where their membership fees would be fixed according to their financial situation. The founders had a special stamp (a circle around the initials *het, daled, lamed,* and *ein; Chevrat Dorshei Leshon Ever*) prepared, and chose the German name of the society (Die Gesellschaft dar Hebräischen Litteraturfreunde), and a postal address in the offices of the Friedländer house of business (Joachim Moses Friedländer & Sons).

From the outset, the society's administrative staff was intended to serve the periodical's editorial board. *Nachal habesor,* the society's manifesto, which included information on the circumstances of its establishment and the exchange of letters with Wessely, was printed in the spring of 1784, and circulated among Jewish communities in Germany and outside it (Copenhagen, Prague, Strasbourg, Vilna) in an attempt to raise funds for the early publication of *Hame'asef.* The Friedländers had provided the initial financial support for the Society ("So that it might be founded, some wealthy men of our community, imbued with the spirit of voluntary deeds, have agreed to donate a certain sum to support the group"), but now at least two hundred annual subscribers were needed to cover the cost of the monthlies in advance and to make their publication worthwhile. The heads of the group also felt it was urgent to purchase new, high-quality lead type to be used in printing the periodical (in Daniel Christoph Kantor's print shop in Königsberg, in the society's Hebrew letters), and to hire a "Hebrew worker" expert in proofreading and printing Hebrew texts.

As soon as the society began its operation, it opened a line of communication by letters between Königsberg and Berlin. Two young tutors were appointed as the society's agents in Berlin: Joel Brill, a childhood friend of Euchel's, who lived in the home of David Friedländer, and Josel Pick of Reichenau, who tutored Mendelssohn's children and lived in Wessely's home. Their addresses were widely circulated for the receipt of letters and literary material to be sent on to the editorial board in Königsberg. Although they lived in Berlin, the two were admitted as full members into Chevrat Dorshei Leshon Ever. This was probably the first move toward the society's expansion into a supra-community body. The society also printed a notice, seeking people to act as its agents to help acquire subscribers in any community. It promised that for every ten subscribers they registered they would receive the cost of the tenth subscriber as a fee. Subscribers living within the bounds of the Königsberg-Berlin, Königsberg-Breslau, and Königsberg-Vilna mail coach line would be exempt from shipping costs.[22]

The society had only a very small number of registered members, and probably these numbered no more than twenty when it was founded. However, although few in number, the aspirations they cherished were passionate and lofty. Like Wessely's *Divrei shalom ve'emet*, *Nachal habesor* was aimed at mobilizing public opinion.[23] However, while Wessely sought broad public support for his modern educational project in keeping with Joseph II's policy, Chevrat Dorshei Leshon Ever sought to establish a Jewish intellectual society, which exceeded geographical and class boundaries, and had a membership of writers and readers who would keep in touch through its periodical and by letters. These anonymous readers were solicited with stirring rhetoric ("Now the age of science has come to all nations . . . ! Arise, our brethren, and we shall revive stones from heaps of dust!") to awaken and to respond to the tidings voiced by the pioneers of the Haskalah in Königsberg.[24] This was a revolutionary clarion call that emphasized the opportune historical moment and the vast cultural momentum taking place in Europe, which also called for the cultural awakening of the Jewish intellectual elite.

Promotion of the Hebrew language, the chief aim of Chevrat Dorshei Leshon Ever, was depicted as a reformist cultural project of the highest order. Jewish culture, including the Hebrew language, was under the control of the rabbinical elite, which represented the "other"—the cause of cultural backwardness and the neglect of Hebrew, the most valuable classical, cultural treasure of the Jewish people. Its liberation from the clutches of representatives of the rabbinical culture ("the little foxes that spoil the vineyard of Israel"), who were impeding a direct encounter with the Bible, for example, was an essential reformist act in view of the criticism of the culture's deplorable state.[25] "Wisdom cries aloud in the streets, she utters her voice in the squares. Hasten to call her, rush to bring her home," was the call sent forth by Chevrat Dorshei Leshon Ever. The knowledge spreading throughout Europe is no longer aristocratic knowledge, the province of scholars only, but is now open to all men of interest and talent. It is democratic knowledge, which draws no distinction between the rich and privileged and the poor and lowborn. It offers an equal opportunity to all seekers of wisdom: "Whether you abide in the castles of kings or in a shepherd's tent, whether you sleep on beds of ivory or lie together upon the earth, whether pomegranate juice and a fatted calf is laid before you, or you eat but a crust of bread and drink water from the well, that is of no import, he will not pass over you, but will consent to sit by you in the smallest of attics."[26] Infused with a profound consciousness of being innovative and pioneering, the "Friends of the Hebrew Language" declared: "A new journal, which has never before been, walks forth in the streets," and they called upon the Jews too to take part in the flourishing of knowledge and culture.[27]

The society's hope was that *Nachal habesor* would fire the readers' enthusiasm and that within a brief time the ranks of the literary republic would swell and a new unprecedented community of "maskilim, lovers of morals and knowledge" would be established, transcending the boundaries of cities, states, wealth, and privilege.

Membership in the society was based on intellect and a shared interest in science, the Jewish sources, and public issues, first and foremost education. This common cause was underpinned by the intimate friendship that existed between the members, at a time when friendship in Germany was in the nature of a cult, which left a strong imprint on belles lettres, sentimental drama, and the content and style of correspondence. It was perceived as a lofty expression of human love and tolerance, free of egoism and prejudice. Personal letters, often read aloud in public and sometimes printed in books, exalted the happiness to be gained from loyal friendship. In Klaus Berghahn's view, friendship during this period was a cosmopolitan bourgeois value that crossed social and class lines, and hence had the potential of engendering social change. On the level of relations between Jews and Christians, friendship enabled Mendelssohn, for example, to gain admission, as an honored member, to the literary republic of the German enlighteners.[28]

It was friendship too that made Chevrat Dorshei Leshon Ever a close-knit group, as well as the source of their self-identity as maskilim and their self-confidence vis-à-vis the traditional society that regarded them with suspicion. "The estate of maskilic comrades" or "the congregation of maskilim," as they called themselves, were first of all a cohesive group of good friends, who were in the habit of publicly displaying their feelings of mutual affection. On the occasion of the society's second anniversary, Shimon Baraz recited for the members an effusive poem about the experience of camaraderie: "Now how I delight in seeing, gathered in the seat of wisdom, friends reasoning and discussing! How glorious is this day for me, and hence I thank my Lord this time!" He described the intimacy forged in the society's meetings: friends generously share knowledge and ideas, seal themselves off, with an invisible wall, from everything around, draw the strength to withstand the "derision of the insensible and the insolent" who regard them with suspicion, and devote themselves unstintingly to "intellect, the mother of happiness."[29]

The custom of composing poems of friendship for various events was very prevalent among maskilim. When Euchel left Königsberg for Copenhagen, the city of his birth, he prepared a special journey album for his friends in Königsberg and those at the stops he made on his trip. The album opened with a farewell poem written for him by "a group of friends who desire all of the best for you." "Pleasing friend," Dorshei Leshon Ever wrote in his album in May 1784, "how sad is our parting," but "the days of peace will return again, for you have not left us forever, after you go in peace to see the land of your birth, you will once again renew your covenant with us."[30]

This was a brotherhood of maskilic men. As in most societies of intellectuals in Europe (with the exception of the salons), women were excluded. The members of the eighteenth-century literary republic almost without exception believed women lacked the ability to contribute to the discourse or creativity of the Enlightenment. For example, in his philosophical-educational book *Emile*, Jean Jacques Rousseau, one of the most eminent spokesmen of the republic of writers, shaped the character of the ideal woman as sensual and emotional, quite the opposite from the rational, moral man, and assigned to her the earthly roles that nature had dictated for her.[31] Immanuel Kant regarded the character of the scholarly, intellectual woman as absurd, asserting that these qualities were opposed to the very nature of the "fair sex." He stated that one of the fundamental differences between the sexes, which preclude the entry of women to the republic of scholars, is that the philosophy of the woman is to feel, not to think rationally.[32] Moses Mendelssohn's view was not substantively different. During his engagement to Fromet Gugenheim of Hamburg, he instructed her from afar in her studies and recommended suitable books to her. However, when he realized she was devoting herself seriously to intensive and diligent study, he rebuked her:

You are very much exaggerating in the diligence of your reading and by doing so, are abusing it. What is it you want to gain from that? To be a scholar? May God save you from that! Reading to a moderate degree is suitable for women, but not scholarship. A girl whose eyes are red from much reading deserves to be scorned. My dear Fromet, you must not find refuge in books, except when you have no company and wish to amuse yourself, or when you need to read to fortify your knowledge of what is good.[33]

Nonetheless, meetings between tutors and their well-born female students often led to deep friendships, love, and in rare cases marriage. For example, the relationship between Isaac Euchel and Rebecca Friedländer (1770–1838) was marked by the tension between the intimate closeness and erotic attraction he felt toward his young pupil and his awareness that the socioeconomic gap put her out of his reach. They became close friends after spending long hours together studying and conversing in her parents' home, and the inner world of love and friendship they shared led them to forget external reality. When Rebecca turned sixteen, Isaac tried to win her heart, but she married her cousin Sanwil Friedländer, Euchel's fellow member of Chevrat Dorshei Leshon Ever—a match far more suited to her social and economic standing.[34] In any event, this friendship with a cultured, adored young woman did not make her a fit candidate for membership in the circle of maskilim.

The stereotypic image of the woman as motivated by emotion and passion, in contrast to the man who is guided by reason, did not allow her to join the "alliance of maskilim." Since in the traditional world Jewish women were excluded from reading the religious texts studied in schools for boys and in the educational settings for talmudic scholars, there was no way they could find a common culture with maskilic men. Hebrew, for example, the focus of Chevrat Dorshei Leshon Ever's research and creativity, was the language of the religious cultural elite. Women, who were not exposed to it in their youth, were unable to write literary or theoretical works in Hebrew, and only a handful of women knew how to read Hebrew.

In the families of the economic elite in Germany, European languages—German and French—were the languages of the women's cultural milieu. They learned these within the framework of their bourgeois education and their profound acculturation to European tastes and fashions. When Euchel wanted to impress his beloved pupil Rebecca Friedländer, he dedicated his German translation of the prayer book to her. This was his way of fulfilling her wish, because she had often complained to him that the experience of prayer had been denied to anyone who knew no Hebrew: "How unfortunate, my dear friend, that nearly all the women and many of the men of our nation are unable to enjoy this happiness."[35] The bourgeois ideal, which assigned to women the domestic roles of wife, housewife, hostess and mother, also left no room for her in the public life that maskilic society aspired to shape. Even more serious, some maskilim regarded women as an obstacle to the young maskil, as a threat to the male intellect, for women spread before men a net of inferior physical temptations and arouse their baser instincts. Against this background, it is clear why women were absent from all spheres of the Haskalah's literary republic, and why hardly any attention was paid them in the Enlightenment project of the Jews until the end of the eighteenth century.[36]

Isaac Satanow, Mendelssohn's contemporary and a key figure among the Berlin maskilim, who maintained close ties with Dorshei Leshon Ever, held an even more radical view regarding the exclusion of women from the world of culture. When Euchel arrived in Berlin in 1784, Satanow recorded some rhymes of love in his album: "Oh, my brother, with affection we have just met one another, but even after so brief a time, you leave me with love so sublime." He also added an astonishing, erotically charged riddle ("Keep this for the days of *niddah* [separation between man and woman due to menstrual impurity] as a man takes leave of his friend"): "Who is that man who lacks a wife to help him reproduce, and yet sows his seed, conceives, suffers the pangs of labor and even gives birth?" And the obvious reply: "A man who writes sows grand ideas, and his pregnant pen gives birth to his writing and produces his offspring—his books."[37] The literary prolificness of the author and the man of letters is purely that of the male of the species, who as far his intellectual activity is concerned has no need to couple with members of the female sex.

These maskilim, "the lovers of the Hebrew tongue," drew much strength and self-confidence from their friendship and social cohesion, which made them feel capable of leading a cultural revolution through the written word. They wanted to communicate their new insights beyond the limits of their own intimate group in order to inspire and educate the ignorant: "to plant the seed of reason in the heart of chaos, to endow the simple with shrewdness, the young with knowledge." A grand, lofty ideal, that of an extensive educational project, intended to spread the light of reason. Our goal is "to teach the confused of mind understanding and the impetuous reason, and the earth shall be as full of knowledge as the waters cover the sea!"[38] A comparison of the utopistic rhetoric of Chevrat Dorshei Leshon Ever to that of other reading circles in Germany reveals a large measure of similarity. For example, the 1789 declaration of intent of the Bonn reading society states that the society is merely a means to a greater end—to influence the public as a whole. Our aspiration, the Bonn maskilim wrote, is to contribute to "progress on the path of light," to disseminate true enlightenment whose enemies are "the friends of darkness," and to promote virtue and the light of reason.[39]

Despite their prayer that God might help them succeed and their focus on the Hebrew language and biblical commentary, the members of Chevrat Dorshei Leshon Ever definitely had no religious agenda. In this early formative stage of the literary republic, they perceived the Haskalah project in secular terms. Their aspiration was to see "the earth as full of knowledge as the waters cover the sea," and they were thinking of universal knowledge and rational thought that members of the Society would endeavor to promote, as a counterweight to the traditional focus on talmudic culture. It is no accident that Shimon Baraz, who wrote a blessing to the Society, changed the messianic verse from Isaiah (11: 9)—"the earth will be filled with the knowledge of God as the waters cover the sea"—by omitting the words "of God."

The paramount aim of the society's activity was to convey its message to the Jewish public. Their private letters became a public "letter" (the contemporary Hebrew word for a journal), and from then on, "the new letter," the journal through which the literary community would be established, was "walking forth in the streets." The society opened its doors wide, much beyond the scholarly-religious elite, which until then had held the monopoly on knowledge and on the public cultural space, and intended to be the cultural home of "every enlightened member of the congregation of Israel who seeks the truth and loves science." *Hame'asef* would try to bring its readers information of general interest, like "innovations being created by our fellow Jews that concern all of us, from their freedom in some countries to the education of their children," as well as information about new books. From time to time, questions on biblical commentary and various riddles would also be printed, to create an ongoing dialogue between the journal and its readership. Occasionally, special notices to the public from Chevrat Dorshei Leshon Ever would appear on *Hame'asef*'s pages. A public notice (Nachricht an das Publikum) printed in 1784 contained a brief, very concise statement of the society's objective: "The sole aim of the editors is to foster Enlightenment (*Aufklärung*) among our people."[40]

The letters that have been preserved show that the Society conducted an intensive and far-ranging correspondence, taking full advantage of improvements in the European postal service introduced at the end of the century. The calendars printed in Berlin for Jews, licensed by the Prussian Academy of Sciences, included the timetables and detailed routes of the various mail coaches that wove a dense, speedy and efficient postal network between the cities of Germany as well as between the states of Europe.[41] Euchel, *Hame'asef*'s first editor, complained about his heavy work load and the constant backlog, which meant it sometimes took a whole year before he could reply to the letters he received.[42] The first question posed to the journal's readers brought over forty replies to the editors within a short time, and they had to apologize to the readers ("young men of our nation, the enlightened among our people") and inform them that only a few of the replies would be published.[43]

The writer of one the first letters to arrive at the home of Sanwil Friedländer in response to *Nachal habesor*, urged the members of Chevrat Dorshei Leshon Ever to volunteer to teach in a new school that would be founded at their initiative in Königsberg. In his view, this step would enhance their public prestige and show they were capable of actually changing reality, not only preaching the need for change. But he also praised Dorshei Leshon Ever for their revolutionary action, since until then Jews had had scarcely any means of presenting their ideas to a broad audience. Very few could afford to print books, and even then they had to overcome the barrier of internal censorship in the form of rabbinical approbations. Now, thanks to Dorshei Leshon Ever, the reality had changed, and "every enlightened Jew who seeks God and loves man" could freely and openly publish his thoughts and proposals: "For who or what can stop him from placing his thoughts on a tablet?"[44]

Chapter Nine
The Maskilim: A Group Portrait

By constructing Moses Mendelssohn's image as a great teacher, a trailblazer, and the embodiment of the Haskalah, historical memory and research have made it difficult to fully depict the nature and scope of the maskilic republic. Mendelssohn's personality eclipses the "Berlin Haskalah" chapter in the sociocultural historiography of German Jews in the second half of the eighteenth century, and appropriates to itself the entire story of the Haskalah. In the predominantly accepted version, the major action of the Haskalah took place in the lively salon held in Mendelssohn's home, at 68 Spandau in Berlin, bustling with many, Jews and non-Jews alike who visited it. It is no wonder, then, that in 1856, when Moritz Oppenheim, the Jewish-German artist with an emancipatory vision, wanted to present the Mendelssohnian era as the quintessence of German-Jewish tolerance, he painted his famous, popular picture of Lessing, Lavater, and Mendelssohn seated around a chess board in his drawing room.[1]

In Mendelssohn's Salon

In the chapter entitled "The Teacher," the fifth in the impressive, most complete biography of Mendelssohn written to date, Alexander Altmann depicted the circle of "Mendelssohn's disciples." He named them one after the other, in the order of their appearance in the Berlin philosopher's salon. The first was the physician Marcus Herz, a student of Kant's and the husband of the well-known salon hostess Henriette de Lemos. Herz was followed by David Friedländer, the teacher; Isaac Satanow, the printer and author from Poland (1732–1805); and Shlomo Dubno, who taught Joseph, Mendelssohn's son, Hebrew, and encouraged Mendelssohn to publish his translation of the Pentateuch. The next to enter Mendelssohn's salon, according to Altmann's narrative, were the poet and Hebrew linguist Naphtali Herz Wessely; the early maskil and *dayan* from Minsk Baruch Schick of Shklov; Herz Homberg (1749–1841), also a tutor in Mendelssohn's home, who was very active in the field of education in the Austrian kingdom; Aaron Friedenthal of Jaroslav, who worked on the *Bi'ur* project—the German translation of and commentary on the Prophets—and returned to his home in Galicia to serve as a teacher in the new Jewish schools; the physician Aaron Joel of Halberstadt (1747–1813), who apparently hoped to find a livelihood in Berlin with Mendelssohn's help; the Lithuanian-German philosopher Solomon Maimon (1753–1800); Joel Brill (1762–1802); and Isaac Euchel (1756–1804), both tutors and editors of *Hame'asef*.[2]

This model of the teacher and his twelve disciples, at first attentively listening to his teaching and then spreading it among the multitudes, tries to put across the idea that it was this direct bond between the "disciples" and the teacher that united the Haskalah movement. Although Altmann does not conceal in his description the fact that they did not form a homogeneous group; from the moment they became associated with Mendelssohn, on their first visit to his home, they accepted the torch of the Haskalah that he had lit and spread its light far and wide. In this approach, Mendelssohn's most important biographer was following a longstanding tradition in Jewish historiography and in the Jewish collective memory of the modern era, a tradition that identified the Haskalah as Mendelssohn's creation, as a movement that operated under the leadership of this "Jewish Socrates." According to this tradition, Mendelssohn was both the rabbi and the founder of the movement, and taught many pupils—known as "Mendelssohn's disciples"—who followed in his footsteps and widely disseminated his teachings.

Peter Gay has defined the European eighteenth-century enlighteners as one small family of *philosophes*, a "small camp" with common beliefs and aims, and has attempted to reconstruct the "family ties" and mutual relations that prevailed among them. At the same time, Gay sketched a more complete picture of the Enlightenment movement, as a whole army flying a common flag, with the philosophers in the center, surrounded by various divisions and a public of consumers, who together created the literary republic of the Enlightenment.[3] In contrast, the Jewish collective of the Enlightenment is usually seen as a kind of maskilic "house of study," a yeshivah or a Hasidic "court," at the center of which there is a teacher, a rabbi, or a *tzadik*. The content of study differs somewhat from traditional religious studies; it has been secularized and its main characters have been replaced by the maskilic philosopher and his pupils, thirsting for knowledge, who sit at his feet. "The first pioneers of the Haskalah," historian Simon Dubnow stated, "were all students of Mendelssohn's."[4] According to Dubnow, the first editors of *Hame'asef*, Isaac Euchel and Mendel Breslau, were Mendelssohn's disciples. He totally ignored the fact that Breslau, a resident of Königsberg, was not among those who frequented Mendelssohn's "court," nor is there any evidence of a direct tie between the two men. Simon Bernfeld, not concealing the analogy with the Hasidic court, was able to provide a precise description of how "Mendelssohn generally sat upon his chair, surrounded by his young friends, who breathlessly awaited his every word; every sentence he uttered seemed to them to be a prophecy . . . they usually asked his counsel in the same manner as men would normally turn to God."[5]

In actual fact, the maskilim who were Mendelssohn's contemporaries deliberately promoted their self-image as "Mendelssohn's disciples." They effusively employed every epithet, epigram, and proverb at their disposal to express their sweeping adoration of their exalted teacher. They described their relations with him based on the model of the relations between a rabbi and his pupils, and related to his dying as to the death of a *tzadik*. They shaped their own image as men supported by Mendelssohn who had been commanded by him, as his consummate disciples, to cherish his teaching and his legacy and to follow in the paths he had paved.[6] The maskilim related to Mendelssohn as the source of their inspiration and nurtured the myth that he was "the great light," sent by God to redeem His people.[7] In 1789, a bust of Mendelssohn, sculpted by Anton Tassaert, had already been installed in the board room of Chevrat Chinukh Ne'arim, the society responsible for Berlin's modern Jewish school.[8] David Friedländer, one of the school's founders, introduced himself throughout his life as one of Mendelssohn's disciples, and even asked to have that epithet carved on his tombstone.[9] The editors of *Hame'asef*, at least the last ones, acceded to Friedländer's demand that he be regarded as Mendelssohn's heir with feelings of esteem. In a paean composed in his honor, they represented him as the defender of Mendelssohn's legacy, as his heir and faithful follower: "In his shadow, you sat . . . gathering the treasures of his wisdom . . . as a babe suckles at the breast, you imbibed of his knowledge. There he taught you the right path to follow, you are happy, David, having observed his commandments, and we are happy in you, his picture before our eyes."[10] This self-image of "Mendelssohn's disciples" was also accepted by maskilim in Eastern Europe in the nineteenth century. Nearly one hundred years after Mendelssohn's death, Abraham Baer Gottlober, a prominent member of the Haskalah movement in Russia, could declare that all maskilim were his disciples: "had it not been for R. Moshe ben Menachem [Mendelssohn] of blessed memory . . . none of us would be here."[11]

We need to ascertain, therefore, what actually took place in Mendelssohn's salon and what exactly was the nature of the nearly daily cultural and social happenings there. Was it the major scene of the Haskalah's events? Were the foundations of the new literary republic laid there? And no less important, what was the connection between the Mendelssohnian salon and the society of young maskilim founded in Königsberg in the winter of 1782?

The replies to these questions expand the social sphere of the Haskalah in the 1780s and sharpen its contours. They also create a certain balance between the excessive weight assigned to Mendelssohn the philosopher in the existing picture of the Haskalah and the decisive influence of the young men who launched the cultural revolution of the Haskalah. It is true that many made the pilgrimage to the house on Spandau Street to spend some time in the company of the renowned, greatly revered philosopher and to hear him speak. Mendelssohn's salon was open to all—Jews and non-Jews, wealthy merchants from the Berlin elite, casual visitors, men and women, rabbis and talmudic scholars from Poland, German academics, physicians, and many, many others. Hardly any foreign scholar or respected tourist, arriving in Berlin on his grand tour, missed the opportunity to visit it and see one of the city's special attractions: the "Jewish Socrates." "Everyone coming to Berlin honored him by paying him a visit, diplomats and nobles traveling from their countries to tour the country, to see new things and valuable objects, will not pass many days in Berlin before visiting his home," Euchel testified effusively.

In 1772, for example, August Hennings of Copenhagen, later to become one of Mendelssohn's admirers and supporters, visited Berlin and, armed with a letter of recommendation, hastened at once to the famous house. The economic and intellectual elite of Jewish Berlin made a particularly strong impression on him. He was especially dazzled by the high living standards of the Itzig and Ephraim families, the beauty and musical talent of the women, and the perspicacity of scholars and physicians like Friedländer, Herz, and Bloch. He was enthralled by the special atmosphere of Mendelssohn's home, where he met quite a few learned intellectuals (*Männer von Geist und Bildung*), some, like him, visitors to Berlin.[12] Many members of the Enlightenment's literary republic in Germany's cultural sphere of influence, like Hennings and others, freely frequented Mendelssohn's home. According to Henriette Herz, a regular visitor, most of the guests arrived without an advance invitation, creating a considerable burden on Fromet Mendelssohn, the hostess, who invariably served them refreshments. Henriette emphasized the distinction between the open house of a scholar, like Mendelssohn's, and the closed, exclusive "salon," which hosted only invitees from high society and had many women among its hostesses and guests. She herself presided over a salon of this type in her home after her marriage to the philosopher and physician Marcus Herz.[13]

Lengthy discussions were held in Mendelssohn's home, on subjects ranging from the world of literature to philosophical questions of particular interest to him—the natural religion, the perfection of man, the fundamentals of morality, and others.[14] Mendelssohn was unquestionably the most famous Jew of the eighteenth century, and since he was a social creature by nature, he never refused to receive anyone who wished to visit him. The more famous he became, the greater the stream of visitors, and some would be waiting for him when he arrived home from work at the business where he was employed.

Euchel, his biographer and great admirer, trying to explain Mendelssohn's great force of attraction, asserted that "Anyone meeting him once and hearing him speak is beguiled by his affection, and greatly pleased by his admonitions and his instruction."[15] All the members of Mendelssohn's family shared the burden of providing hospitality to his visitors. Fromet and her children adjusted to living in a home frequented by many visitors and to a bustling, intensive social life.

The family evidently placed much emphasis on its social life, which took place in their drawing room as well as in the homes of friends and on joint visits to the theater. In a letter from Fromet to her husband, who was away from home on a trip to Königsberg in the summer of 1777, she reported to him at length and in detail about whom she had met, with whom she had drunk coffee, who had visited their home, and what plays she and her daughters had seen.[16] When their eldest daughter, Brendel-Dorothea, married Shimon Veit in 1783, she opened a modest reading society (*Lesegesellschaft*) in her home, intended for family members and close friends, who met once a week to read plays aloud. Henriette Herz and her husband Marcus, David Friedländer, and another of Mendelssohn's children were invited to this society; Mendelssohn himself sometimes attended the meetings, when he was visiting his daughter and son-in-law, and everyone then waited expectantly to hear what he had to say.[17] Solomon Maimon, who would stroll through the streets of Berlin with Mendelssohn, discussing philosophical questions about which they disagreed, described him as a man of society and a brilliant conversationalist. In his view, Mendelssohn was endowed with the ability to know every man's mind, to perceive what he was thinking, and to adapt his conversations to his interlocutory, showing great tolerance and treating everyone amicably.[18]

On Saturdays and holidays, particularly on Friday evenings, only Jewish visitors came to Mendelssohn's drawing room. The subjects of their conversations included Talmud, the Hebrew language, Hebrew books, Jewish education, and the situation of Jews elsewhere in the world. Rabbis, talmudic scholars, and maskilim drank coffee and conversed or argued with the other guests. David Friedländer described a strident argument about the creation of the world according to Genesis. Mendelssohn sat listening without interfering or voicing his opinion, although the disputants were directing their words to the ears of the philosopher they so revered. Mendelssohn, Friedländer emphasized, was not in the habit of lecturing (as Marcus Herz did, for example, in courses on science and philosophy he gave in his home). He was content to play the role of host and guide, welcoming and encouraging his guests. He would sit in an armchair in the corner of the room, near the window, his eyes lowered, occasionally nodding, smiling, or speaking a single word. Sometimes, he would introduce a young visitor and publicly praise him for his wisdom.

One would never hear him utter an authoritative opinion or expound on a theory at these gatherings. Even Friedländer, "the consummate disciple," had to admit that Mendelssohn had no disciples in the normal sense of the word.[19]

In addition to his salon, which served as an open intellectual forum for visitors, most of whom were not Jews, Mendelssohn conducted his social and intellectual life in other circles as well. From the mid-1750s, he was a member of the inner circle of the Berlin Enlightenment republic. He was one of forty scholar and artist members of a reading society founded in 1755, which met once a week for coffee, reading journals, playing billiards, and conversing. On Sunday evenings, he was invited to the home of his friend, the publisher and writer Friedrich Nicolai, who also kept the open salon of a scholar. In 1783, he was admitted as an honorary member to the Wednesday Society, an elitist secret society of intellectuals, among whom were senior government officials, clergymen, physicians, and writers. The highly regarded periodicals of that German literary republic opened their doors to him, and he contributed quite a few articles and book reviews to them. Like the other members of that republic, Mendelssohn carried out much of his activity through the German Enlightenment's widespread social and intellectual network of correspondence, in the second half of the century. A reading of Mendelssohn's letters, which in addition to replies to questions about literature and philosophy, contain many reports about his personal condition and his trips, as well as regards to his friends, shows how deeply rooted he was in this republic.[20]

Within all this extensive activity in which Mendelssohn engaged for nearly thirty consecutive years, he of course also set aside some room for meetings with Jewish maskilim. However, Altmann's portrayal of "twelve disciples," taking their inspiration from Mendelssohn and going out at his behest to disseminate the Haskalah, can be quite misleading. This was not a cohesive group, and certainly its members did not represent the Haskalah movement. Some of them only incidentally, and for a brief time, were in Mendelssohn's orbit, and the attempt to present them as a closely knit group of disciples is quite contrived. The early maskil Baruch Schick, for example, only came to Berlin in 1777 for a few months to print his Hebrew scientific writings.[21] Even Isaac Euchel, who spent several years of his youth in Berlin, made an appearance in Mendelssohn's salon like any other casual visitor, when he was on his way from Königsberg to Copenhagen in the summer of 1784. When he arrived in Berlin, he was already famous in the circle of maskilim as the founder of Chevrat Dorshei Leshon Ever and as the editor of *Hame'asef*, and hence was given an especially warm reception.[22] The physician Aaron Joel of Halberstadt came to Mendelssohn with a letter of recommendation from Immanuel Kant, but returned to his position as the doctor of the burial society in the Königsberg community.[23] Solomon Maimon's visit to Mendelssohn's home was a formative, fascinating experience for him, but he very soon left Mendelssohn and his friends, entered the world of philosophy and distanced himself from both the maskilim and Jewish society.[24]

These men, described as a group, had hardly any contact with one another, since most of their visits to Mendelssohn's home were far apart in time. The most prominent encounter centered on the *Bi'ur* project, which brought Mendelssohn, Dubno, Wessely, Homberg, and Friedenthal together.[25] Only four of the twelve "disciples"—Friedländer, Herz, Satanow, and Wessely—resided permanently in Berlin, near the Mendelssohnian "court," and were regular visitors to it. But these four can hardly be called a group. Marcus Herz was a wealthy, well-known physician, proud of the fact that he had been Kant's student, who frequented the Berlin salons and high society. In contrast, the poor, ascetic maskil from Podolia, Isaac Satanow, devoted his life to writing and printing books in Hebrew. It is very doubtful whether the relations between the two were those of members of a close-knit group; if there were any relations at all between them, Herz would probably have filled the role of Satanow's patron.

Mendelssohn's drawing room, then, differed greatly in its aims and patterns from the organization the young Königsberg maskilim strove to establish in 1782. It is not surprising that Mendelssohn's drawing room and the other societies to which he belonged engaged the interest of his amazed contemporaries and of historians studying the roots of the process of Jewish integration in Europe. Although on several occasions doors were closed in his face, the fact that Mendelssohn was accepted into the German "elite of the intellect" attested to the social, religious, and national neutrality of the intelligentsia and the surprising possibility that "some of [Jewish society's] members were, in some aspects of their existence, transplanted to a common social-cultural milieu with non-Jews."[26] This social neutrality, albeit always partial and very limited, may have been a vital element in the narrative of the exit from the ghetto,[27] but it cannot tell the full story of the cultural revolution that took place in those same years and places. The neutral societies were open to very few Jewish intellectuals, and Mendelssohn's mixed drawing room and the discussions that took place in it were unable to provide an appropriate forum for the formation of the Jewish maskilic republic and the dissemination of its message. In contrast to Chevrat Dorshei Leshon Ever, no voices arose from the Berlin drawing room in an effort to mobilize Jewish public opinion and to shape an intellectual leadership that would constitute an alternative to the rabbis. Moreover, it was totally lacking in revolutionary zeal.

"We are young in years, love morals and knowledge, and lend our ear to hear the truth from any who speak it"—thus the Dorshei Leshon Ever introduced themselves to their readers, alluding to the multidirectional potential inherent in this unprecedented event—the establishment of a new Jewish cultural space.[28] In Königsberg they organized into a reading society of Jewish intellectuals only, who were critical of their people's culture and cherished truly transformative goals. They used rhetoric intended to mobilize, propagandize, and galvanize ("rise up!" "revive!" "build!" "awaken!").[29] From the outset they aspired to expand their ranks, to reach as broad an audience as possible, and openly competed for Jewish public opinion by writing and publishing a journal. In marked contrast to Mendelssohn's drawing room, the sphere of their activity was not limited to the four walls of the room in which members of Königsberg's Jewish "reading society" met, nor did it center on a renowned personality; instead, it extended along lines of communication set up between the writers and readers of *Hame'asef*.

Circles and Boundaries in Maskilic Society

Who were the maskilim that became members of the new literary republic? How many people filled the ranks of the Haskalah movement in the last two decades of the eighteenth century? In actual fact, beyond the twenty or so maskilim that we know fairly well, our knowledge is rather sparse. Very little of their extensive correspondence has been preserved, no archives of the maskilic societies or the *Hame'asef* editorial board are extant, and there were also active maskilim who deliberately tried to hide their identity.

We can use two sources to measure the diffusion, scope, and geographical boundaries of the Haskalah: the number of subscribers to the *Bi'ur* project and the number subscribing to *Hame'asef*.[30] However, most of the 515 subscribers to Mendelssohn's German translation of the Pentateuch (172 from outside the German states, 21 Christians) were consumers of the Haskalah, a sympathetic, supportive outer circle surrounding the Jewish literary republic. Those merchants, bankers, industrialists, accountants, and physicians and their families from the Jewish elite (118 residents in Berlin, 48 in Königsberg, 49 in Frankfort, and 53 in Copenhagen) constituted a cultural bourgeois public interested in a translation of the Bible into high German. Steve Lowenstein's exacting research shows that the Berlin subscribers to the *Bi'ur* came from a high socioeconomic level, and he identifies the upper crust of the Berlin community on the list. It is not surprising, then, that the list also includes eleven women (from Berlin, Vienna, Copenhagen, and Königsberg), most of them from the social elite; since women were very fluent in German, and for some it was their mother tongue, they were naturally interested in a useful German translation of the Bible. What is surprising, however, is the impressive list of fifty-four Jews from Polish and Lithuanian communities, among them four chief rabbis (including the rabbi of Nesvizh, the town of Solomon Maimon's birth), and one woman, Golda Shiskat of Vilna. It was probably Shlomo Dubno who succeeded in signing up these subscribers from Eastern Europe. This literary project, which he represented as a traditional work above any suspicion, was particularly dear to him. Even if some among the 515 subscribers were in favor of the cultural change that the Bi'ur represented and wished to see it carried forward, probably only a very few went to any lengths to promote the cultural revolution beyond making a financial contribution, in the form of a total purchase of 750 copies.[31] This is certainly true of other useful books published by the Haskalah in the 1780s, such as the German translations of the prayer book that came out in Königsberg and Berlin in 1786. For example, 188 men and women subscribed in advance to Euchel's translation, printed in Latin letters, and 416 subscribed to Friedländer's translation, printed in Hebrew letters. About 10 percent of all the subscribers to these two translations were Jewish women. In the translators' view, these educated women, who had been acculturated to a great extent, were in need of an appropriate German translation to help them understand and emotionally identify with the texts. There were 384 subscribers to the German translation (in Hebrew letters) of the five scrolls, printed by Aaron Wolfsohn and Joel Brill in 1789. The best seller was Mendelssohn's translation of the Book of Psalms, published along with Brill's commentary, in 1791: 705 people, who together ordered 1,013 copies, subscribed to it in advance. The purchasers of these translations benefited from the fruit of the maskilim's labors, but they themselves sympathized with the Haskalah only from the outside. They were members of the outer circle of the maskilic republic, whose financial contribution enabled the inner circle of writers to exist.[32]

Many of the 272 subscribers to Hame'asef from 1785 to1788 also belonged to the circle of those who only sympathized with the Haskalah and its aims. Nonetheless, some of them were the maskilim themselves—members of Chevrat Dorshei Leshon Ever and authors who contributed their writing to the periodical.[33] This group was defined as: "Dear men and women, who have subscribed to the issues of Hame'asef, and have given their support to those who collect poems and letters, and engage in their work publishing and distributing everywhere." Only seven of the subscribers were Christians (among them the Berlin publisher Friedrich Nicolai and the Danzig library). They were widely dispersed geographically: 57 in Berlin, 28 in Königsberg, 26 in Vienna, 17 in Amsterdam, 17 in Copenhagen, 17 in Prague, 5 in Strassbourg, 5 in Shklov, 3 in Vilna, and others. The only woman subscriber was Fanny Arnstein (1757–1818), daughter of the Berlin millionaire Daniel Itzig and wife of the banker Nathan Arnstein of Vienna, Wessely's contact in that city during the Divrei shalom ve'emet controversy. "Madame Fanny Arnstein," as her name appears in the 1788 list of *Hame'asef* subscribers, was the same age as the Dorshei Leshon Ever. She also subscribed to the *Bi'ur* and maintained a scintillating literary salon in Vienna, frequented by members of high society, politicians, and men and women of culture.[34] One of the fourteen advance subscribers in Hamburg was Netanel Posner, the main figure in the sharp conflict with Rabbi Raphael Kohen in 1781. Two of the subscribers from the Shklov community in White Russia, the wealthy merchants and Russian court Jews Natan Notkin and Joshua Zeitlin (1742–1821), were also patrons of the small circle of scholars and intellectuals in Shklov.[35] Several subscribers were also distribution agents who purchased a relatively large number of copies: Herz Medelsheim of Strasbourg ordered twelve copies and Joel Wehli of Prague ordered twenty. In all, more than 300 copies of the periodical's issues printed in Königsberg in the mid-1780s were purchased. The editors claimed that many subscribers asked to remain anonymous, and that hence there were more subscribers than the number that appeared on the published lists. In any event, the subscribers to *Hame'asef*, through their financial support and the publication of their names, showed, more than the *Bi'ur* subscribers did, that they were advocates of the new literary project. The *Hame'asef* subscribers responded to the call of the manifesto, *Nachal habesor*, despite the fact that the periodical was obviously nonreligious in character and its editors were by no means representatives of the rabbinical elite that dominated the Hebrew book market. Hence the postal route through which more than 300 copies of *Hame'asef* passed is more helpful than any other source in showing how widely diffused the Haskalah was and in reconstructing its channels of communication. The span of the Haskalah extended in the 1780s from Vilna and Shklov in the east to Amsterdam and London in the west.[36]

Based on these data about all these subscribers (the overlap between those subscribing to the *Bi'ur* and those to *Hame'asef* is only partial), one can estimate, with a high degree of probability, that in the peak years of the maskilic republic's activity more than six hundred people—both sympathizers and activists—belonged to all of its circles. The readership of *Hame'asef* was certainly greater, since more than one reader read each of its issues. The inner circle of the "family of maskilim" itself—writers, entrepreneurs, and agents— was, of course, relatively small, but unquestionably larger and more diversified than the model of "Mendelssohn and his twelve disciples" would suggest. While it is no simple matter to sketch a complete collective portrait of that "maskilic family" by tracing those maskilim who made use of *Hame'asef*'s public forum and participated in the projects initiated by the society of maskilim, one can uncover several of its little-known members.

The oldest member of the maskilic republic (born sixteen years before Mendelssohn) was David Franco-Mendes, a Sephardi poet and dramatist from

Amsterdam, an early maskil and a zealous Hebraist, who collaborated on the compilation of a Hebrew encyclopedia entitled *Ahavat David*. On Wessely's recommendation, Dorshei Leshon Ever wrote to him as soon as the society was founded, in the spring of 1783, asking that he take an active part in their periodical. Franco-Mendes immediately replied in the affirmative, wishing every success to the young men from Königsberg who had founded, in his words, an "academy" of learned Jews. After six years of close collaboration, when he was already seventy-six years of age, they accorded him the status of a full member of Chevrat Dorshei Leshon Ever, and he acknowledged this honor in an emotional letter of thanks.[37] Franco-Mendes, however, was an exception, both because of his advanced age and the fact that he was a Sephardi Jew.

The more typical members of the maskilic republic were young students and tutors, for whom the Haskalah offered a chance to break out of the restricting boundaries of traditional Ashkenazi culture. Shimon Baraz of Königsberg, for example, was one of the most ardent and assiduous activists of Chevrat Dorshei Leshon Ever. An educator who felt compelled to work toward the introduction of reforms in Jewish education, he regularly contributed to *Hame'asef* until his premature death in 1787.[38] David of Hanover read *Hame'asef* even before he reached the age of twenty, and yearned to join the society of maskilim to free himself of the restrictions placed on him by his teachers and close associates to keep him from neglecting his Torah studies.[39] Baruch Lindau (1759–1849), also one of the first to respond to the call put forth in *Nachal habesor* and to join Chevrat Dorshei Leshon Ever, was from Hanover. He moved to Berlin, where he was employed as a private tutor, occasionally wrote poetry and popular Hebrew articles on science, and was a key activist in Berlin's maskilic society.[40] David Theodor, born in Schotland near Danzig, began to study medicine in 1779 and was an admiring student of Kant's in Königsberg. One of the lesser known members of Chevrat Dorshei Leshon Ever, he participated in *Hame'asef* and served as one of its agents, signing up subscribers and selling books published by the Chevrat Chinukh Ne'arim press in Berlin.[41] Another student, Elias Ackord (born in 1757), arrived in Königsberg from Mogilev in White Russia in 1778 and later moved to Berlin to study medicine, where he internalized the values of the Enlightenment and became an admirer of Mendelssohn. After 1783 he returned to Eastern Europe where he worked as a doctor in Warsaw. There he took part in a public debate on the status of Polish Jews held in the years before the end of Polish independence. He advocated religious tolerance according to the Lessing-Mendelssohn model and proposed that Jewish schools of the kind he had seen in Berlin be established.[42]

Many maskilim came to Germany from East European communities; the best known among them, Solomon Maimon. Another was Shabbtai of Janov, who came from Poland to Berlin where he became the administrative director of the Hebrew printing house of the Freischule.[43] At the end of the 1780s, Gedaliah Moshe, the son of a rabbi from Western Poland, joined the later *Bi'ur* project. In 1805, while working as a teacher in Stockholm, he was asked to run a school in Copenhagen structured according to the Berlin Freischule model.[44] Menahem Mendel Lefin (1749–1826), born in Satanow in Podolia, traveled frequently between Germany and Russia. In the 1780s he spent some time in Berlin, where he met Mendelssohn, and then returned to Poland. Lefin, a maskil, wrote in Hebrew and Yiddish under the patronage of the Polish aristocrat and statesman Adam Czartoryski. His Hebrew adaptation of the Swiss Tisso's book on medicine and popular healing, entitled *Refu'at ha'am*, was a best-seller in the Jewish book market of Eastern Europe. At the beginning of the nineteenth century, maskilim from the Brody and Tarnopol communities organized around Lefin in Galicia.[45] Judah ben Zeev (1764–1811), a maskil active primarily at the turn of the century who played an important role as a writer and editor in the printing houses established in various Haskalah centers, came to Berlin from Poland only after Mendelssohn's death and from there continued to Potsdam, Breslau, and finally to Vienna.[46]

David Friedrichsfeld (1755–1810) was a young man when he was sent to Berlin to study Torah in one of the houses of study in the city supported by wealthy Jewish families. To his joy, he was introduced to Mendelssohn, but it was Wessely with whom he became closely associated, and later wrote his mentor's biography, entitled *Zecher tzadik*. In Wessely's home, too, a salon of scholars was held, and on Saturdays and holidays young men came there to discuss literature and linguistics. Friedrichsfeld was a regular visitor to this salon until he moved to Amsterdam in 1781, and in the 1790s he was one of the leaders of the struggle for Jewish emancipation.[47] From Alsace, young Moses Ensheim of Metz arrived in Berlin and became a private tutor to Mendelssohn's children. After he returned to his home community, he sent several brief reports to *Hame'asef* on debates held during the French Revolution on the legal status of the Jews.[48] In 1782, Mendelssohn hired Josel Pick of Reichenau in Bohemia as a tutor for his children, after Herz Homberg left this position to engage in widespread educational activity on behalf of the government in various communities of the Austrian empire. From Berlin, Pick moved to Breslau, and in both cities was a leading member of the society of maskilim and a distributor of their books.[49]

Joseph Ha'efrati of Tropplowitz (1770–1804), who was born in Upper Silesia and lived in Prague in the 1780s, joined the circle of maskilim, contributed articles and poems to *Hame'asef* and gained some fame as the author of the biblical play *Meluchat Shaul* (Saul's Kingdom), printed in Vienna in 1794.[50]

Isaac Satanow's son Dr. Shlomo Schöneman, who worked as a physician in Driesen, wrote a popular chemistry book and published a new edition of Moses Hayim Luzzato's play *Layesharim tehilah* (In Praise of the Honest).[51] Chaim Kesslin, a teacher and scholar of the Hebrew language who was born in Berlin and lived in Hamburg and Stettin, wrote a grammar book, *Maslul bedikduk leshon hakodesh* (A Path in the Holy Language), which was widely circulated.[52] In 1791, Joseph Baran, a key figure in the Berlin circle of writers—a supporter of maskilim as well as a scholar, author, and translator—passed away. He apparently was the scion of a wealthy family, but very little is known about him. The editors of *Hame'asef* printed a moving eulogy upon his premature death, presenting him as a maskil and scholar who had died in the throes of his creative work: "He so indefatigably persevered in much toil and study that he weakened his body, contracted tuberculosis, and died. Many mourned the passing of a dear colleague such as he, our hearts bemoan the fact that an enlightened friend and loyal comrade was taken from us, and also that a tree was felled whose fruit provided much wisdom and moral lessons to our brethren and our periodical, *Hame'asef*."[53]

This partial list represents close to two hundred maskilim identified as activists in the Haskalah movement in the sixteen years between 1782 and 1797. Among them were writers, printers, teachers, book distributors, physicians with a bent for literary or community activity, and official members in the society of maskilim. About two-thirds of them lived in Germany or at least spent some time there, while the rest were dispersed in Jewish communities in Europe outside of Germany. The major centers were, of course, in the Prussian communities—Berlin, Königsberg, and Breslau—where in various years the *Hame'asef* offices were located. However, individual maskilim or small maskilic circles also existed in other cities, such as Hamburg, Dessau, Hanover, Mainz, Cassel, Fürth, Frankfurt-on-Main, Frankfurt-on-Oder, Copenhagen, Stockholm, Trieste, Prague, Vienna, Metz, Strasbourg, London, Amsterdam, Shklov, Warsaw, and Vilna.[54]

One particularly striking aspect of the republic of maskilim was its great mobility. Like the religious scholars and early maskilim, these maskilim also moved from place to place, searching for a livelihood and a residence. Their sojourn in Berlin, if any at all, was for most of them only temporary. The majority belonging to these circles were far away from the neutral settings, like the coffeehouses of scholars, the salons of Berlin or Vienna at the end of the century, or the German reading clubs. In her study of the high-society salons in Berlin, Deborah Hertz found only eight Jewish men, including Mendelssohn, Friedländer, and Marcus Herz, who belonged to the group of maskilim.[55] Between 1796 and 1783, ten Jews, 3 percent of all the participants, were contributors to the German *Berlinische Monatsschrift*: Mendelssohn, Friedländer,

Herz, Maimon, Lazarus Bendavid, Saul Ascher, and the physicians Michael Friedländer (Euchel's private pupil), David Oppenheim, and Marcus Bloch.[56]

The list of Jewish participants in another German periodical, *Berlinische Archiv der Zeit und ihres Geschmacks*, reveals a similar picture in the last five years of the century. Here, too, Herz, Friedländer, Bendavid, Ascher, and Maimon were among the contributors. Other participants were the musician and composer Carl Bernhard Wessely (1768–1826); Abraham Abramson (1754–1811), a medalist at the royal court and a member of the Prussian Academy of Arts; and two representatives of the Berlin circle of romantic salons at the end of the century—Ludwig Robert, Rahel Levin-Varnhagen's brother, and Esther Gad Bernard (1770–1820), a writer and poet born in Breslau, whose fight for women's intellectual rights won her the epithet "the second Wollstonecraft" (after the name of her contemporary, the English author and pioneer in the struggle for equality of the sexes), and who, in 1796, converted to Christianity.[57]

Two Groups of Maskilim

The Jewish intellectuals and writers at the end of the eighteenth century can be divided into at least two subgroups that sometimes overlapped; Mendelssohn, Friedländer, and Herz, for example, moved between them.

The members of the first group aspired to be a prominent part of a German-Jewish intelligentsia in the neutral settings, and hence they usually wrote in German for a general readership. Their commitment to the Jewish religion became more tenuous over time, and quite a few of them embraced deism as a universal religion of reason, which places no barriers between Jew and non-Jew, or converted to Christianity (for example, Moshe Hirschel and Esther Gad Bernard). Many in this group were physicians, graduates of German universities, educated merchants who had received a modern education through the services of private tutors, and members of the learned professions. Nearly all of them were native-born Germans, who had already been extensively acculturated to the German language and culture, as the privileged offspring of the elite of merchants and industrialists or of bourgeois families with ambitions to gain social mobility for their sons. The growth of the Jewish intelligentsia in the eighteenth century was particularly evident in the vibrant cultural center of Berlin. However, Jewish writers, playwrights, and thinkers who maintained a close dialogue with European culture without being involved in the maskilic discourse also lived in cities like Hamburg, Königsberg and Breslau, or even outside Germany—in Vienna, Paris, and London.[58]

The members of the second group, in contrast, established maskilic frameworks that from the outset were intended for Jews only. They aspired to rehabilitate society and culture through internal Jewish literary and educational activity. Their voices were hardly heard in non-Jewish European frameworks; they wrote primarily in Hebrew, although they advocated the parallel study of the state language and culture; and they had a relatively moderate attitude towards the Jewish religion. If they were at all critical of it, their criticism was limited primarily to the rabbinical, in particular the Polish, leadership, and to protest against the fact that knowledge and culture was restricted to the Torah and the Talmud, and scarcely touched upon religious faith and the Halakhah. Many in this group were private tutors, employed in the homes of the wealthy, who engaged in writing prose and poetry. Among the activists of the Haskalah movement were young men who had only been superficially acculturated and whose cultural world was still deeply rooted in the religious culture and talmudic tradition. Nonetheless, they had broken out of this milieu and made their way to European culture, and with their clean-shaven faces and modern garb, most of them did not look much different from the members of the first group.

The maskilim were generally young men in their twenties and thirties. When Chevrat Dorshei Leshon Ever was founded in 1782, Mendelssohn was fifty-three and Wessely fifty-seven. They were an entire generation older than the members of the society, whose average age that year was about twenty-six. The overwhelming majority of the maskilim were born in the 1750s and '60s. There were even some who were not yet twenty, born at the end of the 1760s or the beginning of the '70s, but who asked to be received as members. "We are young in years," the members of Chevrat Dorshei Leshon Ever wrote about themselves, "and most of us are hard at work to earn our daily bread, some engaged in teaching boys and others in commerce."[59] The front page of the first issue of *Hame'asef* carried the emotional appeal of "a young man to Chevrat Dorshei Leshon Ever":

My brothers and friends, Dorshei Leshon Ever! If a young man, halting in speech, yet a boy, like myself, should appear before you, please do not be angry . . . for a society of maskilim have I now seen, and the sweetness of their company to taste I desire, if I should err, you may teach me, for although now I am insignificant compared to you, perhaps in the fullness of time I may become like you; so this time too, my brothers! Please do not scorn me.[60]

Very few of these young men were married, probably because they earned their living as private tutors, a legal status that prohibited them from marrying in cities like Berlin. Half were natives of Germany while the other half were young immigrants who had come there long before the inception of the

Haskalah, like the Jewish teachers who traveled westward from Poland. There were men among these immigrants, as well as among the native Germans, who had not been brought up by their own families. For example, Joel Brill who was probably born in Berlin, was from the age of nine raised in the home of the wealthy banker Aaron Yoresh, Heine Veitel Ephraim's son-in-law. Euchel was sent to Berlin from Copenhagen at the age of thirteen, after his father's death, to study Talmud under his uncle's supervision. Joseph Wolff of Dessau (1762–1826), in later years one of the more prominent members of the Dessau maskilic circle and one of the editors of the German-Jewish periodical, *Sulamith*, was about the same age when he arrived in Berlin, after his father's death, where he was raised by his uncle.[61] David Friedländer was sent to Berlin to study after his father lost all his money. Others ran away from their families because they were dissatisfied with the traditional curriculum and desired to expand their horizons and begin academic studies. That was the case not only with Solomon Maimon, but also Moses Ensheim of Metz, ben Zeev of Cracow, and Aaron Friedenthal of Jaroslav.

This group of men thirsting for knowledge came from the traditional society, from which the elite of *talmidei chakhamim* also emerged. But their future was transformed once they immigrated to Germany, learned German and were exposed to European culture. Since they were so young, cut off from their families and moved from place to place, they had to find patrons to employ them. As young men of letters, even though they lacked a formal education, they were fit to serve as private tutors in the homes of German Jews. These were teachers of a new type, increasingly in demand in the homes of the wealthy elite, since they were fluent in Hebrew and in religious literature as well as in European languages and science. Euchel was a teacher in the home of the family of the court Jew, David of Hanover, and later for the Friedländers of Königsberg; Ansheim taught mathematics in Mendelssohn's home; Homberg taught Hebrew there; Josel Pick replaced him; Joel Brill earned his living as a teacher in the home of David Friedländer; and others served in a similar capacity. Some of the maskilim found employment in Hebrew printing houses in Berlin, Breslau, Vienna, and Prague. Yet others who began as private tutors later were employed as clerks in the business houses of their patrons—a path like the one followed by Mendelssohn in Berlin a whole generation earlier. In any event, these positions assured them of the right to reside in Germany, a privilege that anyone who was not born into the rich families of the elite had a hard time obtaining, and even the rights of residence and marriage of those families were limited.

The maskilim enjoined the heads of the wealthier families to hire those private tutors for their children and to invite them to live in their homes. Moreover, they also demanded that they be treated with special respect, not with disdain, as apparently was sometimes the case. Josel Pick, in demanding that the heads of households employing tutors improve their attitude toward these teachers-servants, gave vent to feelings of frustration and affront:

It is fitting that every father who can afford to do so should seek out an intelligent, upright young man and take him into his home. But he ought not to regard him as one of the lesser servants in his house. Rather he should enter into an alliance with him and treat him with respect, for the sake of his children whom he entrusts to his care, for then the tutor will grow much fond of them, will diligently look after, and treat them amiably.[62]

These maskilim were motivated to seek forums of expression and supportive social settings, as well as to embark on new projects, particularly in the fields of education and literature, owing to several factors: their marginal standing in Jewish society in Germany; their precarious legal status, which often depended on their position that gave them a limited right of residence for the period of their service in wealthy homes; their employment in teaching; their inclination to engage in literary writing; and their ties to families undergoing intense acculturation to their German environment.

These immigrating maskilim were able to obtain assistance from maskilim who were long-time residents of Germany. For example, maskilim arriving in Berlin, like Solomon Maimon, could benefit from Mendelssohn's special status in that city. Mendelssohn recommended Maimon to rich Jews in the community who undertook to provide him with food and other basic needs. In this way, he became a regular guest at their dinner tables and enjoyed the vast libraries he found in their homes. When he left Berlin, Mendelssohn gave him a warm letter of recommendation. However, the gap between Mendelssohn and most of the maskilim who made pilgrimages to his home was all too evident. On Maimon's first visit to Mendelssohn's drawing room, he quaked. When he peeked inside, he nearly fled at once: "the manners and customs of the Berliners were strange to me, and it was with trepidation and embarrassment that I ventured to enter a fashionable house. When I opened Mendelssohn's door and saw him and other gentlefolk there, as well as the beautiful rooms and elegant furniture, I shrank back, closed the door, and had a mind not to go in."[63]

Maimon was well aware that the society of the wealthy families as well as that of most of the visitors to Mendelssohn's home, were far above his social standing. As a result, he soon found a "middle class" for himself, as he put it, comprising Jewish tutors who chose the dissolute lifestyle of young bachelors. Maimon was contemptuous of them because they were incapable of understanding the philosophy on which he lectured to them, and he soon quarreled with them and left their company. Nonetheless, he seemed more comfortable in a society in which he did not need to observe the niceties and manners of high society. Together with these young men, Maimon spent time at parties and taverns, went on excursions, and frequented houses of ill repute. Mendelssohn reproved him harshly for this behavior, after members of this group spread slanderous reports that Maimon was an impious profligate.

Mendelssohn was a patron, an interlocutor, and a mainstay for Maimon in the alien, hostile world in which he took his first steps in an attempt to close the cultural gap between himself and this world. However, when the issue of the maskilic initiative came up, for example, Mendelssohn was quite indifferent. Maimon had undertaken to translate "science books into Hebrew for the enlightenment of Polish Jews who are still living in the darkness."[64] The Berlin group of maskilim promised Maimon that it would see to it that the book was printed. In Mendelssohn's home, but without his direct intervention, a debate took place about whether it was preferable to translate a book of Jewish history or a book on the principles of morality and natural religion, which was David Friedländer's suggestion. Maimon himself, by the way, preferred to write a book on mathematics. Maimon wrote that when Mendelssohn was asked for his opinion, "he refrained from expressing his view, because he believed that whatever was undertaken in this line, though it would do no harm, it would also be of little use."[65] After his friends failed to provide the promised financial support, and the project foundered, Maimon complained to Mendelssohn, who did not offer him any real solution but only advised him to try to finance the project by endeavoring to obtain advance subscribers, which was the usual custom in the Hebrew book culture.[66]

Mendelssohn's somewhat disdainful attitude toward a young maskil is evinced, for example, in two letters relating to Joel Brill's request to print Mendelssohn's German translation of the Book of Psalms with the addition of Brill's commentary. In these letters, Mendelssohn referred to Brill as "a young man" and as "someone" without mentioning his name, and wrote that he had given him permission to translate only because he could not find the strength or the time to do this work himself. It is also apparent from Mendelssohn's reply that he feared Brill might not adhere to his original intent and would interpret it improperly. Brill dedicated the first volume of the translation, which came out in 1785, to Mendelssohn and referred to himself as the "youngest disciple" of the "light of our generation and the glory of his people." However, when the fourth volume appeared in 1790, after Mendelssohn's death, he dedicated it to Isaac Euchel, presenting him too as one of his teachers and mentors, who had led him to great achievements by serving as the exemplar of a militant maskil: "I shall remember your deeds of yore, when, despite all the hardships you bore, you fought the war of science tirelessly, until you embarked on the right path after your victory."[67]

There is no denying, of course, that the "family of the Haskalah" identified itself as being led by Mendelssohn and boundlessly revered him. The maskilim perceived him as an honored, albeit usually remote, father figure. Those who occupied a relatively low economic and social position in Jewish society, as young teachers and writers, felt very close to him. They basked in the great prestige that Mendelssohn enjoyed among non-Jews, in his brilliance as a philosopher, in his rational thought and his ability to preserve the halakhah and Jewish culture and to adhere courageously to his religion, although he was treated as an equal among equals in the very heart of the German intellectual elite. The maskilim nurtured their adoration for him and crowned him as the teacher and founding father of their movement during his lifetime, and even more so after his death. However, the relations between them and Mendelssohn were less those of teacher-students and more those of adored-adorers. It would be true to say that there was no real circle of "Mendelssohn and his disciples," but only a broad, open "league of admirers," whose ranks also included maskilim.

On January 11, 1786, a brief letter from Joel Brill in Berlin reached Chevrat Dorshei Leshon Ever. It informed them of Mendelssohn's death exactly a week earlier. "There is no peace, says the Lord, for the crown of glory has been taken from our head, woe unto us, for we are ruined!" Brill wrote in his letter of lamentation. He compared the death of the father of the Haskalah to the sudden disappearance of the biblical Moses who went up on Mt. Sinai: "For this is Moses, the man about whom we said under his shadow we shall live among the nations, we know not what happened to him, he suddenly left us early in the morning last Wednesday, a day of rebuke and castigation, my father, my father, the chariot of Israel and its horsemen! Here he has risen to the heights, and he is no longer with us, my wound is grievous, I can do nothing."[68] Chevrat Dorshei Leshon Ever hastened to publish a notice of mourning, in the *Hame'asef* issue of the month of Shevat. The words of this notice underscored the sense of loss the editors felt upon Mendelssohn's death, before the fruits of the cultural transformation were evident and before the project of Haskalah had been completed:

Daughter of my people, wrap yourself in sackcloth . . . proclaim a fast . . . your skies have darkened and your light is dimmed . . . the sun had gone down at noon! The days of peace have not yet arrived, years in which nothing is wanted have not yet come, and Moses, the man who raised us up out of the miry pit, from the deep waters of ignorance to the shrines of wisdom and knowledge, has left us.[69]

The maskilim, however, were not the only ones to mourn the death of the most famous, well-connected Jew of the eighteenth century. Newspapers and books in Germany published the news, sparing their readers none of the clinical details of his death, which had been furnished by Mendelssohn's physician, Marcus Herz. Hundreds attended his funeral, the Jewish community of Berlin closed its stores and places of business that day, friends composed lamentations and eulogies and began to collect donations to erect a monument in his memory in the Opera Square of the city that had been blessed with his presence.[70] To the scores of portraits, miniatures, etchings, medals, and sculptures of Mendelssohn created by well-known artists, which had made his likeness an icon of a Jewish intellectual and secular saint during his lifetime, now were added more paintings and portraits, some of which were engraved on china plates and on tea services.[71]

A grandiose memorial event held in Königsberg more than a year after his death marked the acme of the Mendelssohn cult. Chevrat Dorshei Leshon Ever succeeded in organizing an impressive concert, attended by the upper crust of Königsberg society, men and women, Jews and non-Jews. They all joined in lamenting the loss of this great man. The composer and conductor Carl Bernhard Wessely, Naphtali Herz Wessely's nephew, came from Berlin to compose the music for the cantata *Sulamith und Eusebia* based on Karl Ramler's poem. On May 9, 1787, about 500 people crowded together in the splendid main hall in Königsberg to listen to two Jewish singers—Bernice Itzig, who filled the role of Sulamith extolling Mendelssohn in the name of the Jews, and Johanna Seligman, in the role of Eusebia, extolling him in the name of the Christians. The cantata was performed by an excellent orchestra and a choir of twenty-seven students. The press covered this elegant affair, noted the impressive list of invitees, and emphasized the fact that the mayor had personally seen to it that order was maintained outside the hall, when one carriage after another arrived with the guests. At the end of the performance, after the applause, contributions were collected for Jewish and Christian orphans and medals were bestowed upon the artists. It was apparently Isaac Euchel, the founder of Chevrat Dorshei Leshon Ever, who went up on stage, on behalf of the society, to present silver medals coined by Abramson in Mendelssohn's memory to the two singers, and a gold one to the composer. For Euchel, the evening was not only one of the peak moments of Chevrat Dorshei Leshon Ever's activity in Königsberg, it was also one of the momentous events of his own life. Sitting in the audience was his adored teacher, the rector of Königsberg University, the philosopher Immanuel Kant. The press quoted him as saying that no one had managed to drag him into a concert hall or theater for the past eighteen years, but this was one event he did not want to miss. "I was such a close friend of Mendelssohn's," Kant said, "that I could not forgo attending this evening."[72]

Euchel could certainly have drawn much encouragement from this event, shared by Jew and non-Jew alike, which demonstrated the realization of religious tolerance and brought Chevrat Dorshei Leshon Ever to public notice. His personal ambition was to gain a university position, but it finally became clear to him in 1786 that even Kant's intervention would not suffice to open the doors of Prussian academia to him. Hence, he decided to exploit the momentum of the Enlightenment to lead a Jewish maskilic republic, which he had been forming and developing for the past three years. Now he strove to greatly expand its dimensions and the scope of its activity.

Chapter Ten
Euchel Establishes the Haskalah Movement

Moses Mendelssohn was the most famous Jew in the German Enlightenment republic, admired by Jews and non-Jews alike. Isaac Euchel eulogized him and wrote his widely circulated biography, which nurtured the Mendelssohn cult and Mendelssohn's image as the father of the maskilim. It also largely determined Mendelssohn's place for generations in the collective memory of the liberal Jewish camp. But Euchel was not a naive admirer. As an ideologue of the Haskalah, who believed it was the critical maskil mission to seek out the ills of Jewish society and remedy them on the basis of reason and humanistic values, he was not content to follow in Mendelssohn's path. In his view, the "theoretical writer" lacked initiative, for while he cordially received his guests in the drawing room of his home, he failed to deal properly with the urgent problems of the time.[1] And yet, the Mendelssohnian myth that he was instrumental in forging was for Euchel an important element in his self-identity as well as an additional means of reshaping the Jewish public sphere.

Euchel greatly revered the "Jewish-German Socrates," but it was he, more than anyone else, who built the Haskalah movement in the 1780s and brought its fullest flowering. He established institutions, planned actions, disseminated ideas, and in particular aspired to expand the boundaries of influence of the Haskalah's literary republic. In his writing, he made extensive use of the discourse of enlightenment. He believed in the supremacy of reason, humanism, aspiring to truth, and religious tolerance, and he held that men could and must shape their destiny through their own efforts with the help of talented educators. His attitude toward the traditional rabbis and scholars was charged with cynical, acrimonious criticism. On the other hand, he was imbued with profound religious feeling; he had respect and esteem for the ancient Jewish culture that engaged his interest as a researcher, commentator, and translator of the prayer book; and he contemptuously disapproved of shallow-minded heretics. He was the one who initiated quite a few of the steps taken by maskilim to foster the revolution of the Jewish Enlightenment, and he always did so out of the self-consciousness and sense of mission of an intellectual who is also a reformer.[2]

The Genesis of a Maskil

Isaac (Itzik) Euchel was a whole generation younger than Mendelssohn and Wessely. He was born in Copenhagen on October 17, 1756, to a family of merchants who had lived there from at least the beginning of the century.³ Like the Prussian cities of Königsberg and Berlin, from the early seventeenth century, as a result of the state's absolutist policy and its economic interests, Danish Copenhagen also boasted a relatively new Jewish community, which, in the 1780s, already numbered twelve hundred Jews. For a time, Copenhagen was the home of the family of Naphtali Herz Wessely—merchants with close ties to the Danish king, which, for business reasons, moved between Hamburg, Copenhagen and Berlin. Wessely himself moved from Copenhagen to Berlin in 1774. Mendelssohn's brother-in-law Joseph Guggenheim (Fromet's brother), and Moses Fürst, the husband of one of Fromet's sisters, also lived in Copenhagen. The number of Copenhagen Jews who subscribed to *Hame'asef* (17) and the *Bi'ur* (53) attests to the fact that some of them were sympathetic to the Haskalah and its aims. In the year of Mendelssohn's death, the Danish maskil Eliyakim Zoldin, printed a collection of elegies ("Woe to you, Berlin! City of mourning and desolation, a hero has fallen in you who taught the people of Judah warfare") with the title *Bekhi tamrurim* (Bitter Weeping).⁴

In those years, Euchel was no longer in Denmark. In 1767, his father had died, and when his mother became aware that he was a gifted student of Talmud, she began to cherish hopes that he would become a rabbi and join the scholarly elite. Since she had five children to support (the youngest, Yehiel Gottlieb, was born soon after her husband's death), she decided to send Isaac, even before his bar mitzvah, to study in Berlin. His uncle, Rabbi Masos Rintel of Hamburg, had for close to thirty years been one of the directors of the local *talmud torah*. Under his protection, Euchel lived in Berlin as a yeshivah student for five years (1769–73) and won high praise as a promising young prodigy.⁵ In an open letter to his childhood friend Joel Brill, Euchel wrote a fascinating personal testimony about the formative years of his adolescence in Berlin. It affords us a glimpse into the experiences of a youth about to undertake the role of a cultural revolutionary.⁶

Euchel formed a close friendship with the native-born Berliner, Joel Loewe (Brill), although Brill was his junior by five years (born in February 1762). Later the two became major activists in the Haskalah movement and cooperated in establishing the society of maskilim and in editing *Hame'asef*. In 1788, Euchel nostalgically recalled memories of their youth, but in particular, he referred to the changes that had occurred in both their lives. The significant turn that Euchel's life had taken, his success in breaking out of the strictures of traditional education into a world of light, science, and enlightenment, seemed to him almost miraculous, an achievement he would not have dreamed of in those far-off days in Berlin. Brill's path to the Haskalah seemed to be far less precarious, because he had spent his childhood in the care of a family of the economic elite. From the time he was orphaned at the age of nine, Brill lived in the home of Aaron Joresch, a wealthy banker, the father-in-law of Heine Veitel Ephraim, and a friend of Mendelssohn and Lessing. Aaron and his wife Reisel raised Brill as their own son for twelve years and provided him with regular schooling that included a European education.[7] In sharp contrast, Euchel, who was cut off from his family, experienced feelings of loneliness and despair: "I said to myself how good the life of this boy—he will grow into a man, while you will sink lower and lower, and will become a despised, worthless person. For what sort of life can a boy hope to achieve when he has no one to give him support?" He admitted that as an adolescent, he had been a rowdy "immoral youth": "my place was out of doors, like a ram I danced in the streets, young men saw me and approached me jubilantly, old men hid from me."[8]

In retrospect, Euchel would gladly have erased from his memory those days of youthful bawdiness and idleness: "They were no good, they ought not to be counted among the years of my life, they passed in emptiness and vain acts of deceit." He felt his uncle was to blame because he had vigorously opposed Euchel's desire to deviate from the restrictive bounds of religious study. As an adolescent, he was already sharply critical of the limitations and insularity of the traditional culture, and in particular of the dominance of the talmudic text. Euchel began to reveal a bent for languages and sciences, but his uncle prevented him from indulging in any "external learning," insisting that he persevere in his talmudic studies. His uncle was a *talmid chakham*, Euchel wrote in his autobiography, but he had no general education and did not even know how to read and write German. The uncle, who was aware of Euchel's desires and inclinations, cautioned him that he must study only Talmud and that all other areas were merely a waste of time.

Euchel was forced to taste the forbidden fruit of the Haskalah in secret, and in the company of Joel Brill he got some inkling of the activity of the circle of maskilim that centered on Mendelssohn. The two young men sneaked into his drawing room, where they breathed a fresh, enticing, and unfamiliar air: "We came to know this brilliant man, saw him, heard him speak, found pleasure in his writing, and both of us determined to adopt his ethics and to follow in his path."[9] Euchel recalls this chapter of his life in Berlin as a happy time, but these were the last months of his stay there. At the age of seventeen, he decided that he could no longer bear the burden of Rabbi Masos, who was demanding that he make the Talmud his sole preoccupation. Offering a pretext that his uncle accepted, he left Berlin. Euchel describes his lamentable state upon his departure from Berlin, very far from the yearned for enlightenment:

Fifteen years ago, at the age of seventeen I left here to wander about and to live in a foreign country without knowing what the future held in store for me. A youth shaken out and empty, with no knowledge of language or books, not even a trace of wisdom, I learned by rote, understanding nothing. And if I imagined I knew something of the Talmud, of the Bible I understood nothing; I was like a man who goes down to the sea in a boat with but one oar and no compass . . . I stood wretchedly on the road not knowing whether to turn left or right.[10]

Traditional education did not provide the life tools suitable for a young man like Euchel who had rejected the idea of continuing on the routine path of the scholarly elite. With typical maskilic rhetoric, Euchel tells how he reached the decision to devote his life to the intellectual studies that would pave his way to the "temple of reason" he strove to reach.

Euchel told Rabbi Masos that he intended to transfer to a yeshivah in Frankfurt-on-Main to continue his religious studies, but in fact he traveled to Westphalia where he earned his living as a private tutor (*Hofmeister*) for a rich Jewish family. For the first time in his life, he was independent and free to devote his leisure hours to an autodidactic study of nonreligious knowledge.[11] The cultural conversion that the young maskilim underwent was a crucial process in their lives, and Euchel publicly represented his own experience of conversion as a role model and encouragement for young readers. He portrayed his cultural conversion as a heroic tale of deliverance from an inferior economic, social, and cultural opening position, and a breakthrough into the world of Enlightenment. "With all my might and will, I shall explore the ways of wisdom," Euchel swore when he left Berlin. He called on others to follow the same path: "Hear this, young men, if it is your heart's desire to acquire Wisdom, arm yourself against every devil, like a prudent man approach her boundaries, persist at her doors, demand her tirelessly . . . and know that one day her gates will open before you." Euchel likened the passion for knowledge to the desire for a woman who does not respond at once: "Like the refusal of an intelligent maiden who clings to her lover, and yet seems to repel his advances, seals her ears so as not to hear the sound of his pleas, fails to reply to his words of ardor, all this in order to test his heart to find if his love is true."[12]

In 1776, a significant change occurred in Euchel's development as a maskil, when he moved to Hamburg and spent three years with Raphael Levi, an early maskil and scientist. During those years, Euchel studied sciences under the tutelage of this Jewish mathematician, physicist,and astronomer, who was a passionate seeker of knowledge and a devotee of science. In Hanover too, Euchel earned his living as a private tutor, this time in the home of the court Jew Meir Michael David. He tried to organize a small group of maskilim there, which would provide assistance to poor travelers and also hold lectures on Hebrew and the Bible.[13] In 1778, a year before Levi's death, Euchel was sent by Meir David to Königsberg to serve as a tutor to his grandchildren. That is how, at the age of twenty-two, he came to the city in which he would later develop, over the course of a decade, the organizational frameworks of the Haskalah movement in Germany. From the home of the David family, he moved to the home of Meir Friedländer, and in the 1781 winter semester began his studies at the university.[14]

For about five years, he studied Oriental languages, philosophy, and education. Euchel was one of the first Jewish students in German universities permitted to study not only medicine but the humanities as well. Königsberg, which attracted a relatively large number of Jewish students from Lithuania, Kurland, and Danzig, was exceptional in this regard: at the end of the 1780s, four Jews had completed their law studies there, and in 1791 one Jew completed his studies in philosophy. Two teachers who particularly influenced Euchel and also appreciated his talents were Professor Köhler, a lecturer in Oriental languages, and the renowned philosopher Immanuel Kant.[15] The encounter with the university milieu, one of the major centers of the German Enlightenment, gave Euchel his first opportunity to acquire a formal education, but it also provided him an entree into an intellectual circle comprising both Jews and Christians. According to Euchel, he fit into this circle and also made friends among both students and lecturers. Euchel's was one of the eighteen names of students who published, in honor of Kant, their greatly revered teacher, a congratulatory poem on the occasion of his appointment as rector of the University in 1786.[16]

Euchel was also the first Jew who had some chance of being accepted as a member of the junior teaching staff. Professor Köhler was about to retire and in February 1786, Euchel was proposed as a candidate for the position of temporary lecturer in Oriental languages. At the same time, the suggestion was made that he be granted a master's degree, a prerequisite for a teaching position. Representatives of the government in Königsberg asked the University Senate for a report on the candidate and perhaps also suggestions for other candidates. The senate turned to Professor Immanuel Kant, then dean of the faculty of philosophy, asking for his opinion. On February 20, Kant sent the faculty a letter of recommendation, stating that he did not foresee any special problems in relation to this appointment. He wrote that he knew Euchel as an outstanding student as well as the editor of a Hebrew periodical (*Hame'asef*), and since he would be teaching only languages, there could be no reason to fear that some problematic religious interpretations might find their way into his lectures.

But even during the month of March, things changed, and Kant altered his position, joining those opposed to the appointment of a Jew. Although the faculty of philosophy did regard him as an excellent student and extol his knowledge, he stated, the university's laws required candidates for the master's degree to take a Christian oath. Moreover, it was hard to believe that a Jewish teacher would refrain from introducing Jewish interpretation into his lectures, and this would be likely to incite arguments and hostility between Christians and Jews among the students and teaching staff. The university was not interested in such a risk of possible unrest and disorderly behavior that might tarnish its reputation. Moreover, Kant wrote, they had already found other candidates.

On May 24, 1786, a few days after Kant, now rector of the University, participated in the festive memorial concert for Mendelssohn, he sent Euchel the official negative reply that he had been granted neither an academic degree nor a position. In this letter, Kant apologized to Euchel, stating that, while it was true that the modern ideas of the enlightenment were now permitting things that had been forbidden in the past, the heads of the university were bound by the principles of the institution, and so long as these had not changed, only a Christian could receive the post of a lecturer. The affair was frustrating to Euchel and forced him to look for another source of livelihood, but the refusal never lessened the great admiration he felt for Kant throughout his life.[17]

Like Mendelssohn, whose election to the Berlin Academy of Sciences in 1771 had been vetoed by Frederick the Great, Euchel now learned that there were limits to the openness of the enlightened Germans. The realistic Mendelssohn had contented himself with his respected standing in the social settings that accepted him and the salon over which he presided in his home. He dreamed about a future when everyone would come to realize that restrictions of this sort ought to be eliminated.[18] Euchel, in contrast, channeled all his intellectual and social energy, as well as his faith in the values of the Enlightenment, into his efforts to transform Jewry and liberate it from the heavy hand of tradition. Kant closed the doors of Königsberg University to Euchel, but he also provided him with the definition of Enlightenment that guided Euchel in all his endeavors to reform Jewish society and culture. Kant characterized the process of becoming enlightened (*Aufklärung*) as the act of heroic self-liberation of a man capable of shaping his life in the light of critical reason and turning his back on the habits of the past and the dictates of traditional authorities, who had done their utmost to ensure people's ignorance and obedience. As a student of Kant, Euchel conceived of enlightenment in its fullest revolutionary meaning, as that transformative process of criticism, liberation, and the acquisition of intellectual autonomy, which, in his view, had been suppressed for generations.[19]

The Haskalah Project's First Initiatives

As soon as he arrived in Königsberg at the end of 1781, even before he thought about embarking on an academic career, Euchel tried to promote the establishment of a modern Jewish school. The plan was published in an open letter, *Sefat emet*, in which Euchel anonymously appealed to the public to persuade it of the urgent need to reform traditional education in the community. He harshly criticized the lack of a practical purpose in education, neglect of the Hebrew language, and persistence of the old cultural ideal of excelling only in the Talmud. The traditional teachers had forgotten that the Bible and the Mishnah were the source of the Talmud, he asserted. Nor was it enough to observe the commandments. Man, the crowning glory of Creation, also has a duty to gain intellectual and rational knowledge about his creator. If someone could afford to hire a private tutor to guide his children on this true path, all well and good, but the ideal solution would be to establish a community school.

Euchel did not wait for an incentive in the form of Joseph II's legislation; his proposal preceded Wessely's program for a revolution in Jewish education by several months. Although Euchel's plan concerned only the Königsberg community, on the local scene he was presumptuous in appealing directly to public opinion, thus circumventing the authoritative forum of the religious establishment. From this standpoint, his plan was unquestionably subversive. In *Sefat emet*, Euchel urged the community rabbi to abandon his indifference and to express his opinion about the state of education for Jewish youth.[20] Judging from Euchel's own testimony, his plan evoked a favorable response and the support of the Königsberg community, but the project actually failed and apparently was never implemented.[21] In any event, this unprecedented attempt to democratize the decision-making process in the community and the bold initiative of a young maskil to transform the community through the introduction of an innovative enlightened educational system tell us much about Euchel's ambitions and his resourceful strategies.

In marked contrast to the failure of his plan for a modern school, the journal *Hame'asef*, edited by Euchel and his colleagues in Chevrat Dorshei Leshon Ever, was very successful. From the very first issues, the editors endeavored to give their readers a sense of intimacy and of belonging to the literary republic that was taking shape. They addressed their readers directly ("to enlightened sons!"), printed their letters and the maiden works of young maskilim, shared editing and printing problems with them, sought their advice and opinions, posed riddles and questions about biblical commentary to them, and fired them with enthusiasm. The *Hame'asef* project was presented as an heroic endeavor to revive and rehabilitate Jewish culture, as a reformist project aimed at delivering this culture from a prolonged, profound crisis. And the readers did regard *Hame'asef* as the fulfillment of their wishes, made good use of the literary forum, and were glad to join the young literary republic. The letters these maskilim wrote are replete with expressions of a passionate desire for knowledge, of the sort employed by the early maskilim: "the journal you published has reached me; I saw it and was overjoyed! . . . how greatly I had yearned to see some among our people strive to remedy our language . . . nor was there anyone seeking the truth in matters of science and morals (for this I was sick at heart!) and we were like lost sheep that have no shepherd."[22]

Another avid reader, Baruch Lindau of Hanover, hastened to enlist in the camp of maskilim and later became one of the most prolific among them. With the editors and other readers, he shared his experience of initially encountering the innovative journal that offered texts so different from the familiar traditional writings: "I expectantly awaited your words, silent and amazed, until the fruit of your thoughts came into my hands, and with a joyful heart I tasted of your honeycomb . . . and so exhilarated was I that the blazing fire of passion aroused my desire to inscribe on a tablet my plans and ideas as they were engendered by the spirit of our people."[23]

All the issues of *Hame'asef* published in the first year contained high praise for dedication to science and knowledge and the benefits of rational thought. Joel Brill wrote a piece objecting to the belief in dreams and fatalism ("it is not becoming to a wise man to pay heed to dreams and illusions").[24] Euchel exhorted his readers to put their faith in Enlightenment, the supremacy of reason and the possibility of arriving at the absolute truth: "Reason [*Vernunft*] is a royal lady, she will cleanse propositions of all manner of opposition, will strip them of the tin of deception and leave them as pristine and pure as a solid mirror."[25] This sentence appears in a philosophical essay by Euchel, replete with Kantian concepts, which appears to be a coherent summary in Hebrew of a lecture he had heard Kant deliver at the university. However, this was an exception to the type of material that usually appeared in the journal. *Hame'asef* printed mainly original and translated poetry, proverbs, commentaries on biblical verses, riddles, clarifications on Hebrew grammar, historical biographies, and book reviews. The book section played an important role in the construction of the maskilic republic by informing readers of new books and providing a forum for literary criticism based on maskilic criteria. For example, the reviewer of Shlomo Dubno's *Birkat Yosef* criticized the author for having written his book with the rabbinical elite in mind, after he moved to Poland from Berlin, where he had initiated the *Bi'ur* project. He also scornfully pointed out all of the book's literary shortcomings. On the other hand, Rabbi Isaac Alexander of Regensburg earned enthusiastic praise for his German book *Solomon und Joseph II*, which advocated religious tolerance.[26]

The editors and readers of *Hame'asef* immediately realized that the journal had an unprecedented potential for publicizing books, expanding their distribution and promoting those that were germane to the maskilic discourse. *Ha-me'asef* was instrumental in perfecting the method of raising the money needed to cover printing costs. It served as an all-European center for signing up advance buyers, so that it was no longer necessary to travel from place to place. The rabbinical approbations, which had been helpful in boosting sales, were now replaced by the favorable reviews of the *Hame'asef* editors. For example, Chevrat Dorshei Leshon Ever collected advance subscribers for the new book that Elijah Morpurgo wanted to print.[27] They invested an even greater effort to promote Joel Brill's *Sefer Tehilim*, containing his commentary and Mendelssohn's German translation of the Book of Psalms. Euchel printed two sample pages of the book and warmly recommended it to his readers. He also made the services of *Hame'asef* agents in Hamburg, Frankfurt, Berlin, Königsberg, Copenhagen, and London available to all subscribers to the book. "My brethren, of the House of Israel!" Euchel called upon his readers: "Do not tarry, hasten to support the wise-hearted who labor mightily for your benefit and to do honor to our Torah, do not mistrust the pure of heart who ask you to support their [literary] work, for it is your benefit that they seek."[28] When the directors of the Berlin Freischule wanted to provide their students with a *musar* textbook, they published an open tender, offering a financial reward to the author of an original book on the subject. After Sanwil Friedländer visited David Oppenheim's extensive Judaica library, which was then in the possession of a rich Jew and was up for sale, the editors of *Hame'asef* came up with the idea that wealthy Jewish Berliners should jointly purchase it. It would be transferred to Berlin, housed in a special building, and become a cultural center, as an open reference library for scholars. This idea was never implemented, but the public pressure that the editors tried to apply to the wealthy Berliners and their attempt to enlist the journal in a fund raising effort for this purpose is of special interest.[29]

Hame'asef's optimism was manifested in its news section, which reported on historical changes and events, and was undoubtedly the forerunner of a modern newspaper. *Hame'asef*'s first issues contained detailed reports about the success of the Freischule in Berlin and its impact on improving the image of the Jew in the eyes of enlightened Christians.[30] The journal also printed an article about the tolerant policy of the bishop of Mainz, an attitude the writer hoped would lead to a drastic change in Jewish-Christian relations, one that would call for similar tolerance on the part of the Jews. The article, which employed redemptive, quasi-prophetic rhetoric, appealed directly to the reader, adopting the typical stance of a sermonizer:

Now, take heed, my brethren and my people! The Almighty has abolished the hatred of the nations toward us. Now you too must uproot evil thoughts about them from your hearts, so that each day they will become more merciful toward us, and shall enter into a covenant of peace with us as well as with our sons in the future. They shall no longer bear the sword of hatred, and will hammer their swords into ploughshares and their spears into pruning forks, and we shall enjoy peace and blessings.[31]

The cultural alternative that *Hame'asef* offered was expressed in the new concepts of the supremacy of reason, in the advocacy of science and learning, in faith in progress and tolerance, in the production and publication of new texts, and the expanded numbers of readers and writers. In its first year, *Hame'asef* scarcely referred to any adversary. Although both editors and readers were well aware that they were participating in an unprecedented, modern endeavor, they refrained from voicing any militant declarations.

However, in an article by Euchel, the chief editor, printed in the second issue, the rage of the critical maskil exploded with great intensity. Euchel issued a radical call for the maskilim to break away from the traditional rabbinical elite, lashing out at the ignorance of its scholars and asserting that they lacked the most basic knowledge about nature, the world, and human history. With cutting irony, he told of his personal experience in meeting and disputing with "many people, those who consider themselves men well-versed in the Torah, who think they are the fathers of all wisdom, while in truth they are empty and shaken out." They are scornful of all knowledge outside of the religion, but in Euchel's view, they know nothing of the Torah, which they study all their lives: "They open their mouths beyond measure, uttering words devoid of all reason." On this point, Euchel's attack seemed to echo the anti-clerical arguments of the Enlightenment and to reflect his own feeling that the maskilim were being threatened:

They have made no attempt to understand, all of their thoughts deviate from the path of the truth and take such crooked roads that anyone hearing them might conclude that they have no human intelligence. And until now I have wondered whether it was their wickedness or their obstinacy (the outcome of fanaticism) that has falsified their path. But whichever the case may be, the maskil would do well to remain silent, and not dispute with them. He will lose more than he will gain, for they will plan evil against honest men, and He, being compassionate, will forgive their iniquity.[32]

Euchel advised the maskilim to avoid a head-on conflict with the opponents of Haskalah, and instead to concentrate on constructing an alternative to the religious elite, whose members show no interest in extra-religious culture, and some of whom even accuse the maskilim of apostasy.[33] In his *An Essay on the Physical, Moral, and Political Reformation of the Jews*, the French priest Henri Grégoire provided testimony from outside the maskilic camp about the opposition it encountered as soon as it first appeared in the public sphere. He wrote this essay in 1787 and submitted it to a competition held by the Metz Royal Society of Arts and Sciences. In a footnote, based on information he had apparently obtained from a maskil in Alsace, Grégoire informed his readers that young Jews in Berlin, who had been publishing a journal for the past four or five years, were being accused of a horrible crime by the synagogue elders, who claimed that it was evil and harmful to cast doubt on the rabbis, who never erred, and to argue that the study of physics, mathematics, and the like could be of no less benefit than some boring, senseless casuistry in Talmud. He added that these young men had been the object of hatred and the mocking cries of fanatics.[34]

Joel Brill, Euchel's counterpart in Berlin, wrote to him that the orthodox opposition to *Hame'asef* actually attested to its success. In his view, the orthodox reaction should inspire Euchel's faith in the journal's future success and in its maskilic aims: "For the blind small-minded who emerge from their holes will also squabble and bark against this spectacle the likes of which they have never seen . . . and that is the sign that your actions and intentions are desirable."[35] And, indeed, in the first year of the innovative journal's existence, Euchel had already become well known as the head of the maskilim.

His special status as the uncrowned head of the Haskalah republic became manifest in the spring of 1784, when he journeyed from Königsberg to Copenhagen, the city of his birth. Although the purpose of the trip was personal (his mother's death in April and his intention to look into the possibility of settling in Berlin), it turned out to be a trip that evoked much interest and was widely covered in *Hame'asef*. In the course of his journey, Euchel carried out many public duties that he had voluntarily undertaken.[36] This well documented journey took on a special meaning for the maskilim, and Euchel himself thought of it as a kind of tour of supervision. It enabled him to get an up-to-date picture of the diffusion of the Haskalah in the various communities and to make contact with maskilic circles in remote areas. On the aims of the journey he wrote to Michael Friedländer, his former student, now a student in Königsberg: "And now foremost among my aims is to learn the features of each and every city I pass through and the state of the people living in it, particularly about our Jewish brethren who live there, their situation and their character, whether their situation is good or not, whether they have begun to graze in the pastures of wisdom, or have avoided touching it, of their own will, or that of others."[37] It was customary for cultured young men of means in eighteenth-century Europe to go on journeys to acquire knowledge about the world to mold their personalities—visiting museums, meeting writers and scholars and hiking in nature.[38] Euchel was familiar with the custom of taking a grand tour, and he too was imbued with the immense curiosity so typical of Enlightenment culture, to see the wonders of the world and observe human society.

Euchel tearfully parted from his friends and began his journey. Accompanying two ladies from the Friedländer family, he traveled in carriages and was waited on by servants. As was the custom, he took along a travel album (*album amicorum*) in which to record poems, rhymes of friendship, as well as dedications and letters from friends, writers, and scholars he would meet on his way.[39] He kept his travel diary in the form of letters to the young Friedländer, a few of which were printed in *Hame'asef* after his return. However, the route of Euchel's grand tour was rather limited, a round trip from Königsberg to Danzig, Berlin, Hamburg, Kiel, and Copenhagen. The unique aspect of his trip was the special attention he devoted to the situation of the Jews in these cities. Thus the journey from Königsberg to Copenhagen became another fascinating episode in the development of the new maskilic elite, which was striving to achieve a position of leadership.

The journey unquestionably bolstered Euchel's confidence about the path he had chosen and reinforced his self-image as a well-known intellectual. He opened his travel album with a farewell poem written by his fellow members of Chevrat Dorshei Leshon Ever, who depicted him as a leader and the exponent of the vision of the local circle of maskilim. In Brandenburg, Euchel had a moving spiritual-romantic experience. Alone, he went on a stroll through nature, in a pastoral landscape: "Let my spirit live, for I became like a seer, standing in the midst of the Creation observing the work of the Almighty." He sat down on the bank of a lake to record his thoughts about the insignificance of man compared to the Divinity. Elsewhere on his trip, he stopped to give a letter to the elderly parents of one of his classmates at the university, and felt great satisfaction at having done him a good turn by delivering an emotionally moving live message. He hastened to leave a small town he visited after learning that it was a place of backwardness and religious fanaticism: "That city aroused my loathing for it was held in the clutches of folly and the light of wisdom had not shone upon it." In Danzig, he found to his delight that he was already a well-known figure, at least among the Hebrew readers. "Are you the man, Euchel?" an amazed Jew, who did not give his name, asked him. This person, a poet and translator lacking in talent, pressed upon Euchel a poem translated from German that he urged him to print in *Hame'asef*: "I have heard that you are one of the group of *me'asfim* who call themselves Chevrat Dorshei Leshon Ever, and I wanted to show you that my heart is akin to yours and I am in no way inferior to you. So I have come to show you this translation I have done from the book by [Albrecht von] Haller." Upon his return to Königsberg, Euchel printed three stanzas of the translation, to derisively show the mediocre literary quality of the material that landed on the editor's desk from time to time.[40]

The high point of Euchel's journey was his visit to Berlin. He stayed in that city for two months and met its maskilim—Mendelssohn, Wessely, Brill, Isaac Satanow, and others—who received him with great delight and honor. He also collected material for *Hame'asef* and attended gatherings of maskilim in Mendelssohn's home. This time, in contrast to the days of his youth in the 1770s, he came there as a key figure in the Haskalah movement, not as a youth eavesdropping on the conversations of the maskilim. His ties with Mendelssohn grew closer, and when he left Berlin on his way to Copenhagen, Mendelssohn gave him a warm recommendation to his brothers-in-law in that city. Wessely wrote some encouraging rhymes of farewell in Euchel's album, stressing Euchel's personal fame owing to the journal he edited: "People everywhere will welcome you with joy in their hearts, many will wish you godspeed, and *Hame'asef* has made your name well known in these parts."

In July, Euchel continued his journey, pleased with the enjoyable summer he had spent in the company of maskilim, and filled with renewed vigor to embark on new maskilic ventures. In early September 1784, he arrived in Kiel in Danish Schleswig. Martin Ehlers, professor of philosophy at the University of Kiel, wrote words of praise and recommendation in his album. In Kiel, Hamburg and other places he passed through on his journey, Euchel used the opportunity to sign up new subscribers to *Hame'asef*, even among government officials, academicians, and public libraries.

If he had not felt confident of his own abilities and secure in the knowledge that he was a prominent figure in Jewish culture, Euchel would surely not have dared to introduce himself to the king of Denmark as the reformer of the Jews. In October, he arrived in Copenhagen and immediately began to map out the plans for the new maskilic enterprise he had conceived of during his stay in Kiel: the establishment of a Jewish educational institution with state support, to include a modern school and an institute to train teachers and rabbis. This plan, like Euchel's proposal for a school in Königsberg, never materialized. However, although ostensibly a plan for local reform that only concerned the Jews of Denmark and northern Germany, the document he presented to the king was very broad in its scope. Euchel outlined a grandiose maskilic vision, presenting himself as the leader of an elite of enlightened Jews, with the authority to criticize the flaws and shortcomings of Jewry and to propose steps to remedy them. Hence, the thirty-page document, written in German in Copenhagen on October 21, 1784, is of considerable importance. It coherently sets forth the ideology of the critical maskil and his self image as a martyr of the Haskalah, prepared to devote himself to the general good. While in his *Hame'asef* articles, Euchel was careful to avoid provoking the rabbinical elite, in the document he submitted to the King, he did not hesitate to freely speak his mind.[41]

When introducing himself to Frederick VI (actually still the heir to the throne, until the death of the mentally ill Christian VII in 1808), Euchel appropriated Mendelssohn's well-known appellation, a "Jewish Socrates": an educator, philosopher, and teacher of ethics, destined to instruct misguided youth and to lead them to real happiness and moral perfection, the only lofty aim worthy of striving for. He portrayed himself as a true and devoted Jew, but also as an intellectual who was familiar with Christian scholarly circles; the son of a Jewish family from Denmark but also a zealous patriot. In this generation, Euchel asserted, only the enlightened know the path of truth. If the monopoly on education were taken from the rabbis and handed over to the enlightened, and the latter provided with the necessary means, then Jewish society could be delivered from its deplorable state. Hence, Euchel attached his curriculum vitae to his letter. On the one hand, he stressed his bitter experience in encounters with the traditional educational system; on the other, he stressed his own attempts, his education, and his desire to introduce educational reforms. He asked the king for his backing and financial support for the educational project, since without state assistance, his plans and objectives could never be implemented. He argued that his plan merited the endorsement of the king and all Christian lovers of mankind, since its purpose was to free the Jews from the shackles of superstition and ignorance, to make them beneficial citizens of the state, and to remove the social barriers and prejudices that separate them from the Christians.

Candid, but hesitant and somewhat ashamed at having revealed the disgraceful condition of his fellow Jews, Euchel enumerated what he regarded as the "true failures" that stand in the way of the Jewish people's improvement. The present state of Jewry was flawed, he admitted, a fact known to many Christians, among them rulers and enlightened lovers of humanity. They all sought a solution, but until now they had all erred in identifying the cause of this state. Christian Wilhelm von Dohm, who had publicly raised the Jewish question in the Enlightenment era in his *On the Civil Improvement of the Jews*, had not come up with the true reason. The problem was not one with political roots, which could be resolved through immediate political and legislative actions, by granting rights or improving the civil status of Jews in the country. Dohm arrived at his conclusion because he possessed only a partial knowledge of Jewish history and contemporary Jewish society. He looked only at the tortures and persecutions that the Jews had suffered and at the discriminatory civil measures taken against them, the result of anti-Jewish prejudice. He emphasized those aspects of Jewish history that evoked compassion and sought a humane panacea; hence he arrived at a political solution. Moreover, Dohm, in Euchel's view, was acquainted with only a small, atypical group of Jewish society. He had met a number of rich, well-educated Jews in Berlin, and therefore had gained the impression that the problem lay only in the civil sphere, since these men had already been considerably acculturated to German society and culture. If he had been familiar with the picture as a whole, Dohm would have understood that the Jews themselves, and not an external factor, were responsible for the obstacles and flaws that plague their nation. Euchel quoted to the king of Denmark the words of the prophet Isaiah, "Those who laid you waste go forth from you" (49: 17), stating that the problem of the Jews fundamentally stemmed from moral and cultural flaws. Only enlightened Jews living among their people could diagnose its ills and treat them properly. Euchel, like Dohm, was also interested in the rehabilitation and regeneration (*Verbesserung*) of the Jews, but he approached the problem from an internal, cultural vantage point.

The most grievous shortcomings of Jewish society were ignorance (*Unwissenheit*), lack of education, and flawed morality, Euchel argued. Its morality was based on a mechanism of fear and hope; the Jews never do good only because it is good. Euchel, who had internalized Kant's concept of Enlightenment, believed that this approach was both ill-advised and dangerous, because it perpetuated passivity and negligence and prevented people from coping with problems and challenges. In general, he asserted, the Jews failed to see their own faults. It is the role of the enlightened Jew as "the moral physician" of his people, to diagnose this serious illness and to seek out the appropriate means of healing it. The image of the maskil as a physician was a prevalent motif in the self image of the maskilim, in particular those who advocated reforming Jewish society by coercive means, on the assumption that the masses would recognize their shortcomings only after they were rectified. Euchel informed the Danish king, with more than a hint of his self-satisfaction and revolutionary consciousness, that it was only now that several enlightened Jews were beginning to realize that their people were deteriorating and were bitterly lamenting their wretched state.

The Christians also see the ignorance of the Jews, he went on to say, but they believe that at least the rabbis excel in their knowledge of Judaism and the Hebrew language. They are very much mistaken, because the rabbis and teachers, most of whom come from Polish communities, are the most ignorant of all. In his view, this can be easily proven: just ask the most famous rabbi to interpret a biblical verse from a grammatical standpoint, or to show minimal knowledge in the sciences. It is a grievous scandal that in this enlightened century, Jewish pupils are entrusted to coarse, uncultured, ignorant teachers from Poland. Their customs are ridiculous, their religion is fanatic, and they observe the practical commandments without giving any thought to them. The traditional educational system is not methodical, and all it imparts to the pupils are ignorance, mistakes, and false notions. In principle, there can be no objection to the Talmud, on which all study is focused, and there is no cause to belittle it, as some do, but it has to be properly understood. It is really only a sort of encyclopedia, which contains a diversity of opinions and principles. Other than several mystical commentaries or a few offensive remarks about non-Jews, which were directed against pagans, there are many things in the Talmud that are consistent with Evangelical morality. However, in Jewish education, the Talmud is studied in a distorted manner, and for this we can also lay the blame on the Jews. Ignorance, therefore, is the root of the Jewish people's catastrophe. It has to be fought against through education. The greatest effort and the major part of all resources should be devoted to this area, for only by this means would there be any chance of a cultural revolution.

Since the Jews must improve their situation through their own efforts, the proposed educational institution in Denmark must be in Jewish hands, namely, all the teachers and pupils will be Jews. Euchel, who had already envisaged himself as the head of the school, volunteered to examine the candidates for teaching positions. The curriculum would include the study of languages (Danish and German, the languages of speech and culture, and Oriental languages, primarily Hebrew and Aramaic), history and geography (in particular Jewish history), Bible with a critical approach and no mystical interpretations, and Talmud, methodically and scientifically taught by an enlightened teacher. In addition, the pupils would have classes in Jewish theology, based on the rational philosophy of the Middle Ages, and lessons in ethics. Those wishing to prepare to enter the rabbinate would also learn the Jewish laws and the laws of the state. Those wishing to continue to pursue academic studies would be given additional lessons in languages, sciences, and philosophy, and any wishing to engage in commerce would study subjects that would prepare him for that occupation.

Euchel proposed that the institution be established in Kiel for several reasons. The city was in the center of the country; the local population was enlightened and willing to accept an institution of this kind within the city limits; there was a university there with excellent teachers, one of whom might be prepared to serve as an advisor to the Jewish school; the Jews of Denmark could send their children there with relative ease; and it would also be possible to use the university library. A special fund would have to be set up to finance the school, based on donations from individual Jews and perhaps also a budget provided by the government. Euchel was prepared to deal with this matter immediately and to look into operative plans for establishing the school.

Euchel concluded his letter to the king of Denmark with a utopian vision: within ten years after the establishment of the school and the institute for training teachers and rabbis, a leadership elite of enlightened Jews will emerge in Denmark and make an important contribution to the happiness and success of the entire Jewish people.[42]

Hame'asef, 1785–1786

Early in 1785, Euchel returned to Königsberg, having failed to raise the funds needed to implement his ambitious educational project in Denmark. From then on, he invested all of his energies in developing *Hame'asef* and in expanding the maskilic republic. In the second and third years of its operation (1785–86), the maskilic journal firmly established its reputation. Its writers and readers grew in number and became more diversified, the dialogue between Chevrat Dorshei Leshon Ever and its readership became more animated, the German supplement was expanded, and many more new books were reviewed.

For the first time, reports sent from various communities appeared in *Hame'asef*. These items, which gave *Hame'asef* the appearance of a newspaper, helped Euchel and his colleagues foster the maskilic discourse, reinforce optimism, and crystallize the circles of Jews sympathetic to the Haskalah. For example, a report was printed about the permission granted Mainz Jews to send their children to general schools, about a demand that the Jewish children not be harassed; and about the expanded rights of Sephardi and Ashkenazi Jews in Hamburg, including the right to become licensed merchants. The article attributed much significance to this news: "So that we may see how charitable the nations are toward us, and how each day they show us more kindness."[43] When the humiliating transit tax was abolished in France, Wessely composed a paean to Louis XVI and to the wealthy Frenchman Hildesheim of Strasbourg, who had appealed to the king in this matter: "Jacob will no longer pay custom duties at the gate like the duties paid on an ox or a lamb brought to the slaughter; man is far superior to the beasts of the field."[44] Joseph II's policy of tolerance was highly praised in an article that arrived from Bohemia, reporting on the success of government schools for boys and girls.[45] The journal printed the complete text of an open letter by a publisher, who signed it "a Protestant from Saxony," announcing his intent to publish a German periodical that would endeavor to defend the Jews and their image. The editors also enthusiastically recommended to their readers that they subscribe to this new journal and expressed their admiration for the Christian scholar "who is full of unconditional love."[46] Loyalty to the country's rulers was also reflected in an article describing the mourning rites in the Meklenburg community upon the death of Duke Schwerin, and in Wessely's elegy on the occasion of the tragic death of Duke Leopold who drowned when the Oder River flooded in the spring of 1785.[47]

These "articles on progress," which described the growth of tolerance under the benign rule of absolutist kings and the salutary influence of humanistic scholars, reached their highest point in the articles and poems printed in 1786, upon the death of Frederick II, king of Prussia. At first, a mourning notice was printed. The editors already regarded their journal as having a public status as the representative and voice of all the Jews, and urged them to hasten to express their loyalty to the new king, Frederick Wilhelm II. Then the journal printed a detailed biography of the king, in which no fault was found with any of his deeds. An article eulogizing the king, which excessively idealized him, emphasized his merciful treatment of the Jews, and called upon the readers to show their gratitude: "His hands raised you from the rubbish heap; in his time, you were never banned from partaking in the heritage of man as one of his people; in his time, the gates of wisdom were never closed to you, so you might slowly ascend from your wretched state in this bitter exile . . . he has restored the breath of life into your weary body and rejuvenated you so that all who see you will be amazed."[48] The next issue contained reports on the official day of mourning, the mourning ceremonies held by the Königsberg community and the coronation of the new king. At the reception held for the new king in Königsberg, representatives of the community presented him with a declaration of loyalty in the form of an obsequious poem: "God in his wisdom chose you, gave unto you the peace of the nations, witnesses your mercy for the destitute; had it not been for you a scorched desert would have remained here; we weep in gratitude to God, may Jacob rejoice and Israel be glad."[49]

Hame'asef was truly a Jewish-Prussian journal in the enlightened spirit of absolutism, and the maskilic discourse exuded optimism. Euchel and his friends joined the Prussian chorus of loyalty, repressing the well-known fact that Frederick's Jewish legislation, which had been in force since the mid-eighteenth century, was not at all in the spirit of the Enlightenment. Most of the doors of society at large were closed to Jews, and emancipation was still very far off. Only the narrow elite of wealthy Jews were flourishing financially and becoming acculturated, in the framework of the selective, discriminatory, absolutist conception of what was beneficial to the state. Euchel had experienced this kind of discrimination himself, as a private tutor whose legal status as a servant of the house was extremely tenuous, and as a candidate for an academic position who was disqualified because of he was a Jew.

The members of Chevrat Dorshei Leshon Ever devoted their attention primarily to promoting internal rehabilitation and establishing their public status, in keeping with Euchel's ideology. They drew encouragement from readers' letters, in which they were depicted as "men who teach knowledge and explain doctrine, the children of Israel will walk in their light, so that their eyes may be opened to see the path of reason," and from the support of wealthy Jews like Shmuel Wertheimer, who offered to serve as the society's agent in Hamburg. The editors continued to publish various literary projects in the journal, urged their agents to distribute *Hame'asef* and publicize it widely, promised readers engaging issues and quick delivery, and attracted subscribers by offering copper engravings of the two greatly admired personalities in maskilic circles—Wessely and Mendelssohn.[50] The Mendelssohn myth continued to serve the maskilic discourse, and reached its apogee upon his death in 1786. "The light of our generation, the glory of our people and the delight of our eyes, from Moses to Moses no greater sage has arisen than Moses . . . for he is a holy man of God!" Abraham Melodela wrote from Hamburg about Mendelssohn a year before his death. The first lines of the Tammuz issue, which appeared in the summer after his death, were a verse originally attributed to Isaac Newton and now, in the Jewish-Hebrew context, were written about Mendelssohn: "Truth and religion were fettered in darkness from generation to generation, until God spoke: Let there be Moses! Let there be light!"[51]

Hame'asef infused the consciousness of the maskilic republic with rhetoric and constantly repeated slogans in support of the maskilic agenda. "For we were not all created to be talmudists, or to delve into and expand upon the secrets of the Torah," Elijah Morpurgo wrote, objecting to the dominance of the talmudic ethos, in a detailed essay on the ideal education. The translation of the prayer book into German, another maskil wrote, is a major step in improving religious sentiment: "So that the majority of the people of Israel will no longer be speaking ancient languages they do not understand, but will take real pleasure in pouring forth their souls before their Maker." The maskilim also translated Alexander Pope's famous humanistic saying: "The proper study of mankind is man." Others emphasized the Enlightenment ideal of observation and science: "There is no joy like the joy of the inquiring, observing man, thirsting for knowledge." The maskilim also believed there were hardly any barriers still standing between Jews and Christians. "Nothing divides us but the commandments of the Torah that our forefathers have undertaken to keep," was the excessively optimistic view of an article published in installments in 1786.[52] That year, a satirical article, in the style of the radical Enlightenment, printed in the Nisan issue of *Hame'asef*, lashed out at those adamantly clinging to traditional ethics who were browbeating the public, and at mystics who were ruled by superstition:

Those witch doctors who rebuke the public, reviling, cursing and slandering their fellow men with coarse invective, or frightening and intimidating the people with tales of exaggerated punishments, such as cruel beatings and angels of fury with drawn swords who come with iron combs, whips and scorpions. Some comb their victims' flesh, others pull out their hair, others hang on to their nostrils, and other such brutal punishments they have concocted. They also tell of the seven departments of Hell, each with its own name . . . And who is foolish enough to believe this ridiculous nonsense which the deceiving imagination invents or the plots contrived by those who regard themselves as sages to mislead the heart of the masses and frighten them. Or is it their intent in doing so to make themselves renowned in the land as men who have amassed all the hidden secrets in their hands?[53]

During 1785 and 1786, two anonymous readers utilized the *Hame'asef* forum to incite a *Kulturkampf* against the rabbinical elite, with the support of the editors. The first raised again the issue of early burial, in which Mendelssohn had been involved in the early 1770s. Now, the issue was represented as a conflict between the position of progressive science and universal humanism and the position of the rabbis that required burial on the same day death occurred. The anonymous "reader" provocatively called on the rabbis to take part in a public debate, to be conducted on the pages of the maskilic journal. The issues at stake were the benighted image of the Jews in the eyes of the Christians and the openness of the rabbis to modern ideas. "The man who asks about the custom of early burial" praised the editors for refusing to back down in the face of the rabbis' authority ("Your adversaries are those who regard themselves as sages, and refuse to budge, either to the right or the left, from the customs of their fathers") and for printing his article. "The man who asks" was in fact none other than the editor, Isaac Euchel, hiding behind the pseudonym "a reader," a safer way to confront the rabbis.[54] Members of Chevrat Dorshei Leshon Ever, on their part, expressed support for his views. They printed the 1772 letters of Mendelssohn and Emden that Euchel had brought with him from his visit to Berlin, so that the supporters of delaying burial could rely on Mendelssohn and his arguments against those opposed to a change in Jewish burial practices and in favor of the scientific approach. Only one reply was received by the journal, from a Polish rabbi who did not give his name, but there is some suspicion that this reply was forged, because the rabbi supported the maskilim and suggested an original form of symbolic burial in a coffin with air holes for three days, to eliminate the danger of burying a live person.[55]

The second maskil employed more radical rhetoric against a traditional

translation of the Torah about to appear in Prague and compete with Mendelssohn's translation, with an approbation by Rabbi Yehezkel Landau, "It is the
fire of jealousy that burns in my heart and the sword of revenge that pierces,
they shall be a remembrance to the people of the Lord, from me, a man
plagued by the sickness of the time," was how the writer introduced himself,
signing his article as "Amitai HaShomroni." His wish was to fight relentlessly
and uncompromisingly against any dishonor to Mendelssohn's name. The editors hesitated to print this belligerent article in full, which was actually written
by Rabbi Saul Berlin, hiding behind the pseudonym. They finally did print it,
because they shared his desire to block the rival translation and to avert the
danger that its influence on orthodox pupils might destroy the hopes Mendelssohn had pinned on his *Bi'ur*. After they received the text of Landau's approbation, in which he not only criticized, but also was contemptuous of the
Mendelssohnian *Bi'ur* (although he refrained from mentioning it by name),
the editors of *Hame'asef* announced that the truth took precedence over peace.
They had to print the article even though they had wanted to avoid any escala-
tion in the conflict ("Heaven forbid that we should arouse any strife and show
any disrespect for a great rabbi, for our ways are those of peace and truth"),
and were afraid that their opposition to the rabbi might result in a scandal.
Now the readers of *Hame'asef* could see for themselves that Rabbi Landau, one
of the leaders of the rabbinical elite in Europe, was firmly entrenched in the
orthodox camp and was disparaging the project of Mendelssohn, their beloved
hero.[56]

In the meantime, Euchel also publicly settled accounts with his orthodox
critics, who had found flaws in his German translation of the prayer book,
published in 1786. He took umbrage at the criticism that questioned his qualifications and cast doubt on his religious faith. He was also angered by the fact
that this criticism was not voiced in an open forum like the journal, but
secretly, by word of mouth. Hurt and furious, Euchel addressed an emotional
response to those "wagging tongues," which underscored both his self-image
as a man who acted for the general good and his criticism of the traditional
scholars:

Be my witness, before God and His people, whether I have not sanctified His name
among the nations and enhanced the prestige of all Jewry against her enemies. I have
shown the wisdom of her truly devout sages . . . I greatly fear and venerate the Lord
and I love my people unconditionally . . . From the day I had a mind of my own, I
chose to sit among true sages so that I might learn from them to remove the idols
ingrained in me by some of my teachers in the days of my youth . . . all I ever aspired
to do was to improve my mind and intellect each day . . . I shall always honor the God-
fearing and regard the lovers of His Torah with affection, but not every one who grows
a beard is a God-fearing man and not everyone who pores over books is a lover of
Torah.

Euchel concluded this personal confession, printed at the end of the *Hame'asef*'s last issue in 1786, with a prayer, one that could also be easily included in the journal's maskilic discourse: "Allow my heart to know the wonderful deeds you have done, to fear you all the days and to worship you with all my heart . . . Remove the heart of stone from all flesh and be merciful to the blameless, for you know that his ignorance is but his error!"[57]

Euchel was also undoubtedly the author of the maskilic blessing printed in *Hame'asef* toward the Jewish New Year 5547 (1786), which contained optimistic expectations of a transformation of the Jews and the success of the Haskalah:

With joy and praise, the bearer of the sheaves of reason will come. He will dwell in the secret place and teach his flock righteousness, and you, my Lord, be his protector. Strengthen the holder of a pen who teaches the men of Judah knowledge, and endow him with a pure tongue, so his words may be pleasing to his listeners . . . God! Send a blessing through the deeds of your hands. Give the maskil knowledge, the scholar understanding, the judge honesty, the teacher, fine speech, the student eagerness, and modesty to the teacher. Give the wealthy man a good heart and to the generous, give wisdom. From the backs of fools remove the heart of stone, and obstinacy from the minds of simpletons, so that they may not send forth their wrong doings. Open the eyes of the blind, lend an ear to the deaf, so they may hear the instruction of rational men.[58]

These heaven-borne prayers expressed aspirations and yearnings for the triumph of the Haskalah and the spread of reason. Their purpose was not to achieve the traditional religious aims, such as devoutness, atonement, or the redemption of the Jewish people from exile. This blessing, or wish, for the success of the Enlightenment revolution in Jewish society expressed the maskilim's sense that they had been orphaned by Mendelssohn's death, as well as their quasi-messianic zeal for the coming of the secular maskilic redeemer—"the bearer of the sheaves of reason." However, these were more than just ardent wishes for the appearance of a replacement of the same stature as Mendelssohn. Daring organizational steps to change the structure of the Haskalah movement were already in the offing. The man behind these moves was, of course, Isaac Euchel, the indefatigable initiator of the maskilic republic.

Chapter Eleven

The Society for the Promotion of Goodness and Justice

In the last issue of the third volume that came out in the fall of 1786, the readers of *Hame'asef* were informed of changes about to take place in the journal as it began its fourth year of operation. In a notice "to their brethren, the maskilim," Chevrat Dorshei Leshon Ever announced its intent to exploit the journal's success, to double its membership, to foster new maskilic initiatives, and to add another name—"The Society for the Promotion of Goodness and Justice" (Chevrat Shocharei Hatov Vehatushiyah)—to the society's original name. By enrolling new members who showed an interest in the Haskalah project and had financial means at their disposal, the society was able to expand its areas of activity and to open its ranks to members for whom nurturing the Hebrew language, for example, was not a top priority. From now on, "the society would not be based only on exponents of the holy tongue, but every maskil who is a seeker of truth and of good, every scholar with intellectual interests, and every philanthropist among our people will be known as a member of our society." Those interested in joining the new framework were directed in this notice to a new address—Joel Brill, the private tutor who lived in Berlin in the home of his employer and patron, the well-born, wealthy maskil David Friedländer.[1]

The Freischule Printing House

The Berlin address represented a turning point. The Berlin circle of maskilim was joining the society of maskilim in Königsberg as an active partner, and this called for an organizational change to reflect the weight of the Berliners in the movement. At first, there was talk of a kind of federation made up of the two circles, which would bear the name Chevrat Shocharei Hatov Vehatushiyah veDorshei Leshon Ever. The new framework, however, was not established at once, but only a year after the *Hame'asef* announcement. For several months, Euchel was occupied with the organizational preparations for the change and was also planning to move from Königsberg to Berlin, where he was assured of a position as director of a Hebrew printing house, a central, major link in the new organization.

Hame'asef did not come out at all during 1787, and it was only in the summer of that year that the aims and by-laws of the Society for the Promotion of Goodness and Justice were formulated and a decision was taken about its complex, sophisticated modes of operation. The new society was then officially founded and a special manifesto was printed to mark the occasion. It is an interesting document, one unparalleled in its importance as a means of reconstructing the maskilim's grand plan for building their movement in the 1780s. The "Plan of the Society for the Promotion of Goodness and Justice" presents a detailed program of activity that reflects the inner dynamics of the movement and its leaders' great revolutionary dream.[2] The establishment of the Society for the Promotion of Goodness and Justice was the clearest expression of the new elite's attempt to found a well-organized, effective, and ramified maskilic republic. To achieve this aim, all the cultural forces and resources at its disposal in the mid-1780s were unified and centralized—the successful journal, the financial support of a wealthy elite that sympathized with the Haskalah, the registered members of both societies (Chevrat Dorshei Leshon Ever in Königsberg and the new society, Chevrat Matzdikei Harabim [Benevolent Society], in Berlin), and in particular the Hebrew printing press Chevrat Chinukh Ne'arim, which had been under the maskilim's control from its establishment. The integration under one roof of financial means, a journal that had already been published for three years, ties through correspondence, and a printing house was undoubtedly the most important organizational step taken in the framework of the maskilim's Enlightenment revolution.

Late in 1785, Chevrat Matzdikei Harabim was founded in Berlin, with 145 members, largely from Berlin itself, many of them subscribers to *Hame'asef*. This society had totally different character and aims from Chevrat Dorshei Leshon Ever. It was established as a result of an elaborate effort by its founder, Isaac Satanow, to create a support system for himself and the printing house he managed, to ensure that he would have the funds required to print books. The society appointed "collectors" in communities outside Berlin to sign up society supporters on a pledge to purchase new books and to transfer the money to the society's management in Berlin. The members of the management board, Isaac Daniel Itzig, David Friedländer and Isaac Satanow himself, were also "leaders of Chevrat Chinukh Ne'arim," which had established the modern Jewish school in 1778. Matzdikei Harabim undertook to buy in advance, each and every month, a fixed number of publications that Satanow would print in the Freischule printing house. The members were also asked to observe the traditional customs of charity, but to make their donations to a secular philanthropic-cultural cause, rather than to traditional institutions like the synagogue or the talmud torah, as they had in the past. To mark the birth of a son, the marriage of a child, or an *aliyah laTorah* (the honor of being called to read from the Torah in the synagogue) on the Sabbath or a holiday, members of Chevrat Matzdikei Harabim would give a donation to the society. As recompense, Satanow offered them universal fame. The donors' names would be printed in each of the books published by Matzdikei Harabim, "so that the good they have done to safeguard their people will be a memorial throughout all the generations, and the fruit of their charity shall be a source of glory and pride."[3]

Isaac Satanow sincerely believed man could have no greater reward. In the maskilic republic, there was no other man so obsessed with the world of books, writing, and printing as he was. Isaac (Itzik) Halevi, a native of Satanow, was a merchant and early maskil from Podolia and a friend of Mendelssohn's. He settled in Berlin in 1772, where he joined the circle of maskilim, although on his frequent journeys to his family and trade fairs he maintained close ties with Polish Jewry. Satanow was an extraordinary maskil, who produced and invented texts, and the amazing range of his writings attest to this fact. He displayed an astonishing ability to produce books that emulated ancient works (*Zohar taniana* in the language of the Kabbalah, *Mishlei asaf* in the language of the wisdom literature), and contrived enthusiastic approbations supposedly written by rabbis who warmly praised his talents. In addition, he published his own writings as ancient texts, which he said he had found in rare manuscripts only recently discovered in private libraries, and quoted himself in later writings. Satanow's ponderous and turgid works on linguistics, Kabbalah, philosophy, commentary on prayers, and the like are not easy to read. Contemporary as well as later critics accused him of deception, hypocrisy, and literary forgery.

Satanow is unquestionably an enigmatic figure in the eighteenth-century world of Jewish culture, one whose true nature has not yet been plumbed.[4] The scholar of Haskalah literature Shmuel Werses has with great sensitivity succeeded in constructing the historical figure of the "woeful maskil," at least as Satanow saw himself, by listening attentively to Satanow's autobiographical remarks scattered throughout his numerous writings. Satanow was a frustrated intellectual. Throughout his life, he longed for people to recognize his fine qualities, read his books, and admire him as a first-rank scholar who had made an immense contribution to Jewish culture. "The image we get is not so much one of an adventurer and deceiver," Werses wrote, "but rather one of a writer with a mission, a type of piteous sage." Satanow was always disappointed, always dissatisfied, always angry about the declining cultural standards and the dwindling number of Hebrew readers.[5]

Isaac Satanow was a compulsive writer, constantly in the grips of a obsession to write. He devoted all of his time to raising money to finance the printing of books. "I write in the evening and in the morning return to the printing house," Satanow wrote about his ascetic daily routine and his race against death:

And all that for fear that death may snatch me up before I have completed what I have begun. For that reason, I have tried to speedily engage in my sacred work, turning my nights into days. I sleep hardly more than three or four hours a night, I do not partake of delicious food, I do not drink wine or alcohol, I lead an austere life. Material pleasures mean nothing to me.[6]

In his personal life, he was quite lonely because his wife and most of his family remained in Poland. Writing, printing, and publishing were for him a substitute for every pleasure and satisfaction. Like other early maskilim, he employed erotic images to explain the intensity of his irrepressible passion for writing and printing: "Every writer has an intense desire to leave behind some memory in his writing because he wishes some benefit to accrue from it, that he may increase men's wisdom and knowledge so they are not lost in sorry affairs; this is likened to the passion of sexual intercourse whose purpose is to leave some remainder of man behind on this earth." He regarded his literary creation as a means of immortalizing his life and leaving his imprint on the world. He drew an analogy between the sexual drive and the passion for writing, and in his view "The Almighty created in man the passion for the two, to bring things to their appointed end, whether by sowing his seed and bringing forth progeny or planting the seed of wisdom, which is a form of man." However, men ought to channel both these human passions toward a lofty purpose and to avoid giving vent to them in a manner that would bring forth neither the birth of a child nor the publication of beneficial books of wisdom: "Just as can happen in the ardor of sexual intercourse, men of ill will may release their passionate desires in various ways without achieving the end, thus in my view, this may happen with the passion of wisdom."[7]

Thanks to his expertise in the Hebrew book world, his concern for the fate of the Jews, and his good connections with the elite Berlin families of Itzig and Ephraim, in whose home he was employed as private tutor for Jewish studies, Satanow was appointed in 1784 as director of the Freischule printing house. This position provided him with a rare opportunity to make his mark on Jewish culture and, most important of all, to make sure that his own many works were published.

All the recent studies on the construction of the public sphere in modern Europe in general, and on the emergence of the eighteenth-century literary republic in particular, underscore the salient role of printing. It was the focal point for versatile economic, social, and intellectual activity, and the means by which the Enlightenment was disseminated.[8] Among the Jews too, printing played a similar role. The Berlin printing house was the first in Jewish history specifically intended by its founders and directors to serve modern transformative aims, to disseminate knowledge and *chokhmah*, to further the improved education of youth, and to increase the number of readers. While the Hebrew printing press everywhere had been the means of disseminating all streams of religious culture, now, for the first time, it was enlisted in a new cause—to promote the alternative Jewish-maskilic culture and to disseminate a modern ideology.

Six years after the school for boys, the Freischule, was opened in Berlin, the two men who ran it—Isaac Daniel Itzig and David Friedländer—applied to Frederick II for a license to found a printing house, the income of which would finance the philanthropic school, where needy pupils could study tuition-free. Not only would the printing house lighten the financial burden of the donors, it would also print new textbooks for the pupils, thus furthering the school's goal of molding ethical citizens who would be of service to the state. To operate the printing house, intended as a new improved version of the Hebrew printing house already operating in Berlin, the two men also requested a license to hire printing workers—men to cast lead typeface, typesetters and proofreaders, who would come from outside Prussia—and to open a bookstore as well.[9]

Nonetheless, in applying for a license to open a printing house, the two men's intent was not to compete with the printing houses that existed in Berlin. The king's reply was sent within only a day to the state minister, Münchhausen. The Jews, he averred, were already engaged in too much commerce and there was no scarcity of printing houses in Berlin. However, if this was going to be a unique printing house, limited to Hebrew books, he was prepared to grant the request. Münchhausen ruled that the printing house would specialize only in "Oriental languages" (hence its German name—Die orientalische Buchdruckerei), and with his avid support the process of approval moved with relative speed through the various bureaucratic offices. The license was certainly granted owing to the special status of the Itzigs, seven years later the first Jewish family in Prussia to gain full emancipation. But the concepts of the Enlightenment, which since Dohm had made an impact on the public, also affected the decision, because they regarded this sociocultural endeavor of printing as an effective means of bringing enlightenment to the Jews (*Aufklärung*), of improving their morals and rehabilitating them (*Verbesserung, Veredlung*).

On February 3, 1784, Frederick II signed the franchise for the printing house and a bookstore adjacent to the Freischule. It stated the applicants were permitted to sell and trade at fairs, to print in Hebrew and other Oriental languages (Aramaic, for example), to use other alphabets only for purposes of translation, footnotes, or clarification, but not to print an entire book in a non-Oriental language. Another much sought after right in Frederick's Berlin, which was always apprehensive about the growth of the Jewish community, was added to the permit. The printing workers and their families, who had been brought from outside Prussia, were granted resident permits as tolerated Jews. Following further negotiations, the print shop was exempted from most taxes and levies, after being recognized as an enterprise of benefit to the state.[10]

Satanow immediately went to work with enormous zeal. At first, he thought he could make unlimited use of the printing press to print his many manuscripts that he had not succeeded in publishing. He distributed a private prospectus, proposing that the public support the printing of ten of his books. In exchange for a commitment to purchase books, Satanow offered the donors, as was his wont, fame and glory: their names would be engraved in his books "with a pen of iron and lead so they will be a memorial throughout all the generations."[11] In the end, his plan was not fully implemented, because the policy followed in the Freischule press was not based solely on financial considerations, but was set by an editorial board established in keeping with the by-laws of Matzdikei Harabim. This was unquestionably an unprecedented step in the Hebrew book culture. In general, economic considerations (the chances of selling the book or the financing the author provided) as well as the rabbinical authority and approbations had decided whether or not a manuscript would find its way to the printing press. In marked contrast, this modern ideological printing house submitted manuscripts to the critical judgment of maskilim. Its owner and directors decided that no book would be printed before it was judged and had received a positive recommendation from at least three experts:

Every book, new, old, or translated submitted for printing by the leaders of the association (Chinukh ne'arim, Matzdikei harabim) will only be printed after it has been examined by scholars well-versed in all aspects of the science about which the book is written . . . it will be examined by maskilim who have an understanding of the science referred to on the front pages of the book, and the recommendation will be made by three experts to the satisfaction of the leaders of the group who will authorize the printing of the book and provide the necessary funds.

The striking point here is that they circumvented the rabbis' control over the Hebrew book, a trend already apparent in the early Haskalah throughout the eighteenth century. Nonetheless, in one exceptional case the tradition of rabbinical approbations was preserved. Books dealing with the Talmud were submitted for the approval of religious experts—the rabbi of the Berlin community, Zevi Hirsch Levin and his *bet din*, court of law.[12] This was the most salient expression of the sharp division drawn between the sacred and the profane, between the talmudic rabbi and the maskil "who understands science," a division that relegated religious knowledge to the narrow area of the Talmud and to those expert in that field.

The printing house began its work as soon as the suitable approvals were received during the month of April 1784, and in its first year of operation, it published three books, each of which in its own way served the house's maskilic aims. The first was an introduction to philosophy, *Bi'ur milot hahigayon*, a third edition of Mendelssohn's interpretation of Maimonides's work on logic, first published in the 1760s. This time it was prepared for the press by Aaron Friedenthal of Jaroslaw, then a teacher at the Freischule, and a year later one of the directors of the state educational system in Galicia. It was published as a textbook intended for the pupils of the Freischule and was completely financed by Itzig and Friedländer, the directors of the school. In Friedenthal's view, this book, combining medieval Jewish philosophy with the up-to-date terminology of the new philosophy introduced by Mendelssohn, was an invaluable vehicle for shaping orderly rationalist thought, so abysmally lacking in traditional education, as well as an intellectual means for training students to arrive at the truth.[13]

The second book was *Ein mishpat*, the third in the *Divrei shalom ve'emet* series by Wessely, published during his struggle against the rabbinical elite that had attacked his program for reforming Jewish education. It contained letters from Italian rabbis who had come to his defense. *Hame'asef*, which announced the book's appearance, expressed the hope that *Ein mishpat* would silence the critics and provide support for its author, the veteran maskil.[14]

The third book published during the printing house's first year, Satanow's *Sefer hamidot*, was also intended as a textbook for the boys at the Freischule, but unlike *Bi'ur milot hahigayon*, it was an original work printed after having won a tender. In the first pamphlet of *Divrei shalom ve'emet*, Wessely had come out in favor of making ethics a major subject of study in new Jewish education, to be taught methodically with textbooks, based not only on religious texts but also on reason and humanism, as one of the components of the teachings of man: "books of morals based on rational philosophy, with which to teach the pupils *chokhmah* and ethics." Wessely went on to outline the chapter headings of an ethics book of this type: "etiquette, the ways of morality and good character, which are the teachings of man . . . knowledge of the soul and its faculties, which are the qualities implanted in the human soul . . . like wisdom and folly, faith and obstinacy, joy and sadness, love and hate, generosity and miserliness."[15]

The directors of the Freischule issued a tender offering a monetary prize to anyone who would write such a book of ethics. They set the date for the submission of the manuscript as the first day of Nisan 1784 (when the tender was first published, in a German periodical, the date given was October 1783), and appointed Mendelssohn, Wessely, and Marcus Herz as judges. Wessely himself went to work energetically on the book, but was unable to complete it in time because of his involvement in the cultural battle that flared up around him. To Wessely's great disappointment, the prize went to the manager of the printing house, Isaac Satanow.[16]

Satanow's *Sefer hamidot* proposed a personal track of study leading to perfection. Like the authors of traditional *musar* literature, Satanow thought of himself as being responsible for curing "the sicknesses of the soul," namely, identifying the illness and finding the proper balance between mental faculties and moral virtues. However, he attributed particular importance to the intellectual effort he invested in precisely classifying the various virtues and suggesting exact definitions for them. In Satanow's view, this was the major task of the "maskil," whose dominant faculty is the "light of reason" that guides him. *Sefer hamidot*, in its ideas and ponderous baroque style, was actually a book that was characteristic of the early Haskalah. As a matter of fact, the book, along with rabbinical approbations, had been ready ten years earlier (in 1774), and when the Freischule tender was published, Satanow merely retrieved it from the store of his numerous manuscripts.[17]

Satanow's definition of the Haskalah ("for wonderment is the reason for Haskalah in God's verities and deeds") was much closer to the rational thought of the Middle Ages than to Kant's definition, which Euchel had espoused. It is also hard to imagine that the Freischule would offer its pupils a book that recommends, for example, a method of repression to preserve sexual purity like that suggested by the traditional books of morality, which tried to frighten their readers and fill them with a fear of sin and its punishment. And this is what Satanow wrote in *Sefer hamidot*:

When a man is infected by a feeling of passion for a strange woman, he should turn his mind to think of the elements of which she is composed: flesh, blood, sinews and bones, lungs, liver, spleen and intestines, phlegm, smelly bile and filthy urine, and picture them in his mind as disgusting slabs laid out before him, and that organ which he longs for is the most repulsive of all, the place through which urine, the menstrual blood, and the odious discharges pass.[18]

As far as we know, the book was never utilized for the pupils of the Freischule, and its publication only served Satanow in his tireless efforts to get his works into print, in order to gain one more portion of immortal life.

In the following three years, the printing house continued to prosper and grow. Nearly every month, another book was published, and a total of thirty-three titles were published between 1785 and 1787. "To this altar, the authors their offerings will bring, and from the scent of their incense into hearts joy will spring," Wessely's rhymes heaped praise on Isaac Daniel Itzig, who was responsible for establishing "the new altar of print."[19] Satanow continued to print his own works, including a prayer book he had edited, and grammar books. The printing house also received a franchise to print a calendar. It also printed a book of ethics by Wessely (also entitled *Sefer hamidot*), a Hebrew translation of Mendelssohn's *Phädon*; a prayer book translated by Friedländer; Joel Brill's translation of the Satanow edition of the Passover haggadah; *Yaldut vebacharut* (Childhood and Adolescence), a sermon in rhyme advocating the ideal education written by Mendel Breslau, a member of *Hame'asef*'s editorial board; and *Rehovot*, the fourth and last part of *Divrei shalom ve'emet*. All these works that came off the Berlin printing press were added to the Haskalah book shelf. Late in 1787, when a joint organizational framework was established comprising Dorshei Leshon Ever in Königsberg and Matzdikei Harabim in Berlin, the printing house was the major asset that the Berlin group brought to this merger. However, Isaac Satanow was not mentioned at all in the document uniting the two groups, and the Berlin group was apparently represented by Joel Brill and David Friedländer. In any event, Isaac Euchel was about to move to Berlin to replace Satanow as manager of the printing house.

The Haskalah Is Institutionalized

"And there shall be two linked shoulder-pieces to bear the burden of the sacred work that is to begin, God willing, from the month of Tishri, 1787," the founders of the Society for the Promotion of Goodness and Justice proclaimed.[20] The maskilim of Königsberg with their cultural resources, in particular *Hame'asef*, were being amalgamated with the maskilim of Berlin, along with their most important asset, the printing house of the Freischule. This expanded framework also led to close cooperation between three groups. These groups were defined in the new society's regulations: the first as the *toranim* (authors and scholars); the second group as the artists—painters, artisans, and musicians—the third as the philanthropists, the wealthy donors who supported the creators of culture.[21]

In setting forth the aims of the Society, Euchel did not abandon the foundations on which the society in Königsberg had been built four and a half years earlier, first among them the promotion of the Hebrew language. He emphasized, however, that from then on the society's activity would be guided by a more general purpose—to foster enlightenment among the Jews by disseminating knowledge to them, imbuing them with virtues and encouraging them to act for the public good. He did not think of "goodness" in the same sense as Leibniz did—that same optimistic faith that Voltaire mocked in *Candide*, according to which "all is for the best in this best of all possible worlds." In his eyes, goodness was an ideal achieved only through a considerable effort and cultural activism by those truly committed to it. He regarded the members of the Society for the Promotion of Goodness and Justice as dedicated soldiers, prepared to fight for the dissemination and promotion of the good and of morality in all spheres of life. Such ideals were quite prevalent and also appeared in the names of other German intellectual societies. They reflected the aspiration of the German Enlightenment to shape a moral society that would be the best expression of humanism. In fact, the maskilim still conceived of the ideal of enlightenment primarily as a continuation of the endeavor to disseminate knowledge. Hence, even in the broadest program of activity that they tried to implement they never stirred from the three fields they endeavored to foster: expansion of the world of books, improvement of education, and formation of an elite of maskilim. The maskilic agenda contained none of the other possible missions, such as external political activity to gain rights, internal political activity to replace community leadership, or activity to achieve social justice. However, the maskilim who declared their adherence to the idea of fostering wisdom and goodness, no matter how abstract and nebulous it might be, were swept up on a wave of ardor, which revealed a conscious trend of innovativeness, a strong desire to change and improve the existing situation, and a fervent belief in the Enlightenment. This is how Euchel, the architect of the reorganization, defined the aims of the Society (in its German name, Gesellschaft der Beförderung des Edlen und Guten) at the head of its manifesto:

This society undertakes to mightily endeavor to promote good and wisdom among the sons of Israel. And besides the promise of each and every one of its members to gird his loins and to do good himself as best he can, each also has a strong desire to implant good and wisdom in the hearts of their fellow men. And for this, we have on the one side, Dorshei Leshon Ever who are still determined to nurture the holy tongue in order to build their house on a treasured cornerstone; and on the other side, Matzdikei harabim, whose desire it is to make men righteous and to increase among the Jews a love of wisdom, a lust for science and a passion for justice.[22]

In this new umbrella organization, a monopoly was granted to the Freischule printing house. Its regulations stated that all of its and its members' publications, including *Hame'asef*, would from then on be printed only at this printing house after having been judged to be suitable. "At the top of the book," the regulations stated, "it will be written . . . that the contents of the

book were examined by maskilim who found them to be proper and reasonable." A manuscript that was disqualified in this screening process could not
be published by another printing house under the society's name. But a book
selected as meeting maskilic criteria would receive devoted attention and treatment by the society and its author would be invited to sign a generous contract
with it.[23] While the foremost objective of the Society for the Promotion of
Goodness and Justice, which also represented itself as a publishing house, was
to disseminate knowledge and to establish a forum accessible to maskilim who
wished to see their books published, it also wanted to provide a support system
for writers to free them of their economic dependence on the patronage of the
wealthy and socially prestigious elite. In the belief that maskilim deserve to
receive a fitting financial recompense as well as recognition and honor for their
public activity, the society promised to ensure that "each would be paid for
his work both for translating sacred books or writing a book himself, or if he
does some fine act that attests to his generosity, for the good of all Jewry, he
shall be given a reward by the public to thank him for the good he has done
and to publicly acclaim his righteous deeds."[24]

In addition to developing the maskilic book world and furthering the
Chinukh Ne'arim press, Euchel suggested that the members raise any other
ideas that were likely to promote the society's aims and give the members a
sense of satisfaction: "Each and every one of our members who is desirous of
making a new, valuable proposal that will be beneficial to the Jewish people
should bring it to the attention of the heads of the society when they meet."
In addition, the members were assigned various duties, each in keeping with
his function in the society: These *toranim* were given the task of writing articles
and reviews of new books for *Hame'asef* and replying to questions on science
and other scholarly matters. The artists were to contribute an artistic creation
of some kind to the journal every year, an engraving or an illustration ("To
embellish *Hame'asef* or to glorify Jewry among the nations to show that the
wisdom of her sages has not been lost"), while the philanthropists would be
divided into two groups: one to provide regular advance financial support for
the Society's activities by paying a fixed monthly amount, the other to make
contributions from time to time. The members would also enjoy rights: the
writers' works would be printed by the society; the artists would be paid for
their works, and they would all get discounts when purchasing the society's
publications. A detailed, up-to-date report, containing a list of the members
and their activities during that year, would be sent to the members' homes.[25]

The regulations reflect the tendency of the heads of the society to central-
ize its activities. In an attempt to keep the members' activity under close supervision, they adopted for their organization quite a few of the characteristics of
the bureaucratic Prussian state in which they lived. Euchel designed a hier-

archical, centralized structure for the Society for the Promotion of Goodness and Justice, in which a rigid division of powers would be maintained, and which would be operated by a ramified system of bureaucracy. It was the first modern Jewish organization of this type, intended to promote an unprecedented cultural policy, invented at this historical stage by maskilim alone. Hence, it is interesting to examine the general lines of the organization in detail.

Jewish society, particularly in Eastern Europe, was familiar with supra-community organizational frameworks and intra-communal federations. But the typical formal organization in eighteenth-century Jewry was the local community. Hence, the maskilim's aspiration to found, in the late 1780s, a very broad supra-local, supra-communal maskilic republic, and to exploit books and correspondence to unify its members within a single large organization, is particularly striking. The ranks were open to all, "and every man everywhere who desires to join our association and to seek justice wisdom and the good, will be welcome and his company will be pleasing to us, as friends and brethren together, and even if far apart, we will find joy in wisdom and delight in camaraderie." Never before had a broad national, perhaps even international, organization been founded, not even among the hundreds of societies of the enlightened established in Germany, other than the Masonic lodges. The source of inspiration for The Society for the Promotion of Goodness and Justice may well have been the organization of Freemasons, such as the "Asiatic Brothers," in the 1780s, which had a center in Vienna, regional branches in Europe and local offices.[26] However, although there was some similarity in organizational structure, and even if Jews like the head of the Itzig family were Freemasons, the members of The Society for the Promotion of Goodness and Justice were not.

The only other organization, contemporary with and similar in character to the Jewish maskilic society was actually the Deutsche Union. A nationwide movement, founded in early 1788 by the radical intellectual with nationalist leanings Karl Friedrich Bahrdt, it served as a roof organization for reading societies throughout Germany.[27] This time, the founding document of the Society for the Promotion of Goodness and Justice stated, we are not founding another local society of maskilim, like those in Berlin and Königsberg. "The Society for the Promotion of Goodness and Justice is not based, like other groups, on the residents of only one city, but has branches wherever there are truly enlightened men seeking to know the joy that will spring from this society," was the wording of the first clause of the fifth section, outlining the society's organizational structure.[28] Alongside the traditional community organization there had always been voluntary societies, whose members were devoted to the advancement of traditional values, in particular charity and talmudic studies.[29] In this case, not only did this voluntary organization adopt aims that were not the traditional ones, but its purpose was to disseminate the idea of a new type of (maskilic) society to other locations as well and to link the newly established societies in a supra-organization, one in which the communal affiliation would carry no weight.

At the head of the society, Isaac Daniel Itzig was installed as *Überdirektor*. He was the brother-in-law of David Friedländer, the son of the head of the communal establishment in Berlin and Prussia, Daniel Itzig, and one of the directors of the Freischule. This was, however, only a honorary position that did not carry any real executive powers. His appointment at the head of the hierarchy was probably intended to ensure the financial support of donors from the wealthy, well-connected elite as well as to give the movement the honor and status it could hardly expect to gain if it were headed by a private tutor like Euchel or Brill.

Major importance was attributed to the organization's two nationwide operative bodies, one in Königsberg and the other in Berlin. This duality reflected the founding of a federation between the maskilim in these two cities, and perhaps also rivalry over hegemony in the movement. In Berlin, the *Über-direktion*—the organizational and administrative center and the supreme coordinating body of the society—would operate, supervising "the printing and the transmission of letters between the faraway members." It would have six members: a "leader," an "adviser" (Joel Brill and Baruch Lindau), a manager of the printing house, two proofreaders, and a treasurer. The *Hauptdirek-tion*—the body that would manage *Hame'asef* as well as all the activities of the society—would operate in Königsberg. It would be headed by two leaders, Euchel and Mendel Breslau, who would be assisted by an adviser (apparently Sanwil Friedländer), a treasurer, and a secretary. In this way, Euchel ensured the continued control of Chevrat Dorshei Leshon Ever in the new movement and in *Hame'asef*.

On the local scene, there were two possible ways of setting up the organization: in a small cell, with at least ten members, overseen by an *Inspektor*, who served as liaison between the local society of maskilim and the national leadership; or in a *Direktion*, a larger cell, with a membership of at least thirty local maskilim overseen by a *Direktor* assisted by a secretary. Such a large cell would be divided into subgroups of ten, headed by an *Inspektor*. The *Haupt-direktion* would send the movement's seal to each *Direktion*, thus giving an official stamp of approval to its activity in the framework of the organization under the supervision of its institutions. A democratic mechanism was introduced to select the "inspectors" and "leaders" of the local assemblies: the members themselves would elect them, and after they had been approved by the *Hauptdirektion* and given an official letter of appointment, they could be inducted into their respective positions.[30]

In the organization's regulations a great deal of attention was devoted to the link, based mainly on the post, between the various bodies and the many members. For this purpose, a complex, cumbersome bureaucratic system of sending mail, receiving replies, and approving publications was set up. This system maintained the centralized structure and endowed the *Hauptdirektion* in Königsberg with powers of supervisions over everything that went on in the organization. If one of the members wished to send an article, question, or proposal to the organization, he had to submit it in writing to the *Inspektor* of the local cell, who would pass on the material to the *Direktion* in his city or the adjacent one, along with his approval. The *Direktion* would peruse the material and send it to the *Überdirektion* in Königsberg. Only there, at the organization's ideological control center, would the reply be given: approval of the article for publication in *Hame'asef* or an opinion about a specific proposal made by the member. The reply would be returned "downward" through the same bureaucratic channels: from Königsberg to Berlin, from Berlin to the *Direktion*, from there to the local *Inspektor,* and from him to the man who submitted the material or proposal. This procedure, the by-laws stated, had to be strictly observed without any exceptions: "So that everything can be handled in an orderly fashion, no letters will be answered except in the above-mentioned manner, and the *Hauptdirektion* in Königsberg will write only to the *Überdirektion* in Berlin, and they will make their statements to the other assemblies in each and every city."[31] To ensure that manuscripts sent to the organization for publication in *Hame'asef* or to be printed in the Freischule printing house would be objectively judged, the by-laws required that the writer attach two signed letters to the manuscript—one omitting the author's name and bearing the letter S (*Schrift*), the other containing information about the author and bearing the letter N (*Nahme*). The second letter would be opened only if the manuscript were approved for publication. The author would bear the postal expenses for a manuscript that was not accepted.[32]

The regulations of the society required all the local cells to meet at least once a month for the type of ideological literary meeting typical of a "reading society." At these meetings, articles and literary works would be discussed and questions raised by the heads of the society. Leaders of the *Direktion* would convene a weekly meeting, to discuss mainly the activity of the local cells and administrative problems. Once a year, according to plan, a general meeting would be held: "Once a year there will be a large meeting attended by all the members of the organization. All members will be notified of the date set aside for the meeting. Then we shall know how much the organization has grown and how its boundaries have expanded."[33] As far as is known, a meeting of this sort was never actually held.

The breadth of the maskilic vision is amazing. And the optimistic expectations of Euchel and his colleagues that the Haskalah movement would grow to such dimensions, making it possible to hold no less than a supra-national congress of Jews committed to the values of the Enlightenment and cultural reforms in Jewish life, are truly remarkable. The idea of organizing a maskilic republic into a centralized, formal movement, which would create an international forum for meeting and exchanging ideas, had never even occurred to those active in the literary republic of the European Enlightenment.

Intensive Acculturation in Berlin

Euchel expected the organization of the Society for the Promotion of Goodness and Justice to be completed by the middle of Elul, 1787, a month and a half from the publication of its founding document and the regulations binding on its members. With immense optimism, he hoped that by then the center in Königsberg would know the geographical dimensions of the movement and how many members it had.[34]

Late in 1787, the first issue of the new volume of *Hame'asef* was published by the reorganized society, in an expanded format with new sections, printed on the printing press of the Freischule. However, in this brief period of time, Euchel had already moved from Königsberg to Berlin, returning there about three years after having visited the city as the acknowledged head of the Haskalah movement and fourteen years after he had fled it as a boy to embark on his new life.

Euchel's move to Berlin at the end of 1787 disrupted the organizational structure of the Society for the Promotion of Goodness and Justice even before its ability to perform effectively had actually been put to the test. In this structure, the Königsberg circle of maskilim and the *Hauptdirektion* had been given hegemony, but as soon as Euchel arrived in Berlin, several amendments were made regarding the status and power of the organization's bodies, which upset the balance between the maskilim of Berlin and those of Königsberg. The main leadership was transferred to Berlin, headed by Isaac Daniel Itzig and Euchel as general managers (*Hauptdirektoren*), assisted by Brill and Landau. Euchel was appointed manager of the printing house, replacing Isaac Satanow, who had left for Poland on an extended visit to his family. In Königsberg, only a branch of the organization was set up, headed by Yehiel, Isaac Euchel's brother, assisted by the senior members of the organization in that city— Mendel Breslau and Sanwil Friedländer.[35]

As a result of the establishment of the Society for the Promotion of Goodness and Justice and Euchel's move to Berlin, the center of gravity of the Haskalah movement shifted to Berlin. What was the Jewish Berlin that Euchel encountered in 1787 like? One detailed description, from the vantage point of a Christian visitor in the 1780s, reveals a Jewish community intensively acculturating to the European lifestyle and German bourgeois society:

Jewish Berlin is very impressive. Most of the Jews live in the center of the city, particularly on the Jüdenstrasse, Königsstrasse, Spandauerstrasse, and other streets. The splendid home of the banker, Ephraim, is on Unter den Linden Boulevard, while in the Friedrich quarter there are hardly any Jews at all. The Jews in Berlin are very wealthy; Moses, Itzig, and Ephraim are some of the richest among them. Some of them own factories, but most earn their livelihood from commerce. Their behavior is refined and courteous, in particular those who have received a good education. They are no longer stiff-necked, cowardly, and coarse as the members of their nation used to be. Those of noble conduct who act according to worthy principles frequently socialize with Christians, and only rarely do these Christians take note of the fact that they are Jews. The hairstyles of many are similar to those of the Christians and their mode of dress is no different from ours. They no longer think a beard is important because it makes a man look distinguished. One hardly sees any, they no longer feel they are necessary, and if any do keep their beards, it is only to avoid gossip. Among the Jews there are scholars in various fields who devote themselves to the sciences with laudable dedication. Who does not know Moses Mendelssohn? Doctor Bloch is a great expert in the history of nature and in physics, and Doctor Herz is now giving a course of lectures in philosophy. In general, they love to read nowadays much more than ever before. They are developing good taste and a liking for poetry as they begin to read more journals and to attend the theater. The strong tendency to read novels is spreading among them with extraordinary speed, in particular among the women . . . Of all pleasures, the Jews best love the theater, and on Friday evenings they are the ones who fill the balconies. When the weather is fine, one can see them strolling in groups through the Tiergarten Park or along Unter den Linden Boulevard.[36]

Nothing in this description would have been new to Euchel, since he was closely associated with the wealthy and cultured Jewish elite and felt very much at home in this Jewish-German milieu. It seems, however, that soon after he arrived in Berlin Euchel was assailed by many doubts, even though he was still in thrall to the grand vision of expanding the scope of the Haskalah movement in Germany. Until 1786, in particular during Mendelssohn's lifetime, the interests of the rich, well-connected Jews and the circle of maskilim coincided. However, at this particular point in time, a change occurred. This is how Miriam Bodian depicts the process: it is reasonable to assume that the rich, cultured Jews believed the maskilic awakening could be beneficial in the public campaign to improve the status of Jews. On one hand, it had the effect of enhancing Jewish prestige and improving their image in the eyes of Christians; on the other hand, it helped to promote the reform of the Jewish population in regard to employment, culture, and civil behavior. From 1786, and even more so in the 1790s, this situation changed.

Frederick's death roused hopes of liberation from the stifling absolutist centralization, and the leaders of Jewish society looked forward to an improvement in their civil status if they demanded this directly from Frederick and Wilhelm II. However, it soon turned out, contrary to expectations, that Prussia was not embarking on a liberal track and that it was impossible to achieve this sort of change for Jewry as a whole. Hence, they were prepared to demand political rights for themselves, arguing that they were considered an element beneficial to the state, with which they totally identified. Once the wealthy capitalists began to look after their own personal interests, and aspired to find social gratification primarily in German society, the alliance between the maskil and the philanthropist, so vital for the promotion of Jewish enlightenment, since it provided it with economic and social backing, was dissolved. "To justify cutting themselves off from the rest of Jewry," Bodian concluded, "they used the political-moral argument that a citizen's affiliation with the state is the sole collective framework."[37] Needless to say, this position was very far removed from the vision of the future of the Haskalah, which regarded this kind of affiliation as only one of the frameworks, and was not prepared to relinquish the particular affiliations of common Jewish existence.

At the same time, the young cultured elite's connection to the Jewish sources, to Hebrew, to religious faith and its commandments, was growing more tenuous. Many of the sons and daughters of the Berlin tycoons and merchants who grew up in the 1780s no longer concealed their alienation from Jewish religion and customs (in particular after the death of Mendelssohn, who was committed to the tradition). They chose to embrace deism, as the natural, rational religion of the Enlightenment, or Christianity, which was viewed in romantic terms as a religion that gave the soul emotional gratification. These young people no longer had any interest in the maskilim's project to culturally rehabilitate the Jews.[38]

A brief glimpse into the life of Rahel Levin (1771–1833) offers an illuminating picture of the young Berliners who grew up in the 1780s in the homes of affluent Jews. A portrait of fourteen-year-old Rahel and her younger brother Marcus, painted between 1785 and 1786, shows the boy wearing the fashionable clothes of an adult and the girl in a dress with a hoop skirt and décolleté, sitting at a piano holding a delicate flower; both children are looking at the artist with a bored expression. Rahel received a music education and was taught the manners of high society; she was undoubtedly one of the most intellectual young women of her generation. She read incessantly, was familiar with both French and the German Enlightenment culture, quoted Rousseau, Diderot, Wieland, and Lessing in many of her letters and in her diary, strove to gain more and more knowledge, attended the theater, and regarded herself as an enlightened woman. Although she admired Mendelssohn, and knew him and his family who lived nearby, her own conception of Enlightenment was individualistic and cosmopolitan and included neither Jewish tradition nor maskilic texts of the kind that appeared in Hebrew in *Hame'asef*. On a family visit to Breslau, for example, Rahel experienced culture shock when, for the first time, she came face to face with the life of a traditional Jew. She was repelled by the traditional life led by most of Breslau Jewry in the 1790s, and the letters she wrote from that visit reveal her strong feelings of alienation and disgust. It was one of the few occasions in her life that she witnessed Jewish prayer, which to her was ugly and noisy, totally unaesthetic, and lacking in sensitivity. She awoke in the morning, she wrote, to the sound of a commotion that she later learned came from the morning prayer in the synagogue established by her uncle in his home: "I get up and look and hear all too clearly that it was a memorial to *Him* that the Bohemians [traditional Jews] shout every morning in mystical language which they call Holy, all the way to his palace in the clouds."[39]

While it is true that Euchel and other maskilim often harshly criticized traditional Jewish society, the alienation of these young Jews, who aspired to be accepted by the high bourgeois society and break all ties to their Jewish origins, is glaringly evident from their own testimonies. In marked contrast, the maskilim believed their prime mission was to rehabilitate the Jews without expunging their self-identity. In the post-1786 cultural and social reality of Jewish Berlin, it was no longer clear what the Haskalah could hope to accomplish or what the role of the Society for the Promotion of Goodness and Justice was. Ostensibly, the Enlightenment revolution had succeeded in Berlin beyond all expectations, so that Euchel was left with very little work to accomplish there in 1787. However, this would only be true if we viewed this description of Berlin's Jewish high society as a complete, satisfying one, and only if the Haskalah's historical role was limited to secularizing Jewish life and paving the way for the Jews' entry into German society. In truth, neither of these are exact: Jewish Berlin in the late eighteenth century was far more complex than one might gather from the description of the 1786 Christian visitor or Rahel Levin's life.

There was really no need for either the Haskalah movement or the Society for the Promotion of Goodness and Justice to exist for Jewish life in Berlin to become modernized. The maskilic discourse played only a minor, marginal role in this long-term process, which was devoid of all ideology. Secularization and the decline of religious practice were the outcome of a quiet, uninitiated development. There were many affinities between the intellectual elite Rahel Levin represented and the elite of the maskilim, but in the final analysis they were two quite different elites. They were distinguished not only by their socioeconomic status, but also by the fact that the maskilic version of the

Enlightenment discourse was an internal Jewish discourse not intended to serve the tendency to break away from Jewish society and culture. The cultured elite that Rahel Levin belonged to strove to be integrated into the European Enlightenment culture on the basis of its universal values. While the maskilim's aspirations were not always clear-cut and well formulated, they always strove for what was best, most reformed, and most moral for the Jewish collective. Everything the maskilim did was focused on fostering the maskilic republic—a journal, a society of maskilim, and a printing house. Individualistic Jewish-German intellectuals like Rahel Levin showed no interest in these three aims, which manifested a conscious endeavor to build an innovative Jewish sphere and to renew Jewish culture out of a sense of responsibility for Jewry as a whole.

Steven Lowenstein has persuasively demonstrated that the Berlin families that attracted the most attention overshadowed other social groups. In particular, it has been overlooked that even at the end of the eighteenth century, despite a certain weakening of the traditional frameworks, a Berlin community continued to maintain the characteristic patterns of traditional communal life. In general, the modernization of German Jewry reached its peak at the end of the century only in major urban communities like Berlin, Hamburg, and Königsberg. This trend was manifested in use of the German language, abandonment of Yiddish, rising standard of living, bourgeois lifestyle, modern education, adoption of European names, and religious permissiveness. In contrast, for the majority of German Jews, the process of modernization was slow and prolonged and was completed only toward the mid-nineteenth century. Even in the Berlin of the 1780s and 1790s the wealthy elite was merely a minority in comparison to the middle and lower classes, and its lifestyle was not shared by the majority of Jews. Many of the members of this elite continued to support both traditional scholarship and the Haskalah and its projects (the Freischule, the books of the Haskalah) at the end of the 1780s and throughout the '90s.

Berlin's scholarly elite—rabbis, rabbinical judges, and young yeshivah students—still maintained a strong presence and influence. Other than the main synagogue, there were many private congregations in the city, and the rich families—in particular members of the older generation—contributed to the traditional institutions, founded synagogues in their homes, made donations to societies like Machzikei Lomdei Torah (Supporters of Talmud Scholars) and purchased expensive ritual objects. At the end of the 1780s, in a typical orthodox move, Lazarus Bendavid, known as a deist and a proponent of leniency in relation to the commandments, was prevented from serving as a leader in prayer in a synagogue. Jacob Adam, who came to Berlin in the early nineteenth century from a town in Posen to study Torah in a yeshivah, described in his memoirs the world of the young students of Talmud. In their milieu, there were as yet no signs of acculturation, although they were aware that the danger of apostasy was greater in Berlin than elsewhere, and Adam himself had relatives who had abandoned all observance of the commandments.[40] Nor were the "salon women" like Rahel Levin (the best known among them, who after her conversion to Christianity and marriage was called Rachel Varnhagen) representative of the modern Jewish women. Paula Heyman has asserted that new studies on the modernization of Jewish women in Germany indicate they were relatively conservative and committed to the tradition. They related to women like Rahel Levin, who bore her Jewish origin as if it were a mark of disgrace, as fascinating and famous but definitely exceptional.[41]

Consequently, it would be correct to say that after 1786 the Jewish scene became very diversified, particularly in the Berlin community. Alongside the social and economic gaps within the Jewish population, three distinct Jewish intellectual elites began to emerge. One comprised rabbis and traditional scholars with an orthodox orientation; the second, assimilationists who sought to gain the respect of non-Jewish society, and the maskilim. The maskilic project did not go unnoticed, and there were orthodox reactions against *Hame'asef*, which were not printed but became known to the maskilim. And we ought not to forget that when Euchel settled in Berlin and dreamed of fulfilling the grand vision of the Society for the Promotion of Goodness and Justice, he saw a field of activity that extended far beyond the Berlin community. He still could see himself as the head of an avant garde Jewish camp and could try to enlist public opinion in support of the Haskalah and the republic of maskilim.

All these trends reverberated in his belligerent article that opened the society's activities in the summer of 1787, soon after his move to Berlin, and was printed as an introduction to *Hame'asef*'s newest volume. A philosophical-moral article, very typical of the maskilic discourse, its aim was to shore up the self-confidence of the young readers who were just starting or had already begun to undergo a process of cultural conversion to enlightenment and would be the future generation of the movement. Euchel attacked the opponents of *chokhmah* in the traditional society, and asserted that anyone willing to go against the stream would achieve the lofty ideal of humanism ("man, the highest of the earth's creatures, is made sublime by a rational mind"), would gain an intellectual experience, partnership in the Enlightenment project and "true happiness" by attaining perfection. "Wisdom [*chokhmah*]," as Euchel defined it, "embraces all work, all study, every action and behavior that brings man closer to realizing his selfhood," and the *chakham* is "a man who strives diligently to attain true perfection." The concept of human perfection was derived from the perception of God's absolute perfection, and it could be achieved only through rational thought, general knowledge, and humanistic morals. However, Jewish society, in which the potential maskilim grow up, places obstacles in their path. The neglect of *chokhmah* is one of the more grievous historical shortcomings of the religious culture, as a result of which "the enlightened were few and the ignorant many." The intellectual effort also deters those who are "afraid of the intellect," the superficial bourgeoisie, in Euchel's view, who show no interest in the life of spirit and thought. Even more threatening and forbidding is the claim of the "despisers of intellect" that the maskil is suspect of heresy. The orthodox reactions were not limited only to the controversy over *Divrei shalom ve'emet*. From time to time, anonymous vituperative letters were received by the *Hame'asef* editors, denunciations were uttered, and maskilim related instances of slander and schemes against them:

Whenever they see a *chakham* honored and respected among the people, the fire of jealousy is aroused in them and they become quarrelsome and hostile towards him . . . they will despise and slander him saying his taste has left him, his scent has changed, he shall not look upon the sacred, for he has gone astray after lies and has cast off all faith. They will make accusing speeches against him, speaking insolent words, and finally humiliate him and oust him from the congregation of the upright.

Euchel equipped his readers with rebuttals to the hostile orthodox positions. No man has the right to judge the religious faith of another, which is a matter only for his own conscience. The true *chakham* never loses his faith. Those who attack the maskilim are usually stupid and hypocritical, men who only "show themselves outwardly, in their clothing and behavior, to be pious and moral men, but in truth are full of evil and deceit." He suggested that the maskilim should adopt the standard policy of *Hame'asef* and, with disdainful silence, refrain from reacting: "We pay no heed to the whispers spread by many throughout Jewry to utter falsehoods against us and our deeds. We shall not fight with them nor shall we speak their names." And he went on to urge his readers to fearlessly persevere on the path of Haskalah: "So, my brethren, fear no man, seek judgment, study science, learn from men of intelligence and ethics, from the wise, though your beginning was humble, yet your end will be very great."[42]

Early in 1788, when Euchel began to publish Mendelssohn's first Hebrew biography in installments, he again publicly reflected on the Haskalah's target audience. His words carry a certain undertone of disappointment, which will increase even more in the 1790s. He referred to the opposition of the hostile orthodox ("Bats, in the darkness they fly higher and as the sun rises, in the shimmer of dawn they are but creatures that crawl in the dust"), and revealed his fear that the two processes he had witnessed in Jewish Berlin—the rising standard of living and the growing acculturation—would reduce support for the Haskalah. There was in that city, he noted, a group of bourgeois and affluent Jews so intent on the pleasures of life ("They have so glutted their hearts with delights that they have become satiated and disgusted with them, no longer wanting to engage in them, for they have filled their bodies with pleasures without giving any part of their minds") that it was impossible to interest them in the Enlightenment culture. Hence, the target audience was dwindling.

At this point, Euchel referred to the "middle" type, "the true maskil," who chooses a third path on the diversifying social and cultural map: radical European acculturation on the one hand, and an internal *Kulturkampf* on the other. This maskil is in the center, between orthodoxy, which is hostile to the Haskalah, and the bourgeoisie, which is indifferent to it: "Yea to you, the median man! Who stands midway, far from these two battling camps, to you alone I address my speech, go forth my brother! You have known how to find pleasure in the shadow of wisdom and to grow wiser while you engage in pleasures."[43] Although Euchel's encounter with Berlin dimmed his optimism from the early days of the Society for the Promotion of Goodness and Justice, the Haskalah movement was now on the brink of its three most successful years. The years 1788–90 were the time the movement flourished: there was a real growth in the scope of its literary activity, the maskilic republic expanded in Europe and its criticism of the rabbinical elite became more radical.

Chapter Twelve

Growth and Radicalization

On the eve of Rosh Hashanah, the Jewish New Year 5548 (1787), the workers of the Freischule printing house published a special poetic salutation to their employer, the provider of their livelihood, "The famous, exalted officer and minister, Daniel Itzig." This was not merely a gesture of flattery to the Jewish millionaire, but rather a sincere expression of gratitude by the workers, most of whom were of Polish origin and whose employment in the printing house provided them with a license to reside in Berlin.[1] This printing house, then at the peak of its success, operated under the aegis of the Enlightenment project, but was a thriving business in its own right, which also published religious literature against payment.[2]

The Haskalah Library Expands

From the time the Freischule printing house was founded in 1784 until 1790, eighty-four titles came off its press, an average of twelve per year. The peak years of the printing house's output throughout its existence (until 1825) were 1788 (seventeen titles) and 1789 (nineteen titles). Some of these were no more than pamphlets, several pages each, like the congratulatory poems printed to mark the marriages of some of the more outstanding members of the Society for the Promotion of Goodness and Justice,[3] as well as a calendar printed under a special license from the Prussian Academy of Sciences.[4] From 1788 to 1790, however, the printing house enriched the Haskalah library with several books that became the basic books of the movement. The society kept its promise to its members and during those years doubled the size and circulation of *Hame'asef*. The journal came off the presses in Berlin regularly, one issue each month, along with various supplements, including one in German.[5] Each of the volumes for 1788–90 contained about 400 pages, so that more than 1,200 pages were printed of the journal, which was the flagship of the Society for the Promotion of Goodness and Justice.

The basic maskilic books printed during those years included *Shirei tiferet*, the biblical epos of Moses and the exodus from Egypt, written by Wessely, which was still a best-seller in Hebrew poetry in the nineteenth century; *Agadat arba'a kosot*, by the philosopher and scholar Shlomo Pappenheim of Breslau (1740–1814), written after the death of his wife and three sons, as a justification of human fate, which was printed in ten additional editions and was regarded as a literary masterpiece; and Isaac Satanow's brilliant literary work, *Mishlei asaf*, a collection of proverbs and parables, written in the style of biblical wisdom literature and aimed at "instructing man in the paths of knowledge and morality."[6] For students, Aaron Wolfssohn, a private tutor in the home of one of the Friedländers and a key figure of the Haskalah in the 1790s, printed the reader, *Avtalyon*, and in 1788 Baruch Lindau printed the science textbook *Reshit limudim*, which became the most famous, up-to-date book on the Hebrew bookshelf at the end of the eighteenth century.[7] Instead of rabbinical approbations, this popular introduction to science was prefaced by letters of praise and recommendation from the two leading Jewish physicians and scientists in Berlin, Marcus Bloch and Marcus Herz, and not surprisingly, a congratulatory poem penned by Wessely was also appended to the book. Nearly an entire issue of *Hame'asef* was dedicated in 1788 to Euchel's initiative in printing *Givat hamoreh*—Solomon Maimon's commentary on *Guide for the Perplexed*, which was commissioned by the Society for the Promotion of Goodness and Justice. To raise funds for the book's publication, a network of no fewer than twenty agents was set up in the territory between Vilna and London.[8] In the meantime, in 1788, Euchel printed his biography of Mendelssohn, first in installments in *Hame'asef* and then as a book. This work also became one of the maskilic classics of the 1780s, enabling readers who were not fluent in German to read for the first time selected excerpts, in Hebrew, from Mendelssohn's *Jerusalem*.[9]

Joel Brill and Aaron Wolfssohn were the editors of a large collective project that they viewed as the fulfillment of Mendelssohn's last testament and the continuation of the *Bi'ur* project: the publication of German translations, in Hebrew letters, and a commentary on the scriptures that were not included in the *Bi'ur*. No fewer than fifteen maskilim, among them the heads of the society, participated in writing and printing the translation of and commentary on *Haftarot mikol hashanah* (sections from the Prophets recited in the synagogue throughout the year). There was a relatively large demand for these books; for example, 500 copies of the five Scrolls were ordered in advance, and more than 1,000 copies for the edition of Psalms with Mendelssohn's translation.[10] The Society for the Promotion of Goodness and Justice had calculated that an advance order of two to three hundred copies of each of the printed books would cover the minimal costs, and the great demand was unquestionably a measure of success.[11] The books were distributed through a network of agents in the various cities of Europe as well as through the post. Euchel was then simultaneously serving as manager of the printing house, the editor of *Hame'asef,* and the acting head of the society. He was flooded by orders for books, proposals for the publication of new books, and letters.[12]

The list of agents was printed in *Hame'asef.* When the demand for books printed by the Freischule press increased and their distribution became more profitable (the agent's commission was 10 percent of each book's price) people who were impersonating agents would turn up from time to time. One such was Israel Baer, who represented himself as an agent on behalf of the Society for the Promotion of Goodness and Justice. When complaints of his behavior reached the management, it published an open letter in which it denied any association with him, and informed the public that all its agents were supplied with a written endorsement and anyone who failed to present it was surely a fraud.[13] A man by the name of Shimon Kromeneu, from Prague, plagiarized Lindau's book *Reshit limudim,* renamed it *Amud hashachar,* and distributed it in the communities of the Habsburg empire under his own name, but he was finally exposed as a forger.[14]

At least part of the credit for the success of the Freischule books should go to *Hame'asef.* That journal fulfilled several functions simultaneously; it promoted sales, published articles, initiated new activities, signed up subscribers, and reviewed the books published by the printing house, thus stimulating the maskilic republic and promoting its literary activity. In *Hame'asef'*s three peak years (1788–90), the journal doubled in size but the proportion of scholarly articles, biblical commentaries, articles on the Hebrew language, translations, encomiums, and moral parables in the journal gradually decreased. Instead, more space was allotted to news, articles on current events, controversies, reactions, reviews, and dialogue between readers and editors and among readers themselves. Caustic reviews of religious books drew, in broad strokes, the boundary lines between the rabbinical culture and the culture of the Haskalah.[15]

Among the more prominent writers for *Hame'asef* were the two men who in the 1790s took over the editorship of the journal—Joel Brill and Aaron Wolfssohn. Naphtali Herz Wessely continued to contribute to the journal, particularly as the author of poems to mark various occasions, commissioned by community leaders as an expression of loyalty (for example, the illness of England's George III and the vaccinations given to the children of the Prussian king). However, he also acted in a supervisory capacity, moderating any radical statements and rebuking the editors from time to time. In an exceptional theological article, Wessely severely censured the scorn that the author of a 1786 article had heaped on the belief in the punishments of hell. He also used that occasion to remind the editors of his warning in *Nachal habesor* against publishing antirabbinical and antireligious satires. Characteristically, Wessely

lashed out against apostasy and averred that several articles of faith (the spiri-
tuality of the soul, the afterlife, the doctrine of reward) were basic to Judaism.
He tempered the concept of hell that appeared in the terrifying depictions in
the Kabbalistic *musar* literature and represented it as merely a symbolic
expression of abstract punishments that would be visited upon the soul.[16]

Hame'asef began allocating more space to useful knowledge about man
and the world. Detailed articles introduced many readers who had not
received a regular education to the animal world, scientific measuring instruments, the technique of pearl divers in the ocean, an understanding of the
physical forces revealed by Newtonian science, and new pedagogical theories,
as well as to basic concepts in philosophy, cited, for example, from Maimon's
commentary on *Guide for the Perplexed.*[17] The medical student Shlomo Schöneman, Isaac Satanow's son, called on the Jews to revive the Hebrew language,
making it flexible enough for use in scientific texts: "For all others are constantly adding to their language, new verbs and nouns for the actions, results
and sciences that are reviving each and every day . . . while our language is
barren, no longer giving birth."[18]

The mission of acquiring universal knowledge was cloaked in the rhetoric
of the Enlightenment. For example, reading a "nature book" was represented
as the best way of learning to know God: "The observation of everything there
is in the world, from the smallest creatures to the largest . . . the falling of rain,
the blowing of the winds, and the child coming forth from the womb . . . these
will bear witness to the perfection of His wisdom and ability." Moreover, the
"man of science," who yearns to learn the secrets of nature, is the human man
who rises above all other creatures: "The force of the inventor . . . will induce
him to seek to know everything that happens under the sun and to discover
the wonders and secrets of Nature . . . and through the efforts and diligence
of that force . . . the benefits to the existence and glorification of the human
race will greatly multiply."[19] The ideal man is one whose parents and educators
know how to provide him with a free, natural childhood that will strengthen
his body. Well-ventilated rooms, lightweight clothing, games in the open air
("Allow the child to caper and play outside even in the winter months!"),
baths in cold water—all these would ensure health and education "in the paths
of nature," according to the theories of the philosopher Locke, the pedagogue
Campe, and the physician Marcus Herz.[20] The Mendelssohnian myth that
Euchel developed in his biography, published in installments in four whole
issues of *Hame'asef,* shaped the ideal of self-perfection (*Bildung*) and personal
progress. In Euchel's heroic narrative, Mendelssohn's life became an exemplar
of success and a story that symbolized the Enlightenment revolution: the son
of a lowly scribe in Dessau became one of the greats of the generation thanks
to his intellectual faculties.[21]

Mendelssohn, however, was already in the realm of myth. The news sections of *Hame'asef* were intent on the political events of 1788–90 in France and the Austrian empire, which were interpreted as an outcome of the policy of Enlightenment. Moses Ensheim of Metz, in Alsace, was the journal's correspondent on the French Revolution and the debates in the National Assembly on the status of the Jews. Thanks to him, the readers of *Hame'asef* were able to observe from a distance, albeit somewhat belatedly, the dramatic, unprecedented events that took place in Paris. No one censored *Hame'asef*, and an article printed in September 1789 did not hesitate to support unequivocally the revolutionaries' antimonarchic and anti-class system objectives, in marked contrast to the traditional loyalty to the absolutist monarchy that the journal had always maintained. With unconcealed joy, Ensheim reported that "The prison called the Bastille, which terrified every honest man and was loathed by the righteous, was razed to its foundations, all the prisoners were set free, and the warden of the prison was killed by the sword." From then on, he wrote, "There will be no remembrance of the grandeur of the aristocrats, born into noble families, who lord it over the rest of the people, and wickedness is in their midst, and they speak no truth for the general good."[22] A paean to the General Assembly published by Ensheim on the front page of the November 1789 issue contained all the revolutionary slogans, avid support for the basic freedoms and the radical conclusion that "there is no ruler that can imprison the spirit."[23] In the winter of 1790, when news arrived about the emancipation granted to the Jews of Bordeaux, *Hame'asef* raved: "From Paris came a voice heralding redemption for our brethren the children of Israel." From now on, it seemed that "there is no good in this land that the Jew will not partake of as do all its other citizens, and that is the teaching of man!"[24]

Laws obliging Jews to serve in the army were first passed in Europe in 1788 in Joseph II's Habsburg empire. Letters and articles from Prague, Vienna, Trieste, and Lvov conveyed to *Hame'asef* readers the alarmed reactions of the Jews, in particular in Galicia, which had a population of more than 200,000 Jews and until 1772 had been part of the Polish kingdom. Reports also arrived about attempts to moderate their opposition and to explain that these laws actually were a reflection of progress and tolerance, not a decree threatening the Jewish religion. An anonymous open letter addressed to the Jews of Galicia advised Jewish soldiers to divide their time between God and the emperor. It promised them that if they were compelled to violate some religious law, they would not be punished by the Almighty: "Worship God through His commandments in your leisure time, and the emperor through his orders in wartime and in battle."[25] A letter from Trieste, written in the name of the local rabbi, defended Joseph II's tolerant policy and called on the Jews of Galicia to avoid creating the impression that they were ungrateful by opposing the conscription law. Since nothing had changed in Joseph II's policy of tolerance, "Our lord, His Excellency, the Emperor has stated that every man in all the cities of his kingdom shall observe the laws and teachings of their forefathers, there is no religious coercion, and tolerance is steadfast," and the only thing to be done was to reduce as far as possible any conflict between the duties of the soldier and the commandments of the halakhah.[26]

A news item from Prague in the spring of 1789 described the departure of twenty-five Jewish soldiers, attended by crowds and a great commotion: "There was a great pandemonium in the city street, we heard mothers crying for their sons, a sister weeping for her brother, and young women for their husbands, as they left their home city to do battle against our enemies."

Then Rabbi Yehezkel Landau, usually one of the targets of the maskilim's criticism since his involvement in the Wessely controversy, entered the fray, this time to urge moderation and sound judgment. An article from Prague quoted from the moving sermon that the rabbi delivered before Jewish soldiers at a military camp, in which he calmed their fears. He gave every conscript a small prayer shawl, phylacteries, and a prayer book, and gave them advice on how to reconcile their religious obligations, such as prayer, observance of the Sabbath and eating only kosher food, with their civic duties as dictated by the military framework. The emperor, Landau repeated again and again, does not have a policy of impinging upon religion. Landau went even further, and asked the soldiers to regard themselves as exemplary representatives of the Jewish people who through their impeccable service and readiness to give up their lives for their country, would demonstrate the Jews' loyalty to the state. After his sermon, Rabbi Landau gave four gold coins to each Jewish soldier and one to each of the Austrian soldiers who were guarding them, and then everyone parted in tears.[27]

At the end of the year, another article from Prague reported on the thanksgiving ceremony held in the synagogue of the city to mark the capture of Belgrade from the Turks, and on that occasion Rabbi Landau spoke in praise of the emperor.[28] The German supplement of the journal printed the full text of the 1789 Edict of Toleration for the Jews in Galicia, as a political document putting into practice the principles of the Enlightenment. In early 1790, Joseph II died. The journal printed a eulogy that came from Vienna and mourned the emperor as one of the great men of the Enlightenment. It lauded his enormous contribution to advancing the status of the Jews: "He has lifted the dwelling places of Israel from the rubbish heap and led it to the chambers of science and happiness to take part in it as one of his nation."[29]

News items from Austria informed *Hame'asef* readers of historically significant events. Just when the French Revolution was about to apply the principles of the Enlightenment in unprecedented emancipatory legislation, the

Jews learned for the first time the price they would have to pay for recognition by the centralized state as citizens with equal rights and obligations. These two historical developments were depicted in *Hame'asef*'s maskilic discourse as a high point along the road to human progress and were received with much satisfaction. In these articles, the editors uncharacteristically wrote some favorable words about Rabbi Landau for the moderate position he had taken on the issue of military conscription and the attitude toward the state.

The *Kulturkampf* Escalates

During this same period, against the background of Joseph II's policy of tolerance and reform, anticlerical expressions first began to appear in *Hame'asef*. There was nothing new about occasional outbursts against the rabbis, but the fundamental position taken by the editor, Euchel, had been to exercise restraint and to avoid a head-on conflict. Now, from 1788 to 1790, as if this was a coordinated move, the maskilim's rhetoric became sharply defiant, even personal. They challenged the rabbis' authority and mocked the rabbinical elite and its values.

Herz Homberg was the only maskil who in the 1780s held a government position that enabled him to implement a policy of transformation in education under the laws of the state. After leaving Berlin, Homberg traveled between Vienna, Gorizia, Trieste, and Prague. Joseph II's government regarded him as an enlightened Jew, highly motivated to promote the government educational system, which was the core of the Austrian policy of tolerance and reform in the 1780s. In 1788 Homberg was employed in Lvov as the emperor's supervisor of the German-Jewish schools in Galicia. His main task was to overcome the resistance of the traditional communities to any change in traditional education. Many testimonies exist as to the hostility Homberg encountered in Lvov and the stratagems the Jews resorted to in an attempt to evade the obligation to attend a German-Jewish school (which was explicitly set down in the 1789 Edict of Toleration, and the sanction for noncompliance was the withholding of a marriage license).[30]

The readers of *Hame'asef* learned about these things when Homberg published an open letter to the Galician rabbis in an attempt to persuade the rabbinical elite to withdraw its opposition. The letter was also printed separately and distributed in Galicia. Like Wessely in his *Divrei shalom ve'emet* six years earlier, Homberg pointed to the positive aspects of Joseph II's policy and the great advantages that would accrue to the Jews from it, and tried to mitigate the rabbis' fears that Torah study might be seriously impaired. He portrayed a bleak picture of traditional education and its flaws and offered his good services as an experienced and expert educator who had only the interests of the boys at heart. He suggested that an assembly of rabbis be convened to decide on changes in curriculum structure and teacher training.

But a catch appeared at the end of the open letter—a threatening ultimatum in the patronizing tone of someone who sensed he had the power and backing of the ruling government: "You should know, although I began by addressing you meekly, leaving the choice with you, not everything that you find desirous will become the law governing the Jews." What he was actually saying was that he was prepared to hear any ideas they might put forth, but he had the authority to decide, and any suggestions for educational reforms had to meet his approval. Otherwise, he would have no choice but to resort to coercive means: "And if your ideas are not satisfactory, I will compose some of my own . . . and will send them to their excellencies, the government ministers, and whatever they decree is that which will guide us."[31]

That same year, *Hame'asef* subscribers received a special booklet in German, worded as an open letter to all German Jews. It attacked the rabbinical elite, scorning and denigrating the two leading rabbis of the Prague community, Landau and Fleckeles. The author of *Sendschreiben an die deutsche Juden* was none other than David Friedländer, a key figure in the Haskalah movement.[32] Despite his social standing and family connections, Friedländer was not a typical representative of the wealthy elite in that he was a truly cultured man. His command of Hebrew and the religious sources enabled him to appraise the religious culture critically, and he was justifiably accepted in the Society for the Promotion of Goodness and Justice as a member who was one of the *toranim* (writers and scholars), rather than one of the philanthropists. Throughout his life, Friedländer strove to purify the Jewish religion and educate the youth toward a moral life. He was always suspicious of the rabbis' intentions and their intellectual level, and was, of course, one of the organizers of the front that supported Wessely in the 1780s and took steps to silence rabbis Tevele and Landau as well as the others who strongly opposed *Divrei shalom ve'emet*. As a zealous advocate of the German translation of the Bible, he made a contribution of his own.

When he received a copy of Rabbi Eleazar Fleckeles's book *Olat tzibur* (1787), the only anti-maskilic orthodox work published in the 1780s, and read in it the sermon denouncing Mendelssohn's *Bi'ur* project and vigorously objecting to any translations into German, Friedländer was infuriated.[33]

By the end of the 1780s, the maskilim were no longer allowing published religious literature to go uncriticized. Friedländer too decided he could not simply ignore the things Rabbi Fleckeles had written. Instead, he addressed enlightened Jewish public opinion, established by the maskilim, to show how disgraceful Fleckeles's sermon and Rabbi Landau's approbations were. He scornfully exposed them as a reflection of the deplorable state of the religious culture, which was hindering the advancement of Jewish enlightenment. In contrast to the ideal of pure language, Hebrew or German, which was the only medium through which cogent, comprehensible concepts could be taught to schoolchildren, the poor, imprecise rabbinical language was standing in the way of their understanding of the scriptures. The success of the society's translation project and its large number of subscribers attested to the public's sympathy for the maskilim. Rabbi Fleckeles's protests were, in Friedländer's view, no less than a declaration of war against the values of the Enlightenment—reason, science, order, clarity, and the language of culture. It was Fleckeles's desire, Friedländer maintained, to drag the Jews down again into the depths of obscurantism and ignorance, and Rabbi Landau was supporting and praising him. Friedländer's purpose in translating the sermon and approbation into German was to expose the rabbis' inferior language, and in his critical comments on page margins he tried to show, sentence after sentence, how the rabbinical reading distorted the ancient sources and drew conclusions that had absolutely no basis in those sources. Not only was there no prohibition against translating the scriptures and the prayer book, he stated, but it was actually mandatory based on the Talmud, Maimonides, and religious sentiment. Anyone opposed to it was not faithfully reading the sources, was doing an injustice to Judaism and to reason, and was hostile to the Enlightenment.

Friedländer's anticlerical rage intensified and he gave even more radical vent to it in his personal letters. He predicted the total collapse of the rabbinical elite, which was going downhill because it had become so entrenched in orthodox positions. "May God grant," he wrote in the spring of 1789, "that we shall, soon in our own time, sever the reins the rabbis hold around our necks, so that we may worship God shoulder to shoulder with love and awe."[34]

A far less well-known radical maskil followed Friedländer's struggle against Fleckeles with interest, and later that year reprinted excerpts from Friedländer's "open letter" in German in Latin letters, along with his own commentary. This maskil, Moshe Hirschel (born in 1754), was a contemporary of the younger maskilim. A reader of *Hame'asef*, he possessed much knowledge in philosophy that he apparently acquired in academic studies, was fluent in many languages and was well versed in the writings of the French Enlightenment, in particular Voltaire. Hirschel was probably in contact with Friedländer, but he was relatively removed from the circles of maskilim. He preferred to publish his virulent criticism of the rabbinical elite in German journals and books, and hence they aroused very little comment at the time, remaining on the sidelines of the Haskalah's public discourse. He became more and more disgusted with his fellow Jews, who in his view were finding it hard to free themselves from the clutches of the rabbinical leadership and the traditional Jewish lifestyle. And when he realized, greatly frustrated, that they were not ignoring his belligerent voice, he became all the more determined to break away officially from the community framework and to live as an ordinary Prussian citizen. When he found that this was impossible, he chose to convert to Christianity (probably in the mid-1790s).[35]

In 1788, this typical representative of the enlightened free-thinkers published in Breslau one of the most radical works of the Haskalah revolution. It has a telling title that cries out like one of the many revolutionary slogans that are scattered throughout the book: *The Jewish Hierarchy's Struggle Against Reason.*[36] Hirschel conceived of Enlightenment in the French and Voltairean sense. He defined it as liberation from prejudice, as the overthrow of all barriers between nations and religions, and as a struggle for human rights—the freedom of conscience and of faith.[37] "Man is born free and everywhere he is in chains"—this explosive revolutionary statement opened Jean Jacques Rousseau's *Social Contract.*[38] It seems as if the whole of Hirschel's book was inspired by this line, as he applied it to the Jewish reality.

Hirschel's basic premise was that, throughout the generations, the "Jewish hierarchy" had bound the Jews in the shackles of religious laws, customs, worldviews and opposition to the outside world. The result was a dismal fate: their ongoing subjugation and cultural backwardness. The Enlightenment revolution occasioned an all-out war against the "Jewish hierarchy" in the name of reason, in order to bring the Jews happiness and success. Deist and anticlerical aims, as well as a zealous belief in human equality and the power of reason, led Hirschel to publish a series of militant, revolutionary manifestos. The greatest enemy in his eyes was "the forgers of shackles driven by egoism, hungering for power, thirsting for blood and satanic evil, who have created all manner of laws and customs and ceremonies that have brought catastrophe upon entire nations." All history is one vast heroic struggle by philosophers and scholars endeavoring to vanquish superstition and to place reason on the throne: "The order of the day is to light the torch of reason!" And he added:

Walk in the path of reason and you shall be enlightened, happy, and free of those strong and harmful shackles.

I tell you before the omnipresent God, with all of my inner powers of persuasion and those of any intelligent person, that it was they, the forgers of shackles, who have caused men this indescribable suffering through their doctrines, for they have angrily rejected Enlightenment and do so to this very day.

All the religious laws according to which we lived thousands of years ago and which are still valid today are but the fruit of the bellicose endeavors of these people, whose only motivation is a passion for power and the desire to gain personal benefits.[39]

In this revolutionary campaign to enlist others in his cause, Hirschel made public his consuming hatred of the "hierarchy." He openly stated his belief that the rabbinical elite was actually responsible for the humiliating and inferior status of the persecuted Jews: "These evil men have trapped us in a labyrinth of laws, customs, rituals, and baseless views which deprive us of all ability to be useful citizens, possessed of rights and obligations in any state whatsoever, and this has been the cause of the contempt and hatred that all the nations feel toward us." The "theologians" want "to keep the people steeped in stupidity, ignorance, and superstition," by claiming that their suffering is the punishment for the sins of their forefathers. This claim, Hershel averred, was despicable. "Oh, you barbarians, what disgraceful sacrilege is embodied in that claim of yours!" he angrily rebuked them: "How can you so debase God? . . . How can you attribute such a lust for revenge to the infinite goodness of God [and to argue that He] is likely to punish us so severely for the transgressions of our fathers' fathers who lived thousands of years ago?" That is unthinkable. In fact, all the suffering and hatred, the restrictions and the humiliations that the Jews endure arise from "the religious law that dictates our way of life, and from the people who have done their utmost to impose them upon us." The rabbis who did so are "the most stupid of all, for that stupidity has caused an entire nation to be banished for thousands of years to live in insupportable distress, merely to satisfy the prideful drives for power of the hierarchy."[40]

In the great darkness in which "hierarchy" was enveloping Jewish existence and trampling upon reason, Hirschel found but one beam of light. He was fortunate to live in Prussia, as a citizen subject to the government and the law which protected him against the rage of the "hierarchy." Now, in his country, the most important step had been taken toward releasing the Jews from this heavy burden, since Frederick the Great had taken away the rabbis' power by divesting them of the right to exercise excommunication. From now on, the Enlightenment would penetrate into every corner of Jewish society; according to Hirschel's optimistic assessment, about a quarter of the Jews living in Prussia had already openly or secretly turned their backs on orthodoxy. This was the time to destroy the "hierarchy," that horrible monster that had brought such endless suffering to the human species. This could be done by disseminating the idea of religious tolerance, struggling for the recognition of human rights, restraining fanaticism and distributing the writings of the Enlightenment and rational religion. And Hirschel called upon his readers, the enlightened Jews, to join in the revolution:

So that we may act in concert to disseminate the Enlightenment among our fellow Jews, who have been shackled in chains for thousands of years by the usurpative rule of the hierarchy, which has welded them with fanaticism and a distorted religion . . . On you, whom God has endowed with knowledge, talent and sufficient ability to combat this hierarchical body, everything depends. You can bring happiness to an entire people who raise their voices to you in entreaty, and lift their eyes to you in hope![41]

An Attack on Rabbi Raphael Kohen

Hirschel's outspoken, furious *Kulturkampf* failed to reverberate throughout the Jewish world and within a few years he chose to convert to Christianity and disappeared from the public sphere. However, at about the same time, a new tempest was unleashed, with the intent of destroying the reputation and authority of the rabbinical elite, which again placed the "Jewish hierarchy" on the defensive. The author of this attack was Saul Berlin, who in 1789 published his subversive book, *Mitzpeh yokte'el*.[42] Seventeen years earlier Rabbi Raphael Kohen, rabbi of the Altona-Hamburg community, who from the early 1780s had been trying to block the Haskalah and acculturation, had published his book, *Torat yekutiel*. This halakhic work on ritual slaughter, published in Berlin in an ornate folio edition on about 400 densely printed pages, earned its author prestige in the rabbinical elite.[43]

Saul Berlin, an extraordinary figure in the world of the Haskalah, was the maskil who took one of the most radical positions against the religious culture in the *Divrei shalom ve'emet* polemic. He made a thorough study of Kohen's book, which only the truly scholarly could comprehend, and wrote a book to counter it, in which he completely dismantled, piece by piece, this prestigious product of the rabbinical elite, showing it to be merely an empty vessel.

Hiding behind the pseudonym Ovadiah b. Baruch, a Polish talmudic scholar living in Alsace, Berlin mercilessly exposed the true nature of this supposedly reputable and impressive scholarly work and crushed Kohen's pretension of being an authoritative religious leader by dint of his mastery of halakhic texts. On close to eighty double-columned pages of criticism, written in the codes and style prevailing in halakhic literature, Berlin showed how wrong Rabbi Kohen had been throughout his book in his use of scholarly techniques, claiming that a serious talmudic scholar would find in it nothing but nonsense, innumerable errors, and ridiculous conclusions, such as the permission to take bribes and make exemptions in regard to the laws of *kashrut*. Unquestionably, Berlin asserted, Rabbi Kohen had published his book in order to fraudulently move up in the rabbinical hierarchy. He exposed how the rabbi, by exploiting the ignorance of most of the talmudic scholars and heads of the communities, who did not take the trouble to scrutinize the book, had, thanks to it, acquired the respected and profitable position as rabbi of Altona-Hamburg. The author of *Mitzpeh yokte'el* intended it not only as an exposé of Rabbi Kohen's infamy but also as a contribution to the much more significant anticlerical revolution—to purge the Jewish bookshelf of a series of valueless books and to free Jewish society of the encumbrance of mediocre rabbis:

And the prophet stood at the gates, to warn the people lest they permit villains to torment them with their books, or allow those who would lead men astray to raise themselves up as their shepherds to guide the people and to engulf those who follow their guidance. For the Truth has begun to lift its mighty arm against its enemies, thus it will continue to take revenge on its adversaries, to cast iron bars off its neck, and to destroy the fortresses in which it has been imprisoned since Israel has been in exile, where it has been made to dwell in darkness like the dead, and never to see the splendor of light for the sun lives not in that place.[44]

Seven years after the *Divrei shalom ve'emet* controversy, this new campaign was launched in the *Kulturkampf* of the Haskalah. *Mitzpeh yokte'el* was printed on the Freischule printing press. Its directors and founders, Isaac Daniel Itzig and David Friedländer (who were also the principals of the school and officeholders in the Society for the Promotion of Goodness and Justice) decided together with the author, Saul Berlin, to use the book in a radical, sweeping revolutionary move. As was done with Wessely's *Divrei shalom ve'emet*, copies of *Mitzpeh yokte'el* were sent to the most prominent and influential representatives of the rabbinical elite, who were asked to react publicly to Berlin's challenge and to judge whether his criticism was justified.

Fourteen rabbis were asked to respond. Heading the list were Zevi Hirsch Levin of Berlin and Yehezkel Landau of Prague. At the end of the list, in bold letters to indicate his special status, was none other than "the famous, devout genius, the rabbi and teacher, Eliahu of Vilna." This was undoubtedly a well-planned and deliberate provocation, in an attempt to use the opportunity to settle accounts with Rabbi Kohen, who had been a symbol of fanaticism since he had been suspected of having banned Mendelssohn's *Bi'ur*, and since the Netanel Posner affair in Hamburg. Another aim was to inveigle the most senior rabbis at the end of the eighteenth century into a dispute, and by doing so to weaken the rabbinical elite and publicly expose their grievous offenses.

In a provocative open letter printed on the frontispiece of *Mitzpeh yokte'el*, Itzig and Friedländer introduced "Ovadiah b. Barukh" as an authentic representative of pure scholarship, a modest talmudic scholar, a man of virtue, well-versed in science. This educated rabbi, they stated, had asked them to publish his book because its subject matter was of such great public interest. They did not usually publish halakhic literature, nor did they have the tools with which to judge who is right in this rabbinical dispute, Itzig and Friedländer cynically asserted, taking up a righteous position. Then they went on to ask whether it was possible that the crisis in the rabbinical elite was so profound that no one would rise to castigate a rabbi who had been so lax as to publish such an inferior book? Or perhaps "your fury is reserved only for one engaged in *chokhmah* and enlightenment or who seeks the good of his fellow Jews," while their voices were silent when one of their own was guilty of "senseless verbiage and crafty plots."

Like the Wessely polemic in 1782, this affair was regarded by the maskilim as a crucial test of the rabbis. Would they respond to the challenge and join in a debate before public opinion, which also included the new elite of the Haskalah? Would they deviate from their usual behavior and respect the freedom of expression and opinion, and refrain from hurling curses and invective, as they normally did? Would they be courageous enough to admit to the truth, to take sides with *Mitzpeh yokte'el*, and to denounce the rabbi of Altona-Hamburg?[45]

None of the Berlin maskilim's expectations were realized. Nonetheless, probably no one was surprised when, only a few days after the subversive *Mitzpeh yokte'el* arrived in the Altona-Hamburg community, a writ banning it was issued. The fact that everyone knew the true identity of its author—the son of the Berlin community's rabbi, although no one actually mentioned it in public—made the whole affair a much more sensitive one. Once again the *Kulturkampf* raged. This time it was waged not only in letters, banning writs, and handbills, but also in the literary arena established by the maskilim, in particular in *Hame'asef*. Less than four weeks after its publication, *Mitzpeh yokte'el* and its author were banned in the court of justice of the triple community (Altona, Hamburg, and Wandsbeck), whose judges defended the community's rabbi, recognized the threat to the entire rabbinical elite, and declared the book "a libelous and evil piece of writing that must be treated with great contempt and should be burned like heretical books, may they perish now and quickly be destroyed." A day later (the 28th of Adar, 1789) the beadle of the Great Synagogue in Altona read out a special announcement in which the judges publicly proclaimed the ban and denounced the anonymous author who "had attempted to overthrow and destroy the wall of the Torah and had shown contempt and scorn for the honor of the heavens and of the talmudic scholars." One can safely assume that the man behind the announcement was none other than Raphael Kohen, who was not only affronted by the criticism of his book, but was also particularly sensitive to the injury to his status. Such an acrimonious orthodox reaction had not been heard since Rabbi David Tevele's sermon denouncing Wessely:

You, men of the house of Israel, the inheritors of our religion and heritage . . . look closely and see if such a thing has ever been . . . that such an arrogant man would arise in our midst . . . to scoff at a learned Talmud scholar of such great repute, comparable to the Almighty who has laid the foundations of the earth and whose right hand has spanned the heavens, and in particular the greatest man of Torah in our generation . . . lament that such a day has dawned in Jewry, a day of catastrophe, of thick darkness, for he has come forth who would enter into a covenant with a false god and mislead men with mocking speech to insult the Torah of the Lord and to find fault with His holy words . . . for who is the man made of flesh and sound of mind who will not shudder and be horrified upon hearing all the words of such a one . . . and will not smite the hearts of his brethren with screams and shouts upon seeing how greatly we are afflicted by the sacrilege of the Almighty's name and the affront to the honor of the Torah and its sages . . . and that man shall be condemned as a heretic and an apostate, and his writing as a libelous book . . . that does not exist and will not endure, but will be burned as an object no one cares for . . . it will be trampled by the mob at the gate . . . banned and ostracized and excommunicated and separated from all that is sacred in Israel until he acknowledges that he did wrong and removes the veil to repent.[46]

As soon as news of the ban became known in Berlin, Saul Berlin began to defend himself in open letters printed in the Freischule printing house, including some letters of support written by his father, Rabbi Zevi Hirsch Levin. The polemic degenerated into rumor, mutual recriminations, and more libelous writings attacking *Mitzpeh yokte'el*, composed in fiery orthodox rhetoric peppered with curses. Attempts were also made, on Saul Berlin's behalf, to enlist well-known rabbis, in particular Rabbi Landau, to challenge the validity of the ban.[47]

"Ovadiah b. Barukh" argued against those who had excommunicated him, saying that he did not understand why they had been so quick to take this measure before the opinions of the rabbis had been received, or why they had complied with their chief rabbi's demand that they immediately rally to his defense. He asserted that he was still hoping to receive rabbinical support in his war against *Torat yekutiel*, which would prove to the heads of the Altona-Hamburg community that they had erred in hastening to side with their rabbi. He suggested that they urgently apply to Rabbi Zevi Hirsch Levin from Berlin or to the Gaon of Vilna to decide who was right in this affair. In his view, the hasty intervention of the community's judges had thwarted any possibility of holding a rational debate on the book.[48] When Saul Berlin and his father tried to persuade Rabbi Landau to support *Mitzpeh yokte'el*, at first he equivocated, arguing that neither side in the controversy were acting in the public interest. He was finally persuaded that the ban was invalid after he learned the true identity of "Ovadiah b. Barukh" and Rabbi Levin explicitly declared that it had no grounds, but he still failed to make his opinion public.[49]

In the meantime, handbills signed in Berlin were distributed in the major communities (Prague, Hamburg, Amsterdam, Breslau), calling on the Jews, in the name of Rabbi Zevi Hirsch Levin, to ban not only *Mitzpeh yokte'el* but all other books printed by the Freischule press as well. Once again, Isaac Daniel Itzig and David Friedländer had to save the day, this time also out of their concern that the printing house might suffer financial damage. They published a special announcement, sent to various communities and printed in *Hame'asef*: "to assuage the fears of the customers wishing to purchase books printed by us." They denied that the community's rabbi was involved in the affair and quoted him as stating these were fallacious handbills and that he was not responsible for their contents. And in any case, why are we, the directors of the publishing house, who in all fairness decided to print *Mitzpeh yokte'el* only after its author agreed to submit it to a public rabbinical review, now being threatened by a ban on all our books?[50]

Saul Berlin also published a handbill himself in which he defended the printing house, advocated freedom of opinion, represented himself as a fighter for the truth and not a mocker of talmudic scholars, as he had been depicted, and accused the initiators of the ban in Altona- Hamburg of maliciousness and religious fanaticism.[51] In an article under his full name, printed in the Freischule printing house, he laid the blame for the scandal, which had exacerbated the crisis in the rabbinical elite and worsened its image, on the judges who had issued the ban. He demanded that they publicly apologize for the personal affront to him. He gave Rabbi Kohen a month in which to issue a public statement rescinding the ban and admitting there were flaws in his book.[52] In the Sivan 1789 issue of *Hame'asef* the controversy was summed up in an anonymous dialogue, that depicted the rabbis' silence as evidence of the overall crisis affecting the rabbinical leadership. It concluded by calling on the judges to rescind the ban and on the rabbi to respond at long last to Saul Berlin's claims.[53]

This *Kulturkampf* was covered in extremely trenchant articles published by the sharp-tongued art and theater critic H. W. Seyfried (1755–1800), in the local Berlin paper *Chronik von Berlin*.[54] His intimate acquaintance with the maskilim, documents translated from Hebrew to German that were in his possession, and the current news he received from his associates in Hamburg enabled him to inform enlightened German public opinion about the *Mitzpeh yokte'el* affair and to follow it closely through the spring and summer of 1789. The full story of "Ovadiah"'s excommunication by the fanatical rabbi of Altona-Hamburg was printed in the press and, like the *Divrei shalom ve'emet* controversy, became a test case for the degree of religious tolerance and enlightenment to be found among the Jews.

Seyfried conducted a merciless mudslinging campaign against Rabbi Raphael Kohen ("the devil from Hamburg") as well as against all the rabbis who were enemies of the Enlightenment. Blaring headlines in his newspaper described the intolerance of the Jews, the fanaticism and revengefulness of the rabbi, and the grave significance of the penalty of excommunication. Employing demonic images, he provided his readers with an account of the chain of events in the affair, denounced the Jews' superstitions and their insistence on maintaining the power of the religious leadership, and with biting rhetoric, jeered at orthodoxy. He also called upon the Danish government to intervene immediately to punish the rabbi, to force him to rescind the ban, and to save the life of "Ovadiah," who was being unjustly persecuted. Extremely hostile toward the Polish Jews, whom he believed were responsible for such appalling affairs, so unthinkable in a time of Enlightenment, Seyfried placed the blame on Raphael Kohen's Polish origin. In contrast, he devoted several articles to praise the considerable progress made by the enlightened Jews in Berlin and to differentiate between them and the Poles.

Seyfried was convinced that his paper had the power to influence and to tip the scales. It was unimaginable, in his view, that the wheel of history would be turned back; unquestionably, religious fanatics would be subdued and their victims saved. But in the meantime, nothing was happening: "It's now been five months! Mankind, mankind, where is your justice? Is this the result of true enlightenment and pure reason? Are these the fruits of the city that once produced a Mendelssohn? Thank God, there still live—in particular in Berlin—people worthy of the Jewish colony!" He knew them all, Seyfried stated, and urged them to defend the honor of their persecuted fellow Jew and their slandered community, and to act to have the ban rescinded. In one of his reports of the affair, Seyfried addressed an emotional appeal to the enlightened Jews of Berlin, calling on them not to remain silent:

Arise, leaders of the community! Teachers! Scholars! Supporters of the oppressed! Arise! Rip off the treacherous masks! . . . Save the honor of your nation! Release Ovadiah! Know that if you fail to take some serious action, his despicable deed will besmirch your nation! . . . I call upon you: Do your duty! Show your tolerance![55]

Like the Wessely affair in 1782, this one also spilled over from the Jewish public sphere into the general sphere. But in actual fact no steps were taken against Rabbi Raphael Kohen. *Chronik von Berlin* was not powerful enough to induce any government agency to intervene. In any event, Saul Berlin was more concerned about his standing within Jewish society, and he may have been the one who imparted news of the affair to the editor of the *Chronik* and told him how the distressful ban was endangering his life. Throughout the summer of 1789, and more so after a year had gone by since the publication of *Mitzpeh yokte'el*, Saul Berlin began to feel more like the victim of an attack than an attacker. He complained a great deal about his distress, the rabbis' resounding and frustrating silence and the curses and insults he was forced to suffer. The rheumatism that ailed him as he drew near the fiftieth year of his life also did nothing to improve his mood.[56] The news from Lissa that Rabbi

David Tevele, known to us from his war against Wessely, had also joined this
battle in the *Kulturkampf* and had burned *Mitzpeh yokte'el* together with the
chametz (leaven, forbidden during Passover) on Passover eve 1789 brought
home to him the sorry truth that the entire rabbinical elite had risen up against
him with uncompromising resolution.[57]

The campaign against Rabbi Raphael Kohen was never finally resolved,
but Berlin did not give up, and continued to follow closely the actions of his
sworn enemy as well as other manifestations of the rabbinical culture he so
detested. For example, when the Freischule printing house departed from its
usual policy and, in order to realize some profit, printed a distinctly religious
text written by the rabbi of a small community in western Prussia, Saul Berlin
hastened to criticize the book in *Hame'asef* and to rebuke publicly those
responsible for its publication in Berlin. How was it possible, the critic wondered, that the the Society for the Promotion of Goodness and Justice was
acting in total opposition to the worldview of the Haskalah? How could it fight
against ignorance and at the same time provide a forum for a work that
embodied all the flaws of the religious book culture: "he gave voice to words
of folly and stupidity, obscenities and repugnant expressions . . . he opened his
mouth, illegitimately, to admonish and arouse his listeners with words that no
one can hear without finding them bitter, ignorant, and foolish." He publicly
denounced the judges of the Berlin community who had signed the approbation endorsing a book that sullied the reputation of the religious culture.[58]

In the meantime, Rabbi Raphael Kohen published a new book of sermons, in which he not only expressed rigid orthodox positions, but also leveled some implicit criticism at Saul Berlin. In his preface, Rabbi Kohen
declared that he felt caught up in the eye of the storm as the victim of ceaseless
attacks. "I was born to the labor of the Torah," he wrote, "and I shunned all
knowledge that imperiled the purity of the religious sources, as if it were a
strange woman testing the Jewish man's ability to restrain his desires." Without mentioning his name, he condemned Saul Berlin's criticism of *Torat yekutiel* as merely the crafty tactic of a rationalist with noxious intentions, who did
not acknowledge rabbinical authority and whose heart was bereft of faith.[59]

Raphael Kohen completed his *Marpeh lashon* in the middle of the month
of Tammuz 1790, and the following month Saul Berlin's enraged reaction was
ready for the press. He jeered at the rabbi, who in his view had time after time,
published mediocre books and sadly enough was still enjoying the full backing
of the rabbinical elite, which was supporting him in silence. Berlin opened his
review with a critical preface deploring the decline of the rabbinical culture,
reflected not only in halakhic books like *Torat yekutiel*, but also in the rabbis'
flawed understanding of the Bible, and in the *musar* books that did not appeal
to the readers' taste. In his view, this poor state of affairs stemmed from the

rabbis' cultural and social insularity and their isolation from the everyday life of ordinary people. After his introduction, Berlin focused his attention on *Marpeh lashon*, exposing flaws in the author's style, understanding and views, using the same critical method that he had adopted in *Mitzpeh yokte'el*. With satirical mockery, Berlin wrote, "This pious Jew so loathed and detested the *chokhmot* that he did not wish even to take them as his maidservant, hence the Torah alone is his wife, his mother, his sister, his daughter, his spouse, his home, his maidservant, his glory; she is the ornament upon his neck, she bakes for him, she cooks for him, and she does for him all that his heart desires." What is the reader to learn from this? How should one relate to a rabbi and a leader of his people who proudly states that he is "bereft of all sciences"? Should one accept moral lessons from such an ignorant man?

But what Berlin found most perplexing was the fact that a man like Rabbi Raphael Kohen, who seriously damaged the image of the Jew in the eyes of society at large ("they mocked and despised us, calling after us, a nation of scoundrels, a nation without wisdom!"), was not publicly repudiated. Was it the fear of excommunication, a threat the rabbi so often brandished, that deterred everyone? After all, following his critique of *Torat yekutiel*, "every religious man has acknowledged that the critic was right and that truth is on his side, and yet the author has not admitted that, and was not even too ashamed to ban the critic. And the other rabbis see this and remain silent." Perhaps this time, Berlin hoped, following his criticism of the befuddled and ludicrous book *Marpeh lashon*, the true nature of the rabbi of Altona-Hamburg would be obvious to all, and there would be some prospect for the rejuvenation of Jewish culture.[60]

Saul Berlin was a rabbi and a gifted scholar, and hence more capable than others of undermining the reputation of the heads of the rabbinical elite. His motivation was fanned by his identification with the maskilic agenda, stemming also from his feelings of anger and deep revulsion. In any case, Rabbi Raphael Kohen continued in his position as rabbi of the three communities until the end of the eighteenth century without being discredited by maskilic criticism. At the time, Saul Berlin was already busy at work writing another subversive work—the halakhic book *Besamim rosh*, which evoked a scandal in the 1790s, causing him to flee from Germany.

In that last peak year of the maskilim's activity, other voices were heard protesting against the rabbinical elite and its culture and various other religious practices. For example, they censured the group of enthusiastic Hasidim that organized in Frankfurt-on-Main around the Rabbi Nathan Adler, asserting that their ways were opposed to the Haskalah and alien to the path of reason. "We have heard and now we have seen with our own eyes that sanctimonious men have arisen there walking in the path of folly," wrote an anonymous maskil, who had read about them and felt compelled to caution against the danger awaiting anyone who adopted a lifestyle of dreams, visions, and prophecies: "and will not take the measuring line of wisdom and the plummet of reason in everything he does."[61]

In 1790, *Hame'asef* dedicated more and more space in its book review section to attacks on rabbinical literature in order to mark clear boundaries between it and the books written by the maskilic republic. That year, it printed a review by Aaron Wolfssohn of *Bet midot*, by the preacher and early maskil Judah Leib Margolioth. Although Wolfssohn and Margolioth were contemporaries (both were born in the 1750s), the critic regarded Margolioth as an anachronistic figure who represented an obsolete rabbinical elite. Wolfssohn had never heard of Margolioth, and book *Bet midot* came into his possession by chance. He dismissed Margolioth's ornate prose and rhymed figures of speech as "mere frippery" that only repelled the reader, and he lambasted the book's lack of aesthetics, sophistication, and clarity: "so much so that the mind of the enlightened reader is filled with disgust upon reading it." Wolfssohn admitted that it was hard to expect anything better from a Polish rabbi, and regarded his literary style as an expression of that same "old illness" that Polish religious culture was afflicted with.

The Berlin maskil was actually enthralled by Margolioth's "Polishness," because his book provided him with surprising and valuable inside information about the deplorable state of the rabbinate in Eastern Europe. It is no wonder that the only praise *Bet midot* earned was due to Margolioth's social and religious criticism, in particular of the contemporary rabbis and the miracle workers with their presumptuous claims of magical abilities. "Our soul pours out within us" [Job 30: 16], Wolfssohn wrote, "when we hear this dreadful news about what manner of rabbis sit in judgemnt in the land of Poland, may it come about that the words of this rebuker will reach their ears." However, his main criticism of Margolioth touched precisely upon his weakest point, which Wolfssohn easily identified: the early maskilim's constant indecisiveness and their fear that openness to knowledge and the legitimation of social and cultural criticism would have a catastrophic impact on religious faith. Wolfssohn interpreted Margolioth's hesitations as befuddlement and found many internal contradictions in his writing. Margolioth warned against philosophy, but he quoted at length from the words of philosophers. "Most of the ethical statements in this book are taken and copied from the works of those Greek sages!" Wolfssohn exclaimed, and continued to attack the caveats Margolioth inserted in his book to reduce the danger of exposure to the *chokhmot*. He scoffed at the rabbinical book culture and its style, the rabbinical approbations, the profession of a preacher that Margolioth represented, and the preaching of morals. Wolfssohn was enraged by the fact that a book of this sort had been published, and he wrote: "How amazed we were at reading these words emanating from the mouth of a Jewish man, in these very times! . . . it would have been better had this book never been created."[62]

Wolfssohn's criticism of Margolioth underscored the fact that these two men belonged to two disparate historical movements in Jewish culture at the end of the eighteenth century: the early Haskalah and the Berlin Haskalah. Just as Wolfssohn had trouble understanding Margolioth, Margolioth did not really comprehend the nature of that intellectual elite, even though he was exposed to the writings of the young Haskalah and read *Hame'asef*. Amazingly enough, he actually took pride in Wolfssohn's criticism. He noted with great satisfaction that, thanks to the review, the book had been publicized and the entire edition was sold out. "The great men of Israel who have the judgment to distinguish between the good and the bad" have given my book a good name, Margolioth naively claimed, totally insensitive to the critic's harsh appraisal of his work.[63]

In 1790, the maskilim's self-confidence reached its apogee. They were, however, aware that their enlightenment project was met with total opposition by the rabbis. The rabbis' standing as leaders of the public had not been undermined, despite the maskilim's attempts to induce them to engage in an open, public debate on fundamental issues. It was against this background that Mendel Breslau, one of the first editors of *Hame'asef* and a founder of Chevrat Dorshei Leshon Ever in Königsberg, published his open letter: "To the Seekers of Justice and Peace, our Brethren the Sons of Israel, who are the Rabbis and Rabbinical Authorities." He advised the rabbinical elite to take a new look at the face of reality and to change their position, a move he thought was called for in an era in which the prophecies of the End of Days were being fulfilled: "And soon wisdom and knowledge shall be the stability of the times, the abundance of salvation."

In particular, Breslau demanded cooperation in the field of Jewish education, where it was essential to shift the center of gravity from the narrow religious culture to universal humanism ("to awaken love in young boys' hearts for all men, for we are all the children of one God"). Reason and criticism that strove to attain the truth must no longer be obstructed. In his view, the rabbinical style of leadership also needed to undergo radical change—there should be an end to excessive halakhic strictness and to the excommunication of religious deviants. God should be worshipped freely and out of choice, not under the whip of coercion and threats. The time may have come, Breslau suggested, to convene a conference, initiated by the rabbis themselves, to formulate an innovative, tolerant educational and halakhic rabbinical policy that is in keeping with the changing times and the climate of Enlightenment.[64]

The Search for the Ideal Jewish Society

Isaac Euchel, the dynamic leader of the maskilim and the founder of the Society for the Promotion of Goodness and Justice, also joined in the critical offensive on the traditional patterns of life. In the first half of 1790 he anonymously published *Igrot Meshulam ben Uriah ha'Eshtemoi* (The Letters of Meshulam the Son of Uriah the Eshtemoi), a work in which he criticized Jewish society, supposedly viewed from the outside, and suggested ideal models of Jewish life in the private and the social sphere.[65] This was an extraordinary attempt to emulate a literary model that had become a classic in the Enlightenment culture, and to test its applicability to Jewish social-religious life. There is an unmistakable similarity between *Igrot Meshulam* and Montesquieu's *Persian Letters*, a masterpiece of the French Enlightenment, published in 1721.[66]

In both these works, the rational-moral criticism was hidden behind several veils. The author remained in the shadow, an anonymous figure, placing his words of reproof in the mouths of fictional characters—the Persian Uzbek in Montesquieu's book and Meshulam from Aleppo in Euchel's. The choice of the epistolary genre and the claim that the letters were found by chance and prepared for the press by a fictional editor were meant to make the work more credible and to introduce the reader into a distant, exotic, oriental cultural world.

In the book, Euchel hid his identity behind the character of a Spanish Jew, who in 1789 sent to the Society for the Promotion of Goodness and Justice twelve letters that had been in his possession for about twenty years. The letters, originally written in Arabic by an eighteen-year-old man, Meshulam ben Uriah ha'Eshtemoi from the Aleppo community in Syria, and addressed to his friend Baruch ben Albuzagli, were translated into Hebrew by a Spanish private tutor from Majorca and then translated again by the brother-in-law of the man who printed them. Just as Montesquieu sent his hero Uzbek from the East to Europe, on a voyage supposedly to acquire knowledge, to learn to know the wide world and to accumulate life experience, and as Jonathan Swift sent his Gulliver to imaginary realms and Voltaire sent Candide into the world on a journey of adventure that destroyed his naive belief that this is "the best of all possible worlds," so Euchel sent Meshulam "to voyage on the sea to the kingdoms of Europe to see the manners and traits of the people of these lands."[67]

Montesquieu, Swift, Voltaire, and Euchel had a common aim—to hold up a mirror to the reader, in which he could see himself, his culture, and society from a different and supposedly objective vantage point. These protagonists are sent on a rites-of-passage voyage of enlightenment to foreign cultures (in Montesquieu's case, seriously flawed Europe, and in Euchel's case, ideal

Spain and Italy). This encounter provides them with some comparative insights, and by giving them an opportunity to compare the ideal models with the disturbing reality that Enlightenment writers cynically portray, enables them to develop a discriminating critical sense.

Igrot Meshulam was far from being a cogent, sophisticated work, replete with intriguing plots and characters, like *Persian Letters*. It was actually a meager, unfinished literary work (only six of the letters were published) with an uncomplicated plot, hardly on the same literary level as Montesquieu's classic work. However, like all Euchel's maskilic endeavors, it reflected his concern for the future of the Jewish collective and represented the internal maskilic discourse.

In *Igrot Meshulam*, Euchel depicted the Italian Jewry of Livorno as an ideal model of Jewish society, which enjoys religious toleration, has a command of European languages, is open to new knowledge, is economically industrious, modest in its lifestyle, moral, well-mannered, and relatively free of inhibitions in relations between the sexes. He admiringly described the patterns of life of the Italian-Spanish elite, very much in accord with those of Berlin's Ashkenazi Jewry, among whom Euchel lived: "The Jews of Livorno live together in peace and security in comfortable homes among the nobles of the land, their houses are built of granite, most of them are respected merchants, clean-shaven with curly hair; their clothing does not differ from that of the other people, and they speak the vernacular tongue as lucidly and elegantly as their rhetoricians."[68]

Euchel emphatically asserted that the affluent Jews of Berlin had made a grievous error by openly flaunting their wealth and failing to adopt a more modest lifestyle, in contrast to the Italian Jews, who concealed their riches to avoid arousing envy. At a time when Euchel was growing increasingly disappointed by the lack of support by the wealthy elite of Berlin, the people of Livorno were investing in the promotion of culture and showing appreciation for study, books, and fine Hebrew poetry.[69]

But the sharpest barbs in *Igrot Meshulam* were aimed at the "old" Jewish world. From the standpoint of Ashkenazi society and its culture, Livorno Jewry and the young Meshulam, who is becoming enlightened, belong to the utopian domains of the maskilic vision of the future. When Meshulam, brimming over with curiosity and enthusiasm, embarked on his journey of initiation, two generations were concerned about his fate—his grandfather Mordechai ha'Eshtemoi and his father Uriah. Each of them had given the boy different instructions to guide him—one representing the traditional values, the other the maskilic ideals. On his journey, Meshulam examined the surprising reality revealed to him in Spain and Italy in light of the double, contradictory norms presented to him by his father and grandfather. The path of the maskil inevitably led him to an intergenerational rebellion, which in Euchel's literary work is the revolt of the grandson and son against the grandfather.

The worldview of Mordechai ha'Eshtemoi, as reflected in his advice to Meshulam, had a consummately religious orientation, suffused with piety. The study of Torah and observance of the commandments are the absolute values and sole content of Jewish culture:

If you find among the sages one who is inquiring into any of the *chokhmot* other than the wisdom of the Talmud, neither like him nor listen to him, for there is no reason or any wisdom that can compare with the wisdom of the Talmud, and if all the sciences in the world were placed on one pan of the scale, and but one letter of the Talmud on the other, it would tip the scale.

Nor did earthly life have any value in his eyes, and he divested beauty and pleasure of any religious legitimacy. "When you arrive in a large city to spend some time there," the grandfather counseled his grandson, "do not gaze upon the beauty of its buildings, streets, and gardens, for they are but vanities, devoid of any benefit." He cautioned him to be strict about washing his hands, "for a man who eats without washing his hands is likened to a man who comes to a whore." "Crush the evil instinct that is inherent in you by fasting," he advised. The grandfather's religious world was shrouded in "wondrous secrets," "a union with the forces of heavenly creatures," and the fear of magical spells. Meshulam's worldview, in contrast, was one of harmonious and ideal perfection, and he is described as:

A pure-minded maskil, who knows the language of his people and those of other nations, and from the day his wise father began his education, he taught him science and knowledge, rhetoric, music and logic, astronomy and surveying, and the other qualities a person must have to stand before great men . . . handsome and goodhearted, pleasing to all his acquaintances, and very God-fearing throughout his life.

His grandfather has an entirely different, and much narrower, concept of perfection: "Take unto your heart my Torah, study the Torah, seek good deeds, and be at one with your God."

The father Uriah, unlike the grandfather, has already cut himself off from this mentality and has properly educated his son. The world he presented to Meshulam was a secular, open, rational, and friendly world. Indeed, his letter of advice to his son was a distinctly maskilic text, in which Euchel summarized the maskilic discourse, using the model of a letter of morals. The perfection that God had intended for mankind could, in his view, be attained in this world. The world of nature, man, and the holy scriptures are open to rational observation and study, and the perception of God shapes morality. Whoever conceives of God as a jealous, angry god, who desires to conspire against man and punish him, "he too will be prone to anger, resentful and avengeful, and will act with evil intent." But he who perceives God as the source of mercy and justice will be a moral person of virtue. The grandfather is afraid to observe the commandment to give charity for fear that the poor man will cast a magic spell on the giver of alms ("Take care not to give a coin or a crust to a poor man whom you do not know for fear of sorcery"). Uriah's advice, derived from his rational, empirical, good, and moral world, is unequivocal: "To the beggar, give, for God has bestowed his blessing upon us, and why should we not also grant some of it to others?"[70]

Equipped with the excellent education he had received from his father, Meshulam was easily able to make the transition from the rigid, pessimistic, traditional views about man's innate nature to the liberal, rational, optimistic, humanistic views of the Enlightenment culture. His grandfather Mordechai, the representative of the religious culture, is totally vanquished. The future, so it seems, belongs to Uriah and Meshulam, the revolutionaries of the Enlightenment, and the buds of this future are already flowering, at least in Italian Jewish communities such as Livorno.

But we need to bear in mind that all of this takes place in the fictional and propagandistic literary world that Euchel created in *Igrot Meshulam*. In the real world of the Haskalah republic, signs of crisis were becoming evident late in 1790. Only three years had passed since Euchel, as head of the Haskalah movement, had come forth with the far-reaching program of the Society for the Promotion of Goodness and Justice and now he had lost his central place in the movement. Certainly the main problem was the failure of the heads of the maskilic republic to ensure public support broad enough to provide the budget necessary to finance its activity.

At the end of the last issue of *Hame'asef* in 1790, the leaders of the Society for the Promotion of Goodness and Justice informed their readers of the crucial state of affairs. Although no one questioned the great success of the journal and the decisive contribution it made in spreading the Enlightenment among the Jewish people, the leaders could no longer conceal the fact that they were unable to continue financing the costs of printing it. The decline in the number of subscribers to less than two hundred, and the fraud of agents who failed to transfer the money they collected to the society, had obliged them, they reported, to conduct a thorough examination and to come up with a recovery program. They could no longer publish *Hame'asef* on a regular basis, so it would not be a monthly but would come out only four times a year. The transfer of monies from the agents would be more closely supervised, and they would be required to submit receipts and lists of the subscribers' names. The large quantity of material sent to the journal by anonymous writers, requiring the addressee to pay the postage, also increased its deficit, so from then on, writers would have to bear this cost themselves.

The heads of the society added that the Society for the Promotion of Goodness and Justice would continue to exist and was looking forward to contributions from intellectuals and donors as it had in the past. It was opening its ranks to new members, and promised to publish *Hame'asef* in the seventh year, too, if there were at least 200 subscribers as well as a precise financial statement. But probably the most important change is the one noted in the fourth paragraph of the recovery program: the Society for the Promotion of Goodness and Justice has chosen Aaron Wolfssohn to edit *Hame'asef* and to be responsible for finances and correspondence."[71]

Wolfssohn, Euchel's friend and contemporary, shared his worldview and commitment to the Enlightenment revolution. A scholar and a talented writer, he was the ideal candidate to carry on the activity of the Haskalah movement in the 1790s. Euchel was still an active member of the Society for the Promotion of Goodness and Justice. But it soon turned out that the change in personnel had many implications. Within two years, Wolfssohn moved to Breslau, invested most of his efforts in the modern school he ran there, and showed relatively little interest in organizing the movement. *Hame'asef* did not appear in the following three years, and in 1794 the editorial offices moved from Berlin to Breslau.

"I have remained the only one writing here in Berlin and I am preoccupied with several affairs," Euchel wrote about himself, still as the representative of the Society for the Promotion of Goodness and Justice.[72] The interest the literary republic took in the Haskalah in general and in *Hame'asef* in particular never flagged. But the fact that Euchel no longer initiated new projects, along with other changes that occurred in the centers of the organization and the dissemination of the Haskalah in Germany, began to take the wind out of the sails of the great vision. The report printed on the last pages of the sixth volume of *Hame'asef* in 1790, only eight years from the time Chevrat Dorshei Lashon Ever was founded in Königsberg, signaled the downfall of the maskilic republic.

PART IV

On Two Fronts

Chapter Thirteen

Crisis at the Turn of the Century

For the young Haskalah movement, the century came to a close in a series of strident, worrisome chords, attended by a profound sense of crisis. The maskilim's optimistic belief that the Jewish public sphere could be reshaped by modern intellectuals was replaced by their anxiety in the face of the secularization gaining in momentum among the Jewish bourgeoisie in urban communities—a process neither intended by the maskilim nor controlled by them. The disappointing and futile struggle to change the legal status of Prussian Jewry was accompanied by voices expressing deep alienation from tradition and the Jewish community and calling on the elite to withdraw completely from the backward Jewish society. The internal quarrels among the modern intelligentsia between moderates and radicals and between reformists and assimilationists impeded the momentum of the maskilic republic at the very time when the orthodox protest was growing stronger. Frustrated maskilim, making no attempt to hide their disappointment, left the movement. Maskilim from the periphery who knocked at the gates of the Haskalah in Berlin and Königsberg got no response. The final closure of *Hame'asef* and the disbanding of the Society for the Promotion of Goodness and Justice in 1797, marked, more than anything else, the collapse of the movement and in one stroke led to the downfall of the organized literary republic constructed in the 1750s. It would be true to say that the end of the eighteenth century brought with it the end of the first chapter in the history of the Jewish Enlightenment movement.

Voices of Despair and Protest

Four episodes that occurred at the turn of the century vividly symbolize the crisis affecting the Haskalah: the resignation of one of the maskilic teachers in the Freischule; an abortive attempt to revive *Hame'asef*; a voice of protest against David Friedländer's betrayal of the Haskalah, and the disgraceful burial of Solomon Maimon.

In 1800 Naumann Simonsohn, a senior member of the administrative staff of the Freischule, decided to move from Berlin to Lissa as a declaration of his disillusionment and protest.[1] According to the maskilic worldview, this move from Berlin, the city of Enlightenment, to traditional Poland was in a direction opposite to the one in which history was moving. Naumann Simonsohn, who became a maskil in his twenties, had fully espoused the ethos of the Haskalah, revered Mendelssohn, belonged to a group of Berlin maskilim, regarded Joseph II as the historical hero of tolerance, and served as an *Inspektor* in the Freischule. And now, he decided to slam the door behind him and move to, of all places, the Polish community of Lissa (then under Prussian rule), the city from which Rabbi David Tevele had issued his unforgettable, sharp orthodox protest against the new maskilic elite in 1782. "All is lost!" the frustrated maskil cried out in anguish: a son rises against his father, a pupil rules over his teacher, and every hedonistic, fashionable, freedom-seeking youth nurtures some third-rate sort of "wild Haskalah" which goes completely out of control:

A young man who has scarcely read any books calls out "I am a hero!" and all those who have a watch in their pocket and spectacles in their hands, a braid behind them and a fool in front, think themselves wise and intelligent, and carry their heads high . . . they violate all the commandments, desecrate the Sabbath, eat unclean bread and do not call upon God, they anoint their flesh with wine, eat rich food without saying the blessing, go to bed and rise in the morning without prayers . . . and all of this they call a generation of knowledge, a wise and clever people.[2]

Naumann Simonsohn was one of the few idealistic teachers in the Freischule in the 1790s. He tried hard to implement a balanced curriculum, which combined *Torat haShem* and *Torat ha'adam* according to Wessely's formulation. When he urged one of the wealthy elite in the Berlin community, which supported the modern school for indigent boys, to introduce lessons in Mishnah and Talmud into the school, he encountered opposition: "What is the purpose of such studies and what good will it bring to Jewry to confuse their minds with such nonsense, to waste their time by neglecting the study of science and beneficial knowledge for the sake of learning casuistry and irrelevant issues from the halakhic disputes between Abbayeh and Raba?"[3] Simonsohn tried to argue by explaining that even the emergence of the modern maskilic elite would have been impossible without the foundation of the religious knowledge that was the heritage of all the maskilim from Mendelssohn and Wessely and up to Aaron Wolfssohn and Lazarus Bendavid. It turned out, however, that the support of the Haskalah by the elites that were aspiring to become citizens of Europe was dwindling. In Simonsohn's view, the process in which the maskilim had emerged was characterized by a revolt against the rigid talmudic education they had received in their youth, and this revolt had led them to the knowledge and culture of Europe without totally eradicating their link to the religious texts. In contrast, the revolt of young men for whom the only educational foundation was the *chokhmot* would inevitably lead to religious permissiveness and hedonism at the expense of their intellectual development. Hence, he saw no possibility of a future for the Haskalah in Berlin. "False people"—private tutors, spreading heresy, who had deviously gained access to the homes of the Berlin bourgeoisie, replacing the "true maskilim," were taking over the Haskalah and giving it a bad name. In Lissa, where the Jewish *Kulturkampf* had begun in the 1780s, the erstwhile maskil cut himself off almost completely from the maskilic republic. With the support of his rich father-in-law, he devoted himself to scholarship and became one of the orthodox opponents of religious reform in the second and third decades of the nineteenth century.[4]

Simonsohn's protest was quite typical and reflected the prevailing mood among many maskilim, both the older and the younger, who had been avid partners in the establishment of the maskilic republic. *Hame'asef*, the flagship of the maskilic revolution for fourteen years, sank toward the end of the century. Isaac Euchel, the driving force behind the revolution, was no longer on the editorial board in the 1790s. He lost his place at the head of the movement and was also affected by the despondent atmosphere of the Haskalah in crisis. Euchel was replaced by Aaron Wolfssohn, and the center of the movement along with the *Hame'asef* editorial board moved from Berlin to Breslau.

Shalom Hacohen (1773–1845), a Hebrew poet and dynamic maskil from the Prussian-Polish district of Posen, who had just arrived in Berlin to join the teaching staff of the Freischule, advised Euchel two years after *Hame'asef* closed down to reconsider opening it again. Euchel's response was one of despair and skepticism, completely at odds with his optimistic approach and energetic policy of cultural transformation in the 1780s. His reply to Hacohen in the summer of 1800 reads like a bitter lament over his failure:

I suffer for you my friend. You have a precious gem in your hand that no one wants, you have brought forth balm and myrrh, a remedy and cure for all who seek morals, and no one pays heed to it. Why have your steps come so late? Why have you waited until now, when you call out and no one replies? The days of love have passed, gone are the days of the covenant between me and the sons of Israel, when the buds of wisdom were seen and the Hebrew language flowered in glorification, and the young men of Israel went forth each day to pick the fruits of its reason.

The maskilim had missed the opportune moment in the 1780s, he asserted. From the time of Mendelssohn's death, the historical developments that occurred had left behind the intellectuals in general and the maskilim, the advocates of Jewish culture and literature, in particular. Euchel regarded the failure of *Hame'asef* as his personal failure. He lamented his lonely state and his relegation to the margins of Jewish public life: "I too have tasted of the goblet of poison that has been the lot of the Jewish people and its maskilim . . . I too have been forgotten and abandoned like a juniper plant in the wilderness," Euchel wrote woefully to the young maskil, informing him that at the end of the eighteenth century only a very few had remained from the Dorshei Leshon Ever group, and that "the downfall of the language and the book," was absolute and irremediable.[5]

But Hacohen was not prepared to concede defeat. He was convinced that Euchel was not reading the map correctly, and that in the broad periphery of the "Berlin Haskalah," which had emerged in the 1780s and '90s, there were still many thirsting for a periodical like *Hame'asef*. He did not renounce the vision of the Haskalah or the maskilic republic, and four years after Euchel's untimely death, he founded the Society of the Lovers of the Hebrew Language (1808) in Berlin and for a short time revived *Hame'asef* under his editorship. After he too left the moribund Haskalah center in Berlin, Hacohen became an extremely important link between the first chapter of the Haskalah and its second chapter, one of whose centers in the first quarter of the nineteenth century was Austria.[6]

In early September 1800, only a few weeks after Euchel had given vent to his despair and frustration about the crisis in the Haskalah, the physician from Driezen, Shlomo Schöneman, Isaac Satanow's son, published an open letter to David Friedländer, who had claimed to be Moses Mendelssohn's heir. In it, he cried out to him: "You have betrayed the Haskalah!"[7] His was one of the vociferous reactions to Friedländer's radical step. In 1799 Friedländer had sent an controversial anonymous letter to the distinguished Protestant pastor Wilhelm Abraham Teller. In the name of "a number of heads of families of the Jewish faith," he made an extraordinary, unprecedented proposal: that the Jewish elite, which was estranged from its religion, would join the church on the basis of the principles of the natural religion. "Within the wide circle of the true spirit of Protestantism," he wrote to Teller, "we and our system can also find shelter and protection."[8] Friedländer, the founder of Chevrat Chinukh Ne'arim, the author of the first reader for the school's pupils, one of the owners of the Freischule printing house, and a key figure in the Haskalah movement who had been close to Mendelssohn and had supported all the Haskalah's projects, was now being attacked publicly on the pages of the *Berlinische Monatsschrift* by a maskil of the new generation, the son of an early maskil, who was the first manager of the printing house.

Schöneman's worldview was not very far from Friedländer's anticlerical criticism and his vision of the integration of European Jewry. Nonetheless, he accused Friedländer of egoism and alienation. "You have thought only of yourself, you have disregarded the nation whose fate you share and taken a hasty step that will lead to bitter results for your co-religionists. You are not interested only in removing the oppressive burden of the commandments," Schönemann lashed out at him in his frustration and rage. "You also want to cut yourself off from the Jewish nation and to abandon the Jewish circle of solidarity. If this had been merely a personal step, perhaps we could have accepted it. But because of your status as one of the leaders of the Enlightenment revolution among the Jews, this step is tantamount to a betrayal of the ancient cultural heritage, of the community and the Haskalah, a step that can destroy any chance of its success." The wheel will turn back—the Jewish nation will regress culturally a hundred years, to the era that preceded the maskilic revolution, and orthodoxy will take hold of the letter to Teller and win the *Kulturkampf* that has just begun. Its spokesmen will justifiably claim that this is the disastrous outcome of all the innovations they have jealously fought against. The transition from tradition to enlightenment will be halted at once. "Not only have you egoistically betrayed the Jewish nation and shown concern only for the narrow interests of the Jewish upper class, but you are also indirectly serving the orthodox."

With great anxiety, Schöneman conjured up a dreadful picture: the cultured Jews of the intellectual elite, which was supposed to be at the forefront of the struggle for the transformation of the Jews, were withdrawing from the fray at the very time when victory was at hand, leaving behind them an exulting orthodoxy, religious permissiveness, low morals, and a leadership vacuum: "Can one commit a greater sin against a nation then to take away its instructors and guides?"[9] "Where is your sense of public responsibility and that of your friends?" Schöneman bitterly chastised Friedländer, and then asked with reluctance, as if he did not want to believe in the possibility,"Can it be that you have reached such a state of utter despair that you no longer want to be Jews?"

Two months after Schöneman's article was printed, in the winter of 1800, Solomon Maimon's tragic and trouble-plagued life drew to a close. At least in his case, he had explicitly declared his chosen path: in his well-known and influential autobiography, Maimon openly stated his view that a member of the "philosophical religion" was entitled to withdraw from the "Jewish state," in which membership was conditional upon submission to the laws of religion, and to become a subject of the political state only.[10]

Solomon Maimon was the greatest loss of the Haskalah movement in the eighteenth century. This young, talented Lithuanian scholar and talmudist became a philosopher and man of the Enlightenment. Inspired by reason, he experienced a "spiritual reawakening" and overcame the difficult obstacles of penury, solitude, and the lack of formal education. His fine intellectual capacities made him the best candidate for the role of the "Jewish Voltaire" in the Haskalah movement. He could have made an immense contribution to the Jewish Enlightenment movement, owing to the blunt, defiant anticlerical stance he took vis-à-vis the rabbis, his independence of thought revealed in his debates with Mendelssohn and Kant, and his readiness to participate in the Haskalah project in order "to illuminate the path of our people, raise them up from the sea of ignorance, and to awaken them from the slumber of stupidity." His book, *Ta'alumot chokhmah*, was meant to help the maskilim in their efforts to expand knowledge and to rationalize Jewish culture. However, it remained in manuscript form, one more proof of Maimon's failure to become an active partner in the Haskalah project and further evidence of the failure of the Berlin maskilim to recognize Maimon's immense potential.[11]

This was unquestionably a double loss. The maskilim did not go to any lengths to support Maimon and missed the opportunity to bring into their ranks a philosopher of his stature who was committed to the maskilic agenda. And Maimon himself treated the maskilim with arrogance and contempt that later turned into indifference. Only at the end of the 1780s, when Isaac Euchel discovered Maimon and urged that he be invited to write for the Society for the Promotion of Goodness and Justice, was one of his Hebrew works published.[12] However, by then Maimon was already investing all his energies in his effort to gain acceptance into the German Enlightenment republic, acquiring Christian friends among the scholars he met, and publishing articles in German periodicals.

When he returned to Berlin from Breslau in 1787, Maimon wrote that Mendelssohn was no longer among the living, his former friends did not want to know him, and only Lazarus Bendavid collected some donations for him to keep him from starving. But Euchel persisted. At first, he succeeded in persuading Maimon to write a brief article for *Hame'asef* in 1789, in the hope that it would be followed by others.[13] Later, after a vigorous publicity campaign and an effort to sign up advance subscribers,[14] he also managed to print the first half of *Givat hamoreh*, Maimon's commentary on *Guide for the Perplexed*.[15] This book, published anonymously in Berlin in 1791, was an exceptional work. Its preface is worthy of special attention; it was the first systematic survey in Hebrew of the history of philosophy, from the pre-Socratic philosophers to Descartes, Newton, Leibniz, Kant, and Maimon himself, with a stress on the challenges of the scientific revolution. An enlightenment text of this kind was unprecedented in the works produced by the Haskalah and hence was of momentous importance. Maimon tried to imbue his readers with his ideal of philosophical truth and passion for Enlightenment. He introduced into *Givat hamoreh* up-to-date discussions on the sciences, described a series of experiments and discoveries, refuted old scientific theories, criticized Maimonides's scientific knowledge in comparison to the new science, and dealt with the issue of materialism and many other topics.

Publication of the book could have enhanced the prestige of the Haskalah after Mendelssohn's death and stimulated interest in the new philosophy. But Maimon himself did little to avail himself of this opportunity, because of his shifting moods and his skepticism about the entire Haskalah project. At the time, particularly after the publication of his German book on transcendental philosophy in 1790, which won Kant's praise, Maimon had already shut the door of the Haskalah behind him, despite Euchel's efforts to enlist him in the movement. He turned to the extra-Jewish reference group of scholars and philosophers, among whom he sought a sympathetic and attentive audience. In his autobiography, Maimon referred skeptically to the Berlin maskilim's plan to commission him to translate books of science, history and philosophy from German to Hebrew:

My friends began, though too late, to see that their ill-considered project must of necessity collapse, because they had no assurance of a market for such voluminous and expensive works. From the religious, moral and political condition of the Jews up to this time, it was easy to foresee that the few enlightened men among them would certainly give themselves no trouble to study the sciences in the Hebrew language, which is very ill-adapted for the exposition of such subjects; they will prefer to seek science in its original sources. The unenlightened, on the other hand—and these form the majority—are so swayed by rabbinical prejudices that they regard the study of the sciences, even in Hebrew, as forbidden fruit, and persistently occupy themselves only with the Talmud and the enormous number of its commentaries.[16]

In Maimon's estimation, the Haskalah project had lost its relevance for the modernists and had no chance of being accepted by traditional Jews.

In the 1790s, Maimon's estrangement from Jewry and the Haskalah grew. On November 22, 1800, he passed away at the estate of his Christian patron, Graf Kalkreuth, in Silesia. His ignominious burial as a despised apostate, outside the Jewish cemetery in Glogau—in an unmarked grave with no eulogies—was a potent symbol of this German-Jewish philosopher, talmudist, brilliant rationalist critic of rabbinical culture, mysticism and Hasidism, and former early maskil's deliberate withdrawal from the Jewish religion, the Haskalah, and the Jewish people. This rebellious individualist left Judaism in stages: at first exchanged the traditional Judaism of "obscurantist Poland" for Berlin and the Enlightenment culture; then he abandoned the "Jewish state" and the synagogue because they had lost all meaning for a man who adhered to the natural religion; and finally he left the Haskalah, too, because he no longer believed in its ability to make a revolution.[17]

Decline in the 1790s

These four episodes, which occurred in 1800, expressed—from different directions—lack of faith in the power and future of the Haskalah project. The teacher Naumann Simonsohn lost all hope that the Freischule would bring about the fulfillment of Wessely's vision of the future and would shape a new generation of young Jews with a balanced Jewish-European culture. He was assailed with anxiety in the face of the secularization of members of the Berlin elite, and in protest, fled to seek refuge in the Polish-Prussian town of Lissa. Solomon Maimon voiced his skepticism about the importance of the Haskalah for the German-Jewish intelligentsia, which had been largely acculturated, and doubted whether it was capable of presenting a real threat to the rabbinical elite, which he felt was as powerful and authoritarian as ever. Isaac Euchel despaired of the possibility of fostering Hebrew culture through a forum like *Hame'asef*; he was faced with the ruins of the organization he had founded, and pessimistically witnessed the waning of the Haskalah. And Shlomo Schöneman was astounded to find Friedländer, leader of the maskilim, at the head of an elitist sectoral group that in his view was betraying the nation and the Haskalah, deserting them in an unforgivable hypocritical act that was egotistically and irresponsibly derailing the Haskalah revolution.

How was it that the great dream cherished by Euchel, who only fourteen years earlier had proposed a grandiose plan for the maskilic republic, crumbled in 1800? How did this evolving movement, which had already become institutionalized, with a printing house, a journal, and subscribers and patrons who assured its financing, fall apart? How did such a movement, which had not been defeated in cultural battles and had endeavored to expand more and more the periphery of its readers, writers, and subscribers, collapse?

The financial crisis that had been ongoing since 1790 and the decline in the number of subscribers to *Hame'asef* can explain only the closing down of the journal in 1797, particularly after its irregular publication discouraged many of its subscribers in peripheral communities outside the cities of Prussia. To understand the crisis of the Haskalah, we need to look at a series of processes that occurred in the 1790s within three groups: the Jewish bourgeoisie and the wealthy elites of Berlin, Breslau, and Königsberg; the radical German-Jewish intelligentsia of Berlin; and the maskilim themselves and their activity in the last decade of the century.

A careful scrutiny of the history of the Haskalah in its second chapter, which opened after 1797, shows that in various communities in Germany and outside it, the movement continued to develop. The crisis in the Haskalah, which led to the collapse of the organized movement founded in the 1780s, was first of all a crisis in the "Berlin Haskalah." The rapid processes of modernization and secularization that occurred in the 1790s, and the replacement of the discourse on the enlightenment and reform of the Jews and their culture by the political discourse of emancipation and the ethos of "the citizen," turned the maskilim into fighters of past wars. The societies of maskilim were eclipsed by the salons, *Hame'asef* by the German journals, Hebrew culture by German culture, maskilim of the middle and lower classes of teachers and clerks by the high intelligentsia of physicians, members of the learned professions, and wealthy merchants; and the shared Jewish fate by more and more cases of alienation and desertion.

Noting the disparate pace at which modernization progressed along different paths, Jacob Katz offered an overall historical reply to the question of what caused the Haskalah crisis: "The interrelation between change in social reality and in social thinking is too complicated to be neatly spelled out by the historian who seeks to establish the sequence of cause and effect. Sometimes, however, development on one of the two planes becomes so accelerated that it leaves the course of events on the other far behind."[18]

What Katz meant was that in the eighteenth century the ideas and future vision of the Enlightenment outpaced the social reality, which was not yet ripe. However, in the story of Berlin Jewry's modernization in the 1790s, the process was reversed: the maskilim represented intellectual and educational modernization and an internal cultural revolution, but the social changes and the trends of acculturation in Jewish Berlin at the end of the century, which began long before the Haskalah revolution, left the maskilim behind, so that the option for modernization they proposed was hardly exercised. And since Berlin was the center, where the key maskilim and the Haskalah's institutions were located, the collapse in that city engendered a crisis in the entire movement. Hence maskilim like Shalom Hacohen, Judah ben-Zeev, Mendel Lefin, and many others had to exert much effort in the early nineteenth century to rebuild the movement outside Berlin.[19]

The turbulent 1790s throughout Europe were marked by the French Revolution. It was not only the military conflicts of the political coalitions against France, but primarily the ideological conflict that underpinned them—between the modernist principles of the revolution and the principles of the old absolutist order, between innovators and conservatives, that shook Europe. The sense of stability had been shaken, and the more extreme events became, the more anxious became even those who had earlier supported the revolution. In 1793, Louis XVI was executed, and this act was followed by the Reign of Terror imposed by the Jacobeans and the Cult of Reason introduced by Robespierre as a secular substitute for religion and the church. The revolution began to fanatically destroy its own sons, and by the end of the century, Napoleon had become a sole ruler.

The great debate that the revolution evoked finally also led to the end of the Enlightenment. Although trends of "counter-Enlightenment" had existed beforehand, and enemies of the Enlightenment among the conservatives and the clergy had repeatedly attacked the philosophers, claiming that Enlightenment was leading to heresy and anarchy, this time the conservatives blamed the Enlightenment for the revolution, which they regarded as overwhelming proof that they had been in the right. In 1790 the Irishman Edmund Burke opened the great debate about the path taken by the revolution, in his influential and widely circulated book *Reflections on the French Revolution*, and raised some penetrating questions about the dangers that freedom would pose for morality, religion, and political and economic stability. In Germany, more and more conservative voices were heard from enlightened intellectuals. Reason was placed on the defensive in face of the claim that blood was spilled at the foot of the guillotine in the name of the rationalist ideology. The Romantic trend in literature and philosophy rejected the Enlightenment, and responded to the longing for emotional self-expression and for a return to religious faith instead of the abstract universal ideas of reason.[20]

Berlin itself, in the transitional period of the 1790s, experienced a remarkable cultural flourishing, and the general atmosphere in the city encouraged secularization and acculturation among the Jews. Frederick William II (r. 1786–97), who led Prussian absolutism to a crisis, is generally depicted as a king who neglected the affairs of state, instead investing his energies to make Berlin a center of culture and art on the same level as the capitals of France, England and Austria. One report about him states:

The King remained faithful to his preference for the theater, the concert, to his old and new mistresses. One was astonished also that for hours he could examine paintings, furniture, shops, or play the violincello or listen to the intrigues of the ladies at court, while having obviously so very little time to listen to his ministers who under his eyes guided the interests of the state.[21]

The middle class grew more powerful and many of its members filled positions in the bureaucracy. During this period, Berlin was characterized by neoclassical architecture (the famous Brandenburg Gate at the end of the Royal Mile, near the Tiergarten amusement park), plastic art (Schadow's sculpture), literary clubs, and in particular the Nationaltheater, which flourished under the management of Wilhelm Iffland. It mounted operas and plays by Schiller, Lessing, and Goethe, and also served as a public stage for its audience's ostentatious show of wealth and social class and a place for vanity and flirtation. All these created a vibrant city with an abundance of opportunities and temptations.[22]

The Jews of Berlin were mindful of these new trends and often took an active part in them. Berlin Romanticism emerged from the literary salons of the intellectual bourgeoisie, and assimilated Jewish women were at the center of some of the more sought-after salons. In 1798, the *Athenaeum* journal edited by the brothers August and Friedrich Schlegel first came out and proclaimed the Romantic revolution. In its first issue, its editors depicted it as literature that unites all genres, literature in an eternal state of becoming that can never be completed.[23] According to Friedrich Schlegel, who later became the adored lover and then husband of Mendelssohn's daughter Dorothea, God is the god within us. He is not a transcendental god, who demands the fulfillment of obligations, and a person is religious if he is full of God and does everything out of love, not duty. Dorothea first met Schlegel in the salon presided over by Henriette Herz, the young wife of the physician and philosopher Marcus Herz, Kant's student. Another visitor to the salon and a close friend of Henriette's was the theologian Friedrich Schleiermacher, who at the turn of the century developed a Romantic doctrine of the Christian faith as a personal emotional experience.[24]

An overview of Jewish life in 1790s Europe shows how a high wall of cultural and social variance was rising between East and West (historical Polish Jewry on one side and the Jews of Germany, Austria, France, England, and Holland on the other), as well as between the Jews in the large, developing cities and those in the towns and villages.[25] The recent partitions of Poland (1793–95) completed the boundaries of the Pale of Settlement of Russian Jewry, under the constantly tightening control of the absolutist czar.

The Hasidic movement that began to coalesce in the 1790s grew stronger in Russia and Galicia. New episodes were added to the religious-social struggle between the *mitnaggedim*, the representatives of the ethos of talmudic scholarship, and the Hasidim, who cast themselves as alternative religious leaders, in the form of the *tzadik*, with an emphasis on the religious experience. The Gaon of Vilna, the great opponent of Hasidism, published a letter in 1796, shortly before his death, in which he denied rumors that he had withdrawn his opposition. With unwavering resolution, he repeated his ruling that "Anyone who calls himself a Jew and has a God-fearing heart is obliged to repel and harass them with all manner of persecutions and to subdue them . . . for they are sinful and as afflicting as parasites to Israel."[26] At the end of the century, Rabbi Schneor Zalman of Lyadi, leader of the Hasidim in White Russia, was thrown into a Russian jail twice, after the opponents of Hasidism informed on him to the authorities.

Nonetheless, there were intellectuals in Eastern Europe who felt an affinity to the Haskalah. Several early maskilim continued to grapple with their passion for science and philosophy, disinclined to remain committed to the norms of rabbinical culture and averse to the ecstatic and mystical religion of the Hasidim. One such maskil was the physician from Mitau and Grodno, Judah Hurwitz (1734–97).[27] Pinhas Hurwitz of Vilna, author of *Sefer haberit* (The Book of the Covenant) (1797), also provided his readers with a diverse selection of scientific and philosophical knowledge, from Copernicus to Kant, and reacted to several books of the Haskalah that he had read, although in the final analysis he identified with the orthodox anxiety.[28] In contrast to him, several other individuals drew closer to the Enlightenment revolution. For example, Shimon Ben Wolf of Vilna, a key figure in the internal politics of Lithuanian Jewry in the 1790s, applied to the Polish Sejm requesting that it rescind Jewish autonomy, based on the Enlightenment discourse and a reformist program.[29] In commercial cities like Shklov a wealthy bourgeoisie had already emerged, which attempted to adopt European patterns of life and maintained ties with German maskilim. However, the voices of modernist Jews had very little impact until the early nineteenth century, and the debate about the patterns of the spiritual leadership and the ritual customs was dominant in Jewish public life, in which the control of the rabbinical and Kabbalist elite went unchallenged. As we shall see later, the maskilim also had a hand in sharpening the boundaries between East and West, because they continued to construct their self-image as modernists while strongly disapproving of Jewish "Polishness," which in their eyes represented a culture that was badly in need of reform.

The boundary between East and West grew even sharper, until in the 1780s and '90s, the polemic between the Hasidim and *mitnaggedim* in Eastern Europe hardly resonated at all in the "Western" maskilic discourse. In the Western part of the continent, events took a totally different course and were characterized by accelerated modernization. The National Assembly in Paris passed the first emancipation law in the world, in September 1791, after a lengthy debate, and it became—for good or bad—a model for any discussion of the Jewish question from then on. Although the value of this law depreciated somewhat in the Napoleonic era, its fundamental importance was of no little significance—the Enlightenment's principles of freedom, equality, and civil rights led to a radical political shift in the status of Jews in the state. In the cities of Berlin, Hamburg, Königsberg, London, Vienna, and Amsterdam, a bourgeois Jewish lifestyle evolved, and more ambitious and well-to-do Jews took advantage of the opportunities and temptations European life offered. They adopted its language, fashions, books, and leisure activities, and in doing so expanded the areas in which they rubbed shoulders with gentile society and shared in its culture. This process took place without being induced by any ideology of modernization.[30] In the 1790s, there was also no dearth of Jews who remonstrated against the drastically changing Jewish world, against religious laxity and the tendency slavishly to follow the latest fashions. And these instances of secularization became more and more evident and frequent.[31] To illustrate how distant and culturally estranged the East was from the West, we can compare two episodes that occurred in 1799, one in the East of Europe and the other in the West. In Berlin, Jewish rationalism reached its apogee with Friedländer's revulsion at the religion of his forefathers and his attempt to cut himself off from it and his community. At the same time, in the East, Nahman of Bratslav, the prominent figure of the Hasidic movement whose radical anti-rationalistic views would later provide ammunition for the orthodox in their *Kulturkampf* against the Haskalah, left for Palestine on a mysterious mystical mission, set against the roar of Napoleon's cannons.[32]

Jewish-German Intelligentsia

The radical conclusions that David Friedländer reached in the last year of the eighteenth century were not shared by Berlin Jewry at large. Nonetheless, at that time, Berlin's Jewish bourgeoisie's appetite for the pleasures of urban life reached an all-time high and their ambitions to gain citizenship soared.[33] Paintings and sculptures depict the men and women of Berlin's Jewish elite in fashionable dress, the men clean-shaven and bareheaded. In the literature and the press, we find images of the nouveaux riches, of young women swept up by the cult of Kant and Goethe, women pushing their way into the front rows at the theater, and others involved in tempestuous liaisons with Christians. For example, there is the character, in a Berlin story of 1797, of a young cultured Jewish dandy, an outstanding billiard player, who goes horseback riding, appreciates Mozart's music, and has many love affairs with Christian girls.[34]

Until then, the secular life of Jewish high society in Berlin and in other German cities had been regarded by the enlightened as an intriguing novelty, and they also saw it as evidence of the Enlightenment's success because so many Jews in modern dress and European hairstyles were seen on the city boulevards and in particular in the theaters, and Jewish women were known as admired hostesses and guests in the salons of high society. However, as this process escalated, it became a source of concern for Jews and Christians alike.[35] Anti-Jewish writings expressed opposition to the advance of the Jews from the fringes to the center of society, depicting their acculturation with scorn and indignation. For example, among other complaints, Friedrich Grattenauer[36] accused the Jews of moral corruption, since young men behave dissolutely in the brothels and young women associate with Christians without their families' knowledge and maintain intimate relations with them.

Taking a more optimistic view of the situation, Moshe Hirschel of Breslau wrote that, while he admitted that cases of this kind did occur, they did not reflect a general trend. He cited as evidence the fact that out-of-wedlock births, the murder of unwanted infants, and prostitution were not widespread phenomena among Jews. Moreover, he regarded romantic attachments between Jews and Christians as a desirable innovation, since it was preferable to the mutual hatred of the past.[37] Even Jewish intellectuals like David Friedländer, Saul Ascher, Wolff Davidson, and Lazarus Bendavid, who aspired to full citizenship for Jews, were greatly perturbed by this "surge of luxury." In their view, it was in poor taste, bordering on the immoral, and they felt that those indulging in it were taking ill advantage of the Enlightenment and culture.

The Berlin physician Davidson, who in 1798 described the escalating acculturation of Berlin Jewry, also reported on the establishment of a special committee of community leaders to curb this ostentatious behavior. As a result of the rise in the standard of living and the growing wealth of Jewish merchants, many new families entered the acculturation race, and the children of these merchants, both men and women, were in Davidson's view the leaders in purchasing luxury items and fashionable clothing, strolling on the promenades, and attending the theater.[38]

Davidson was somewhat disapproving of the altered lifestyle of the Jewish bourgeoisie. In contrast, when he introduced the contemporary Jewish-German intelligentsia, among whom he counted himself, to enlightened public opinion he did not conceal his pride. It had all started of course with the "German Socrates" who was no longer among the living. Inspired by him, a diversified and impressive group of freethinking Jews emerged, many of them artists or members of the free professions—physicians, philosophers, teachers, writers, sculptors, painters, musicians, and architects. They were dispersed in various Prussian cities, but the majority were residents of Berlin. Davidson enumerated a detailed roster of well-known names in the Jewish intelligentsia: the physicians Marcus Bloch and Marcus Herz, the scholars and philosophers David Friedländer, Lazarus Bendavid, Solomon Maimon, and Saul Ascher, the musician and conductor Bernhard Wessely, and other men and women known as outstanding instrumentalists, singers, medalists, and painters of miniatures. In only two lines, in the category of teachers, Davidson noted the names of four maskilim: Joel Brill and Aaron Wolfssohn, teachers at the Breslau school, Isaac Euchel, and the poet Wessely. He counted about forty men and women, some of them outstanding figures in their fields, who were socially and economically integrated into high society, were well known to society at large, and in Davidson's opinion, had made a significant contribution to Jewish prestige. Above all others, he lauded the physician and philosopher Marcus Herz, Kant's student and the husband of Henriette, who presided over a salon. He was accorded a special place of pride in the Berlin intelligentsia, since he had been awarded the title Professor by Frederick William II, the first Prussian Jew to receive this title.[39]

In view of the success of the German-Jewish intelligentsia in the overall public sphere, Davidson expected to see the Jews fully accepted into Christian society, and he called on the state to permit intermarriage between Jews and Christians without requiring their conversion. Davidson's book *Über die bürgerliche Verbesserung der Juden* bore a title similar to that of Dohm's book published seventeen years earlier, but the conclusions he drew in it differed totally from Dohm's. Davidsohn ended his book with a fervent wish for maximum integration: "We hope that the religion will not be a hindrance to talented men and women and those who are of benefit [to the state], and that every citizen who fulfills his civil duties will also be able to enjoy rights, and that the splendid time will come when Jews and Christians, citizens of the Prussian state, will have only one God, one King, and one homeland."[40]

There is no way of knowing whether all of the forty men and women on Davidson's list shared this three-part vision of the future. However, Davidson himself and many of the people he included in his list were unquestionably among the eighteenth-century "freethinkers" in the German-Jewish intelligentsia, a group that only partially overlapped with the supporters of the Haskalah. Even if that intelligentsia maintained its affinity for the values and concepts of the European Enlightenment, it had at the top of its agenda issues such as social and economic success and acceptance as citizens, rather than the balanced education of youth and the promotion of Jewish culture. The Jewish enlightened intelligentsia had emerged in Germany before the 1790s, and it also had parallels elsewhere, in London, for example.[41] Since they had the self-confidence to write in European languages, to form intellectual and social ties with Christians, to join scholarly societies, and to appear in public in general literary forums, the members of this intelligentsia became a part of the general republic of intellectuals. Even when they wrote about the current problems of Jewish society and Judaism, their words were not addressed solely to a Jewish audience.

However, in 1790s Berlin the process was far more extreme. Not only was the presence of that intelligentsia more visible, but the alienation of some of its leading spokesmen from Jewish society and religion was particularly excessive. The last barrier they declined to cross was religious conversion. Their fear of mass desertion induced them to propose a new legal relationship between Jews and the state (emancipation, annulment of the autonomy and collective responsibility for debts incurred by members of the community) and a new concept of Judaism that would not run counter to the natural religion.

The members of this group tried again and again to define their place in Jewish society, drawing internal boundaries in it based on an ideological cross-section and the level of acculturation. One of these attempts was made by Lazarus Bendavid (1762–1832), a prolific and extremely dynamic intellectual, who in the nineties lived in Vienna and Berlin, where he wrote his books and articles and disseminated Kantian philosophy in writing, lectures and in conversations held in salons. Between 1789 and 1800, Bendavid published thirteen books—in mathematics, philosophy and studies on Jewish society. In addition twenty articles that he penned were printed in major journals in Prussia and Austria.[42] In his 1793 book, *Etwas zur Charackteristick der Juden* (Something on the Characteristics of the Jews), Bendavid described Jewish society facing the challenges of modernization, and proposed his own radical solution. Representing himself as an objective intellectual looking at the Jews from the outside, he wrote, in a tone of haughty condescension:

Dear friends! . . . You know that I am not dependent on you, and I have no expectations of you nor do I fear you or anyone else, and that I can look upon your play with the same degree of indifference as a man watches small puppets twirling in a music box. I spent the first years of my life among you, and I received many good things from you; and I wish you all possible good, and would like to see you happy to the extent that human beings can be happy.[43]

Bendavid characterized the four groups that in his view made up contemporary Jewish society: the majority group made up of those totally faithful to the religious tradition who he believed were unreformable ("its gradual demise is the only hope for its offspring"); the group of libertine sons of the wealthy ("a rabble of profligates"); the group of decent moral Jews who were not enlightened; and the group of "truly enlightened." Bendavid viewed himself as a representative par excellence of the latter group, but it would be a mistake to think, in his view, that this group defined the maskilim; it would be more correct to see it as the German-Jewish intelligentsia of the 1790s. Bendavid defined its members as "equally distant from both Judaism and (religious) apathy; persons faithful to the true natural religion who feel the need to fervently believe that it influences the intelligent man."[44]

In fact, Bendavid was very far removed from Judaism. His radical criticism of the Jews of his time diverged considerably from that of the Haskalah and was totally at odds with the maskilic discourse. The maskilic critical discourse adopted Dohm's formulation, which blamed the flaws of Jewish society on its social insularity, inadequate education, and low moral standards, as well as on the oppression and restrictions imposed by the Christian state. In contrast, Bendavid's deist and alienated discourse portrays the Jews out of a sense of profound shame and revulsion, blaming them for their insularity and their negative image as shysters and swindlers. He held talmudic and rabbinical

Judaism, along with the practical commandments, responsible for the social and cultural perversion of the Jews. Still, Bendavid was very apprehensive about the vulgar modernization that was indifferent to enlightenment and morality and was disgracing decent Jews: "a riffraff of wanton men who abandon the commandments because they are an encumbrance and prevent them from devoting themselves entirely to their wild passions." When such men convert to Christianity, they become asocial people—apathetic, lacking in values, and injurious to the state.

Indeed, enlightened deists like Bendavid were confronted by a difficult dilemma: on the one hand, the state continued to discriminate against them as Jews and failed to view them as a separate enlightened group; on the other, the Jews regarded them as apostates. In Bendavid's view, there was only one solution: the emancipation of the Jews depended on their willingness to revolutionize their religious concepts and to abrogate the obligation of observing the commandments. Only if the Jewish religion were limited to the pure Mosaic doctrine, identical with natural religion, and only if the inner core of the religion were preserved on the basis of "the greatest teaching of our religion . . . love thy brethren as thyself," could the character of the Jews be improved. Then Bendavid's group could also regard themselves as members of the Jewish community at large. This goal could best be achieved if the state too would wield its power. In desperation and frustration, Bendavid called upon his Jewish brethren:

For how long will this stupidity of disgraceful and unfounded ritual commandments be continued, for how long will the Jew believe that God in his heaven will bestow a prize on him for observing them . . . surely there will be no end to this unless someone dares to address the Jews clearly and firmly, to explain the illogic in preserving their customs. But at the same time, he must ask the state to annul the ritual commandments, since their observance inevitably has an effect on the Jews' character . . . this is the hydra, all of whose heads must be chopped off at one fell swoop.[45]

Bendavid was one of Mendelssohn's great admirers, but in these words of his he expressed an approach that was the exact opposite of Mendelssohn's. His was a Kantian approach—seeking in the Jewish religion its inner moral essence and totally rejecting its rituals. Precisely ten years after Mendelssohn, in his *Jerusalem*, had stated that the unique essence of Judaism lay in the obligation to observe the practical commandments, Bendavid was the first Jewish intellectual to publicly put forth the radical idea of totally annulling the commandments as an essential step to ensure the existence of the Jews in the modern world. His suggestion to utilize the state's power of coercion to circumvent the adamant persistence of the Jews, who did not know themselves how to choose what was good for them, was of course totally contradictory to Mendelssohn's liberal worldview. Indeed, when Kant read Bendavid's book, he concluded from it (albeit erroneously) in his book *Der Streit der Fakultäten* (1798), that the enlightened Jews had already totally abandoned their religious heritage and were prepared to accept the religion of Jesus.[46]

Saul Ascher (1767–1822) also took a step in contradiction to Mendelssohn's approach. This Berlin Jew, owner of a bookshop, was a radical intellectual who advocated religious reform. In his 1792 book, *Leviathan*, he proposed a religious revolution as a prerequisite for acceptance of the Jews as full citizens of the state. Ascher, following Kant, also stated that the law-based character of Judaism was opposed to the "true autonomy of the will," and irrelevant to the new generation. In contrast to Mendelssohn, Ascher proposed a list of dogmas as an obligatory basis for the Jewish religion—a new set of laws that would preserve the essence of the religion and relinquish its traditional form. Unlike Bendavid, Ascher portrayed Jewry as a society split into two large groups, becoming more and more differentiated—the reformists on the one hand and the orthodox on the other. He felt compelled to find a formula that would preserve the Jewish collective, among other reasons, because of the crisis he perceived in the Berlin community: He noted that many were Jews in name only, and that from day to day, the number of converts to Christianity was growing.[47]

Certainly Bendavid and Ascher's close acquaintance with the salons of Berlin, which represented the ambition of Jewish men and women to climb the social ladder, contributed to their sense of urgency. Many of the Jewish women who were part of that high mixed society were particularly estranged from Jewish tradition and the community. They found no outlet for their interest in European culture in the traditional Jewish milieu, and the culture of the Haskalah was also foreign to them. "Why was I born a Jewess?" Rahel Levin complained in a well-known letter in 1795. She lamented her bitter fate, blamed Judaism for all her tribulations, and claimed that because of it her life was akin to death.[48] The salon culture did not include the Haskalah discourse, nor in fact any other Jewish discourse. Even a radical proposal like Bendavid's, calling for annullment of the commandments, was irrelevant to those Jews who found satisfaction in the Romantic culture and in their close friendships with the aristocracy, high officials, and intellectuals. In the end, most of the salon women chose conversion as an escape route from the Jewish fate, and marriage with upper-class Christians as a means of social mobility.[49] At the turn of the century, conversion was for many regarded as "cultural adaptation." As Jacob Katz wrote:

Going from one community to the other no longer seems the hazardous leap over a gulf . . . Those belonging to the enlightened Jewish upper class were attracted by the splendor, the freedom and the greater spiritual amplitude of Christian society. The children of court Jews, who had received some secular education and had the means to adopt the expensive habits of high society, were most likely to observe the discrepancy between their material affluence and their low social standing. With greater freedom for contact with Gentiles, these children became an easy prey to intermarriage and conversion. If the encounter with non-Jewish society ended in joining it, the convert had no difficulty in justifying his step.[50]

The demonized image of the salons, which was prevalent in Jewish historiography from the days of Heinrich Graetz, is no longer found in the new research. Recent studies have shown much more sensitivity, as well as the ability to penetrate the world of ambitious young women, who acquired social standing and prestige in late eighteenth-century and early nineteenth-century Berlin. Deborah Hertz, for example, writing from a feminist point of view, explained the motivations of Rahel Levin, Dorothea Mendelssohn, Henriette Herz, Rivkah Friedländer, and several other salon hostesses, arguing that their desire to gain personal emancipation and to achieve self-fulfillment and a high social status through conversion and intermarriage were connected ("conversion out of temptation").[51] Michael Meyer has shown that these women were seeking love, an authentic expression of their feminism, and in particular a gratifying personal religious experience. They found these in the salons, in the company of enlightened Christian men, and in Romantic Christianity.[52] While there is no reason not to accept these sensitive and empathetic interpretations, from the vantage point of Jewish society in general and of the maskilim in particular, the phenomenon signified a path of abandonment. Conversion had an especially erosive effect on the Jewish elite of Berlin. The number of converts in Berlin in the 1790s rose to 136, from 77 in the previous decade. This figure does not reflect the trend in full, because there were men and women from the community who converted outside Berlin, but it does provide an indication of how widespread it became in the 1790s.[53]

In contrast to the small group of about twenty women, who climbed the social ladder via the glittering salons and Jewish-German society, "freethinking" (*Freidenker*) Jewish men, only a few of whom had access to the salons, sought a supportive social framework for themselves. With this purpose in mind, over a hundred modern men, employed as tutors or clerks by wealthy Jews, founded an association in 1792, known as Gesellschaft der Freunde (Society of Friends). It was actually an association of protest against the community in which they no longer felt at home as they had in the past. As their number grew, so did their self-confidence, and they decided to establish their own mutual aid and burial institutions of as an alternative to those of the community.[54]

The association's first meeting was opened by one of its founders, Joseph

Mendelssohn (1770–1848), Moses Mendelssohn's son, then a young accountant embarking on a business career, who later became a wealthy banker. Mendelssohn opened his speech with the optimistic rhetoric typical of the Haskalah:

The light of Enlightenment that has shone on all of Europe in our century has also cast its blessed influence on our nation for the last thirty years. Among us too, each day the number increases of those who separate the kernel from the husk in the religion of our forefathers. In particular in the state in which we live the number of our brethren who are enlightened and thinking men is greater than the number of our "old" brethren who denounce the light of reason in matters of religion.[55]

The dichotomy between the modernists and the orthodox, which nearly all the spokesmen in the 1790s referred to, reflected the reality of Berlin life, in Mendelssohn's view. Unlike Bendavid, who argued that the freethinkers were still a minority group, he believed that the majority of Prussian Jews were already enlightened. Hence the time had come to organize and to break the monopoly of the orthodox, who were hostile to the Enlightenment and persecuted anyone who thought differently than they did. It was during these years that orthodoxy was first perceived as a separate camp, for example by Moshe Hirschel and Saul Ascher. In setting up their own alternative institutions, the Gesellschaft chose to clash with the orthodox on the issue of early burial. It established its own burial society, which would preserve human dignity, in keeping with medical recommendations, and avoid any risk of premature burial.[56]

Several maskilim joined the association as soon as it was founded. The most prominent among them was Isaac Euchel, who also served as its chairman from 1797 to 1801. The association declared that it was basing itself on Mendelssohn's legacy and on Enlightenment values. The Gesellschaft, however, was not a continuation of the Haskalah societies. It did not represent intellectuals who aspired to nurture Jewish culture and guide the public in making the changes necessitated by modernization. Rather, it was a new social group in the Berlin bourgeoisie (together with members of branches in Breslau and Königsberg), whose members wished to join together in struggling to achieve an independent status and to establish a supportive social framework. Euchel joined the association after having left his positions at *Hame'asef* and the Society for the Promotion of Goodness and Justice, resigning as a teacher and taking on a new position as an accountant in Meir Warburg's business. It is symbolic that toward the end of his life Moses Mendelssohn wrote to Herz Homberg that his son Joseph, in whose education he had invested considerable effort, had already forgotten the Hebrew language he had taught him.[57]

Joseph Mendelssohn, the son of the most famous and highly revered maskil of all, was unable to find any relevance in the Haskalah, first of all because he, like many of his generation, had already realized a large part of the Haskalah's vision: he had received a balanced education, was fluent in European languages, was able to maintain social and economic relations with Christians, had a modern lifestyle, and was conscious of belonging to a period of Enlightenment and progress in modern Europe. All these had been goals of the Haskalah in the early 1780s, as expressed, for example, by Wessely and Euchel. Joseph Mendelssohn had fully internalized this optimistic rhetoric, and hence for him the Haskalah as an ideology advocating the transition of Jewry from traditional culture and patterns of living to the modern, secular world, had already fulfilled its role. More important, he had lost his religious faith and adopted deist concepts, and hence had lost all interest in nurturing a particular Jewish culture. From these standpoints, he exemplified Solomon Maimon's argument that for the enlightened Jews the Haskalah had lost its relevance in the 1790s. If for the maskilim the world of external knowledge had been a temptation and an enormous challenge, for the young Mendelssohn and his sisters that knowledge was an inseparable part of their cultural world, so there was no need to struggle to acquire it. The new temptations were the life of the modern city and the possibility of totally abandoning Jewish society. In the face of these challenges, intellectuals like Bendavid and societies like Gesellschaft der Freunde emerged, seeking a formula that would still preserve the Jewish collective in the future.[58]

Solomon Maimon was one of the members of the Gesellschaft. He had won a name for himself in the German intellectual republic thanks to his autobiography, published in two parts in 1792–93, which was a personal, moving test case of Kant's general definition of Enlightenment: man's heroic liberation from dependence on authority, his intellectual autonomy and free use of reason. In Breslau, around 1787, Maimon severed the last tie connecting him to Poland, when he divorced his wife, who had come there with his son to demand that he return home. His portrait, painted in the 1790s, shows us a German intellectual in a fashionable hairstyle, clean-shaven and bareheaded. Maimon in the 1790s was a freethinker like Bendavid, Joseph, and Friedländer.

In the 1790s, Maimon the philosopher had no ideological agenda, nor was he a party to the program to reform the Jews or gain civil rights for them. Gideon Freudenthal wrote that Maimon, as a philosopher, "advocated the autarchy of the spirit, and the historical events occurring before his eyes had no real effect on his thinking. It would therefore seem that the philosophical life of the spirit is a substitute, of equal value, to the worthy life of the perfect man."[59] A list of Maimon's impressive works from 1789 to 1799 reflects an outpouring of philosophical creativity whose speculative topics, with the exception, of course, of his autobiography, do not address Jewish or any social or political issues.[60] Maimon, like Bendavid, believed that contemporary rabbinical Judaism was a distorted version of a religion that had originally been a natural religion congruous with reason.

Maimon was by then indifferent to the question of his Jewishness, and showed no special interest in the internal Jewish discourse. When he was in Hamburg, in a moment of despair, he did consider converting to Christianity, if he would not be required to relinquish his faith in the natural religion. In Berlin he lived on the margins of the salon society which was then at its zenith, and the Jewish men and women of this high society regarded him as an exotic figure. They helped him occasionally, but he never actually gained an entree into their milieu. He was also a member of the Gesellschaft for only a brief period. As an independent philosopher who had no vocation, Maimon never fit into any communal framework and showed no interest in the association's activities in the sphere of mutual socioeconomic aid. With an air of intellectual arrogance, he regarded it with contempt, put off by its formalism and indifferent to its aims.[61]

Maimon tried only once to escape his isolation and loneliness. After he left the Gesellschaft, he initiated the establishment of a social circle of intellectuals, one that had nothing on its agenda but the abstract, individualistic, and philosophical goal of advancing human understanding. In effect, Maimon's intent was to take an informal circle of friends, who had been meeting for some time in cafes to discuss philosophical subjects, and to found a reading society (*Lesegesellschaft*), where lectures would be given, articles would be read aloud, and discussions would be held. According to the by-laws, each month the elected chairman would present a special topic, on which articles would be written competing for a prize. The topic would be published in the press and the winner's article would be printed in the society's publication. Unlike the circles of the Haskalah or the Gesellschaft, Maimon's society was not committed to any social or cultural aim whatsoever, nor did it wish to serve as a spearhead to realize any ideology. "Nothing is more important for a man, for the expansion of his understanding, the improvement of his moral character and the promotion of his happiness," Maimon wrote at the head of the society's regulations, "than his self-knowledge." Hence, the society's aim would be "to promote human understanding."

Following the festive opening ceremony, the society did embark upon its activities, but very soon its membership dwindled, Maimon himself lost interest in it, and it became defunct.[62] In 1794, when Maimon was in difficult straits and unable to publish his philosophical works, he appealed to Goethe for help, describing himself as a forty-two-year-old man living on the fringes, with prematurely gray hair, who had nothing but his philosophy and lived a very lonely life. A year later, Maimon left Berlin, the city where he had so longed to live, and moved to a remote estate in Silesia, and almost completely severed the few ties he still had with Berlin's Jewish-German intelligentsia.[63]

Friedländer and the Letter to Teller

In marked contrast to Maimon's quiet disappearance from the public sphere of intellectual Jewry, in 1799 David Friedländer's letter to Teller, publicly declaring that he wished to officially sever his ties to Judaism and join the Protestant church, provoked a scandal.[64] Friedländer was presumptuous in casting himself as Mendelssohn's successor, but he unquestionably filled a major role in the story of the Jewish Enlightenment in the last quarter of the eighteenth century, and was one of the leading Jews in Prussia after Mendelssohn's death. In the 1790s, Friedländer was involved in a wide variety of activities, in particular Prussian Jewry's struggle to have the legal restrictions annulled and to gain their yearned for emancipation. Moreover, as a rich merchant and an enlightened intellectual he belonged, at one and the same time, to both groups of the Jewish elite: that of the wealthy Jews who were the communal leaders and that of the Jewish-German intelligentsia.

Friedländer entered Jewish historiography primarily in his negative, infamous image as the radical maskil who had been on the verge of converting to Christianity. He was perceived as a man who was servile toward the authorities, as "Mendelssohn's monkey" who desecrated his legacy, as an assimilationist who endeavored to promote the interests of his class of capitalists at the expense of his co-religionists, and as a maskil who brought shame upon his nation. It was this kind of assessment that determined Friedländer's place in history.[65] In the new research, however, we find a more balanced view. It is not only the letter to Teller that comes under its purview, but also the entire range of his activity and life prior to 1799 and thereafter. A residual identification with Judaism can be discerned in the letter, and it is read not as a total renunciation of Judaism but rather as a defense of it, out of a lingering Jewish self-consciousness, or at least is read with a sensitive understanding of Friedländer's sorely divided soul.[66]

What was Friedländer's position in the Haskalah crisis of the 1790s? On the one hand, his views and his social class aligned him with the group of German-Jewish intellectuals who no longer saw any point in preserving the tradition and felt estranged from it. On the other hand, his deep involvement in the Haskalah movement from its inception, his attempts to direct the modernization of Prussian Jewry, and his claim to the title "keeper of Mendelssohn's legacy" grant him a special place in the events of the 1790s.

On January 9, 1791, Friedländer addressed a speech to the maskilim of the

Society for the Promotion of Goodness and Justice, at a memorial assembly marking the fifth anniversary of Mendelssohn's death. He urged them to continue adhering to the legacy of their revered teacher, in particular in view of the worrisome phenomenon of the "pseudo-enlightened," who were relegating science and the intellect to the sidelines, interested only in a glamorous, ostentatious lifestyle. Moreover, Friedländer utilized Mendelssohn's memory to enlist the maskilim in a struggle for the emancipation of Prussian Jewry: "I am aware, the wise scholar said on many occasions to his friends, that many difficulties stand in the way of our acceptance into civic society, some of our own doing and some created by others. But my motto is—do not give up."[67] The attempt to portray the continued struggle for Jewish citizenship as part of Mendelssohn's testament was part and parcel of Friedländer's intensive activity during those years to persuade the Prussian government to introduce some real change in the Jews' legal status. However, these endeavors were defeated by bureaucratic red tape and fears that the Jews might penetrate into the social and political systems of the state.[68]

Friedländer's letter to Teller, therefore, seems to be one of the paradoxical results of the struggle for emancipation that he and his fellow members of the wealthy elite waged. It is correctly explained as an act of frustration and despair, after the efforts to gain emancipation came up against the stone walls of Prussian conservatism and failed. The insupportable gap between the social class, complete identification with the civil ethos and high level of acculturation of these Jews, on one hand, and their humiliating legal status on the other, remained in force, unchanged since the infamous decree of 1750. This gap led Friedländer and his friends to exert pressure on the government to fundamentally alter this situation, and it also induced them to cultivate a detached class consciousness, to break away from the communal institutions, and to become an insular elite concerned only with its own interests. "They were painfully aware," Michael Meyer succinctly summed up their situation, "of the wide gulf between what they thought of themselves and what they were considered by the state."[69]

To understand the case of David Friedländer one must look beyond the socioeconomic and class interests that induced him to try to close the gap between his self-image and the legal reality. His political activity and his involvement in the *Kulturkampf* from its inception in the early 1780s were underpinned by the worldview of a radical maskil. From Friedländer's point of view, the Enlightenment revolution was basically a Voltairean, anticlerical revolution, with the aim of overthrowing the rabbinical culture and destroying the status and authority of the rabbinical elite. His enlightenment discourse in the 1790s, reflected in the official memoranda he sent to the government and particularly in his letter to Teller, shows that he shared the views of Bendavid,

Ascher, and Davidson, who advocated the annulment of the religious ritual—or at least profound reforms in it—and the preservation of the deist
essence of the pure Mosaic religion. This is, however, but one part of the whole
picture.

An invaluable key to an understanding of Friedländer's worldview is
found in several polemical personal letters extant from the correspondence he
maintained for years with a religiously observant Jew, Meir Eger of the Glogau
community in Silesia.[70] The letters are written in a mixture of Hebrew, Yiddish, and German. Unlike other maskilim such as Wolfssohn or Saul Ascher,
Friedländer did not compose any biting critical satires, but in his letters to
Eger in the 1790s, personal letters never meant to be published, Friedländer
felt particularly free to reveal his true feelings. In them, he expressed himself
in a language far more common and much coarser than the one he used in his
numerous letters in German, using internal Jewish codes known only to scholars familiar with the religious sources and the traditional lifestyle. He acerbi-
cally criticized the rabbinical elite, recording a plethora of cynical remarks on
the ridiculous aspects of the rabbinical culture and giving free rein to his rage
and frustration at what was happening in Jewish society—ranging from the
strict adherence to the finer points of the halakhah to the libertine behavior of
young Jews in Berlin.

In response, Eger argued that Friedländer's political activity vis-à-vis the
Prussian government had the effect of worsening the situation of the Jews and
trampling on the religion. Friedländer rejected these arguments, claiming that
everything he did was actually for the good of his co-religionists. In his view,
those who were endangering them and putting the religion to shame were the
leaders of the rabbinical elite, such as Raphael Kohen and Yehezkel Landau,
whose ludicrous books were treating reason, God's most noble gift, as if it were
a base handmaiden. The perpetuation of ignorance and the base morals of rabbinical Judaism will lead to mass conversions, Friedländer warned, and that
ought to be the greatest fear of anyone concerned about the fate of Jewry.
Friedländer told his correspondent from Glogau about his public agenda: "I
have been watching all this for the last twenty years, and I have found only
one possible solution: to throw off the heavy yoke under which the King and
the judges of this country, who are not of our people, have harnessed us; to
throw off, furthermore, that other yoke which we have taken upon us with the
rule of our own rabbis and communal leaders."[71] Friedländer believed in the
two goals of the Enlightenment revolution: liberation from the restrictions of
the state and liberation from the authority of the communal leadership and
the rabbinical elite. He was skeptical about the possibility—advocated by
Wessely, Euchel and other maskilim—of merging traditional Judaism and
Enlightenment values and finding a balance between them. When translating

Wessely's *Divrei shalom ve'emet* into German, Friedländer had changed the author's intention, for example, by upsetting the delicate balance Wessely had constructed between the Jew as a man and the Jew as a citizen. In the German adaptation, he stated: "To be a man is of a higher degree than to be a Jew."[72] Friedländer saw no point in trying to introduce a two-part curriculum for Jewish youth—a half day of religious studies taught by a rabbi and a half day of general and business studies in a Christian school. A program of that kind is a contradiction in itself and such a balance is unfeasible, he maintained. Any attempt to combine the contents and approaches of talmudic study (such as the belief that the Jews are the chosen people or that exposure to external knowledge is harmful) and the universal contents of the Enlightenment is doomed to failure from the outset.

Friedländer resolutely held that the time for observing the commandments had already passed and that the status of the rabbis was an anachronism. The youth, he asserted, should be educated to think freely and to integrate into civil society. In his vision of the future, which he outlined for Eger in a letter written early in 1799, at the time he wrote his letter to Teller, a radical Enlightenment revolution was about to take place in Jewry as a whole. The freedom the Jews enjoyed would be expanded, they would no longer study Talmud, there would be no more yeshivot, the halakhah would be forgotten, and the rabbis would no longer have any authority. In Berlin, there were hardly any Polish teachers, and "within ten years," Friedländer added to his vision of the decline of talmudic culture, "no one in Berlin will know what is leaven found over Passover or what is a growth on the lung."[73] What happened in Berlin in ten years would take place in Glogau within fifteen years, and the same would undoubtedly be true in Breslau, Amsterdam, and Königsberg. No one will be able to arrest this historical process, and the obsolete rabbis are the only ones who cannot see it. The philosophical religion is the religion of the modernists and the members of the upper class, while the popular religion of the practical commandments is the religion of the superannuated conservatives and of the lower classes.

The letter to Teller expressed Friedländer's radical world view and vision of the future from a different angle. In the intra-Jewish discourse with Eger, he gave vent to his anticlerical rage provoked by the Jews' serious shortcomings. In the letter to Teller, in contrast, he addressed general public opinion, expressing his frustration at the fact that the future vision had not yet been realized and the enlightened Jews were fed up with the Judaism of Talmud and commandments. Other than his main argument, that the Jews should be accepted into civil society through the mediation of the enlightened Church and on the basis of the pure Mosaic faith, the rhetoric in Friedländer's letter was replete with his sense of insult, the affront to his self-respect, and humiliation. The Judaism of his time is harshly contrasted to the Enlightenment: "There is nothing more humiliating to a man of reason than this situation of eternal immaturity."[74] The educational and cultural foundation on which Friedländer and members of his group were raised is depicted in the letter as foreign, mystical and embarrassing; he also finds that it is contrary to modern life and makes it hard for Jews to integrate into it: "The commandments . . . have turned us into foreigners in the everyday circle of life; the scrupulous observance of meaningless customs . . . have embarrassed us, often causing us to feel discomfort in the company of persons of a different religion, even in the company of servants."[75] The Jewish customs are frightening and repugnant, and they impair social relations. The Jewish people has undergone a serious historical process of degeneration, the messianic idea has clouded their minds. The profound sense of shame that this form of Jewish religion evokes can easily lead one to skepticism, the total abandonment of religious practices, and conversion. However, he asserted, this is a line the Jew should not cross; a decision of this kind, the letter claimed, would bid our conscience pause and be damaging to our self-respect.

As he did in his letter to Eger, here too Friedländer expresses his expectation that Judaism in its present form would disappear: "The study of Hebrew and the Talmud declines among us day by day, and with the neglect of the ceremonial ritual laws it must continue to diminish. In every country the government, with great justice, has taken from these rabbis all power to make binding judgments and enforce the halakhah."[76] However, the present situation was a particularly irksome one, since not many from within the community shared his view that the salvation of Judaism depended on a deliberate abrogation of the practical commandments, and the yearned for rights as citizens could not be obtained from outside the community. To avoid the possibility that he and his like-minded friends would become an isolated sect, an intermediary body between Christians and Jews, Friedländer made his proposal to Teller in 1799. It had a twofold advantage: the acquisition of Prussian citizenship with all the rights that implies, on the one hand, and preservation of the self-respect of Jews who had not converted, but had found in several principles of the natural religion a common denominator with the enlightened Christian world, on the other.

Eger did not hide from Friedländer his suspicion that he was the author of the letter to Teller. Nonetheless, only one day later, he urgently sent him another letter to assure him that, on second thought, he was retracting his accusation. Friedländer's reply indicates that he was all too aware of the scandal his letter had aroused in 1799, and in particular of the fierce attack against its author and his denunciation as a heretic, who had desecrated God and colluded with evildoers. Feigning innocence, Friedländer wrote that he believed the exact identity of the man who was behind the letter to Teller was of less interest and import than a relevant discussion of the significant matters the letter had had sincerely and rationally brought to the public's attention.

Is it possible that Friedländer wrote the letter to Teller solely to underscore the severity of the problems and to induce both Jews and Christians to seek a solution? There is no way of knowing for certain. However, we ought not to forget that Friedländer continued to engage in extensive intellectual, communal and political activity to promote his worldview in the first decades of the nineteenth century as well. In any event, he reacted with his typical cynicism to the news that "Great talmudic scholars and sages of our time, first and foremost among them, the renowned rabbinical authority, the rabbi of Glogau, have joined together to compose an illustrious tract against the author of the above-mentioned wretched letter," referring, of course, to his letter to Teller. He asked for a copy of the tract and concluded his letter by saying: "It is to your joy, the people of Glogau, that a great man in Israel has emerged from your midst to uproot the thistles from the vineyard using a soft stick and a book full of goodness and knowledge," rather than with the weapon of excommunication which had been the custom until then.[77]

As far as we can reconstruct from his descriptions, David Friedländer's collection of books exemplified the ideal maskilic library. Arranged on its shelves alongside one another were books in German and Hebrew, German periodicals to which Friedländer frequently contributed articles, books published by the Freischule Hebrew printing house, many of which were written by maskilim, the writings of Jewish-German intellectuals, like Marcus Herz, Bendavid, and Davidson, the *Hame'asef* periodical, as well as rabbinical literature, which Friedländer continued to take an interest in. And yet, Friedländer had pronounced a death sentence on the religious Hebrew culture and on the Haskalah project. The crisis of the Haskalah was for him a process he had anticipated, one from which there was no return.

In that same turbulent year in which the scandal surrounding his letter to Teller erupted, Friedländer wrote to Aaron Wolfssohn, the last editor of *Hame'asef*, rejecting the idea—so central in the Haskalah's vision—of reforming and regenerating (*Verbesserung*) the Jews. He expressed a total lack of faith in the Haskalah project: "I consider the nation, in its present state, with all its appearance of culture, taste and learning, to be in general irremediably bad and all enlightenment through the *"me'asfim* to be useless." Fifteen years after he had been concerned enough about the education of Jewish youth to found the Freischule, in despair, he cynically declared that the age of the Haskalah had drawn to a close: "No one reads any of the books written in Hebrew . . . For whom are they written? I would propose that a sign be placed on all the Hebrew printing houses: Here books are printed that are never read!"[78]

Chapter Fourteen

Tensions and Polemics in the Shadow of Crisis

The death sentence that David Friedländer pronounced on the Haskalah exemplified the sense of crisis that reached its height in the last two years of the eighteenth century and was manifested in the movement's almost total waning. Until then the Haskalah had continued to develop, despite the relative decline of the 1790s, and Friedländer himself had been one of its chief patrons. Along with the political campaign waged by the German-Jewish intelligentsia in the general public arena to achieve civil rights, efforts to stabilize the Haskalah republic continued. The hunger for enlightenment and the passion for knowledge, which in the Berlin community was no longer hard to gratify, were still as strong as ever among young Jews elsewhere, and these were the ideal new recruits to fill the ranks of the maskilim.

David Hanover, for example, waited impatiently for two years until an article he had sent to *Hame'asef* was printed. From his youth, he had followed with interest the organization of maskilic groups; in the second decade of his life he had already rebelled against the religious education he had received, and longed to join the Society for the Promotion of Goodness and Justice. As soon as he reached adulthood, he "converted" to the culture of the Haskalah and left the authority of his parents. Describing this liberation from bondage, he wrote, "Three years have gone by since I severed the fresh bowstrings with which they had bound my arms, I broke down brass gates and cut through the iron bars put upon me, I pursued men of science and seekers of justice; I rushed after lovers of wisdom and integrity."[1] The editor of *Hame'asef*, Aaron Wolfssohn, together with his colleague Joel Brill, went to great lengths to keep the movement alive and continue its activity, even when the number of its activists and supporters dwindled. Isaac Euchel too once again contributed articles to *Hame'asef* early in 1797 (about three years before he told Shalom Hacohen that in his view *Hame'asef* had failed and there was no chance of reviving it), and with guarded optimism, tried to buoy the spirits of Joel Brill, the friend of his youth. The periodical he had founded together with Chevrat Dorshei Leshon Ever fourteen years earlier had been for many young Jews a gateway to Enlightenment, and now too, when circumstances had changed and Hebrew was no longer an effective tool in achieving the aims of the Haskalah, *Hame'asef* could, in his view, be infused with new life, particularly if it were printed in German.[2]

Satanow and the Haskalah Library in the 1790s

In the 1790s, the Haskalah movement continued to expand its innovative and subversive library, utilizing the Freischule press to print its publications. In 1790 Euchel resigned from his positions in the Haskalah institutions, and the printing house came again under Isaac Satanow's management. This prolific writer, publisher, and printer, as we have seen, related in an extraordinarily obsessive and erotic manner to his work as a writer and publisher. As a fervent believer in the power of the printed book and its ability to influence readers' patterns of thought and behavior, Satanow constantly reiterated the important role of the professional educated author, who served the society as "a physician who specializes in giving healing medicines to the illnesses of the enlightened soul as one does to the illnesses of the body." He devoted all his time and energy, until the day of his death, to printing the many works he wrote and to developing the printing house.

On the covers of the works printed by the Freischule press, Satanow published the catalog of books for sale and urged buyers to send in their orders by mail. Until he lost his sight in 1799, he sent requests for support to the wealthy Jews of the large communities in Europe, traveled three times a year to sell books in Frankfurt-on-Oder, and frequently visited the homes of Berlin's financial elite to persuade them—with no small measure of success—to purchase books from the printing house. He lived in an apartment above the printing house, in a building that belonged to Daniel Itzig, the chief patron of the printing house and the Freischule, a philanthropist who unceasingly gave his support to the Haskalah projects.[3] Satanow's apartment also served as a bookstore, selling mainly the books printed by the publishing house. Satanow never stopped hatching schemes to obtain financing to print the many books he planned to publish, and from time to time he also threatened he would close down the Freischule press unless he received immediate financial support.

For this purpose, in 1794 Satanow founded Chevrat Marpeh Lanefesh (Cure for the Soul Society). The twenty-two members each contributed between five to twelve talers to the society's coffers, in order to set up an initial fund for printing the science and philosophy books and textbooks Satanow insisted were important and necessary. Among the supporters were Isaac

Euchel, Marcus Herz, and others from Königsberg, Dessau, and Frankurt-on-
Oder, as well as David Friedländer, who also published a personal letter of
support for this project. In total opposition to the image of Friedländer that
was prevalent in the 1790s, it seems that even when he was engrossed in the
struggle for emancipation and increasingly estranged from traditional Jewish
life, he continued to support the development of the maskilic library. Friedländer praised the varied literary works published under Satanow's management and urged the wealthy Jews to strengthen their commitment to the
enlightened scholars.[4]

In the last decade of the century, a total of seventy-three titles were
printed at the Freischule press. While this number included calendars, circu-
lars issued by the community and polemical brochures, the majority were titles
that enriched the shelves of the Haskalah library. Other than a few religious
works, printed in order to realize some profit, Satanow, faithful to maskilic
criteria, did not print the books of the rabbinical elite. In this sense, the Haskalah library printed in Berlin was subversive in the 1790s as well. From some of
the books, voices of protest resonated, decrying the inadequacies of the rabbis
and the rabbinical culture. Textbooks in algebra and geometry, chemistry and
Hebrew grammar contributed to expanding knowledge in the Hebrew language.[5] Poems printed in both Hebrew and German, written to mark state
events such as the military and political achievements of Prussia (for example
Prussian occupation of Polish territory in the second partition of Poland in
1793) and events in the lives of the royal family, reflected the community's
patriotism; and congratulatory poems like one printed on the occasion of
Daniel Itzig's birthday reflected the maskilim's dependence on wealthy Jewry.[6]
The collective project of translating *Haftarot* into German, in which Baruch
Lindau, Isaac Euchel, David Friedländer, Josel Reichenau, Joel Brill, and Aaron
Wolfssohn participated, was completed early in the decade.[7] In 1792, the Freischule press printed an extraordinary work by Samuel Romanelli of Mantua,
who in the early 1790s, after returning to Europe from a journey to North
Africa, lived in Berlin under Friedländer's patronage. His travel book was not
a witty satire like Montesquieu's *Persian Letters*, nor did it resemble Euchel's
Igrot meshulam. Nonetheless, from the perspective of the European Enlightenment, it examined the customs and beliefs of Moroccan Jewry, harshly and
arrogantly criticizing the oriental way of life, with the intent of reaffirming the
accepted values of the Haskalah. From Romanelli's European point of view,
in his *Masa be'Arav* (Journey in Arab Lands), the Jews of Morocco were the
embodiment of a primitive society which was nearly irremediable: "The lack
of books and knowledge sinks their hearts into the mire of stupidity and gullibility . . . the light of wisdom has never reached them to eradicate the errors
of their morals and their youthful follies. A veil of ignorant belief distorts their

hearts and vision."[8] The closest comparison Romanelli could find to their backward culture was that of Polish Jews, although he admitted in some areas, particularly in the study of Talmud, the Moroccan Jews surpassed them.

A literary project of long duration that the Society for the Promotion of Goodness and Justice initiated but never succeeded in completing was the serial publication of Wessely's great biblical epic, *Shirei tiferet*. How was it possible that the market for Hebrew literature had so dwindled that the income did not cover the printing costs? "Self-acknowledged scholars" believe they have already learned enough and no one has anything to teach them ("there is no remedy for the illness of those simpletons, and they will die of their stupidity"), and the "sanctimonious" prefer to flee "from all words of science and wisdom, as a man runs from a bear robbed of her cubs." These words of rebuke, uttered by Wolfssohn and Brill, who were responsible for the publishing house, may not have been pleasing to Wessely's ears, but he too was forced to admit that it was truly difficult to expand the readership of maskilic literature at the end of the century.[9]

The number of books produced by the Freischule press was about 40 percent less in the last decade of the eighteenth century than in the previous decade (from 12 books a year in 1784–90 to an average of 7 in 1791–1800).[10] In 1794, only twenty-two men responded to Satanow's initiative and joined Chevrat Marpeh Lanefesh, whose purpose was to provide regular financial support to print books on the Freischule press. Only eight years before, when he had adopted a similar method of financing and founded Chevrat Matzdikei Harabim, 145 members had undertaken to contribute for this purpose.[11] One could not expect scholars, admitted the disappointed Satanow, to show any interest in books of the Haskalah since "they learn to receive a prize and a reward in the next world" and do nothing to expand their horizons beyond the traditional books in their libraries. But, he added, to his sorrow "most of the wealthy Jews are also closefisted when it comes to buying books and would rather spend money on vain pleasures, as it is written 'and the lyre, the lute, the tambourine and pipe, and wine are in their feasts, but they regard not the work of the Lord.' With the exception of but a few, I have not seen the elite volunteering to spend money on books."[12]

As a result of the weakened state of the Society for the Promotion of Goodness and Justice, one of whose aims had been to establish a public framework to support the republic of writers and to raise money for printing books, Satanow once again took up the role of chief publisher of the Haskalah library. Unquestionably, in the 1790s the printing house was occupied mainly with books written by its manager; more than one-fourth of all the books it printed were penned or edited by Satanow. The most original and striking work he published in the 1790s was his *Divrei rivot*. In the literary style of an inter-religious debate, like that of *Sefer hakuzari* (The Kuzari), concealing the author's real name, Satanow dared more than ever before to reveal his world-view. Most of his writings had been marked by verbosity, sagacious, moralistic sayings reminiscent of the early Haskalah, and a strong emphasis on the ideal figure of the rationalistic and knowledgeable *choker*, who is also the true believer. But apparently *Divrei rivot* was the only one of Satanow's books in which he integrated the two elements of the maskilic ideology: a message of tolerance and religious freedom for all peoples, on one hand, and a demand for the thorough revision and reform of the educational system, communal organization, and economic life of the Jews, on the other. In Satanow's maskilic utopia, the intellectuals and the scientists would be assigned a special status, exempt from all civil duties and payment of taxes, and the only rabbis who would be granted the authority to judge (without the right of coercion) would be enlightened rabbis. In this reformed state, "there will no longer be any difference between Jews and Christians unless the laws of their religions divide them, for we, like them, are members of one human species." The religious fanatics, the ignorant masses, and the libertines who take the name of philosophy in vain were, in his eyes, enemies of the Enlightenment.[13]

Satanow's most important contribution to the maskilic library was to reprint books of Jewish thought from the medieval and Renaissance periods. Most of these books in philosophy, literature, historical research, and linguistics had never been reprinted after the sixteenth century. Within several years, Satanow prepared annotated editions, usually with the addition of commentaries, of several key works: Maimonides's *Bi'ur milot hahigayon* with Mendelssohn's commentary in a fourth edition, two additional parts of *Guide for the Perplexed*, Judah Halevi's *haKuzari*, the historical studies of Azariah de Rossi, *Ma'or einayim*, and *Machbarot Immanuel* by Emanuel of Rome.[14] Satanow imputed much importance to their publication, both as a service to Hebrew literature and as a part of the Haskalah project. He deemed Maimonides's logic as interpreted by Mendelssohn important in shaping philosophical thought, and regarded Emanuel's love poems (which he was able to publish after having persuaded Isaac Daniel Itzig to purchase, for a very high price, a rare copy of the book's first edition) as a model of superb literary writing in Hebrew that also provided readers with a pure aesthetic pleasure. All these could be a source of gratification for those thirsting for enlightenment: "I have placed them upon the printing press to satisfy all those imbibing the waters of science from the well of wisdom."[15]

Satanow never tried to conceal his wish to leave for posterity his own personal stamp on all the editions he published, and he underscored his mediating role as an editor and commentator, without which most of these important books would have no meaning for scholars. On more than one occasion,

Satanow pursued his ambition to be at the center of the revival of Hebrew culture. One example is his 1794 publication of the Book of Psalms with Rabbi Shmuel ben Meir's commentary, on the frontispiece of which he claimed that he had found the manuscript in the Prussian king's royal library in Berlin; he admitted only in a footnote on the last page that he was actually the author of the work: "The handwritten commentary from which I copied was decaying, half or sometimes whole pages having been eaten away, so the reader ought to know that most of this is my own commentary."[16] His utter dedication to writing and publishing reached its peak in the last years of his life. Even after he was blind and partially paralyzed, he persevered at his work, and he dictated to an amanuensis at least two of his books, a German translation and a commentary on the Book of Job.[17]

Isaac Satanow's literary endeavor burgeoned against the background of the weakness of the Society for the Promotion of Goodness and Justice, which had failed to realize its plan to serve as an organizational framework for the Haskalah library. However, the Society continued to exist until 1797, although its scope of activity was greatly reduced, certainly in comparison to the grand plan conceived by Isaac Euchel in the 1780s. From time to time, special meetings of the Society were convened, for example, the meeting in memory of Moses Mendelssohn in 1791, at which David Friedländer was the key speaker. It maintained its ties with maskilim in other cities primarily through the agents who distributed the Freischule's books. The bonds of friendship between the Society's activists were expressed in the special congratulatory poems printed in honor of Baruch Lindau and Joel Brill's weddings, and in the eulogy for "our dear departed friend of blessed memory, Joseph Baran," a member of the Society who passed away at the early age of twenty-four, printed in *Hame'asef* in 1796.[18]

The seventh and last volume of *Hame'asef* was published by the Society for the Promotion of Goodness and Justice, and the first booklet of the four it contained was printed in 1794 on the Freischule press, according to the Society's regulations. But in 1794 the Society and the journal underwent considerable change. The slowdown in the Haskalah's momentum, which reached its peak in 1789–90, was manifested in the lengthy period during which *Hame'asef* ceased to appear. Its publication was renewed only four years later, and from 1794 to 1797 only one booklet came out each year, and that containing only about 100 pages, with a considerable reduction in the number of its participants, as well as of its purchasers and readers. The new editors, Wolfssohn and Brill, whose own writings filled most of the pages of the fourth volume, were conscious of this crisis. They did try, from time to time, to hearten themselves and their readers into thinking that *Hame'asef* still had a bright future, but in 1797, at the end of the fourth booklet, they finally conceded defeat. Frustrated and despairing, they announced that, unless at least two hundred people were found at once in Germany, each prepared to pay the nominal fee of two talers a year, they could no longer meet the printing expenses and the project of "true enlightenment," so important to the Jews, would be consigned to the limbo of lost dreams.[19]

Hame'asef, 1794–1797

The seventh volume of *Hame'asef* marked the transfer of the Haskalah movement's center from Berlin to Breslau and the nearly absolute control of its editors, Wolfssohn and Brill, over the movement's agenda. From 1795, the journal's booklets were printed in Breslau, a breach of the monopoly that had been granted to the Freischule press. The two men, who, in Berlin, had earned their livelihood as private tutors for the sons of the Friedländer families, were hired to teach in and direct the first Jewish government school founded in Prussia—the Wilhelm II Royal School. They moved to Breslau, a city southeast of Berlin with a Jewish community that then numbered about 2,500. There was already a branch of the Haskalah in Breslau, and in 1780 several maskilim had founded the Society of Love and Brotherhood, which later became the Breslau branch of the Society of Friends founded in Berlin. Nonetheless, most of the community members were relatively conservative and had been considerably influenced by their Polish environment. The school was founded at the initiative of maskilim and enlightened government officials, in particular the governor of the Silesia district, Carl Georg Heinrich von Hoym, with the involvement of local Prussian educators. It opened its doors to about 130 pupils at the end of the winter of 1791, and immediately became a bone of contention among the community members. One issue was whether the Talmud would be included in the curriculum and who would be responsible for teaching it. Wolfssohn and Brill, who had no compunctions about standing at the forefront of the *Kulturkampf*, regarded the school they had been engaged to run as an invaluable tool in achieving the aims of the Haskalah.[20]

The struggle against the rabbinical elite had been a hallmark of the maskilic revolution from its inception, but Wolfssohn and Brill's anticlerical positions were particularly provocative, and they left their imprint on the seventh volume of *Hame'asef*, arousing internal polemics. From the opening page of the volume it was evident that Wolfssohn had espoused Friedländer's views and regarded the unfaltering war against the rabbis as the major aim of the maskilic revolution.[21] In a poem in honor of David Friedländer's birthday, Wolfssohn flattered him, naming him Mendelssohn's successor. Employing militant rhetoric, he referred to the ignorance and religious fanaticism of the leaders of orthodoxy:

Those priests of the people sit upon their seats, preserving vanities and iniquities, they have made Jacob and Israel the object of curses, for they have shut their eyes so they may not see and closed their hearts so they may not understand, they are like a rider in the wilderness, searching the innermost being and penetrating hearts, to condemn a man if his thoughts are not like theirs. Theirs is a vengeful sword drinking the blood of their rage, for in their fury they have overthrown many, they show no mercy for the aged, they call what they do an offering of zealousness to the Lord, but it is an abomination, God never commanded man to judge the ideas of others. A curse be on their anger, for it is fierce, a curse on their wrath.

In his view, only Friedländer was capable of taking a courageous stand, like the biblical David against Goliath, especially when he lambasted the rabbis of Prague for their criticism of Mendelssohn's *Bi'ur*:

Who shattered those who rose up like the swelling sea? You, and only you, David, seeing there is no one to bring salvation, you gave breath to your spirit, then all grew calm, and do no more harm. Just like the son of Yishai, who putting his faith in God, drew encouragement to confront the giant from Gat . . . he felt no fear of them, and the stone hit [Goliath] in the forehead . . . not by sword and not by stone, but with your pen, with your swift author's pen, you vanquished them.[22]

Hame'asef's book review section was particularly important as a forum for internal polemics. The journal underscored the fact that it was carrying on the project begun by Mendelssohn and Wessely, and in particular it commended Wessely's bold war against the rabbis during the *Divrei shalom ve'emet* controversy.[23] Hardly any new men joined the ranks of writers during the 1790s, and occasionally the journal printed old material that had been sitting in its office for some time.

Naturally, *Hame'asef* also gave major coverage to events in the life of the Breslau community.[24] A lengthy article gave a detailed description of the ceremony inaugurating the Wilhelm II Royal School, and quoted excerpts from the key speeches in a Hebrew translation of the German original. However, it was only printed three years after the event.[25] The maskilim in Breslau were particularly elated by the link between the vision of the transformation of Jewish society through education and the representatives of the Prussian government, which gave the school an added public, political dimension. Not only was Wessely's program being realized in the school's curriculum, but the government was encouraging and supporting it, thus proving that maskilic optimism was justified. Josel Reichenau, author of the article, did his utmost to impart to his readers the excitement that had gripped those attending the festive ceremony, nor did he conceal his great delight upon hearing the message of friendship expressed by the Christian speakers: "I could not restrain myself; I wept tears of joy for having been fortunate enough to see and to hear these good words from a man who is not of our people nor of our faith."[26] In translating the speech delivered by Professor Freidrich Gedike, one of the men in charge of the school, Reichenau took great liberties, adding phrases couched in the finest maskilic rhetoric, brimming with optimism and confidence in the redemption that the Enlightenment would bring:

Merciful God has removed the cloud of folly and has dispersed the darkness so that our eyes may see and our minds may be uplifted, to enhance the perfection of man and to record our society in the book of brotherhood and friendship. Joy has shone on his face and his mouth proclaims: the time of redemption draws near, for the supreme wisdom has revived our souls and has awakened the dear government that it governs to raise our prestige . . . the terrors of the nations are ended, the rods of iron are destroyed, the copper chains placed upon us by the earlier cruel kings of Europe are broken . . . superstition has been abandoned and the power of tyrants weakened . . . peace and tranquillity reign now in most parts of Europe, and as a resident and a citizen, every man will now worship the Supreme Being according to his beliefs.[27]

Apparently it was this faith that also fueled the impatience of the editors of the seventh volume towards what they saw as an obstacle to the full realization of enlightenment in Jewish society. In two caustic critiques, one directed at Baruch Jeiteles (1762–1813), an outstanding figure among the Prague maskilim, and the other at Isaac Satanow, the manager of the Freischule press, Aaron Wolfssohn seemed to be filling the role of Robespierre, zealously determined to defend the maskilic revolution even against the maskilim themselves. The eulogy (*Emek habakha*) that Jeiteles composed in 1793 upon the death of Rabbi Yehezkel Landau of Prague, a leader of the rabbinical elite in the *Kulturkampf*, was regarded by the editors of *Hame'asef* as a betrayal of the Haskalah. This man "is our brother and our friend," so we, the editorial board of *Hame'asef*, have decided, with a heavy heart, to print the critique which reveals Jeiteles's true nature, as a man lacking in knowledge of science and the religious culture, as well as a fool. "This eulogy," Wolfssohn wrote at the beginning of his article, "is brimming with stupidity and evil spirit, and devoid of any good." It is hard to believe, he stated, that any man of our group would so flatter the rabbinical culture and ally himself with the rabbis; hence it is our duty to expose his hypocritical face, cunningly springing from one camp to another.[28]

A no less sharp critique was printed in 1796 in the third booklet of the seventh volume. It lashed out at *Mishlei asaf*, a series of wisdom and *musar* books which Isaac Satanow regarded as one of his finest works. Wolfssohn's criticism, which reminded the readers of the author's Polish origin ("the rabbi and maskil, our master and teacher, Isaac Satanow, a man from Poland") was a personal affront to one of the central pillars of the Haskalah's literary republic. It also reflected a schism between two focal points of the Haskalah movement—the Freischule printing house in Berlin and the *Hame'asef* editorial board in Breslau. Moreover, it emphasized the large gap between what these two perceived to be the essence of the maskilic revolution. In Wolfssohn's opinion, Satanow's literary artifices, in particular the device he employed of disguising his identity and hiding behind a supposedly earlier poet, showed that he attributed greater wisdom to the earlier generations and was perpetuating the "modernists'" sense that they were inferior to their predecessors. He held that there could be no greater damage to the maskilic revolution, which was striving to do the very opposite—to give the Jews the sense that they were making scientific progress and that the "modernists" were superior, as well as to weaken the supremacy of tradition and faith in the supposedly sanctified authority of the "ancients."[29]

In the leading text of the seventh volume of *Hame'asef*, Wolfssohn articulated his revolutionary policy. His play *Sicha be'eretz hachayim* (A Conversation in the Land of the Living) was published in installments in the four booklets of that volume, and with its many lengthy footnotes it took up about a fourth of these booklets.[30] In one of the most radical literary works produced by the maskilic revolution in the eighteenth century, Wolfssohn took the antagonistic conflict between the new intellectual elite and the rabbinical elite to new heights. At its end, he declared that the Haskalah had emerged triumphant from the *Kulturkampf* and the authority of the rabbis had crumbled. The play was first represented as a subversive piece of writing by an anonymous author who, in his will, had asked Wolfssohn to print it. However in *Hame'asef*, Wolfssohn admitted that he had penned the play himself.

In *Sicha be'eretz hachayim*, the culture war is brought before the supreme divine court for decision, but first the case is presented to the medieval philosopher, Maimonides. The play takes place in the land of immortal souls (based on Mendelssohn's concept in *Phädon*) and is centered around the character of the nameless rabbi, who, to Wolfssohn, represented both the great enemy of the maskilim, Rabbi Raphael Kohen of Altona-Hamburg, and the contemporary rabbinical elite as a whole.[31] In vain the rabbi tries to get Maimonides to recognize him, but as he describes the worldview of the rabbinical elite, which presumes to hold a monopoly on the Torah and its interpretation, on the bookshelf and knowledge, Maimonides becomes more and more repelled by him: "I pity the generation whose leader you are! Oh, people of God, how you have fallen and been horribly degraded!"[32]

In his anticlerical play, Wolfssohn levels an unremitting barrage of criticism at the limitations, fanaticism, and ignorance of the rabbinical elite, with the aim of challenging its presumption that it can continue to hold the reins of leadership. He introduced into the play Moses Mendelssohn, the earthly enemy of Rabbi Raphael Kohen in the polemic over the *Bi'ur* and the revered personification of the Jewish Enlightenment. Unquestionably, Wolfssohn, who had reacted so sharply to Jeiteles's eulogy for Rabbi Yehezkel Landau, must also have read *Alon bakhut*, the literary eulogy for Landau by Joseph Ha'efrati, an Austrian maskil.[33] In Ha'efrati's harmonistic eulogy, a florid, emotional conversation about reconciliation takes place in the "eternal world" between Rabbi Landau and Mendelssohn. Each of the two expresses his deep esteem for the other and grants him legitimation—from the rabbinical viewpoint on the one hand and from the maskilic on the other.

It may have been this work that inspired Wolfssohn to write his *Sicha be'eretz hachayim*. In any event, Wolfssohn hastened to destroy the harmony that Ha'efrati had constructed between the rabbi and the maskil. In his play, Mendelssohn reconstructs for Maimonides the first campaign in the *Kulturkampf* of the 1780s, in which Wessely was harshly attacked by the fanatic rabbis, who refused "to listen to the voice of reason whose only wish is to open blind eyes and to turn darkness into light." If the rabbis of Italy had not come to Wessely's aid, who knows what might have been his fate.[34] In contrast to the harmony introduced by Ha'efrati, Wolfssohn's play ends in an irreversible rupture. Even after his death, the rabbi still clings to rigid anti-maskilic orthodox positions, and Mendelssohn has received the full support of Maimonides, as well as his friendship as a kindred soul. In the universal world of souls, the two have joined the great Greek philosophers. God himself decides in favor of the maskilim in the *Kulturkampf* and declares: "My dear son, Moses [Mendelssohn], shun the counsel of the wicked [the rabbis], for they do not regard the works of the Lord or what His hands have done."[35] At the conclusion of the play, the rabbi is left standing alone on the stage, and the message is crystal clear: soon the rabbinical elite will admit its failure and, utterly confused, will leave the stage of history, and that will signify the ultimate victory of the Haskalah.

The Early Burial Controversy

This victory was not merely a case of wishful thinking, expressed in the play in a fictional situation in the world of souls, where everything is possible. In the Jewish public, several cultural campaigns were being vigorously waged, throwing into sharper focus the rifts between the Enlightenment revolutionaries and the defensive orthodoxy. The most intensive and stormy campaign was around the issue of early burial, which reached its peak in the 1790s. Maskilim, physicians, rabbis, communal leaders, and Prussian government officials were involved in this controversy, in which the head-on clash between the Enlightenment and the Jewish religion seemed particularly bitter and unrelenting.[36]

The maskilim, who advocated deferring burial, clamored for the acceptance of the scientific and medical opinion that certainty of death could not be established for at least three days. They intimidated their adversaries with horrifying stories of cases from medical research and the press describing people considered dead who had been buried hastily and later revived in their graves, but were unable to get out. This was one of the methods of persuasion employed by the physician and philosopher, Marcus Herz, for example. In his influential work on this polemic, he asked readers to conjure up the picture of a man awakening in his dark, narrow grave, unable to make his way out, remaining there until he dies a horrible death: "His face grows red and his blood rushes, pouring out of all his orifices, he grows more and more agitated, begins to pull out his hair, to scratch at his flesh, wallows in his blood, and flounders in the clay."[37] The cover of the German edition of his book opposing the early burial of Jews bears the picture of a dead man trying to get out of his grave in Berlin's Jewish cemetery.[38] Members of the Society of Friends in Berlin and Breslau went to great effort to establish an alternative burial society, to enable enlightened Jews in favor of delayed burial to assure themselves and their families that they would never run the risk of such a horrifying experience. It was a very significant step in the Haskalah revolution, because it created a social split within the communities, drew concrete boundaries between the enlightened and the orthodox, and for the first time questioned whether it was at all possible to continue a common way of life.

Nearly every maskilic text in the 1790s related to this issue. The opposition of the rabbis, including prominent representatives of the rabbinical elite like Rabbi Yehezkel Landau, was cited as an example of their lack of compassion and tenacious adherence to "our forefathers' custom," even at the cost of burying people alive and cruelly contradicting reason, the science of medicine, humanism, and the essence of the Torah as a "doctrine of life." In 1794, Joel Brill composed a special booklet on the subject, which was published under the auspices of the Breslau Society of Friends and financed by it. The booklet was sent free of charge to all the burial societies in various communities, in an attempt to persuade them once and for all to support the practice of delayed burial.[39] Once again, the maskilim tried to circumvent the rabbinical leadership, as they had done on the issue of education in 1782, and to convince those directly responsible for burial of the rightness of their position. Would it be thinkable to act otherwise when it was a question of saving lives? Can you fail to understand that the present practice can lead to bloodshed? Does not the value of life take precedence over every other value? And, in any case, Brill pleaded with the members of the burial society, why do you believe that the requirements of the religion cannot be compatible with the requirements of reason and humanity?

The public appeal of "the professor and headmaster of the Wilhelm Royal School in Breslau" evoked numerous reactions and inflamed the controversy. One of the sharpest reactions was printed in Berlin in 1796, on the Freischule press, and was intended to provide talmudic-halakhic support for Brill's argument, which he badly needed.[40] However, its author, Abraham Ash, a former talmudic scholar who turned into an anticleric, reacted by writing a militant text that amounted to an indictment of the rabbinical elite and the *posekim* (halakhic authorities) who rejected the demand to introduce delayed burial. The revolutionary rhetoric of his book *Torah kullah* (The Whole Torah) was interspersed with emotional outbursts: "Rabbinical authorities of the land! You are not only striking at our Torah but you also refuse to listen to our master, Moses. You are defying the Almighty and wisdom. Shall I hold my tongue upon seeing this? Go then, and see how you are obstructing justice because of your exorbitant pride."[41]

Since the issue of early burial led to a clash between the halakhic norms and life itself, this raised a crucial question—was the rabbinical elite capable of adapting the religion to a world in which reason, science, and humanism dictate the way of life of individuals and society? Ash depicted the Judaism of the rabbinical elite as insular and perverted and accused it of turning a blind eye to the challenges of the modern era. Educating youth solely on the basis of the Talmud was perpetuating economic and cultural backwardness, and Ash viewed that as a terrible offense against the young generation: "They prepare their sons for slaughter, they hand them over to Molech in a vision, and when they awake, they see it was but a dream! Daughter of my people, daughter of my people, how have you become a whore! . . . see how you have behaved in the valley of the Hebrews who sacrifice the children!"[42] Abraham Ash was clearly giving vent to all his frustrations and anger from the time he had spent as a pupil of the rabbinical elite. When he arrived in Berlin at an early age and became a maskil under Friedländer's patronage, he developed a strong antipathy to the rabbinical culture that he was brought up on. In his view, "The purpose of the Torah is the success of human society," and hence it is incumbent on the rabbis to do all they can for this purpose, in particular on the crucial issue of early burial. He was certain that the rabbinical elite was sticking adamantly to its position against delayed burial only in order to retain its honor and its preferred status, and to do so was even prepared to distort the true meaning of the Torah, which calls upon the Jews to do everything possible to save human lives.[43]

In the last booklet of *Hame'asef*, Isaac Euchel also returned to the public arena. In a long article, he revealed the leading role he had played in the 1780s in placing the issue of early burial on the Jewish public agenda. In it, he also summed up the various arguments that had been raised until then during the controversy, and pointed to the fundamental questions that were still unresolved as a result of the orthodox opposition.[44] In a public letter of support for his friend Brill, he once again depicted early burial as a barbaric practice, but also admitted that after struggling for ten years, the maskilim had not really been able to effect any change on this issue. Perhaps, Euchel suggested, we ought to show more understanding for the rabbis' position. If they really believe they are unable to give in without violating the halakhah, "then the philosopher too, who relies on reason alone and believes the rabbis' reasoning is untenable, ought to modestly withdraw and admit, out of his love of man, that this is the custom based on the laws of the nation. That is the boundary line at which philosophy ceases to quarrel with theology, and although it does not justify it, must yield to it."[45] Of course, this was not a declaration of defeat, but a preface to Euchel's detailed argument that the prohibition against delayed burial originated in a halakhic error that stemmed from a misinterpretation of the biblical language.[46] Euchel invited the rabbinical elite to a public debate on the issue, to deliberate about the various commentaries on the biblical sources themselves. He believed that was the only way to avoid a head-on collision between the religion and the Enlightenment.

Euchel was concerned about the possibility of a total schism, so he proceeded carefully, suggesting ways of reaching a compromise on this issue to mitigate the tension between the camps. In marked contrast, Aaron Wolfssohn, Euchel's successor in the leadership of the Haskalah movement, resolutely demanded that the rabbis relent, just as he had imagined them doing in *A Conversation in the Land of the Living*. In a long response, printed in *Hame'asef* in 1797, to a critique of his play sent in by an anonymous scholar from Vienna, Wolfssohn also became embroiled in the controversy over early burial.[47] Wolfssohn was less interested in the possibility of finding support for delayed burial in the religious sources, and far more concerned that the shameful position of the rabbinical elite might mar the image of the Jews in the eyes of enlightened Christians. He blamed that elite for the prolonged *Kulturkampf* and demanded that it show flexibility in its halakhic rulings. In his view, the earlier generations of rabbis, unlike their present-day successors, had been more lenient and had tried to avoid laying down rules that the public could not live with. "Until when, my brethren who sit in judgment," Wolfssohn publicly pleaded with the rabbis, "until when will there be quarrel and strife among the children of Israel and the sword of a holy war (which is the name you would give it) stand between brothers? Until when will you shut your ears so that you hear not the cries of your people calling out to you for delayed burial?" Furthermore, he added, there is a real danger in their unshakable obstinacy: "For you know, this will lead to a bitter end . . . Please! For the honor of God before whom our forefathers walked and the honor of our Torah, so that the people will not be divided in two or that Heaven forbid, there will be two Torahs, do not spurn their plea!"[48] In Wolfssohn's opinion, there was but one satisfactory solution for the issue of delayed burial: the rabbinical elite must submit and come to terms with the fact that scientific conclusions are superior to "our forefathers' custom." Wolfssohn advised the rabbis to sign a writ of submission, in which they were invited to concede that medical science was in the right and to agree to refrain from intervening in the matter and to grant the Jews complete freedom to fix the date of burial according to the opinion of the physicians.[49] This was not merely a vision of the future, in the spirit of Wolfssohn's revolutionary maskilic view that greater validity and authority should be ascribed to the values and knowledge of the "modernists" than to those of the "traditionalists." In this case, his approach reflected a reality that was taking shape toward the end of the eighteenth century, in light of the country's laws, which in Germany compelled the Jews to refrain from early burial.

The debate over the time of burial elicited much furor, particularly in the Breslau community, where the tension between the camps was very high.[50] To protest early burial, Aaron Wolfssohn's came to the rabbi's home during the Purim repast, disguised as a dead man who had climbed out of his grave. But this was just one provocative episode in this battle.[51] In September 1798 the Prussian king, Frederick William III issued an order divesting the religious establishment of the right to determine time of burial and transferring it to the professional field of medicine, also requiring a burial license that would be issued by the police.[52] At least on the subject of early burial, Wolfssohn's prediction that the power of the rabbinical elite would be forcibly weakened came true, although the passage of the laws did not put an end to all the quarrels on the subject.

The *Besamim Rosh* Affair

The renewed furor over early burial was preceded by another affair, alarming the rabbinical elite, which felt the Haskalah was seriously threatening it and challenging its status. Saul Berlin, who had touched off a tempest in 1793, was once again at the epicenter of the affair. Before the reverberations of his attack on Rabbi Kohen of Altona-Hamburg and his subversive book *Mitzpeh yokte'el* had died down, his halakhic and no less subversive book *Besamim Rosh* came off the Freischule press.[53] To give it credibility and an aura of exotic distance, the book pretends to be an authentic manuscript. In this sense, its frame story resembles other frame stories of the Haskalah culture. Maskilim such as Euchel, Wolfssohn and Satanow, as well as Berlin himself in his *Ktav yosher* and *Mitzpeh yokte'el*, used a similar literary vehicle. But in this case, the level of sophistication was particularly high.

According to the story, Rabbi Isaac de Molina had found an unknown manuscript in the library of a wealthy Alexandrian Jew in the sixteenth century. It allegedly contained halakhic responsa of the famous fourteenth-century *posek* of Spain, Rabbi Asher ben Yehiel, who had never published this invaluable book. Rabbi de Molina's book, which contained Rabbi ben Yehiel's responsa, came into the possession of a Jewish scholar from Turkey by the name of Yonah Zeevi in the eighteenth century. Zeevi had once been in Saul Berlin's company at a hotel in Piemonte, Italy, and had sold him the manuscript of *Besamim Rosh*. Eleven years later, Berlin had it printed in Berlin under the title *Kasa deharsana*, after adding to this collection of responsa his own halakhic annotations, under the title. In the spring of 1792, an open letter was printed singing the praises of the book and appealing to all talmudic scholars to subscribe to it in advance to help cover the printing costs.[54] The 127 people who responded to his call ordered 272 copies of the book. Although this number was far lower than Berlin had expected, *Besamim Rosh* was published within less than a year.

The book attracted a great deal of attention at the time, and also aroused the interest of rabbis and scholars in later generations for several reasons. First of all, the outward appearance of the book—with 110 folio-size double-columned pages—was typical of volumes of questions and responsa. Second, it bore the approbations of Rabbis Yehezkel Landau and Zevi Hirsch Levin. Third, the book was written in rabbinical style and the 392 responsa in it displayed an erudite knowledge of halakhic issues. All of these qualities gave the impression of authenticity, which ran counter to the loud voices that accused Saul Berlin of forging the book.[55] Some scholars regarded *Besamim Rosh* as the beginning of the reform of Judaism. Others accepted the author's explanation that he published the book to placate the many enemies he had made in the *Mitzpeh yokte'el* affair, so that he could once again take his rightful place among the top-ranking members of the rabbinical elite.[56]

Indeed, an examination of the book from the perspective of the techniques of halakhic literature, on one hand, and the unavoidable assumption that the entire work was penned by Berlin, on the other, leads one to the conclusion that "Saul Berlin attempted to reform aspects of rabbinic culture from the inside by forging Jewish memory."[57] Nonetheless, this conclusion cannot obscure the fact that the work was written in the public arena of the 1790s in connection with the maskilic revolution. Hence, we are obliged to see it as one more step in the overall endeavor to erode the authority of the rabbinical elite by employing the type of literature it regarded as the crowning glory of its intellectual achievement. Unquestionably, Berlin wanted to display his amazing erudition in rabbinical literature to the scholars, but his subversive aim is unmistakable. Not only was his book printed by a publishing house under maskilic control, and probably under Isaac Satanow's close supervision, but the list of subscribers to it was almost identical to the usual roster of supporters of the Freischule press in the 1790s. Contrary to Berlin's expectations, with the exception of a relative, Rabbi Alexander Sender of Satanov, no rabbis were among the advance subscribers. On the other hand, a striking number of heads of the economic and communal elite, such as members of the Itzig and Ephraim families of Berlin, as well as David Friedländer, subscribed to the book. Abraham Peretz (1771–1833), Saul Berlin's cousin, who was also the father-in-law of the wealthy Jew, and supporter of science and Haskalah in White Russia, Joshua Zeitlin, ordered fifty copies.[58] Peretz, a prominent figure in the circle of Shklov maskilim, who converted early in the nineteenth century, certainly was aware of the subversive power of the book when he subscribed in advance to such a large number of copies, which he planned to distribute.

A cursory examination of *Besamim Rosh* aroused the suspicion of contemporary scholars. They found in it a series of rulings that were contrary to the accepted halakhah regarding observance of the Sabbath, *niddah*, and the dietary laws. In several instances, *Besamim Rosh* suggested leniency: If a man was on his way home and had no money left, and might miss the last leg of his journey in the wagon to avoid travelling on the Sabbath, it would be better for him to travel on the Sabbath than to become a burden on others and in need of their charity (no. 375); it is permitted to mourn for a man who has committed suicide because one ought to acknowledge the genuine despair of a poor man who is sick of life, and to justify his action (no. 345); a man who "embraced and kissed his impure [menstruating] wife in public" should not be excommunicated (no. 175).

But the real explosives lay in a series of questions and responsa that depicted the rabbinical culture as ludicrous, intolerant, and antithetical to enlightenment—exactly as Saul Berlin had done in *Ktav yosher* and *Mitzpeh yokte'el*. Is it permissible to whip a woman who has refused to accept a religious judgment in a case in which the king had forbidden the rabbis to excommunicate offenders (no. 25)? Is the marriage of man binding if his testicles have been cut off? In determining the ruling in his case, cannot we learn from the custom of the Hottentots, who remove one testicle from every boy at the age of nine, that this defect does not render him infertile (no. 340)? Shall someone who has lost all his teeth eat a matza soaked in water on Passover or swallow it whole (no. 114)? Was that fanatic rabbi correct in ruling that the nose of a young widow, who admitted having slept with a centile, be cut off (no. 192)?

Number 251 is especially important, and its inclusion in *Besamim Rosh* may have been Berlin's main reason for writing the book, while all the other sections are there as window dressing. Berlin was not satisfied with the rather radical statement he made about the supremacy of reason over tradition ("a man will not learn about the essence of the Torah and the commandments from the knowledge he may derive from the literary meaning of the scriptures or the words of our ancient sages, but rather from the books of the scholars of the nations, who know how to delve into these matters"). He also related to the rising tension between the religion and its commandments and everyday life. In his book, he introduced an idea, which, from the standpoint of the rabbinical culture, was subversive and destructive in the extreme:

If, heaven forbid, the time should ever come when the Torah, its laws and commandments, bring misfortune to our nation as a whole, or if it should transpire that they bring us no happiness whatsoever, we should then cast its yoke from our necks. For the axis upon which all the laws of the Torah turn is that God in His love commanded them to make those laws, for He wanted to show men mercy. (no. 251)

Since the purpose of the Jewish religion is to support the life of those who observe it and it is unthinkable that "God, who made heaven and earth, should hate His creatures," it is equally unthinkable that its representatives, the members of the rabbinical elite, should lead it into such a conflict, causing harm and suffering, without totally losing all its validity.

The orthodox, ever vigilant and sensitive, went into action immediately, and as soon as the danger posed by this subversive book of halakhah became obvious, an organized effort was made to denounce it and warn against it. At first a small pamphlet with the provocative title *Ze'ev yitrof* was printed in Frankfurt-on-Oder. In it a scholar from Berlin cautioned Jews not to attribute the book to Rabbi Asher ben Yehiel, nor to accept the erroneous halakhic rulings it contained.[59] Before long, Berlin's long-time enemy Rabbi Kohen from Altona-Hamburg took up his position at the forefront of the battle against *Besamim Rosh* and its author. We learn from the correspondence about the affair between members of the rabbinical elite in 1793 that Rabbi Raphael Kohen asked his father-in-law, Rabbi Jacob Katzenellenbogen of the Oettingen community, who was in Altona to attend his son's wedding, to enlist additional rabbis in the struggle. Katzenellenbogen's letter to Rabbi Meshullam Igra of Tysmenitsa in eastern Galicia was sent about two months after the publication of *Besamim Rosh*. It reveals a plan for an all-out battle against Saul

Berlin, very similar to the struggle that the rabbinical elite attempted to organize against Wessely a decade earlier in the *Divrei shalom ve'emet* affair. This
time too, the orthodox rhetoric reached a high pitch of anxiety:

Here I have seen a thing that has revolted my soul and dissolved my heart, and
trembling took hold of my flesh . . . On hearing of this, we wail, Alas! Such a day of
sorrow and darkness, a tribulation that the sons of Jacob have never known before . .
. for he is a heretic who uproots the foundations of our religion leaving not one trans-
gression he has not permitted . . . and the name of this doer of abomination is a man
infamous for his evil and profanity, R. Saul, son of the chief rabbi of Berlin . . . and
this is not a time to remain silent for before long the entire House of Israel, heaven
forbid, will be misled by him . . . and the Torah will be forgotten by Israel and the
words of the living God will be perverted, heaven forfend, for he has revolted against
the Lord . . . and has injected a venom that seeps into every element of the principles
of our religion.[60]

Rabbi Katzenellenbogen, agitated and alarmed, urged a whole list of rabbis to declare war on Saul Berlin to prevent him from carrying on his destructive campaign. His son Lazar Katzenellenbogen was more pragmatic; he
suggested they ought to publish excommunication notices and burn copies of
Besamim Rosh. He added that if more rabbis known as great scholars would
join in the fray, victory would be assured. Saul Berlin's subversive intentions,
already exposed in his *Mitzpeh yokte'el*, were overwhelming proof, he opined,
of his malicious designs in his new book as well.[61]

Rabbi Kohen was unprepared to lead the struggle himself, because of his
personal involvement and because his hands were tied, since after the last affair
in which he played a role he had been deprived of the right to issue a public
writ of excommunication. But we know he did join in the campaign, since we
have a letter he sent to Rabbi Meshullam Igra, in which he heaped invective
on Saul Berlin and expressed his anxiety that a terrible catastrophe was in the
offing:

And now this loathsome man has wounded many, uprooting the foundations of the
Torah, and in particular has deceived the children of Israel in his instructions, some of
which he has fabricated himself and some he has brought forth in the name of Rabbi
ben Yehiel . . . this is a time of misfortunate the likes of which has never been before,
when the enemies of the Lord have attempted to deny His existence. The Almighty will
overturn his counsel and what he has brought forth from his spirit, a spirit of confusion which lies within him, will have no existence.[62]

Rabbi Mordechai Benet of Nikolsburg filled a more central role in the
struggle. Sensitive to enormity of the threat to the rabbinical elite, he clearly
conveyed its distress as well as its determination to resolutely ward it off:
"There are no more heroes in the land who will step into the breach, we have

remained standing steadfast like a masthead at the top of the mountain, we sit
alone. This is a day of trouble, a day of reproof, the daughter of my people is
wounded, and there is no strength to withstand the war against the scurrilous
enemies of the Lord."63

The leaders of the struggle brought great pressure to bear on Rabbi Zevi
Hirsch Levin of Berlin, Saul Berlin's father, to denounce his son in order to
ensure the victory of orthodoxy and the salvation of the rabbinical elite. Rabbi
Benet sent him a detailed critique of the book, pointing out all the subversive
parts, which in his view, were a disgrace to the Jews and to the Torah. He
offered Rabbi Hirsch an honorable way out. He was prepared to assume that
no malice was intended and that the author had erred in thinking that he had
an original manuscript in his hands, if Rabbi Levin would admit that the book
was offensive.64 But the chief rabbi of Berlin had no intention of accepting this
offer. He publicly sided with his son and scornfully dismissed the harsh criticism that had been leveled at Besamim Rosh. He supported the frame story
that Saul Berlin had brought the manuscript from Italy, took the responsibility
himself for the publication of the book, and adamantly insisted that his son's
expertise as a talmudic scholar was a proven fact. He argued that the entire
affair was the result of a plot contrived by Raphael Kohen, who was constantly
inciting other rabbis against his son, to take revenge on him and harm his
family.65 He also had a special open letter about the book printed on the Freischule press, claiming that while there were halakhot in the book which had
never actually been ruled and others that were not really fit for publication,
this was not an exceptional occurrence in the rabbinical literature. He called
on readers of the letter to refrain from being incited by the slanderous words
of Rabbi Benet: "And I caution every man who has in him but a spark of the
fear of God . . . not to listen to those who would instigate and incite them . . .
and he who suspects worthy men will be smitten with disease."66

As he had in the previous polemic centering on his Mitzpeh yokte'el, Saul
Berlin felt grievously threatened. Although he thought of writing an indignant
reply to all his critics, he never did so, deciding instead, probably at his father's
advice, to leave Berlin. It seems that despite Rabbi Levin's resolve to defend
his son, he felt somewhat uneasy about provoking Rabbi Kohen and wanted
to restore some calm and peace to the rabbinical elite. In 1793, just before Rosh
Hashanah, Saul Berlin departed on a journey that took him through Amsterdam to London, where he died a year later in the winter of 1794. During a
stopover in the city of Halle, he wrote a letter containing his last will, expressing the full depth of his misery: through his rabbinic family and his own traditional orientation, this maskil was held captive in the bonds of the rabbinical
elite, but never publicly renounced it despite his great aversion to it. Lonely
and despairing, suffering from the pains of his illness, Saul Berlin cautioned

whoever found his body not to read the writings he had left in his suitcase, but to send them in a sealed envelope to his father or to "loyal friends in Berlin." They would know what to do with them. He also asked that no eulogies be delivered at his funeral, and signed the letter with the words: "These are the words of an embittered man to whom God has given a cup of poison to drink."[67]

However, his comrades in the Enlightenment revolution did not forget his contribution to their struggle. Immediately following his death, the Freischule printing house published *Ktav yosher*, the satire he had written in 1784, lambasting the position taken by the rabbinical elite against Wessely. In *Hame'asef*, a very favorable review of the book was printed, praising Saul Berlin (without mentioning his name) as one of the greats of the generation who had joined the maskilim, risking his life and reputation, and been persecuted and banned by men "seeking a vain revenge."[68]

Chapter Fifteen

On Frivolity and Hypocrisy

The picture of Jewish society and culture in the 1790s is a very complex one, as we have learned from the previous chapters. Only a few years after the maskilim first made their appearance in the public arena, they found themselves embroiled in a series of conflicts, from within and from without. The accelerated pace of secularization, so evident in the city streets, led the orthodox to harden their opposition to the Haskalah. The Haskalah's prominent spokesmen, headed by Wolfssohn and Friedländer, no longer hesitated to launch even more formidable anticlerical assaults on the rabbinical elite. Moderate maskilim, who were observing with concern the growing radicalization of the group leading the movement, and were displeased with what they viewed as a digression from the path of their revered teacher, Mendelssohn, were also attacked and accused of hypocrisy. An internal maskilic polemic soon developed, which further reduced the ranks of the maskilic republic, eroded the public and financial support it had received, and helped hasten its demise.

The maskilim, then, were compelled to struggle on two fronts. On the one hand, they escalated their attacks on the rabbinical elite, who they perceived as the enemy of Enlightenment, and on the other, they had to defend the "true Haskalah" against the "pseudo-Haskalah," which both radical and moderate maskilim regarded as a manifestation of a substandard secularity. The processes of cultural and moral decline taking place in the bourgeois Jewish family were viewed as perversions and caused much concern. The orthodox rigidity and religious hypocrisy of Jewish Tartuffes, on one hand, and the frivolity of young men and women, hungering for the free life outside the ghetto, on the other, compelled the revolutionary maskilim to redefine their role. In the new balance of power, they had to choose between right and left, as the critics and overseers of Jewish modernization, who wanted to see it realized, in spite of the opposition of the rabbis of the old elite, but without dissolving the collective Jewish identity.

The Enemies of Enlightenment

The *Besamim Rosh* controversy subsided a short time after Saul Berlin fled to London. However, it left a significant mark on Jewish society. It particularly affected the orthodox, always on guard to identify any new threats. Indeed, another provocation, apparently directed at Rabbi Raphael Kohen, evoked an immediate response. In April 1796, an amazing account was planted in a local newspaper in Altona, reporting that a synod of Italian rabbis, meeting in Florence, had allegedly decided to abolish a list of halakhic prohibitions: to transfer the weekly day of rest from Saturday to Sunday, to permit work on holidays, and to allow the use of a razor in shaving and the eating of pork. Many Jews, the account claimed, were interested in these reforms and had been expecting them for a long time. Rabbi Kohen was convinced that this was an attempt to exploit the Italian rabbinate, known for its relatively moderate positions since it had sided with Wessely in the 1780s, and to attack the Ashkenazi rabbinical elite. He sent an urgent letter to Livorno to ascertain the truth of the newspaper account and to demand that a denial be published. After a short time, the rabbis of Italy did publish letters of denial, printed in a special pamphlet in Hebrew and in German translation. Whoever had published the false account, the pamphlet said, "was one of the mockers of the angels of the Lord. This is their way in their folly to be free of the commandments and to be content with licentiousness, Oh, who would have believed such things could be? Never before has there been such an abomination in Israel . . . the rest of Israel would not cancel even one half of a commandment from our holy Torah."[1]

In this case, even more than in the *Besamim Rosh* affair, it was not very difficult to defend the orthodox positions, since in the 1790s the leaders of the rabbinical elite had a growing pessimistic sense of being under siege. Rabbi Kohen's sermons from the 1790s, for example, which were compiled in the book *Da'at kedoshim*, expressed neither despair nor the admission of defeat. Instead, they reflected recognition of the need to resolutely counter the "evil ones" and at the same time strengthen the self-confidence and the conviction of the "righteous ones"—in his view, still the majority of the public—that their path was the right one.[2] He continued to deride the value of external knowledge and totally rejected any rationalistic interpretation of the religion as heresy in disguise. Clearly alluding to Saul Berlin, Rabbi Kohen vented his anger at scholars who misuse their knowledge of the Torah to vex the religious establishment. Furthermore, he reiterated the worldview he had held throughout all the controversies he had been embroiled in as the rabbi of Altona-Hamburg, that the authority to employ coercion in relation to religious offenders was one of the foundations of the Torah ("anyone who has seen the splendors of the Torah knows that a cornerstone, a sure foundation of the Torah and the commandments, is the power to punish the transgressor").[3] Hence the maskilim who are opposed to coercion are distorting the Torah and exposing their true countenance, as Jews who reject anything that is not compatible with reason. Rabbi Kohen quoted Maimonides, who stated that it is desirable to maintain one's distance from apostates. He cautioned his audience to avoid being tempted by their inclination "to follow the path of reason," and "to shun those who would interfere with our people's worship of God, for today there are many who break away from the people and have filled the earth with their corrupt words, to strengthen their pure faith, in view of the severe tribulations with which God is testing them, and to study the Torah for its own sake." In his eyes, the crisis stemmed from the fact that Jews were daring to attack the rabbinical elite and criticize it publicly: "Alas, how lowly we have fallen," the rabbi of Altona-Hamburg lamented in one of his sermons:

Woe to those who seek to hide their plans from God, and what they have done until now in the dark, they do now openly, they brazenly enact unjust laws and draft oppressive edicts. Alas, what will be our final end . . . Woe to the generation in whose time this has transpired . . . They show contempt for the talmudic scholars, these base men who follow idle pursuits . . . They mock the messengers of the Lord, scorn His words, and deceive His prophets.[4]

With these words, he voiced his feelings that those few still standing in the breach were struggling to stem the tidal wave of modernism. This was also the mood in which Rabbi Eleazar Fleckeles eulogized Rabbi David Tevele of Lissa, one of the first orthodox fighters in the *Kulturkampf*, in the Meisel synagogue in Prague in the summer of 1792.[5] Just as the maskilim had kept alive the legacy of Wessely's battle in the cultural war in 1782, Flekeles extolled the figure of the heroic rabbi who had been at the forefront of the war against the philosophers. Referring to *Divrei shalom ve'emet*, the preacher denied the distinction Wessely had drawn between religious knowledge and human knowledge, and spoke highly of Rabbi Tevele's crusade against the dangerous concept that "the teaching of man takes precedence over the teaching of God." Now, Rabbi Fleckeles eulogized, "we have lost a great man, a mighty hero, the talmudic authority, Rabbi Tevele of Lissa," who had taken a courageous stand against the maskilim who were plotting to "cause the Torah of the Almighty to be forgotten and to revoke His laws." Rabbi Tevele's death had left a void in the camp of the scholarly elite, which was waning in any case. The number of *yeshivot* was dwindling and the scholars, "the guardians of the walls, who spend their nights and days poring over the Torah, are growing fewer in each generation." Although there are still quite a few *tzadikim* and great talmudic scholars at the head of the camp, their power has been weakened; because they have been deprived of the authority to coerce transgressors, their hands are tied—"we have no power to blot out the evildoers who commit their offenses in public." Fleckeles's views had not changed in the slightest. In his sermons, as opprobrious as they had been in the past, he attacked the maskilim who criticize Jewish society, saw no benefit for Jews in science or philosophy, spoke out against the study of "foreign subjects" in Jewish education, and jeered at the maskilic writers: "who spend their days and nights writing pernicious letters in a lofty language, in which they omit all things fine and leave in all that is unfit."[6] His anxiety about the Frankist apostasy, underground cells of which were already planted in the Prague community at the time, undoubtedly heightened his apprehension about various types of threats, including that posed by the Haskalah.

The early maskilim, who toward the end of the century were mindful of the reverberations of the Enlightenment revolution, without necessarily taking part in it, were clearly perturbed by the stormy events that were changing Jewish life and society. One of them was the physician Judah Hurwitz, an intellectual of the early Haskalah, who in the 1760s had been instrumental in gaining entry for writers into the public arena and injecting rationalist patterns of thought into Jewish culture. In the 1790s, Hurwitz was a member of the old generation, and from his home in the Lithuanian communities of Vilna and Horodno he observed the rapid and intensive historical changes that the members of the new generations were introducing. It is no wonder, then, that in his later books the literary setting changed. He still wrote in ponderous, rhymed baroque prose and never stopped believing in the efficacy of preaching morals. But the conversations he described were no longer conducted by a harmonious group of writers and scholars, as they were in his book *Amudei bet yehudah* of the 1760s. Now they were held by fathers and sons, between whom there was a generation gap marked by tension and misunderstandings. The threat of heresy, which he inveighed against in his books, still troubled Hurwitz in the 1790s, but this concern was now joined by the fear of a split in Jewish society caused by Hasidism and the Haskalah. The polemical rhetoric he employed in denouncing heresy became all the more strident as he became convinced that their number was rising: "the rebellious scoundrel," "the despicable fool," the frivolous hedonist who defiles "his mind with the words of apostates and heretics," and the libertine who casts off "the burden of the religious laws at first, and then the commandments and good deeds he is obligated to perform by virtue of his humanity."[7]

The most plastic literary description of heresy is Hurwitz's characterization of the "subverted city," a kind of modern Sodom, full of all types of heretics. This fictional city appears in his *Megilat sedarim*, printed in Prague in 1793. It is depicted as a relatively new city, all of whose residents base their heresy on science and philosophy. Their leader is a man who adheres to a materialistic worldview and blatantly mocks the obligation of observing the commandments.[8] He does not believe that humans differ in any way from the other living creatures in nature, denies the existence of the soul, and sees no point in observing the commandments. Of course, Hurwitz does not fail to provide readers with his own reaction to the heretic city. He employs it in the story to persuade his readers that one can turn back even from such a radical heresy, just as, in the 1760s, he showed how the "savage" became a proper Jew. At the same, Hurwitz was disturbed by the growth of the camp of mystics and enthusiasts, who, in his view, were causing serious harm not only to the study of the Torah but to the observance of the commandments as well. However, he regarded the emergence of sects, which threatened to destroy all unity among Jews, as the major obstacle. "And now the bonds of love have been broken," Hurwitz lamented, "and the nation from its great holiness, from its good unity, has fallen into quarrels and disputes, jealousy and hostility, and into great desolation . . . See the community of the Jews! Who in their love were once united . . . and now in their hatred are divided, like demons and devils."[9]

Hurwitz realized that, in order to mend the rifts, it was important to clarify the areas of agreement and disagreement within the Jewish elite. For this purpose, in *Megilat sedarim* he invited the representatives of the three sects to a literary debate, at the end of which each sect acknowledged the legitimacy of the others. At first the representatives of each camp, the Kabbalists, talmudists, and maskilim, claimed an absolute monopoly on religious truth. Hurwitz felt it was urgent to ease the tension between the three, all members of the new generation. Their father, "Yedidyah" (God's friend), a Jew of the old generation, regards these trends as intensely innovativ, and views them all as a form of religious radicalization. The three characters faithfully represent historical figures in eighteenth-century European Jewry: "Ovadiah"(God's worshipper) joins a group of Kabbalists, attracted by their zeal, asceticism and piety, and becomes a disciple of Pietist and enthusiastic religiosity. "Chashaviah" (he who reflects on God) joins a circle of talmudic scholars and so excels in his yeshivah studies that he becomes a rabbi and brilliant scholar. "Hodiyah" (he who thanks God) is enthralled by "pure doctrines and sciences" and studies medicine at the university of "Athens."

After the first two sons fervently hold forth on their positions and defend their choice, Hurwitz places quite surprising words of summary in their father's mouth. Not only is he pained by their bickering, but he points out that both the Kabbalah and the Talmud originate from a divine source and that their argument is not between truth and falsehood or between faith and heresy. However, he says, one must also consider whether there is any point in the argument and what implications it has for the Jews. First Yedidyah suggests to the Hasid and the talmudic scholar a common basis in "virtues free of all abominations," which transcend any theological controversy or difference in modes of worship. Afterward, an agreement of compromise is signed between the parties, which, Hurwitz believes, can dispel the tension between them and preserve unity. Although the contract is represented as a compromise, as a "happy medium," it does not provide a balance between the two religious alternatives. However, the solution Hurwitz wants to offer his readers does finally emerge from it. The contract, a kind of legal judgment, bears signatures and a date (1791) and imposes strict limitations on the scope of mystic activity of the Kabbalistic elite, in particular among the young. It obliges the Kabbalists to relate cautiously and seriously to the path taken by the talmudic scholars, while the scholars do not undertake to make any concessions or to retract any of their positions.[10]

Although his declared aim is to suggest a compromise between two legitimate streams in Judaism, in the 1790s Hurwitz unequivocally took exception to the mystical trends, one of whose manifestations was, of course, the Hasidic movement. In Hurwitz's contract, the Kabbalists agree to remain inside their *yeshivot* and not to neglect their mainstream religious studies. Hurwitz admitted that in his generation both Jews and Christians were taking an interest in mysticism, but in his view it should be kept apart from public religious life and within the confines of select circles. Hurwitz took a dim view of the intellectual abilities of the masses and felt they ought to live a life of virtue, leaving halakhic studies and Kabbalistic piety to special individuals.

After the Kabbalistic threat was "removed" in this literary-polemic fashion, and its adverse effect as the cause of a social-religious schism was wiped out, the *choker* (the scientist and philosopher), the representative of the new intellectual elite, came onto the scene. This type, personified by the character of "Hodayah," is described as "intelligent, enlightened, and a doctor," a graduate of a European university with an education in philosophy. It turns out that Hodayah is Hurwitz's ideal type. Although in the argument between the scholar and the Kabbalist, their creator sides with the former, he does not conceal his criticism of the flaws that mar both of them. The character of the *choker*, in contrast, is highly idealized. If the savage, Ira HaYe'ari, who converted to Judaism out of free choice, is the ideal of the 1760s, then the Jew who has studied science and philosophy is the ideal of the 1790s. Hodayah is "handsome and comely, clearly a superior being." He is a graduate of a university "in the noble city of Athens," who within a short time excelled in "the useful arts and skills, in the lore of medicine" and was destined to be "a glory to his community, a splendor to his family."[11]

And yet, exposure to science and philosophy entails dangers. The clash between reason and religion is apt to lead to heresy. When Hodayah returns to his family and to the Jewish social and cultural sphere, a cloud of suspicion hangs over his head. A short time later, it turns out the suspicion of the *choker*'s heresy is unfounded, and he is actually the ideal believer, no less God-fearing, and perhaps even more so than the others, far removed from esoteric learning and religious enthusiasm.[12]

Nonetheless, it would be a mistake to regard Hurwitz as a maskil who recommends inquiry and science as desirable paths to religious knowledge and learning, or who would turn them into an educational program open to all. On the contrary, Hurwitz never stops warning against the danger of philosophical heresy. However, in his apologetic attempts to come up with persuasive rebuttals to the atheists and at the same time to curtail the legitimacy of mystic religiosity, in the 1790s Hurwitz shaped the ideal model of the intellectual elite: a man steeped in science and inquiry, who also has high moral virtues and faithfully observes the commandments.[13]

At the end of the eighteenth century, the intellectual map of European Jewry was so diverse and complex that it contained some apparent paradoxes, for example, the case of the enemy of Enlightenment Pinhas Hurwitz, the author of *Sefer haberit*. His ardor for knowledge, the many areas of his interest, his immense dedication to his work on an encyclopedic book, and his life story full of wandering between the east and west of Europe (he was born in Vilna in 1765)—were all characteristics usually associated with the maskilic writer.[14] His worldview was influenced by the Lurianic Kabbalah, and his attitude toward the Enlightenment's cultural aims was a distinctly orthodox one. In his book, Hurwitz included the best knowledge available at the time, and his surveys of new developments in science and philosophy were more impressive than any to be found then in the maskilic library. He was also an avid reader of the maskilic library and made wide use of it in writing his book. One of his sources of scientific knowledge was Baruch Lindau's *Reshit limudim*, and in Solomon Maimon's *Givat hamoreh* he found terminology and up-to-date philosophical methods. But his reading was definitely orthodox and polemical; he was not sympathetic to the contents of these books, nor did he internalize their messages.

Sefer haberit, written in Galicia and Holland and first printed in Bruenn in Moravia in 1797, was popular in the Jewish book world. It attacked "philosophical inquiry," which in Hurwitz's view was fueling the growing heresy in his generation. In the field of science, he even denied Copernicus's heliocentric cosmology, arguing that the Jewish sources, which had divine authority, contradicted science, which was based on reason and experimentation, and that they should be given preference ("Whom ought I to heed, Copernicus or he whose wisdom and science has been given to him by the Almighty in the heavens?").[15] In the field of philosophy, Hurwitz understood Kant's revolution as an affirmation of his own skeptical view that philosophy could never present absolute truths:

Beloved man, enlightened reader, man of understanding, now pay heed whether there has ever been anything that so overthrows philosophy and its teachings as this book by Kant [*Critique of Pure Reason*]. When I learned of this book and its content, I raised my hands to the Almighty and blessed Him, for the time has come to expel the ways and teachings of philosophy from the land, and they will be cast out even among the nations.[16]

Although from many standpoints *Sefer haberit* resembles Isaac Satanow's writings and advocates the study of science (although only from books written in Hebrew), Pinhas Hurwitz was extremely critical of the Haskalah project, in particular of Satanow's literary "forgeries" in *Mishlei asaf* and Saul Berlin's in *Besamim Rosh*. In *Sefer haberit*, he depicted the Haskalah project, including *Hame'asef*, as a plot to spread heresy and to destroy the status of the rabbis, who, in his view, were showing weakness:

They arrogantly publish their words, sinning themselves and leading many others to transgress, sending letters to Jewish youth in which they praise the ways of philosophy and human reason, and their intent in doing so is to capture souls and attract them to apostasy . . . and the elders of Israel, the men of Torah, are fearful, not fear of the Almighty, but for fear they will lose their high positions and earn less, and they turn their faces to the ground and do nothing to stop them.[17]

Another erstwhile early maskil, Rabbi Judah Leib Margolioth, who had moved from Poland to the Frankfurt-on-Oder community in Prussia, stood at the threshold of the nineteenth century, gripped with fear at the spread of heresy. The reader will recall that Margolioth wrote a critique on Mendelssohn's *Jerusalem*, and was attacked, in *Hame'asef*, by Aaron Wolfssohn. He was particularly concerned by the religious laxity he perceived among the young men of the scholarly elite, evidence of which he had seen in Poland as well as in Germany. As a result, he adopted an anti-maskilic position, far removed from his views in the 1790s, and warned against the noxious implications of the Enlightenment. "And there are some people, young and old, who scorn the commandments," Margolioth wrote, "our spirit drinks their poison, and young men fall in their iniquity, casting off the burden of the Torah and wearying themselves with mere vanity, spending their days in studying philosophy from the books of the nations that are not drawn from the wellsprings of Judaism."[18]

Margolioth used a three-stage model to depict the downhill path that heresy unavoidably follows, the final stage of which demonstrates the dangers of embarking upon it. At first there is the strong temptation to acquire external knowledge, in order to overcome the cultural inferiority of the Jews ("In our generation, we lack wisdom, we speak in a barbarous tongue, and the gentiles regard us as beasts"). Then the "spark of philosophy" is kindled in the heart of religious skepticism, until it provides a pretext for religious laxity ("and hence he will find it pleasing to abandon several commandments whose observance is burdensome, like the Sabbath or forbidden foods"), although that permissiveness is really motivated by their evil inclination. Philosophy is only called upon, after the fact, to justify it. In the final stage of this sweeping atrophy, Margolioth cautioned, total anarchy will reign. The sons of those permissive skeptics will cut themselves off from any ties to their Jewish brethren and will rebel not only against the Torah and the commandments, but against every moral norm. They will fall into libertinism and extreme sexual permissiveness, the destructive effects of which threaten to tear the very fabric of human civilization.[19]

From his turn-of-the-century vantage point, Margolioth viewed the danger of heresy as a phenomenon that threatened not only the Jews. The propaganda of the atheists resonated from every corner in Europe, bearing Voltaire's dreadful message. That "well-known atheist from a foreign land" is the enemy of all religions wherever they be, a viper who exudes its poison on all things:

The land was like a paradise before him, and now it is a wasteland . . . with deep contempt he took all the religions of Europe and gathered them like sheaves to the threshing floor, to flog them with thorns and briars . . . to tear them from their roots, and whosoever does not draw strength from the fortress of his religion and drinks of the evil waters, putrid with poison, the viper's tongue shall slay him.[20]

This horrifying, apocalyptic picture, of poisonous snakes and demonic philosophers who leave behind them a scorched earth, tells us more about Margolioth's view of things than it does about the historical reality. However, it also opens a window through which we can see and begin to understand the mortal fear that the new Europe aroused in the enemies of Enlightenment. Indeed, in his book *Atzei eden*, Margolioth confessed to his readers, publicly repenting his youthful sin when he had been misled into embarking on the first stages of that graded process that leads to heresy and libertinism. He too had read "the books of the gentiles," and he too had eagerly become engrossed in books of philosophy. However, he learned from his own bitter experience that their sole intent was to uproot faith from men's hearts, and the prudent man would do well to flee from them.[21]

Only when he understood heresy as libertine behavior, and not an intellectual criticism of religion, did he finally choose to flee from it, and this realization enabled him to successfully cope with the paradox of the early Haskalah in which he had become inveigled. It also enabled him to choose a dual approach: to continue to praise science and philosophy and to defend them against their attackers, as well as to adopt an orthodox position in an attempt to curb the potential temptation of philosophy—that same "long-forgotten harlot from among the Jewish nation" who spreads her net to entangle men possessed of evil inclinations. If in the past, Margolioth said, he permitted his students to study some philosophy, although only in books written by Jews, in these days one could no longer permit this. As long as the moral crisis, which is at the root of religious laxity, goes on, it was imperative to lock all the doors.

At a low point when the gates of religious rationalism were being locked, Margolioth chose to rely on a revered source of authority—Rabbi Eliahu, the Vilna Gaon. Rabbi Eliahu, a prominent figure in the rabbinical elite had been opposed to philosophy, and hence he was a source of support to Margolioth in his orthodox struggle. According to him, the Gaon of Vilna regarded man's very passion for knowledge as a negative trait, a product of the original sin. Already in the Garden of Eden, Adam had rebelled against God and expressed his desire for autonomy. Margolioth asserted that the Gaon s legacy was opposed to the Enlightenment and urged all Jews to stay as far away as possible from "inquiry": "From his words I have learned that the innocent would do well to be wary of climbing the mountain of philosophy and touching its peak, even though some of its teachings appear to be beneficial in the worship of the Almighty."[22]

Internal Rifts

As if the attacks by enemies of the Enlightenment were not enough to weaken the Haskalah movement, in the 1790s internal quarrels arose within the small circle of maskilim. The internal rift began with two fierce attacks, printed in *Hame'asef*, in which Aaron Wolfssohn accused Baruch Jeiteles of having betrayed the Haskalah and criticized the literary project of the manager of the Freischule press, Isaac Satanow.

Baruch Jeiteles's rejoinder was a particularly sharp one. In 1795 he published his *Sefer ha'orev* in Prague, in which he took a stand against the heads of the Haskalah movement and stated they could no longer be acknowledged as its legitimate heirs.[23] He was not the one who had betrayed the Haskalah; rather it was Wolfssohn, Brill and all those then leading the movement and presuming to carry on the Society for the Promotion of Goodness and Justice. Like other books of the Haskalah, *Sefer ha'orev* also had a fictional frame story, designed to hide the author's identity and the place where it was printed, as well as to lend credibility to his delegitimization of the editors of the seventh volume of *Hame'asef*. To invest his judgment with objectivity and to distance it from the scene of the events, Jeiteles placed his criticism in the mouth of an

Italian Jew from Mantua, who had come into possession of the seventh volume by chance when he was staying in Ferrara. Supposedly without knowing anything about the Haskalah, he compared that volume, in particular Wolfssohn's play *Sicha be'eretz hachayim* (Conversation in the Land of the Living), with the first five praiseworthy volumes of *Hame'asef*, and reacted angrily: "How infuriated I became upon seeing that they are opening their mouths without measure, and charging with folly the scholars of God's people in words of scorn and mockery."

That same Jew received confirmation of the fact that the Haskalah was declining into frivolity and radical criticism from one "Signore Herschel." The writer met this gentleman, who had been born near Berlin and was familiar with all the persons involved in the Haskalah, at dinner in the home of a wealthy Jew in Trieste. Herschel told him about the great deception that Wolfssohn and Brill were perpetrating:

The first editors of *Hame'asef* have gone on their way . . . and some young men have founded a society, which they have called The Society for the Promotion of Goodness and Justice, for the purpose of dishonest gain. Since *Hame'asef* was a pleasing journal in these parts, those young men called their journal *Hame'asef* on the name of the original *Hame'asef*, but they are not the ones who published the first editions.[24]

Now that the deception was exposed, Baruch Jeiteles took on the role of the *orev* (the ambusher) who would not permit them to persist in their ways. If they continued to distort the Haskalah, he would be the first to rise up from his lair and strike at them, but if they returned to the original maskilic public arena, he would be the first to support and bless them. With the sense of being a betrayed maskil, Jeiteles proclaimed his goal: "I will reveal the shame of these *me'asfim*, and they will no longer act so presumptuously and will no longer call it *Hame'asef* but rather its name in Israel will be *ha'asafsuf* [riffraff]."[25]

This internal rift had implications that went far beyond the quarrel between the Prague circle of relatively moderate maskilim and the radical Wolfssohn and Brill in Breslau. Added to the sense that the *Hame'asef* was controlled by imposters were the fears of maskilim like Jeiteles that the concept of Enlightenment was being perverted, and was serving as a label to justify heresy and libertine behavior. These fears were aired when Baruch Jeiteles summed up the changes in Jewish culture and society that had occurred by the end of the eighteenth century. Writing under the disturbing impression left by the exposure of the Frankist underground sect in Prague, in the very midst of "the generation of intellect and reason," Jeiteles's words reflected his feelings of crisis and confusion:

In our own time, they no longer look, neither upon the Talmud, the Bible, the wisdom literature, nor the literature of *musar*, and they lack all faith. And this is the cause of all the evils among the young men nowadays, for the foundations of faith have been weakened by them, they turn to every driven leaf, chasing after passion and sexual desire . . . for encrustations have spread upon the word *Aufklärung,* and every youth nowadays thinks he understands it without thoroughly knowing its true meaning . . . For this word teaches us to understand the difference between truth and falsehood, good and evil, knowledge and ignorance, and happy is he who chooses it, but they would overturn the meaning, and would consider that they have done much if they take a private tutor for their children . . . the teacher generally (but not all of them) is ignorant, lacking both in knowledge of the Torah and in good manners.[26]

Naumann Simonsohn, the *Inspektor* of the Freischule in Berlin, was plagued by similar worries. As we have seen, he was about to leave Berlin and the Haskalah to settle in the Polish community of Lissa. In 1796, he decided to speak out openly against the trends of secularization of Berlin Jewry and Aaron Wolfssohn's policy for the Haskalah. First he asked Isaac Daniel Itzig to intervene, and it was only at Itzig's personal instruction that Simonsohn's critical book *Ein mishpat* was printed on the Freischule press.[27] As Jeiteles did in his *Sefer ha'orev,* Simonsohn also claimed that the leaders of the Haskalah in the 1790s were too extreme in their behavior, taking the name of Mendelssohn and the other "true" maskilim in vain, so that it was no wonder that the Haskalah was facing a crisis. Immediately after Mendelssohn's death, which he compared to the destruction of the Temple, new *me'asfim* took control of his legacy and were taking the Haskalah down a ruinous path. The man at their head— "evil and profane" Aaron Wolfssohn—had already demonstrated his digression from Mendelssohn's path in his play *Sicha be'eretz hachayim. Ein mishpat* was, then, one more lament over the decline of the Haskalah:

From the time of Moses' death, many have arisen, like locusts and flies, like jesters they stand philosophizing in the camp and call out in the city: this is the Torah that Moses has given us, and the people see that Moses is delayed in coming and they quickly stray from the path and gather together and come unto Aaron, that Aaron [Wolfssohn] who has taken the gold from them and out of that came this calf, sin and abomination in Judah and Israel, and a new king reigns over them . . . and they are called by the name of *me'asfim* . . . and they presumed to surpass the heads and elders of our people, shattering the wind with the blowing of horns, shouting their vain nonsense . . . to overthrow the sacred wall that our sages of blessed memory have raised around the Ark of the Covenant and the Torah, and the little foxes have broken down the wall of our forefathers, and many of our brethren have gone forth like the beasts of the forest without bridle or rein and speak of the Lord and His Messiah.[28]

Based on Simonsohn's description, this was no less than a coup d'etat, as a result of which radicals took over the leadership, to the great dismay of Mendelssohn's disciples. On the frontispiece of *Ein mishpat,* Simonsohn recorded some pessimistic rhymes about the death of *Hame'asef.* Since it is in such a sorry state and in such poor hands, it is no wonder that it no longer is a worthy address for the maskilim.[29]

Isaac Satanow, the manager of the Freischule press, understood that if he were to publish the manuscript of *Ein mishpat* that Simonsohn had brought him, he would become embroiled in a conflict with the editors of *Hame'asef*. At first he refused, but was forced to print it when Daniel Itzig explicitly instructed him to do so. Wolfssohn and Brill, suspecting that Satanow was the author of *Ein misphat,* made him the target of their attacks. At least that is how Shlomo Schöneman, Satanow's son, explained the background to Wolfssohn's slander of his father on the pages of *Hame'asef*. Schöneman, unable to brook the insult, wrote a rejoinder to the criticism of his father's literary project, in a pamphlet entitled *Minhat bikurim*, which was also printed by the Freischule press.[30] Attacking the effrontery of a man who, lacking knowledge of the religious sources, presumed to criticize Satanow's books, he jeered at Wolfssohn's stupidity and dismissed all of his arguments. He also added a withering critique of Wolfssohn's textbook *Avtalyon* and pointed out all the errors that appeared in *Hame'asef* under his editorship.

Schöneman, like Simonsohn and Jeiteles, asserted that the present editors of *Hame'asef* were not the authentic representatives of the Haskalah, nor were they carrying on the work of the Society for the Promotion of Goodness and Justice, although they were boldly presuming to do so. He stated that "The members of the group are not the same people who were in it before, and this is surely close to the truth, for we see that many worthier than they have left the group, and now only the younger ones have remained . . . and they are wanting in all matters of wisdom and understanding."[31] From his point of view, the Haskalah movement was already in an advanced stage of disintegration. It is not surprising, then, that Schöneman was so sensitive to the slightest shift or fluctuation in the intellectual elite, and reacted so sharply, as we have seen, to Friedländer's letter to Teller. In his view, the ongoing extremism of the intellectuals and their betrayal of the Haskalah were likely to hand the orthodox a victory and to quash the maskilic revolution.

In the last years of *Hame'asef*'s existence its editors were under siege. The orthodox denounced them as spreaders of heresy who were deriding talmudic scholars, and anxious maskilim were challenging their status as leaders of the movement. They had no choice but to conduct a polemical dialogue with their critics in the last two issues of the expiring journal. They jeered at their parochialism, hurled counterattacks at them and defended their own legitimacy. Wolfssohn and Brill totally dismissed *Ein mishpat*, which they attributed to Isaac Satanow, and scoffed at its whining tone: "Here is the baby crying bitter tears over *Hame'asef* and its author, and his voice of that of a child for he calls loudly on the Almighty to remove the shameful rule of *Hame'asef* from the land."[32] They depicted Baruch Jeiteles, the author of *Ha'orev*, as their worst enemy, because he had declared all-out war on them: "He has proclaimed his intent to wipe *Hame'asef* off the face of the earth and to expunge its memory, not to leave us a name or a remnant in the land. This man of war has drawn his sword from its sheath and with it will judge to the ends of the earth and not sheathe it again until *Hame'asef* falls at his feet."[33]

The next issue of *Hame'asef* was supposed to contain a detailed polemical article against "the ambusher," but it never came out. In the meantime, Wolfssohn had exposed Jeiteles's identity as the author of *Sefer ha'orev*, had contemptuously censured him for trying to conceal it, and written that he was obviously deranged, and hence deserved compassion, not anger.[34] Wolfssohn's rebuttal to *Minhat bikurim* was very brief compared to the detailed pamphlet in which Schöneman had defended his father's life work. Wolfssohn was certain that Satanow, taking advantage of his son's naivete, had written the pamphlet himself. Schöneman was known as a well-educated physician, but not as a man skilled in Hebrew writing. In an attempt to drive a wedge between father and son, Wolfssohn tried to prove to Schöneman that his father had also concealed from him the truth about his other books.[35]

However, between the lines of the sarcastic, scoffing rhetoric employed by Wolfssohn to dismiss the criticism of *Hame'asef*'s extremism, there is a real sense of distress. Among his arguments, Wolfssohn asks: Who knows the motive behind Satanow's claim that we are not faithfully carrying on the work of the Society for the Promotion of Goodness and Justice? Perhaps he was influenced by Jeiteles? Perhaps he lied, as is his wont? Perhaps he so hated Wolfssohn for daring to criticize his *Mishlei asaf* that he was prepared to toady to the rabbis "to whom he was always opposed and always jeered at"? Or perhaps he was representing several of the Berlin maskilim, who were displeased with the Breslau maskilim? In any case, Wolfssohn hastened to declare that to the best of his knowledge the editors of *Hame'asef* were faithfully continuing to further the aims of the Haskalah movement. Several of the writers for *Hame'asef* under his editorship were founders of the Society (Euchel, for example), and in general, "the Society . . . is as strong as it was then in speech and action, where has he learned that it is falling apart, that can only be because a lying spirit has seduced him."[36] However, the reality proved Wolfssohn wrong. At the end of 1797, shortly after he published this declaration of his faith in the movement's continuity, *Hame'asef* was closed down, the Society for the Promotion of Goodness and Justice was dissolved, and the internal polemic was broken off.

Rabbi Josephche and Jettchen in the Brothel

We have seen that at the end of the eighteenth century, the veteran maskilim were in dire straits. Isaac Satanow, attacked from within and without, pondered whether he ought to continue his literary project and whether he still had any readership:

> To whom shall I speak, to tell how I have seen two houses of Israel. One is pious and scoffs at science, and the other scoffs at piety and studies the sciences . . . but where are those in whom both piety and science reside together. They are superior beings, but are few in number. Hence, it is a time to keep silent, and it is a pity that no one demands or seeks these printed books.[37]

Naphtali Herz Wessely's voice was no longer heard in public, and in the Berlin of the 1790s he was lonely, forgotten, and despairing. As the rift between modernists and orthodox traditionalists widened, it was harder for him to find his place: "The traditional ones suspect me being of being an innovator and the modern ones suspect me of being traditional."[38] Was it only the internal squabbles that were impeding the Haskalah movement? Were the attacks of the orthodox preventing it from developing further? Was it the betrayal of the intelligentsia, as Schönemann claimed in his reaction to Friedländer, that was depriving it of its potential leaders? Or perhaps the French Revolution had influenced the maskilim into becoming more extreme and shedding their responsibility toward the whole of Jewish society?[39]

Isaac Euchel and Aaron Wolfssohn, the leaders of the Jewish Enlightenment revolution in the 1780s and 1790s, apparently saw things differently. Closely and sensitively observing events in Jewish society toward the end of the century, they blamed the movement's failure on the character of the young generation as well as on their social and family situation. Of course, these two men did not concur with the criticism that the moderate maskilim leveled at the Haskalah's radicalism, but they did find themselves fighting on two fronts: against the influence of the rabbinical elite and the orthodox, who were indifferent to the messages of Enlightenment and against the misuse of the Enlightenment as a cover for frivolous libertine behavior.

In the mid-1790s Euchel and Wolfssohn were the authors of plays that were exceptional in the Haskalah culture. The purpose of the Haskalah library, in Hebrew and German, was to disseminate knowledge and to criticize the rabbinical culture and its lifestyle. These two social satires, however, were directed at the bourgeois Jewish families in German cities, to compel them to see their true selves through the plays' outlandish characters and improbable plots. They were written in the vernacular (in the plays the traditional Jews spoke Yiddish and the modern Jews, German), rather than in the elitist language of the Haskalah culture (Hebrew and High German). The plot underscored the tensions between the generations and the crises that were threatening the Jewish family, torn between the "orthodox" and the "modernists," between the "sinners of Israel" and the "philosophers." The plays presented the questions of modernization in all their urgency and depicted the formula of Haskalah as the only one offering redemption.

Euchel's play, *Reb Henoch oder was tut me damit*, was circulated in manuscript from 1793. Wolfssohn's play, *Leichtsinn und Frömmelei: Ein Familien Gemälde in drei Aufzügen*, was printed in 1796, and a Hebrew version was published at the same time. These two plays furnish invaluable historical evidence of the social processes German Jewry was undergoing at the end of the century. They both dramatically describe the crisis of the bourgeois Jewish family: on the one hand, a lack of communication between the generations and sexual and religious permissiveness, and on the other, confusion about the best education to provide to their children, and growing orthodox rigidity in relation to anything new, ranging from wearing modern hats to studying Hebrew grammar.[40] The plays also reflect the *Kulturkampf* in the street and the home, although the authors undoubtedly greatly intensified the sense of confusion and bewilderment in that historical hour, in which the maskilim feared that their gloomy predictions about the results of Jewry's encounter with modernity were coming true.

Euchel's and Wolfssohn's work as private tutors in the homes of the wealthy bourgeoisie provided them with a view from both within and without. They had an intimate knowledge of the family dynamics and were adept at depicting the dilemma facing the father, a rich merchant and communal leader. On one hand, he showed great respect to the rabbinical elite and attempted to educate his children to continue the traditional patterns of life. On the other, he brought enlightened tutors into his home, to give his sons and daughters the general education they needed. The plays also describe the young women, who so yearn to enjoy all the opportunities the modern city has to offer. They long to attend the theater and frequent the dance halls, they dream of romantic love affairs and are repelled by the religious norms, and often by their Jewish husbands as well. They also describe the younger members of the family: they no longer observe the practical commandments, have been exposed to Christian society and culture, engage in sexual relations with the family's Christian servants, and have sometimes even converted—practices that are shocking to the traditional heads of the household.[41] These two maskilim had depended on their employment as tutors for their livelihood, and as intellectuals they also knew how to look it with a critical eye, as outside observers. The two plays are very similar in the characters and situations they describe and in the messages they convey.

In Euchel's play, which takes place "at the end of the enlightened century," the outer layers covering Reb Henoch's family are gradually peeled away. He is a wealthy merchant, father to two sons and two daughters, and a communal leader. On one catastrophic Sabbath, his children's moral corruption is exposed, along with their attempts to abandon the Jewish way of life. By depicting Reb Henoch's rigid orthodox positions and his blindness to what is happening around him, Euchel is able to point out the weaknesses of the orthodox, reducing them to absurdity, and he also enables someone observing the scene from a distance of over two hundred years to experience the intensity of Reb Henoch's fears and anguish. His deep mistrust of philosophers, enlightened physicians, students, and innovators borders on obsession. Even the slightest change in accepted dress encounters an extreme reaction and awakens a suspicion of heresy. Reb Henoch, for example, wishes to sign a communal regulation threatening punishment to anyone coming to the synagogue on the Sabbath wearing boots or wrapped in a black silk shawl, because "one can conclude from this that they are preparing to become *chokrim* and philosophers, who favor lax morals and are forgetting Israel and Judaism."[42]

The *Kulturkampf* takes the form of a fierce internal controversy about the reform that enlightened Jews want the Prussian government to introduce—to abolish the community's collective responsibility for payment of monies owed by thieves and tax delinquents and to make each individual Jew subject to the state institutions. The orthodox, who, in Euchel's play, hold most of the ruling positions in the community, do all they can to prevent this. The enlightened Jews, on the other hand, regard the reform as an opportunity to induce the government to bring about an overall transformation of Jewish life, and to free themselves of their dependence on the community. Secularization even creeps into Reb Henoch's home. His daughter Hedwig speaks about him behind his back with disgust: "That orthodox man! How repugnant he is to me!"[43] His son Samuel, who at first is portrayed as a righteous young man, a future scholar who will bring honor to the family, turns out to have made their gentile maid pregnant. The married daughter, Elizabeth, is unfaithful to her husband with a Prussian army officer and on the Sabbath goes to parties, while the son Hartwig is even more dissolute than the others and threatens to drag the entire family into disgrace.[44]

The situations depicted in Wolfssohn's *Leichtsinn und Frömmelei* are very similar to those in Euchel's satire. But criticism of the talmudic scholars reaches a new height in the grotesque character of the religious hypocrite Rabbi Josephche. He pretends to be a rabbi and a scholar well versed in the Talmud, a pious Jew who is strongly opposed to the maskilim who authentically represents the values and norms of the rabbinical elite. The naive father of the fictional family, who greatly admires talmudic scholars, brings him into his home and even promises him the hand of his daughter Jettchen in marriage, without realizing how deeply corrupt the rabbi is. Wolfssohn portrays Rabbi Josephche as a lecher who invests most of his energy in finding an outlet for his sexual drives. This description has its parallel in the radical and pornographic underground literature of the French Enlightenment culture, in which a hypocritical priest seduces young innocent girls to have sex with him for religious purposes.[45] Indeed, Rabbi Josephche does have sex with the maid Sheindel, and when he is caught in the act by the head of the household, he delivers a sanctimonious speech of repentance about his struggle against his evil instincts ("But it is as our Sages have said, every man greater than his fellows has a greater appetite than they").

Rabbi Josephche courts Jettchen with her naive father's consent and boasts to her about his sexual prowess: "So long as I have strength in my loins and power in the muscles of my belly, my tail [male organ] is as rigid as a cedar, the sinews of my flanks are tightly knit, like a man of valor, I shall come to you to lie with you." Scoffing at him, she rejects his advances, and he becomes violent and smashes her musical instrument. Only toward the end of the play, is his true face revealed, when the whore Lemgin testifies that he is a regular client of hers ("that Jew, a hairy man, with a leather belt about his loins, clad in a robe, whose member is like those of donkeys and whose seed came in floods like that of stallions"). She says that when he wanted to satisfy his desires but lacked the money to cover his heavy debts, he would leave his phylacteries with her as security.[46]

In this play too, the daughter, Jettchen, deceives her father and behaves frivolously, neglecting all her duties. She is not a consumer of the Haskalah library but avidly reads shallow romances in German that she borrows from the local library, takes pleasure in music and the theater, and enters into secret romantic liaisons with Christian men. Her father, who knows about her lax behavior, a digression from the norms of conduct he regards as suitable for a young Jewish woman, lashes out furiously at his wife, who tries to defend Jettchen:

Does she say the blessing on the food, does she pray, does she read from *Tse'enah u-re'enah* like the good daughters of Zion? All day long we hear only voices singing, the sound of violins and the trilling of harps . . . and when the Sabbath comes its sanctity is forgotten and nothing holy is on her mind or in her heart, Heaven forbid, and that will be counted as her wickedness, and she goes down into the garden to seek lovers.[47]

Her father tries to force her to marry Josephche, but she loathes him and has no choice but to turn to the Prussian aristocrat who lusts after her and ask for his protection. To her great sorrow, she soon finds herself penniless and betrayed, locked in Lemgin's brothel, waiting in despair for her first customer.[48]

What was it, in Euchel and Wolfssohn's view, that led to that "pseudo-Haskalah"? We need to listen carefully to Hartwig's long confession, in which he recounts his life story to an enlightened doctor. There were three stages in his life: a traditional, rigid education in the home of his "obscurantist" parents, a brief encounter with the Enlightenment through study and book reading—cut short by the vigorous objection of his parents—and an irreversible decline into a corrupt, hedonist lifestyle, which ended in much suffering for the man himself and all those around him. The interruption of his cultural conversion to enlightenment was, in Euchel's eyes, the root of all evil, and had led directly to his deterioration. It was the traditional Polish education that had paved the way to a dissolute life:

Today I am twenty-two. Until the age of sixteen, I studied, as is the custom . . . A Polish rabbi tried to teach me things which God in heaven knows that he himself knew nothing about. I was not so stupid that I wasn't able to realize that this meant merely a waste of time. Hence only rarely did I listen to his babbling in Yiddish. He succeeded in gaining my attention only with coarse words, curses and beatings . . . At the end of this chapter in my life I hardly knew how to read a bit of German and understood even less.

At this stage, he had an opportunity to begin a process of cultural conversion to enlightenment by reading books that were not to be found in the religious library:

My older sister . . . to her great misfortune, was forced . . . to marry a man whose lifestyle and way of thought were totally antithetical to hers. Consequently, she began a downhill path that led to the lowest point, which she has now reached . . . she loved me especially, brought me close to her, taught me to read and write. She taught me German and French and saw to it that I had good books to read. In a short time, I learned so much that I probably could have developed into a decent man.

But his parents' orthodox opposition blocked this process in its infancy. The young man's frustration and distress grew, various ways of earning a decent living by learning a profession were out of the question, and he began a downhill slide:

Her husband, that scoundrel, informed on me to my father . . . They said I was becoming an atheist and an apostate . . . not only did they take all the books away from me, but they made sure I had no possibility of acquiring others. Time went by. More than half a year. And during that time I never managed to spend more than half an hour by myself. They tried to keep me busy with chores at home and at the business, and you can imagine that I did what they told me to without any desire . . . I wasn't capable of continuing with that kind of lifestyle. I asked my father to let me learn a trade. You should have heard how he reacted to that request. "What do you want to do?" my father asked. I would have liked to learn the building trade. "A builder? And what about the risks? And what will you do on the Sabbath? You'll desecrate the Sabbath, won't you?" I suggested that I might learn sculpting. My father began to yell: "To sculpt idols? Nothing will come of you. If you had only wanted, you could have been a decent family man by now." What does one do? In the meantime, time passes by and I still sit here idle. In my sister's home, I met some Christians and began to go about in their company. My parents did not object, because they thought in this way I might acquire some customers for the business. These Christian friends drew me into their style of life and their pranks. They took me to taverns and coffee houses where we played cards. There I met several young Jews from good families and they joined me. We became friends and they began to teach me the practical philosophy of life. Before too long, I became as enlightened in this doctrine as they were. It was from this period of time that my downfall began taking on momentum. We took frivolity for enlightenment and licentiousness for freedom. I forgot all my family inhibitions. I jeered at my parents and at my people . . . My Enlightenment took a wrong direction and I have the profound feeling that I am totally corrupt in my morals.[49]

Wolfssohn's and Euchel's plays brought the crisis to the fore and warned against its implications, but in no sense did they convey a message of despair. In all that confusion and disarray, they emphasized the figure of the maskil as the only one capable of leading those who have lost their way to the right path. In Euchel's case, he is the enlightened physician, who successfully mediates between the furious Rabbi Henoch who denies his son, and Hartwig who discovers he has sunk into pseudo-enlightenment. In Wolfssohn's play, it was Jettchen's uncle, the private tutor Marcus, who throws a life preserver to the girl and her family. He is the only one who has perceived Josephche's true nature, that he is nothing but a dangerous scoundrel and hypocrite, and dares to take a stand against him, despite the mask of rabbinical authority with which he has so skillfully hidden his face; he is the only one who warns Jettchen's parents that the neglect of her education will lead to a bad end, and supports her opposition to the match. Throughout the entire play, the enlightened Marcus's voice is the voice of reason. Deeply concerned, he correctly reads the cultural and social processes taking place in the bourgeois family. Although he is attacked as a "sinner against Israel" for having identified with the innovators and because of his appearance (he grows a lock of hair over his forehead and wears a bowler hat), he comes to Jettchen's aid, finally saves her from her shameful fate in the brothel, provides her with an opportunity to rehabilitate her life, and is revealed as a savior of Israel. In the brothel, toward the end of the play, Marcus, in an impassioned monologue, explains reality from a maskilic point of view, and like an ancient prophet rebukes those who are responsible for Jettchen's fall into "the rogues' lair":

Here is your blind faith. And here is your fruit. For like a robber you lie in wait and they are but bitter clusters . . . The flesh of your sons will not satisfy you. Your jealousy is as cruel as the grave, even though you bring your sacrifices and burnt offerings year after year. You have prepared a slaughterer for your sons, because of their fathers' sins their flesh will rot . . . but I cannot cleanse her [Jettchen] of her sin of gullibility, she was wrong to follow them and she despised reproof, hence her bad end. Did she not betray, this faithless woman? Folly is held in high esteem and many girls in these times follow in the paths of vanity; you have outdone them all. And after these true things, I have seen that her parents have found much wrongdoing in her and have grievously blamed her. Why do you not discipline your children, why do you not remove the folly from their hearts, and instruct them properly. Forego caring to clothe their naked bodies and turn your attention to clothing their naked souls. Teach them well, instruct them in the virtues and inscribe them upon their hearts. Accustom them to come among persons who love God and man, and then you will no longer have to bear the disgrace of your children and their shame will not be upon you.[50]

At the end of the century, the leaders of the Enlightenment revolution still believed they possessed the solution to the many-sided crisis of "the blind faith," religious hypocrisy, and the libertinism of the youth. Only they exposed the flaws of the rabbinical elite and demanded they be removed from their positions of leadership and education, and only they were capable of preparing the young generation for an easier encounter with the challenges of modernity and proposing an honorable path that did not call for debauchery or moral turpitude. Of course, the plays did not reflect the reality. Their extreme and flagrant portrayal of Jewish life was intended as a warning against the disastrous results of continuing to accept the leadership of the rabbinical elite, on the one hand, and of the sweeping secularization of the young generation, on the other. Unable to come to terms with the pervasive excesses he saw, the deeply concerned maskil did not know with whom to side. "Reb Josephche" was the traditional enemy of the Haskalah, while the maskilim regarded "Jettchen" as a perversion of the Haskalah. Both Wolfssohn and Euchel saw her as representing the pseudo-Enlightenment, which was an obstacle in the way of the true Enlightenment. Libertine behavior, the maskilim contended, is not enlightenment, but a lamentable and unforeseen dialectic result of rigid orthodox obstinacy.

These two maskilic playwrights did not spare the traditional society their biting criticism. They warned against the implications of the breakdown of the family framework and the total abandonment of tradition. They derided those people who fancied themselves maskilim but in actual fact were a long way from the intellectuals of the maskilic republic. Their imagined enlightenment, Euchel cynically comments, boils down to nothing but drinking wine in taverns, sitting in coffee houses, befriending Christians, engaging in loose behavior and "practical philosophy, which means hedonism."[51]

The existence of this "pseudo-enlightenment" was also confirmed by people outside of the Haskalah. For example, Professor Köhler, an expert on Semitic languages from the University of Königsberg, who was very familiar with the local circle of maskilim, warned against this trend. In an article entitled "On the Enlightenment of the Jewish Nation," he commended the progress of Jewish acculturation, their close ties with Christian families, their fashionable dress and refined cultural taste. However, he inveighed against slackening of religious commitment, loss of faith, and loosening of ties to the ancient tradition. This, the writer stressed, is not worthy of being called Enlightenment:

The Jewish nation should aspire to Enlightenment of the type . . . that Moses Mendelssohn delineated. I am referring to true Enlightenment that must be absolutely differentiated from pseudo-Enlightenment. It will be a pseudo Enlightenment of the Jewish nation if it rejects the Mosaic laws and adopts the laws of freedom in their stead. In other words, it will amount to anarchy if the ancient religion is trampled upon and naturalism or atheism are preferred instead.[52]

The maskilim laid the blame not only on the frivolity of the young generation and the temptations they were succumbing to. In particular, they blamed the generation of the parents, who did not know how to properly educate their children according to the "true Haskalah," in an age of great change and exposure to "low" European culture. They believed that the grave crisis, with all of its extreme manifestations, was a result of the sharp transition from rigid traditional norms to the total abandonment of all restraint, attended by the dissolution of family ties and the disavowal of religion and morality. The maskilim saw themselves as the bearers of moderate, controlled modernization, which combined Jewish culture and values with universal knowledge and humanism and legitimized cultural and social regeneration. Hence, they held that the movement's failure was the fault of the guardians of tradition, whose carelessness, poor education and misreading of the future were responsible for the spread of the "pseudo-Haskalah."

The Jewish enlightenment revolution did not restrict itself only to the public struggle that the maskilic republic was waging against the authority and status of the rabbinical elite. It also strove to gain the right to shape the Jewish family. Alongside their criticism, the maskilim wanted to protect it in that crucial hour at the end of the century, when the tension between the heavy hand of tradition and the temptations of the "new world" was at its height threatening to smash the foundations of Jewish life, at least in the urban communities of German, the major arena of the maskilim's activity.

Afterword: Haskalah and Secularization

To what extent did the eighteenth-century Enlightenment change the face of Europe? From a balanced historical perspective, which no longer holds that the French political revolution stemmed from philosophical ideas or which underestimates the value of the Enlightenment culture, one can state that the Enlightenment was unquestionably a revolution, even a radical one. It rejected the world of knowledge, the concepts and *Weltanschauung* that had prevailed until then under the authority of the Church's doctrine and instruction, and suggested a new system of values, through which men and society would set new goals. With unflinching criticism, the enlightened investigated and reexamined the nature of man and human society. Everything perceived as a superfluous vestige of the past, as immoral and inhumane, as superstition and prejudice, became an obstacle to progress and an affront to reason. While only a small number of the enlightened were atheists or deists, from an overall perspective the Enlightenment contributed, more than any other factor, to the secularization of European thought. The Christian religion did not disappear, of course, but it was no longer the dominant shaper of culture, education, literature, the vision of the human future, of the imagination or of thought.

The Enlightenment in Europe offered an alternative to the religious elite, which until then had held a monopoly on the dissemination of knowledge, the education of the young, the guidance of the public, and all branches of culture. This alternative was in the form of men of letters, who became more and more independent in their opinions and actions. The new media of communication, in particular the press, altered the world of literature and knowledge. They appealed to a growing readership and disseminated new, often subversive ideas. The radical, most striking move in the Enlightenment's secular revolution was the emergence of a new intellectual elite at the expense of the traditional elite of the spokesmen of religion, and its evolution into a group that strongly influenced society, politics and culture. In this sense, all of modern Western culture is the daughter of the Enlightenment.[1]

Postmodern criticism of the Enlightenment justifiably points to the failings and shortcomings of the enlightened. Their range of vision of human society hardly included, for example, questions such as ethnic rights, status of the common people, exclusion of women, and acknowledgment of multiculturalism. But it seems that neither the enemies of the Enlightenment, nor the counter-enlightened or the postmodern critics have shaken the dominance of the basic values of the Enlightenment. These values still serve as cornerstones in government and legislation as well as in the liberal and humanistic cultural discourse.[2]

The Haskalah as a Revolutionary Event

Were the Jews also participants in this immensely significant historical process in the eighteenth century? This book argues that the Haskalah was indeed an unprecedented, revolutionary historical event in Jewish history. This is evinced by a reconstruction of the course of the Jewish Enlightenment, from the early Haskalah among the first Jewish students in German universities at the beginning of the century, and to the collapse of its well-developed organizational framework at its demise. The Haskalah was one instance of the all-European Enlightenment. The maskilim were familiar with many of the ideas and slogans of the Enlightenment, but even if one occasionally finds evidence of the influence of the French Enlightenment (particularly Voltaire), they were really much closer to the German Enlightenment. They were familiar with its literature and periodicals, and some of them even actively participated in them.

The interest that European enlightened public opinion showed in the Haskalah is of particular importance. Much of this interest was due to Mendelssohn's fame, his direct ties to the German Enlightenment and his acceptance into several of its circles. Many of the values of the Enlightenment and its patterns of organization and activity were adopted by the maskilic societies. The struggle they waged against the punitive authority of the rabbinical leadership, against excommunication and in favor of the adoption of religious tolerance in Jewish society was one campaign in the overall struggle for the recognition of human rights and freedom of conscience in eighteenth-century Europe. However, the maskilim had interests of their own to promote and a specific agenda, which stemmed from the years-long neglect of everything that had been pushed to the sidelines in the pre-modern traditional culture, in particular science and philosophy, the external *chokhmot*. The maskilim were active in a Jewish framework, separate from all other enlightened. One of their aims was to expand the boundaries of Hebrew writing, to create an all-embracing cultural renaissance, and they hurled their criticism, first and foremost, at the rabbis of their generation.

In this book, in contrast to other descriptions of the Haskalah, an attempt has been made to depict it in its full scope, to trace, step by step, along the axis of time, the various stages of its development, to include many minor characters who until now have been relegated to the sidelines or had remained anonymous. A glimpse into the emotional and experiential world of the cast of characters reveals a rich, dramatic picture, arrived at through an analysis of the maskilim's rhetoric, so important in their appeal to their readers. Only through such an analysis can one, in my view, probe the full depth of their world.

Young Jews well-versed in talmudic studies exerted much effort to acquire some knowledge of European culture or of Jewish philosophy, which evoked scant interest at the time. These efforts were attended by inner torment and an irrepressible quasi-erotic passion for new and forbidden knowledge, and were often perceived as an blatant crossing of boundaries and personal cultural conversion, which had a signifying and defining meaning in Jewish society. It is no wonder that some early maskilim tasted the "honey" of science and philosophy, and after much soul-searching about benefit versus harm, recoiled from it. New documents and an analysis of the reactions of the rabbinical elite to the challenges of the Haskalah, starting from the early Haskalah but more particularly from the *Divrei shalom ve'emet* affair, indicate that the orthodox fear of the "new" was an inseparable part of the story of the Jewish Enlightenment. An examination of several of the episodes of the Haskalah from various vantage points—the maskilic, orthodox and external—has enabled me to reevaluate the great public impact they had at the time.

From the first clash between the Haskalah intellectual elite and the rabbinical elite it was clear that a culture war was flaring up between them. The anxiety of the orthodox and their readiness to fight an uncompromising battle, already apparent in their initial reactions to any threats to the status of the elite and the religion, also characterize orthodox society and the rabbinical leadership in the modern era.

This book has focused on the maskilim themselves and their opponents, their activity in the public arena and on the various affairs in which they were involved, not only on an analysis of the diverse texts they left behind. When all is said and done, the essence of the Haskalah revolution did not lie only in ideas or in the contents of their books, but also in the appearance of the modern, secular, independent Jewish literati in Jewish society: in their criticism of the flaws in the lifestyle and culture of the Jews, in their declared aim of leading the Jews toward modernization, and in their attempts to gain a place for themselves in the leadership. On more than one occasion, the maskilim deliberately antagonized the heads of the rabbinical elite by taking an especially revolutionary and subversive action. For example, in 1789, the managers of the Freischule press sent Saul Berlin's book, which challenged the authority and scholarly prestige of the rabbi of Altona-Hamburg, to the rabbis of the generation, demanding that they publicly respond to the maskilic criticism. It is symbolic that this provocative and rebellious step was taken the very same year that the French Revolution broke out. For this reason, it was also so important to define the role played by Mendelssohn, the most famous Jew in the eighteenth century, in the full historical story of the Haskalah. By greatly expanding the scope of the story, I was able to examine Mendelssohn's role, more as a revered figure whom the maskilim took as their model than as a revolutionary leader, as the man who founded the Haskalah movement or shaped its path.

Indeed, the Haskalah revolution was one event within the totality of stormy events in the eighteenth century that the Jews were caught up in. Here and there, general processes are mentioned in the book, to avoid losing the overall context and the synchronous view of the changes that occurred. To arrive at a sober evaluation of the Haskalah movement, it was particularly important to reconstruct the scope of the maskilic republic and its geographical dispersion. We need to bear in mind that the Haskalah as an elitist historical phenomenon was relatively limited in the number of people who took an active part in it, in contrast to far broader, more popular events, especially the emergence of the Hasidic movement in the last quarter of the century. Only a small portion of European Jewry, mainly from Germany, were aware at first of the evolution of the new type of maskil, and the real influence of the maskilic revolution on Jewish life in the eighteenth century was still rather slight. Nonetheless, in several urban Jewish communities in Europe one could already clearly identify the enlightened Jewish intellectual. Several members of the literary republic of the German Enlightenment were conscious of this development and reported on it. They sensed the change that was taking place in the landscape of Jewish society from the moment they first saw intellectuals, Western in their dress and appearance, some of whom even took part in the general literary forums and clubs and published writings in Hebrew and German.

The Haskalah revolution took place in the scholarly elite that had close ties to the wealthy elite, which recognized the importance of exposure to European culture. The revolution was given expression in the world of the book and journals, schools and groups of intellectuals. It affected norms, frameworks, texts, and methods of influencing the public, all of which had until then been under the absolute control of the religious scholars in Jewish society. The maskilim did not confine their activities to the closed circles of writers, hungering for knowledge and thirsting for books. Rather, they attempted to make their voices heard by as broad a public as possible. The ideology of the Haskalah was to introduce sweeping change in all spheres of Jewish life: by imparting the new knowledge in properly run schools, by extricating the Jews from their cultural backwardness, by dictating the content of the public discourse, by instilling the principles of liberal thought, by rejuvenating the Jewish book-shelf, and shaping the "new Jew."

The astute historian Jacob Katz has already noted that the emergence of the new type of the maskil in the last quarter of the eighteenth century marked a decisive turning point in modern Jewish history. However, he regarded this historical process as a sign of the collapse of the systems of the "traditional society"—a structural crisis that entailed a loss of the power and authority of leadership in exchange for the social and psychological integration of Jews into non-Jewish circles and their "exit from the ghetto." It is not difficult to interpret his "tradition and crisis" model in light of the fundamental experience of the Jewish historian who grew up in Europe in the early decades of the twentieth century and was greatly perturbed by the problem of assimilation.[3]

If we conceive of the Haskalah as an internal revolution affecting Jewish society and culture, and not as a crisis or a milestone in the course of the Jews' integration, assimilation, or abandonment of the "ghetto" for the sake of the temptations "outside," we arrive at a different picture. In an intensive process of criticizing, rebelling, sketching a vision, and struggling for a central place in the public sphere, the revolution did not lead the Jews out of the ghetto, but rather attempted to renew the face of the Jewish collective. The majority of the maskilim were not assimilating intellectuals intent upon destroying the collective; rather, they were transformationists, intent upon rehabilitating it. They instilled liberal values into the Jews, advocated a new order and demanded that their voice be heard so that the Jews could live in an age of change and revolution as European men of culture who are also committed to nurturing their particular Jewish culture and improving the frameworks of Jewish life. However, a reconstruction of the historical development of the Haskalah movement shows that the revolution with its hopes and successes, its disappointments and failures, also mirrored the "modern condition" of the Jews, marked by dilemmas, qualms, retreats, fears, inflamed passions, and cultural battles. The representatives of the ancien régime on their part tried to maintain their power and the existing patterns of life; they shaped a militant opposition, inimical to the Enlightenment and hostile toward the innovators.

The Haskalah was not active in a historical vacuum filled only with books and ideas. It was a historical, social, cultural, even political phenomenon, and this was expressed in the demands it made on the rabbinical leadership and in its transformative pretensions. It reflected a response to many diverse challenges of the time, like the marked growth of Kabbalistic and ecstatic trends, the neglect of the Hebrew language, the objection to the study of "external *chokhmot*" at the very time when the new science was emerging, and the challenge of rationalistic heresy. Of course, it responded to the various challenges of the Enlightenment—tolerance, rational religion, the "noble savage," the superiority of medicine to religion (the early burial controversy), and others. The Haskalah existed in the historical context of the emergence of the wealthy elite, the government's (for example, Joseph II's) reform policy, the acculturation of European Jewry, the intergenerational tension evoked by the many material temptations offered by the surrounding society, the control wielded by Polish teachers and rabbis over the education of youth, and many other events and processes.

The early Haskalah was rooted in the Jews' feelings of inferiority and affront because of their backwardness in relation to their contemporaries in acquisition of knowledge, rational shaping of life, and expansion of their intellectual horizon. Over time, new motives were added, such as the desire to regenerate the Jews and the belief that it was possible to reshape the society and culture and heal all its ills. The maskilim also strove to normalize the relations between Jews and the state and to accept the ethos of economic benefit, new scientific and medical innovations, and rationalism.

The story line of the Haskalah reached its climax in the twenty years between the beginning of the *Bi'ur* project and the establishment of the Freischule in 1778 and the closure of *Hame'asef* in 1797. This was the only period, however brief, during which one can say with certainty that the movement existed. But these intensive years left deep, ineradicable impressions. As we have seen in the fourth part of this book, in the 1790s a crisis was already gripping the Haskalah, which had just reached maturity. At the end of the crisis, its organizational systems had totally crumbled and veteran maskilim were eulogizing the project they believed had already drawn its last breath.

Was this truly a failure? Does the fact that the Haskalah was a movement of the few, which was nipped in the bud, inevitably lead to the conclusion that it was a passing episode? Should one accept the view of Euchel, a founder of the Haskalah movement and a shaper of its path and vision in its formative years, who proclaimed its demise in 1800? The rapid dismantling of its frameworks was certainly a surprising and very significant event. However, from an historical perspective, it does seem that the maskilim succeeded in carrying out their enlightenment revolution despite the voices of disillusionment that were heard at the time. At the turn of the century, a new generation of maskilim had already emerged in various cities in and outside Germany, who regarded themselves as the successors of the eighteenth-century maskilim. Moreover, several attempts were made to revive *Hame'asef* and to establish societies to replace the Society for the Promotion of Goodness and Justice. The Haskalah movement was renewed, and an especially bright future was in store for maskilim in Eastern Europe throughout the nineteenth century.[4] The liberal discourse of the Enlightenment had an enormous impact on Jewish public opinion from then on, and permeated nearly all the ideological movements that appeared in the following two hundred years. The subversive trends that underpinned the independence of the maskilic writers, their criticism and the new library they created did indeed gradually weaken what the radical maskil from Breslau, Moshe Hirschel, called the "Jewish hierarchy." Even if the *Kulturkampf* did not end in a decisive defeat or victory for either side, without a doubt the new intellectual elite of the maskilim broke the monopoly on knowledge and guidance of the public that had been held by the religious elite in Ashkenazi society.

Secular Revolution

The enlightenment revolution in eighteenth-century Jewish society was a secular one. One must, of course, be more precise: most of the maskilim did not declare a cultural war on the religion itself. They did not wish to sever their followers' ties to the religious sources, the sacred tongue or the observance of the commandments and the holidays according to the Jewish calendar, as some of the enemies of enlightenment claimed they did from the very first clash that erupted between the two camps. The Bible, the Hebrew language, and Jewish philosophy were at the center of the maskilim's study and inquiry. Of course, they were selective in the way they related to the Jewish sources, and they tried to shape a Jewish tradition that was compatible with the Enlightenment and emphasized moral values and reason. It was, however, a secular revolution, because it weakened the public standing of religion and of the clergy and established, alongside them or in their place, a secular culture and institutions. This process was parallel to the secularization of thought, culture, and society in Christian Europe. A long drawn-out process, it began with the Renaissance and the scientific revolution, reached its peak with the religious radicalism and skepticism of the seventeenth century and the Enlightenment of the eighteenth, and spread to broad sectors only in the nineteenth century. Secularization was expressed in many fields of thought and lifestyle, but in essence, one broad and diverse development took place, in the course of which the sacred and the profane were separated. In this way, two blocs of knowledge, institutions, and patterns of behavior were created, and each of them gained autonomy. They drew upon different sources of authority—one from the sanctity of divine authority, the other from the reason, experience, and human will himself.[5]

The revolution of the Haskalah was therefore manifested in two interrelated dimensions: the secularization of knowledge, values, and worldview, and the ingress of the secular writer into the public arena. The alternative posed by the maskilim was different and particularly subversive compared to the pre-modern situation in Ashkenazi Jewish society in regard to knowledge and its inculcation as well as to thought and the book world. *Torat ha'adam*, the teaching of man, namely everything that is neither religious nor divine, was introduced from the early Haskalah, into the Jewish library. *Torat ha'adam* also increasingly pushed aside traditional texts and confined them to the limited area of *Torat haShem*, the teaching of God, thus separating the sacred from the profane. It also enhanced the value of man and his right to realize the full potential of his abilities in this world. Knowledge about the world (science, history, geography) outside Jewish culture was perceived as essential and useful for the functioning of Jews in civil, economic, and political life, the improvement of their image in the eyes of society at large, the molding of the individual Jew into a moral person, beneficial to society, successful and happy in his own life. Reformed education had a key role to play; hence, the maskilim invested so much effort in that direction.

The modernist doctrine of the Haskalah encompassed values such as religious tolerance, contempt for superstition, the self-consciousness of living in a modern era, an optimistic view of the course of human history, and faith in man's power to shape his life by means of his reason. It was also employed to criticize many flaws in the communal organization and rabbinical authority, which were seen as an obstacle to the Jews' entrance into enlightened Europe. The maskilim did not conceal their hope that the profound change in Jewish life would also help the state and the society to overcome their prejudices against the Jews, although they directed most of their energies to the internal problems of Jewish society.

The group of young men who launched the enlightenment revolution in Jewish society were quite diversified. Although the rabbinical elite was the main target of their criticism, and from the end of the 1780s their propaganda became much more extreme in its anticlerical tendencies, these men did have divergent attitudes to the religion itself. Mendelssohn, we will recall, stated unequivocally that in the absence of an additional divine revelation there was no justification for abrogating any of the commandments, and other maskilim, such as Wessely and Satanow, shared his opinion. On the other hand, at the end of the century, maskilim like Friedländer and Bendavid expressed deist views. They regarded the practical commandments as an obstacle, and believed that only after it was removed could the full regeneration of the Jews be achieved, allowing them to be accepted into society at large. And yet, in the final analysis, they objected to the path of secularization that attracted young men and women in end-of-the-century Berlin, which led them to totally abandon the religious lifestyle and to succumb to the temptations of the city and its culture, a path that culminated in acculturation, even assimilation and conversion to Christianity. To the maskilim this way of life was ostentatious, hedonistic, lacking any moral backbone, and a disgrace to Jewish society. They wanted to base social change on ideals, ideas and principles that would provide a firm foundation for the process of modernization.

If this was the essence of the secular intellectual revolution, then, as we have stated many times, it was the maskil himself—the secular writer—who stood at the forefront of this social and cultural revolution. The literary republic was decidedly the most important achievement of the eighteenth-century Haskalah and its most important contribution to the modernization of the Jews. The maskil constructed in Jewish society (to which he remained connected even after he underwent cultural conversion to the Enlightenment) institutions that had never before existed, like the first modern school, the first publishing system, the first journal, and the first organization of intellectuals. He also invented a narrative of the progress and freedom of Jewish history and instilled in many the optimistic belief in life in "the modern era."[6] Above all, he established the Jewish literary republic, the basic framework for the growth of a vibrant and keenly involved Jewish public opinion.

Toward the end of the century two subtypes of writers emerged. The first retained close ties to the sources, the language and the readership of the rabbinical elite, and sought their audience solely within Jewish society. The other maintained ties with the German Enlightenment as well and took an active part in its literary frameworks in the German language. However, they both took the major revolutionary step of joining the Haskalah. At their own initiative, without any institutional backing and without having been an organic part of the traditional elite, they assumed the right to "speak" to the Jewish public (in fact, only to their readers, since at this stage they did not intervene at all in the synagogue or in preaching), to propose their worldviews to it and to set forth their plans for the regeneration of Jewry. The rabbinical elite regarded this as an intolerable provocation and as a revolutionary step to undermine their authority. From this historic moment, the separation between the orthodox leadership and the secular intellectual was determined. And even though the maskil may have continued to observe the religious norms in his personal life and as a member of the community, in his public literary life he drew his authority and ideas from his new reading of all aspects of Jewish tradition, from his analysis of reality and his rational judgment.

In this way, the maskilim simultaneously waged the secular revolution and the culture war that broke out as soon as they were identified as a threatening challenge. From these standpoints, the roots of the liberal intellectual elite as well as the roots of the complicated dilemmas created by the Jews' encounter with modern Western culture lie in the Haskalah. From the vantage point of the twenty-first century, it would then be correct to say that the Jews, to one extent or another, are also the children of the Enlightenment.

Notes

Introduction: The Jews and the Enlightenment

1. See Shmuel Feiner, "Towards a Historical Definition," in *New Perspectives on the Haskalah*, ed. Feiner and David Sorkin (London, 2001), 184–219.

2. See Immanuel Kant, "What Is Enlightenment?" in *On History*, ed. Lewis W. Beck (New York, 1986).

3. See Jürgen Habermas, *The Structural Transformation of the Public Sphere*, trans. T. Burger (Cambridge, Mass., 1998); Dena Goodman, *The Republic of Letters: A Cultural History of the French Enlightenment* (Ithaca, N.Y., 1994); Margaret C. Jacob, *Living the Enlightenment: Freemasonry and Politics in Eighteenth-Century Europe* (New York, 1991); Thomas Munck, *The Enlightenment: A Comparative Social History, 1721–1794* (London, 2000).

4. See Peter Gay, *The Enlightenment, an Interpretation: The Rise of Modern Paganism* (New York, 1996); Norman Hampson, *The Enlightenment: An Evaluation of Its Assumptions, Attitudes and Values* (London, 1968); Dorinda Outram, *The Enlightenment* (Cambridge, 1995).

5. Isaiah Berlin, *Against the Current: Essays in the History of Ideas* (Princeton, N.J., 1979). The classical work on Enlightenment thought is still Ernst Cassirer, *The Philosophy of the Enlightenment* (Princeton, N.J., 1963).

6. See Roy Porter, *The Enlightenment* (London, 1990).

7. Robert Darnton, *The Great Cat Massacre* (New York, 1985), 201–2.

8. Voltaire, *Candide, Zadig, and Selected Stories*, trans. Donald M. Frame (New York, 1981), chaps. 19, 21, 23.

9. Kant, "What Is Enlightenment?" On similar trends in German Enlightenment, see David Sorkin, *The Berlin Haskalah and German Religious Thought* (London, 2000).

10. Moses Mendelssohn, Über die Frage: Was heisst aufklaeren?" *Berlinische Manatsschrift* 4 (1784): 193–200.

11. See Jacob Katz, *From Prejudice to Destruction: Anti-Semitism, 1700–1933* (Cambridge, Mass., 1980).

12. See Michael Meyer, *The Origins of the Modern Jew: Jewish Identity and European Culture in Germany, 1749–1824* (Detroit, 1979), 11–18; Shmuel Ettinger, "The Beginnings of the Change in the Attitude of European Society Toward the Jews," *Scripta Hierosolymitana* 7 (1961): 193–219; Jacob Katz, *Out of the Ghetto: The Social Background to the Jewish Emancipation, 1770–1870* (Cambridge, Mass., 1973).

13. See Shmuel Ettinger, "Jews and Judaism as Seen by English Deists of the Eighteenth Century," in *Anti-Semitism in the Modern Era* (Tel-Aviv, 1978), 57–88 (Hebrew); idem, "The Attitude of the Deists Toward Judaism and Their Influence on the Jews," in *History and Historians* (Jerusalem, 1992), 215–24 (Hebrew); Katz, *From Prejudice to Destruction*, 25–33.

14. John Toland, *Reasons for Naturalizing the Jews in Great Britain and Ireland . . . Containing also a Defence of the Jews against all Vulgar Prejudices in all Countries* (London, 1714).

15. Voltaire, "The Jews," in *The Works of Voltaire*, trans. William F. Fleming (Akron, Ohio, 1904), 283–84. See Katz, *From Prejudice to Destruction*, 34–45; Arthur Hertzberg, *The French Enlightenment and the Jews* (New York, 1970); and recently Adam Sutcliffe, *Judaism and Enlightenment* (Cambridge, 2003).

16. Voltaire, *Treatise on Tolerance*, trans. B. Masters (Cambridge, 2000), 54–63.

17. See Richard I. Cohen, "The Rhetoric of Jewish Emancipation and the Vision of the Future," in *The French Revolution and Its Impact*, ed. Cohen (Jerusalem, 1991), 145–70 (Hebrew).

18. See Jacob Katz, "Kant and Judaism," *Tarbiz* 41 (1971): 219–37 (Hebrew).

19. See Yosef Kaplan, *An Alternative Path to Modernity: The Sephardi Diaspora in Western Europe* (Leiden, 2000); idem, "The Portuguese Jews in Amsterdam: From Forced Conversion to a Return to Judaism," *Studia Rosenthaliana* 15 (1981): 37–51; idem, "The Social Function of the *Herem* in the Portuguese Jewish Community of Amsterdam in the Seventeenth Century," *Dutch Jewish History* 1 (1984): 111–55; Yirmiyahu Yovel, *Spinoza and Other Heretics* (Princeton, N.J., 1989); Steven Nadler, *Spinoza: A Life* (Cambridge, 1999).

20. See Jacob Katz, *Tradition and Crisis* (New York, 1961); Mendel Piekarz, *The Beginning of Hasidism: Ideological Trends in Derush and Musar Literature* (Jerusalem, 1978) (Hebrew); Rachel Elior, "Natan Adler and the Frankfurt Pietists: Pietist Groups in Eastern and Central Europe During the Eighteenth Century," *Zion* 59 (1994): 31–64 (Hebrew); C. Abramsky, "The Crisis of Authority Within European Jewry in the Eighteenth Century," in *Studies in Jewish Intellectual and Religious History Presented to A. Altmann*, ed. S. Stein and R. Löwe (University, Ala., 1979), 13–28; Azriel Shohet, *Changing Eras: The Beginning of the Haskalah Among German Jewry* (Jerusalem, 1960) (Hebrew); Jonathan Israel, *European Jewry in the Age of Mercantilism, 1550–1750* (Oxford, 1991).

21. Solomon Maimon, *Lebensgeschichte*, ed. K. Ph. Moritz (Berlin, 1792–93).

22. See Jacob Katz, "The Eighteenth Century as a Turning Point of Modern Jewish History," in *Vision Confronts Reality*, ed. R. Kozodoy and K. Sultanik (New York, 1989), 40–55.

23. Katz, *Tradition and Crisis*; Katz, *Out of the Ghetto*; Meyer, *Origins of the Modern Jew*; Raphael Mahler, *Chronicles of Jewish History*, vol. 1 (Rehavia, 1956), 13–88 (Hebrew), trans. as *A History of Modern Jewry* (London, 1971); Michael Graetz, "The Jewish Enlightenment," in *German Jewish History in Modern Times*, ed. Michael Meyer, trans. W. Templer (New York, 1996–98).

24. Alexander Altmann, *Moses Mendelssohn: A Biographical Study* (Philadelphia, 1973).

25. Joseph Klausner, *History of Modern Hebrew Literature*, vol. 1 (Jerusalem, 1952–54) (Hebrew).

26. See Lois C. Dubin, *The Port Jews of Habsburg Trieste: Absolutist Politics and Enlightenment Culture* (Stanford, Calif., 1999); David Fishman, *Russia's First Modern Jews: The Jews of Shklov* (New York, 1995); Ruth Kestenberg-Gladstein, *Neuere Geschichte der Juden in den böhmischen Ländern: Das Zeitalter der Aufklärung, 1780–1830* (Tübingen, 1969); J. Hillel Kieval, "Caution's Progress: The Modernization of Jewish Life in Prague, 1780–1830," in *Toward Modernity: The European Jewish Model*, ed. Jacob Katz

(New Brunswick, N.J. 1987), 71–105; Michael Silber, "The Historical Experience of German Jewry and Its Impact on the Haskalah and Reform in Hungary," in *Toward Modernity, 107–57;* Joseph Michman, *"The Impact of German-Jewish Modernization on Dutch Jewry," in Toward Modernity, 171–87;* idem, *Dutch Jewry During the Emancipation Period, 1787–1815* (Amsterdam, 1995), chap. 7; David B. Ruderman, *Jewish Enlightenment in an English Key: Anglo-Jewry's Construction of Modern Jewish Thought* (Princeton, N.J., 2000); idem, "Was There a Haskalah in England?" *Zion* 62 (1996): 109–31 (Hebrew); Shmuel Feiner, "Isaac Euchel: Entrepreneur of the Haskalah Movement in Germany," *Zion* 52 (1987): 427–69 (Hebrew); Liliane Weissberg, "Erfahrungsseelenkunde als Akkulturation: Philosophie, Wissenschaft und Lebensgeschichte bei Salomon Maimon," in *Der ganze Mensch: Anthropologie und Literaturwissenschaft im achtzehnten Jahrhundert,* ed. Hans Jürgen Schings (Stuttgart, 1994), 298–328; idem, "1792–93, Salomon Maimon Writes his Autobiography: A Reflection on His Life in the (Polish) East and the (German) West," in *Yale Companion to Jewish Writing and Thought in German Culture 1096–1996,* ed. Sander Gilman and Jack Zipes (New Haven, Conn., 1997), 108–15; Christoph Schulte, "Haskala und Kabbala, Haltungen und Strategien der jüdischen Aufklärer beim Umgang mit der Kabbala," in *Aufklärung und Esoterik,* ed. Monika Neugebauer-Woelk (Hamburg, 1999), 335–54; Edward Breuer, "Napthali Herz Wessely and Cultural Dislocations of an Eighteenth-Century Maskil," in *New Perspectives on the Haskalah,* ed. Shmuel Feiner and David Sorkin (London, 2001), 27–47; Martin L. Davis, *Identity or History? Marcus Herz and the End of the Enlightenment* (Detroit, 1995); Nancy Sinkoff, "Tradition and Transition: Mendel Lefin of Satanow and the Beginnings of the Jewish Enlightenment in Eastern Europe 1749–1826," Ph.D. dissertation, Columbia University, 1996.

27. See Moshe Pelli, *Struggle for Change: Studies in the Hebrew Enlightenment in Germany at the End of the Eighteenth Century* (Tel-Aviv, 1988) (Hebrew); idem, "When Did the Haskalah Begin?" *Year Book of the Leo Baeck Institute* 20 (1975): 109–27; Yehudah Friedländer, *Studies in Hebrew Satire* (Tel Aviv, 1979) (Hebrew); Allan Arkush, *Moses Mendelssohn and the Enlightenment* (New York, 1994).

28. See David Sorkin, *Moses Mendelssohn and the Religious Enlightenment* (London, 1996); Arkush, *Moses Mendelssohn and the Enlightenment.*

29. Steven M. Lowenstein, *The Berlin Jewish Community: Enlightenment, Family and Crisis, 1770–1830* (Oxford, 1994).

30. David Sorkin, *The Berlin Haskalah and German Religious Thought* (London, 2000).

31. Simon Bernfeld, *Dor Ta'hapukhot* (Warsaw, 1897). On the historical context of this book, see Shmuel Feiner, "Like a Suckling Babe—Post Haskalah at the End of the Nineteenth Century," *Alpayim* 21 (2000): 59–94 (Hebrew).

32. See Azmi Bishara, ed., *Enlightenment—An Unfinished Project? Six Essays on Enlightenment and Modernism* (Tel Aviv, 1997) (Hebrew); Michel Foucault, "What Is Enlightenment?" *The Foucault Reader,* ed. Paul Rabinow (New York, 1984), 32–50; Theodor Adorno and Max Horkheimer, *Dialectic of Enlightenment* (New York, 1972).

33. Robert Darnton, "George Washington's False Teeth," *New York Review of Books,* 27 March 1997, 34–38.

34. Tod M. Endelman, *The Jews of Georgian England (1714–1830): Tradition and Change in a Liberal Society* (Philadelphia, 1979; Ann Arbor, 1999).

35. Shulamit Volkov, "The Jewish Project of Modernity: Diverse and Unitary," in

Zionism and the Return to History: A Reappraisal, ed. S. N. Eisenstadt and M. Lissak (Jerusalem, 1999), 239–305 (Hebrew).

36. Robert Darnton, *The Business of Enlightenment: A Publishing History of the Encyclopédie, 1775–1800* (Cambridge, Mass., 1979); idem, *The Forbidden Best-Sellers of Pre-Revolutionary France* (New York-London, 1995); idem, *The Literary Underground of the Old Regime* (Cambridge, 1982).

37. See Habermas, *Structural Transformation of the Public Sphere.*

38. Roy Porter and Mikulis Teich, eds., *Enlightenment in National Context* (Cambridge, 1981).

39. Darnton, "George Washington's False Teeth."

40. See Shulamit Volkov. "Prussian Jewry: Myth and Reality," *Braun Lectures in the History of the Jews in Prussia*, vol. 1 (Bar-Ilan University, 1993), 11–12 (Hebrew).

Chapter 1. Intellectual Inferiority: The Affront

1. For the best summary on Jews in German academic institutions, see Monika Richarz, *Der Eintritt der Juden in die akademischen Berufe* (Tübingen, 1974).

2. The correspondence between the two is cited in A. Freimann, "Briefwechsel eines Studeneten der Medizin in Frankfurt a.d. Oder mit dem in Halle Medizin studierenden Isak Wallich im Jahre 1702," *Zeitschrift für Hebräische Bibliographie* 14 (1910): 117–23.

3. On Hoffman, see Roy Porter, *The Greatest Benefit to Mankind: A Medical History of Humanity from Antiquity to the Present* (London, 1997), 247–48.

4. See Richarz, *Der Enritt der Juden*, 78–79; Gershon Hundert, *The Jews in a Polish Private Town: The Case of Opatow in the Eighteenth Century* (Baltimore, 1992), 72; Mordechai Eliav, *Jewish Education in German During the Haskalah and the Emancipation* (Jerusalem, 1961), 19. On Jewish students in Frankfurt-on-Oder University, see Louis Lewin, "Die Jüdische Studenten an der Universität Frankfurt an der Oder," *Jahrbuch der jüdisch-literarischen Gesellschaft* 14 (1921): 217–38; 15 (1923): 59–63; 16 (1924): 43–86.

5. Isaac Wetzlar, *Libes briv*, ed. and trans. Morris M. Faierstein (Atlanta, 1996), 70. And see Stefan Rohrbacher, "Isaak Wetzlar in Celle—Ein jüdischer Reformer vor der Zeit der Aufklärung," in *Juden in Celle: Biographische Skizzen aus drei Jahrhunderten* (Celle, 1996), 33–66. The text of *Kohelet musar* was published in an annotated edition with a lengthy introduction, in Meir Gilon, *Mendelssohn's "Kohelet musar" in Its Historical Context* (Jerusalem, 1979) (Hebrew).

6. Ephraim Epstein, *Gevurot haAri* (Vilna, 1870), 11–12.

7. Solomon Maimon, *Lebensgeschichte*, ed. K. Ph. Moritz (Berlin, 1792–93), 117–19. For more on the rabbi from Slonim, see Israel Zinberg, *A History of Jewish Literature*, vol. 3 (New York, 1975). On the knowledge of foreign languages in eighteenth-century Poland, see Daniel Stone, "Knowledge of Foreign Languages Among Eighteenth-Century Polish Jews," *Polin* 10 (1997): 200–218.

8. Epstein, *Gevurot haAri*, 12.

9. The approbation of Rabbi Shimshon ben Mordechai of Slonim to Barukh Schick's translation to Hebrew of Euclid's *Geometry*. On Barukh Schick, see David Fishman, *Russia's First Modern Jews: The Jews of Shklov* (New York, 1995).

10. Tobias Cohen, *Ma'aseh Tuvyah* (Cracow, 1707), author's preface, 1–2; Intro-

duction, 25. On Tobias and *Ma'aseh Tuvyah,* see David Ruderman, *Jewish Thought and Scientific Discovery in Early Modern Europe* (New Haven, Conn., 1955), chap. 8.

11. See Joseph Melkman, *David Franco Mendes: A Hebrew Poet* (Jerusalem, 1951); David Friedrichsfeld, *Zekher tzadik* (Amsterdam, 1808); Joseph Michman, "The Impact of German-Jewish Modernization on Dutch Jewry," in *Toward Modernity: The European Jewish Model,* ed. Jacob Katz (New Brunswick, N.J., 1987), 171–87; Wagenaar's letter to Mendelssohn (apparently in 1775) is printed in Moses Mendelssohn, *Gesammelte Schriften,* vol. 19 (Stuttgart, 1974), 206–7. See also Shlomo Berger, "Amadores das Musas," *Scripta Classica Israelica* 15 (1996): 274–88.

12. Judah Hurwitz, *Amudei bet Yehudah* (Amsterdam, 1766), before the author's preface, no page number. On Hurwitz's meeting with this circle, see Zvi Malachi, "Isaac Cohen Belinfante: A Poet Preacher and Publisher in 18th Century Amsterdam," in *Studies on the History of Dutch Jewry,* vol. 1 (Jerusalem, 1975), 139 (Hebrew); idem, "N. H. Ulman, Maskil and Philosopher," in *Studies on the History of Dutch Jewry,* vol. 2 (Jerusalem 1979), 77–88 (Hebrew). On Hurwitz and his book *Amudei bet Yehudah* as a central book of the early Haskalah, see Shmuel Feiner, "Between the 'Clouds of Foolishness' and the 'Light of Reason': Judah Hurwitz, an Early Eighteenth-Century Maskil," in *Within Hasidic Circles: Studies in Hasidism in Memory of Mordechai Wilensky,* ed. I. Etkes, D. Asaf, I. Bartal, and E. Reiner (Jerusalem, 1999), 111–60 (Hebrew).

13. Wessely's 1768 letter to Mendelssohn; Mendelssohn, *Gesammelte Schriften,* vol. 19, 121.

14. See comprehensive discussion on this question in Uzi Shavit, "Luzzatto's *Layesharim tehilah*: A New Approach," in *Studies on the History of Dutch Jewry,* vol. 4 (Jerusalem, 1984), 179–218 (Hebrew).

15. This argument has been put forward by, among others, S. W. Baron, *A Social and Religious History of the Jews,* vol. 2 (New York, 1936), 205–12. It is also mentioned in his article, "New Approaches to Jewish Emancipation," *Diogenes* 29 (1960): 56–58. For an attempt systematically to examine points of similarity and disparity between the Berlin Haskalah and the "Haskalah of Italy," see Isaac Barzilay, "The Italian and Berlin Haskalah (Parallels and Differences)," *Proceedings of the American Academy for Jewish Research* 29 (1960–61): 17–54.

16. Azriel Shohet, in his *Changing Eras: The Beginning of the Haskalah Among German Jewry,* described the rabbis Emden and Eybeschütz as Mendelssohn's precursors, and 1721, the year in which the second edition of *Ma'aseh Tuvyah* was published in Jesnitz, as the year in which the Haskalah began.

17. Baruch Schick, *Sefer Uklides* (Euclid's Elements) (The Hague, 1780), author's introduction.

18. This was the main point in Jacob Katz's criticism of Shohet's argument suggesting an earlier date for the beginning of the Haskalah. See Jacob Katz, *Out of the Ghetto: The Social Background to the Jewish Emancipation, 1770–1870* (Cambridge, Mass., 1973), chap. 3 and notes.

19. See, inter alia, Zeev Yavetz, "The Tower of the Century," *Knesset yisra'el* 1 (1886): 89–152 (Hebrew); A. H. Weiss, "The Beginning of the Haskalah in Russia," *Mimizrach umima'arav* 1 (1894): 9–16 (Hebrew); Ben-Zion Katz, "The Enlightenment of the Jews in Russia," *HaZeman,* vol. 1 (Petersburg, 1903), 77–105 (Hebrew); idem, *Rabbinate, Hasidism, and Haskalah,* vol. 1 (Tel-Aviv, 1956) (Hebrew); Jacob Raisin, *The Haskalah Movement in Russia* (Philadelphia, 1913); J. Eschelbacher, "Die Anfänge allgemeiner Bildung unter den deutschen Juden vor Mendelssohn," in *Festschrift zum*

70 Geburtstage Martin Philippsons (Leipzig, 1916), 168–77; Josef Meisel, *Haskalah, Geschichte der Aufklärungsbewegung unter den Juden in Russland* (Berlin, 1919); Yitzhak Barzilay, *Menasseh of Ilya, Precursor of Modernity Among the Jews of Eastern Europe* (Jerusalem, 1999); Jacob Shatzky, *Kultur-Geschichte fun der Haskalah in Lita* (Buenos Aires, 1950); Ben-Zion Dinur, "The Question of Redemption at the Beginning of the Haskalah," in *At the Turn of the Generations* (Jerusalem, 1954), 248–69 (Hebrew); Azriel Shohet, *Changing Eras: The Beginning of the Haskalah Among German Jewry* (Jerusalem, 1960), chap. 10 (Hebrew); Raphael Mahler, *History of the Jewish People*, vol. 4, 14–68 (Hebrew); Isaac Eisenstein-Barzilay, "The Background of the Berlin Haskalah," in *Essays on Jewish Life and Thought, Presented in Honor of Salo W. Baron* (New York, 1959); Alexander Altmann, *Moses Mendelssohn: A Biographical Study* (Philadelphia, 1973), 21–25; Mordechai Breuer and Michael Graetz, *Deutsch-Jüdische Geschichte in der Neuzeit*, vol. 1 (Munich, 1996), 223–33, 254–55.

20. See Moses Mendelson-Frankfurter, "Mendelssohns und Wesselys Zeit," *Der Orient* 9 (1848): 27–29, 45–46, 122–25, 140–44, 165–70; idem, *Pnei Tevel* (Amsterdam, 1871), 241–52. On him, see Noah Rosenblum, " Moses Mendelson-Frankfurter, Among the Last Maskilim in Germany," in *Studies in Literature and Thought* (Jerusalem, 1990), 52–66.

21. Isaac Baer Levinsohn, *T'eudah beYisra'el* (Vilna-Horodno, 1828). On Levinsohn and his aims, see Shmuel Feiner, *Haskalah and History* (Oxford, 2002), 178–92.

22. Samuel Joseph Fuenn, *Safah lene'emanim* (Vilna, 1881). The work first appeared on the pages of the monthly *HaCarmel* 4 (1778–79); Zvi Hirsh Rabinowitz, *Yesodei chokhmat hateva hakelalit* (Vilna, 1867), xxi–xviii.

23. Yosef Kaplan, *An Alternative Path to Modernity: The Sephardi Diaspora in Western Europe* (Leiden, 2000), 16.

24. Yosef Kaplan, *The Western Sephardi Diaspora* (Tel Aviv, 1994), chap. 10 (Hebrew).

25. Immanuel Etkes, *The Gaon of Vilna: The Man and His Image* (Jerusalem, 1998), 192–217 (Hebrew).

26. Immanuel Etkes, "On the Question of the Precursors of the Haskalah in Eastern Europe," in *Religion and Life: The Jewish Enlightenment in Eastern Europe*, ed. Etkes (Jerusalem, 1993), 95–114 (Hebrew); idem., *The Gaon of Vilna.*

27. See Fishman, *Russia's First Modern Jews*; idem, "A Polish Rabbi Meets the Berlin Haskalah: The Case of R. Baruch Schick," *AJS Review* 12 (1987): 95–121.

28. Jacob Schacter, "Rabbi Jacob Emden: Life and Major Works," Ph.D. dissertation, Harvard University, 1988, chap. 6, 499–662.

29. See David Sorkin, "From Context to Comparison: The German Haskalah and Reform Catholicism," *Tel Aviver Jahrbuch für deutsche Geschichte* 20 (1991): 27–41; idem, *The Transformation of German Jewry, 1780–1840* (Oxford, 1987), chap. 2; idem, "Preacher, Teacher, Publicist: Joseph Wolf and the Ideology of Emancipation," in *Between East and West: Jews in Changing Europe, 1750–1870*, ed. Frances Malino and David Sorkin (Oxford, 1990), 107–11; idem, *The Berlin Haskalah and German Religious Thought* (London, 2000).

30. See David Sorkin, *Moses Mendelssohn and the Religious Enlightenment* (London, 1996); idem, "The Early Haskalah," in *New Perspectives on the Haskalah*, ed. Shmuel Feiner and Sorkin (London, 2000), 10–26.

31. Ruderman, *Jewish Thought and Scientific Discovery*, 340.

32. Jacob Emden, *Megilat sefer* (Altona, 1740), Abraham Bick edition (Jerusalem, 1978), 126.

33. See, inter alia, Horst Möller, *Vernunft und Kritik: Deutsche Aufklärung im 17. Und 18. Jahrhundert* (Frankfurt am Main, 1986), 19–40; Rudolph Vierhaus, *Germany in the Age of Absolutism, 1600–1790* (Cambridge, 1988), 79–84; John Gagliardo, *Germany Under the Old Regime* (London, 1991), chap. 15; Thomas P. Saine, "Who's Afraid of Christian Wolff?" in *Anticipations of the Enlightenment in England, France, and Germany*, ed. Alan Charles Kors and Paul J. Korshin (Philadelphia, 1987), 102–33. On the question of the "precursors" of the Enlightenment in Europe, see the introduction to that volume, and the introduction to Margaret C. Jacob, *The Enlightenment: A Brief History with Documents* (Boston, 2001).

34. See Michael Heyd, *"Be Sober and Reasonable": The Critique of Enthusiasm in the Seventeenth and Eighteenth Centuries* (Leiden, 1995).

35. See Edward Shils, "Intellectuals," *International Encyclopedia of the Social Sciences*, vol. 7 (1968): 399–415. For a comprehensive discussion of the various definitions and their significance in the Jewish context, see Paul R. Mendes-Flohr, "The Study of the Jewish Intellectuals: Some Methodological Proposals," in *Essays in Modern Jewish History: A Tribute to Ben Halpern*, ed. Franco Malino and Phyllis Cohen Alber (London, 1982), 142–72.

36. On this, see B. Wilson, "Secularization: The Inherited Model," in *The Sacred in a Secular Age*, ed. Philip E. Hammond (Berkeley, Calif., 1985), 9–20.

37. See Kors's introduction to *Anticipations of the Enlightenment*, in particular Mitchell's article. And see Peter L. Berger, *The Sacred Canopy* (New York, 1967), chap. 5. As Robert Darnton has recently shown, the Enlightenment culture was characterized, first and foremost, by the emergence of the new social type, "the philosophe," the critical man of letters and thinker, who demonstrated commitment and involvement, fought against negative phenomena in the society and culture and strove for intellectual autonomy. See Darnton, "Washington's False Teeth."

38. Katz, in his *Tradition and Crisis*, chap. 24, noted the decisive importance of this historical process. And Michael Graetz also noted its social significance in "The Jewish Enlightenment," in *German Jewish History in Modern Times*, ed. Michael Meyer, trans. W. Templer (New York, 1996–98).

Chapter 2. The Early Haskalah and the Redemption of Knowledge

1. Jacob Emden, *Sefer she'ilat yavetz*, vol. 1 (Lvov, 1884), 41.

2. Judah Leib Margolioth, *Tal orot* (Frankfurt-on-Oder, 1811). Although the book was printed in the last year of Margolioth's life, it contains ideas and stories from his earlier years.

3. See Daniel Boyarin, "Thinking with Virgins: Engendering Judeo-Christian Difference," *Historia* 3 (1999): 5–32 (Hebrew); Abraham Melamed, "Woman as Philosopher: The Image of Sophia in Y. Abravanel's *Dialoghi d'Amore*," *Jewish Studies* 40 (2000): 113–30 (Hebrew). On Rabbi Emden's attitude toward philosophy, see Jacob Emden, *Mitpachat sefarim* (Altona, 1768), chap. 9, 53, 121.

4. Shlomo Chelm, *Mirkevet hamishneh* (Frankfurt-on-Oder, 1751), 3, 1. On him see Abraham Brik, "Rabbi Shlomo Chelm, the Author of *Mirkevet hamishneh*," *Sinai* 61 (1966): 168–84 (Hebrew). The division of time between the holy and the profane and the allocation of secular time to nonreligious knowledge was a well-known tactic to legitimize the "sciences." Rabbi Jacob Emden adopted this approach in a perfected

manner by setting aside certain times and places for the various spheres of knowledge. See Jacob Schacter, "Rabbi Joseph Emden: Life and Major Works," Ph.D. dissertation, Harvard University, 1988.

5. Baruch Schick, *Sefer amudei shamayim* (Berlin, 1777).

6. Meir Neumark's manuscripts are in the Bodlean Library at Oxford. On him see Moritz Steinschneider, "Mathematik bei der Juden 1551–1840," *Monatsschrift für Geschichte und Wissenschaft des Judentums* 30 (1905): 590–95.

7. Shlomo Z. Hanau, *Binyan Shlomo* (Frankfurt a.m., 1708), Introduction.

8. The text of Hanau's apology is cited in *Zeitschrift für Bibliographie* 7 (1904): 93–94.

9. Shlomo Z. Hanau, *Tzohar hateivah* (Berlin, 1733), Introduction.

10. Raphael Levi, *Luchot haibur* (Leiden, 1755–56) (all copies of the book, including one that is in the National and University Library in Jerusalem, were signed in the author's handwriting, so that the tables could not be printed without his approval); idem, *Luach alot hashachar* (Hanover and Amsterdam, 1765).

11. Raphael Levi, *Tekhunat hashaymayim*, vol. 1 (Amsterdam, 1755), 1.

12. See Alexander Even-Chen, "Two Messianic Texts at the Beginning of the Haskalah," *Da'at: A Journal of Jewish Philosophy and Kabbalah* 35 (1995): 87–97 (Hebrew).

13. See the picture in the article surveying Raphael Levi's life, which depicts him as an early maskil in Germany: Steven Schwarzchild and Henry Schwarzchild, "Two Lives in the Jewish Frühaufklärung: Raphael Levi Hannover and Moses Abraham Wolff," *Year Book of the Leo Baeck Institute* 29 (1984): 229–76. Also compare the portrait of the physician Tobias Cohen that appears on the frontispiece of his book *Ma'aseh Tuvyah*, which shows the figure of a scholar holding in his one hand an open book and in the other a pine cone, behind him bookshelves. On portraits of Jews in Baroque art, see Richard Cohen and Vivian Mann, "Melding Worlds: Court Jews and the Art of the Baroque," in *From Court Jews to the Rothschilds*, ed. Mann and Cohen (Munich, 1997), 97–104.

14. Levi, *Tekhunat hashaymayim*, Introduction, 1.

15. See Alexander Altmann, *Moses Mendelssohn: A Biographical Study* (Philadelphia, 1973), 161–63; Moses Mendelssohn, *Gesammelte Schriften*, vol. 12/1 (Stuttgart, 1971–78), 148–51.

16. See Theodor Danzel, *Gottsched und sein Zeit: Auszüge aus seinem Briefwechsel* (Leipzig, 1855), 333–38; Jacob Katz, *Die Enstehung der Judenassimilation in Deutschland und deren Ideologie* (Frankfurt a.m., 1935), 43–44.

17. Aaron Solomon Gumpertz, *Megaleh sod* (Hamburg, 1765). On him, see Max Freudenthal, *Die Familie Gomperz* (Frankfurt a.m., 1907); Selma Stern-Taeubler, "The First Emancipated Jews," *Year Book of the Leo Baeck Institute* 15 (1970): 9–11; Altmann, *Mendelssohn*, 23–35; Miriam Bodian, "The Gumpertz Family in Germany in the 17th–18th Centuries: Toward Emancipation," *Proceedings of the Tenth World Congress on Jewish Studies, Div. B*, vol. 1 (Jerusalem, 1990), 177–82 (Hebrew); Ruderman, *Jewish Thought and Scientific Discovery in Early Modern Europe* (New Haven, Conn., 1995), 334–35.

18. Moses Mendelssohn, *Bi'ur Milot hahigayon leharav hehakham beyisrael . . . rav moshe midesau* (Berlin, 1765).

19. Shlomo Dubno's 1780 letter to Mendelssohn, in Mendelssohn, *Gesammelte Schriften*, vol. 19, 258–59. Shlomo Chelm, *Sefer sha'arei ne'imah* (Frankfurt am Oder, 1766).

20. Shlomo Dubno, List of Books (1771) Manuscript in the Rosenthaliana Library, Amsterdam.

21. On the existence of books of the early Haskalah in private libraries and houses of study, see Pinhas Katzenelbogen, *Sefer yesh manchilin* (written in the eighteenth century, published Jerusalem, 1986), 41–51 (among the books in his library, which in 1747 numbered more than 400, were also *Ma'aseh Tuvyah, Mafteach ha'algebrah, Tzohar hateivah*); Gershon Hundert, "The Library of the Study Hall in Volozhin, 1762: Some Notes on the Basis of a Newly Discovered Manuscript," *Jewish History* 14 (2000): 225–44.

22. Yonathan ben Yosef, *SeferYeshuah beYisrael* (Frankfurt a.m., 1720), author's introduction.

23. Chelm, *Mirkevet hamishneh*, vol. 3, 1.

24. Hanau, *Tzohar hateivah*. See also Iris Parush, "A Different Look at the Life of the 'Dead' Hebrew Language: The Deliberate Ignorance of Hebrew in East European Jewish Society in the Nineteenth Century and Its Influence on the Literature and Its Readers," *Alpayim* 13 (1996): 95 (Hebrew).

25. Naphtali Herz Wessely, *Gan na'ul* (Amsterdam,1765–76).

26. Meir Gilon, *Mendelssohn's "Kohelet musar" in Its Historical Context* (Jerusalem, 1979), 160–64.

27. Ibid., 158. Gilon shows (126–27) that in *Kohelet musar* the "autonomous man" of the Haskalah, who knows his value, has confidence in himself and in human reason and acknowledges the value of human pleasures, is revealed.

28. Zevi Hirsh Koidonover, *Kav hayashar* (Frankfurt a.m., 1705; Jerusalem, 1993), chap. 1. On the widespread distribution of the book, see Yeshayahu Shachar, *Criticism of Society and Leadership in the Musar and Drush Literature in Eighteenth-Century Poland* (Jerusalem, 1992) (Hebrew). On its context in the popular culture of Polish Jewry, see Gershon Hundert, "Jewish Life in Poland-Lithuania in the Eighteenth Century," in *The Broken Chain: Polish Jewry Throughout the Ages*, ed. Israel Bartal and Israel Gutman (Jerusalem, 1997), 230–32 (Hebrew).

29. Other than these two books, David Gans's science book *Nechmad vena'im* (1742) and Bahya Ibn Paquda's *Chovot halevavot* (1743) were printed in Jesnitz in the 1740s. On Hebrew printing in Germany, see Menahem Schmelzer, "Hebrew Printing and Publishing in Germany 1650–1750," *Year Book of the Leo Baeck Institute* 33 (1988): 369–83.

30. Israel Zamosc, *Netzach Yisrael* (Frankfurt-am-Oder, 1740), 1–3.

31. Israel Zamosc, *Ruach chen*, vol. 15 (Jesnitz, 1744), 2. On his aim to purify talmudic thinking and to correct the method of scholarship, see Jay M. Harris, *How Do We Know This? Midrash and the Fragmentation of Modern Judaism* (New York, 1995), 138–41.

32. Zamosc, *Ruach chen*, 12–15.

33. Emden, *She'ilat yavetz*, vol. 13, 1.

34. Asher Anshel Worms, *Mafte'ach ha'algebra hachadashah* (Offenbach, 1722), introduction. In his image of Algebra as a maiden, Worms was undoubtedly influenced by the sixteenth- and seventeenth-century emblems, which gave a visual expression to concepts such as arts and sciences (for example, "Madame Philosophy"). See David Ruderman, trans., *A Valley of Vision: The Heavenly Journey of Abraham ben Hananiah Yagel* (Philadelphia, 1990).

35. Asher Anshel Worms, *Sayeg laTorah* (Frankfurt a.m., 1766). On him see Edward Breuer, *The Limits of the Enlightenment: Jews Germans, and the Enlightenment Study of Scripture* (Cambridge, Mass., 1996), 112–15; David Sorkin, *The Berlin Haskalah and German Religious Thought* (London, 2000), 45–48.

36. Worms, *Seyag leTorah*, general introduction. On Johann Christian Edelmann, a radical German deist who lived in Berlin, see Thomas P. Saine, *The Problem of Being Modern; or, The German Pursuit of Enlightenment from Leibniz to the French Revolution* (Detroit, 1997), 205–12.

37. This has already been noted by Mendel Piekarz in *The Beginning of Hasidism: Ideological Trends in Derush and Musar Literature* (Jerusalem, 1978), 331–33 (Hebrew).

38. Judah Hurwitz, *Amudei bet Yehudah* (Amsterdam, 1766), 1:2.

39. See Daniel Defoe, *Robinson Crusoe* (1716); Jonathan Swift, *Gulliver's Travels* (1726); Dorinda Outram, *The Enlightenment* (Cambridge, 1995), 63–79, 114–17; Roy Porter and G. S. Rousseau, *Exoticism in the Enlightenment* (Manchester, 1990); Paul Hazard, *The European Mind: The Critical Years, 1680–1715* (New York, 1990), 3–28.

40. For Occum's story, see Isaac Backus, *The Diary of Isaac Backus*, ed. William McLoughlin (Providence, R.I., 1979), 550–51.

41. Hurwitz, *Amudei bet Yehudah*, 2:2. Compare to the character of the savages as cruel, naked barbarians, as portrayed in the memoirs of Glikel of Hamelin in the early eighteenth century, *The Memoirs of Glückel of Hameln*, trans. Marvin Lowenthal (New York, 1977). This description of savages appears only in the Hebrew version, *Glikel miHamlin, Zikhronot*, trans. A. Z. Rabinowitz (Tel-Aviv, 1928), 17–18.

42. Hurwitz, *Amudei bet Yehudah*, 2:2.

43. Ibid., 4:1; 3:1.

44. Ibid., 3:2.

45. Based on the 1703 English edition: Baron de Lahontan, *New Voyages to North America*, vol. 2 (London, 1703), 517–618. The discussion is in Hurwitz, *Amudei bet Yehudah*, 53:1.

46. Ibid., 27:1.

47. On this see Altmann, *Mendelssohn*, 218–19.

48. Moses Mendelssohn, "Schreiben an den Herrn Diaconus Lavater" (1769), in *Gesammelte Schriften*, vol. 7, 12. In *Jerusalem* (1783), trans. Alfred Jospe (New York, 1969), Mendelssohn again used this test, and as part of his polemic in relation to Christianity he wrote: "If, therefore, mankind must be corrupt and miserable without revelation, why has the far greater part of mankind lived without true revelation from time immemorial? Why must the two Indies wait until it pleases the Europeans to send them a few comforters to bring them a message without which they, according to this opinion, live neither virtuously nor happily? To bring them a message which, in their circumstances and state of knowledge, they can neither rightly comprehend nor properly utilize?" (*Jerusalem*, 94). Mendelssohn also found this argument in Jean-Jacques Rousseau's book *Emile* (1762); see trans. Barbara Foxley (London, 1993), 321–22. Elsewhere in *Jerusalem* Mendelssohn discusses the specific case of the Philantrophin school that Johann Basedow established in Dessau, and states that neither his reason nor his inexperience enabled him to comprehend the abstract worship of God being conducted there. For this purpose, he cites the well-known example of Omai, a savage brought to England by Captain Cook in 1772: "Imagine a second Omai who, knowing nothing of the secret art of writing, and without being gradually accustomed to our

ideas, would be suddenly removed from his part of the world to one of the most image-free temples in Europe" (114).

49. Hurwitz's statement about the possible union with the Christians is quite far-reaching: "If it were within our power to unite them with us, they would be like us, for we have one God, one father to us all, and not to hate them because they are somewhat opposed to the religion of our God" (*Amudei bet Yehudah*, 27:1).

50. Ibid., 28:1.

51. Ibid., 28:2.

52. See Judah Hurwitz, *Sadeh tevunah*. Compare to Olaf Gerhard Tychsen, the first to write a critique of Hurwitz's books, *Bützowische Nebenstunden* 5 (1769): 47–53.

53. Judah Leib Margolioth, *Tov veYafeh* (Frankfurt-am-Oder, 1770). On Margolioth as an early maskil, see Shmuel Feiner, "The Dragon Around the Bee-Hive: Judah Leib Margolioth and the Paradox of the Early Haskalah," *Zion* 63 (1998): 41–74 (Hebrew).

54. Margolioth, *Tov veYafeh*, 6:1.

55. See Kant, *What Is Enlightenment?* in *On History*, ed. Lewis W. Beck (New York, 1986).

56. Margolioth, *Tov veYafeh*, 7:1; 22:1.

57. Inter alia, "Love of the Creator and the joys of the next world, which is the consummation of passion that exists nowhere in this world, whose pleasures have no value and in no way resemble the perfect pleasure that a man enjoys in the world to come" (*Tov veYafeh*, 21:1).

58. Margolioth, *Tov veYafeh*, 10:2

59. Ibid., 16:2.

60. Ibid., 11:12.

61. Moshe Steinhardt, *Chovot halevavot* (Fuerth, 1764), Introduction and German translation, 161.

62. Judah Leib Minden, *Milim leElohah* (Berlin, 1760).

63. Steinhardt, *Chovot halevavot*, introduction to the German translation, chap. 1. In Raphael Levi of Hanover's *Tekhunat hashamayim* (Amsterdam, 1756), Copernicus's method is cited along with a drawing of the heliocentric solar system. It was presented as a latest innovation in astronomy with complete agreement (32:1–2). On how the Jews met the challenge of Copernican astronomy, see Ruderman, *Jewish Thought and Scientific Discovery*; Hillel Levine, "Paradise Not Surrendered: Jewish Reaction to Copernicus and the Growth of Modern Science," in *Epistemology, Methodology, and the Social Sciences*, ed. Robert Cohen and Marx Wartofsky (Dordrecht, 1983), 203–25; André Néher, "Copernicus in the Hebraic Literature from the Sixteenth to the Eighteenth Century," *Journal for the History of Ideas* 38 (1977): 211–26.

64. "And my son Moshe has added something of his own, an interpretation in the lucid language of Ashkenaz that their philosophers use, and there he clarifies several matters relating to the course of the sun, some of the planets and Orion and their dominion over the earth" (Steinhardt, *Chovot halevavot*, approbation to the Fuerth edition, 1768).

65. In a letter Wessely sent to Mendelssohn in 1768, he informed him that he was trying to prove, based on Jewish sources as well, that Copernicus's method was acceptable: "For in those generations, what [the Sages] had rejected was accepted, namely Copernicus's view that the constellations revolve in the ether and are not held fast in the heavenly sphere." The letter is from Mendelssohn, *Gesammelte Schriften*, 19: 120–21.

66. Joseph Steinhardt, *Zikhron Yosef* (Fuerth, 1773), Introduction.

67. From 1738 to 1778, a total of 62 Jewish students from Poland (Zamosc, Brody, Lisa, Vilna, Cracow, Lvov) and the Habsburg Empire (Pressburg, Prague) studied at this school, but Hakaliri, as a Jerusalemite, is undoubtedly an exception. See list of students: Monika Richarz, *Der Eintritt der Juden in die Akademischen Berufe* (Tübingen, 1974), 227. In the list, his name appears as Shimshon Kalix, graduate of the Collegium in 1761 with a master's degree in medicine from the University of Frankfurt-on-Oder in 1764.

68. Hakaliri's introduction to the Berlin edition (1765), in Mendelssohn, *Gesammelte Schriften*, vol. 14, 298–300.

69. Dov Baer wrote about his aims in reprinting the book and its importance in his introduction, "In Praise of Philosophy," Mendelssohn, *Gesammelte Schriften*, vol. 14, 303–4.

70. "It would be desirable for those young men zealously pursuing their Torah studies to set aside one or two hours a week to peruse these matters, for they are also of great benefit to the study of Talmud, Rashi's commentaries, and the *Tosefoth*) as well as in *pilpul*, since they clear the mind and guide it in a reasonable, correct path, and also improve speech which is man's glory and his advantage over the beasts of the land" (Mendelssohn, *Gesammelte Schriften*, vol. 14: 25–31). See lengthy discussion in David Sorkin, *Moses Mendelssohn and the Religious Enlightenment* (London, 1996).

71. On him, see Ruderman, *Jewish Thought and Scientific Discovery*, chap. 12; Heinz Moshe Graupe, "Mordechai Shnaber Levison: The Life, Works and Thought of a Haskalah Outsider," *Year Book of the Leo Baeck Institute* 51 (1996): 3–20.

72. Mordechai Gumpel Schnaber Levison, *Ma'amar haTorah vehachokhmah* (London, 1771), 1–11; Ruderman, *Jewish Thought and Scientific Discovery*, 335–68.

73. On the Enlightenment and medicine, see Peter Gay, "The Enlightenment as Medicine and as Cure," in *The Age of Enlightenmen: Studies Presented to Theodor Besterman* (Edinburgh, 1967), 375–86; Roy Porter, *The Greatest Benefit to Mankind: A Medical History of Humanity from Antiquity to the Present* (London, 1997), chap. 10; and in the book on the Berlin physician and philosopher, Marcus Herz: Martin L. Davis, *Identity or History? Marcus Herz and the End of the Enlightenment* (Detroit, 1995).

74. Tobias Cohen, *Ma'aseh Tuvyah* (Cracow, 1707), 98–99.

75. Ibid.

76. The physicians are Benjamin De Lamos, Hirschel, and Mordechai Bloch. See Benjamin De Lamos and Mordechai Bloch, *Atzirat hamagefah* (Frankfurt-am-Oder, 1770).

77. See Khone Shmeruk, *Yiddish Literature: Aspects of Its History* (Tel-Aviv, 1978), 187–96 (Hebrew); Alexander Gutterman, "Dr. Moses Marcuse's Proposal for Reforms in the Life of the Jews," in *Gal-Ed: On the History of the Jews in Poland*, 4–5 (1978): 35–53 (Hebrew). Marcus Herz, the Berlin doctor and student of Kant (1747–1803), was a classmate of Marcuse's at Königsberg University. See list of Jewish university graduates: H. J. Krüger, *Die Judenschaft von Königsberg in Preußen 1700–1812* (Marburg, 1966).

78. See Moshe Rosman, "The History of an Historical Source: On the Editing of *Shivchei haBesht*," *Zion* 58 (1993): 213 (Hebrew), which includes a bibliography on this topic of physicians versus popular healers.

79. See Gutterman, "Dr. Moses Marcuse's Proposal," 52.

Chapter 3. The Secular Author in the Public Arena

1. See Meir Gilon, *Mendelssohn's "Kohelet musar" in Its Historical Context* (Jerusalem, 1979), particularly 97–106 (Hebrew).

2. Israel Zamosc, *Netzach Yisrael*, vol. 2 (Frankfurt-am-Oder, 1740), Introduction, 1.

3. Ibid. Portions of the book with the addition of comments and an introduction appear in Y. Friedländer, *Hebrew Satire in Europe*, vol. 2, *The Eighteenth and Nineteenth Centuries* (Ramat Gan, 1989) (Hebrew).

4. Israel Zamosc, *Nezed hadema*, vol. 3 (Dyhernfurth, 1773), 2.

5. Ibid., vol. 18, 1–2.

6. Shlomo Chelm, *Mirkevet hamishneh* (Frankfurt-am-Oder, 1751), Introduction. This description, like a similar one in *Nezed hadema*, was a subject of controversy between scholars, against whom the criticism was leveled. See Haim Lieberman, "How Hasidism Is Studied in Israel," in *Ohel Rahel*, vol. 1 (New York, 1979) (Hebrew); Gershom Scholem, "The Controversy About Chasidism and Its Leaders in *Nezed hadema*," *Zion* 20 (1955): 73–81; Mendel Piekarz, *The Beginning of Hasidism: Ideological Trends in Derush and Musar Literature* (Jerusalem, 1978), 331–33 (Hebrew).

7. Judah Hurwitz, *Amudei bet Yehudah* (Amsterdam, 1766), Introduction.

8. Ibid. About the significance of the polemic against the ecstatic religious phenomena, see Rachel Elior, "Natan Adler and the Frankfurt Pietists: Pietist Groups in Eastern and Central Europe During the Eighteenth Century," *Zion* 59 (1994): 31–64 (Hebrew).

9. Baruch Schick, *Sefer Euclids* (The Hague, 1780), Introduction. See Yosef Salmon, "Anti-Hasidic Polemic in Rabbi Barukh Schick of Shklov's Introduction to Uklides," in *Studies in Hasidism*, ed. David Assaf, Yosef Dan, and Immanuel Etkes (Jerusalem, 1999), 57–64 (Hebrew).

10. Judah Leib Margolioth, *Beit midot* (Shklov, 1786).

11. From the manuscript "Sela machloket," quoted here from Zevi Malachi's article "N. H. Ullman, Maskil and Philosopher," *Studies on the History of Dutch Jewry*, vol. 2 (Jerusalem, 1979), 77–88 (Hebrew). On Ullman, see A. Even-Chen, "Haskalah, Pragmatism, and Faith: The Philosophical Teachings of Naphtali Herz Ullman," Ph.D. dissertation, Hebrew University of Jerusalem, 1992, (Hebrew).

12. Judah Hurwitz, *Sadeh tevunah.*

13. Asher Anshel Worms, *Seyag laTorah* (Frankfurt a.m., 1766), general introduction.

14. Mordechai Gumpel Schnaber-Levison, *Ma'amar haTorah vehachokhmah* (London, 1771), 9.

15. Quotations taken from Malachi, "The Maskil and Philosopher N. H. Ullman."

16. N. H. Ullman, *Sefer chokhmat hashorashim* (The Hague, 1781).

17. Ibid., "The Author's Apology in Lieu of the Approbations."

18. The criticism of Gumpertz is included in Jacob Emden, *Mitpachat sefarim* (Lvov edition, 1871), 70–75.

19. Ibid., 75.

20. Jacob Emden, *Igeret bikoret*, vol. 1(first editions, 1736, 1765) (Zhitomir, 1867), 1.

21. On this matter and its later ramifications, see Moshe Samet, "Early Burial:

The History of the Controversy on Determining Time of Death," *Asufot* 3 (1988): 413–65 (Hebrew).

22. The correspondence is in Moses Mendelssohn, *Gesammelte Schriften*, vol. 19 (Stuttgart, 1971–88), 161–68, in particular 161–63.

23. On patrons, see M. Bodian, "The Jewish Entrepreneurs in Berlin and the Civil Improvement of the Jews in the 1780s and 1790s," *Zion* 49 (1983): 159–84 (Hebrew); Monika Richarz, *Der Eintritt der Juden in die akademischen Berufe* (Tübingen, 1974), 67–82; David Sorkin, "The Problem of Patronage and Institutionalization: Some Reflections on Haskalah and Some Remarks on the Armenians," in *Enlightenment and Diaspora: The Armenian and Jewish Cases*, ed. Richard G. Hovannisian and David N. Myers (Atlanta, 1999), 131–.;4. Meir Neumark wrote science books under the patronage of David Oppenheim; Isaac Wallich studied medicine in Halle under the patronage of the banker Asher Markus; Solomon Zalman Hanau was given patronage in Frankfurt-on-Main by Michael Oppenheim, the son of David Oppenheim of Vienna; Yonathan ben-Yosef lived in the home of the son-in-law of the court Jew Shimshon Wertheimer; Shimshon Hakaliri and Israel Zamosc found patrons in Berlin in the Ephraim and Itzig families; Raphael Levi was employed as a clerk by Shimon Wolf Oppenheimer in Hanover; Mendelssohn worked in Isaac Bernard's house of commerce; Ginzburg, the medical student in Göttingen, received housing and patronage, in the 1730s, in the home of the "community leader Eliah of Edinburgh"; and in the 1790s, Baruch Schick lived in the home of Joshua Zeitlin, a merchant and supplier to the government who had close ties to the ruling circles in Russia, at his estate in the Mohilav district.

24. See lists of subscribers: Abraham Joseph Mentz, *Reshit limudim* (Berlin, 1777); Baruch Schick, *Sefer yesod olam* (Berlin, 1776).

25. Naphtali Herz Wessely, *Shir dodim* (Berlin, 1777).

26. Solomon Maimon, *The Autobiography of Solomon Maimon*, trans. J. C. Murray (London, 1954), 189–90.

27. Mendelssohn, *Gesammelte Schriften*, vol. 19, 134–36 (the letter is dated February 9, 1770).

28. See Shmuel Feiner, "Isaac Euchel: Entrepreneur of the Haskalah Movement in Germany," *Zion* 52 (1987): 435 (Hebrew).

29. Correspondence in Mendelssohn, *Gesammelte Schriften*, vol. 19, 120–23.

30. Jacob Katz, *Tradition and Crisis* (New York, 1961), 302.

31. Mordechai Gumpel Schnaber-Levison, *Sefer tokhachat megillah*, vol. 1 (Hamburg, 1784), 1r.

32. *Hama'asef* 1 (1784): 163–66.

33. See Martin L. Davis, *Identity or History? Marcus Herz and the End of the Enlightenment* (Detroit, 1995).

34. See Gershom Scholem, "The Career of a Frankist: Moses Dobrushka and His Metamorphoses," in his *Studies and Sources Concerning the History of Sabbatianism and Its Metamorphoses* (Jerusalem, 1974), 160–63.

35. See Shmuel Feiner, "Mendelssohn and Mendelssohn's Disciples: A Re-examination," *Year Book of the Leo Baeck Institute* 40 (1995):133–67.

36. See Gerhard Alexander, "Isachar Falkensohn Behr," in *Aufklärung und Haskalah*, ed. Karlfried Gründer and Nathan Rotenstreich (Heidelberg, 1990), 57–66.

37. See Arthur Galliner, "Ephraim Kuh: Ein jüdisch-deutscher Dichter der Aufklärungzeit," *Bulletin des Leo Baeck Institute* 5 (1962): 189–201.

38. See Moritz Stern, "Jugendunterricht in der Berliner jüdischen Gemeinde wäh-

rend des 18. Jahrhunderts," *Jahrbuch der jüdisch-literarischen Gesellschaft* 19 (1928): 39–67; 20 (1929): 379–80.

39. See Frances Malino, *A Jew in the French Revolution: The Life of Zalkind Hurwitz* (Oxford, 1996).

40. The quotations are from *Divrei binah*, a book in manuscript form completed in 1780, and are taken from A. Y. Brawer, *Studies in Galician Jewry* (Jerusalem, 1956) (Hebrew),197–209, and from Dov Baer of Bolichov, *Zichronot R. Dov miBolichov* (Berlin, 1921), 45–46.

41. Judah Leib Margolioth, *Tal orot* (Frankfurt-am-Oder, 1810).

42. From Wessely's introduction to *Phädon*. See Moses Mendelssohn, *Phädon oder über die Unsterblichkeit der Seele in drey Gesprächen* (Berlin, 1767); trans. into Hebrew by Isaiah Beer of Metz as *Pha'edon: Hu sefer hasharat hanefesh* (Berlin, 1787).

Chapter 4. The Wessely Affair: Threats and Anxieties

1. The text of the sermon was first printed in an article by Louis Lewin: "Aus dem Jüdischen Kulturkampfe," *Jahrbuch der jüdisch-literarischen Gesellschaft* 12 (1918): 165–97. One of the copies distributed in manuscript from was copied in The Hague. See David Tevele, *Haderasha*, MS in Columbia University Library (photocopy in the National and University Library in Jerusalem, no. 16563). Rabbi Tevele's sermon was recently printed in Israel Nathan Heschel, "The View of the Great Rabbis of the Generation in Their War Against the Maskil, Naphtali Hertz Wessely, II" *Kovetz Beis Aaron ve'yesroel* 44 (1993): 121–31 (Hebrew). Heschel's article, written with an anti-maskilic Orthodox bias, does contain important documents, and in five installments reviews the chain of events in the polemic evoked by *Divrei shalom ve'emet*.

2. See Heinrich Graetz, "Wessely's Gegner," *Monatsschrift für Geschichte und Wissenschaft des Judentums* 20 (1871): 466–68.

3. On the possible involvement of the Vilna Gaon in the burning of *Divrei shalom ve'emet*, see Lewin, "Aus dem Jüdischen Kulturkampfe," 194–97; Moshe Samet, "M. Mendelssohn, N. H. Wessely, and the Rabbis of Their Generation," in *Research into the History of the Jewish People and the Land of Israel*, ed. A. Gilboa, B. Mevorach et al. (Haifa, 1970), 233–57 (Hebrew). On the struggle against the Hasidim in Vilna, see Mordechai Wilensky, *Hasidim and Mitnagedim: A Study of the Controversy Between Them in 1772–1815* (Jerusalem, 1970), 1–2 (Hebrew); Immanuel Etkes, *The Gaon of Vilna: The Man and His Image* (Jerusalem, 1998), chap. 3 (Hebrew).

4. Landau's (undated) letter to Vienna was printed from a manuscript by Heschel in "The View of the Great Rabbis, I," *Kovetz Beis Aaron ve'yesroel* 43 (1993): 162–65. The letter was written some time between the first day of Shevat and the beginning of Nisan, 1782.

5. Naphtali Hertz Wessely, *Divrei shalom ve'emet*, parts 1–4 (Berlin, 1782). The references here are to Kalman Schulman's edition, which includes all four parts of the book, including *Rav tuv livnei Israel* (Berlin 1782); *Ein mishpat* (Berlin, 1784); *Rechovot* (Berlin, 1785), and was published in Warsaw in 1886.

6. See Elisheva Carlebach, *The Pursuit of Heresy: Rabbi Moshe Hagiz and the Sabbatian Controversies* (New York, 1990).

7. On this see Shmuel Feiner, "The Dragon around the Bee-Hive: Judah Leib Margolioth and the Paradox of the Early Haskalah," *Zion* 53 (1998): 41–74 (Hebrew);

idem, "Between the 'Clouds of Foolishness' and the 'Light of Reason': Judah Hurwitz, an Early Eighteenth-Century Maskil," in *Within Hasidic Circles: Studies in Hasidism in Memory of Mordechai Wilsensky*, ed. I. Etkes, D. Asaf, I. Bartal, and E. Reiner (Jerusalem, 1999) (Hebrew).

8. Azriel Shohet, *Changing Eras: The Beginning of the Haskalah Among German Jewry* (Jerusalem, 1960) (Hebrew).

9. See Louis Lewin, *Geschichte der Juden in Lissa* (Pinne, 1904), 120–23, 192–201; Shlomo Tal, "The Cleves Divorce," *Sinai* 24 (1949): 152–67, 214–30 (Hebrew).

10. The Shabbat HaGadol sermon of Rabbi Tevele of Lissa, in Lewin, "Aus dem Jüdischen Kulturkampfe," 184.

11. Wessely, *Divrei shalom ve'emet*, 34–35.

12. See Jacob Katz, *Tradition and Crisis* (New York, 1961), chap. 18.

13. On the ideal of *Bildung* and its adoption by the maskilim, see David Sorkin, *The Transformation of German Jewry, 1780–1840* (Oxford, 1987), 15–18, 126–27.

14. Wessely, *Divrei shalom ve'emet*, 21–24. On the maskilic *musar* literature, see Harris Bor, "Enlightenment Values, Jewish Ethics: The Haskalah's Transformation of the Traditional Musar Genre," in *New Perspectives on the Haskalah*, ed. Shmuel Feiner and David Sorkin (London, 2001), 48–63.

15. Isaac Euchel, "Introduction," *Hame'asef* 4 (1787): 1–12.

16. Wessely, *Divrei shalom ve'emet*, 17–21.

17. Ibid., 5–6.

18. Rabbi Tevele's sermon, 185.

19. Ibid., 188.

20. On the significant change that occurred in the meaning of the term "man" (Mensch), see Jacob Katz, *Exclusiveness and Tolerance: Studies in Jewish-Gentile Relations in Medieval and Modern Times* (London, 1961), 170.

21. Wessely, *Divrei shalom ve'emet*, 5–6.

22. On Wessely's consciousness of an historical shift and the maskilim's invention of the "modern era," see Shmuel Feiner, *Haskalah and History: The Emergence of a Modern Jewish Historical Consciousness* (Oxford, 2002), chap. 1; idem, "The Invention of the Modern Age: A Chapter in the Rhetoric and Self-Image of the Haskalah," *Dappim: Research in Literature* 11 (1998): 9–29 (Hebrew).

23. Feiner, *Haskalah and History*, chap. 1.

24. Ibid., 32.

25. Ibid., 6.

26. Rabbi Tevele's sermon, 182–83.

27. Ibid., 188, 194.

28. Rabbi Hurwitz's sermon, in Heschel, "The View of the Great Rabbis," *Kovetz Beis Aaron ve'yesroel* 46 (1993): 150–51.

29. Rabbi Tevele's sermon, 188.

30. See Isser Woloch, *Eighteenth Century Europe: Tradition and Progress, 1715–1789* (New York, 1982); Jeremy Black, *Eighteenth Century Europe, 1700–1789* (London, 1992); John Merriman, *Modern Europe*, vol. 1, *From the Renaissance to the Age of Napoleon* (New York, 1996), part 3; Horst Möller, *Vernunft und Kritik, Deutsche Aufklärung im 17. Und 18. Jahrundert* (Frankfurt am Main, 1986).

31. See H. M. Scott, ed., *Enlightened Absolutism: Reform and Reformers in Late Eighteenth Century Europe* (London, 1990).

32. See Moshe Pelli, "Naphtali Hertz Wessely: Moderation in Transition," in

Pelli, *The Age of Haskalah: Studies in Hebrew Literature of the Enlightenment in Germany* (Leiden, 1979), 113–30; Edward Breuer, "Naphtali Hertz Wessely and Cultural Dislocations of an Eighteenth-Century Maskil," in *New Perspectives on the Haskalah*, 27–47.

33. Wessely, *Rav tuv livnei Israel*, 96–99.

34. The poems were not preserved, but Wessely writes about their composition in his letter to Elijah Morpurgo. See Isaac Rivkind, "Eliahu Morpurgo: Wessely's Aide in the Haskalah War, in Light of New Documents (with Introduction and Comments)," in *Studies in Jewish Bibliography and Related Subjects in Memory of Abraham Solomon Freidus* (New York, 1929), 138–59 (Hebrew).

35. The location and inscription on his grave: Yochanan Witkover, *Agadat perachim* (Altona, 1880), 303–4.

36. Wessely, *Rav tuv livnei Israel*, 83–86.

Chapter 5. Projects of Enlightenment and Tests of Tolerance

1. See Arthur Ruppin, *Die soziale Struktur der Juden* (Berlin, 1930), 67–75; Sergio Dellapergola, "Changing Patterns of Jewish Demography in the Modern World," *Studia Rosenthaliana* 23, 2 (1989): 154–67; Jonathan Israel, *European Jewry in the Age of Mercantilism, 1550–1750* (Oxford, 1991), chap. 10, actually notes negative demographic trends, although these only relate to the overall population in Central and Western Europe, and ignore the constant growth in the number of Jews in the important urban centers of Europe.

2. On these trends in eighteenth-century Jewry, see inter alia Azriel Shohet, *Changing Eras: The Beginning of the Haskalah Among German Jewry* (Jerusalem, 1960) (Hebrew); Steven M. Lowenstein, *The Berlin Jewish Community, Enlightenment, Family and Crisis, 1770–1830* (Oxford, 1994); T. M. Endelman, *The Jews of Georgian England (1714–1830): Tradition and Change in a Liberal Society* (Philadelphia, 1979; Ann Arbor, 1999); Israel, European Jewry.

3. See Shmuel Feiner, "The Modern Jewish Woman: A Test Case in the Relationship Between the Haskalah and Modernity," in *Sexuality and the Family in History*, ed. Israel Bartal and Isaiah Gafni (Jerusalem, 1998), 253–304 (Hebrew); Deborah Hertz, *Jewish High Society in Old Regime Berlin* (New Haven, 1988); Fromet's letter to Moses Mendelssohn, July 18, 1777, in Moses Mendelssohn, *Gesammelte Schriften*, vol. 19 (Stuttgart, 1974), 217–18.

4. On the Freischule, see Shmuel Feiner, "Educational Agendas and Social Ideals: Judische Freischule in Berlin, 1778–1825," n *Education and History, Cultural and Political Contexts*, ed. Rivka Feldhay and Immanuel Etkes (Jerusalem, 1999), 247–84 (Hebrew); Mordechai Eliav, *Jewish Education in Germany During the Haskalah and Emancipation* (Jerusalem, 1960), 71–79, 209–15 (Hebrew). All the documentation on the school and its broad historical contexts are collected in Ingrid Lohmann, *Die jüdische Freischule in Berlin (1778–1825), im Umfeld preußischer Bildungspolitik und jüdischer Kultusreform*, 2 vols. (Munich, 2001).

5. See F. Gedike, "Über Berlin," *Berlinische Monatsschrift* 1 (1784): 556–64; J. S. Krünitz, "Jude," *Ökonomisch-technologische Encyclopaedia*, vol. 21 (Berlin, 1784), 371–72.

6. See Friedrich Nicolai, *Beschreibung der königlichen Residenzstädte Berlin und Potsdam* (Berlin, 1786), 699–700; Selma Stern, *Der Preussische Staat und die Juden* (Tübingen, 1971), 345–48, 356–61; Ludwig Geiger, *Geschichte der Juden in Berlin*, vol. 2 (Berlin, 1871), 134–37; Jacob Jacobson, "Jüdische Spitzenklöpplerinnen im Netzedistrikt," *Zeitschrift für der Geschichte der Juden in Deutschland* 1 (1929): 154.

7. See an analysis of the interests of the wealthy elite, in M. Bodian, "The Jewish Entrepreneurs in Berlin and the Civil Improvement of the Jews in the 1780s and 1790s," *Zion* 49 (1983) 171–75 (Hebrew).

8. On the Itzig family, see Steven M. Lowenstein, "Jewish Upper Crust and Berlin Jewish Enlightenment: The Family of Daniel Itzig," in *From East and West: Jews in Changing Europe, 1750–1870*, ed. F. Malino and David Sorkin (Oxford, 1990), 182–201.

9. On Friedländer, see Michael Meyer, *The Origins of the Modern Jew: Jewish Identity and European Culture in Germany, 1749–1824* (Detroit, 1979), chap. 3; Eliav, *Jewish Education in Germany*, 61–67; Steven M. Lowenstein, *The Jewishness of David Friedländer and the Crisis of Berlin Jewry*, Braun Lectures in the History of the Jews in Prussia 3 (Bar-Ilan University, Ramat Gan, 1994).

10. See David Friedländer, *Lesebuch für jüdische Kinder: Zum Besten der jüdischen Freyschule* (Berlin, 1779). On the aims of the reader and the German models used in it, see Zohar Shavit, *D. Friedländer: Lesebuch für jüdische Kinder* (Frankfurt am Main, 1991); idem, "1779, David Friedländer and Moses Mendelssohn Publish the *Lesebuch für jüdische Kinder*," in *Yale Companion to Jewish Writing and Thought in German Culture, 1096–1996*, ed. Sander Gilman and Jack Zipes (New Haven, Conn., 1997), 68–74.

11. See Moritz Stern, "Die Konzession zur Errichtung der orientalischen Buchdruckerei und Buchhandlung in Berlin 1784," *Zeitschrift für die Geschichte der Juden in Deutschland* 6 (1935): 169.

12. Friedländer's translation: Wessely, *Worte der Wahrheit* (1782, another edition in 1798).

13. Naphtali Herz Wessely, *Rav tuv livnei Israel* (Berlin, 1782), 83–84.

14. *Hame'asef* (1784): 42–45, 61–63.

15. Cranz' sreport first appeared in German: Friedrich August Cranz, "Nachricht von dem Erziehungs-Institute der Jüdischen Nation," *Berlinische Correspondenz* 1, 4 (Berlin, 1782): 58–62.

16. John Locke, "A Letter Concerning Religious Toleration," trans. William Popple, 1689.

17. See Ernst Cassirer, *The Philosophy of the Enlightenment* (Princeton, N.J.,1979), 160–82.

18. Voltaire, *Philosophical Dictionary*, trans. T. Besterman (Harmondsworth, 1985), 387–89.

19. See Shmuel Ettinger, "The Beginnings of the Change in the Attitude of European Society to the Jews," in Ettinger, *Anti-Semitism in the Modern Era* (Tel-Aviv, 1978), 57–88; Meyer, *Origins of the Modern Jew*, 14–19; David Sorkin, "Jews, Enlightenment, and Religious Toleration: Some Reflections," *Year Book of the Leo Baeck Institute* 37 (1992): 3–16.

20. Locke, "Letter Concerning Toleration."

21. Jacob Katz, *From Prejudice to Destruction: Anti-Semitism, 1700–1933* (Cambridge, Mass., 1980), chaps. 3, 4.

22. Jacob Katz, *Tradition and Crisis* (New York, 1961), chap. 23.

23. Heinrich Graetz, *Geschichte der Juden von ältesten Zeiten bis auf Gegenwart*, vol. 9 (Leipzig, 1863–1902), 1–92.

24. Jacob Katz, *Exclusiveness and Tolerance: Studies in Jewish-Gentile Relations in Medieval and Modern Times* (London, 1961).

25. Jacob Katz, *Out of the Ghetto: The Social Background to the Jewish Emancipation, 1770–1870* (Cambridge, Mass., 1973), chap. 4.

26. On friendship as a value of the Enlightenment culture in Germany and about Mendelssohn and his friends, see L. Klaus Berghahn, "On Friendship: The Beginnings of a Christian-Jewish Dialogue in the Eighteenth Century," in *The German-Jewish Dialogue Reconsidered: A Symposium in Honor of George Mosse*, ed. Klaus L. Berghahn (New York, 1996), 5–24.

27. See Mendelssohn's letter to Aaron Gumpertz (June 1954), *Gesammelte Schriften*,. 12, 9–14; Alexander Altmann, *Moses Mendelssohn: A Biographical Study* (Philadelphia, 1973), 40–43.

28. The most detailed, in-depth survey of the Lavater affair is in Altmann, *Mendelssohn*, chap. 3. And see L. Klaus Berghahn, "Lavater's Attempt to Compel the Conversion of Moses Mendelssohn Abuses the Friendship Cult Surrounding Jewish and Christian Intellectuals," in *Yale Companion to Jewish Writing and Thought*, ed. Gilman and Zipes, 61–67.

29. Mendelssohn's letter to Lavater, in Mendelssohn, *Jerusalem and Other Jewish Writings*, trans. and ed. Alfred Jospe (New York, 1969), 113–27.

30. Ibid., 116.

31. Ibid., 117. See Jacob Katz, "The Vicissitude of Three Apologetic Passages," *Zion* 23–24 (1957–58): 175–93; idem, *Exclusiveness and Tolerance: Studies in Jewish-Gentile Relations in Medieval and Modern Times* (London, 1961), chap. 14.

32. Mendelssohn, letter to Lavater, *Jerusalem*, 120.

33. Ibid., 118.

34. Isaac Euchel, *Toledot rabbenu Moshe ben Menachem* (Berlin, 1789). Here from the 1813 Vienna edition, 39. On the end of the Lavater affair and Mendelssohn's illness, see Altmann, *Moses Mendelssohn*, 223–95.

35. Mendelssohn, *Gesammelte Schriften*, 12/2, 200 (letter to Peter Adolph Winkopp, dated July 28, 1780).

36. The translation and commentary were printed only at the end of the nineteenth century by Issac Fuchs. See Wessely's translation of Mendelssohn's letter to Lavater, in *Mikhtav leHacohen Lavater*, with introduction and comments by Isaac Solomon Fuchs (Berlin, 1892). See also *Magid Mishneh*, supplement to issue 37 (1890), letter by Solomon Mandelkern to Fuchs.

37. Gotthold Ephraim Lessing, *Nathan der Weise* (Stuttgart, 1990), Act II, 50.

38. On *Nathan the Wise*, see Altmann, *Mendelssohn*, 569–82; Chaim Shoham, *"Nathan the Wise" Among His Own* (Tel-Aviv, 1981) (Hebrew).

39. See Robert Liberles, "From Toleration to Verbesserung: German and Jewish Debates on the Jews in the Eighteenth Century," *Central European History* 22, 1 (1989): 8.

40. The letter is quoted in Altmann, *Mendelssohn*, 453.

41. Wessely, *Rav tuv livnei Israel*, 97.

42. On Dohm and his work, see Altmann, *Mendelssohn*, 474–49; Robert Liberles, "Dohm's Treatise on the Jews: A Defence of the Enlightenment," *Year Book of the Leo Baeck Institute* 33 (1988): 29–42; Peter Erspamer, "1781, The Publication of Christian Wilhelm von Dohm's *On the Civic Improvement of the Jews* Prompts Widespread Public Debate on the Jewish Question by Both Jews and Gentiles," in *Yale Companion to Jewish Writing and Thought*, ed. Gilman and Zipes, 75–83.

43. See Dohm, *Übur die bürgerliche Verbesserung,* 2: 151–52.

44. Ibid., 1: 39.

45. Ibid., 1: 26–28.

46. Ibid., 1: 119.

47. Preface to Menasseh ben Israel, *Teshu'at Israel,* in Moses Mendelssohn, *Gesammelte Schriften,* 8: 1–25.

48. Altmann, *Mendelssohn,* 455–57.

49. The Edicts of Toleration were printed in Francois A. Pribram, *Urkunden und Akten zur Geschichte der Juden in Wien* (Wien-Leipzig, 1918). See Altmann, *Mendelssohn,* 461–63; Joseph Karniel, *Der Toleranzpolitik Kaiser Josephs II* (Stuttgart, 1986).

50. The letter is quoted in Altmann, *Mendelssohn,* 462. Mendelssohn's letter to Nicolai, February 8, 1782, in Mendelssohn, *Gesammelte Schriften,* 13: 131.

51. Naphtali Herz Wessely, *Divrei shalom ve'emet* (Berlin, 1782), 15–16.

52. Mendelssohn, Preface to *Teshu'at Israel,* in *Gesammelte Schriften,* 13: 4.

53. Ibid., 5.

54. Ibid., 16–25.

55. Ibid., 24–25.

56. See Jacob Katz, "Rabbi Raphael Cohen: Moses Mendelssohn's Opponent," in *Divine Law in Human Hands: Case Studies in Halakhic Flexibility* (Jerusalem, 1998), 191–215.

57. Mendelssohn's letter to Avigdor Levi, May 25, 1779, Mendelssohn, *Gesammelte Schriften,* 19: 251–53.

58. Mendelssohn's letter to Hennings, June 29, 1779, Ibid., 12/2,: 149.

59. On the *Bi'ur,* see Altmann, *Mendelssohn,* 368–83; Perez Sandler, *Mendelssohn's Edition of the Pentateuch* (Jerusalem, 1984) (Hebrew); Edward Breuer, *The Limits of the Enlightenment: Jews, Germans, and the Enlightenment Study of Scripture* (Cambridge, Mass., 1996). David Sorkin, *Moses Mendelssohn and the Religious Enlightenment* (London, 1996), 53–89.

60. Mendelssohn, *Or lanetivah;* here, according to Mendelssohn, *Gesammelte Schriften,* 15: 243–47.

61. See Steven M. Lowenstein, "The Readership of Mendelssohn's Bible Translation," *Hebrew Union College Annual* 52 (1982): 179–213.

62. Wessely, *Mehalel re'a,* printed at the beginning of *Netivot hashalom* (Berlin, 1783), but already written in 1778. See Mendelssohn, *Gesammelte Schriften,* 15: 8–15.

63. Wessely, *Mehalel re'a,* 9–10.

64. Mendelssohn's letter to Avigdor Levi, May 25, 1779, Mendelssohn, *Gesammelte Schriften* 19: 251–253.

65. Mendelssohn's letter to Avigdor Levi, 1781, 278–79; Altmann, *Mendelssohn,* 396–97. Moshe S. Samet, "M. Mendelssohn, N. H. Wessely, and the Rabbis of Their Generation," in *Research into the History of the Jewish People and the Land of Israel,* ed. A. Gilboa, B. Mevorach, et al., vol. 1 (Haifa, 1970), 233–57 (Hebrew), tends to downplay Landau's opposition (240–41). However, the content of Landau's approbation for the five Books of the Torah that Shlomo Dubno attempted to publish himself, in 1783–84, indicates that he was apprehensive about Mendelssohn's *Bi'ur.* In it, Landau claims that Mendelssohn did ask him for an approbation and he refused because "In that work, the sacred and the secular were conjoined, since a commentary in a foreign tongue was appended to the Torah, which the author called a German translation, and we were fearful that this would create an obstacle for Jewish children and lead them to neglect their study of Torah" (Sandler, *Mendelssohn's Edition of the Pentateuch,* 196).

66. Correspondence between Hennings and Mendelssohn, Mendelssohn, *Gesammelte Schriften*, 12/2: 145–65; Altmann, *Mendelssohn*, 383–86.

67. *Staats und Gelehrte Zeitung des hamburgischen unpartheyischen Corresponden-ten*, July 17, 1779, 4. On the denial issued from Berlin see Altmann, *Mendelssohn*, 387–88.

68. Mendelssohn to Hennings, September 20, 1779, ibid., 166; Altmann, *Mendelssohn*, 392.

69. Wessely, manuscript (Ginzburg Collection, Moscow; Department of Manuscripts, National and University Library in Jerusalem), 228–35.

70. On the Posner affair, see Katz, "Rabbi Raphael Cohen"; Altmann, *Mendelssohn*, 473.

71. The writ of excommunication dated the 8th day of Tamuz, 1780 is quoted in Katz, "Rabbi Raphael Cohen,"Appendix C.

72. It is hard to accept Katz's opinion that Rabbi Kohen had in this case come up against a breaker with tradition who had already been influenced by maskilic trends. Public criticism like that voiced by Posner about some of the Sages' instructions was not typical of the Haskalah, but much more characteristic of the Jewish bourgeoisie that had become accustomed to religious permissiveness.

73. The memorandum was published anonymously in Berlin in 1781 like many of Cranz's polemic and critical writings. See August Friedrich Cranz, *Über den Missbrauch der geistlichen Macht oder der weltlichen Herrschaft in Glaubenssachen durch Beispiele aus dem jetsigen Jahrhundert ins Licht gesetst* (Berlin, 1781).

74. Ibid., 52–59.

75. Moses Mendelssohn, Preface to *Menasshe ben Israel*, in *Gesammelte Schriften*, 8.

76. Ibid.

77. Ibid.

Chapter 6. The Rabbinical Elite on the Defensive

1. See Jacob Katz, "To Whom Was Mendelssohn Replying in *Jerusalem*?" *Zion* 29 (1964): 112–32 (Hebrew).

2. Shmuel Feiner, "Isaac Euchel: Entrepreneur of the Haskalah Movement in Germany," *Zion* 52 (1987): 427–69 (Hebrew).

3. The pamphlet was published anonymously. See Isaac Euchel, *Sefat emet* (Königsberg, 1782). Euchel revealed his authorship and the date of publication in his autobiographical letter to the king of Denmark in 1784.

4. Euchel, *Sefat emet*, 9–10.

5. On this affair, see Alexander Altmann, *Moses Mendelssohn: A Biographical Study* (Philadelphia, 1973), 474–89; Moshe S. Samet, M. Mendelssohn, N. H. Wessely, and the Rabbis of Their Generation," in *Research into the History of the Jewish People and the Land of Israel*, ed. A. Gilboa, B. Mevorach, et al. (Haifa, 1970) (Hebrew); Israel Nathan Heschel, "The View of the Great Rabbis of the Generation in Their War Against the Maskil, Naphtali Herz Wessely, II," *Kovetz Beis Aaron ve'Yisrael* 8 (1993): 121–31; Mordechai Eliav, *Jewish Education in Germany During the Haskalah and Emancipation* (Jerusalem, 1960), chap. 1 (Hebrew).

6. The first sermon has not been preserved, but Rabbi Landau mentioned it on several occasions and there is no doubt that it was delivered. Rabbi Landau's letter,

intended to enlist other rabbis in the struggle, is an extremely harsh one, containing derogatory remarks about Wessely. It is published in Heschel, "The View of the Great Rabbis, II."

7. The sermon was printed years later; see Yehezkel Landau, *Derushei hatzelach* (Warsaw, 1886), Sermon 39, 53: 1–54.

8. For Rabbi Tevele's sermon, see Louis Lewin, "Aus dem Jüdischen Kulturkampfe," *Jahrbuch der jüdisch-literarischen Gesellschaft* 12 (1918): 182–84.

9. Naphtali Herz Wessely, *Ein mishpat* (Berlin, 1784), 130.

10. Naphtali Herz Wessely, *Rav tuv livnei Israel* (Berlin, 1782), 44. Wessely only mentioned the names of these rabbis in a personal letter to the heads of the Trieste community sent on May 7, 1782. The letter was printed in *Kerem chemed* 1 (1833): 5–7. Supplements containing the names of the three rabbis are in M. Güdemann, "Die Gegner Hartwig Wessely," *Monatsschrift für Geschichte und Wissenschaft des Judentums* 19 (1870): 478–80. See Altmann, *Mendelssohn*, 482; Isaac Rivkind, "Eliahu Morpurgo, Wessely's Aide in the Haskalah War, in Light of New Documents (with Introduction and Comments)," in *Studies in Jewish Bibliography and Related Subjects in Memory of Abraham Solomon Freidus* (New York, 1929), 150–52 (Hebrew).

11. Zedlitz's letter to Daniel Itzig, dated March 30, 1782, is cited in M. Kayserling, *Moses Mendelssohn: Sein Leben und Wirken* (Leipzig, 1888), 311. A second letter was transmitted by Zedlitz to the heads of the Berlin community about a month later (June 4, 1782), in which he continued to request information in the hope that no harm would be done to Wessely (312).

12. In a special article written as a reply to the question as to how best to grapple with prejudice, he objected to the use of Voltairean methods and the weapon of satire, arguing that the origin of all evil can be blocked through *Aufklärung*, not by strong-arm tactics. See "Soll man der einreissenden Schwaermerey durch Satyre oder durch äussere Verbindung entgegenarbeiten?" Moses Mendelssohn, *Gesammelte Schriften*, 6/1: 135–41.

13. Mendelssohn's letter to David Friedländer, April 17, 1782, *Gesammelte Schriften*, 13: 178.

14. On the Italian context of the Wessely affair, see Lois C. Dubin, "Trieste and Berlin: The Italian Role in the Cultural Politics of the Haskalah," in *Toward Modernity: The European Jewish Model*, ed. Jacob Katz (New Brunswick, N.J., 1987),189–224; idem, *The Port Jews of Habsburg Trieste, Absolutist Politics and Enlightenment Culture* (Stanford, Calif., 1999).

15. Wessely, *Rav tuv livnei Israel*, 76–77.

16. Ibid., 44, 58.

17. Ibid., 46–47.

18. Ibid., 113–15.

19. Ibid., 116–18.

20. Mendelssohn's letter to Galico was first published in Ben Zion Dinaburg (Dinur), "Mendelssohn and the Quarrel About Wessely's Book *Divrei shalom ve'emet*," *Kiryat Sefer* 2 (1925): 155–57 (Hebrew). The letter is also contained in *Gesammelte Schriften* 19: 281–82.

21. Wessely, letter to the leaders of the Trieste community, May 7, 1782, printed in *Kerem Chemed* 1 (1833): 5–7.

22. Hennings's letter to Mendelssohn, April 27, 1782, in Mendelssohn, *Gesammelte Schriften*, 13: 35.

23. See "Hartwig Wessely in Berlin," in *Charackteristik edler und merkwürdiger Menschen nebst einzelnen schönen Charackterzügen*, ed. Friedrich Wilhelm Wolfrat, vol. 1 (Halle, 1791), 202.

24. Yehezkel Landau's letter from Prague to Rabbi Zevi Hirsch Levin in Berlin, June, 1782, was published in Heschel, "The View of the Great Rabbis," 123–24.

25. Wessely's letter to Trieste, 6.

26. Letter to the Lissa congregation in the collection of the Rosenthaliana Library in Amsterdam (Hs.Ros. 549).

27. Wessely's letter to Trieste, June 28, 1782: "And leading members of this community have already written to the congregations of Lissa and Posen protesting severely the actions of their rabbis." The letter is published in Rivkind, "Eliahu Morpurgo, Wessely's Aide in the Haskalah War," 152.

28. See Josef Meisl, *Protokolbuch der jüdischen Gemeinde Berlin (1723–1854)* (Jerusalem, 1962), 324–26.

29. On Lissa and the aristocratic Polish family that ruled it, see Louis Lewin, *Geschichte der Juden in Lissa* (Pinne, 1904).

30. All these quotations are from "the letter of the seven" from Berlin to the Lissa community.

31. See Friedrich August Cranz, *Das Foreschen nach Licht und Recht, in einem Schreiben an Herrn Moses Mendelssohn auf Veranlassung seiner merkwürdigen Vorrede zu Menasse Ben Israel* (Berlin, 1782). On Cranz and his pamphlet see Altmann, *Mendelssohn*, 513–16.

32. See Cranz, *Über den Missbrauch der geistlichen Macht und der weltlichen Herrschaft in Glaubenssachen durch Beispiele aus dem jetsigen Jahrhundert ins Licht gesetst*, vol. 2 (Berlin, 1781).

33. On Cranz see *Allgemeine Deutsche Biographie*, vol. 4 (Leipzig, 1876), 564–65. And compare Jacob Katz, "To Whom Was Mendelssohn Replying in *Jerusalem*?" *Zion* 29 (1964): 112–32 (Hebrew); idem, "To Whom Was Mendelssohn Replying in *Jerusalem*?" (Continuation) *Zion* 36 (1971), 116–17 (Hebrew); Altmann, *Mendelssohn*, 511–13.

34. Cranz, *Über den Missbrauch der geistlichen*, 2: 4.

35. Ibid., 32–33, 56–60.

36. "To the honorable . . . lay leaders of the Berlin community, and at their head, the exalted Rabbi . . . Zevi Hirsch, head of the rabbinical court, state rabbi, and chief of the community . . . from R. Tevele here at the Lissa community," undated, Rosenthaliana library. The letter was printed in "Igrot," *Tzefunot* 5, 2 (1993): 100–101.

37. "I call upon you men . . . men of renown and wealthy lay leaders . . . of the Berlin community and first among them the great light . . . head of the religious court and state rabbi . . . from your beloved friend R. Yehezkel Landau," apparently July 1782. A copy of the letter is in the Rosenthaliana library. The letter was printed in Heschel, "The View of the Great Rabbis, III," and in Simcha Asaf, *Sources for the History of Jewish Education* (Tel-Aviv, 1954), 239–40 (Hebrew). See Marc Saperstein, "1782 ('Shabbat ha-Gadol,' 5542) Chief Rabbi Ezekiel Landau Responds to the Austrian Emperor's Edict of Toleration (Toleranzpatent)," in *Yale Companion to Jewish Writing and Thought in German Culture, 1096–1996*, ed. Sander Gilman and Jack Zipes (New Haven, Conn., 1997), 84–87.

38. All the quotations are from Landau's letter to Berlin.

39. Wessely's letter to the leaders of the Trieste community, 1781, in Rivkind, "Eliahu Morpurgo, Wessely's Aide in the Haskalah War," 151–52.

40. Excerpts from Rabbi Hurwitz's sermon have been published in various places: first in Heinrich Graetz, "Wessely's Gegner," *Monatsschrift für Geschichte und Wissenschaft des Judentums* 20 (1871): 466–68; recently in Israel Nathan Heschel, "The View of the Great Rabbis, V," *Kovetz Beis Aaron ve'Yisrael* 8 (1993): 150–51.

41. Rabbi Hurwitz's letter to Rabbi Tevele, 6th of Tammuz, 1782, first printed in Akiva Yosef Schlesinger, *Lev ha'ivri*, vol. 2 (Lvov, 1870), 29, and again in Heschel, "The View of the Great Rabbis, V," 154–55. On Rabbi Hurwitz's involvement in the affair, see also Samet, "M. Mendelssohn, N. H. Wessely, and the Rabbis of Their Generation," 246–48; Altmann, *Mendelssohn*, 485–86.

42. Mendelssohn's letter to Wolf Dessau, July 11, 1782, in *Gesammelte Schriften* 13: 69–70.

43. "Countless felicitations to the exalted sirs . . . lay leaders of the Berlin community, from your loyal servant, Zevi Hirsch, 13th day of Av, 1782" (no date appears on the letter but it is dated according to the letter of reply sent to Rabbi Levin). A complete copy of the letter is in the Rosenthaliana Library in Amsterdam.

44. A copy of this letter, too, which was sent by the heads of the Berlin community to Rabbi Levin, on the 11th day of Elul, 1782, is in the collection of letters found in the Rosenthaliana Library. The letter has been printed in "Igrot," *Tzefunot* 5, 2 (1993): 101–2 (with several slight errors). The delay in the reply to Rabbi Levin (about four weeks after he left Berlin) was probably due to the absence from Berlin of several heads of the community who were away on business.

45. Letter from Berlin to Rabbi Levin.

46. Peter Adolph Winkopp, "Fortsetzung der Karakteristik der Sitten Berlins," *Bibliothek fuer Denker* 2, 1 (1783): 3–19.

47. See Gedalia Yogev, *Diamonds and Coral: Anglo-Dutch Jews and Eighteenth-Century Trade* (Leicester, 1978), 268.

48. Rabbi David Tevil Schiff's letter to his brother, the *dayan* Meir, 20th of Elul, 1782, printed in Charles Duschinsky, *The Rabbinate of the Great Synagogue, London from 1756–1842* (London, 1921), 177–78.

49. "To lay leaders of the Berlin community . . . from your brother who seeks your welfare and good in all times, is greatly troubled and awaits salvation, Rabbi Zevi Hircsh," undated, apparently at the end of Elul, 1782; a copy is in the Rosenthaliana Library. The letter has been printed in "Igrot," *Tzefunot* 5, 2 (1993): 102–3.

50. On this consequence of the Wessely affair, which marked a turning point in relations between the well-established conservative leadership and its new rivals, and deepened the chasm between them, see Jacob Katz, *Out of the Ghetto: The Social Background to the Jewish Emancipation, 1770–1870* (Cambridge, Mass., 1973), 140–57, in particular 146–48.

Chapter 7. On Religious Power and Judaism

1. For a bibliography of Saul Berlin's writings and studies on him, see Moshe Samet, "Rabbi Saul Berlin and His Works," *Kiryath Sefer* 43 (June 1968) (Hebrew). Many studies on Berlin and his writings have been published by Moshe Pelli. He also referred in his notes to many other writings dealing with this issue. See Pelli, "Saul Berlin's *Ktav Yosher*: The Beginning of Satire in Modern Hebrew Literature of the Haskalah in Germany," *Year Book of the Leo Baeck Institute* 20 (1975); idem, "Aspects

of Hebrew Enlightenment Satire—Saul Berlin: Involvement and Detachment," *Year Book of the Leo Baeck Institute* 22 (1977): 93–107; idem, *The Age of Haskalah: Studies in Hebrew Literature of the Enlightenment in Germany* (Leiden, 1979), 171–89; Idem, *Struggle for Change: Studies in the Hebrew Enlightenment in Germany at the End of the 18th Century* (Tel-Aviv, 1988), 141–65 (Hebrew).

2. Saul Berlin, *Ktav Yosher* (Berlin, 1794). Since it was mentioned by Wessely in *Rehovot* (the fourth pamphlet he published in his *Divrei shalom ve'emet* series), *Ktav Yosher* was written in 1785 at the earliest. The satire was printed again in an annotated edition with an introduction: Yehudah Friedlander, *Studies in Hebrew Satire*, vol. 1 (Tel-Aviv, 1979), 66–119 (Hebrew). The writer of an anonymous review in *Hame'asef* gave clear hints as to the author's identity in "A Review of New Books, *Ktav Yosher*," *Hame'asef* 7 (1796): 267–71: "The author of this book remains anonymous . . . but the reviewer knows who he is, for he is one of the greats of the generation, a rabbi, a rabbinic scholar, and a great *chakham*." He did not print the book during his lifetime "because he feared for his life lest he be penalized with excommunication" and hence he fled to London (signed "D"). See an analysis of Berlin's satire in Meir Gilon, "The Riddle in Saul Berlin's *Ktav Yosher*, Trying to Solve It," *Proceedings of the Eleventh Congress on Jewish Studies*, Div. C, 3 (Jerusalem, 1994), 69–76 (Hebrew).

3. For an analysis of Saul Berlin's literary methods, see Friedlander, *Studies in Hebrew Satire*, 65–85.

4. All quotes are from *Ktav Yosher*, the Friedlander edition.

5. For a detailed interpretation of the allegory in the last chapter of *Ktav Yosher* (for example, Mendelssohn as the Kabbalistic rabbi), see Gilon, "The Riddle in Saul Berlin's *Ktav yosher*."

6. Moses Mendelssohn, *Jerusalem*, in *Gesammelte Schriften*, 8: 99–204. Here, from English edition, *Jerusalem and Other Jewish Writings*, trans. and ed. Alfred Jospe (New York, 1969), 109–10. In a letter to Herz Homberg (September 22, 1783), Mendelssohn's skepticism reached its peak and he expressed the fear that a secret plot to attract the Jews to Christianity lay behind the Edicts of Toleration. See Mendelssohn, *Gesammelte Schriften*, 13: 132–34.

7. Mendelssohn, *Jerusalem* (English), 108; Preface to *Menassah ben Israel*, in *Gesammelte Schriften*, 13: 3. His concerns were exacerbated by news from America that the Church was asking for special rights in Virginia: "Alas, we can hear even the American Congress intone the old song once again when it speaks of a "dominant religion" (168, n. 43).

8. August Cranz, *Das Foreschen nach Licht und Recht, in einem Schreiben an Herrn Moses Mendelssohn auf Veranlassung seiner merkwürdigen Vorrede zu Menasse Ben Israel* (Berlin, 1782), 40–41.

9. Mendelssohn, *Jerusalem* (English), 57.

10. Hennings's letter to Mendelssohn, April 27, 1782, in Mendelssohn, *Gesammelte Schriften*, 13: 35–41.

11. Alexander Altmann, *Moses Mendelssohn: A Biographical Study* (Philadelphia, 1973), 489–513.

12. Jacob Katz, "To Whom Was Mendelssohn Replying in *Jerusalem*?" *Zion* 29 (1964): 112–32 (Hebrew); idem, "To Whom Was Mendelssohn Replying in *Jerusalem*?" (Continuation), *Zion* 36 (1971): 116–17 (Hebrew).

13. Arkush stated that Cranz did not intend to persuade Mendelssohn to acknowledge the truths of Christianity. See Allan Arkush, *Moses Mendelssohn and the Enlightenment* (New York, 1994), 161.

14. Cranz, *Das Foreschen nach Licht und Recht.* The footnote in which he refers to his tract against Rabbi Kohen, which also helps to indubitably identify him as the author, appears on pp. 20–21.

15. Mendelssohn, *Jerusalem* (English), 23.

16. Ibid., 106.

17. Ibid., 57.

18. Ibid., 100–102.

19. Ibid., 61.

20. Ibid., 71.

21. See ibid., 104: "Indeed, I cannot see how those who were born into the household of Jacob can in good conscience exempt themselves from the observance of the law. We are permitted to reflect on the law, to search for its meaning, and occasionally, where the Lawgiver himself provides no reason [for a particular law], to surmise that it must perhaps be understood in terms of a particular time, place and set of circumstances. Therefore, the law can perhaps also be changed according to the requirements of a particular time, place, and set of circumstances, but only if and when it pleases the supreme Lawgiver to let us recognize His will—to make it known to us just as openly, publicly, and beyond any possibility of doubt and uncertainty, as He did when He gave us the law itself. As long as this has not happened, as long as we can show no such authentic dispensation from the law, no sophistry of ours can free us from the strict obedience we owe to it. Reverence for God must draw a line between speculation and observance, beyond which no conscientious person may go."

22. Ibid., 104. Several different interpretations have been given to *Jerusalem*; among the most interesting are: Michael Meyer, *The Origins of the Modern Jew, Jewish Identity and European Culture in Germany, 1749–1824* (Detroit, 1979), chap. 2.; Altmann, *Mendelssohn*, 514–52; Arkush, *Mendelssohn and the Enlightenment*; David Sorkin, *Moses Mendelssohn and the Religious Enlightenment* (London, 1996), chaps. 8–9. See also David Sorkin, "The Mendelssohn Myth and Its Method," *New German Critique* 77 (1999): 7–28; Allan Arkush, "The Questionable Judaism of Moses Mendelssohn," *New German Critique* 77 (1999): 29–44.

23. Mendelssohn's letter to Johann Zimmermann, September 1, 1784, in *Gesammelte Schriften*, 13: 221–23; Mendelssohn's letter to Herz Homberg, November 20, 1784, ibid., 233–234.

24. See Altmann, *Mendelssohn*, 517.

25. He spoke of this in a letter to Herz Homberg dated June 14, 1783. See Altmann, *Mendelssohn*, 516.

26. Abraham Meladola, "Likhvod HaRambman (Moses Mendelssohn)," *Hame'asef* 2 (1785): 81–84.

27. Judah Leib Margolioth, *Atzei eden* (here from the Königsberg edition, 1858).

28. The biography appeared in 1789 in Isaac Euchel's book *Toledot rabbenu Moshe ben Menachem.*

29. Margolioth, *Atzei eden*, 1: 2.

30. Ibid., 7: 2.

31. Ibid., 7: 2–8: 1.

32. Ibid., 8: 1.

33. Ibid., 8:2.

34. The sermons are contained in two collections: Eleazar Fleckeles, *Olat chodesh rishon* (Prague, 1785) and idem, *Olat chodesh sheni* (Prague, 1793). On Fleckeles, see

Jacob Katz, *Out of the Ghetto: The Social Background to the Jewish Emancipation, 1770–1870* (Cambridge, Mass., 1973), 145–47; S. H. Lieben, "Rabbi Eleaser Fleckeles." *Jahrbuch der jüdisch-literarischen Gesellschaft* 10 (1913), 1–33.

35. Sermon delivered during the Ten Days of Penitence, 1784 in the Klois Synagogue in Prague, in Fleckeles, *Olat chodesh sheni*, sermon 1, section 5.

36. The approbation was printed in *Hama'asef* 3 (1786): 142–44.

37. Fleckeles, *Olat chodesh sheni*, section 3.

38. Ibid.

39. Ten Days of Penitence sermon, 1784, *Olat chodesh sheni*, sermon 5, section 14.

40. Ibid.

41. [David Friedländer], *Sendschreiben an Seine Hochwürden, Herrn Oberconsistorialrath und Probst Teller zu Berlin von einigen Hausvätern jüdischen Religion* (Berlin, 1799); see chapter 12 below.

42. See *Isaak Alexander. Schriften, Ein Beitrag zur Frühaufklärung im deutschen Judentum*, ed. Anja Speicher (Frankfurt am Main, 1998); Altmann, *Mendelssohn*, 831, n. 27.

43. See M. Kayserling, "Ein vergessener Zeitgenosse Mendelssohns," *Monatsschrift für Geschichte und Wissenschaft des Judentums* 16 (1867): 161–67.

44. *Salomo und Joseph II: Mit einer Einleitung von Isaak Alexander zu Regensburg, Wien, 1782*, in Speicher, *Isaak Alexander*, 161–202.

45. Review of *Salomo und Joseph II*, by Isaac Alexander, *Hame'asef* 1 (1784): 19–20 (German supplement).

46. Elijah Morpurgo's letter to Rabbi Jacob Danon of Constantinople, 28th of Tevet, 1784, Isaac Rivkind, "Eliahu Morpurgo, Wessely's Aide in the Haskalah War, in Light of New Documents (with Introduction and Comments)," in *Studies in Jewish Bibliography and Related Subjects in Memory of Abraham Solomon Freidus* (New York, 1929), 158–59 (Hebrew).

47. Wessely, *Ein mishpat* (Berlin, 1784), "Third Epistle, written to our brethren, the Israelites, in all their places of habitation . . . it includes some words of truth, by seven men of reason, all great scholars, rabbinical authorities, rabbis, and teachers in the sacred communities of the cities of Italy . . . We have given this epistle the name 'The Fountain of Judgment' . . ." (here based on the 1886 Warsaw edition).

48. Ibid., 129, 132.

49. Ibid., 133.

50. See Lois C. Dubin, *The Port Jews of Habsburg Trieste: Absolutist Politics and Enlightenment Culture* (Stanford, Calif., 1999).

51. Wessely, *Ein mishpat*, 139.

52. Ibid., 200–201.

53. Wessely, *Rehovoth* (Berlin, 1785): "Fourth Epistle, also written to our Jewish brethren . . . it will elucidate what is written in my epistle, and show the rightness of all that was said . . . Hence I have called it Rehovoth." The epistle was signed by Wessely on the 22nd day of Sivan, 1785 (here, based on the 1886 Warsaw edition).

54. Ibid., 360–61.

55. Ibid., 363–65.

56. Wessely's letter to Elijah Morpurgo (probably 1784), manuscript (Ginzburg Collection, Moscow; Department of Manuscripts at the National and University Library in Jerusalem), 218.

57. Letter from Wessely to Elijah Morpurgo, 18th day of Shevat 1786, in Meir Letteris, ed., *Avnei nezer*, vol. 3 (Vienna, 1853), 3–5.

Chapter 8. The Society of Friends of the Hebrew Language

1. Letter from Chevrat Dorshei Leshon Ever, from Königsberg, to Wessely in Berlin, 21st day of Tevet, 1782, printed in *Nachel habesor* (Königsburg, 1782): 4–6.

2. See Lynn Hunt, ed., *The New Cultural History* (Berkeley, Calif., 1989); Joseph Mali, "The Poetics and Politics of Modern Historiography: An Introduction," in *Literature and History*, ed. Raya Cohen and Joseph Mali (Jerusalem, 1999), 9–32 (Hebrew); Ouzi Elyada, "The 'Annales' School and the Culture of the Book," in *Literature and History*, ed. Cohen and Mali, 299–323.

3. See Jürgen Habermas, *The Structural Transformation of the Public Sphere*, trans. T. Burger (Cambridge, Mass., 1998); Keith M. Baker, "Defining the Public Sphere in Eighteenth Century France: Variations on a Theme by Habermas," in *Habermas and the Public Sphere*, ed. Craig Calhoun (Cambridge, Mass., 1994), 181–211; Dena Goodman, *The Republic of Letters: A Cultural History of the French Enlightenment* (Ithaca, N.Y., 1994); Dorinda Outram, *The Enlightenment* (Cambridge, 1995), chap. 2; Margaret C. Jacob, *Living the Enlightenment: Freemasonary and Politics in Eighteenth-Century Europe* (New York, 1991); James van Horn Melton, *The Rise of the Public in Enlightenment Europe* (Cambridge, 2001).

4. Quoted in Roger Chartier, *The Cultural Origins of the French Revolution*, trans. Lydia G. Cochrane (Durham, N.C., 1991), 30–31.

5. See David Sorkin, "Emancipation and Assimilation: Two Concepts and Their Application to German-Jewish History," *Year Book of the Leo Baeck Institute* 35 (1990): 17–33. For two important attempts to investigate the texture of the inner life of the Berlin community from a social and cultural standpoint, see Steven M. Lowenstein, *The Berlin Jewish Community: Enlightenment, Family and Crisis, 1770–1830* (Oxford, 1994); Deborah Hertz, *Jewish High Society in Old Regime Berlin* (New Haven, Conn., 1988).

6. Wessely's letter to Dorshei Leshon Ever, 4th day of Shevat, 1782, published in *Nachal habesor*, 6–10.

7. See Otto Dann, *Lesegesellschaften und bürgerliche Emanzipation* (Munich, 1981); Herbert G. Göpfert, "Lesegesellschaften im 18. Jahrhundert," in *Aufklärung, Absolutismus und Bürgertum in Deutschland*, ed. Franklin Kopitzsch (Munich, 1976), 403–11; Richard van Dülmen, *Die Gesellschaft der Aufklärer: Zur bürgerlichen Emanzipation und aufklärerischen Kultur in Deutschland* (Frankfurt am Main, 1986).

8. See Horst Möller, "Enlightened Societies in the Metropolis: The Case of Berlin," in *The Transformation of Political Culture: England and Germany in the Late Eighteenth Century*, ed. Hellmuth Eckhart (Oxford, 1990), 219–33; Ulrich Im Hof, "German Associations and Politics in the Second Half of the Eighteenth Century," in *The Transformation of Political Culture*, 207–18.

9. See Fania Oz-Saltzberger, "Republic of Letters or Tower of Babel? The Transmission of Ideas Across Linguistic and Culture Barriers in the Age of Enlightenment," *Historia* 5 (2000): 7–37 (Hebrew).

10. Jacob Katz, *Tradition and Crisis* (New York, 1961), 184–94.

11. Meir Benayahu, "Contracts of Association of the Jerusalem Kabbalists," *Asufot* 9 (1995): 9–126 (Hebrew); Arie Morgenstern, *Mysticism and Messianism: From Luzzatto to the Vilna Gaon* (Jerusalem, 1999), 94–103 (Hebrew); Elchanan Reiner, "Wealth, Social Position, and the Study of the Torah: The Status of Kloiz in Eastern European Jewish Society in the Early Modern Period," *Zion* 58 (1993): 287–328 (Hebrew); Moshe

Rosman, The History of an Historical Source: On the Editing of *Shivhei HaBesht*," *Zion* 58 (1993): 175–214 (Hebrew); Chavivah Pedaya, "On the Development of the Social, Religious, Economic Model in Chasidism: The Pidyon, the Chavura, and the Pilgrimage," in *Religion and Economy, Connections and Interaction*, ed. Menahem Ben-Sasson (Jerusalem, 1995), 311–73 (= David Asaf, ed., *Zaddik and Devotees: Historical and Social Aspects of Chasidism* [Jerusalem, 2001], 343–97) (Hebrew).

12. Meir Gilon, *Mendelssohn's Kohelet musar in Its Historical Context* (Jerusalem, 1979), 176–77 (Hebrew) . Even if this was a literary invention, it was undoubtedly based on a new sociocultural reality in the circles of the early maskilim.

13. See Shlomo Berger, "Amadores das Musas," *Scripta Classica Israelica* 15 (1996): 274–88.

14. Isaac Euchel, "Letter to the King of Denmark," October 21, 1784, Schleswig Archive Acta A 18, no. 439, photocopy in the General Archives of Jewish History, Jerusalem, HM2/1062a, also printed in Ingrid Lohmann, ed., *Die Jüdische Freischule in Berlin (1778–1825), im Umfeld preußischer bildungspolitik und jüdischer Kultusreform*, 2 vols. (Munich, 2001); Max Erik, "The History of Euchel's Hebrew Docent at Königsberg University," *Die Yiddische Sprache* 3, 4–5 (1929): 51–54 (Yiddish); H. J. Krüger, *Die Judenschaft von Königsberg in Preußen, 1700–1812* (Marburg, 1966), 96–97; Monika Richarz, *Der Eintritt der Juden in die Akademischen Berufe* (Tübingen, 1974), 55–58.

15. Solomon Maimon, *The Autobiography of Solomon Maimon*, trans. J. C. Murray (London, 1954), 189–90.

16. See Ernst Friedländer, *Das Handlungshause Joachim Friedländer et Söhne zu Königsberg in Preussen* (Hamburg, 1913).

17. See Krüger, *Die Judenschaft von Königsberg*, 96–97; Selma Stern, *Der Preußische Staat und die Juden* (Tübingen, 1971) 3, 2b, 1121; H. Jolowicz, *Geschichte der Juden in Königsberg* (Posen, 1867); Michael Meyer, *The Origins of the Modern Jew: Jewish Identity and European Culture in Germany, 1749–1824* (Detroit, 1979), chap. 3.

18. On the importance of the patrons' support, see Miriam Bodian, "The Jewish Entrepreneurs in Berlin and 'The Civil Improvement of the Jews' in the 1780s and 1790s," *Zion* 49, 2 (1984): 159–84 (Hebrew); Meir Gilon, "Hebrew Satire in the Age of Haskalah in Germany: A Rejoinder," *Zion* 52 (1987): 214 (Hebrew); Steven M. Lowenstein, *The Berlin Jewish Community: Enlightenment, Family and Crisis, 1770–1830* (Oxford, 1994), 25–32.

19. See Über die Aufklärung der jüdischen Nation," *Magazin für die biblisch-orientalische Literatur und gesammte Philologie* (Königsberg, 1789), 193–200, 196–98.

20. Isaac Euchel, *Sefat emet* (Königsberg, 1782).

21. *Nachal habesor*, 3–4, 14–15; Shimon Baraz, *Ma'arakhei lev* (Königsberg, 1784). See Moshe Pelli, "*Hame'asef*, Introduction and Opening of a Published Letter," *Kesher* 24 (1998): 48–55 (Hebrew). For keys to references in *Hame'asef*, see Pelli, *A Gate to Haskalah: An Annotated Index to Hame'asef, the First Hebrew Journal* (Jerusalem, 2000) (Hebrew).

22. *Nachal habesor*, 14–17; "Notice," *Ha-me'asef* 1 (1784): 15–16.

23. On *Nachal habesor*, see Moshe Pelli, *Struggle for Change: Studies in the Hebrew Enlightenment in Germany at the End of the 18th Century* (Tel Aviv, 1988) (Hebrew); Zemach Tsamriyon, *Hame'asef: The First Modern Periodical in Hebrew* (Tel Aviv, 1988), 33–71 (Hebrew).

24. *Nachal habesor*, 11.

25. On the Hebrew language in the eighteenth-century Haskalah, see Yaacov

Shavit, "A Duty Too Heavy to Bear: Hebrew in the Berlin Haskalah, 1783–1819: Between Classic, Modern and Romantic," in *Hebrew in Ashkenaz: A Language in Exile*, ed. Lewis Glinert (New York, 1993), 111–28.

26. *Nachal habesor*, 11.

27. *Nachal habesor*, 1. See Shmuel Feiner, *Haskalah and History* (Oxford, 2002), 9–11.

28. See Klaus L. Berghahn, "On Friendship: The Beginnings of a Christian-Jewish Dialogue in the 18th Century," in *The German-Jewish Dialogue Reconsidered: A Symposium in Honor of George Mosse*, ed. Bergahn (New York, 1996), 5–24.

29. Baraz, *Ma'arakhei lev.*

30. See H. Vogelstein, "Handschriftliches zu Isaak Abraham Euchels Biographie," in *Festschrift zum 70. Geburtstage Martin Philippsons* (Leipzig, 1916), 227–28.

31. See Jean Jacques Rousseau, *Emile*, trans. Barbara Foxley (London, 1993), book 5.

32. Immanuel Kant, "The Fair Sex" (1765), in Isaac Kramnic, *The Portable Enlightenment Reader* (New York, 1995), 580–86.

33. Mendelssohn's letter from Berlin to Fromet Gugenheim in Hamburg (November 11, 1761), *Gesammelte Schriften* 19: 64.

34. See Euchel's letter of dedication at the beginning of his German prayer book, Isaac Euchel, *Gebete der hochdeutschen und polnischen Juden* (Königsberg, 1786).

35. Euchel's letter, 4–5. In 1785, a German translation of the Passover Haggadah was printed in Hebrew letters. According to the introduction by the translator, Joel Brill, and his dedication to Bleimchen Friedländer (the wife of David Friedländer, Brill's patron), it was meant for women whose mother tongue was German. Isaac Satanow, *Hagadah shel Pesach im tirgum Ashkenazi* (Berlin, 1785).

36. See at length in Shmuel Feiner, "The Modern Jewish Woman: A Test Case in the Relationship Between the Haskalah and Modernity," in *Sexuality and the Family in History*, ed. Israel Bartal and Isaiah Gafni (Jerusalem, 1998), 253–304 (Hebrew).

37. Vogelstein, "Handschriftliches zu Euchel," 229–30.

38. Baraz, *Ma'arAkhei lev.*

39. See Dülmen, *Die Gesellschaft der Aufklärer*, 85–86.

40. *Nachal habesor*, 1, 5, 11; *Hame'asef* 1 (1784): German supplement, "da der Wunsch der Herausgeber blos zur Beförderung der Aufklärung der Nation bezielt."

41. See, for example, Wolf Landsberg, *Lu'ach mishenat 5547* (Berlin, 1788).

42. Euchel's letter to Solomon Rosenthal, Adar, 1790, in Judah Arye Blau, "An Exchange of Letters Between Solomon Rosenthal and Isaac Euchel," *HaTzofeh lechokhmat Israel* 5 (1921): 51–52.

43. *Hame'asef* 1 (1784): 9, 106.

44. Anonymous, signed Pili, "A Word to *Chevrat Dorshei Leshon Ever* and to Every Reader of Their Letter, *Hame'asef*," *Hame'asef* 2 (1785): 40–43.

Chapter 9. The Maskilim: A Group Portrait

1. Moritz Oppenheim, *The First Jewish Painter: Catalogue of the Israel Museum Exhibition* (Jerusalem, 1983) (Hebrew); Ismar Schorsch, "The Myth of Sephardic Supremacy," in *From Text to Context: The Turn to History in Modern Judaism* (Hanover, 1994), 71–92.

2. See Alexander Altmann, *Moses Mendelssohn: A Biographical Study* (London, 1973), chap. 5.

3. Peter Gay, *The Enlightenment: An Interpretation, the Rise of Modern Paganism* (New York, 1966), 3–19.

4. Simon Dubnow, *History of the Jews*, vol. 6 (1925–29; South Brunswick, N.J., 1967–73).

5. Simon Bernfeld, *Dor tahapukhot*, vol. 2 (Warsaw, 1897), 11.

6. Moshe Pelli, "The Image of Moses Mendelssohn as Reflected in the Early German Hebrew Haskalah Literature," *Proceedings of the Fifth World Congress of Jewish Studies*, vol. 3 (Jerusalem, 1972), 269–82; David Sorkin, *Moses Mendelssohn and the Religious Enlightenment* (Berkeley, Calif., 1996), 147–55.

7. Saul Levin-Berlin, who hid behind the sobriquet "Amitai haShomroni," wrote about his experience of cultural conversion: "Indeed, I turned into a different person after the great light of the contemporary luminaries, the scholar R. Moses of Dessau and the poet R. Herz Wessely, shone upon us" (*Hame'asef* 3 [1786]: 67).

8. *Hame'asef* 5 (1789): 51. On Mendelssohn as a myth of German Jewry, see Max Freudenthal, *Zum Zweihundertjährigen Geburtstag Moses Mendelssohns* (Berlin, 1929); Alexander Altmann, "Moses Mendelssohn as the Archetypal German Jew," in *The Jewish Response to German Culture*, ed. J. Reinharz and W. Schatzberg (Hanover, 1985), 17–31; Jacob Katz, "Moses Mendelssohn's schwankendes Bild bei der jüdischen Nachwelt," in *Moses Mendelssohn und die Kreise seiner Wirksamkeit*, ed. Michael Albrecht et al. (Tübingen, 1994), 349–62.

9. For the wording on the tombstone in the Jewish cemetery, see Immanuel Ritter, *David Friedländer: Sein Leben und sein Wirken*, vol. 2 (Berlin, 1861), 174.

10. Aaron Wolfssohn, "Al yom holedet hechakham R. David Friedländer," *Hame'asef* 7, 1 (1784): 14–19.

11. Abraham Baer Gottlober, "Et la'akor natu'a," *Haboker or* 2 (1876): 225–33.

12. See Ludwig Geiger, *Berlin 1618–1840: Geschichte des geistigen Lebens der Preußischen Haupstadt* , vol. 1 (Berlin, 1893).

13. Isaac Euchel, *Toledot harav hachoker elohi rabbenu Moshe ben Menachem* (Berlin, 1789; Vienna, 1814; Lvov, 1860) 116; Henriette Herz, *In Erinnerungen, Briefen und Zeugnissen* (Frankfurt am Main, 1984), 61ff.; Deborah Hertz, *Jewish High Society in Old Regime Berlin* (New Haven, Conn., 1988).

14. Solomon Maimon, *The Autobiography of Solomon Maimon*, trans. J. C. Murray (London, 1954), 226.

15. Euchel, *Toledot rabbenu Moshe ben Menachem*, 116.

16. Fromet's letter, dated July 18, 1777, Moses Mendelssohn, *Gesammelte Schriften*, vol. 19 (Stuttgart, 1974), 217–18.

17. Herz, *In Erinnerungen*, 48.

18. Maimon, *Autobiography*, 224.

19. Euchel, *Toledot rabbenu Moshe ben Menachem*, 127–28; Meir Gilon, *Mendelssohn's Kohelet Musar in Its Historical Context* (Jerusalem, 1979), 18–19 (Hebrew); David Friedländer, *Moses Mendelssohn: Fragmente von ihm und über ihm* (Berlin, 1819), 31ff.; Mendelssohn, *Gesammelte Schriften*, 23: 390–92.

20. Altmann, *Mendelssohn*, 74–76; Jacob Katz, *Out of the Ghetto: The Social Background to the Jewish Emancipation, 1770–1870* (Cambridge, Mass., 1973), chap. 4; Horst Möller, *Aufklärung in Preussen: Der Verleger, Publizist und Geschichtsschreiber Friedrich Nicolai* (Berlin, 1974), 232–36.

21. David Fishman, "A Polish Rabbi Meets the Berlin Haskalah: The Case of R. Baruch Schick," *AJS Review* 12 (1987): 95–112.

22. Shmuel Feiner, "Isaac Euchel: Entrepreneur of the Haskalah Movement in Germany," *Zion* 57 (1991): 444–45.

23. He studied medicine in Königsberg (1773) and Berlin (1778). For details on him, see H. J. Krüger, *Die Judenschaft von Königsberg in Preußen, 1700–1812* (Marburg, 1966), 93.

24. See below, Chapter 13. Another visitor of this type was the Polish skeptic Abba Glusk. On him, see Hayim Shoham, *In the Shadow of the Berlin Haskalah* (Tel Aviv, 1966) (Hebrew).

25. Peretz Sandler, *Mendelssohn's Edition of the Pentateuch* (Jerusalem, 1984) (Hebrew).

26. Jacob Katz, *Tradition and Crisis* (New York, 1961), 254.

27. Katz, *Out of the Ghetto*, chap. 4; idem, *Jews and Free Masons in Europe, 1723–1939* (Cambridge, Mass., 1970) chaps. 1–5.

28. *Hame'asef* 1 (1784): 16–17.

29. See Feiner, "The Invention of the Modern Age: A Chapter in the Rhetoric and Self-Image of the Haskalah," *Dappim: Research in Literature* 11 (1998): 9–29 (Hebrew).

30. See Steven M. Lowenstein, "The Readership of Mendelssohn's Bible Translation," *Hebrew Union College Annual* 52 (1982): 179–213.

31. See Steven M. Lowenstein, "Jewish Upper Crust and Berlin Jewish Enlightenment: The Family of Daniel Itzig," in *From East and West, Jews in Changing Europe 1750–1870*, ed. F. Malino David Sorkin (Oxford, 1990), 187.

32. Isaac Euchel, *Gebete der hochdeutschen und ponischen Juden* (Königsberg, 1786); David Friedländer, *Gebete der Juden auf das ganze Jahr* (Berlin, 1786); Aaron Wolfssohn and Joel Brill, *Chamesh megiloth im tirgum Ashkenazi vebi'ur* (Berlin, 1789); Joel Brill, *Sefer tehilim* (Prague, 1834).

33. The names of *Hame'asef* subscribers were published in four installments: *Hame'asef* 2 (1785): front page; *Hame'asef* 3 (1786): 64, 211; *Hame'asef* 4 (1788): front page.

34. Mendelssohn, *Gesammelte Schriften* 23: 140–42; Reuven Fahn, *Tekufat Hahaskalah beVina* (Vienna, 1918) (Hebrew).

35. See David Fishman, *Russia's First Modern Jews: The Jews of Shklov* (New York, 1995), chap. 3.

36. The figures are based on the list of subscribers printed in *Hame'asef* between 1785 and 1788. Compare to the inexact data cited by Walter Röll, "The Kassel *Hame'asef* of 1799," in *The Jewish response to German Culture*, ed. J. Reinharz and W. Schatzberg (Hanover, 1985), 34–37. The German periodicals published at the same time had a circulation of 1,000 to 2,000 copies and even more. See Möller, *Aufklärung in Preussen* (Berlin, 1974), 203–4. Compare to the number of subscribers to the *Encyclopédie*, the flagship project of the French Enlightenment: Robert Darnton, *The Business of Enlightenment: A Publishing History of the Encyclopédie, 1775–1800* (Cambridge, Mass., 1979), 287–94.

37. David Franco-Mendes, *Kinor David*, manuscript in the Etz Hayim Library, Institute for Photocopies of Manuscripts, National and University Library in Jerusalem, reference number 3514, 150–51; idem, *Sukat David*, "Upon my admission as a member of Chevrat Dorshei Leshon Ever in Berlin" (Iyar 1789): 30–31, manuscript in the Etz Hayim library, reference number 3527. See Joseph Melkman, *David Franco Mendes: A Hebrew Poet* (Jerusalem, 1951).

38. *Hame'asef* 4 (1788): 43.

39. David of Hanover's 1791 letter: *Hame'asef* 7, 1 (1793): 9–14.

40. Baruch Lindau, *Hame'asef* 1 (1783): 75–76. See Joseph Klausner, *History of Modern Hebrew Literature*, 6 vols. (Jerusalem, 1952–54), 1: 191–92 (Hebrew); Tal Kogman, "The Creation of Images of Knowledge in Texts for Jewish Children and Young Adults Published During the Haskalah Period," Ph.D. dissertation, Tel-Aviv University, 2000, chap. 3 (Hebrew).

41. H. J. Krüger, *Die Judenschaft von Königsberg in Preußen, 1700–1812* (Marburg, 1966), 95–96.

42. See Fishman, *Russia's First Modern Jews*, 60.

43. Shabbtai of Janov published, among others, Wessely's book *Chikor hadin* (Berlin, 1788).

44. Moses Shulvass, *From East and West: The Westward Migration of Jews from Eastern Europe during the Seventeenth and Eighteenth Centuries* (Detroit, 1971),154; M. Rosenmann, *Isak Noa Mannheimer* (Vienna, 1922), 15–24. In 1805, the Freischule was founded in Copenhagen at the initiative of Mendel Levin Nathansohn. A similar proposal had been raised in 1796 by Yehiel-Gottlieb Euchel, Isaac Euchel's brother (23–24).

45. On Menahem Mendel Lefin, see Nancy Sinkoff, "Tradition and Transition: Mendel Lefin of Satanow and the Beginnings of the Jewish Enlightenment in Eastern Europe, 1749–1826," Ph.D. dissertation, Columbia University, 1996; idem, "Strategy and Ruse in the Haskalah of Mendel Lefin of Satanow, in *New Perspectives on the Haskalah*, ed. Shmuel Feiner and David Sorkin, 86–102. (London, 2001).

46. Klausner, *History of Modern Hebrew Literature*, 1: 178–90 (Hebrew).

47. Dan Michman, "David Friedrichsfeld: A Fighter for Enlightenment and Emancipation of the Jews," *Studies on the History of Dutch Jewry*, vol. 1 (Jerusalem, 1975):151–97 (Hebrew).

48. See Altmann, *Moses Mendelssohn*, 725–27.

49. Ibid., 724.

50. Joseph Ha'efrati of Tropplowitz, *Meluchat Shaul* (Vienna, 1794), Gershon Shaked's edition (Jerusalem, 1968). See Shmuel Werses, "From Change of Words to Change in Meaning: The Play 'Saul's Kingdom' in Yiddish," *Chulyot* 6 (Fall 2000): 55–78 (Hebrew).

51. *Hame'asef* 4 (1788): 84. And see Moshe Pelli, *Struggle for Change: Studies in the Jewish Enlightenment in Germany at the End of the 18th Century* (Tel Aviv, 1988), 90–91 (Hebrew).

52. Chaim Kesslin, *Maslul bedikduk leshon hakodesh* (Hamburg, 1788), published in about twenty editions over a period of one hundred years; G. Kressel, *Encyclopedia of Modern Hebrew Literature*, vol. 2 (Merchavia, 1964–66), 784–85 (Hebrew).

53. *Hame'asef* 7, 3 (1795), 274–75. After the eulogy, a lament written by Joel Brill was printed: "We grieve for you, our brother Joseph, for you have left us in your youth, and have been ensnared in the sorrows of death. Indeed, your memory among us shall not fade, your labors that have brought much knowledge to our brethren, and the science you have imparted to our people are engraved forever on the pages of *Hame'asef*."

54. In the absence of any "census of maskilim" or orderly lists of members of the maskilic societies, the number of maskilim and their geographical dispersion is estimated here based on the names of the Haskalah activists that appear in *Hame'asef*, on the extant correspondence in the records of the Chevrat Chinukh Ne'arim printing

house, and on studies conducted on maskilim in various European cities. Heinrich Graetz, in his *History of the Jews*, vol. 5 (1853–75; Philadelphia, 1949), 411, estimated that after Mendelssohn's death about one hundred young maskilim remained in Berlin alone, but this figure is based on the number of members of Gesellschaft der Freunde, only a few of whom were in fact maskilim. On the Haskalah in Scandinavia, see D. Simonsen, "Mendelssohniana aus Dänemark," *Festschrift zum 70. Geburstage Martin Philippsons* (Leipzig, 1916), 213–24; Wilhelm Kurst, "The Influence of German Jewry on Jewish Communities in Scandinavia, *Year Book of the Leo Baeck Institute* 3 (1958): 224–313. On the Haskalah in France: Jonathan I. Helfand, "The Symbolic Relationship between French and German Jewry in the Age of Emancipation," *Year Book of the Leo Baeck Institute* 29 (1984): 331–50. See also the articles devoted to various centers in Europe, including Galicia, Prague, Hungary, and Trieste, contained in the anthology: Jacob Katz, *Toward Modernity: The European Jewish Model* (New Brunswick, N.J., 1987). On the circle of maskilim in White Russia, see Fishman, *Russia's First Modern Jews*. On the maskilim of Russia, Mordechai Zelkin, "The Jewish Enlightenment in Russia, 1800–1860, Social Aspects," Ph.D. dissertation, Hebrew University of Jerusalem, 1995 (Hebrew). On the circles of maskilim in Holland, see Michman's studies, in Jozeph Michman (Melkman), *Michmanei Yosef: Studies on the History and Literature of Dutch Jews* (Jerusalem, 1994) (Hebrew). On the maskilim in Hungary: Michael Silber, "The Roots of the Split in Hungarian Jewry: Cultural and Social Changes from the time of Joseph II Until the Eve of the 1848 Revolution," Ph.D. dissertation (Hebrew University of Jerusalem, 1985). On the Haskalah in Bohemia, particularly in Prague, see Ruth Kestenberg-Gladstein, *Neuere Geschichte der Juden in den böhemischen Ländern: Das Zeitalter der Aufklärung 1780–1830* (Tübingen, 1969) . Compare to the data on the number of writers in France and Germany during the Enlightenment. In 1750 France, Darnton found 434 writers (Robert Darnton, *The Great Cat Massacre* [New York, 1985], 141–83), and according to the estimate of Franklin Kopitzsch (*Aufklärung, Absolutismus und Bürgertum im Deutschland* [Munich, 1976], 60–61), the number of writers in the German-speaking countries reached nearly 5,000 in 1784. See also Horst Möller, "Wie aufgeklärt war Preußen?" in *Preußen im Rückblick*, ed. H. J. Puhle and H. U. Wehler (Göttingen, 1980), 176–201.

55. Hertz, *Jewish High Society*, 147–50.

56. Ursula Schulz, *Die Berlinische Monatsschrift (1783–1796): Eine Bibliographie* (Bremen, 1968); Möller, *Aufklärung in Preussen*, 246–54; idem, *Vernunft und Kritik: Deutsche Aufklärung im 17. Und 18. Jahrundert* (Frankfurt am Main, 1986), 295–96.

57. Gunter Schulz and Ursula Schulz, *Das Berlinische Archiv der Zeit und ihres Geschmacks* (Bremen, 1967); Jacob Toury, *Prologema to the Entrance of Jews into German Citizenry* (Tel Aviv, 1972), 68 (Hebrew); Hertz, *Jewish High Society*, 176–77. On Esther Gad, see Karin Rudert, "Die Wiederentdeckung einer 'Deutschen Wollstonecraft': Esther Gad Bernard Domain für Gleichberechtigung der Frauen und Juden," *Quaderni* 10 (1988): 213–61.

58. This can be found, for example, in memoranda sent by the Jews to the French national assembly, supporting the demand for emancipation and the principles and values of the Enlightenment. See Michael Graetz, *The French Revolutin and the Jews: The Debates in the National Assembly, 1789–1791* (Jerusalem, 1989), 80–84 (Hebrew).

59. From the introduction written by Isaac Euchel for the fourth volume of *Hame'asef* in 1788 (unpaginated).

60. *Hame'asef* 1 (1784): 2. The German non-Jewish enlightened were generally

born in the 1730s and 1740s, a whole generation older than the maskilim and closer to Mendelssohn's and Wessely's generation. See Möller, *Vernunft und Kritik*, 295–96, and note on 344.

61. See David Sorkin, "Preacher, Teacher, Publicist: Joseph Wolf and the Ideology of Emancipation," in *Between East and West: Jews in Changing Europe, 1750–1870*, ed. Frances Malino and David Sorkin (Oxford, 1990), 107–25.

62. *Hame'asef* 5 (1789): 180–81.

63. Maimon, *Autobiography*, 215.

64. Ibid., 265.

65. Ibid., 266.

66. Ibid., 268.

67. Shocharei hatov vehatushiyah, *Sefer Zemirot Israel, including a Book of Psalms in German and a Commentary*, vol. 4, *Introduction* (Berlin, 1790).

68. *Hame'asef* 3 (1787): 66.

69. "A Dirge Instead of Poetry," *Hame'asef* 3 (1786): 65–66.

70. See Euchel, *Toledot rabbenu Hechakham Moshe ben Menachem* (Berlin, 1788), 106–11; Mendelssohn, *Gesammelte Schriften*, 24: 295–305; Altmann, *Moses Mendelssohn*, 729–59.

71. See the special volume dedicated to portraits of Mendelssohn, *Gesammelte Schriften*, 24.

72. On the concert in Königsberg, see Louis Weyl, "Sulamith und Eusebia." *Literaturblatt des Orients* 11 (1850): 413–15; Isaac Euchel, *Toledot rabbenu Moshe ben Menachem*, 109–10; Altmann, Mendelssohn, 754–55. For a photograph of the memorial medals, see Mendelssohn, *Gesammelte Schriften*, 24, 73.

Chapter 10. Euchel Establishes the Haskalah Movement

1. Euchel refrained from publicly criticizing Mendelssohn, but in his letter to the king of Denmark, dated October 21, 1784, an invaluable source of information about Euchel's biography and worldview, his opinion is explicit. Selected excerpts from the letter have been published by Moritz Stern, "Euchel's Plan zur Errichtung eines jüdischen Erziehungsinstitutes und Lehrerseminars 1784," *Israelitische Monatsschrift* 1–2 (1900): 45–46; 3 (1901): 10–11. The full letter in Euchel's handwriting is in the Schleswig state archives. See Isaac Euchel, Letter to the King of Denmark, October 21, 1785, Schleswig archives, Acta A XVIII, No. 439, photocopy in the General Archives on Jewish History in Jerusalem, HM2/1062a.

2. For a comprehensive discussion on Euchel as a key figure in the Haskalah movement; see Shmuel Feiner, "Isaac Euchel: 'Entrepreneur' of the Haskalah Movement in Germany," *Zion* 52 (1987): 427–69 (Hebrew).

3. In his biography, he commends his grandfather, Israel Levin Euchel (1717–63), who was also a cantor, and his father, the merchant Abraham Israel Euchel (1731–67), for their knowledge of the fine arts; his grandfather was also well known on this account and one of the nobles extended his auspices to him. See *Stamtavlen Eichel*, ed. J. Fischer (Copenhagen, 1904).

4. See I. N. Bamberger, "A Cultural History of the Jews of Denmark," Ph.D. dissertation, Yeshiva University, New York, 1975, 12–78; D. Simonsen, "Mendelssohniana

aus Dänemark," in *Festschrift zum 70. Geburstage Martin Philippsons* (Leipzig, 1916), 213–24; Eliyakim Zoldin, *Bekhi tamrurim* (Copenhagen, 1786).

5. Euchel, Letter to the King of Denmark. On Masos Rintel, see Josef Meisl, ed., *Protolbuch der jüdischen Gemeinde Berlin (1723–1854)* (Jerusalem, 1962), 208, 235, 254, 262, 274, 318, 325, 343, 379 (Hebrew and German). On the duties of the managers of synagogue affairs, see the introduction, 29.

6. Isaac Euchel, letter to Brill (1788), included as a dedication to *Toledot harav hackoker elohi rabbenu Hechakham Moshe ben Menachem* (Berlin, 1789).

7. Joel Brill dedicated his commentary on the Book of Psalms to his adoptive parents and paid a glowing tribute to them (Brill, *Sefer Tehilim* [Prague, 1834]: 33: 2–34: 2. On Aaron Joresch, see Alexander Altmann, *Moses Mendelssohn: A Biographical Study* (Philadelphia, 1973), 282. He was among the subscribers to the *Bi'ur* and ordered twenty copies.

8. Euchel, letter to Brill, 3; Isaac Euchel, Letter to the King of Denmark.

9. Euchel, letter to Brill, 7; Brill, *Sefer Tehilim*, dedication to his adoptive parents, 32: 1.

10. Euchel, letter to Brill, 3.

11. Euchel, letter to the king of Denmark.

12. Euchel, letter to Brill, 5.

13. Euchel, letter to the King of Denmark. On Raphael Levi, see Altmann, *Mendelssohn*, 161–63; above, Chapter 2. On Meir David, see M. Zuckermann, *Dokumenta zur Geschichte der Juden in Hannover* (Hanover, 1908), 16–20, 28, 44–45.

14. See Euchel, letter to the King of Denmark; Max Erik, "The History of Euchel's Hebrew Ducent at Königsberg University," *Die Yiddische Sprache* 3, 4–5 (1929): 51–52, 54 (Yiddish); H. J. Krüger, *Die Judenschaft von Königsberg in Preußen, 1700–1812* (Marburg, 1966), 44–66, 96–97; Monika Richarz, *Der Eintritt der Juden in die Akademischen Berufe* (Tübingen, 1974), 55–58.

15. Euchel, letter to the King of Denmark. On Köhler, professor of Oriental languages at the universities of Kiel and Göttingen, and at Königsberg University from 1781 to 1786, see *Allgemeine Deutsche Biographie* 16 (Leipzig, 1882), 444–45.

16. See Euchel et al., *An Herrn Professor Kant, da er erstenmal Rector der Königsbergschen Universität wurde, Von einigen Seiner Schüler* (Königsberg, 1786).

17. For sources on the Euchel affair and his appointment to Königsberg University, see G. von Selle, *Geschichte der Albertus: Universitaet zu Königsberg in Preussen* (Würzburg, 1956), 198–99; Immanuel Kant, *Gesammelte Schriften*, vol. 12 (Berlin und Leipzig 1922), 426–27, 429–30; vol. 11, 435; "Ein Brief Kant's über Isaak Euchel," *Juedisches Literaturblatt* 11 (1882): 129–130.

18. See Jacob Katz's discussion on the limitations of the "semi-neutral society" in Jacob Katz, *Out of the Ghetto: The Social Background to the Jewish Emancipation, 1770–1870* (Cambridge, Mass., 1973), chap. 4.

19. See Immanuel Kant, "What Is Enlightenment?" in *On History*, ed. Lewis W. Beck (New York, 1986), 465–81.

20. Isaac Euchel, *Sefat emet* (Königsberg, 1782). On this, see also Chapter 6.

21. Euchel, letter to the King of Denmark.

22. Sh . . . S . . . , "Mikhtav el bachurei chemed limudei hasekhel" (A Letter to the Enlightened Youth), *Hame'asef* 1 (1784): 70.

23. Baruch Lindau, "Igeret lebachurei chemed Chevrat Dorshei Lashon Ever" (A Letter to the Youth of the Society of Friends of the Hebrew Language) *Hame'asef* 1 (1784): 75.

24. J. L. [Joel Brill], "Mikhtavim: hachalomot hemah hirhurei deliba" (Letters: Dreams Are But Wishful Thinking), *Hame'asef* 1 (1784): 104.

25. A . . . P [Isaac Euchel] "Davar el hakore mito'elet divrei hayamim hakadmonim vehayediot hamechubarim lahem" (About History), *Hame'asef* 1 (1784): 13.

26. "Mishpat al sefer chadash," *Hame'asef* 1 (1784): 47–48; E-P, Review of *Solomon und Joseph II, Erste Zugabe zu der hebraeischen Monatsschrift dem Sammler* (January 1784): 19–20.

27. Isaac Euchel, "Besorat sefarim chadashim," *Hame'asef* 1 (1784): 15, 45–46.

28. Ibid., 92–96.

29. Ibid., 63–64, 78–80.

30. Anon., "Toledot hazeman," *Hame'asef* 1 (1784): 11–112; 42–44, 61–63.

31. Ibid. On the maskilim's redemptive faith in the historical shift in relations between Jews and non-Jews, see at length Shmuel Feiner, *Haskalah and History* (Oxford, 2002), chap. 1. The same anonymous maskil who reported on the news from Mainz also opened the Shevat issue of *Hame'asef* with a paean marking the birthday of Frederick II. He lauded the religious tolerance that characterized the king's policy toward the Jews. *Hame'asef* 1 (1784): 65–69.

32. Euchel, "Davar el hakore," 27–28.

33. Compare the editor's comment to the article in *Hame'asef* 1 (1784): 125.

34. See Henri Grégoire, *Essai sur la régénération physique et politique des Juifs* (Paris, 1789).

35. Letter from Joel Brill to Isaac Euchel, 5th of Iyar, in Letters, *Hame'asef* 1 (1784): 136.

36. See Meir Gilon, *Mendelssohn's "Keholet musar" in Its Historical Context* (Jerusalem, 1979), 17–20 (Hebrew).

37. *Hame'asef* 2 (1785): 118.

38. See Paul Hazard, *The European Mind: The Critical Years, 1680–1715* (New York, 1990), 5–8.

39. For extant excerpts of the album, see Vogelstein, "Handschriftliches zu Isaak Abraham Euchel's Biographie," in *Festschrift zum 70. Geburtstage Martin Philippsons* (Leipzig, 1916), 225–31.

40. The experiences of Euchel's journey are contained in his letters to Michael Friedländer, *Hame'asef* 2 (1785): 116–21, 137–42.

41. Euchel, Letter to the King of Denmark.

42. Ibid.

43. *Hame'asef* 2 (1785): 16, 27.

44. *Hame'asef* 3 (1786): 33–34, 49–50.

45. "Deutsche Schulanstalten zur besseren Ausbildung der hierlaendischen Juden," *Zweyte Zugabe des zweyten Jahrganges zu der hebraeischen Monatsschrift dem Sammler* 2 (1786): 28–34.

46. *Hame'asef* 2 (1785): 106–9.

47. Ibid., 122, 145–52.

48. *Hame'asef* 3 (1786): 177–82.

49. Ibid., 193–201.

50. *Hame'asef* 2 (1785): 33–35; 1 (1784): 192; 2 (1785): 127–28; 46–48.

51. Abraham David Melodela, "Shirim likhvod HaRamban ner dorenu" (Songs in Honor of Mendelssohn), *Hame'asef* 2 (1785): 61–64; 2 (1786): 65–66, 82–85, 161.

52. Elijah Morpurgo, "Mikhtav meEliahu" (Letter from Elijah), *Hame'asef* 3 (1786): 73; "Bikoret sefarim chadashim" (Book Reviews), 139; "Mikhtavim" (Letters), 203; Yosef Baran, "Raiyonei ish be'alot hashachar" (Man's Thoughts in the Early Morning), 119; "Chakirah shishit," 169.

53. M..K . . . , "Besorat sefarim chadashim" (New Books), *Hame'asef* 3 (1786): 164–65.

54. Euchel, *Hame'asef* 7 (1787): 365–91.

55. *Hame'asef* 2 (1785): 87–90, 152–54; 3 (1787): 79–81, 183–92, 202–5.

56. Amitai HaShomroni [Saul Levin-Berlin], "Igeret bikoret" (Letter of Criticism), *Hame'asef* 3 (1787): 95; Chevrat Dorshei Lashon Ever, "Hitnatzlut" (Apology), 95–96, 141–44.

57. Isaac Euchel, *Hame'asef* 3 (1786): 205–10.

58. *Hame'asef* 3 (1786): 211–12.

Chapter 11. The Society for the Promotion of Goodness and Justice

1. *Hame'asef* 3 (1786): 210–11.

2. *Tavnit Chevrat Shocharei hatov vehatushi'ah (Plan zu einer Gesellschaft der Beförderer des Edlen und Guten)* (Königsberg and Berlin, 1787). The bilingual by-laws were printed in Hebrew and German on facing pages, and a form for membership registration was attached. A photocopy of the by-laws is in the Chaim Bar-Dayan collection in the National Library of the Hebrew University of Jerusalem. The Hebrew portion was printed in part in Abraham Meir Haberman, "The First Hebrew Journals in the Haskalah Period," in Haberman, *Literary Works: Studies in Jewish Culture and LIterature* (Jerusalem, 1981), 37–46 (Hebrew).

3. Isaac Satanow, *Pinkas vektav hadat* (Berlin, 1786).

4. See Yosef Klausner, *History of Modern Hebrew Literature*, vol. 1 (Tel Aviv, 1952), 165–77 (Hebrew); Nehama Rezler-Bersohn, "Isaac Satanow, the Man and His Work: A Study in the Berlin Haskalah," Ph.D. dissertation, Columbia University, 1975; Rezler-Bersohn, "Isaac Satanow: An Epitome of an Era," *Year Book of the Leo Baeck Institute* 25 (1980): 81–100; Moshe Pelli, *The Age of Haskalah* (Leiden, 1979), 151–70; Moshe Pelli, *Struggle for Change: Studies in the Hebrew Enlightenment in Germany at the end of the 18th Century* (Tel Aviv, 1989), 83–139 (Hebrew).

5. Shmuel Werses, "On I. Satanow and his Work *Mishlei Asaf*," in Werses, *Trends and Forms in Haskalah Literature* (Jerusalem, 1990) (Hebrew).

6. Isaac Satanow, commentary on Judah Halevi, *Sefer haKuzari* (Berlin, 1795), 40.

7. Isaac Satanow, *Gam eleh divrei Asaf* (Berlin, 1792). And see Shmuel Feiner, "The Modern Jewish Woman: A Case Study in Relations Between the Haskalah and Modernity," in *Eros, Sexuality, and the Family in History*, ed Israel Bartal and Yeshayahu Gafni (Jerusalem, 1998), 262–63 (Hebrew).

8. See the studies of Robert Darnton, in particular, *The Business of Enlightenment: A Publishing History of the Encyclopédie 1775–1800* (Cambridge, Mass, 1979. In the German context of the eighteenth century see Rudolf Schenda, *Volk ohne Buch, Studien zur Sozialgeschichte der populären Lesestoffe 1770–1910* (Munich, 1977); Paul Raabe, *Bücherlust und Lesefreuden: Beiträge zur Geschichte des Buchwesens im 18. und Frühen 19. Jahrhundert* (Stuttgart, 1984).

9. Letter dated January 8, 1784. The archival material on the history of the Berlin

printing house and its 1784 establishment is now in the document volumes Ingrid Loh-mann, ed., *Die Jüdische Freischule in Berlin (1778–1825), im Umfeld preußischer bildungs-politik und jüdischer Kultusreform*, 2 vols. (Munich, 2001). See also Moritz Steinschneider, "Hebräische Drucke in Deutschland." *Zeitschrift für die Geschichte der Juden in Deut-schland* 5 (1892): 166–82; Moritz Stern, "Die Errichtung der orientalischen Buchdruck-erei und Buchandlung in Berlin 1784," *Zeitschrift für die Geschichte der Juden in Deutschland* 6 (1936): 168–71 ; Chaim Dov Friedberg, *History of the Jewish Press* (Antwerp, 1935), 95–97 (Hebrew).

10. The archival documents are from the Berlin collection, Jerusalem, the Central Archives for Jewish History; Stern, "Die Errichtung," 170; David Friedländer, "Hebräische Buchhandlung der hiesigen jüdische Freischule." *Berlinische Monatsschrift* 7 (1786): 503–10.

11. Isaac Satanow, *Sefer hagilui vehachitum* (Berlin, 1784).

12. Isaac Satanow, *Pinkas vektav hadat* (Berlin, 1786).

13. Moses Mendelssohn, *Bi'ur milot hahigayon im peirush mehatorani morenu harav Moshe miDesau* (Berlin, 1784). (The book was printed as soon as the franchise was received, but the name of the printing house did not yet appear on the front page.) the book's publication was announced in *Hame'asef* 1(1784): 174–75, with an explicit mention that it had been printed in the new printing house.

14. Naphtali Herz Wessely, *Ein mishpat* (Berlin, 1784). The following words were printed on the front page: "A third epistle written to our brethren the people of Israel wherever they reside, may God protect them. It contains true statements by seven men of reason . . . Talmud authorities and rabbis . . . from the cities of Italy . . . on our epistle *Divrei shalom ve'emet*." The book was printed in the month of Iyyar, 1784, and for the first time, the front page bore the inscription: "At the printing house of the Chinukh Ne'arim Institute." The announcement about the book's publication: *Hame'asef* 1 (1784): 158–60.

15. Naphtali Herz Wessely, *Divrei shalom ve'emet* (Berlin, 1782–85; Vienna, 1826).

16. *Hame'asef* 1 (1784): 156–58.

17. Isaac Satanow, *Sefer hamidot* (Berlin, 1784).

18. Ibid., 113. Cf. Itamar Hacohen, *Shevet musar* (1712; Jerusalem, 1988), 74–75. Cf. Moshe Idel, "Female Beauty: A Chapter in the History of Jewish Mysticism," in *Within Hasidic Circles: Studies in Hasidism in Memory of Mordechai Wilensky*, ed. Immanuel Etkes, David Asaf, Israel Bartel, and Elchanan Reiner (Jerusalem, 1999), 317–34.

19. Naphtali Herz Wessely, *Hame'asef* 3 (1786): 145–46.

20. *Tavnit Chevrat Shocharei hatov vehatushi'ah*, Introduction.

21. Ibid., section 2: "On membership in the Society."

22. Ibid., section I: "Aims and Scope."

23. Ibid., section 3, clause 4: Regulations; section 4, clause 1.

24. Ibid., section 1: "Rewards."

25. Ibid., section 1; section 3, clauses 1–4; section 4, clauses 1–3.

26. See Jacob Katz, *Jews and Freemasons in Europe 1723–1939* (Cambridge, Mass., 1970), chap. 3.

27. See Günter Mühlpfordt, "Radikale Aufklärung und nationale Leserorganiza-tion: Die Deutsche Union von Karl Friedrich Bahrdt," in *Lesegesellschaften und bürger-liche Emanzipation*, ed. Otto Dann (Munich, 1981), 103–22.

28. *Tavnit Chevrat Shocharei hatov vehatushi'ah*, section 5.

29. See Jacob Katz, *Tradition and Crisis* (New York, 1961), chap. 16.

30. *Tavnit Chevrat Shocharei hatov vehatushi'ah*, sections 5 and 8. Appointments of secretaries, advisers, and treasurers are made by the leaders of the local societies, but these also require the approval of the *Hauptdirektion*.

31. Ibid., section 6: "Communications by letter," clauses 1–2.

32. Ibid., section 6, clauses 4–6.

33. Ibid., Section 9, clauses 1–3: "Meetings."

34. Ibid., Section 10, clause 9.

35. The source for the changes entailed in Euchel's move to Berlin is an article reviewing the fourth volume of *Hame'asef* : "Über die Aufklärung der jüdischen Nation," *Magazin für die biblisch-orientalische Literatur und gesammte Philologie* (Königsberg-Leipzig, 1789): 193–200.

36. This description of 1786 Jewish Berlin, even before Mendelssohn's death, appeared in an anonymous work entitled *Bemerkungen eines Reisenden durch die königlichen Preußischen Staaten* (Altenburg, 1799). The description is included in Franz Eyssenhardt, *Berlin im Jahre 1786* (Leipzig, 1886), and is quoted here in English translation from a citation in Stefi Jersch-Wenzel's article, "Die Juden im gesellschaftlichen Gefüge Berlins um 1800," in *Bild und Selbstbild der Juden Berlins: Zwischen Aufklärung und Romantik*, ed. Marianne Awerbuch & Stefi Jersch-Wenzel (Berlin, 1992), 153–54. See also Nicolai's description of the art collections of wealthy Jews and the collections of Jewish physicians and men of science: Friedrich Nicolai, *Beschreibung der königlichen Residenzstädte Berlin und Potsdam* (Berlin, 1786).

37. See Miriam Bodian, "The Gomperz Family in Germany in the 17th and 18th Centuries: Towards Emancipation," *Proceedings of the Tenth World Congress on Jewish Studies*, vol. 2 (Jerusalem, 1990), 177–82 (Hebrew).

38. See Michael Meyer, *The Origins of the Modern Jew: Jewish Identity and European Culture in Germany, 1749–1824* (Detroit, 1979).

39. Heidi Thomann Tewarson, *Rahel Levin Varnhagen: The Life and Work of a German Jewish Intellectual* (Lincoln, 1998), 84.

40. See Steven M. Lowenstein, "The Pace of Modernization of German Jewry in the Nineteenth Century," *Leo Baeck Institute Year Book* 21 (1976): 41–56; Lowenstein, *The Berlin Jewish Community: Enlightenment, Family and Crisis, 1770–1830* (Oxford, 1994), chaps. 5, 6. On Jacob Adam, see Adam Jacob, *Zeit zur Abreise: Lebensbericht eines jüdischen Händlers aus der Emanzipationszeit*, ed. Jörg Fehrs and Margret Heitmann (Hildesheim, 1993). On the incident in the synagogue related by Bendavid, see Lazarus Bendavid, *Selbstbiographie*, in *Bildniss jetztlebender Berliner Gelehrten mit Ihren Selbstbiographie* (Berlin, 1806).

41. Paula E. Heyman, *Gender and Assimilation in Modern Jewish History: The Roles and Representation of Women* (Seattle, 1995).

42. Y. Z., "Chevrat Shocharei hatov vehatushi'ah, Introduction," *Hame'asef* 4 (1788), unpaginated.

43. Isaac Euchel, "Toledot rabbenu Moshe ben Menachem," *Hame'asef* 4 (1788): 114. Compare with Euchel's letter to his former student, urging him to adhere to the Haskalah and to resist the temptations of the good life, *Hame'asef* 4 (1788): 65–71.

Chapter 12. Growth and Radicalization

1. *Birkat poalim* (Berlin, 1787).

2. For example, Zevi Mirlesh, *Sefer mispar tzva'am* (Berlin, 1789).

3. Among others, *Shocharei hatov Vehatushiyah, Shir kelulot* (On the Occasion of Sanwil Friedländer's Marriage to His Cousin . . . Rivkah Friedländer) (Berlin, 1788); *Shocharei hatov Vehatushiyah, Shir yedidut* (On the Occasion of Baruch Lindau's Marriage) (Berlin, 1790).

4. For example, Wolf Landsberg, 1789 calendar (Berlin, 1789).

5. On the German supplement, see Shmuel Werses, "The Inter-Lingual Tensions in the Maskilic Periodical *Hame'asef* and Its Time in Germany," *Dapim: Research in Literature* 11 (1998): 29- 69.

6. Naphtali Herz Wessely, *Shirei tiferet*, vol. 1 (Berlin, 1788); Shlomo Pappenheim, *Agadat arba kosot* (Berlin, 1790); Isaac Satanow, *Mishlei asaf* (Berlin, 1788).

7. Aaron Wolfssohn-Halle, *Avtalyon* (Berlin, 1806); Baruch Lindau, *Reshit limudim* (Berlin, 1788).

8. Isaac Euchel, *Hame'asef* 4 (1788): 241–63; Solomon Maimon, *The Autobiography of Soloman Maimon* (London, 1954), 288.

9. Isaac Euchel, *Toledot rabbenu Moshe ben Menachem.*

10. Aaron Wolfsohn and Joel Brill, *Megilat shir hashirim*, translated into German by R. Moses ben Menahem with a commentary by the editors, members of the Society for the Promotion of Goodness and Justice (Berlin 1788); idem, *Chamesh megilot*, with a Hebrew translation and a commentary by members of the Society (Berlin, 1789); *Haftarot mikol hashanah*, with German translation and commentary, Chevrat Shochar Hatov Vehatushiyah (Berlin, 1790–91).

11. *Hame'asef* 4 (1788), 112.

12. Judah Arye Blau, "Exchange of Letters between Shlomo Rosenthal and Isaac Euchel," *Hatzofeh lechokhmat Israel* 5 (1921): 48–52 (Hebrew).

13. "Nachricht," *Hame'asef* 5 (1789): 256.

14. *Hame'asef* 6 (1790): 265–68.

15. See, e.g., *Hame'asef* 5 (1789): 262–68.

16. Naphtali Herz Wessely, "Chikur din," *Hame'asef* 4 (1788): 97–111, 145–65.

17. Joseph Baran, "Divrei hayamim lemamlekhot ha'artzot," *Hame'asef* 4 (1788): 369–85; idem, "Divrei hayamim lemalkhei ashur madei ubavel," *Hame'asef* 4 (1789): 76–88; Aaron Wolfssohn, "Toledot haminim hativiyim," *Hame'asef* 4 (1788): 49–57, 274–80; Baruch Lindau, "Toledot haminim hativiyim," *Hame'asef* 4 (1788): 211–18; idem, "Biber o fiber o kastar," *Hame'asef* 5 (1789): 234–43; idem, "Maslul hateva," *Hame'asef* 4 (1788): 226–34; Josel Pick Reichenau, "Chinukh ne'arim," *Hame'asef* 4 (1788): 176–87; Aaron Wolfssohn, "Sichat shnei anashim al odot rabot vechisaron hamayim," *Hame'asef* 6 (1790): 73–80, 108–22; Isaac Euchel, "Besorot," *Hame'asef* 4 (1788): 241–63.

18. Shlomo Schöneman, "Midarkei halashon vehamelitzah," *Hame'asef* 4 (1788): 85.

19. Shimon Baraz, "Chaviv adam shenivra betzelem," *Hame'asef* 5 (1789): 171; Lindau , "Toledot haminim hativiyim," 211.

20. Shimon Baraz, "Chinukh ne'arim," *Hame'asef* 4 (1788): 33–43.

21. The biography was printed in the issues of the months of Shevat, Adar, and Av in 1788 and the Cheshvan issue.

22. Moses Ensheim, "Toledot hazeman," *Hame'asef* 5 (1789): 365–72. See Shmuel Werses, "The French Revolution as Reflected in Hebrew Literature," *Tarbiz* 58 (1989): 567–602 (Hebrew); Reuven Michael, "Did the Triumph of the Ideas of the Enlightenment at the Start of the French Revolution Cause the Demise of the 'Berlin Enlightenment'?" *Zion* 56 (1991) (Hebrew).

23. Moses Ensheim, "Al havaad hagadol asher bemedinat Tzarfat," *Hame'asef* 6 (1790): 33–36. Other news items: *Hame'asef* 6: 30–32.

24. "Toledot hazeman," *Hame'asef* 5 (1789): 167–68.

25. "Toledot hazeman," *Hame'asef* 4 (1788): 331–34.

26. "Igeret rabanei Trieste le'ir habirah Vina," *Hame'asef* 4 (1788): 366–68; see Lois C. Dubin, *The Port Jews of Habsburg Trieste: Absolutist Politics and Enlightenment Culture* (Stanford, Calif., 1999), 148–52.

27. "Toledot hazeman," *Hame'asef* 5 (1789): 252–55. See Ruth Kestenberg-Gladstein, *Neuere Geschichte der Juden in den böhmischen Ländern: Das Zeitalter der Aufklärung, 1780–1830* (Tübingen, 1969), 69–73.

28. "Toledot hazeman," *Hame'asef* 6 (1790): 62–64.

29. Ibid., 188–89; "Edict . . . Joseph des Zweiten die Juden in Galizien betreffend," *Deutsche Zugabe zum sechsten Jahrgang der hebräischen Monatsschrift der Sammler* (April 1790): 1–23.

30. See M. Balaban, "Herz Homberg in Galizien," *Jahrbuch für jüdische Geschichte und Literatur* 19 (1916): 186–221; Joseph Klausner, *History of Modern Hebrew Literature*, 6 vols. (Jerusalem, 1952–54) (Hebrew).

31. Herz Homberg, *Hame'asef* 4 (1788): 227–36.

32. David Friedländer, "Sendschreiben an die deutsche Juden" (special supplement to *Hame'asef*, 1788). See Michael Meyer, *The Origins of the Modern Jew: Jewish Identity and European Culture in Germany, 1749–1824* (Detroit, 1979), chap. 3; Steven M. Lowenstein, *The Jewishness of David Friedlander and the Crisis of Berlin Jewry*, Braun Lectures in the History of the Jews in Prussia 3, Bar-Ilan University (Ramat Gan, 1994).

33. Eleazar Fleckeles, *Olat tzibur* (Prague, 1786).

34. Joseph Meisel, "Briv fun David Friedländer," *Historishe Shriften* 2 (Vilna, 1937): 390–412, quote 401. Euchel, who was much moderate in his criticism than Friedländer, also berated the rabbis for their idleness, in his biography of Mendelssohn, *Hame'asef* 4 (1788): 178–79.

35. See Raphael Mahler, *History of the Jewish People in Modern Times* (Tel Aviv, 1960–80) (Hebrew).

36. See Moshe Hirschel, *Kampf der jüdischen Hirarchie mit der Vernunft* (Breslau, 1788).

37. Ibid., 68–69.

38. Jean Jacques Rousseau, *The Social Contract and Discourses and Other Essays* (1762), trans. G. D. H. Cole (New York, 1955), 322.

39. Moses Hirschel, *Kampf der jüdischen Hirarchie mit der Vernunft* (Breslau, 1788), 3–11.

40. Ibid., 11–15, 32.

41. Ibid., 36.

42. Saul Levin-Berlin, *Mitzpeh yokte'el* (Berlin, 1789).

43. Raphael Kohen, *Torat yekutiel* (Berlin, 1772).

44. *Mitzpeh yokte'el*, author's preface, unpaginated. On Saul Berlin, see also Chapter 7 above. On the *Mitzpeh yokte'el* affair, see Eliezer Landshut, *Toledot anshei shem vepeulatam be'adat Berlin* (Berlin, 1884), 87–99; Simon Bernfeld, *Dor tahapukhot* (Warsaw, 1897), 68–77; Moshe Samet, "Rabbi Saul Berlin and His Writings," *Kiryat Sefer* 43 (1967): 430 (Hebrew); Moshe Pelli, *Struggles for Change: Studies in the Hebrew Enlightenment in Germany at the End of the 18th Century* (Tel-Aviv, 1988), 147–49 (Hebrew).

45. Isaac Daniel Itzig and David Friedländer, "Divrei hamevi'im leveit hadefus . . ." on the frontispiece of the Saul Berlin's book *Mitzpeh yokte'el.*

46. The two documents, the court's verdict and the proclamation read out in the Great Synagogue of Altona, were printed in Landshut, *Toledot anshei Shem*, 89–91.

47. Most of the various documents can be found in Landshut, *Toledot anshei Shem.*

48. [Saul Berlin] Ovadiah b. Barukh, *Leha'alufim ketzinim . . . kahal Altona vekahal Wandsbeck*, 4th of Nisan, 1789; [Saul Berlin] Ovadia b. Barukh, *Amar hatza'ir Ovadia b. Barukh*, 9th of Nisan, 1789.

49. Rabbi Landau's two letters, the first dated the 17th of Elul, 1789 and the second the 29th of Sivan, 1790, are printed in Landshut, *Toledot anshei Shem*, 98–99. The first letter was printed by Saul Berlin in *Hame'asef* 6 (1790): 223.

50. *Hame'asef* 5 (1789): 223–24. The date on the announcement is the first day of the month of Nissan 1789, and it states that the handbills have already been distributed over the past three weeks.

51. [Saul Berlin] Ovadiah b. Barukh, *Amar hatza'ir Ovadia b. Barukh*, 9th day of Nissan, 1789.

52. Saul Berlin, *Teshuvat harav hagaon Shaul leharav . . . al devar cherem hasefer Mitzpeh yokte'el hana'asah be'Altona* (Berlin, 1789).

53. *Hame'asef* 5 (1789): 261–73 (the author may have been Saul Berlin himself).

54. See *Allgemeine Deutsche Biographie* 34 (Leipzig, 1892): 111–13.

55. See *Chronik von Berlin*, August 8, 1789, 967–68. Other articles on the affair appeared on the following pages of 1789 issues of the newspaper: 484–88, 520–24, 574–81, 680–82, 768–74, 791–802, 867–92, 932–72.

56. Saul Berlin, *Hame'asef* 6 (1790): 222–23; Saul Berlin's letter, 15th day of Sivan, 1790, *Jahrbücher für Jüdische Geschichte und Literatur* 7 (1887): 44–49.

57. See *Chronik von Berlin*, August 8, 1789, 954–68.

58. Amitai HaShomroni (Saul Berlin), *Hame'asef* 6 (1790): 201–7. The book referred to is Joel Ben-Meir, *Yetedot ohalim.*

59. Raphael Kohen, *Sefer marpeh lashon* (Altona, 1790). The quotation is from pages 39: 2–40: 1. On the orthodox role of the book, see Jacob Katz, "Rabbi Raphael Cohen, Moses Mendelssohn's Opponent," in idem, *Divine Law in Human Hands: Case Studies in Halakhic Flexibility* (Jerusalem, 1998), 191–215.

60. *Hame'asef* 6 (1790): 362–80.

61. *Hame'asef* 6 (1790): 28–30. See Rachel Elior, "Nathan Adler and the Chasidic Community in Frankfort: The Affinity Between Chasidic Groups in Eastern and Central Europe in the 18th Century," *Zion* 59 (1993): 31–64 (Hebrew).

62. *Hame'asef* 6 (1790): 177–86.

63. Judah Leib Margolioth, *Atzei eden* (Frankfurt-am-Oder, 1802).

64. Mendel Breslau, *Hame'asef* 6 (1790): 301–314.

65. *Igrot Meshulam ben Uriah ha'Eshtemoi*, *Hame'asef* 6 (1790): 38–50, 80–85, 171–76, 245–49. Based on the annotated edition edited by Yehudah Friedlander, *Studies in Hebrew Satire* (Tel Aviv, 1979), 19–61 (Hebrew).

66. Charles-Louis de Secondat, Baron de Montesquieu, *Persian Letters*, trans. C. J. Betters (New York, 1993).

67. *Igrot Meshulam*, ed. Friedlander, 41.

68. *Igrot Meshulam*, fourth letter, 53. On the maskilic image of Italian and Spanish Jewry, see Lois C. Dubin, "Trieste and Berlin: The Italian Role in the Cultural Poli-

tics of the Haskalah," in *Toward Modernity: The European Jewish Model*, ed. Jacob Katz (New Brunswick, N.J., 1987), 189–224; Ismar Schorsch, "The Myth of Sephardic Supremacy," in *From Text to Context: The Turn to History in Modern Judaism* (Hanover, 1994), 71–92.

69. *Igrot Meshulam.*

70. All the quotes are from "A Letter from My Grandfather" and "A Letter from My Father," contained in the second letter of *Igrot Meshulam*, 46–48.

71. *Hame'asef* 6 (1790): 380–84.

72. Letter from Isaac Euchel to Shlomo Rosenthal (27th of Iyyar, 1784), in "Correspondence Between Solomon Rosenthal and Isaac Euchel," ed. Judah Arye Blau, *Ha-Tzofeh lechokhmat Israel* 5 (1921): 48–52 (Hebrew).

Chapter 13. Crisis at the Turn of the Century

1. On Naumann Simonsohn, see Louis Lewin, *Gesichte der Juden in Lissa* (Pinne, 1904), 238–39; Moshe Samet, "The Social and Historical Teachings of R. Nachman Berlin," in *Society and History: The Annual Conference on Jewish Thought*, ed. J. Cohen (Jerusalem, 1979), 125–36 (Hebrew); Shmuel Feiner, "Educational Agendas and Social Ideals: Jüdische Freischule in Berlin, 1778–1825," in *Education and History: Cultural and Political Contexts*, ed. R. Feldhay and Immanuel Etkes (Jerusalem, 1999), 274–77 (Hebrew).

2. Nachman Berlin (Naumann Simonsohn), *Ein mishpat* (Berlin, 1796), [2], 10–13.

3. Nachman Berlin (Naumann Simonsohn), *Et ledaber* (Breslau, 1819), 21–23.

4. See Naumann Simonsohn, *Juda, oder freimüthige Aeusserungen über Religion und Bürgerglück* (Berlin, 1817); S. Plessner, *Ein Wort zu seiner Zeit oder über die Autorität der rabbinischen Schriften* (Breslau, 1826), 6–12; Moshe Samet, "Changes in Synagogue Arrangements: The Rabbis' Position Against the Reformist 'Innovators'," *Asufot* 5 (1990): 367–69 (Hebrew). When an attempt was made in 1808–11 to revive the publication of *Hame'asef* in a new format with a moderate worldview, presented by the editor, Shalom Hacohen, Naumann Simonsohn supported it; see *Hame'asef* (1808), List of Subscribers.

5. Euchel's letter, dated the 20th of Av, 1800, was printed in Shalom Hacohen, *Ktav yosher* (Vienna, 1820), 97–99. Meir Letteris corrected the date to 1799 in Letteris, ed., *Hame'asef be-1784* (Vienna, 1862), 45–47.

6. See Shmuel Feiner, "Educational Agendas and Social Ideals," 277–78; idem, "Out of Berlin: The Second Phase of the Haskalah Movement 1797–1824," in *Meah She'arim: Studies in Medieval Jewish Spiritual Life in Memory of Isadore Twersky*, ed. E. Fleischer, G. Blidstein, C. Horowitz, and B. Septimus (Jerusalem, 2001), 403–31 (Hebrew).

7. See Shlomo Schönemann, "An die Hrn. Verfasser des Sendschreiben an Hrn. K. Rath Teller," *Neue Berlinische Monatsschrift* 5 (1800): 208–25.

8. See David Friedländer, "Open Letter to His Reverence, Probst Teller" (Berlin, 1799); here quoted from the translation by S. Weinstein, in *The Jew in the Modern World*, ed. Paul R. Mendes-Flohr and Jehuda Reinharz (New York, 1980), 99.

9. Schönemann, "An die Hrn. Verfasser des Sendschreiben," 216. Also see

Michael Meyer, *The Origins of the Modern Jew: Jewish Identity and European Culture in Germany, 1749–1824* (Detroit, 1979), 87–88.

10. Solomon Maimon, *The Autobiography of Solomon Maimon*, trans. J. C. Murray (London, 1954), 230. Bibliography up to the mid-1960s: N. J. Jacobs, "The Literature on Solomon Maimon—Annotated Bibliography," *Kiryat Sefer* 41 (1965) (Hebrew): 245–62. Some recent studies: Liliane Weissberg, "1792–93, Salomon Maimon Writes His Autobiography, A Reflection on His Life in the (Polish) East and the (German) West," in *Yale Companion to Jewish Writing and Thought in German Culture, 1096–1996*, ed. Sander Gilman and Jack Zipes (New Haven, Conn. 1997), 108–15; idem, "Erfahrungsseelenkunde als Akkulturation: Philosophie, Wissenschaft und Lebensgeschichte bei Salomon Maimon," in *Der ganze Mensch: Anthropologie und Literaturwissenschaft im achtzehnten Jahrhundert*, ed. Hans Jürgen Schings (Stuttgart, 1994), 298–328; Dagmar Barnouw, "Enlightenment, Identity, Transformation: Salomon Maimon and Rahel Varnhagen," in *The German-Jewish Dialogue Reconsidered: A Symposium in Honor of George Mosse*, ed. Klaus L. Berghahn (New York, 1996), 25–58; Zwi Batscha, "Nachwort," in *Salomon Maimon Lebensgeschichte: Von ihm selbst geschrieben*, ed. Batscha (Frankfurt a.M., 1984), 331–92; Christoph Schulte, "Salomon Maimons Lebensgeschichte: Autobiographie und moderne jüdische Identität," in *Sprache und Identität im Judentum*, ed. Karl E. Grözinger (Weisbaden, 1998), 135–49.

11. Solomon Maimon, *Sefer ta'alumot chokhmah* (Breslau, 1787), manuscript in the Bodleian library, Oxford (Department of Manuscripts, National Library and Hebrew University of Jerusalem, S-19346).

12. See Raphael Mahler, *History of the Jewish People in Modern Times*, vol. 2 (Tel-Aviv, 1960–80), 152–55 (Hebrew).

13. Shlomo ben Yehoshua of Lithuania, *Hame'asef* 5 (1789): 140–46. The article was previously published in German in *Berlinische Monatsschrift.*

14. Euchel spread a network of agents in the territory between Vilna and Lvov and to London and Amsterdam to enlist subscribers. See Isaac Euchel, *Hame'asef* 4 (1788): 241–63.

15. Maimonides, *Guide for the Perplexed*, Commentary by Solomon Maimon (Berlin, 1791); Solomon Maimon, *Givat hamoreh*, new ed. by S. H. Bergman and Nathan Rotenstreich (Jerusalem, 1965).

16. Maimon, *Autobiography*, 269.

17. On Maimon's death, see Lazarus Bendavid, "Über Salomon Maimon." *National-Zeitschrift für Wissenschaft, Kunst, und Gewerbe in den Preussischen Staaten* 1 (1801): 88–104; and Sabattia Joseph Wolff, *Maimoniana, oder Rhapsodien zur Charackteristik Salomon Maimon's* (Berlin, 1813), 79–81, 251–54.

18. Jacob Katz, *Out of the Ghetto: The Social Background to the Jewish Emancipation, 1770–1870* (Cambridge, Mass., 1973), 57.

19. On this, see at length Feiner, "Out of Berlin."

20. See Edmund Burke, *Reflections on the French Revolution*, ed. L. G. Mitchell (1790; Oxford, 1993); Ford Franklin, *Europe, 1780–1830* (London, 1989), 144–71; Frederick C. Beiser, *Enlightenment, Revolution and Romanticism: The Genesis of Modern German Political Thought, 1790–1800* (Cambridge, Mass., 1992). On the question of the historical link between the Enlightenment and the Revolution, see Dorinda Outram, *The Enlightenment* (Cambridge, 1995), 114–32. On the periodization of the German Enlightenment and the date it ended, see Horst Möller, *Vernunft und Kritik, Deutsche Aufklärung im 17. Und 18. Jahrhundert* (Frankfurt a.M., 1986), 19–40.

21. H. W. Koch, *A History of Prussia* (London, 1978), 141–42.

22. See Ronald Taylor, *Berlin and Its Culture: A Historical Portrait* (New Haven, Conn., 1997).

23. Ibid., 93–94.

24. See Meyer, *Origins of the Modern Jew*.

25. On the major changes in the history of European Jewry in the eighteenth century, see Jacob Katz, "The Eighteenth Century as a Turning Point of Modern Jewish History," in *Vision Confronts Reality*, ed. R. Kozodoy and K. Sultanik (New York, 1989), 40–55.

26. See Mordechai Wilensky, *Hasidim and Mitnaggdim: A Study of the Controversy Between Them from 1772 to 1815*, 2 vols. (Jerusalem, 1970) (Hebrew).

27. See Shmuel Feiner, "Between the 'Clouds of Foolishness' and the 'Light of Reason': Judah Hurwitz, an Early Eighteenth-Century Maskil," in *Within Hasidic Circles: Studies in Hasidism in Memory of Mordechai Wilensky*, ed. Immanuel Etkes, David Asaf, Israel Bartal, and Elchanan Reiner (Jerusalem, 2000), 111–60 (Hebrew).

28. Pinhas Eliahu Hurwitz, *Sefer haberit* (Bruenn, 1796; Jerusalem, 1990).

29. See Israel Klausner, "The Internal Struggle in the Communities of Russia and Lithuania and R. Shimon Ben Wolf's Proposal for Reforms," *Ha'ever* 19 (1972): 54–73 (Hebrew).

30. On this path of secularization and one instance of it in English Jewry, see T. M. Endelman, "The Englishness of Jewish Modernity in England," in *Toward Modernity: The European Jewish Model*, ed. Jacob Katz (New Brunswick, N.J., 1987), 225–46.

31. See, e.g., the anonymous booklet *Zeh hakontras nikra olam chadash venikra olam hafukh* (London, 1789).

32. See Arthur Green, *Tormented Master: A Life of Rabbi Nahman of Bratslav* (Univeristy, Ala., 1979).

33. See in particular Steven M. Lowenstein, *The Berlin Jewish Community: Enlightenment, Family and Crisis, 1770–1830* (Oxford, 1994), 43–54.

34. See Och Gunnar, "Ess- und Teetisch: Die Polemik gegen das Akkulturierte Berliner Judentum im ausgehenden 18. Und frühen 19. Jahrhundert," in *Musik und Ästhetik im Berlin Moses Mendelssohns*, ed. Anselm Gerhard, Wolfenbütteler Studien zur Aufklärung 25 (Tübingen, 1999), 77–96.

35. See Lowenstein, *The Berlin Jewish Community*, 104–33; Meyer, *Origins of the Modern Jew*, 96–130; Deborah Hertz, *Jewish High Society in Old Regime Berlin* (New Haven, Conn., 1988).

36. Katz, *Out of the Ghetto*, 85–86.

37. See Moses Hirschel, *Apologie der Menschenrechte* (Zurich, 1793), 204–5.

38. See Wolff Davidson, *Über die bürgerliche Verbesserung der Juden* (Berlin, 1798).

39. Ibid., 90–109. On Marcus Herz, see Martin L. Davis, *Identity or History? Marcus Herz and the End of the Enlightenment* (Detroit, 1995).

40. Davidson, *Über die bürgerliche Verbesserung*, 114–15, 119.

41. On this, see David B. Ruderman, "Was There a Haskalah in England? Reconsidering an Old Question," *Zion* 62 (1996): 109–32 (Hebrew); idem, *Jewish Enlightenment in an English Key: Anglo-Jewry Construction of Modern Jewish Thought* (Princeton, N.J., 2000).

42. Julius Guttmann, "Lazarus Bendavid: Seine Stellung zum Judentum und seiner literarische Wirksamkeit," *Monatsschrift für Geschichte und Wissenschaft des Judentums* 61 (1917): 26–50, 176–211.

43. See Lazarus Bendavid, *Etwas zur Charackteristick der Juden* (Leipzig, 1793), 56–57.

44. Ibid., 45–52. On him, see Dominique Bourel, "Eine Generation später: Lazarus Bendavid (1762–1832)," in *Moses Mendelssohn und die Kreise seiner Wirksamkeit*, ed. Hinske Norbert (Tübingen, 1994), 363–80.

45. Bendavid, *Etwas zur Charackteristick der Juden*, 54–55.

46. Jacob Katz, "Kant and Judaism," *Tarbiz* 41 (1971): 232–35 (Hebrew).

47. Saul Ascher, *Leviathan oder über Religion in Rücksicht des Judentums* (Berlin, 1792). On Saul Ascher, see Michael Graetz, "The Formation of the New 'Jewish Consciousness' in the Time of Mendelssohn's Disciples: Saul Asher," *Studies in the History of the Jewish People and the Land of Israel* 4 (1976): 219–37 (Hebrew); Katz, *Out of the Ghetto*, 133–36; Walter Grab, "Saul Ascher, Ein jüdisch-deutscher Spätaufklärer zwischen Revolution und Restauration," *Jahrbuch des Instituts für Deutsche Geschichte* 6 (1977): 131–79; Christoph Schulte, "Saul Ascher's *Leviathan*, or The Invention of Jewish Orthodoxy in 1792," *Year Book of the Leo Baeck Institute* 45 (2000): 25–34.

48. See Dagmar Barnouw, "Enlightenment, Identity, Transformation: Salomon Maimon and Rahel Varnhagen," in *The German-Jewish Dialogue Reconsidered: A Symposium in Honor of George Mosse*, ed. Klaus L. Berghahn (New York, 1996), 25–58.

49. See Meyer, *Origins of the Modern Jew*; Hertz, *Jewish High Society*; Lowenstein, *Berlin Jewish Community*. On the ethos of the salon society, see Davis, *Identity or History?* 163–69.

50. Katz, *Out of the Ghetto*, 109–10.

51. Hertz, *Jewish High Society*, 204–50.

52. Meyer, *Origins of the Modern Jew*, 130.

53. For a detailed discussion of the dimensions of conversion, see Lowenstein, *Berlin Jewish Community*, 120–33.

54. See Ludwig Lesser, *Chronik der Gesellschaft der Freunde* (Berlin, 1842).

55. Ibid., 8–10.

56. On this subject, see Davidson's ardent words, *Über die bürgerliche Verbesserung*, 111–13.

57. See Meyer, *Origins of the Modern Jew*, 57; "Isaac Euchel, Entrepreneur of the Haskalah Movement in Germany," *Zion* 52 (1987): 464–65 (Hebrew).

58. Meyer, *Origins of the Modern Jew*, 98–99.

59. See Gideon Freudenthal, "Solomon Maimon's Autarchy," *Metaphora* 4 (1996): 67 (Hebrew).

60. Friedrich Küntze, *Die Philosophie Salomon Maimons* (Heidelberg, 1912), 1–18.

61. See Wolff, *Maimoniana*, 151–53.

62. Ibid., 143–50.

63. See Shmuel Feiner, "Solomon Maimon and the Haskalah," *Aschkenas* 10, 2 (2000): 337–59; Christoph Schulte, "Salomon Maimons Lebensgeschichte: Autobiographie und moderne jüdische Identität," in *Sprache und Identität im Judentum*, ed. Karl E. Grözinger (Weisbaden, 1998), 135–39.

64. See David Friedländer, *Sendschreiben an Seine Hochwürden: Herrn Oberconsistorialrath und Probst Teller zu Berlin von einigen Hausvätern jüdischer Religion* (Berlin, 1799).

65. See in particular Raphael Mahler, *History of the Jewish People in Modern Times* (Tel Aviv, 1960–80), 96–107, 144–51, 342–48 (Hebrew).

66. See Meyer, *Origin of the Modern Jew*, 79–88; Steven M. Lowenstein, *The Jew-*

ishness of David Friedländer and the Crisis of Berlin Jewry, Braun Lectures in the History of the Jews in Prussia 3 (Bar-Ilan University, Ramat Gan, 1994).

67. David Friedländer, "Vorlesung bey der erneuerten Todesfeyer Mendelssohns," in Moses Mendelssohn, *Gesammelte Schriften, Jubiläumsausgabe,* vo. 23 (Stuttgart, 1998), 296–305.

68. See Ismar Freund, "David Friedländer und die politische Emanzipation der Juden in Preussen," *Zeitschrift für die Geschichte der Juden in Deutschland* 6 (1936): 77–92.

69. Meyer, *Origin of the Modern Jew,* 65.

70. The original and full wording of the letters was published in Josef Meisl, "Briv fun David Friedländer," *Historishe Shriften* 2 (Vilna, 1937): 390–412.

71. Friedländer's letter to Eger, March 19, 1792, ibid., 404; here the translation by J. Hessing in *The Jew in the Modern World,* ed. Paul R. Mendes-Flohr and J. Reinharz (New York, 1980), 79–80.

72. Feiner, "Educational Agendas and Social Ideals," 262–63.

73. Friedländer's letter to Eger, March 30, 1799, in Meisl, "Briv fun David Friedländer, 406–8.

74. Friedländer, *Sendschreiben an Seine Hochwürden,* 10.

75. Ibid., 5.

76. Ibid., 62.

77. Friedländer's letter to Eger, August 4, 1799, in Meisl, "Briv fun David Friedländer, 411.

78. The 1799 letter is quoted in Leopold Stein, *Die Schrift des Lebens,* vol. 2 (Strassburg, 1877), 444–45. See Meyer, *Origin of the Modern Jew,* 198, n. 41.

Chapter 14. Tensions and Polemics in the Shadow of Crisis

1. David Hanover, *Hame'asef* 7, 1 (1794): 9–14.

2. Isaac Euchel, *Hame'asef* 7, 4 (1797): 361–91 (his words relate to the path of *Hame'asef,* 361–66).

3. Satanow noted his addresses at the end of the catalog of books he offered for sale, printed on the cover of the work, Nachman Berlin, *Ein mishpat* (Berlin, 1797).

4. Isaac Satanow, *Mikhtav marpeh lanefesh* (Berlin, 1795).

5. David Friesenhausen, *Sefer klil hacheshbon* (Berlin, 1797); Shlomo Schönemann, *Chimiah* (Berlin, 1795)(German, in Hebrew letters); Joel Brill, *Amudei halashon* (Berlin, 1794); Isaac Satanow, *Lu'ach binyanei hape'alim* (Berlin, 1794).

6. See, inter alia, Samuel Romanelli, *Hakolot yachdelun* (Berlin, 1791); David Friedrichsfeld, *Divrei habrit vehahavah* (Berlin, 1792); *Shir renan vesimcha* (Berlin, 1793; *Shir yedidut al shoshanim* (Berlin, 1794); Isaac Satanow, *Shir yedidut* (Berlin, 1799); Baruch Schotlander, *Kol zimrah* (Berlin, 1799).

7. *Haftarot mikol hashanah,* 1791.

8. Samuel Aaron Romanelli, *Masa be'Arav,* in *Selected Works* (Jerusalem, 1968), 31–32 (Hebrew). He described their marriage customs and the status of women and a whole list of superstitions as an abomination, and throughout his book cried out emotionally against them in the spirit of the maskilic rhetoric. See also his work dedicated to David Friedländer, also printed on the Freischule press: Romanelli, *Ruach nakhon* (Berlin, 1792).

9. Naphtali Herz Wessely, *Shirei tiferet* (Berlin, 1789–91).

10. The decline of the Freischule printing house was accelerated even further in the first quarter of the nineteenth century, in particular after it was no longer run by the maskilim after 1806 and was leased to new management. In all the years of the printing house's existence, it published 226 books. In the first decade of the nineteenth century, only 36 books were published by it, including calendars. See Haim Dov Friedberg, *History of the Jewish Press* (Antwerp, 1935), 94–96 (Hebrew); Josef Meisl, "Berliner Jüdische Kalender." *Soncino Blätter* 2 (1927): 41–54.

11. See Isaac Satanow, *Pinkas vektav hadat* (Berlin, 1786).

12. Satanow recorded his reflections on the state of the literature at the end of 1793 in a note at the end of the book, *Bi'ur milot hahigayon* (Berlin, 1795).

13. Isaac Satanow, *Divrei rivot*, 1: 47–48. See Moshe Pelli, *Studies in the Jewish Enlightenment in Germany at the End of the Eighteenth Century* (Tel Aviv, 1988), 129–39 (Hebrew).

14. Among the editions published by Satanow between 1793 and 1798: Satanow, *Sefer igeret hakodesh* (Berlin, 1793); Satanow, *Ma'or einayim* (Berlin, 1794); Satanow, *Sefer haKuzari* (Berlin, 1795); Satanow (editor and publisher), *Moreh nevukhim*, Parts 2, 3 (Berlin, 1796); Satanow, *Machbarot Immanuel* (Berlin, 1796); Satanow, *Sefer hagedarim* (Berlin, 1798).

15. Satanow's note at the end of the fourth edition of *Bi'ur milot hahigayon*.

16. Isaac Satanow, *Sefer tehilim im perush haRashbam* (Berlin, 1794).

17. Isaac Satanow, *Sefer i'yov* (Berlin, 1799); idem, *Megilat chasidim* (Berlin, 1801).

18. *Shir yedidut*, on the occasion of Baruch Lindau's wedding, from his friends in the Society for the Promotion of Goodness and Justice (Berlin, 1790); *Rinat dodim*, on the occasion of Joel Brill's wedding, from his friends in the Society for the Promotion of Goodness and Justice (Berlin, 1792); *Hame'asef* 7, 3 (1796): 274–75.

19. *Hame'asef* 7, 4 (1797): 399–404. This issue opened with a pessimistic letter by Joel Brill admitting the failure of the Haskalah: "Wisdom will rejoice outside, will uplift her voice in the street, but there is no one to answer, to listen to hear her. Thus was it in the days of Solomon, and until this day there is no one to gather her into his home" (278).

20. On the school in Breslau, see Mordechai Eliav, *Jewish Education in Germany During the Haskalah and Emancipation* (Jerusalem, 1960), 80–87 (Hebrew); Andreas Reinke, "Zwischen Tradition, Aufklärung und Assimilation: Der Königliche Wilhelmsschule in Breslau, 1791–1848," *Zeitschrift für Religions und Geistesgeschichte* 43 (1991): 193–214; Max Freudenthal, "Die ersten Emanzipationsbestrebungen der Juden in Breslau," *Monatsschrift für Geschichte und Wissenschaft des Judentums* 37 (1893): 41–48, 92–100, 188–97, 238–47, 331–41, 409–29, 467–83, 522–36, 565–78.

21. On Wolfssohn, see Jutta Strauss, "Aaron Halle-Wolfssohn: Ein Leben in drei Sprachen," *Wolfenbütteler Studien zur Aufklärung* 25 (1999): 57–75.

22. Aaron Wolfssohn, "Al yom huledet hechakham R. David Friedländer," *Hame'asef* 7, 1 (1794): 14–19.

23. *Hame'asef* 7, 3 (1796): 191.

24. Ibid., 99–103. News of the death of the rabbi of Breslau, 78.

25. Josel Reichenau, *Hame'asef* 7, 1 (1794): 68–77; 7, 3 (1796): 229–51.

26. Ibid., 72.

27. Ibid., 229–30.

28. *Hame'asef* 7, 1 (1794): 79–91. On Jeiteles and the Prague circle of maskilim,

see Ruth Kestenberg-Gladstein, *Neuere Geschichte der Juden in den böhmischen Ländern: Das Zeitalter der Aufklärung 1780–1830*, vol. 1 (Tübingen, 1969), 115–35; J. Hillel Kieval, "Caution's Progress: The Modernization of Jewish Life in Prague, 1780–1830," in *Toward Modernity: The European Jewish Model*, ed. Jacob Katz (New Brunswick, N.J., 1987), 71–105.

29. Heiman [Aaron Wolfssohn], "Review of New Books—*Mishlei Asaf*, Parts I and II; *Zemirot Asaf*, Part III," *Hame'asef* 7, 3 (1796): 251–66.

30. [Aaron Wolfssohn], *Sicha be'eretz hachayim, Hame'asef* 7 (1794–96): 93–67; 120–58; 203–28; 279–98; Yehuda Friedlander, *Studies in Hebrew Satire* (Tel Aviv, 1979) (Hebrew), 123–200.

31. See Wolfssohn's third footnote, *Sicha be'eretz hachayim*, 176.

32. Ibid., 151.

33. Joseph Ha'efrati, *Alon bakhut* (Vienna, 1793).

34. Wolfssohn, *Sicha be'eretz hachayim*, 172–73.

35. Ibid., 176.

36. See Moshe Samet, "Early Burial: The History of the Controversy on Determining Time of Death," *Asufot* 3 (1988), (Hebrew), in particular pp. 433–49, which reconstruct the events of the 1790s in the early burial controversy; Gerda Heinrich, "Haskala und Emanzipation, Paradigmen der Debatte zwischen 1781 und 1812," *Das Achtzehnte Jahrhundert* 22 (1999): 152–75.

37. Marcus Herz, *Mikhtav* (letter to *Hame'asef*) (Berlin, 1788).

38. See Marcus Herz, *Über die frühe Beerdigung der Juden* (Berlin, 1788).

39. Joel Brill, *Schreiben an die . . . chevrot gemilut chasadim bechol hakehitlot hakedushot* (Berlin, 1794).

40. Abraham Ash, *Sefer Torah kullah* (Berlin, 1796). In 1805 Ash published a book in German advocating religious reform. See Katz, *Out of the Ghetto: The Social Background to the Jewish Emancipation, 1770–1870* (Cambridge, Mass.), 137.

41. Ash, *Sefer Torah kullah*, 7.

42. Ibid., 17–18.

43. Ibid., 25–26

44. Isaac Euchel, *Hame'asef* 7, 4 (1797): 361–91.

45. Ibid., 381–82.

46. See Samet, "Early Burial."

47. Aaron Wolfssohn, *Hame'asef* 7, 4 (1797): 347–60.

48. Ibid., 357.

49. Ibid., 353.

50. See Freudenthal, "Die ersten Emanzipationsbestrebungen der Juden," 570–78.

51. See Shlomo Rosenthal's description, which, although it does not provide an accurate picture, unquestionably reflects the tension in the community around the question of burial, in M. Roest, *Catalog der Hebraica und Judaica aus der L. Rosenthalischen Bibliothek*, vol. 2 (Amsterdam, 1785, facsimile edition , Amsterdam, 1966), 176.

52. See Samet, "Early Burial," 449–51; Siegfried Silberstein, "Mendelssohn und Mecklenburg," *Zeitschrift für die Geschichte der Juden in Deutschland* 1 (1929): 233–90.

53. Saul Berlin, *Besamim Rosh* (Berlin, 1793).

54. Saul Berlin, *Arugot habosem* (Berlin, 1792)

55. Moshe Samet, "Rabbi Saul Berlin and His Works," *Kiryat Sefer* 43 (June 1968): 429–43 (Hebrew); idem, "Rabbi Saul Berlin's *Besamim Rosh*: Bibliography, Historiography, and Ideology," *Kiryat Sefer* 48 (1973): 509–23 (Hebrew); Pelli, *Studies in the Jewish Enlightenment*; idem, *The Age of Haskalah* (Leiden, 1979), 171–89.

56. Saul Berlin, *Besamim Rosh*, introduction by the editor.

57. Talya Fishman, "Forging Jewish Memory: *Besamim Rosh* and the Invention of Pre-Emancipation Jewish Culture," in *Jewish History and Jewish Memory: Essays in Honor of Yosef Hayim Yerushalmi*, ed. Elisheva Carlebach, John M. Efron, and David N. Myers (Hanover, 1998), 81.

58. On him, see David Fishman, *Russia's First Modern Jews: The Jews of Shklov* (New York, 1995).

59. Wolf Landsberg, *Ze'ev yitrof* (Frankfurt-am-Oder, 1797).

60. Jacob Katzenellenbogen to Meshullam Igra. 22nd of Sivan, 1793, in Abraham Berliner, *Veshema baketuvim* (Lvov, 1909), 13–16.

61. Lazer Katzenellenbogen to Meshullam Igra, 22nd of Tammuz, 1793, in Berliner, *Vehema baketuvim*, 17–18.

62. Raphael Kohen to Meshullam Igra, 23rd of Tammuz, 1793, in Samuel Klein, "Zur Geschichte des Literarischen Streites über die Werke *Mitzpe Yoktiel* und *Besamin Rosh*," *Israelitische Manatsschrift, Wissenschaftliche Beilage zur Jüdischen Presse* 4–6 (1909).

63. Mordechai Benet to Jacob Katzenellenbogen, 3rd of Tammuz, 1793, in Berliner, *Vehema baketuvim*, 19–20.

64. Mordechai Benet to Hirsch Lewin (Av 1793), in Shimon Büchler, *Shai lamoreh* (Budapest, 1894), 11–17.

65. Zvi Hirsch Levin to Mordechai Benet (probably Elul 1793), in Büchler, *Shai lamoreh*, 18–19.

66. Zevi Hirsch Levin, *Ish anav* (Berlin, 1793), also printed in Eliezer Landshuth, *Toldot anshei hashem ufe'ulatam be'adat Berlin* (Berlin, 1884), 102–4.

67. See Joseph Meyer, "Mittheilungen über den Verfasser der Gutachten *Besamim Rosh*" *Literaturblatt des Orients* 5 (1844): 712–13.

68. *Hame'asef* 7, 3 (1797): 266–71.

Chapter 15. On Frivolity and Hypocrisy

1. On this affair, see *Letters of the Italian Rabbis* (Hamburg, 1796); Hayim Joseph David Azulai, *Yosef ometz*, reply 7 (Livorno, 1798); *Hame'asef* 7, 3 (1796): 271–73 (letter of denial from Mantua sent at the request of Baruch Jeiteles of Prague); Abraham Meir Vaaknin, "Letter from Italian Rabbis Against German Reformists in 1796," *Tzfunot* 5 (1990): 83–88 (Hebrew); Jacob Katz, *Out of the Ghetto: The Social Background to the Jewish Emancipation, 1770–1870* (Cambridge, Mass.), 136–37.

2. Raphael Kohen, *Sefer da'at kedoshim* (Altona, 1797). See Jacob Katz, "Rabbi Raphael Kohen, Moses Mendelssohn's Adversary," in *Halakkah in Straits* (Jerusalem, 1992), 260–61 (Hebrew).

3. Kohen, *Sefer da'at kedoshim*, 6, 18, 28, 49, 81–82.

4. Ibid., 4, 15, 41, 48, 82.

5. Eleazar Fleckeles, *Olat chodesh hashelishi* (Prague, 1793).

6. Ibid., 61–68. See Shmuel Werses, *Haskalah and Sabbatianism: The Story of a Controversy* (Jerusalem, 1988), 64–65 (Hebrew).

7. Judah Hurwitz, *Chayei nefesh venitzchiyota* (Poritzk, 1787).

8. Judah Hurwitz, *Megillat sedarim* (Prague, 1793), 25–26. See Shmuel Werses, "The Sermonizing of a Maskil in the Guise of Rhymed Prose: A Study of *Megillat Sed-*

arim of Judah Hurwitz," in *Trends and Forms in the Haskalah Literature*, ed. Shmuel Werses (Jerusalem, 1990), 187–205 (Hebrew).

9. Hurwitz, *Megillat sedarim*, Introduction.

10. Ibid., 13–14.

11. Ibid., 4: 2.

12. Ibid., 31: 2.

13. Ibid., 29: 1

14. Pinhas Hurwitz, *Sefer haberit* (Bruenn, 1797); Noah Rosenblum, "The First Hebrew Encyclopedia: Its Author and Its Development," *Proceedings of the American Academy for Jewish Research* 55 (1988): 15–65.

15. Hurwitz, *Sefer haberit*, 156.

16. Ibid., 364.

17. Ibid., 358.

18. Judah Leib Margolioth, *Atzei eden* (here according to the 1858 Königsberg edition), 15: 2.

19. Ibid., 16: 1.

20. Ibid., 16: 2.

21. Ibid.

22. Judah Leib Margolioth, *Tal orot* (Frankfurt-am-Oder, 1811). The words of the Vilna Gaon are quoted from the 1843 Pressburg edition of this book, 61: 1.

23. Baruch Jeiteles, *Sefer ha'orev* (Prague, 1795); Ruth Kestenberg-Glastein, *Neuere Geschichte der Juden in den böhmischen Ländern: Das Zeitalter der Aufklärung 1780–1830* (Tübingen, 1969), 135–146.

24. Jeiteles, *Sefer ha'orev*, 5: 1.

25. Ibid., 5: 19–20.

26. Baruch Jeiteles, *Sicha bein shnat, 5560 ve-5561* (Prague, 1800), 2–3. See Shmuel Werses, *Haskalah and Sabbatianism: The Story of a Controversy* (Jerusalem, 1988), 74–81 (Hebrew).

27. Naumann Simonsohn, *Ein mishpat* (Berlin, 1796). On him, see above, Chapter 13.

28. Simonsohn, *Ein mishpat*, 4.

29. Ibid. Another case of a maskil who chose to abandon Berlin (in 1796) and to move to Hungary, in view of his disillusionment with the radicalization of the Haskalah, was David Friesenhausen, described in Meir Gilon, "R. David Friesenhausen Between the Haskalah and Chasidism," in *The Rabbinical Seminary of Budapest, 1877–1977* (New York, 1985), 19–44.

30. Shlomo Schönemann, *Minhat bikurim* (Berlin, 1797).

31. Ibid., 4. See also, on page 41, a general criticism of the policy of *Hame'asef*'s editors and suggestions for improving the journal, which Schönemann continued to regard as a useful forum.

32. Joel Brill, *Hame'asef* 7, 3 (1796): 192; Aaron Wolfssohn, *Hame'asef*, 7, 4 (1797): 301–2.

33. Ibid., 299–304.

34. Wolfssohn dedicated most of his polemical words against critics of *Sicha be'eretz hachayim* to Dov Berl of Vienna, who he claimed had sent him a harsh letter of criticism, which he had printed nearly in its entirety. This was probably a text written by Wolfssohn himself, which he used to expand the polemic with the rabbinical culture that he began in the play. See Wolfssohn, *Hame'asef* 7, 4 (1797): 299–360.

35. Ibid., 397–99.

36. Ibid., 397–98.

37. Schönemann, *Minhat bikurim*, 46: 1 (quotation from his conversation with his father, Isaac Satanow).

38. Moses Mendelssohn (Hamburg), *Pnei tevel* (Amsterdam, 1871), 241.

39. See Reuven Michael, "Did the Triumph of the Ideas of the Enlightenment at the Start of the French Revolution Cause the Demise of the 'Berlin Enlightenment'?" *Zion* 56 (1991): 275–98 (Hebrew), and Shmuel Feiner's rebuttal in Feiner, "Did the French Revolution Influence the Development of the 'Berlin Enlightenment'?" *Zion* 57 (1991): 89–92 (Hebrew).

40. See Aaron Halle-Wolfssohn, *Leichtsinn und Frömmelei: Ein Familien Gemälde in drei Aufzügen*, in *Lustpiele zur Unterhaltung beim Purim-Feste* (Breslau, 1796), 1: 33–111; Bernardd Weinryb, "An Unknown Hebrew Play of the German Haskalah," *Proceedings of the American Academy for Jewish Research* 24 (1955): 165–75. See also Dan Miron's Introduction to the Hebrew edition: "On Aaron Wolfssohn and His Play," *Frivolity and Hypocrisy*, ed. R. Chanoch and Rabbi Josephche (Tel Aviv, 1977), 5–55 (Hebrew)—an excellent historical and literary study on the two plays.

41. On the family crisis in the Berlin community, see Steven M. Lowenstein, *The Berlin Jewish Community: Enlightenment, Family and Crisis, 1770–1830* (Oxford, 1994), chap. 5.

42. Isaac Euchel, *Reb Henoch oder was tut me damit* (Vilna, 1930), 94–106.

43. Ibid., Act 1, scene 3.

44. Elizabeth goes out to spend an evening at the Vauxhall dance hall, which was in fact one of the popular entertainment spots in Berlin, next to which there was a brothel. See Deborah Hertz, *Jewish High Society in Old Regime Berlin* (New Haven, Conn., 1988).

45. See Robert Darnton, *The Forbidden Best-Sellers of Pre-Revolutionary France* (New York, 1995).

46. Aaron Wolfssohn, *Leichtsinn und Frömmelei*, 71–73, 84–87, 110–13 (from Miron ed.). Schönemann disputed with Wolfssohn and defended his father's books. He denounced the play because it audaciously depicted a Jew frequenting a brothel: Schönemann, *Minchat Bikurim*, 5: 2.

47. Wolfssohn, *Leichtsinn und Frömmelei*, 63 (Miron ed.).

48. Ibid., 103.

49. Euchel, *Reb Henoch*, Act 5, scene 7, 129–33.

50. Wolfssohn, *Leichtsinn und Frömmelei*, 105 (Miron ed.).

51. At the end of the eighteenth century, the pseudo-Enlightenment was also a problem for the German Enlightenment. See G. E. Patri, "Aufklärung," *Allgemeine Encyclopädie der Weissenschaften und Künste*, ed. J. S. Ersch and J. G. Gruber, vol. 6 (Leipzig, 1821), 307; Horst Stuke, "Aufklärung," *Geschichtliche Grundbegriffe*, ed. O. Brunner, W. Conze, and R. Koselleck (Stuttgart, 1979) 283–86.

52. Professor Köhler, "Über die Aufklärung der jüdischen Nation," *Magazin für die biblische-orientalische Literatur und gesammte Philologie* (Königsberg, 1789), 193–200.

Afterword: Haskalah and Secularization

1. See Roy Porter, *The Enlightenment* (London, 1990), 70–75.

2. See Daniel Gordon, ed., *Postmodernism and the Enlightenment: New Perspec-*

tives in Eighteenth-Century French Intellectual History (New York, 2001); Robert Darnton, *George Washingtons falsche Zähne, oder noch einmal: Was ist Aufklärung?* trans. H. Ritter (Munich, 1996).

3. Jacob Katz, *Tradition and Crisis*, trans. Bernard Cooperman (New York, 1993); idem, *Exclusiveness and Tolerance: Studies in Jewish-Gentile Relations in Medieval and Modern Times* (London, 1961).

4. See at length in Shmuel Feiner, "Out of Berlin: The Second Phase of the Haskalah Movement," in *Meah She'arim: Studies in Medieval Jewish Spiritual Life in Memory of Isadore Twersky*, ed. Ezra Fleischer, Gerald Blidstein, Carmi Horowitz, and Bernard Septimus (Jerusalem, 2001), 403–31 (Hebrew).

5. See, inter alia, Peter Burke, "Religion and Secularization," in *The New Cambridge History* (Cambridge, 1980), 13: 293–317.

6. On the shaping of the modern historical consciousness in the Haskalah, see Shmuel Feiner, *Haskalah and History: The Emergence of a Modern Jewish Historical Consciousness* (Oxford, 2002).

Index